W9-AWT-465

Finding cures.
Saving children.

ARGENTINA
4th Edition

**Where to Stay and Eat
for All Budgets**

**Must-See Sights
and Local Secrets**

Ratings You Can Trust

Portions of this book appear in *Fodor's South America*.

Fodor's Travel Publications   New York, Toronto, London, Sydney, Auckland
www.fodors.com

FODOR'S ARGENTINA

Editors: Laura M. Kidder, lead editor; Carissa Bluestone; Michael Nalepa

Editorial Production: Tom Holton

Editorial Contributors: Eddy Ancinas, Brian Byrnes, Joyce Dalton, Robin Goldstein, Satu Hummasti, Victoria Patience

Maps: David Lindroth, *cartographer*; Rebecca Baer and Bob Blake, *map editors*

Design: Fabrizio La Rocca, *creative director*; Guido Caroti, *art director*; Moon Sun Kim, *cover designer*; Melanie Marin, *senior picture editor*

Production/Manufacturing: Colleen Ziemba

Cover Photo (Andes Mountains, Patagonia): John Warden/Superstock

Fourth Edition

ISBN: 1–4000–1665–7

ISBN-13: 978–1–4000–1665–5

ISSN: 1526–1360

SPECIAL SALES

This book is available for special discounts for bulk purchases for sales promotions or premiums. Special editions, including personalized covers, excerpts of existing books, and corporate imprints, can be created in large quantities for special needs. For more information, write to Special Markets/Premium Sales, 1745 Broadway, MD 6-2, New York, New York 10019, or e-mail specialmarkets@randomhouse.com.

AN IMPORTANT TIP & AN INVITATION

Although all prices, opening times, and other details in this book are based on information supplied to us at press time, changes occur all the time in the travel world, and Fodor's cannot accept responsibility for facts that become outdated or for inadvertent errors or omissions. So **always confirm information when it matters,** especially if you're making a detour to visit a specific place. Your experiences—positive and negative—matter to us. If we have missed or misstated something, **please write to us.** We follow up on all suggestions. Contact the Argentina editor at editors@fodors.com or c/o Fodor's at 1745 Broadway, New York, NY 10019.

PRINTED IN THE UNITED STATES OF AMERICA

10 9 8 7 6 5 4 3 2 1

Be a Fodor's Correspondent

Your opinion matters. It matters to us. It matters to your fellow Fodor's travelers, too. And we'd like to hear it. In fact, we *need* to hear it.

When you share your experiences and opinions, you become an active member of the Fodor's community. That means we'll not only use your feedback to make our books better, but we'll publish your names and comments whenever possible. Throughout our guides, look for "Word of Mouth," excerpts of your unvarnished feedback.

Here's how you can help improve Fodor's for all of us.

Tell us when we're right. We rely on local writers to give you an insider's perspective. But our writers and staff editors—who are the best in the business—depend on you. Your positive feedback is a vote to renew our recommendations for the next edition.

Tell us when we're wrong. We're proud that we update most of our guides every year. But we're not perfect. Things change. Hotels cut services. Museums change hours. Charming cafés lose charm. If our writer didn't quite capture the essence of a place, tell us how you'd do it differently. If any of our descriptions are inaccurate or inadequate, we'll incorporate your changes in the next edition and will correct factual errors at fodors.com *immediately.*

Tell us what to include. You probably have had fantastic travel experiences that aren't yet in Fodor's. Why not share them with a community of like-minded travelers? Maybe you chanced upon a beach or bistro or B&B that you don't want to keep to yourself. Tell us why we should include it. And share your discoveries and experiences with everyone directly at fodors.com. Your input may lead us to add a new listing or highlight a place we cover with a "Highly Recommended" star or with our highest rating, "Fodor's Choice."

Give us your opinion instantly at our feedback center at www.fodors.com/feedback. You may also e-mail editors@fodors.com with the subject line "Argentina Editor." Or send your nominations, comments, and complaints by mail to Argentina Editor, Fodor's, 1745 Broadway, New York, NY 10019.

You and travelers like you are the heart of the Fodor's community. Make our community richer by sharing your experiences. Be a Fodor's correspondent.

¡Buen Viaje!

Tim Jarrell, Publisher

CONTENTS

MAPS

ABOUT THIS BOOK

Our Ratings

Sometimes you find terrific travel experiences and sometimes they just find you. But usually the burden is on you to select the right combination of experiences. That's where our ratings come in.

As travelers we've all discovered a place so wonderful that its worthiness is obvious. And sometimes that place is so unique that superlatives don't do it justice: you just have to be there to know. These sights, properties, and experiences get our highest rating, **Fodor's Choice,** indicated by orange stars throughout this book.

Black stars highlight sights and properties we deem **Highly Recommended,** places that our writers, editors, and readers praise again and again for consistency and excellence.

By default, there's another category: any place we include in this book is by definition worth your time, unless we say otherwise. And we will.

Disagree with any of our choices? Care to nominate a place or suggest that we rate one more highly? Visit our feedback center at www.fodors.com/feedback.

Budget Well

Hotel and restaurant price categories from ¢ to $$$$ are defined in the opening pages of each chapter. For attractions, we always give standard adult admission fees; reductions are usually available for children, students, and senior citizens. Want to pay with plastic? **AE, D, DC, MC, V** following restaurant and hotel listings indicate whether American Express, Discover, Diners Club, MasterCard, and Visa are accepted.

Restaurants

Unless we state otherwise, restaurants are open for lunch and dinner daily. We mention dress only when there's a specific requirement and reservations only when they're essential or not accepted—it's always best to book ahead.

Hotels

Hotels have private bath, phone, TV, and air-conditioning and operate on the European Plan (aka EP, meaning without meals), unless we specify that they use the Continental Plan (CP, with a Continental breakfast), Breakfast Plan (BP, with a full breakfast), or Modified American Plan (MAP, with breakfast and dinner) or are all-inclusive (including all meals and most activities). We always list facilities but not whether you'll be charged an extra fee to use them, so when pricing accommodations, find out what's included.

Many Listings
- ★ Fodor's Choice
- ★ Highly recommended
- ✉ Physical address
- ✦ Directions
- ✇ Mailing address
- ☎ Telephone
- 🖷 Fax
- ⊕ On the Web
- ✎ E-mail
- ✑ Admission fee
- ☉ Open/closed times
- ⚑ Start of walk/itinerary
- Ⓜ Metro stations
- ▭ Credit cards

Hotels & Restaurants
- 🏨 Hotel
- Number of rooms
- Facilities
- Meal plans
- ✕ Restaurant
- Reservations
- Dress code
- Smoking
- BYOB
- ✕ Hotel with restaurant that warrants a visit

Outdoors
- Golf
- Camping

Other
- Family-friendly
- Contact information
- ⇨ See also
- ✉ Branch address
- ☞ Take note

Argentina

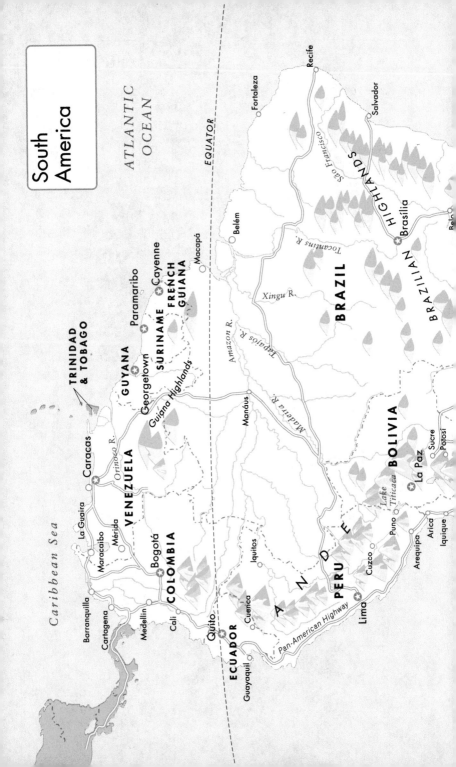

South America

ATLANTIC OCEAN

Caribbean Sea

EQUATOR

TRINIDAD & TOBAGO

Caracas
La Guaira
Maracaibo
Mérida
Barranquilla
Cartagena
Medellin
Cali
Bogotá

VENEZUELA

COLOMBIA

Orinoco R.

GUYANA
Georgetown

SURINAME
Paramaribo

FRENCH GUIANA
Cayenne

Guiana Highlands

Macapá

Belém

Amazon R.

Xingu R.

Tapajós R.

Tocantins R.

São Francisco R.

Fortaleza

Recife

Salvador

BRAZIL

Brasilia

BRAZILIAN HIGHLANDS

Belo

Manáus

Madeira R.

Iquitos

ECUADOR
Quito
Cuenca
Guayaquil

PERU

Lima

Cuzco

A N D E S

Pan-American Highway

Lake Titicaca

Puno

BOLIVIA
La Paz
Sucre
Potosí

Arica
Iquique
Arequipa

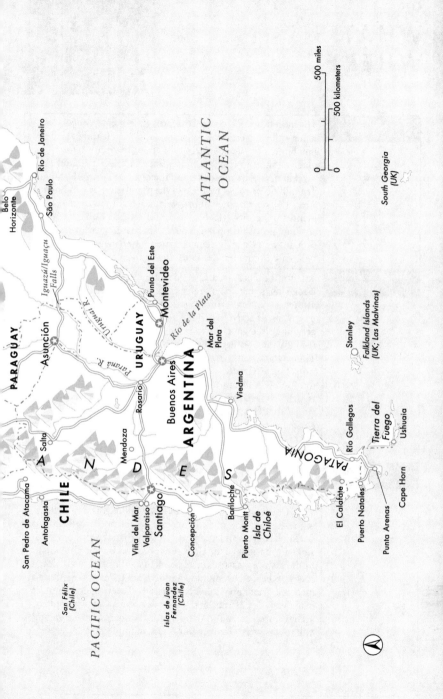

WHAT'S
WHERE

BUENOS AIRES	The most beautiful women, the most gallant men, the best foot-ballers, the juiciest steak: superlatives always feature when the inhabitants of Buenos Aires talk about their city. This is *the* place to shop in chic boutiques, dine in eclectic restaurants, revel in first-class museums and theaters, and learn the tango. Ten million people (one-third of the population) live in Buenos Aires's 48 *barrios* (neighborhoods), each with its own distinct identity. The city's leafy parks and elegant boulevards are reminiscent of European capitals; its chaotic traffic and passionate hordes staging demonstrations or on their way to a football match bring a more Latin flavor to things.
EXCURSIONS FROM BUENOS AIRES	Atlantic beaches are crowded with Buenos Aires locals on weekends; some spots are casual and family-friendly, others attract jet-setters. Worlds apart are the flat, expansive Pampas. Signs of active ranch life are everywhere, from the cattle grazing to the gauchos working the grasslands. Just north of the city, the Río Paraná splinters into a lush delta known as Tigre, where waterways, rather than roads, take you to luxurious lodges. The Río Paraná meets the Río Uruguay to form the Río de la Plata. A short hop over this from Buenos Aires is the sleepy Uruguayan town of Colonia, full of cobbled streets shaded by huge trees and crumbling colonial mansions. Much farther north, surrounded by subtropical forests, are the Cataratas del Iguazú, the mind-blowing system of waterfalls that straddle Argentina and Brazil.
CÓRDOBA	Córdoba Province is at the nation's geographical heart. Architectural reminders of its colonial past abound, notably in the Jesuit *estancias* (estates)—declared UNESCO World Heritage Sites. Córdoba City itself has colonial buildings as well as thriving restaurant and nightlife scenes. To the north, hills dotted with golf courses and estancias give way to the rugged red sandstone formations of the Cerro Uritorco and Parque Ongamira. In the far northeast, natural pigments adorn the rust-colored rocks of the Cerro Colorado national park, one of Argentina's most important pre-Columbian art sites. Landscapes are milder in the Valle de Calamuchita, south of Córdoba City, where alpine architecture lets you know that the founders of these mountain towns were German and Austrian immigrants.

THE NORTHWEST	Few venture beyond the northwestern cities—Catamarca, Jujuy, Salta, and Tucumán—to the high-mountain passes, deep red gorges, peaceful valleys, and subtropical jungles. In Jujuy Province, a palette of reds, greens, and yellows washes across the slopes of the Quebrada Humahuaca (Humahuaca Gorge) as it follows the Río Grande north. The great high plateau of the Puna stretches along the borders with Bolivia and Chile. Pre-Columbian and Spanish cultures are apparent in the architecture, traditions, and handicrafts. In sunny Calchaquí Valley, between Tucumán and Salta, former colonial settlements dot the landscape amidst Torrontés vineyards, and in the cities, the plazas and churches recall Spain. Even pre-Inca civilizations have left their marks on ghostly menhirs.
WINE REGIONS	Argentina's innovative vintners use desert sun, mountain snow, and extreme altitudes to craft distinctive wines—especially Malbec, the area's signature red. Mendoza's wineries enjoy the greatest reputation, while those in the Valle de Uco grow their grapes higher than almost anyone else. Family-owned wineries in tiny San Rafael focus on quality, and the wine-tourism industry in San Juan is starting to take off. The Pan-American Highway passes through Mendoza, heading west over spectacular Uspallata Pass to Chile. Along the way are hot springs, Inca ruins, and incomparable views of Aconcagua Mountain. Near the city of San Rafael, you river raft, horse pack in the Andes, or ski at the super resort of Las Leñas near Malargüe.
PATAGONIA	Patagonia really is the end of the world: Tierra del Fuego is closer to Antarctica than to Buenos Aires, and Ushuaia is the Earth's southernmost city. But the region is about a lot more than just a latitude. Patagonia is home to the Perito Moreno glacier, Argentina's most spectacular natural sight; on the Chilean side of the Andes, Parque Nacional Torres del Paine competes in grandeur. Well to the north the district of lakes and ski slopes around Bariloche attracts the jet set. On the Atlantic coast, marine life is abundant, exotic, and entertaining, with its epicenter at the Peninsula Valdés and nearby Puerto Madryn. There are some less-than-exciting aspects of Patagonia, too—inconvenient plane schedules, border-crossing bureaucracy, uninteresting transit cities like Comodoro Rivadavía and Río Gallegos, and roads through nothing. Witness the R40: "the loneliest road in the world" is a drive of days upon days on unpaved terrain between Bariloche with El Calafate. For some, though, Patagonia's romance lies in just such desolation.

QUINTESSENTIAL ARGENTINA

The Beef

Argentina is cow country. The beef is so good, most Argentines see little reason to eat anything else, though Patagonian lamb and chicken are tasty alternatives, as is *chivito* (kid). *Carne asado* (roasted cuts of beef) might be done on a grill over hot coals (*a la parrilla*), baked in an oven, or slowly roasted on a metal spit stuck in the ground aslant on a bed of hot coals. A *parrillada mixta* (mixed grill) is the quintessential Argentine meal for two in a restaurant. A family *asado* (barbecue), where men show off their barbecuing skills is the classic way to spend a Sunday afternoon. Expect different cuts of beef—both on and off the bone and usually roasted in huge pieces and served dripping—as well as chorizo sausage, roasted sweetbreads, and less bloodthirsty accompaniments like provolone cheese and bell peppers.

Vino

Given the high consumption of beef, Argentines understandably drink a lot of *vino tinto* (red wine). Although most of the wine consumed is nondescript table wine, in recent years the industry has boomed and Argentine vineyards (especially so-called boutique vineyards) are firmly on the map. The most popular grapes are Cabernet Sauvignon and Malbec, which Argentina is famed to do better than anywhere else. Tempranillo, Tannat, Merlot, and Shiraz (known as Syrah) are also on the rise. If you prefer *vino blanco* (white wine), try a sauvignon blanc or chardonnay from Mendoza, or lesser-known wineries from farther north, such as La Rioja and Salta, where the Torrontés grape thrives. This varietal produces a dry white with a lovely floral bouquet.

It's easy to partake of Argentina's daily rituals during your trip. Among other things, you can simply enjoy some fancy footwork—on the field or in the ballroom—or savor the rich flavors (and conversation) of a leisurely meal.

Futbol

In a country where Diego Maradona is revered as a god, nothing unites and divides Argentines as much as their passion for soccer. Local teams are the subject of fiery dispute and serious rivalry; the national team brings the country together for displays of unrivaled passion and suicidal despair, especially during the World Cup. Argentina's blue-and-white striped jerseys have flashed across TV screens since it won the 1978 and 1986 World Cups, and nothing can lift—or crush—the spirits of the nation like the result of a soccer match. Every weekend, stadiums across the country fill to bursting with screaming fans toting drums and banners and filling the air with confetti and flares in their team's colors which—together with the play on the field—make for a sporting spectacle second to none.

Tango

There's no question as to what the soundtrack of Buenos Aires is: the city and the tango are inseparable. From its beginnings in portside brothels at the turn of the 19th century, tango has marked and reflected the character of Buenos Aires and its inhabitants. Although visitors associate tango with dance, for locals it's more about the music and the lyrics, and you can't help but cross paths with both forms. You may hear strains of tango on the radio while sipping coffee in a boulevard café or see high-kicking sequined dancers in a glitzy dinner show or listen to musicians in a cabaret. Regardless, you'll experience the best of this broody, melancholic, but impassioned, art form.

IF YOU LIKE

The Wild, Wild World

Climates range from tropical to subarctic and altitudes descend from 22,000 feet to below sea level, so every conceivable environment on Earth is represented. Plants, birds, and animals thrive undisturbed in their habitats. Along the south Atlantic coast, sea mammals mate and give birth on empty beaches and in protected bays. To the north, guanaco, rhea, and native deer travel miles over Andean trails and across windswept plains, while birds pass above in clouds of thousands or descend on lagoons like blankets of feathers.

- **Glaciar Perito Moreno, Patagonia.** Tons of ice regularly peel off this advancing glacier and crash into Lago Argentino.

- **Cataratas de Iguazú, Northeast.** Iguazú Falls National Park protects 275 waterfalls and countless species of bird, mammal, insect, and amphibia. Trails disappear into a greenhouse of lianas, creepers, epiphytes, bamboo, orchids, and bromeliads.

- **Península Valdés, Patagonia.** This is the best place to view southern right whales as they feed, mate, give birth, and nurse their offspring.

- **Parque Nacional Nahuel Huapi, Bariloche.** Rich forest surround the sapphire-blue waters of Lake Nahuel Huapi. Smaller bodies of water nearby make this Argentina's lake district.

- **Quebrada de Humahuaca.** Vibrant pinks, yellows, and greens color the walls of this northwestern canyon like giant swaths of paint.

- **Reserva Faunística Punta Tombo, Patagonia.** It's home to the world's largest colony of Magellanic penguins.

Adrenaline Rushes

If an eyeful of natural beauty doesn't make your heart race in the way you'd like, why not try an adventure sport? Argentina is great for winter rushes—skiing, snowboarding, and dogsledding among them. When temperatures soar, you can cool down by white-water rafting or leaping (with a parachute) into the breeze.

- **Ice Trekking on the Perito Moreno Glacier.** You can trek over the glacier's 1,000-year-old ice, then celebrate your ascent with cocktails served over cubes of it.

- **Hang gliding and paragliding at Cuchi Corral.** Argentina's top jumping spot is a natural 1,320-foot-high parapet in northwest Córdoba Province with spectacular Río Pinto valley views.

- **White-water rafting in the Río Mendoza.** This river's medium to difficult rapids course through Andean foothills. You can combine one- or two-day descents with horseback riding in the mountains.

- **Skiing and snowboarding at Las Leñas, Catedral, and Chapelco ski areas.** Las Leñas near Mendoza, Catedral near Bariloche, and Chapelco near San Martín de los Andes offer groomed runs, open bowls, and trails that follow the fall line to cozy inns or luxurious hotels.

- **Tierra Mayor, Patagonia.** This family-run Nordic center near Ushuaia has such novelties as dogsled rides, snowcat trips, and wind skiing.

- **Mountain climbing at Aconcagua, Mendoza Province.** Close to the Chilean border, this 6,959-meter (22,831-foot) peak is the highest in the western and southern hemispheres and is surrounded by a host of other climbable mountains.

Culture & History

Buenos Aires is a city of Paris-inspired boulevards and historical neighborhoods. Beyond the city, gauchos work ranches that sprawl over every horizon, and old Jesuit estancias evoke Argentina's colonial days in Córdoba Province. The Andes tower above the age-old vineyards of Mendoza and San Juan, while Salta and Jujuy retain traditions that stretch back to before the arrival of Europeans. The windswept reaches of Patagonia roll on forever and a few miles more.

- **Museo de Arte Latinoamericana de Buenos Aires (MALBA).** One of the world's few museums specializing in Latin American art is in a stunningly simple building.

- **Camino de la Historia, Córdoba.** Five-hundred-year-old Jesuit estancias, a reminder of Argentina's colonial past, dot the countryside around Córdoba City.

- **Festival de Tango, Buenos Aires** The world's most important tango festival is a nine-day-long extravaganza culminating in a huge *milonga* (dance session) along Corrientes Avenue.

- **Festival de La Vendimia, Mendoza.** At the grape-harvest festival, during the first week of March, parades, folk dancing, and fireworks take place. The crowning of a queen marks the grand finale.

- **Museo Marítimo, Ushuaia.** A museum in Tierra del Fuego's penal colony sheds light on Patagonia's past.

- **Museo Paleontológico, Trelew.** You can marvel at dinosaur bones and watch archaeologists at work at this impressive paleontology museum.

Shopping

Argentines love to shop. On weekends, town squares become *ferias* (open-air markets); street performers wind their way between stalls of hand-made offerings. Big shopping malls stock local and international brands. Wine, chocolate, cookies, and preserves are some of the consumables.

- **Handmade jewelry and housewares, Buenos Aires.** Artisans sell wares for you and your home in alpaca, wood, and leather.

- **Gaucho goods, San Antonio de Areco.** Modern-day gauchos can stock up on saddles, bridles, asado knives, belts, and handbags in this town of artisans.

- **Ceramics and weavings, Salta and Jujuy.** Salta is famed for its rich red and black ponchos. Woven wall-hangings and alpaca knitwear are ubiquitous in Jujuy. Red-clay figures and cookware abound.

- **Jams and cookies, Córdoba.** If it grows on a tree, chances are that you'll find it made into a preserve. The province's *alfajores* (cookies) are delightful.

- **Wine, Mendoza and Salta.** Tour the vineyards, sampling Malbecs, Cabernets, and Torrontéses at leisure, before stocking up on those you liked most.

- **Young designer clothing, Buenos Aires.** In trendy Palermo Viejo, cobbled streets are lined with the boutiques of up-and-coming designers.

- **Chocolate, Bariloche.** Many of Bariloche's original inhabitants were German, hence the thriving chocolate industry. The most famous is *en rama*, sticks of folded flaky chocolate.

GREAT ITINERARIES

PORTEÑOS & PAMPAS

Day 1: Arrival

Arrive in Buenos Aires and pick up a city map from the tourist office right before you enter the main terminal. Get cash at the ATM before taking a taxi to your hotel. Ignore the drivers asking if you need a cab; head straight for the taxi booth, pay up front for your ticket (about 48 pesos) and let staffers assign you a driver, who will take you straight to a car. Spend the first afternoon in La Recoleta, whose famous cemetery contains Eva Peron's tomb. Make your first meal a memorable one at La Brigada, a top downtown *parrilla* (grill) for *bife de chorizo* (steak).

Day 2: San Telmo & El Centro

Have your morning coffee at Bar Dorrego on San Telmo's Plaza Dorrego, then wander around this characteristic old neighborhood. Move on to El Centro, and have a lunch at a traditional pizzeria. Take in the Plaza de Mayo, Teatro Colón (on a tour), and other downtown sights during the afternoon. Before dinner see musical or tango performances. Dinner at an innovative restaurant, such as Sucre or Resto (you'll need a reservation a week in advance) might give you the fortitude to hit the bars. Try the strip in Recoleta near the cemetery, a famous expat scene. Buller, the microbrewery, is a standout.

Day 3: Palermo Viejo

Hop a cab to MALBA and spend the morning viewing Latin American art. Afterward take a short taxi ride to the Japanese Garden. From there, it's a short hop to the cutting-edge Palermo Hollywood neighborhood, where you can lunch on sushi, Vietnamese, or far-out fusion. Afterward wander leisurely over to Palermo Soho, browsing the city's coolest clothing and shoe stores (don't miss the strip on Gurruchaga). When night falls, have coffee or a cocktail on Placita Serrano, and finish with dinner at a modern restaurant: Casa Cruz or Bar Uriarte. If you're up for a nightcap, you're already right where all the action is.

Day 4: La Boca

Begin with a taxi ride to La Boca, the old tango neighborhood. The main strip is Caminito, which though colorful and iconic, is too touristy to merit more than an hour or two of your time. Lunch at El Obrero is a classic. So is an all-out evening wine experience at the Gran Bar Danzón in the Retiro neighborhood. In between you can revisit Palermo Viejo (a day is hardly enough), El Centro, or San Telmo.

Day 5: Buenos Aires to the Pampas

After getting a sense of the city, hit the highway for gaucho country. The town of San Antonio de Areco, in the heart of the Pampas, is home to several *estancias,* country inns that also function as working farms with gauchos who tend to the horses (and to the guests). La Bamba and El Rosario de Areco are two of our favorites. After arriving, you'll be treated to a lavish dinner, likely an *asado*; most estancias include three or even four meals per day in the room price.

If you don't want to drive yourself, arrange ground transportation through estancias. Some can orchestrate a 20-minute flight to an airstrip in San Antonio—now that's arriving in style. If you drive, reserve a rental car downtown, not at the airport. Take the Acceso Norte to the Panameri-

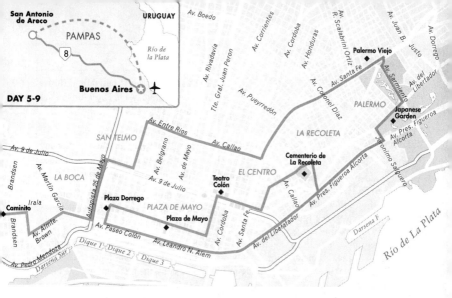

cana (RN-9) to Pilar and then RN-8, a much slower road, to San Antonio. Leave after lunch for the hour-long drive.

Day 6: San Antonio de Areco

Spend your first morning in the Pampas on horseback, roaming across the grassland with a resident gaucho. This, like other activities, should be included with the estancia price. No riding experience is necessary; seasoned riders can gallop while beginners walk or trot. After lunch—and this is one reason you'll be glad to have a car—head into downtown San Antonio. Check out the gaucho museum, wander the sleepy streets, and try one of the excellent meat restaurants, such as the Almacén de Ramos Generales. Finish with a Quilmes or two at Las Ganas, a dusty old gaucho hangout. One caveat: Beware of driving in the rain, which can turn San Antonio's streets into deep rivers of sorrow

Day 7: San Antonio de Areco

This is a day to relax. If there's a day-trip group coming in, the midday meal might be accompanied by a song and dance performance with whooping gauchos—cheesy, but fun. Take an afternoon swim in the pool, where someone will probably serve you empanadas and drinks, then have dinner at the estancia, perhaps followed by a game of pool with other guests, who by now may be good friends.

Days 8–9: To Buenos Aires and Home

Return to Buenos Aires after one last lunch. Spend the last afternoon shopping and strolling, revisit your favorite neighborhood, and have a blowout meal. Good splurge restaurants are Tomo I, Le Mistral at the Four Seasons, and La Bourgogne.

On Day 9, allow an hour to get to Ezeiza for your flight home. Don't forget to stash some of that superb red wine in your carry-on baggage—it's a sure way to impress your friends at home. Q, a range of wines by Zuccardi, is one of the more impressive labels of late, with an impressive Tempranillo and a powerful Malbec. If you kept your rental car, so that you can drive yourself to the airport, make sure your hotel has a garage and allow an extra half hour before your flight to return the car (it's not as easy in Argentina as it is in some countries).

ALTERNATIVES: If you're a soccer fan and Boca Juniors are playing during your stay in Buenos Aires, don't miss it. Just show up at the stadium and buy tickets at the window.

You can combine this itinerary with a trip to Uruguay or replace the San Antonio excursion with it. Montevideo and the port town of Colonia are both easily accessible by the Buquebus, a fast ferry. Spending two or three days in Uruguay isn't just a fun way to get an extra passport stamp—it's a window into a country whose economic and cultural differences from Argentina (their heightened obsession with *mate*, for instance) are readily apparent.

Another add-on or replacement side trip is to Iguazú Falls, in Argentina's northeast corner on the border with Brazil. The Argentines say that to see Iguazú Falls is to come face to face with God. Spend one day on the Argentine side of things, in the Parque Nacional Iguazú. Spend another day in the Parque Nacional Foz do Iguaçu, Brazil's national park.

Aerolineas Argentinas has three daily flights between Buenos Aires and Iguazú. Note that Americans need a visa to enter Brazil. At the falls, however, they don't always stamp you in and out, but rather just note your name and passport number, especially if you're with an organized tour. To be safe, go with a tour and/or allow a couple of days for processing. In Puerto Iguazú, the Brazilian consulate is open weekdays 8–12:30, and in Buenos Aires from 10–1.

TIPS

1 This itinerary works best if Day 1 (Arrival) is on a Saturday and Day 9 (On to Home) is the following Sunday.

2 If you plan to shop in Buenos Aires, stay in the same place before and after any excursions so you can leave extra bags with your hotel while traveling.

3 You can save a lot of money if you opt for an eight-day apartment rental in Buenos Aires.

4 In towns the many intersections without traffic lights or signs function like four-way stops: the first vehicle to the intersection crosses first. In the countryside, don't count on good signage leading to the estancias. Do as the locals do: pull over and ask directions.

5 Flights to and from Iguazú use the Aeroparque, the downtown airport; international flights leave from Ezeiza. If you're flying from Iguazú and home on the same day, allow at least five hours between your arrival in one airport and departure from the other.

GREAT ITINERARIES

IN PATAGONIA

Day 1: Arrival and on to Bariloche

Reaching Patagonia isn't easy. Your long flight to Buenos Aires will be followed by a transfer from Ezeiza International to the downtown Aeroparque and a flight to Bariloche. Rent a car at Bariloche's airport, and drive to your hotel (consider a place on the Circuito Chico outside of town). If you could use a beer after all that, there's no better place than the Map Room, a laid-back downtown pub with a deep commitment to local brews.

Day 2: Bariloche and Circuito Chico

Spend the day exploring the Circuito Chico and Península Llao Llao. Start early so you have time for a boat excursion from the dock at Puerto Pañuelo on the peninsula's edge as well as for some late afternoon shopping back in Bariloche. Spend the evening devouring delicious Patagonian lamb *a la cruz* (spit-roasted over an open fire) wherever you can find it—for example, Don Molina.

Day 3: Circuito Grande to Villa La Angostura

Villa La Angostura is the Lakes region's most up-and-coming destination—a tranquil lakeside retreat that marks the beginning of the legendary Circuito Grande. Getting there is a gorgeous experience as you'll hug the shores of the Lago Nahuel Huapi on R237 and R231. Check into a hotel in Puerto Manzano, a little outside Villa, whose hotels aren't as nice. The sparkling Puerto Sur is a good choice, with its endless water views. Or try the even more isolated and wonderful Las Balsas. Neither hotel is more than 10 minutes from town;

either one will give you the chance to fully relax.

Day 4: Villa La Angostura

You can spend your second day in Villa La Angostura skiing at Cerro Bayo, if it's winter and that's your thing; exploring the Parque Nacional los Arrayanes, the only forest of these myrtle trees in the world or simply relaxing by the lake, which, if you're staying at Puerto Sur or Las Balsas, might be the most appealing option. Regardless, reserve for dinner at Las Balsas, whether or not you're staying there; it has one of Patagonia's best restaurants.

Day 5: Seven Lakes Road to San Martín de los Andes

Head out of Villa La Angostura onto the the unbelievable Seven Lakes Road (R234), which branches right and along the way passes Lago Correntoso, Lago Espejo, Lago Villarino, Lago Falkner, and Lago Hermoso. The drive is today's main event; take the road all the way to San Martín, where you can spend the rest of the afternoon shopping, trying trout and other delicacies at the smoke shops, and enjoying an asado feast at Restaurante Kú. Note that the Seven Lakes Road is closed in winter; you'll have to go through Junín de los Andes to get to San Martín.

Day 6: San Martín de los Andes

If you're here in winter, and you're a skier, you will no doubt want to spend one full day in San Martín at Cerro Chapelco. Otherwise, spend the day relaxing on the beach, fishing, horseback riding, rafting, or otherwise outdoors.

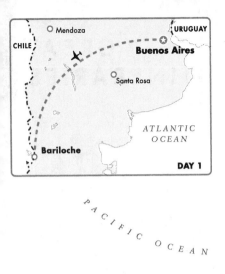

Day 7: Flight to El Calafate

Get an extremely early start from San Martín de los Andes for the five-hour drive back to Bariloche, where you'll catch a flight to El Calafate. Be sure to take the fast route through Junín from San Martín to Bariloche. If you follow the winding Seven Lakes Road you'll have little chance of catching an early afternoon flight.

It's a mere 1¾ hours from Bariloche to the Parque Nacional Los Glaciares. Grab a taxi to your hotel, have dinner, and get some sleep in preparation for glacier-viewing tomorrow. If you're on a no-holds-barred budget, stay at Los Notros, the only hotel within the park and in view of the glacier. It's also a place where all excursions will be taken care of for you. Otherwise, stay at a hotel in El Calafate and book your glacier visits through El Calafate tour operators—preferably before 7 PM today.

Day 8: El Calafate and Perito Moreno Glacier

Perito Moreno is one of the world's most impressive glaciers. Spend two days taking it in from different angles. Devote today either to the Upsala Glacier tour, which traverses the lakes in view of an impressive series of glaciers, or the hour-long

"Safari Náutico" on a boat that sails as close as possible to the front of the glacier. Enjoy a well-deserved dinner back in El Calafate, perhaps at the funky Pura Vida. Again, remember to arrange tomorrow's activities by 7 PM. Tonight, this means organizing an ice trek.

Day 9: El Calafate and Perito Moreno Glacier

It's all about one of Argentina's unique and most memorable activities: ice trekking. You'll don crampons and actually walk across Perito Moreno's surface. The trip is expensive, but worth every penny. (Note that ice treks are included in the rates if you stay at Los Notros.) You'll crawl through ice tunnels and hike across ice ridges that seem to glow bright blue. After all this, dinner—and everything else—will seem insignificant.

Day 10: Departure

Board a bus or taxi for El Calafate's gleaming new airport, and take a flight back through Buenos Aires and home. You'll be dreaming of glaciers for weeks to come. Note that if you are not connecting to another Aerolíneas flight home, you may have to spend an additional night in Buenos Aires on the way back.

ALTERNATIVES: Sports and outdoors enthusiasts can really customize this itinerary. Skiers, for example, can skip southern Patagonia, spending a day or two in Cerro Catedral, near Bariloche and a day at Cerro Chapelco. Rafters can work with Bariloche operators to create trips that range from those down the Río Manso—an eight-hour outing with easy rapids through a unique ecosystem—to 13-hour excursions to the Chilean border. Serious hikers can boat across Masacardi Lake to Pampa Linda, then hike to the black glaciers of Tronodor, continuing up above timberline to Otto Meiling hut, spending the night, walking along the crest of the Andes with glacier views, then returning to Pampa Linda. Day hikes to the foot of Tronodor leave more time for a mountain bike or horseback ride in the same area.

The most adventurous travelers drive from Bariloche to El Calafate instead of flying. It adds, oh, about a week to the itinerary, but it involves an unforgettable trip down the largely unpaved RN 40. Don't attempt this route without a 4WD vehicle that has two spares. And pack plenty of extra food and water as well as camping gear. Getting stuck in a place where cars and trucks pass only once every day or two is dangerous.

TIPS

❶ Don't try to follow the full itinerary in the dead of winter; limit yourself to the ski resorts in the Lakes district. That said, Bariloche is teeming with kids on high-school vacation trips in July.

❷ Book your flight to Argentina and your round-trip ticket to Bariloche at the same time. (Chances are you'll have to fly Aerolíneas Argentinas to do this). Booking a separate flight with another carrier will mean you won't be able to check your luggage through and you'll have to work really hard to get the timing right and avoid missing your connection.

❸ You can't tour the Lakes region without a rental car. If you don't want to drive, confine your visit to southern Patagonia, spending more time in El Calafate, and perhaps extending the trip into Ushuaia and Tierra del Fuego.

WHEN TO GO

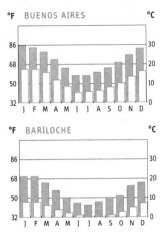

°F BUENOS AIRES °C

°F BARILOCHE °C

Because of Argentina's great variety of latitudes, altitudes, and zones, you can encounter many different climates in any given month. The most important thing to remember is the most obvious—when it's summer in the northern hemisphere, it's winter in Argentina. Winter in Argentina stretches from July through October, and summer settles in from December through March.

If you can handle the heat, Buenos Aires is wonderful January through February. During these months, as well as in July (for school holidays), Argentines crowd resorts along the Atlantic as well as inland around Córodoba and in the Pampas. Meanwhile traffic-free Buenos Aires has a host of city-sponsored events and concerts that bring city dwellers out into the sun and moonlight.

Spring and fall are temperate: it's usually warm enough for just a light jacket, and it's right before or after the peak (and expensive) season. The best time for trips to Iguazú Falls is August–October, when temperatures are lower, the falls are fuller, and the spring coloring is at its brightest.

Ski resorts such as Bariloche and San Martín de los Andes are obviously packed in winter. If you're heading to the Lake District or Patagonia, visit during the shoulder seasons of December and March. The Patagonia coast is on the infamous latitude that sailors call the "Roaring Forties," with southern seas that batter the region year-round. Thirty-mile-per-hour winds are common, and 100-mile-per-hour gales aren't unusual. In Tierra del Fuego fragments of glaciers cave into lakes with a rumble throughout the thaw from October to the end of April—the best time to enjoy the show.

🌦 Forecasts Servicio Meteorológico Nacional (National Weather Service for Argentina) ☎ 11/4514-4248 automated information ⊕ www.meteofa.mil.ar has information in Spanish. **Weather Channel Connection** ☎ 900/932-8437, 95¢ per minute from a Touch-Tone phone ⊕ www.weather.com.

ON THE CALENDAR

		Any of Argentina's top seasonal events can provide the stuff of lasting memories. Just remember that Argentina's seasons are the reverse of those in North America.
WINTER	December	Trelew, in Patagonia, celebrates the **Fiesta Provincial del Pingüino** (Provincial Festival of the Penguin).
	January	Cosquín, near Córdoba, is the home of the country's most prestigious local music festival, the **Festival Nacional de Folklore** (National Festival of Folklore), held the last week of January in the Plaza Próspero Molina.
	February	Scores of performances, concerts, and classes mark the **Festival Buenos Aires Tango,** the world's biggest tango festival, which culminates in a massive outdoor *milonga* along Avenida Corrientes.
		Carnaval comes in many guises in Argentina throughout February. Andean rituals prevail in Jujuy, while in Buenos Aires urban dance and drumming troupes known as *murgas* take to the streets.
SPRING	March	In Viedma and Carmen de Patagones, March 7 begins the annual, weeklong **Fiesta de Soberanía y la Tradición,** during which the towns celebrate their defeat of Brazil in an 1827 incursion, with music, food, crafts, and cultural exhibits.
		Mendoza celebrates the **Festival de La Vendimia,** the grape-harvest festival, during the first week of March. Parades, folk dancing, and fireworks take place; the crowning of a queen marks the finale.
	April	Independent, arty flicks are the order of the day at **Festival Internacional de Cine Independiente de Buenos Aires,** which attracts a handful of top international actors and directors.
SUMMER	June	In the Northwest, **Inti Raymi** (Festival of the Sun) is celebrated on June 20, the night before winter solstice, when the sun is thanked for last year's harvest.
		On June 17, when the **Salta Gaucho Parade** takes place, hundreds of gauchos ride into Salta in full regalia: wraparound leather chaps; black boots; *bombachas* (baggy pants); knife tucked into their belts; and red-and-black ponchos.
	July	The weeklong **Fiesta del Poncho** (Gaucho Festival) takes place in Catamarca. Artisans from all over the province sell their best weavings, ceramics, and wood carvings; folk singers perform in the evening.
		In Tucumán, **Día de Independencia** (Independence Day) is celebrated with much fervor. Lesser festivities taking place all over the country.

	In July, Bariloche hosts the Fiesta de las Colectividades (Party of Different Communities), a celebration of the town's diversity; dancing, music, handicrafts, and food from Europe, Scandinavia, the Middle East, Central Europe, and South America are represented.
	In the last two weeks of July all the country action is in Buenos Aires, at La Rural. Argentina's biggest agricultural show includes displays of gaucho riding skills and even horses trained to dance the tango.
August	Pachamama, a pre-Columbian rite celebrating Mother Earth, is celebrated on August 1 in Humahuaca and other towns in Jujuy Province.
	On August 22, Jujuy celebrates the Semana de Jujuy (Jujuy Week) with a reenactment of the great 1812 exodus: citizens dress in period costumes and ride their horses or carts through town; hotels are usually booked up during this week.
	The Fiesta Nacional de la Nieve (National Snow Festival) is a month-long winter carnival that takes place in August all over Bariloche and at the Catedral ski area.
FALL September	One of Trelew's major cultural events is the Eisteddfod de la Juventud in early September, which celebrates the music, food, and dance of Welsh tradition.
	During Bariloche's Semana Musical Llao Llao (Llao Llao Musical Week) in September, international soloists and orchestras perform classical, jazz, and tango music at the Llao Llao Hotel & Resort.
October	The Festival Nacional de la Cerveza (National Beer Festival, or Oktoberfest) takes place in the town of Villa General Belgrano, in Córdoba Province, which was originally settled by Bavarian and Alsatian immigrants.
	The second half of October marks Trelew's Eisteddfod de Chubut, a Welsh literary and musical festival, first held in Patagonia in 1875.
November	In mid-November, San Antonio de Areco hosts the weeklong Fiesta de la Tradición, a celebration of the area's gaucho past. Lesser celebrations are held at Buenos Aires's Feria de Mataderos market.
	Some of the world's best polo players and the snooty jet set gather every year for chukkas and sundowners at the Abierto Argentino de Polo, played out on the hallowed turfs of the Argentine Polo fields in Buenos Aires.

SMART TRAVEL TIPS

AIR TRAVEL

If your national airline doesn't fly directly into Buenos Aires, it's possible to fly into Brazil or Chile and take a two- to three-hour flight on Aerolíneas Argentinas into Ezeiza, Argentina's international airport, 42 km (26 mi) from central Buenos Aires. To go elsewhere in the country, you will have to fly out of Jorge Newbery Airport (aka *Aeroparque*), about 15 minutes from downtown. This often requires an overnight stay in Buenos Aires.

Aerolíneas Argentinas, Air Canada, American Airlines, Delta, LAN Chile, and Varig are the major carriers from the United States and Canada—they all have daily flights to Argentina. Miami and New York are the primary departure points, as well as Atlanta (Delta), Toronto (Air Canada), and Washington, D.C. (United). Passengers from Vancouver, Seattle, San Francisco, and Los Angeles have the option of flying LAN Chile Airlines from Los Angeles to Buenos Aires via Santiago, Chile. This flight stops in Lima, and the actual flying time to Buenos Aires is not much different from flying via Miami. Air Canada from Toronto also stops in Santiago. Varig flies to Buenos Aires from Los Angeles via São Paulo, Brazil. Other airlines flying from Los Angeles go through Miami or Dallas.

LAN Chile has direct flights from Santiago to the Argentine cities of Mendoza, Cordoba, Bariloche, and Ushuaia, thus avoiding the airport transfer (and probable overnight) in Buenos Aires.

From London, United and American fly via Miami, Varig via São Paulo, and Aerolíneas Argentinas via Madrid. Aerolíneas Argentinas has a 19-hour flight from Sydney, Australia, to Buenos Aires, stopping in Auckland, New Zealand, and Ushuaia in southern Argentina.

Major destinations within Argentina are often far apart, and although overland transportation can be more economical, it is much slower. You'll save a lot of time and energy traveling by air. Aerolíneas Argentinas/Austral is the major domestic carrier.

BOOKING

When you book, look for nonstop flights and remember that "direct" flights stop at least once. Try to avoid connecting flights, which require a change of plane. Two airlines may operate a connecting flight jointly, so ask whether your airline operates every segment of the trip; you may find that the carrier you prefer flies you only part of the way. To find more booking tips and to check flight reservations and make online flight reservations, log on to www.fodors.com.

To & from Argentina Aerolíneas Argentinas ☎ 800/333-0276 in U.S., 0/810-2228-6527 in Buenos Aires ⊕ www.aerolineas.com.ar. **Air Canada** ☎ 888/247-2262 in U.S. and Canada, 11/4327-3640 in Buenos Aires ⊕ www.aircanada.com. **American Airlines** ☎ 800/433-7300 in U.S., 0345/789789 in the U.K., 11/4318-1111 in Buenos Aires ⊕ www.aa.com. **British Airways** ☎ 0345/222111 in the U.K., 11/4320-6600 in Buenos Aires ⊕ www.britishairways.com. **Delta** ☎ 800/241-4141 in U.S., 800/221-1212 in Canada, 11/4894-8170 in Buenos Aires ⊕ www.delta.com. **LAN Chile Airlines** ☎ 866/435-9526 in U.S, 306/670-9999, 11/4378-2200 in Buenos Aires. ⊕ www.lan.com. **United Airlines** ☎ 800/538-2929 in U.S., 11/4316-0777 in Buenos Aires ⊕ www.united.com. **Varig Airlines** ☎ 800/468-2744 in U.S., 11/4329-9211 in Buenos Aires ⊕ www.varig.com.

Within Argentina Aerolíneas Argentinas ☎ 800/333-0276 in U.S., 0/810-2228-6527 in Buenos Aires ⊕ www.aerolineas.com.ar. **Austral** ☎ 11/4340-7800 in Buenos Aires ⊕ www.austral.com.ar.

CHECK-IN & BOARDING

Airports in Argentina are mostly small and easy to get around. Security is not as stringent as in the USA—computers stay in cases, shoes stay on your feet, and there are no random searches. Air travel is expensive for Argentines, so airports are less crowded.

Always find out your carrier's check-in policy. Plan to arrive at the airport about two hours before your scheduled departure time for domestic flights and 2½ to 3 hours before international flights. You may need to arrive earlier if you're flying from one of the busier airports or during peak air-traffic times. To avoid delays at airport-security checkpoints, try not to wear any metal. Jewelry, belt and other buckles, steel-toe shoes, barrettes, and underwire bras are among the items that can set off detectors.

CUTTING COSTS

It's smart to call a number of airlines and check the Internet; when you are quoted a good price, book it on the spot—the same fare may not be available the next day, or even the next hour. Always check different routings and look into using alternate airports. Also, price off-peak flights and red-eye, which may be significantly less expensive than others. Travel agents, especially low-fare specialists (⇨ Discounts & Deals), are helpful.

Consolidators are another good source. They buy tickets for scheduled flights at reduced rates from the airlines, then sell them at prices that beat the best fare available directly from the airlines. (Many also offer reduced car-rental and hotel rates.) Sometimes you can even get your money back if you need to return the ticket. Carefully read the fine print detailing penalties for changes and cancellations, purchase the ticket with a credit card, and confirm your consolidator reservation with the airline.

Many airlines, singly or in collaboration, offer discount air passes that allow foreigners to travel economically in a particular country or region. These visitor passes usually must be reserved and purchased before you leave home. Information about passes often can be found on most airlines' international Web pages, which tend to be aimed at travelers from outside the carrier's home country. Also, try typing the name of the pass into a search engine, or search for "pass" within the carrier's Web site.

Consolidators AirlineConsolidator.com ☎ 888/468-5385 ⊕ www.airlineconsolidator.com; for international tickets. **Best Fares** ☎ 800/880-1234 ⊕ www.bestfares.com; $59.90 annual membership. **Cheap Tickets** ☎ 800/377-1000 or 800/652-4327 ⊕ www.cheaptickets.com. **Expedia** ☎ 800/397-3342 or 404/728-8787 ⊕ www.expedia.com. **Hotwire** ☎ 866/468-9473 or 920/330-9418 ⊕ www.hotwire.com. **Now Voyager Travel** ☎ 212/459-1616 ⊕ www.nowvoyagertravel.com. **Onetravel.com** ⊕ www.onetravel.com. **Orbitz** ☎ 888/656-4546 ⊕ www.orbitz.com. **Priceline.com** ⊕ www.priceline.com. **Travelocity** ☎ 888/709-5983, 877/

282-2925 in Canada, 0870/111-7061 in the U.K. ⊕ www.travelocity.com.

DISCOUNT PASSES

You can save money on regional flights if you purchase your tickets in Argentina. (Note that if you're traveling during holidays or peak times you should always buy your tickets in advance.)

For travel between multiple destinations within Argentina, consider a **Visit Argentina Pass** offered by Aerolíneas Argentinas. This pass can only be purchased in your home country, not in Argentina. You'll get a bigger discount if you purchase the pass in conjunction with a full-fare international Aerolíneas Argentinas ticket. You can change the dates you fly as needed, but once you pick a route, you have to stick to it.

For multiple destinations within South America, Aerolíneas Argentinas offers a **South America Pass,** which can be used by passengers visiting two to five countries and includes two stopovers in Argentina.

For current information, contact Aerolíneas Argentinas or visit ⊕ www. aerolineas.comand select *US* and *Special Offers*

FLYING TIMES

Flying times to Buenos Aires are 11–12 hours from New York, 10 hours from Atlanta, 9 hours from Miami, and 13 hours from Chicago. Flights from Los Angeles routed through Lima, Miami, Dallas, or Washington, D.C., are 16–17 hours, and 16 hours via São Paolo, Brazil. Canadians can fly from Vancouver on Air Canada, connecting with Lan Chile in Santiago; the total trip to Buenos Aires takes 19 hours. Flights from Montreal and Toronto are 13–14 hours. The shortest flights from London are 16 hours, on British Airways, Air France, Iberia, or Varig. In 19 hours you can fly the polar route from Sydney, Australia.

HOW TO COMPLAIN

If your baggage goes astray or your flight goes awry, complain right away. Most carriers require that you file a claim immediately. The Aviation Consumer Protection Division of the Department of Transportation publishes *Fly-Rights,* which discusses airlines and consumer issues and is available online. You can also find articles and information on mytravelrights.com, the Web site of the nonprofit Consumer Travel Rights Center.

🔳 **Airline Complaints** Aviation Consumer Protection Division ☎ 202/366-2220 ⊕ airconsumer.ost.dot.gov. **Federal Aviation Administration Consumer Hotline** ☎ 800/322-7873 ⊕ www.faa.gov.

AIRPORTS

The major gateway to Argentina is Buenos Aires's Ezeiza International Airport (EZE), 47 km (29 mi) and a 45-minute drive from the city center. Ezeiza, also known as Aeropuerto Internacional Ministro Pistarini, is served by a variety of foreign airlines, along with domestic airlines running international routes. Though Argentina has other international airports, they generally only serve flights from other South American countries. You can fly directly to some cities from Santiago, Chile (⇨ Air Travel, *above*). Flights from Buenos Aires to other points within Argentina depart from the Aeroparque Jorge Newbery (AEP), a 15-minute cab ride from downtown. On leaving Argentina, Bariloche and Igazú are the only airports from which you can fly directly to Ezeiza, thus avoiding the airport transfer in Buenos Aires.

🔳 **Airport Information** Aeroparque Jorge Newbery AEP ☎ 11/4130-4100. Ezeiza Airport EZE ☎ 11/5480-6111 ⊕ www.aa2000.com.ar.

BOAT & FERRY TRAVEL

Buquebus provides frequent ferry service between Argentina and Uruguay and has several packages and promotions. Round-trip rates for economy travel range 100–300 pesos from Buenos Aires to the cities of Colonia, La Paloma, Montevideo, Piriápolis, and Punta del Este, all in Uruguay. All destinations, except Colonia, include bus transfers; the duration of the trip varies from 45 minutes to around 3 hours. You can order tickets by phone or on the Web site.

The more modest Ferry Lineas Argentina also serves the Buenos Aires–Uruguay route on a smaller scale with fewer boats per day; they sometimes work in conjunction with Buquebus.

🚢 **Boat & Ferry Information Buquebus** ✉ Antártida Argentina 821, at Av. Córdoba, Buenos Aires ✉ Patio Bullrich in Unicenter [Martínez] shopping mall, Buenos Aires ☎ 11/4316-6550 ⊕ www. buquebus.com. **Ferry Lineas** ✉ Maipú 866, Buenos Aires ☎ 11/4311-2300 ⊕ www.ferrylineas.com.uy.

BUSINESS HOURS

BANKS & OFFICES

Official business hours are weekdays 9–noon and 2–7 for offices and 9–3 for banks; some currency exchange offices remain open until 7 PM. Offices in larger cities remain open all day.

GAS STATIONS

Most gas stations in cities are open 24 hours.

MUSEUMS & SIGHTS

Museums are usually closed on Tuesday. Many close for one month during the summer. In small towns and more rural areas, museums may close for lunch.

PHARMACIES

Pharmacies, marked by a green cross, are open 8–1 and 2–9 in all of Argentina. In Buenos Aires and large cities, they remain open during lunchtime. *Farmácias de turno* take turns providing 24-hour service for prescriptions and emergency supplies. Your hotel will know which one is open and if they deliver.

POST OFFICES & TELEPHONE CENTERS

Post offices are open weekdays from 9 to 8 and Saturday 9–1. Telephone centers generally stay open daily 8–8.

SHOPS

In Buenos Aires street shops are open weekdays 10–8 to compete with the malls, which remain open until 10 daily. On Saturday, street shops remain open until 1 PM, and almost all are closed Sunday. In the provinces, store hours are weekdays 9–noon and 2–7. The larger, more modern supermarket chains are open daily until 9.

BUS TRAVEL

Frequent and dependable bus service links Buenos Aires to towns and cities in all of the provinces of the country, as well as to neighboring countries. With airline prices out of reach for many Argentines, long-distance bus travel has become the conveyance of choice. Snack bars, toilets, videos, air-conditioning, attendants, meal service, and seats that recline into beds have raised the bar on bus travel. Smoking is not allowed. For short trips, it's a good idea to bring your own food and beverages, though *paradas* (food stops) are made en route, and some companies have snack bars or catering services on board. Travel light, dress comfortably, and keep an eye on your belongings. Keep in mind that when crossing the border you will need to present your passport and visa at customs and immigration checkpoints.

Buenos Aires's **Estación Terminal de Omnibus** in the Retiro district is the gateway for bus travel to bordering countries and within Argentina. Within the four levels of this modern center, you will find restrooms, restaurants, banks, a tourist office, public telephones, lockers, and ticket sales (*boleterías*) (third level). Stands arranged in order by the destinations served, allow for easy price comparison. *See* individual chapters' A to Z sections for information about local bus stations. For information on the bus terminal and which company goes where, see ⊕ www. tebasa.com.ar. Click on the red circle to open, then click on the province you wish to visit—or select *buscar* (look for) and select your destination from the dropdown list which gives names of bus companies, their telephone numbers, and location of ticket booths.

CLASSES

Two types of buses, *común* and *diferencial,* are the most common. On común buses, the cheaper option, there may not be air-conditioning or heating. Diferencial, only marginally more expensive, usually have reclining seats (some even have *coche-camas,* bedlike seats), an attendant, snacks, and videos. To get between neighboring towns, you can generally get a local city bus ("*collectivos*"). For overnight trips, sleeper buses offer full reclining beds.

PAYING

Tickets can be purchased at bus terminals right up until departure time. Note that in larger cities there may be different terminals for buses to different destinations. Arrive early to get a ticket, and be prepared to pay cash. On holidays, buy your ticket as far in advance as possible and arrive at the station extra early.

RESERVATIONS

Bus lines generally don't accept reservations for short trips, but you can purchase your tickets in advance at the terminal. Usually, there are no assigned seats, so arrive well in advance of boarding time, especially on weekends and holidays, if you have your heart set on a window seat. You can purchase tickets over the phone with a credit card. Andesmar and Via Bariloche are the only companies that allow online reservations.

🚍 **Bus Information Estación Terminal de Omnibus** ✉ **Antártida Argentina and Calle 10, Buenos Aires** ☎ 11/4310-0700 ⊕ www.tebasa.com.ar. **Andesmar** ☎ 11/4313-3650 ⊕ www.andesmar.com. **El Rapido** ☎ 11/4313-3757 ⊕ www.elrapidoint.com.ar. **La Veloz del Norte** ☎ 11/4315-2482 ⊕ www.lavelozcallcenter.com.ar. **T.A.C.** ☎ 11/4312-7012. **Via Bariloche** ☎ 11/4315-7700 ⊕ www.viabariloche.com.

CAR RENTAL

Renting a car in Argentina is expensive (around US$65 per day plus tax for a midsize car). Extras such as car seats drive the fee even higher. Ask about special rates; a better price can usually be negotiated. Keep in mind that almost all cars have manual transmission, so if you need an automatic, be sure to request it in advance.

All cities and most areas that attract tourists have car-rental agencies. You can also rent cars at airports and through some hotels. If the rental agency has a branch in another town, arrangements can usually be made for a one-way drop off. Offices in Buenos Aires can make reservations in other locations; provincial government tourist offices also have information on car-rental agencies.

Europcar in Buenos Aires has good rates that are even lower if you fly on Aerolíneas Argentinas. Cell phone and laptop rentals are optional add-ons.

An alternative to renting a car is to hire a *remis,* a car with a driver, especially for day outings. Hotels can make arrangements for you. Remises are more comfortable and cheaper than taxis for long rides. You'll have to pay cash, but you'll often spend less than you would on a rental car. In cities, remises cost about 25–30 pesos per hour; sometimes there's a three-hour minimum and an additional charge per kilometer when you go outside city limits. In smaller towns, the rate is often much less (perhaps 20–25 pesos for the entire day). Some local car agencies offer chauffeur-driven rentals as well. Refer to individual chapters for more information on hiring remises.

🚗 **Major Agencies Avis** ☎ 800/331-1084 in the U.S., 800/879-2847 in Canada, 0870/606-0100 in the U.K., 11/4130-0130 in Buenos Aires ⊕ www.avis.com. **Dollar** ☎ 800/800-6000, 0800/085-4578 in the U.K., 11/4315-8800 in Buenos Aires ⊕ www.dollar.com. **Europcar** ✉ Maipú 965, Buenos Aires ☎ 11/4311-1000 ⊕ www.europcar.com.ar. **Hertz** ☎ 800/654-3001, 800/263-0600 in Canada, 0870/844-8844 in the U.K., 11/4129-7777 in Buenos Aires ⊕ www.hertz.com. **National Car Rental** ☎ 800/227-7368, 11/4811-6903 in Buenos Aires ⊕ www.nationalcar.com.

🚗 **Local Agencies ABC Rent a Car** ✉ Embassy Gallery, Marcelo T. de Alvear 628, Buenos Aires ☎🚗 11/4315-0313 ⊕ www.abc-car.com.ar. **AI International** ✉ Marcelo T. de Alvear 678 ☎ 11/4311-1000 or 11/4313-1515 ⊕ www.airentacar.com.ar. **Localiza** ✉ 1126 Rivadavia, Buenos Aires ☎ 800/999-2999, 11/4382-9267 in Buenos Aires ⊕ www.localiza.com.ar.

INSURANCE

When driving a rented car you are generally responsible for any damage to or loss of the vehicle. You also may be liable for any property damage or personal injury that you may cause while driving. Before you rent, see what coverage you already have under the terms of your personal auto-insurance policy and credit cards.

REQUIREMENTS & RESTRICTIONS

Your own driver's license may be valid in Argentina, though you may want to take out an International Driver's Permit; contact your local automobile association (⇨ Auto Clubs *in* Car Travel). These international permits, valid only in conjunction with your regular driver's license, are universally recognized; having one may save you a problem with local authorities. The minimum driving age is 18. You'll need to present a major credit card at the agency counter in order to rent a car.

SURCHARGES

Before you pick up a car in one city and leave it in another, ask about drop-off charges or one-way service fees, which can be substantial. Also inquire about early-return policies; some rental agencies charge extra if you return the car before the time specified in your contract while others give you a refund for the days not used. Most agencies note the tank's fuel level on your contract; to avoid a hefty refueling fee, return the car with the same tank level. If the tank was full, refill it just before you turn in the car, but be aware that gas stations near the rental outlet may overcharge. It's almost never a deal to buy a tank of gas with the car when you rent it; the understanding is that you'll return it empty, but some fuel usually remains. Note that airport rental agencies may charge an airport concession fee of 10%.

CAR TRAVEL

AUTO CLUBS

The Automóvil Club Argentino (ACA) provides complete mechanical assistance, including towing, detailed maps and driver's manuals, and expert advice (often in English). The ACA can help chart your itinerary, give you gas coupons, and even set you up with discounted accommodations in affiliated hotels and campgrounds. Present your own auto-club membership card to enjoy these benefits. Note that ACA service is also available at many of the YPF service stations throughout Argentina.

7 **American Automobile Association (AAA)** ☎ 800/564-6222 ⊕ www.aaa.com. **Automobile Association (AA)** ☎ 0870/550-0600 in the U.K. **Automóvil Club Argentino (ACA)** ☎ 11/4802-6061 ⊕ www.aca.org.ar. **Canadian Automobile Association (CAA)** ☎ 613/247-0117 ⊕ www.caa.ca. **Royal Automobile Club (RAC)** ☎ 0870/572-2722 ⊕ www.rac.co.uk.

GASOLINE

You'll find Esso, Shell, and national YPF service stations throughout Buenos Aires, in the provinces, and along major highways. The stations usually include full service, convenience stores, snack bars, and ATMs. In rural areas, gas stations are few and far between and have reduced hours; when traveling in the countryside, it's a good idea to start looking for a station when your tank is half empty.

Gas is expensive (around 1.50 pesos per liter, or about 6 pesos per gallon) and may run you 80 pesos to fill a midsize car. There are several grades of unleaded fuels, as well as diesel.

INTERNATIONAL TRAVEL

Paved highways run from Argentina to the Chilean, Bolivian, Paraguayan, and Brazilian borders. If you do cross the border by land you'll be required to present your passport, visa, and documentation of car ownership at immigration and customs checkpoints. It's also common for cars and bags to be searched for contraband, such as food, livestock, and drugs.

ROAD CONDITIONS

City streets throughout Argentina are notorious for potholes, and lanes are generally poorly marked and flagrantly ignored by local drivers. Ultramodern multilane highways connect the major cities, and more are being built and improved throughout the country. You must pay tolls on many highways, and even on some unpaved roads. Tolls come frequently and can be steep (one toll, for instance, on the five-hour drive between Buenos Aires and Mar del Plata, is around 13 pesos).

As you travel farther into the countryside, highways become narrow county routes that are not divided, and often not in particularly good condition. Street signs are often hard to see and sometimes nonexistent.

Night driving can be hazardous: some highways and routes are poorly lit, routes sometimes cut through the center of towns, cattle often get onto the roads, and in rural areas *rastreros* (old farm trucks) seldom have all their lights working. Beware of *guardeganado*s (cattle guards). They are often raised so that your car flies into the air if speeding. For highway-condition reports, updated daily, and basic routes in Spanish, contact La Dirección Nacional de Vialidad.

F **La Dirección Nacional de Vialidad** ☏ 0800/ 333-0073 ⊕ www.vialidad.gov.ar.

RULES OF THE ROAD

Don't drive after dark. Obey speed limits (marked in kilometers per hour) and traffic regulations. If you do get a traffic ticket, don't argue. Although you'll see Argentines offering cash on the spot to avoid getting a written ticket, this isn't a good idea.

Seat belts are required by law, as are car lights at daytime on highways. The use of cellular phones while driving is forbidden, and turning left on two-way avenues is prohibited unless there's a left-turn signal; likewise, there are no right turns on red. Traffic lights turn yellow before they turn red, but also before turning green, which is interpreted by drivers as an extra margin to get through the intersection, so take precautions.

In Buenos Aires, drivers in general, and buses and taxis (which cruise slowly on the right-hand side to pick up passengers), often drive as though they have priority, and it's a good idea to defer to them for your own safety. If you experience a small accident, jot down the other driver's information and supply your own. A police officer will not assist you; you must go down to the police station in the area to file a report. Contact your rental agency immediately.

In towns and cities, a 40-kph (25-mph) speed limit applies on streets, and a 60-kph (37-mph) limit is in effect on avenues. On expressways the limit is 100 kph (62 mph), and on other roads and highways out of town it's 80 kph (50 mph). These limits are enforced by strategically placed cameras triggered by excessive speed.

COMPUTERS

Internet access is inexpensive or free in most hotels throughout the country—either in your room, on a lobby computer or in a business office. High-speed or wireless connections can be found in major cities, less so the farther you go into the countryside. Internet cafés are popular and plentiful, and many *locutorios* (telephone centers) offer high-speed Internet and full business services. If you've brought your own laptop or palm pilot, you can access **Arnet Wi-Fi** through Telecom (Argentina's telephone company) in hotel lobbies, libraries, cafés, bars, business and event centers, some airports, and any public Wi-Fi zones. Look for the little black-and-white **WiFi** logo. At Ezeiza and Aeroparque airports, Arnet has kiosks where you can buy a card for 30 pesos that gives you 24 hours of Internet access, or you can sign up for a month's service.

F **Arnet Wi-Fi** ☏ 800/888-27638 ⊕ www.arnet. com.ar/wifi.

CUSTOMS & DUTIES

When shopping abroad, keep receipts for all purchases. Upon reentering the country, be ready to show customs officials what you've bought. Pack purchases together in an easily accessible place. If you think a duty is incorrect, appeal the assessment. If you object to the way your clearance was handled, note the inspector's badge number. In either case, first ask to see a supervisor. If the problem isn't resolved, write to the appropriate authorities, beginning with the port director at your point of entry.

IN ARGENTINA

Upon arriving in Buenos Aires by air or ship, you'll find that customs officials usually wave you through without close inspection. International airports have introduced a customs system for those with "nothing to declare," which has streamlined the arrival process. If you enter the country by bus, take the time to have the border officials do a proper inspection of your belongings and documents. This could prevent problems later when you are trying to leave the country.

Personal clothing and effects are admitted duty-free, provided they have been used, as are personal jewelry and professional equipment. Fishing gear presents no problems. Up to 2 liters of alcoholic beverages,

400 cigarettes, and 50 cigars are admitted duty-free.

IN CANADA

Canadian residents who have been out of Canada for at least seven days may bring in C$750 worth of goods duty-free. If you've been away fewer than seven days but more than 48 hours, the duty-free allowance drops to C$200. If your trip lasts 24 to 48 hours, the allowance is C$50; if the goods are worth more than C$50, you must pay full duty on all of the goods. You may not pool allowances with family members. Goods claimed under the C$750 exemption may follow you by mail; those claimed under the lesser exemptions must accompany you. Alcohol and tobacco products may be included in the seven-day and 48-hour exemptions but not in the 24-hour exemption. If you meet the age requirements of the province or territory through which you reenter Canada, you may bring in, duty-free, 1.5 liters of wine *or* 1.14 liters (40 imperial ounces) of liquor *or* 24 12-ounce cans or bottles of beer or ale. Also, if you meet the local age requirement for tobacco products, you may bring in, duty-free, 200 cigarettes, 50 cigars or cigarillos, and 200 grams of tobacco. You may have to pay a minimum duty on tobacco products, regardless of whether or not you exceed your personal exemption. Check ahead of time with the Canada Border Services Agency or the Department of Agriculture for policies regarding meat products, seeds, plants, and fruits.

You may send an unlimited number of gifts (only one gift per recipient, however) worth up to C$60 each duty-free to Canada. Label the package UNSOLICITED GIFT—VALUE UNDER $60. Alcohol and tobacco are excluded.

🇨🇦 **Canada Border Services Agency** ☎ 800/461-9999 in Canada, 204/983-3500, 506/636-5064 ⊕ www.cbsa.gc.ca.

IN THE U.K.

From countries outside the European Union, including Argentina, you may bring home, duty-free, 200 cigarettes, 50 cigars, 100 cigarillos, or 250 grams of tobacco; 1 liter of spirits or 2 liters of fortified or sparkling wine or liqueurs; 2 liters of still table wine; 60 ml of perfume; plus £145 worth of other goods, including gifts and souvenirs. Prohibited items include meat and dairy products, seeds, plants, and fruits.

🇬🇧 **HM Customs and Excise** ☎ 0845/010-9000 or 0208/929-0152 advice service, 0208/929-6731 or 0208/910-3602 complaints ⊕ www.hmce.gov.uk.

IN THE U.S.

U.S. residents who have been out of the country for at least 48 hours may bring home, for personal use, $800 worth of foreign goods duty-free, as long as they haven't used the $800 allowance or any part of it in the past 30 days. This exemption may include 1 liter of alcohol (for travelers 21 and older), 200 cigarettes, and 100 non-Cuban cigars. Family members from the same household who are traveling together may pool their $800 personal exemptions. For fewer than 48 hours, the duty-free allowance drops to $200, which may include 50 cigarettes, 10 non-Cuban cigars, and 150 ml of alcohol (or 150 ml of perfume containing alcohol). The $200 allowance cannot be combined with other individuals' exemptions, and if you exceed it, the full value of all the goods will be taxed. Antiques, which U.S. Customs and Border Protection defines as objects more than 100 years old, enter duty-free, as do original works of art done entirely by hand, including paintings, drawings, and sculptures. This doesn't apply to folk art or handicrafts, which are in general dutiable.

You may also send packages home duty-free, with a limit of one parcel per addressee per day (except alcohol or tobacco products or perfume worth more than $5). You can mail up to $200 worth of goods for personal use; label the package PERSONAL USE and attach a list of its contents and their retail value. If the package contains your used personal belongings, mark it AMERICAN GOODS RETURNED to avoid paying duties. You may send up to $100 worth of goods as a gift; mark the package UNSOLICITED GIFT. Mailed items do not affect your duty-free allowance on your return.

To avoid paying duty on foreign-made high-ticket items you already own and will take on your trip, register them with a local customs office before you leave the country. Consider filing a Certificate of Registration for laptops, cameras, watches, and other digital devices identified with serial numbers or other permanent markings; you can keep the certificate for other trips. Otherwise, bring a sales receipt or insurance form to show that you owned the item before you left the United States.

For more about duties, restricted items, and other information about international travel, check out U.S. Customs and Border Protection's online brochure, *Know Before You Go*. You can also file complaints on the U.S. Customs and Border Protection Web site, listed below.

U.S. Customs and Border Protection ⊕ www.cbp.gov ☎ 877/227-5551, 202/354-1000.

DISCOUNTS & DEALS

Be a smart shopper and compare all your options before making decisions. A plane ticket bought with a promotional coupon from travel clubs, coupon books, and direct-mail offers or purchased on the Internet may not be cheaper than the least expensive fare from a discount ticket agency. And always keep in mind that what you get is just as important as what you save.

Note that most museums are free one morning or afternoon per week and movies are half price on Wednesday and for matinees.

DISCOUNT RESERVATIONS

To save money, look into discount reservations services with Web sites and toll-free numbers, which use their buying power to get a better price on hotels, airline tickets (⇨ Air Travel), even car rentals. When booking a room, always call the hotel's local toll-free number (if one is available) rather than the central reservations number—you'll often get a better price. Always ask about special packages or corporate rates. When shopping for the best deal on hotels and car rentals, look for guaranteed exchange rates, which protect you against a falling dollar. With your rate locked in, you won't pay more, even if the price goes up in the local currency.

The Automóvil Club Argentino (ACA) recognizes your auto-club card for discounts on gas within Argentina (⇨ Auto Clubs *in* Car Travel).

Hotel Rooms Accommodations Express ☎ 800/444-7666 or 800/277-1064. **Hotels.com** ☎ 800/246-8357 ⊕ www.hotels.com. **Steigenberger Reservation Service** ☎ 800/223-5652 ⊕ www.srs-worldhotels.com. **Turbotrip.com** ☎ 800/473-7829 ⊕ w3.turbotrip.com.

PACKAGE DEALS

Don't confuse packages and guided tours. When you buy a package, you travel on your own, just as though you had planned the trip yourself. Fly/drive packages, which combine airfare and car rental, are often a good deal. In cities, ask the local visitor's bureau about hotel and local transportation packages that include tickets to major museum exhibits or other special events.

EATING & DRINKING

The restaurants we list are the cream of the crop in each price category. Properties indicated by a ✕🏠 are lodging establishments whose restaurant warrants a special trip. See individual chapters for price charts.

MEALS & SPECIALTIES

Argentina is known for its quality beef, which has always been a big part of its cuisine and culture. The *asado* (barbecue) refers both to the grilling of beef, lamb or goat and to the event itself. If you are invited to an asado at an *estancia* (ranch) or restaurant, be prepared for abundant servings of various beef cuts, tripe, sweetbreads, kidney, chorizos, and empanadas. A *parrilla* is not only the grill upon which meats are cooked but also a restaurant serving grilled meat and chicken as a main attraction. Robust Argentine *tintos* (red wines) are excellent accompaniments, as are the white varietals; smaller ¼ bottles (*media-botello*) can be ordered.

Argentina's strong Italian heritage manifests itself in the cuisine; you'll find delicious pastas served with a variety of sauces, crusty pizzas, polenta, and creamy *helados* (ice cream).

Mate is a strong tea-like beverage drunk in Argentina as well as Uruguay, Paraguay, and southern Brazil. The word *mate* derives from the native Quechua for "drinking vessel"; the tea is served in a carved-out gourd and is sipped through a metal *bombilla* (filter-straw).

MEALTIMES

Breakfast is usually served until 11 AM; lunch runs from 12:30 to 3:30; dinner is from 8 to around midnight. Several restaurants in Buenos Aires and other large cities stay open all night, or at least well into the morning, catering to the after-theater and nightclub crowd. Unless otherwise noted, the restaurants listed in this guide are open daily for lunch and dinner.

RESERVATIONS & DRESS

Reservations are always a good idea; we mention them only when they're essential or not accepted. Book as far ahead as you can, and reconfirm as soon as you arrive. (Large parties should always call ahead to check the reservations policy.) We mention dress only when men are required to wear a jacket or a jacket and tie. Even when it's not required, you may want to wear a jacket and tie or dress up for evening dining at the formal restaurants in the top price category; casual-chic or informal dress is fine for most other restaurants.

ELECTRICITY

The electrical current in Argentina is 220 volts, 50 cycles alternating current (AC); wall outlets usually take Continental-type plugs, with two round prongs, though newer hotels are moving to plugs with three flat, angled prongs. To use electric-powered equipment purchased in the United States or Canada, bring a converter and adapter; some high-end accommodations provide these, but you're better off bringing them if you're unsure.

If your appliances are dual-voltage, you'll need only an adapter. Don't use 110-volt outlets marked FOR SHAVERS ONLY for high-wattage appliances such as blow-dryers. Most laptops operate equally well on 110 and 220 volts and only require an adapter. Power outages can happen anywhere, so it's a good idea to unplug your laptop when leaving your hotel for the day.

EMBASSIES

American Embassy ⊠ Colombia 4300, Buenos Aires ☎ 11/5777–4533 ⊕ www.usembassy.state.gov. **British Embassy** ⊠ Luis Agote 2412 ☎ 11/4803–7799 or 11/4576–2222, 15/5331–7129 for an emergency ⊕ www.britain.org.ar. **Canadian Embassy** ⊠ Tagle 2828 ☎ 11/4808–1000 ⊕ www.dfait-maeci.gc.ca/argentina.

EMERGENCIES

Emergency numbers are the same nationwide, so wherever you find yourself you can call the numbers below to be connected to a local emergency unit.

Ambulance & Medical ☎ 107. **Fire** ☎ 100. **Police** ☎ 111 or 4346–5770.

ETIQUETTE & BEHAVIOR

Argentines are very warm and affectionate people, and the way they greet each other reflects this. The customary greeting between both friends and strangers is one kiss on the right cheek. This is done by both men and women. If you don't feel comfortable kissing a stranger, a simple handshake will suffice.

When arriving at parties, Argentines will often have something in hand to offer the hosts: a bottle of wine or a cake or other goodies, but there is certainly no rule about giving gifts. When you leave a party it's normal to say good-bye to everyone in the room (or, if you're in a restaurant, to everyone at your table), which means kissing everyone once again. Argentines are never in a hurry to get anywhere, so a formal good-bye can certainly take awhile.

Smoking is very common in Argentina, so be prepared for some smoke with your steak. Most restaurants offer nonsmoking sections (*sin fumar*), but make sure to ask before you are seated. If you are at a dinner party, don't be surprised if the room fills up with smoke right after the main course; if it bothers you, you should excuse yourself—don't ask others to smoke outside.

BUSINESS ETIQUETTE

Arriving late for social occasions may be normal and acceptable among Argentines, but arriving late for a business appointment is not. Business cards are always appreciated.

Traditionally, Argentines don't like to discuss business during a meal. However, since many hours of the day are spent eating, this tradition seems to be fading slowly—at least for the new generation of businesspeople. There are occasions when spouses (particularly women) are not included in a dinner; to avoid embarrassment for all involved, ask if you can bring your spouse along. At a typical business dinner, the flow of conversation is much like it is in the U.S.—discussing common interests such as sports, hobbies, family, travel, and even politics are all part of the ritual of getting to know and trust an individual. Professionals, especially men, dress conservatively for business events, and women like to dress up.

Note that asking someone what they do for a living is almost the same as asking how much money they make.

HEALTH

ALTITUDE SICKNESS

Soroche, or altitude sickness, which results in shortness of breath and headaches, may be a problem when you visit high altitudes in the Andes. To remedy any discomfort, walk slowly, eat lightly, and drink plenty of fluids (avoid alcohol). If you have high blood pressure or a history of heart trouble, check with your doctor before traveling to high elevations. If you experience an extended period of nausea, dehydration, dizziness, or severe headache or weakness while in a high-altitude area, seek medical attention.

FOOD & DRINK

Buenos Aires residents drink tap water and eat uncooked fruits and vegetables. However, if you've got just a week, you don't want to waste a minute of it in your hotel room. It's best to drink bottled water, which can be found throughout Argentina for about 1.50 pesos for a half liter.

Each year there are cases of cholera in the northern part of Argentina, mostly in the indigenous communities near the Bolivian border; your best protection is to avoid eating raw seafood.

OVER-THE-COUNTER REMEDIES

Travelers will find familiar medicines in *farmácias* (pharmacies) and modern markets throughout the country. Aspirin (*Aspirina* aka *Geniol* is sometimes available in restaurants and kiosks. **Farmacity** is a supermarket-style drugstore chain with 69 locations in Buenos Aires. Locations and directions are available on their Web site (in Spanish) ⊕ www.farmacity.com.ar. If you think you'll need to have prescriptions filled while you're in Argentina, be sure to have your doctor write down the generic name of the drug.

PESTS & OTHER HAZARDS

Outdoor recreation at high altitudes and in all kinds of weather is an important component of travel in Argentina. Awareness and precautions for altitude sickness, heat stroke, dehydration, sunstroke, frostbite, and insect bites are the best antidotes. In southern Patagonia, the ozone layer is said to be thinning, causing severe sunburn even during short exposures, especially during October through January. Piz Buin, H Tropic, and Dermaglos are a few of the many varieties of sunscreens sold in markets and farmácias. The same SPF system applies.

OFF, sold in aerosol, cream, and spray, and Ultrathon are dependable repellants for mosquitoes and the pesky black flies found around horses and in the mountains. More repellants can be found in fly shops and some sporting goods stores in resort towns like Bariloche.

SHOTS & MEDICATIONS

No specific vaccinations are required for travel to Argentina. According to the Centers for Disease Control (CDC), however, there's a limited risk of cholera, hepatitis B, and dengue. The local malady of Chagas' disease is present in remote areas. If you plan to visit remote regions or stay for more than six weeks, check with the CDC's International Travelers Hot Line. In areas with malaria (in Argentina, you are at risk for malaria only in northern rural areas bordering Bolivia and Paraguay) and dengue, which are both carried by mosquitoes, take mosquito nets, wear clothing that covers the body, apply repellent containing DEET, and use a spray against flying insects in living and sleeping areas. The hot line recommends chloroquine (analen) as an antimalarial agent; no vaccine exists against dengue or Chagas. Children traveling to Argentina should have current inoculations against measles, mumps, rubella, and polio.

A major health risk is traveler's diarrhea, caused by eating unfamiliar foods or contaminated fruit or vegetables or drinking contaminated water. Mild cases may respond to Imodium (known generically as loperamide) or Pepto-Bismol (not as strong), both of which can be purchased over the counter; paregoric, another antidiarrheal agent, does not require a doctor's prescription in Argentina. Drink plenty of purified water or tea—chamomile is a good folk remedy. In severe cases, rehydrate yourself with a salt-sugar solution (½ teaspoon salt and 4 tablespoons sugar per quart of water). Note that many medications that require a prescription in the United States and elsewhere, including some antibiotics, are available over the counter in Argentina.

🔃 **Health Warnings National Centers for Disease Control and Prevention** (CDC) ☎ 877/394–8747 international travelers' health line, 800/311–3435 other inquiries, 404/498–1600 Division of Quarantine and international health information 🖷 888/232–3299 ⊕ www.cdc.gov/travel. **Travel Health Online** ⊕ tripprep.com. **World Health Organization** (WHO) ⊕ www.who.int.

HOLIDAYS

January through March is summer holiday season for Argentines, and the second and third weeks of July are winter school holidays.

New Year's Day; Day of the Epiphany (January 6); Veteran's Day (April 2); Labor Day (May 1); Anniversary of the 1810 Revolution (May 25); Semana Santa (Holy Week; 4 days in April leading up to Easter Sunday); National Sovereignty Day (June 10); Flag Day (June 20); Independence Day (July 9); Anniversary of San Martín's Death (August 17); Día de la Raza (Race Recognition Day) (October 12); Day of the Immaculate Conception (December 8); and Christmas. Some holidays that fall on

weekdays may be moved to Monday to create a three-day weekend. Note that all banks and most commercial and entertainment centers are closed on these days.

INSURANCE

The most useful travel-insurance plan is a comprehensive policy that includes coverage for trip cancellation and interruption, default, trip delay, and medical expenses (with a waiver for preexisting conditions). Without insurance you'll lose all or most of your money if you cancel your trip, regardless of the reason. Default insurance covers you if your tour operator, airline, or cruise line goes out of business—the chances of which have been increasing. Trip-delay covers expenses that arise because of bad weather or mechanical delays. Study the fine print when comparing policies.

If you're traveling internationally, a key component of travel insurance is coverage for medical bills incurred if you get sick on the road. Such expenses aren't generally covered by Medicare or private policies. U.K. residents can buy a travel-insurance policy valid for most vacations taken during the year in which it's purchased (but check preexisting-condition coverage). British citizens need extra medical coverage when traveling overseas.

Always buy travel policies directly from the insurance company; if you buy them from a cruise line, airline, or tour operator that goes out of business you probably won't be covered for the agency or operator's default, a major risk. Before making any purchase, review your existing health and home-owner's policies to find what they cover away from home.

🔃 **Access America** ☎ 800/284–8300 ⊕ www.accessamerica.com. **Association of British Insurers** ☎ 020/7600–3333 ⊕ www.abi.org.uk. **RBC Insurance** ☎ 800/387–4357 or 905/816–2559 in Canada ⊕ www.rbcinsurance.com. **Travel Guard International** ☎ 800/826–1300 or 715/345–1041 in the U.S. ⊕ www.travelguard.com.

LANGUAGE

Argentines speak *Castellano,* Castilian Spanish, which differs slightly from the Spanish of most other Latin American countries. For example, the informal *vos* (you) is used instead of *tu,* in conjunction with the verb *sos* (are) instead of *eres.* The double "L" found in words like *pollo* phonetically translates to the ZH-sound, rather than a Y-sound. English is considered the second most widely used language. Services geared toward tourism generally employ an English-speaking staff. It's also common to find English-speaking staff at commercial and entertainment centers.

LANGUAGE SCHOOLS

A wide selection of language courses can be found in the classifieds of Argentina's English-language daily newspaper, the *Buenos Aires Herald.* The list includes schools as well as private tutors. If you prefer to arrange for Spanish classes prior to your arrival in Argentina, try Berlitz International School of Languages, Instituto de Lengua Española para Extranjeros, Languages Abroad, or Latin Immersion, all of which specialize in teaching Spanish to foreigners and have classes beginning every week. Most of these schools arrange home stays or independent living and include cultural outings.

Berlitz International School of Languages ✉ Av. de Mayo 847, fl. 1, Buenos Aires ☎🖷 11/4342-0202 ⊕ www.berlitz.com. **Instituto de Lengua Española para Extranjeros** ✉ Av. Callao 339, fl. 3, Buenos Aires ☎🖷 11/4372-0223 ⊕ www.argentinailee.com. **Languages Abroad** ☎ 015/0921-1612 in the U.K. ⊕ www.languagesabroad.co.uk/argentina. **Latin Immersion** ☎ 866/577-8693 in the U.S. and Canada, 11/4802-0794 in Buenos Aires ⊕ www.latinimmersion.com.

LANGUAGES FOR TRAVELERS

A phrase book and language-tape set can help get you started. *Fodor's Spanish for Travelers* (available at bookstores everywhere) is excellent.

LODGING

The lodgings we list are the cream of the crop in each price category. We always list the facilities that are available—but we don't specify whether they cost extra: when pricing accommodations, always ask what's included and what costs extra. Properties marked ✕🖾 are lodging establishments whose restaurants warrant a special trip. See individual chapters for price charts.

Assume that hotels operate on the European Plan (EP, with no meals) unless we specify that they use either the Continental Plan (CP, with a Continental breakfast), Breakfast Plan (BP, with a full breakfast), Full American Plan (FAP, with all meals), or the Modified American Plan (MAP, with breakfast and dinner) or are all-inclusive (including all meals and most activities).

APARTMENT & VILLA RENTALS

If you want a home base that's roomy enough for a family and comes with cooking facilities, consider a furnished rental. Called *apart-hotels* in Argentina, these can save you money, especially if you're traveling with a group.

International Agents Hideaways International ☎ 603/430-4433 or 800/843-4433 ⊕ www.hideaways.com, annual membership $185.
Local Agents Apartments BA ☎ 646/827-8796 in the U.S., 11/5254-0100 in Buenos Aires ⊕ www.apartmentsba.com. **B&T Travel & Housing** ☎ 11/4804-1783 ⊕ www.bytargentina.com. **Buenos Aires Habitat** ☎ 305/586-7698 in the U.S., 11/4812-3296 in Buenos Aires ⊕ www.buenosaireshabitat.com.

BED & BREAKFASTS

A B&B in Argentina can be anything from an upscale hostal to a residential, posada, or small hotel. Some are new and modern, some homey and old-fashioned, some city- or country-chic. Many will serve afternoon tea or wine as part of the price. An assortment of fresh baked breads and rolls accompany homemade jams and local fruits for breakfast, plus cereals, cold cuts and cheeses. Posadas and small hotels often include lunch or dinner.

Reservation Services Reservation services are limited mostly to Buenos Aires, as everything outside of the city that isn't a hotel could be considered a B&B, and, therefore, a central reservations system would be hard to maintain. Check out ⊕ bedandbreakfast.com.ar for listings in Buenos Aires.

CAMPING

Campgrounds can be found in popular tourist destinations, including some beach areas. They usually have running water, electricity, and bathroom facilities with toilets and showers; some even provide tent rentals for spur-of-the-moment camping. Rates are generally 10–15 pesos per person per night. The Automóvil Club Argentino (⇨ Auto Clubs *in* Car Travel) can provide a list of campgrounds nationwide. Provincial tourist offices in Buenos Aires have lists of campgrounds in their regions.

ESTANCIAS

In Patagonia, the Pampas, the Northeast, and the Northwest you can stay at *estancias* (working ranches). Unique activities include horseback riding and *asados* (barbecues). They range from rustic structures to mansions, and provide a memorable experience.

HOME EXCHANGES

If you would like to exchange your home for someone else's, join a home-exchange organization, which will send you its updated listings of available exchanges for a year and will include your own listing in at least one of them. It's up to you to make specific arrangements.

🚪 **Exchange Clubs HomeLink USA** ☎ 954/566-2687 or 800/638-3841 ⊕ www.homelink.org; $75 yearly for a listing and online access; $45 additional to receive directories. **Intervac U.S.** ☎ 800/756-4663 ⊕ www.intervacus.com; $128 yearly for a listing, online access, and a catalog; $68 without catalog.

HOSTELS

No matter what your age, you can save on lodging costs by staying at hostels. In some 4,500 locations in more than 70 countries around the world, Hostelling International (HI), the umbrella group for a number of national youth-hostel associations, offers single-sex, dorm-style beds and, at many hostels, rooms for couples and family accommodations. Membership in any HI national hostel association, open to travelers of all ages, allows you to stay in HI-affiliated hostels at member rates; one-year membership is about $28 for adults (C$35 for a two-year minimum membership in Canada, £15 in the U.K., A$52 in Australia, and NZ$40 in New Zealand); hostels charge about $10–$30 per night. Members have priority if the hostel is full; they're also eligible for discounts around the world, even on rail and bus travel in some countries.

Hostels in Argentina charge about 10–25 pesos per night.

🚪 **Organizations Hostelling International–Argentina (RAAJ)** ☎ 11/4511-8712 ⊕ www.hostels.org.ar. **Hostelling International–Canada** ☎ 613/237-7884 or 800/663-5777 ⊕ www.hihostels.ca. **Hostelling International–USA** ☎ 301/495-1240 ⊕ www.hiusa.org. **YHA England and Wales** ☎ 0870/870-8808, 0870/770-8868, 0162/959-2600 ⊕ www.yha.org.uk.

HOTELS

Amenities in most nice hotels—private baths, 24-hour room service, heating and air-conditioning, cable TV, dry cleaning, minibars, and restaurants—are above average. The less expensive the hotel, the fewer amenities available, though you can still find charm, cleanliness, and hospitality. You may or may not have a television and a phone in your room, though they are usually provided somewhere in the hotel. Rooms that have a private bath may only have a shower, or in some cases, you'll share a bath in the hall. In all but the most upscale hotels, you may be asked to leave your key at the reception desk whenever you leave. Many small hotels have a curfew, so if you arrive after the reception desk closes, you may have to ring to get in. Most hotels in all categories include a Continental breakfast in the room rate, whether or not there is a full restaurant in the hotel; the pricier hotels offer buffet-style breakfasts, some at an extra charge.

🚪 **Toll-Free Numbers Best Western** ☎ 800/528-1234 ⊕ www.bestwestern.com. **Choice** ☎ 800/424-6423 ⊕ www.choicehotels.com. **Four Seasons** ☎ 800/332-3442 ⊕ www.fourseasons.com. **Hilton** ☎ 800/445-8667 ⊕ www.hilton.com. **Holiday Inn** ☎ 800/465-4329 ⊕ www.ichotelsgroup.com. **Howard Johnson** ☎ 800/446-4656 ⊕ www.hojo.com. **Hyatt Hotels & Resorts** ☎ 800/233-1234 ⊕ www.hyatt.com. **Inter-Continental** ☎ 800/327-0200 ⊕ www.ichotelsgroup.com. **Marriott** ☎ 800/228-9290 ⊕ www.marriott.com. **Ramada** ☎ 800/228-2828, 800/854-7854 international reservations ⊕ www.ramada.com or www.ramadahotels.com. **Sheraton** ☎ 800/325-3535 ⊕ www.starwood.com/sheraton.

MOTELS

Family-oriented motels can be found through the Automóvil Club Argentino (⇨ Auto Clubs *in* Car Travel). Generally these motels are inexpensive (40–50 pesos a night) and more than adequate.

You may want to avoid *albergues transitorios* (temporary lodgings), the euphemistic term for drive-in motels used for romantic trysts. They're also known as *telos*. Very common in this country where people often live with their parents until marriage, they are easily recognizable by their pink or purple neon exterior lights. Room rates are by the hour.

RESIDENCIALES

Residenciales can be either family-run pensions or bed-and-breakfasts. These are generally found in smaller towns.

MAIL & SHIPPING

Mail delivery is quite dependable and should take around 6–15 days from Buenos Aires to the United States and 10–15 days to the United Kingdom, but like many things in Argentina, this is not guaranteed. Put postcards in envelopes and they will arrive more quickly. An international airmail letter or card costs 4 pesos (up to 20 grams).

EXPRESS MAIL

Express mail is available in major cities throughout the country. It'll take 2 to 5 days for express mail to reach international destinations, but the cost can be steep (for instance, a letter to the United States via FedEx can cost upwards of $30). ⚑ **Major Services Correo Argentino** ✉ Sarmiento 151, Buenos Aires ☎ 11/4316-3000 ⊕ www.correoargentino.com.ar. **DHL** ☎ 0800/222-2345 ⊕ www.dhl.com.ar. **Federal Express** ☎ 0810/333-3339 ⊕ www.fedex.com. **UPS** ☎ 0800/2222-2877 ⊕ www.ups.com.

RECEIVING MAIL

You can receive mail in Buenos Aires at the Correo Central (Central Post Office). Letters should be addressed to your name, A/C Lista/Poste Restante, Correo Central, 1000 Capital Federal, Argentina. You will be asked to present an ID and pay 1.50 pesos for handling when recovering your mail.

American Express cardholders can have mail sent to American Express. Some embassies allow mail to be delivered to their consulate address; inquire beforehand. ⚑ **Locations American Express** ✉ c/o American Express, Arenales 707, 1061 Buenos Aires ☎ 11/4310-3000. **Buenos Aires Correo Central** ✉ Sarmiento 151, fl. 1, Buenos Aires ☎ 11/4316-3000.

SHIPPING PARCELS

Purchases or personal effects can be shipped home by any international shipping company. Allow ten days to two weeks for anything not sent by express mail.

MONEY MATTERS

If you're traveling from a country with a strong currency like the U.S. dollar or the euro, Argentina is still very inexpensive. Sumptuous dinners, in the finest restaurants, can run as high as 100 pesos per person with appetizers, wine, dessert, and tip—the equivalent of around $35. A large wood-grilled sirloin with salad, potatoes, dessert, wine, and an espresso will run around 30 pesos at steak houses in Buenos Aires and much less in the hinterlands.

In Buenos Aires you're likely to pay 1.50–2 pesos for a *cafecito* (small cup of coffee) in a café. A soda costs 1.50 pesos. A taxi ride will run you 4–8 pesos in the larger cities. A tango show dinner with a couple of drinks costs about 100 pesos. A double room in a moderately priced, well-situated hotel costs $100–$130 dollars, including taxes. Many hotels are now in the habit of charging strictly in dollars. Make sure that the rate you are paying is valid for both tourists and Argentines; some hotels have been known to take advantage of foreigners who are unaware of the favorable exchange rate by charging them an increased price.

When ordering alcoholic drinks, ask for Argentine liquors, or suffer the import fees. A bottle of Chivas Regal costs 80 pesos in shops, for instance. When ordering drinks, specify your preference for whiskey or vodka *nacional,* for example.

Prices throughout this guide are given for adults. Substantially reduced fees are almost always available for children, students, and senior citizens. For information on taxes, *see* Taxes.

ATMS

ATMs are easy to find, especially in major cities and resort towns. The Banelco ATM system is the most widely used, indicated by a burgundy-colored sign with white lettering.

Before leaving home, make sure that your credit cards have been programmed for ATM use in Argentina. Your local bank card may not work overseas; ask your bank about a MasterCard–Cirrus or Visa–Plus debit card, which works like a bank card but can be used at any of the ATMs displaying their logo.

Although fees charged for ATM transactions may be higher, Cirrus and Plus exchange rates are excellent because they are based on wholesale rates offered only by major banks.

🖪 **ATM Locations** **Banelco** ⊠ Mexico 444, Buenos Aires ☎ 11/4334–5466. **Cirrus** ☎ 800/424-7787 ⊕ www.mastercard.com. **Plus** ⊕ www.visa.com/pd/atm.

CREDIT CARDS

If you choose to bring just one card, Visa is recommended, as it is the most readily accepted. American Express, Diners Club, and MasterCard are the most commonly accepted after Visa. It may be easiest to use your credit card whenever possible—the exchange rate only varies by a fraction of a cent, so you won't need to worry whether your purchase is charged on the day of purchase or at some point in the future. Note, however that you may get a better deal if you pay with cash.

Throughout this guide, the following abbreviations are used: **AE**, American Express; **DC**, Diners Club; **MC**, MasterCard; and **V**, Visa.

🖪 **Reporting Lost Cards** **American Express** ☎ 11/4310-3000 ⊕ www.americanexpress.com. **Diners Club** ☎ 0810/444-2484 toll free ⊕ www.dinersclub.com.ar. **MasterCard** ☎ 0800/555-0507 toll free ⊕ www.mastercard.com. **Visa** ☎ 114379-3333 ⊕ www.visa.com.

CURRENCY

Throughout its history, Argentina has had one of the most volatile economies in the world, and that tradition continues today. After a decade of relative calm, the Argentine economy crashed in 2001, when the country defaulted on billions of dollars in foreign debt. The economic uncertainty sent citizens scurrying to the banks to withdraw their savings, only to be denied access because of government-imposed banking restrictions known as *el corralito*. Angry, and sometimes bloody, protests followed, as many middle-class Argentines joined the lower-class in a revolt against the government and the banks. The banking sanctions have since been lifted and most Argentines once again have access to their money, but the value of their savings has been greatly diminished.

One peso equals 100 centavos. Peso notes are in denominations of 100, 50, 20, 10, 5, and 2. Coins are in denominations of 1 peso, and 50, 25, 10, 5, and 1 centavos. When giving change, the cashier may round your purchase to the nearest 5 or even 10 centavos. Always check your change.

CURRENCY EXCHANGE

During the 1990s the Argentine peso was pegged to the U.S. dollar. This policy provided Argentina with a decade of unparalleled prosperity, when foreign products were available and affordable for the first time. This 1:1 peg eventually proved fatal for Argentina, and in 2002 the peso was unhinged on the open market. It has since lost around 60 percent of its value. This currency meltdown wiped out many Argentines' life savings, but has proved to be advantageous for tourists. Once one of the most expensive countries on the planet, Argentina is now a bargain for travelers.

If possible, exchange your local currency for pesos before you travel, but check to make sure you are getting a good rate. Once you arrive in Buenos Aires, there are many places where you can get pesos. Ask in your hotel or visit a *casa de cambio* (money changers) in El Centro, where you should be prepared to show your passport to complete the transaction.

There are two exchange desks at Buenos Aires's Ezeiza Airport, on the upper level in Terminal A, and a desk at the city's domestic Jorge Newbery Airport. Keep in mind that banks charge exchange fees, as do some hotels. Plan ahead, since it's often hard to change large amounts of money at hotels on weekends, even in cities.

Banks, ATMs, and Casas de Cambio all charge a fee. As a rule, banks charge the least, and hotels the most. Although ATM transaction fees may be higher abroad than at home, ATM rates are excellent because they are based on wholesale rates offered only by major banks. To avoid lines at airport exchange booths, get a bit of local currency before you leave home.

You may not be able to change currency in rural areas at all, so don't leave major cities without adequate amounts of pesos in small denominations.

At this writing, the rate of exchange was 2.9 pesos to the U.S. dollar, 2.2 pesos to the Canadian dollar, 5.48 pesos to the pound sterling, 3.66 pesos to the euro, 2.26 pesos to the Australian dollar, 2 pesos to the New Zealand dollar, and 0.44 pesos to the South African rand.

🗷 Exchange Services International Currency Express ☎ 888/278-6628 orders ⊕ www. foreignmoney.com. **Travel Ex Currency Services** ☎ 800/287-7362 orders and retail locations ⊕ www.travelex.com.

TRAVELER'S CHECKS

Most large stores in Buenos Aires accept traveler's checks, but smaller shops and restaurants are leery of them. When using traveler's checks, remember to carry a valid ID with you for any purchases or when changing them at a bank or the American Express office. You'll have trouble changing traveler's checks outside of Buenos Aires, so if you want to bring them plan on changing them before you leave the city.

PACKING

Argentines are very fashion- and appearance-conscious. If you're doing business in Argentina, bring the same attire you would wear in U.S. and European cities: for men, suits and ties; for women, suits for day wear and cocktail dresses or other suitable dinner clothes. In Buenos Aires, people dress stylishly, whether casual or elegant, for dinner, depending on the restaurant. For sightseeing and leisure, casual clothing and good walking shoes are desirable and appropriate. Note, though, that if you walk around Buenos Aires in shorts, a T-shirt, sneakers, and a baseball hat, you will definitely be spotted as a tourist and may draw some unwanted attention. In smaller towns and villages, dress is more conservative.

For beach vacations, bring lightweight sportswear, and sweaters, a windbreaker, or a jacket for evenings when the temperatures drop. You can purchase all of these items here, but they are more expensive than they are in the United States. Travel in the tropical rain forest requires long-sleeve shirts, long pants, socks, sneakers, a hat, a light waterproof jacket, a bathing suit, and plenty of insect repellent with DEET.

If you're visiting high altitudes or southern Patagonia, bring a fleece jacket, thermal underwear, and thick sweaters—you'll need even heavier clothing in winter months. Local markets often carry hand-knit sweaters, ponchos, and Andean headgear. Depending on where you go, you may also want to pack a screw-top water bottle, a money pouch, a travel flashlight, extra batteries, a pocketknife with a bottle opener, a medical kit, and binoculars. Don't forget to check camera batteries and bring along your favorite film; though these items are readily available in major cities, they may be harder to find elsewhere.

In your carry-on luggage, pack an extra pair of eyeglasses or contact lenses and enough of any medication you take to last a few days longer than the entire trip. You may also ask your doctor to write a spare prescription using the drug's generic name, as brand names may vary from country to country. In luggage to be checked, never pack prescription drugs, valuables, or undeveloped film. And don't forget to carry with you the addresses of offices that handle refunds of lost traveler's checks. Check *Fodor's How to Pack* (available at online retailers and bookstores everywhere) for more tips.

To avoid customs and security delays, don't pack any sharp objects in your carry-on luggage, including knives of any size or material, scissors, nail clippers, and corkscrews, or anything else that might arouse suspicion. To avoid having your checked luggage chosen for hand inspection, don't cram bags full. The U.S. Transportation Security Administration suggests packing shoes on top and placing personal items you don't want touched in clear plastic bags.

CHECKING LUGGAGE

Baggage allowances vary by carrier, destination, and ticket class. On international flights, you're usually allowed to check two bags weighing up to 70 pounds (32 kilograms) each, although a few airlines allow checked bags of up to 88 pounds (40 kilograms) in first class. Some international carriers don't allow more than 66 pounds (30 kilograms) per bag in business class and 44 pounds (20 kilograms) in economy. If you're flying to or through the United Kingdom, your luggage cannot exceed 70 pounds (32 kilograms) per bag. On domestic flights, the limit is usually 50 to 70 pounds (23 to 32 kilograms) per bag. In general, carry-on bags shouldn't exceed 40 pounds (18 kilograms). Most airlines won't accept bags that weigh more than 100 pounds (45 kilograms) on domestic or international flights.

Airline liability for baggage is limited to $2,500 per person on flights within the United States. On international flights it amounts to $9.07 per pound or $20 per kilogram for checked baggage (roughly $640 per 70-pound bag), with a maximum of $634.90 per piece, and $400 per passenger for unchecked baggage. You can buy additional coverage at check-in for about $10 per $1,000 of coverage, but it often excludes a rather extensive list of items, shown on your airline ticket.

At check-in, make sure each bag is correctly tagged with the destination airport's three-letter code. Because some checked bags will be opened for hand inspection, the U.S. Transportation Security Administration recommends that you leave luggage unlocked or use the plastic locks offered at check-in. TSA screeners place an inspection notice inside searched bags, which are re-sealed with a special lock.

If your bag has been searched and contents are missing or damaged, file a claim with the TSA Consumer Response Center as soon as possible. If your bags arrive damaged or fail to arrive at all, file a written report with the airline before leaving the airport.

🔁 Complaints **U.S. Transportation Security Administration Contact Center** ☏ 866/289-9673 ⊕ www.tsa.gov.

PASSPORTS & VISAS

When traveling internationally, carry your passport even if you don't need one. Not only is it the best form of ID, but it's also being required more and more. As of December 31, 2005, for instance, Americans need a passport to re-enter the country from Bermuda, the Caribbean, and Panama. Such requirements also affect re-entry from Canada and Mexico by air and sea (as of December 31, 2006) and land (as of December 31, 2007). Make two photocopies of the data page (one for someone at home and another for you, carried separately from your passport). If you lose your passport, promptly call the nearest embassy or consulate and the local police.

U.S. passport applications for children under age 14 require consent from both parents or legal guardians; both parents must appear together to sign the application. If only one parent appears, he or she must submit a written statement from the other parent authorizing passport issuance for the child. A parent with sole authority must present evidence of it when applying; acceptable documentation includes the child's certified birth certificate listing only the applying parent, a court order specifically permitting this parent's travel with the child, or a death certificate for the nonapplying parent. Application forms and instructions are available on the Web site of the U.S. State Department's Bureau of Consular Affairs (⊕ travel.state.gov).

ENTERING ARGENTINA

U.S., Canadian, and British citizens do not need a visa for visits of up to 90 days, though they must carry a passport at all times. Upon entering Argentina, you'll receive a tourist visa stamp on your passport valid for 90 days. If you need to stay longer, exit the country for one night; upon reentering Argentina, your passport will be stamped allowing an additional 90 days. The fine for overstaying your tourist visa is $50 dollars, payable upon departure at the airport. If you do overstay your visa, plan to arrive at the airport several hours in advance of your flight so that you have ample time to take care of the fine.

PASSPORT OFFICES

The best time to apply for a passport or to renew is in fall and winter. Before any trip, check your passport's expiration date, and, if necessary, renew it as soon as possible.

🗗 **American Citizens National Passport Information Center** ☎ 877/487-2778, 888/874-7793 TDD/TTY ⊕ travel.state.gov.
🗗 **British Citizens U.K. Passport Service** ☎ 0870/521-0410 ⊕ www.passport.gov.uk.🗗 **Canadian Citizens Passport Office** ☎ 819/994-3500 or 800/567-6868 ⊕ www.ppt.gc.ca.

RESTROOMS

Public restrooms are found only in hotels, restaurants, and public buildings. Perhaps for this reason, proprietors in restaurants or bars seldom complain if you ask to use the facilities and don't patronize the establishment. Gas stations have clean restrooms.

SAFETY

Buenos Aires is one of the safer cities in the world; however, recent political and economic instability has produced an increase in robberies and petty theft, so you should be aware of your surroundings at all times and don't take any unnecessary chances. House and car break-ins continue to plague locals as well as visitors. Do your best to blend in with the locals and you will not attract attention. Police constantly patrol any areas where tourists are likely to be, and violent crime is rare. Smaller towns and villages in Argentina are even safer.

Generally you'll find that people are friendly and helpful. That said, there are a few precautions worth taking—here as in any place else. Don't wear any jewelry you're not willing to lose. Don't dangle purses or cameras from your shoulders—pull the straps across your body—and carry briefcases or bags firmly. Always remain alert for pickpockets, especially on buses, trains, or subway. Tickets and other valuables are best left in hotel safes. Don't wear a money belt or a waist pack, both of

which peg you as a tourist. Distribute your cash and any valuables (including your credit cards and passport) between a deep front pocket, an inside jacket or vest pocket, and a hidden money pouch. Do not reach for the money pouch once you're in public.

Buenos Aires taxi drivers are notorious for, literally, taking you for a ride. Call or hail only metered taxis and make sure the meter is turned on. It helps to have an idea where you are going and how long it will take. If you're hailing a taxi, make sure it says "radio taxi"; this means that the driver works for a licensed company and is required to call in every new fare over the radio. Also look for the driver's photo ID, which should be well displayed inside the car. Better yet, call a licensed *remis,* which is always safer and usually cheaper, as you agree on a fixed price beforehand.

Argentines like to speak their minds, and there has been a huge increase in strikes and street protests in recent years. *Piquiteros* (picketers) clog streets and plazas in downtown Buenos Aires causing major traffic jams. Most of them have to do with government policies, but there has been an increase in anti-U.S. and anti-British sentiment, stemming primarily from Argentina's strained relationship with the International Monetary Fund (IMF) and the war in Iraq. Avoid these demonstrations if you can. If you do get caught up in one, don't panic—the overwhelming majority of them are peaceful—but leave the area as soon as you find an opportunity.

LOCAL SCAMS

When asking for price quotes, always confirm whether the price is in dollars or pesos. Some salespeople, especially street vendors have found that they can take advantage of confused tourists by charging dollars for goods that are actually priced in pesos. If you're in doubt about that beautiful leather coat, don't be shy about asking if the number on the tag is in pesos or dollars.

WOMEN IN ARGENTINA

Women are safer in Buenos Aires than in many other major cities in the world, but crimes still occur. It's best to dress modestly and avoid wearing flashy jewelry on the street. Women can expect pointed looks, the occasional *piropo* (a flirtatious remark, usually alluding to some physical aspect), and some advances. Act confident, avoid eye contact, and ignore the comments.

TAXES

Sales tax (IVA) in Argentina is 21%. The tax is usually included in the price of goods and noted on your receipt. The IVA tax is entirely refundable for purchases exceeding 70 pesos at stores displaying a duty-free sign. Request a tax form from the store and keep your receipts. The IVA is also included in the price of hotels. When you depart, plan enough time to visit the return desk at the airport to obtain your refund. The $18 departure tax must be paid in U.S. dollars. Domestic airport taxes are usually included in the ticket price.

TELEPHONES

The country code for Argentina is 54. To call Argentina from overseas, dial 00 + the country code (54) + the area code (omitting the first 0, which is for long-distance calls within Argentina). The area code for Buenos Aires is 11. For information, dial 110. For the time, dial 113. For information about international calls, dial 19 or 000.

Telecom's *telecentros* and Telefónica's *locutorios* offer a variety of services, including metered phone calls, faxes, telegrams, and access to the Internet; some even provide wire transfers. They are convenient to use and abound throughout all cities; some are specially equipped for people with hearing impairments. Telecom has white and yellow pages on their Web site, plus postal code information.

◪ Telecom ☎ 0800/555-0112 ⊕ www.telecom. com.ar. **Telefónica** ☎ 0800/222-4262 ⊕ www. telefonica.com.ar.

CELL PHONES

To call the cell phone number of a Buenos Aires resident, dial 15 before the number (unless you're also calling from a cell phone with a Buenos Aires number). Local cell phone charges vary depending on certain factors, such as the company and time of day, and can cost up to 2 pesos per call;

the fee is charged to the caller, not the recipient, unless on a pay phone.

Cellular phones can be rented at the airport, or through your hotel—sometimes they can be added on to a car rental package. Delivery is free in Buenos Aires. You can compare prices online and makes reservations in advance.

◪ Mobile Phone Rental Phonerental ☎ 0800/ 335-3705, 11/4311-2933 ⊕ www.phonerental.com.ar. **Unifon** ✉ Av. Corrientes 645, Buenos Aires ☎ 0800/333-6868 ⊕ www.unifon.com.ar.

LOCAL CALLS

Hotels charge steep rates for local calls; before dialing, ask at the front desk about phone charges. Public phones are reliable and abundant. They operate with coins or cards, which are called *tarjetas chip*. Simply slide the card in, wait for the reading of how many minutes you have, then dial.

Cards are available at kiosks, pharmacies, and phone centers. Cards range 4–10 pesos; rates are 23¢ for every two minutes during peak hours (weekdays and Sunday 8–8, Saturday 8 AM–1 PM), and half rate off-peak. You can use the cards for local, long-distance, and international calls, though you're better off calling long distance from a phone center.

LONG-DISTANCE CALLS

When calling from one area code to another in Argentina, add a 0 before the area code, then 1 for Capital Federal and Greater Buenos Aires, 2 for the Southern region, and 3 for provinces in the North. Charges increase with distances, beginning at 30 km (18½ mi) outside of the city. Many hotels charge up to 4 pesos per call on top of the regular rate. It's best to call from a public phone or telephone center.

Hotels have *DDI*, international direct dialing, but may charge up to 3 pesos for a long-distance call. You're best off calling from telecentros or locutorios, where your call is metered and will run around 95 centavos for the first minute, and 68 centavos each additional minute, during peak hours to the United States. Rates are much higher for England (starting at 1.40 pesos for the first minute and 1.25 pesos for each additional minute) and Australia

(2.85 pesos for the first minute and 2.30 pesos for each additional minute).

The country code is 1 for the United States and Canada and 44 for the United Kingdom. To call out from Argentina, dial 00 + country code + area code + number.

AT&T, MCI, and Sprint access codes make calling long-distance relatively convenient, but you may find the local access number blocked in many hotel rooms. First ask the hotel operator to connect you. If the hotel operator balks, ask for an international operator, or dial the international operator yourself. One way to improve your odds of getting connected to your long-distance carrier is to travel with more than one company's calling card (a hotel may block Sprint, for example, but not MCI). If all else fails, call from a pay phone. If you are traveling for a longer period of time, consider renting a cell-phone from a local company.

Access Codes For local access numbers abroad, contact **AT&T Direct** ☎ 0800/555-4288, **MCI WorldPhone** ☎ 0800/222-6249 or 0800/555-1002, or **Sprint International Access** ☎ 0800/222-1003.

TIME
New York is one time zone behind Buenos Aires from April through October (it's two hours behind the rest of the year, as Argentina does not observe daylight savings time). There's a two-hour difference for Chicago and four-hour difference between Los Angeles and Buenos Aires. Buenos Aires and most of the country, most of the time, is three hours behind London GMT.

TIPPING
Propinas (tips) range 10%–15% in bars and restaurants (10% is enough in a casual café or if the bill runs high). Note that some restaurants charge a *cubierto,* covering table service, not the waiter's tip. Argentines round off a taxi fare, though some cabbies who frequent hotels popular with tourists seem to expect more. Hotel porters should be tipped at least 3 pesos or the equivalent of one dollar, 5 pesos for more than one bag. Three pesos per night is adequate for chambermaids, and anything up to 20 pesos for a concierge is good, depending on what you ask of them. Give door-

men and ushers about 2 pesos, restroom attendants change under a peso, and beauty and barbershop personnel around 5%. Depending on the extent of their service, anything from a beer to 5 to 10 pesos a day should be fine for local guides.

TOURS & PACKAGES
Because everything is prearranged on a prepackaged tour or independent vacation, you spend less time planning—and often get it all at a good price.

BOOKING WITH AN AGENT
Travel agents are excellent resources. But it's a good idea to collect brochures from several agencies, as some agents' suggestions may be influenced by relationships with tour and package firms that reward them for volume sales. If you have a special interest, find an agent with expertise in that area. The American Society of Travel Agents (ASTA) has a database of specialists worldwide; you can log on to the group's Web site to find one near you.

Make sure your travel agent knows the accommodations and other services of the place being recommended. Ask about the hotel's location, room size, beds, and whether it has a pool, room service, or programs for children, if you care about these. Has your agent been there in person or sent others whom you can contact?

Do some homework on your own, too: local tourism boards can provide information about lesser-known and small-niche operators, some of which may sell only direct.

BUYER BEWARE
Each year consumers are stranded or lose their money when tour operators—even large ones with excellent reputations—go out of business. Ask several travel agents about an operator's reputation, and try to book with a company that has a consumer-protection program. In the United States, members of the United States Tour Operators Association are required to set aside funds (up to $1 million) to help eligible customers cover payments and travel arrangements in the event that their chosen company defaults. It's also a good idea to choose a company that participates in

the American Society of Travel Agents' Tour Operator Program; ASTA will act as mediator in any disputes between you and your tour operator.

Remember that the more your package or tour includes, the better you can predict the ultimate cost of your vacation. Make sure you know exactly what is covered, and beware of hidden costs. Are taxes, tips, and transfers included? Entertainment and excursions?

▶ Tour-Operator Recommendations American Society of Travel Agents (⇨ Travel Agencies). **CrossSphere–The Global Association for Packaged Travel** ☎ 859/226-4444 or 800/682-8886 ⊕ www.CrossSphere.com. **United States Tour Operators Association** (USTOA) ☎ 212/599-6599 ⊕ www.ustoa.com.

TRAIN TRAVEL

Argentina's rail system, which was built by the British, no longer plays an important role in the national transportation system. It's often not as comfortable as traveling by luxury bus. The most popular routes are from Buenos Aires to Mar del Plata and Bariloche. There are also two special tourist-oriented trains: the Tren a las Nubes (Train of the Clouds), which goes through the Andes, and the Tren de la Costa (Coast Train), which runs from Buenos Aires to the river delta area of Tigre.

Train tickets are inexpensive. Usually there are two classes. Plan to buy your tickets a few days ahead of your trip (two weeks in advance in summer months), and arrive at the station well before departure time. Reservations must be made in person at the local train station. Refer to the Essentials sections in individual chapters for more information about train service.

TRAVEL AGENCIES

A good travel agent puts your needs first. Look for an agency that has been in business at least five years, emphasizes customer service, and has someone on staff who specializes in your destination. In addition, make sure the agency belongs to a professional trade organization. The American Society of Travel Agents (ASTA) has more than 10,000 members in some 140 countries, enforces a strict code of

ethics, and will step in to mediate agent-client disputes involving ASTA members. ASTA also maintains a directory of agents on its Web site; ASTA's TravelSense.org, a trip planning and travel advice site, can also help to locate a travel agent who caters to your needs. (If a travel agency is also acting as your tour operator, *see* Buyer Beware *in* Tours & Packages.)

▶ Local Agent Referrals American Society of Travel Agents (ASTA) ☎ 703/739-2782 or 800/965-2782 24-hr hotline 🖷 703/684-8319 ⊕ www.astanet.com and www.travelsense.org. **Association of British Travel Agents** ☎ 020/7637-2444 ⊕ www.abta.com. **Association of Canadian Travel Agencies** ☎ 613/237-3657 ⊕ www.acta.ca.

VISITOR INFORMATION

Learn more about foreign destinations by checking government-issued travel advisories and country information. For a broader picture, consider information from more than one country.

The city of Buenos Aires has a tourist office representing each province of Argentina. These offices can provide you with maps and regional information. Ask at your hotel for their locations throughout the city. Check out the Argentine Government Tourist Offices.

Tourist information is also available at Embassies and Consulates in the U.S., Canada, Australia, New Zealand, and the U.K.

▶ Argentina Government Tourist Offices Los Angeles ✉ 5055 Wilshire Blvd, Suite 201, Los Angeles, CA 90036 ☎ 323/954-9155. **Miami** ✉ 2655 Le Jeune Rd., Miami, FL 33134 ☎ 305/442-1366. **New York** ✉ 12 W. 56th St., New York, NY 10019 ☎ 212/603-0400. **Canada** ✉ 90 Sparks St., Suite 910, Ottawa, Ontario K1P5B4 ☎ 613/236-2351. **U.K.** ✉ 65 Brooke St., London, 4AH ☎ 020/7318-1300.

▶ Government Advisories U.S. Department of State ☎ 202/647-5225, 888/407-4747 or 317/472-2328 for interactive hotline ⊕ www.travel.state.gov. **Consular Affairs Bureau of Canada** ⊕ www.voyage.gc.ca. **U.K. Foreign and Commonwealth Office** ☎ 0870/606-0290 or 020/7008-1500 ⊕ www.fco.gov.uk/travel.

WEB SITES

Do check out the World Wide Web when planning your trip. You'll find everything from weather forecasts to virtual tours of famous cities. Be sure to visit Fodors.com (⊕ www.fodors.com), a complete travel-planning site. You can research prices and book plane tickets, hotel rooms, rental cars, vacation packages, and more. In addition, you can post your pressing questions on the travel forum. Other planning tools include a currency converter and weather reports, and there are loads of links to travel resources.

Don't rule out foreign-language sites; some have links to sites that present information in more than one language, including English.

Web Sites **Argentina Secretary of Tourism** ⊕ www.turismo.gov.ar. **Buenos Aires Herald** ⊕ www.buenosairesherald.com. **Embassy of Argentina** ⊕ www.embajadaargentinaeeuu.org. **Tango** ⊕ www.abctango.com.

Buenos Aires

WORD OF MOUTH

"Buenos Aires is one of the most vibrant big cities on the planet. . . ."

—drdawggy

"Buenos Aires . . .is a wonderful city. And this from a person who never thought she wanted to go. I can't wait to go back. The people are wonderful and the shopping—wow!"

—SharonG

"Amazing city. We discovered it by *barrio* (neighborhood). Our favorites were San Telmo (loved the Sunday market) and Palermo Viejo. Some drawbacks though: lots of noise and pollution. And the taxi drivers are crazy. Aside from that, we loved every minute of it."

—rozelle

THIS CITY IS REALLY HOT. INCREDIBLE FOOD, FRESH YOUNG DESIGNERS, and a cultural scene that's thriving despite tough economic times—all these Buenos Aires has. Yet less tangible things are at the heart of the city's sizzle—namely the spirit of its often divided but never indifferent inhabitants. Here, a flirtatious glance can be as passionate as a tango; a heated sports discussion as important as a world-class soccer match. It's this zest for life that's making Buenos Aires Latin America's hottest destination.

The world's ninth-largest city rises from the Río de la Plata and stretches more than 200 square km (75 square mi) to the surrounding pampas, Argentina's fertile plains. With more than one-third of the country's 39 million inhabitants living in or around the city, it's clearly the country's hub as well as it's main gateway.

ORIENTATION & PLANNING

Orientation

By Victoria Patience

Buenos Aires's identity lies in its 48 *barrios* (neighborhoods)—each with its own character and history. Several generations of many families have lived in the same barrio, and traditionally people feel more of an affinity to their neighborhood than to the city as a whole.

Try to take things one neighborhood at a time, exploring on foot and by *colectivo* (bus), *subte* (subway), and/or relatively inexpensive taxis. Streets are basically laid out in a grid, though a few transverse the grid diagonally; these are helpfully called *diagonales. Avenidas* are broader, often two-way, streets, while regular streets (officially *calles* but actually referred to just by their name) are generally one-way. Streets and avenues running north–south change names at Avenida Rivadavía. Each city block is 100 meters (328 feet) long, and addresses are based on the building's measured position from the corner (for instance, 180 Calle Florida is 80 meters from the corner, and 100 meters, or one block, from 80 Calle Florida).

El Centro
The term *el centro* is confusing: although people tend to say *"Voy al centro"* or *"Trabajo en el centro"* (without the capitals), meaning "I'm going downtown" or "I work downtown," they're using the term generally. The official barrio names of the downtown area are San Nicolás and Monserrat, though few people use these either. Suffice to say that "el centro" is really an umbrella term to cover several action-packed districts at the city's heart. In it are theaters, bars, cafés, bookstores, and the crowded streets you'd expect to find in any major city center.

THE MICROCENTRO & TRIBUNALES The *microcentro* is the unofficial name for the barrio of San Nicolás: the area north of Avenida Rivadavia, west of Avenida 9 de Julio, and south of Avenida Santa Fe. This is effectively Buenos Aires's central business district, and the action focuses on the pedestrian-only street Florida. The next district west is Tribunales, meaning law courts, so called because of the supreme court and other civic buildings that are here; it's also where you'll find the world-famous Colón Theater.

Top Reasons to Visit

Dance the Night Away. OK. This *is* the capital of tango, that most passionate of dances. But *porteños* (as locals are called) also dance to the pulsating beats of samba and salsa or to sounds mixed by DJs. Regardless of the type of beat, rest assured it goes on until the wee hours.

Shop Till You Drop. High-quality silver and leather goods as well as fashionable clothing and accessories are available at world-class malls and boutiques. Open-air markets carry regional and European antiques and objets d'art as well as provincial handicrafts, such as dried gourds for drinking *mate* (strong tea) or gaucho ponchos.

Best of Both Worlds. The architecture, wining-and-dining, and arts activities rival similar offerings in European capitals. But the lifestyle, low prices, and warm locals are more typical of Latin America.

Meat-ing Your Destiny. Argentines eat twice as much meat per capita as Americans, and after your first steak you'll know why. The capital of cow country has enough *parrillas* (traditional grill restaurants) to satisfy even the most bloodthirsty.

The Beautiful Game. Some of the world's best players and most passionate fans make soccer in Argentina much more than just a game. Top matches play out in Buenos Aires's colorful stadiums, stuffed to bursting with screaming *futbol* addicts.

PLAZA DE MAYO This square was where Buenos Aires started: it once sat right on the river and, in keeping the traditions of Spanish colonies, was home to the city's central institutions, both governmental and religious. The Plaza de Mayo is not technically a district, but few people use the area's official handle, Monserrat. Regardless, the square has enough worthy offerings for you to treat it as a neighborhood for the purpose of sightseeing. West along Avenida de Mayo is Congreso, a part-residential, part-commercial barrio named for the nation's congress, which is at its heart.

Almagro

One of Buenos Aires's traditional tango districts, Almagro, is west of the center and south of La Recoleta and Palermo, but was until recently seedy and run down in comparison with its posher neighbors. Its old buildings are beginning to get the Palermo recycling treatment, thanks to both the huge rise in tango tourism and also the pioneering presence of the Abasto shopping mall, in a beautiful old building that once held Buenos Aires's main food market. Almagro is easily accessible by the subte (Line B).

San Telmo

Highlights of bohemian San Telmo include Sunday strolls, antiques shopping at Feria de San Pedro and surrounding stores, and the tango halls that come to life nightly. Cobblestone streets teem with 19th-century buildings, once inhabited by affluent Spaniards. Thanks to preser-

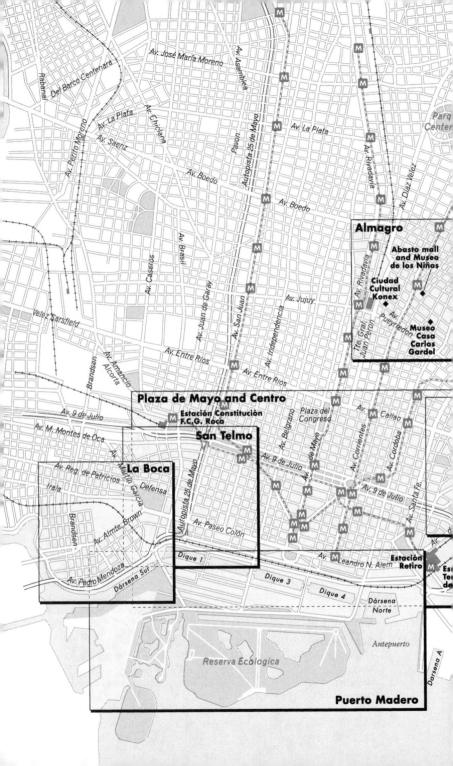

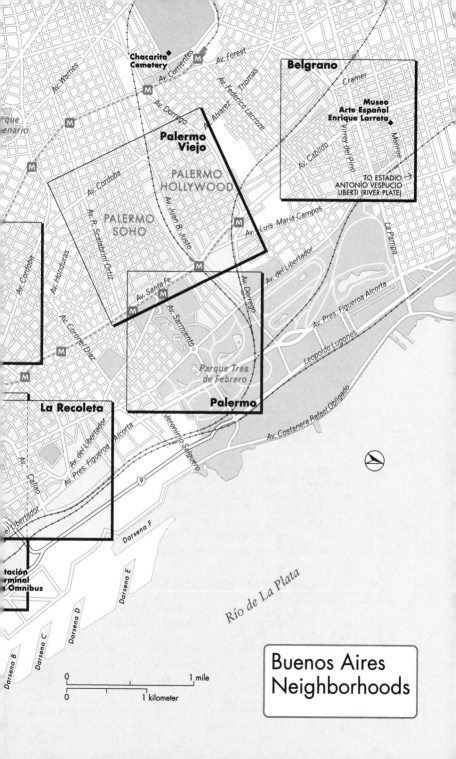

Chacarita Cemetery

Av. Forest

Av. Corrientes

Av. Warnes

Av. Federico Thomas

Av. Alvarez Thomas

Av. Forest

Belgrano

Cramer

Av. Dorrego

Palermo Viejo

Av. Federico Lacroze

Museo Arte Español Enrique Larreta

Virrey del Pino

Monroe

Av. Cabildo

PALERMO HOLLYWOOD

Av. Cordoba

Av. Juan B. Justo

TO ESTADIO
ANTONIO VESPUCIO
LIBERTI (RIVER PLATE)

PALERMO SOHO

Av. R. Scalabrini Ortiz

Av. Honduras

Av. Luis María Campos

La Pampa

Av. del Libertador

Av. Santa Fe

Av. Sarmiento

Av. Dorrego

Av. Coronel Díaz

Av. Cordoba

Av. Pres. Figueroa Alcorta

Leopoldo Lugones

Parque Tres de Febrero

Palermo

La Recoleta

Av. del Libertador

Av. Pres. Figueroa Alcorta

Jerónimo Salguero

Av. Costanera Rafael Obligado

Av. Callao

el Libertador

9

**tación
rminal
Omnibus**

Darsena F

Darsena E

Darsena D

Río de La Plata

Darsena C

Darsena B

0   1 mile

0   1 kilometer

Buenos Aires
Neighborhoods

vation efforts, the area is now a cradle of history and culture, and all its landmarks have been declared national monuments.

La Boca

The vibrant working-class neighborhood of La Boca, just south of San Telmo, served as the first port of Buenos Aires. Many who settled here were immigrants from Genoa, Italy, and the district retains much of its Italian heritage although time as a tourist center is taking its toll on La Boca's authenticity. You can still enjoy inexpensive Italian fare in a cantina along Avenida Patricios.

Puerto Madero

The newest barrio has a view of the sprouting skyline on one side and the exclusive yacht club on the other. Once an abandoned port area, its multimillion dollar facelift imitated that of London's Docklands. Its main draw is a chic riverside promenade, which has become *the* place to go for a casual stroll, elegant dining, and nightlife.

La Recoleta

This neighborhood to the east of El Centro has seen it all. It was settled in the 1700s by the Franciscan Recoleto friars. The needs of the spirit eventually gave way to those of the flesh, and the neighborhood became home to brothels and tango halls. In the late 1800s, the elite swarmed here to escape yellow fever, and the district remains upscale and European in style. People-watching at sidewalk bars and cafés here is an art.

Palermo & Las Cañitas

Palermo not only has the honor of being the largest barrio, but also the one with the most subneighborhoods. The city's gastronomic, design, and shopping scenes revolve around its districts, and families flock to its parks on weekends to picnic, sunbathe, bicycle, and jog. The polo field and hippodrome also make Palermo the city's nerve center for equestrian activities.

Nowadays "Palermo" tends to refer to the area's more generic parts; that is, those outside of Palermo Viejo (Old Palermo, itself subdivided into Palermo Soho and Palermo Hollywood) and Las Cañitas. It includes the area around the Museo de Arte Latinoamericano de Buenos Aires (MALBA), which is known as Palermo Chico; the area around Parque Las Heras and the Alto Palermo shopping mall, bordering on Barrio Norte; and the areas around Plaza Güemes, the Jardín Japonés, and the Jardín Zoológico.

A brash conversion transformed the formerly sketchy neighborhood of Palermo Viejo into two very trendy districts. The streets surrounding Plaza (also known to locals as Plazoleta Cortázar) form an area now known as Palermo Soho. The other half of Palermo Viejo, across Avenida Juan B. Justo from Palermo Soho, took the name Palermo Hollywood for all the young film and video producers that have opened studios here, looking to leverage the low peso to sell their services abroad. Las Cañitas—a hip little area on the northern edge of Palermo—is full of hopping nightspots, modern restaurants, and a youthful buzz.

Belgrano

Once a far-flung northwestern suburb, Belgrano is now as bustling as downtown. It's home to many wealthy porteños as well as Buenos Aires's diminutive Chinatown. The main thoroughfare, Avenida Cabildo, buzzes with people round the clock. Shady squares and narrow cobbled streets are leftovers from quieter times.

Costanera Norte

The northern riverside has long been a traditional place for Sunday strolls and picnics for people anxious for some fresh air. These days, as well as traditional *choripan* (chorizo sausage in a roll) and steak vendors, it's also home to a golf course, the Jorge Newbery airport (for domestic flights), and a range of top nightclubs.

Planning

When planning your trip, remember that when it's summer in the United States, it's winter in Argentina, and vice versa. Winters (July–September) are chilly and rainy, though temperatures never drop below freezing. Summer's muggy heat (December–March) can be taxing at midday but makes for wonderful, warm nights. Spring (September–December) and autumn (April–June), with their mild temperatures—and blossoms or changing leaves—are ideal for urban trekking.

Take It All In

3 Days: You can appreciate the city at breakneck speed. Allow a half day each for Plaza de Mayo, El Centro, San Telmo, La Boca, Palermo, and La Recoleta. If possible visit La Recoleta on Saturday and San Telmo and La Boca on Sunday to browse their respective markets. Plan museum time in advance as opening days vary, though shops tend to be open seven days a week. Schedule time for an evening siesta to allow you late dinner and a lengthy night out at a club, bar, or tango hall.

5 Days: With five days you can enjoy all the sights listed in the three-day itinerary above at a more leisurely pace. You'll also have more time to tour the riverside promenade of Puerto Madero or head north to the neighborhood of Belgrano.

7 Days: With a week you can fully enjoy all the sights suggested in the three- and five-day itineraries above and venture beyond the city. You could take a day trip just outside town to San Antonio de Areco or up the river delta to Tigre. A day trip to the picturesque and historic city of Colonia del Sacramento, Uruguay, 45 minutes away by ferry is also another option.

10 Days: Spend six or seven days touring Buenos Aires and its immediate environs. Then add on a two- or three-day trip northeast to the breathtaking Cataratas del Iguazú (Iguazú Falls) on the border with Brazil. Alternatively, you make a three- or four-day trip west to Córdoba and/or the wine regions of San Juan, Mendoza, San Rafael, or San Luis.

Tango

"The tango is macho, the tango is strong. It smells of wine and tastes like death."

So goes the famous tango "Why I Sing Like This," whose mix of nostalgia, violence, and sensuality sum up what is truly the dance of Buenos Aires. The tango was born at the end of the 19th century in the *conventillos* (tenement houses) of the port neighborhood of La Boca, although its roots aren't known for sure: theories place its origins in Spain, Italy, and even Africa. Nevertheless, the tango swept from the immigrant quarter to the brothels and cabarets of the whole city, and by the 1920s had become respectable enough to fill upper-class salons and drawing rooms. In the 1930s, with the advent of Carlos Gardel, tango's great hero, it became known outside Argentina. (Gardel, who died in a plane crash at age 40 in 1935, is buried in Chacarita Cemetery; you can visit his grave there.) Since then, tango has had its ups and downs but remains a key part of the city's culture.

Today, you can experience tango culture all over Buenos Aires in many different guises. More than 170,000 people attended the city's fortnight-long tango festival in 2005, testament to the big business that is tango tourism. Several travel agents can arrange everything from tango-themed accommodation and excursions, through dance classes, Spanish lessons, tango shopping trips, and introductions to the *milonga* (dancehall) scene. If you're serious about the dance of Buenos Aires, get in touch with the Web-based company **Argentina Tango** (⊕ www.argentinatango. com). Run by a British devotee, it offers highly organized, tailor-made tango tours.

Look for the English-language publication *El Tangauta,* and multilingual listings mag *Guía Trimestral—B.A. Tango* at newsstands; both give information on milongas and classes. Online, check out www.todotango. com.ar, a bilingual site devoted to the dance, or try the government-run www.tangodata.com.ar. For information about classes and teachers, contact the **Academia Nacional de Tango** (✉ Av. de Mayo 833, Plaza de Mayo ☎ 11/4345–6968 ⊕ www.anacdeltango.org.ar).

On the Town

When a date at 7 PM is considered an afternoon coffee break, you know you're in a city that likes to party. Porteños wouldn't want to be seen in a disco before 2 or 3 AM. Tango, too, gets going after midnight and never seems to stop. The best neighborhoods are La Recoleta (for bars) Costanera Norte (for clubs), and Palermo (for a little of everything). The long nights give you enough time to tango, have a midnight dinner, and then relax in a tony café or jazz club or continue the revelry pub-hopping or clubbing. Your "evening" may not wind down until 9 AM.

Buenos Aires has a busy schedule of world-class arts happenings. Except for some international short-run performances, tickets to most events are surprisingly easy to get. Note that, like many Argentine businesses, theaters take a summer vacation (January–February). Men usually wear jackets and ties to theater performances, and women also dress accordingly.

CLUB & SHOW   The English-language daily, *Buenos Aires Herald*; the major (Spanish-
INFO   language) papers' Friday supplements: Vía Libre in *La Nación* and Sí in *Clarín*; www.dondevamos.com and www.vuenosairez.com for gen-

eral going out suggestions; and www.buenosaliens.com for clubbing information *La Nación* and *Clarín* both publish weekly events booklets in addition to their Friday paper supplements.

ADVANCE TICKETS
You can buy discount tickets for music-hall revues, plays, concerts, and movies through **Cartelera Baires** (✉ Av. Corrientes 1382, Local 24, Microcentro ☎ 11/4372–5058). **Entrada Plus** (☎ 11/4324–1010) sells tickets for theater, dance performances, and concerts; tickets can be sent to your hotel or picked up at the box office. **Ticketmaster** (☎ 11/4321–9700 ⊕ www.ticketmaster.com) handles tickets for events at the Colón, the Teatro San Martín, and other venues. **Ticketek** (✉ Alto Palermo Shopping Center, Av. Santa Fe 3251 ☎ 11/4323–7200 ⊕ www.ticketek.com.ar) sells tickets for concerts, local theaters, and music halls from several locations. Tickets for international gigs are often available at branches of **Dromo** (✉ Florida 665 ☎ 11/5779–4080).

Eat Right, Sleep Well

Dining in Buenos Aires is an art, a passion, and a pastime. *Sobremesa* (chatting over wine or coffee long after the table has been cleared) is as much of an event as the meal itself. World-renowned beef is a staple, cooked on a *parrilla* (grill), or sometimes over quebracho wood for a savory *asado* (barbecue). A typical meal consists of steak, fries, salad, and a robust *tinto* (red wine), followed by *flan* (crème caramel) with *dulce de leche* (a gooey caramel-like spread).

Buenos Aires has hotels, inns, *apart-hotels* (short-term rental apartments), B&Bs, hostels—you name it. World-class facilities include the majestic Alvear Palace Hotel, the ultra-hip Faena Hotel + Universe, and the luxurious Four Seasons—all celebrity favorites. High season includes the summer months of mid-December through February and the winter holidays that fall in July. As a rule, hotel prices don't vary between high and low seasons; however, book ahead during high season, especially at upscale places, which fill up months in advance.

WHAT IT COSTS In Argentine Pesos					
	$$$$	$$$	$$	$	¢
RESTAURANTS	over 32	25–32	17–24	9–16	under 9
HOTELS	over 550	401–550	251–400	100–250	under 100

Restaurant prices are for one main course at dinner. Hotel prices are for two people in a standard double room in high season.

Get Around Just Fine

PUBLIC TRANSIT
The *subte,* Latin America's oldest subway system (dating from 1913), has five underground lines and the *premetro,* which runs above ground in the southwest of the city. Líneas (Lines) A, B, D, and E fan out from downtown; Línea C connects them all, as will the new H line. Service is efficient and inexpensive. Single-ride tickets cost 70¢ to anywhere in the city; you can buy passes for 1, 2, 5, or 10 trips or a no-contact-necessary rechargeable card. The subte shuts down around 11 PM and reopens at 5 AM.

Colectivos (city buses; 80¢ within the city, 1.25 to 1.65 pesos outside the city) connect the city's barrios and the greater Buenos Aires area. Carry small change as the ticket machines on board only accept coins. Bus stops are on every other block but you may have to hunt around for the small metal signs that mark the route numbers: they could be stuck on a shelter, lamppost, or even a tree. Stop at a news kiosk and buy the *Guía T,* a handy route guide.

TAXIS   Black-and-yellow taxis fill the city streets and take you anywhere in town and short distances into greater Buenos Aires. Fares start at 1.98 pesos with 22¢ per ¼ km (⅛ mi). You can hail taxis on the street or ask hotel and restaurant staffers to call for them.

TOURS   Consider having an Argentine travel agent book your tours and flights within the country. It's not uncommon for domestic airlines to have two ticket prices, one for residents and one for foreigners. Although this may seem unfair, try to see it from the point of view of someone whose currency is as weak as the Argentine peso and who's paying for flights priced in the same dollar amounts as before devaluation.

Argentinago (☏ 11/4372–7268 ⊕ www.argentinago.com) organizes hotels and tours in Buenos Aires and tours elsewhere, including all-inclusive two- and three-week packages to Argentina's top destinations. A dynamic way to see the city's sights is on two wheels through **La Bicicleta Naranja** (☏ 11/4362–1104 ⊕ www.labicicletanaranja.com.ar). You can either rent a bicycle (with helmet, lock, and water bottle) and follow one of the routes on their excellent maps or go with a fun young guide who'll talk you through it all—in Spanish or English—on general or themed trips.

Eternautas (☏ 11/4384–7874 ⊕ www.eternautas.com) offers cultural and historical tours (in Spanish or English) led by highly informed guides who are historians from the University of Buenos Aires. The company can organize basic city orientation tours as well as themed ones (e.g., Evita, the literary city, Jewish Buenos Aires). Eternautas can also organize side trips to San Antonio de Areco and Tigre. The small Web-based company, **Tour Experience** (☏ 11/4383–0717 Ext. 36 ⊕ www.tourexperience.com.ar) is taking tourism to new extremes with its alternative city tours. During its explorations of Villa 20, a shantytown in the Lugano neighborhood, a resident shows you around precarious corrugated-iron housing and a cooperative that residents have started. Tour proceeds go to the villa inhabitants.

For tailor-made tours contact **Wow! Argentina** (☏ 11/5239–3019 ⊕ www.wowargentina.com.ar). Cintia Stella and her team design packages and arrange for flights, lodging, transfers, and organized excursions/activities all over Argentina.

VISITOR INFO   Tourist information centers at the airports and in six locations around the city provide maps, though few brochures, and have English-speaking personnel. Look for centers at/on the Caminito; Calle Florida; Centro Cultural General San Martín (Avenida Sarmiento 1551); the Obelisk; Puerto Madero; and the Retiro bus station (corner of Avenida Antártida Argentina and Calle 10). For friendly guidance and brochures, maps, and even planning tips, try the information counter on the second floor of the Galerías Pacífico shopping center at Calle Florida 753.

To see things from a local's perspective, contact the **Cicerones de Buenos Aires** (☎ 11/4431–9892 ⊕ www.cicerones.org.ar), a free service that pairs you with an enthusiastic Porteño to show you parts of town—and parts of life in Argentina—you might not see otherwise.

You can get information over the phone weekdays from 9 to 5, from the **Dirección de Turismo del Gobierno de la Ciudad de Buenos Aires** (☎ 11/4313–0187 ⊕ www.buenosaires.gov.ar). Its excellent Web site has printable walking tours and other suggestions. The **Secretaría de Turismo de la Nación** (✉ National Secretary of Tourism; Av. Santa Fe 883, Microcentro ☎ 11/4312–2232 or 0800/555–0016 ⊕ www.turismo.gov.ar) has a 24-hour hotline that's toll-free from any point in Argentina.

Safety

Although Buenos Aires is safer than most Latin American capitals, thanks to the country's economy, crime is on the rise. Pickpocketing and mugging are common so avoid wearing flashy jewelry and be discreet with and mindful of cameras and bags. Go out at night in pairs or, better yet, in groups, and take taxis as much as possible. Although police patrol the areas where you're likely to go, they have a reputation for corruption, so locals try to avoid contact with them.

Protests are a fact of life in Buenos Aires. They often take place in the Plaza de Mayo, in the square outside the Congreso, or along the Avenida de Mayo connecting the two. Demonstrations are calmer than those at the height of the economic crisis in 2001 and 2002, but if you happen upon one, exercise caution.

EXPLORING

Revised by Victoria Patience

Buenos Aires locals refer to themselves as *porteños* because many of their immigrant forebears arrived by ship to this *port* town. Known as thinkers, porteños launch readily into philosophical discussions and psychoanalysis (Buenos Aires has the largest number of psychoanalysts per capita of any city in the world). People here take their beliefs seriously, be they about politics, food, or sport, and passions (and voices) run high at dinner-table discussions. With 85% of the Argentine population of European origin, there's a blurred sense of national identity in Buenos Aires—South American or European? Residents are often concerned with how outsiders perceive them, and they also scrutinize one another—with casual, appreciative glances or curious stares—making many of them deeply image-conscious.

Unlike most other Latin American cities, where the architecture reveals a strong Spanish influence, little remains of Buenos Aires's colonial days. This is due in part to the short lifespan of the *adobe* (mud and straw) used to build the city's first houses, and also to the fact that Buenos Aires's elite have always followed Europe's architectural trends closely. The result is an arresting hotchpotch of building styles that hints at many

Who *Are* These People?

BUENOS AIRES might not have as many museums or monuments as other capitals, but it does have some of the liveliest inhabitants. Here are a few things you can expect of them:

It's All in the Hands. Like their Italian ancestors, many porteños gesture, rather than speak, half of their conversation. Brushing your chin outward with your hand means "I have no idea." Bunching up your fingers is "What on earth are you talking about?" Pulling down the skin under one eye says "Watch out."

Getting Physical. Porteños greet each other with an effusive kiss on the cheek (always to the left) and look for other opportunities that allow physical displays of affection. Even men follow this pattern and laugh at foreign males who refuse to do so, saying that they are obviously insecure in their masculinity.

Hey Good-Looking. Locals claim porteño women are the most beautiful in the world, and, in tribute, the men have perfected the *piropo* (cat-call). Comments range from corny compliments to highly witty—and mildly offensive—word-plays. Follow local girls' cues and take it in stride.

Bigger, faster, better. "How do you make a quick buck in Argentina? Buy a porteño for what he's worth, and sell him for what he says he's worth." So goes a local joke lampooning the extremely high esteem in which Buenos Aires's residents hold themselves.

Sweets for the Sweet. Even the tiniest espresso arrives with four packets of sugar (or sweetener), just one testament to the local sweet tooth. Dulce de leche (a gooey milk-caramel spread) is another. It's practically a food group. Not only does it come in many desserts, but porteños also spread it on toast and—in the privacy of their kitchens—eat spoonfuls straight from the jar.

A Different Language. Porteños speak a very local version of Spanish. Instead of *"tú"* for "you," the archaic *"vos"* form is used, and "ll" and "y" are pronounced like "sh." A singsong accent owes a lot to Italian immigrants; indeed, an Italian-influenced slang—called *lunfardo*—is ever present.

Up in Smoke. Cigarettes cost a song, and much of the population indulges in the habit. No-smoking areas are nominal in restaurants and unheard of in bars and clubs. Buses, subway cars, and cinemas are the only smoke-free areas around.

Doggy Style. Porteños are big dog-lovers. Professional *paseaperros* (dogwalkers) wander with packs of well-dressed hounds anchored to their waists. Most porteños seem to have excellent poop radar, too: though the streets are filled with dog mess, you rarely see anyone step in it.

Driving You Crazy. Crossing the street is an extreme sport: roads are packed, traffic rules are openly flaunted, drinking and driving is practically a norm, and porteños think seat belts are for sissies. Sadly, traffic accidents are the biggest cause of death in the city, but that hasn't caused local habits to change.

far-off cities—Rome, Madrid, Paris, Budapest—but resembles none. With their boulevards lined with palatial mansions and spacious parks, Palermo, La Recoleta, Belgrano, and some parts of the downtown area are testament to days of urban planning on a grandiose scale (and budget), whereas San Telmo and La Boca have a distinctly working-class Italian feel.

EL CENTRO: MICROCENTRO & TRIBUNALES

Porteños love to brag that Buenos Aires has the world's widest avenue (Avenida 9 de Julio), its longest street (well, not really—but locals refuse to admit that Toronto's Yonge Street is longer than Rivadavia), its best steak, and its prettiest women. The place to decide if they're right is unquestionably downtown, where traffic noise and driving tactics also reach superlative levels. The Microcentro is the central business district, lying between Avenidas L.N. Alem and 9 de Julio and north of Avenida de Mayo. It includes Calle Florida, a pedestrian-only street with discount leather stores and a top mall.

Illuminated by flashing billboards, the Obelisk, at the intersection of Avenida Corrientes and Avenida 9 de Julio, rises above the hubbub. At 221½ feet, the Obelisk is one of Buenos Aires's most prominent landmarks, built in 1936 on the site where the nation's flag was first raised. Inescapably phallic, the Obelisk is both the butt of local jokes about male insecurity in this oh-so-macho city and the subject of serious theorizing. Open-air concerts are sometimes staged in the area surrounding it, and during elections or major soccer matches, huge crowds of porteños converge here to rejoice in the outcome of the day's events.

More highbrow cultural events are celebrated a few blocks away in the spectacular Teatro Colón, a world-class opera house, on Avenda 9 de Julio and Viamonte. The legal district, behind the opera house, revolves around the Palacio de Justicia (Supreme Court), home to some of Argentina's biggest scandals. Buenos Aires's theater district is Avenida Corrientes, whose sidewalks overflow on weekends with dolled-up locals. All of the Microcentro and Tribunales is easily accessible by subte Líneas B, C, and D; it's also easy to walk around both areas.

Timing & Precautions
Half a day in the Microcentro and Tribunales is enough to take in the sights and have your fill of risky street-crossing, though you could spend a lot more time caught up in shops or seeing shows.

Walking along Florida, with its countless salesmen and money changers, can feel like running the gauntlet, but a purposeful look and *"No, gracias"* gets you past them. Many stores close in the evenings and on weekends, leaving things deserted; wander with care at these times. Although Lavalle is a commercial hub, it is also peppered with adult entertainment and a mega-bingo hall; again, use caution here. Corrientes is usually packed with theatergoers, but keep an eye out for purse snatchers.

Always use ATMs within bank hours (weekdays 10–3) as they're common target areas for thieves. Hail taxis far from banks and ATMs in this part of town. Robbers have been known to pose as taxi drivers and search for potential victims—that is visitors who have just withdrawn money. In general, looking aware is enough to make someone else a better target than you. In the unlikely event that you are held up, comply with the perpetrator's requests quickly and quietly.

Top Sight

Calle Florida. When porteños talk about Florida (pronounced flo-*ree*-da, they aren't referring to a vacation but rather a pedestrian street that crosses the Microcenter's heart. This downtown axis is a riot of office workers, fast-food chains, boutiques, and vendors selling (and haggling over) leather goods. The commercial institutions that line the street are battered and paint-splattered—unhappy customers have been taking out their anger at these *corralitos* (banks retaining their savings) since the economic crisis of 2001–02. You'll also find souvenir, food, and bookstores. The closer you get to Plaza San Martín, the better the offerings.

Milan's Galleria Vittorio Emanuele served as the architectural model for **Galerías Pacífico** (Pacific Gallery), designed during Buenos Aires's turn-of-the-20th-century golden age. Once the headquarters of the Buenos Aires–Pacific Railway, it's now a posh shopping mall and cultural center. Head to the central stairwell to see the allegorical murals painted by local greats Juan Carlos Castagnino, Antonio Berni, Cirilo Colmenio, Lino Spilimbergo, and Demetrio Urruchúa. The Centro Cultural Borges, which hosts small international exhibitions and musical events, is on the mezzanine level. ⊠ *Florida 753, Microcentro* ☎ *11/ 5555–5100* ⊕ *www.galeriaspacifico.com.ar; www.ccborges.org.ar* Ⓜ *B to Florida.*

If all the activity of Florida becomes too much, just steps away is **Plaza San Martín** (San Martín Square), a great place to put down your shopping bags and rest your feet. French landscape architect Charles Thays designed the square in the 1800s, juxtaposing local and exotic trees. An imposing bronze equestrian monument to General José de San Martín watches over lunching office workers. The Monumento a los Caídos en las Malvinas is a more somber presence. Guarded by a grenadier, the monument's 25 black marble slabs are engraved with the names of those who died in the 1982 Falkland Islands War. ⊠ *Av. Libertador and Calle Florida, Microcentro* Ⓜ *C to San Martín.*

NEED A BREAK?
More than just a coffeehouse, **Florida Garden** (⊠ Florida 899, at Paraguay, Microcentro ☎ 11/4312–7902), a '60s-style bordering-on-kitsch café, is a landmark because of its association with the intelligentsia of yesteryear. Among other cultural icons, writer Jorge Luis Borges hung out here. Sit elbow to elbow along the 20-foot bar or in a room upstairs and enjoy afternoon tea or an ultra-rich hot chocolate.

Top Experiences

A Night at the Opera

Fodor'sChoice ★ Its magnitude, magnificent acoustics, and opulence (grander than Milan's La Scala) position the **Teatro Colón** (Colón Theater) among the world's top five operas. An ever-changing stream of imported talent bolsters the well-regarded local lyric and ballet companies. After an eventful 18-year building process involving the death of one architect and the murder of another, the ornate Italianate structure was finally inaugurated in 1908 with Verdi's *Aida*. It has hosted the likes of Maria Callas, Richard Strauss, Arturo Toscanini, Igor Stravinsky, Enrico Caruso, and Luciano Pavarotti, who has said that the Colón has only one flaw: the acoustics are so good, every mistake can be heard.

The theater's sumptuous building materials—three kinds of Italian marble, French stained glass, and Venetian mosaics—were imported from Europe to create large-scale lavishness. The seven-tier main theater is breathtaking in size, and has a grand central chandelier with 700 lights to illuminate the 3,000 mere mortals in its red-velvet seats.

The opera and ballet seasons run from April through December, but many seats are reserved for season-ticket holders. Throughout the year you can buy tickets for any performance from the box-office in Pasaje Toscanini. If seats are sold out—or beyond your pocket—you can buy standing-room tickets on the day of the performance for a fraction of the cost. These are for the lofty upper-tier *paraíso*, from which you can both see and hear perfectly, although three-hour-long operas are hard on the feet.

Shorter options in the main theater include symphonic cycles by the stable orchestra, as well as international orchestral visits. The Colón also holds chamber music concerts in the U-shaped Salón Dorado (Golden Room), so named for the 24-karat gold leaf that covers its stucco molding. Underneath the main building is the ultra-minimal Centro Experimental, a tiny theater showcasing avant-garde music, opera, and dramatic performances.

You can see the splendor up close and get in on all the behind-the-scenes action with the theater's extremely popular guided tours. The whirlwind visits take you up and down innumerable staircases to rehearsal rooms and to the costume, shoe, and scenery workshops, before letting you gaze at the stage from a sought-after box. Arrive at least a half hour before the tour starts as places fill up very quickly. You can while away time before a tour or a performance at the small but very classy café opposite the box office. There's also a gift shop selling souvenirs like totes and aprons; CDs; and, surprisingly, a small selection of tableware.

✉ *Main entrance: Libertad between Tucumán and Viamonte; Box office: Pasaje Toscanini 1180, Microcentro* ☎ *11/4378–7100 tickets, 11/4378–7132 tours* ⊕ *www.teatrocolon.org.ar* ☉ *Tours in English: weekdays 11, noon, 1, and 3; Sat. 9, 11, 1, and 3; Sun. 11, 1, and 3* Ⓜ *D to Tribunales.*

Broadway of the South

On Avenida Corrientes, performances of Shakespeare, Chekhov, and Pinter rub shoulders with revues starring dancing *vedettes* (scantily clad showgirls) wearing a few strategic sequins. Although Buenos Aires's answer to Broadway is nowhere near as glamorous as it once was, the

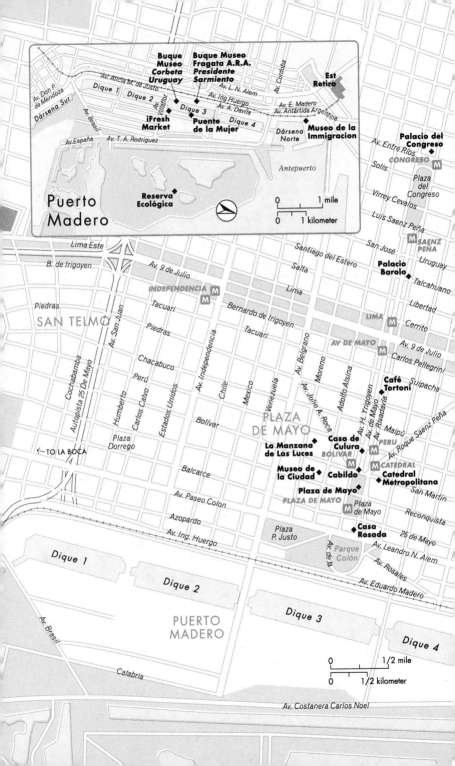

Buque Museo Corbeta Uruguay

Buque Museo Fragata A.R.A. Presidente Sarmiento

Est Retiro

Palacio del Congreso

Av. Alicia M. de Justo

Av. Don P. de Mendoza

Dársena Sur

Dique 1

Dique 2

Av. Brasil

Av. L. N. Alem

Av. Ing Huergo

Av. A. Dávila

Av. Córdoba

Dique 3

Dique 4

Av. E. Madero

Av. Antártida Argentina

Av. Entre Ríos

iFresh Market

Puente de la Mujer

Dársena Norte

Museo de la Immigracion

Av. España

Av. T. A. Rodriguez

Antepuerto

CONGRESO Ⓜ

Solís

Plaza del Congreso

Virrey Cevalos

Reserva Ecológica

Luis Saenz Peña

San José

Uruguay

SAENZ PEÑA Ⓜ

0   1 mile

0   1 kilometer

Puerto Madero

Santiago del Estero

Salta

Lima Este

B. de Trigoyen

Lima

Palacio Barolo

Talcahuano

Libertad

Tacuari

INDEPENDENCIA Ⓜ

Bernardo de Irigoyen

LIMA Ⓜ

Cerrito

Piedras

SAN TELMO

Piedras

Tacuari

Av. 9 de Julio

Carlos Pellegrini

Chacabuco

Av. Independencia

Chile

Mexico

Venezuela

Av. Julio A. Roca

Morena

Adolfo Alsina

Av. H. Yrigoyen

AV DE MAYO Ⓜ

Café Tortoni

Suipacha

Perú

Av. San Juan

Av. Belgrano

Av. de Mayo

Av. Rivadavia

Maipú

Av. Roque Saenz Peña

Cochabamba

Autopista 25 de Mayo

Humberto

Carlos Calvo

Estados Unidos

Bolívar

PLAZA DE MAYO

PERU Ⓜ

Plaza Dorrego

La Manzana de Las Luces

Casa de Cultura

BOLÍVAR

CATEDRAL Ⓜ

Museo de la Ciudad

Cabildo

Catedral Metropolitana

Balcarce

Plaza de Mayo

San Martin

← TO LA BOCA

Av. Paseo Colon

PLAZA DE MAYO Ⓜ

Plaza de Mayo

Reconquista

Azopardo

Plaza P. Justo

Casa Rosada

25 de Mayo

Av. Ing. Huergo

Av. de la

Parque Colón

Av. Leandro N. Alem

Dique 1

Dique 2

Av. Rosales

Av. Eduardo Madero

PUERTO MADERO

Dique 3

Dique 4

Av. Brasil

Calabria

0   1/2 mile

0   1/2 kilometer

Av. Costanera Carlos Noel

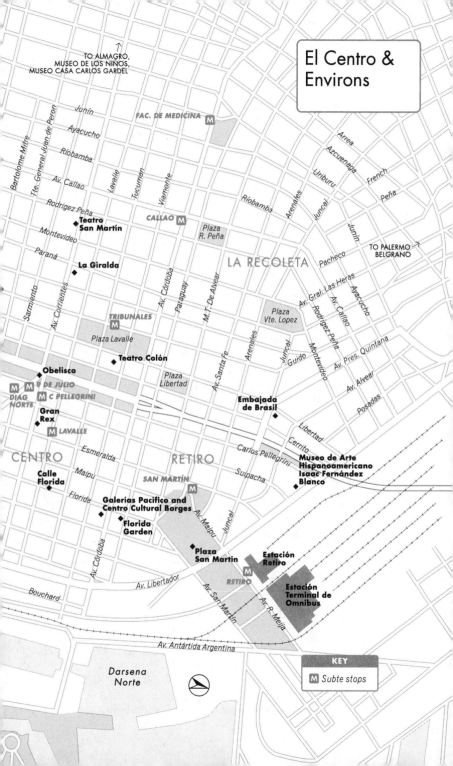

El Centro & Environs

TO ALMAGRO,
MUSEO DE LOS NIÑOS,
MUSEO CASA CARLOS GARDEL

FAC. DE MEDICINA M

Junín
Ayacucho
Ríobamba
Av. Callao
Rodriguez Peña

Bartolomé Mitre
Tte. General Juan de Perón
Lavalle
Tucuman
Viamonte

CALLAO M
Plaza R. Peña

Arrea
Azcuenaga
Uriburu
French
Peña

Ríobamba
Arenales
Juncal

Teatro San Martín
Montevideo
Paraná

LA RECOLETA

Pacheco
Junín

TO PALERMO
BELGRANO

La Giralda

Sarmiento
Av. Corrientes

Av. Córdoba
Paraguay
M.T. De Alvear

Av. Gral. Las Heras
Rodriguez Peña
Av. Callao
Ayacucho

TRIBUNALES
Plaza Lavalle

Plaza Vte. Lopez

Av. Pres. Quintana

Teatro Colón

Arenales
Juncal
Guido
Montevideo

Av. Santa Fe

Av. Alvear

Obelisco

Plaza Libertad

Posadas

M M 9 DE JULIO
DIAG NORTE
M C PELLEGRINI

Embajada de Brasil

Libertad
Cerrito

Gran Rex

M LAVALLE

CENTRO
Esmeralda
Maipu

RETIRO

SAN MARTÍN M

Carlos Pellegrini
Suipacha

Museo de Arte
Hispanoamericano
Isaac Fernández
Blanco

Calle Florida
Florida

Galerias Pacifico and
Centro Cultural Borges

Florida Garden

Av. Córdoba

Plaza San Martín

Av. Maipu
Juncal

Estación Retiro

RETIRO M

Estación Terminal de Omnibus

Bouchard

Av. Libertador

Av. San Martín
Av. R. Mejía

Av. Antártida Argentina

Darsena Norte

KEY
M Subte stops

crowds of porteños that fill the street's sidewalks each evening are testament to a thriving theater scene. If there aren't any shows that take your fancy, watch the theatergoers over an evening drink in one of the street's many cafés.

The **Teatro San Martín,** a three-stage municipal complex, hosts a wide range of theater productions as well as world-class contemporary dance performances, mime, and puppet shows. It's also the site of year-round classical music performances by top Argentine performers; many concerts are free. ⊠ *Av. Corrientes 1530, Microcentro and Tribunales* ☎ *11/4374–9680* ⊕ *www.teatrosanmartin.com.ar* Ⓜ *B to Callao or Uruguay.*

All along Avenida Corrientes are exquisite art deco theatres like the **Gran Rex,** a favorite venue for rock, pop, and jazz musicians. Recent performances include Brazilian Caetano Veloso and Oscar-winning Uruguayan Jorge Drexler, who love the acoustics as much as the enthusiastic audiences. ⊠ *Corrientes 857* ☎ *11/4322–8000* ⊙ *Box office daily 10–10* Ⓜ *B to Carlos Pellegrini.*

NEED A BREAK? Beret-wearing intellectuals and perfumed theatergoers alike love **La Giralda** (⊠ Av. Corrientes 1453 ☎ 11/4371–3846), one of Av. Corrientes's most famous cafés. Don't let the small tables or surly waiters put you off; its signature *chocolate con churros* (hot chocolate with crisp cigar-shape donuts) are to die for.

Also Worth Some Time

Museo de Arte Hispanoamericano Isaac Fernández Blanco. The distinctive Peruvian neocolonial-style Palacio Noel serves as the perfect backdrop for the Isaac Fernández Blanco Hispanic-American Art Museum. It was built as the residence of architect Martín Noel in the late 18th century. He and museum founder Fernández Blanco donated most of the silver items, wood carvings, furnishings, and paintings from the Spanish colonial period that are on display. Concerts are held in the lush, Spanish-style garden, and there's a library. Guided tours in English can be arranged with prior notice. The museum is an easy five-block walk from Estación San Martí on Línea C: from there go west along Avenida Santa Fe and then turn right into Suipacha and continue four blocks. ⊠*Suipacha 1422, at Av. Libertador, Retiro* ☎ *11/4327–0228* ⊠ *3 pesos, free Thurs.* ⊙ *Tues.–Fri. 2–7, weekends 3–7* Ⓜ *C to San Martín.*

EL CENTRO: IN & AROUND PLAZA DE MAYO

Many historic events transpired around the axes of Plaza de Mayo (May Square), though outsiders perhaps best know it from the balcony scene in the 1996 film *Evita.* Although it's not technically speaking a city district, there are enough sights around the square for you to treat it as such. Government workers, businesspeople, and protesters crowd the area on weekdays; on weekends it becomes a haven for pigeons and swallows, as well as the children who delight in feeding them.

West along Avenida de Mayo are several architectural wonders of yesteryear—French-inspired domes and towers with Iberian accents—as well as numerous cafés. The avenue runs from the Casa Rosada all the way up to the legislative Palacio del Congreso (Congressional Building), whose facade resembles that of the U.S. Congress, except for the trumpet-wielding angels of revelation. The monumental 1906 structure marks Km 0 for routes leading out of the city. You can reach Plaza de Mayo by Líneas D and E, as well as line A, which runs under Avenida de Mayo.

Timing & Precautions

A leisurely walk through the Plaza de Mayo area should take two or three hours, but allow up to a day if you plan to visit all the sights here. The area can be very busy on weekdays, but given that weekend opening hours are erratic—indeed, most of the government-owned sights are closed on Saturday—it's best to brave the chaos and visit the area midweek and see it as most porteños do. The area is very quiet at night as there isn't much to do here; visit during the day.

Top Sights

★ **Plaza de Mayo.** Dating from 1580, the Plaza de Mayo itself has been the stage for many important events throughout the nation's history, including the uprising against Spanish colonial rule on May 25, 1810—hence its name. The square was once divided in two by a *recova* (gallery), but this reminder of colonial times was demolished in 1883 and the square's central monument, the Pirámide de Mayo, was later moved to its place. The pyramid you see is actually a 1911 extension of the original, erected in 1811 on the anniversary of the Revolution of May, which is hidden inside. The bronze equestrian statue of General Manuel Belgrano, designer of Argentina's flag, dates from 1873 and stands at the east end of the plaza.

The plaza remains the traditional site for ceremonies as well as mass protests, including the bloody clashes in December 2001, as testified by ongoing heavy police presence and lots of crowd control barriers. The white headscarves painted round the Pirámide de Mayo represent the Madres de la Plaza de Mayo (Mothers of May Square) who have marched here every Thursday at 3:30 for more than two decades. Housewives and mothers turned militant activists, they demand justice for *los desaparecidos,* the people who were "disappeared" during the military government's reign from 1976 to 1983. Here, too, you can witness the changing of the Grenadier Regiment guards; it takes place weekdays every two hours from 9 until 7, Saturday at 9 and 11, and Sunday at 9, 11, and 1.

The eclectic Casa de Gobierno, better known as the **Casa Rosada** (⊠ Hipólito Yrigoyen 219, Plaza de Mayo ☎ 11/4344–3802 or 11/4344–3600 ⊕ www.museo.gov.ar) or Pink House, is at the plaza's eastern end, with its back to the river. The building houses the government's executive branch—the president works here but lives elsewhere—and was built in the late 19th century over the foundations of an earlier customhouse and fortress. Swedish, Italian, and French architects have since modified the structure, which accounts for the odd mix of styles.

Its curious hue dates from the presidency of Domingo Sarmiento, who ordered it painted pink as a symbol of unification between two warring political factions, the *federales* (whose color was red) and the *unitarios* (represented by white). Local legend has it that the original paint was made by mixing whitewash with bull's blood.

The balcony facing Plaza de Mayo has served as a presidential podium. From this lofty stage Evita rallied the *descamisados* (the shirtless—meaning the working class), Maradona sang along with soccer fans after winning one World Cup and coming second in another, and Madonna sang her filmed rendition of "Don't Cry for Me Argentina." Check for a small banner hoisted alongside the nation's flag, indicating "the president is in." Behind the structure, you can find the brick-wall remains of the 1845 Taylor Customs House, discovered after being buried for almost a century. Enter the Casa Rosada through the basement level of the Museo de la Casa Rosada, the only area open to the public, which exhibits presidential memorabilia along with objects from the original customhouse and fortress. Admission to the museum is free. It's open weekdays 10–6 and Sunday 2–6. Call ahead to arrange an English-language tour. To reach the Plaza de Mayo and the Casa Rosada, take Línea A to Plaza de Mayo, D to Catedral, or E to Bolívar.

La Manzana de Las Luces (The Block of Illumination). Constructed by the Jesuits in the early 1800s, prior to their expulsion, La Manzana de Las Luces, a cluster of buildings southwest of Plaza de Mayo, was an enclave meant for higher learning. The metaphorical *luces* (lights) of its name refer to the "illuminated" scholars who lived within. This was the colonial administrative headquarters for the Jesuits' vast land holdings in northeastern Argentina and Paraguay. In 1780 the city's first School of Medicine was established here, and it became home to the University of Buenos Aires early in the 19th century. Among the historic buildings still standing are the Parroquia de San Ignacio de Loyola and the neoclassic Colegio Nacional, a top-notch public school and a hotbed of political activism.

You can tour parts of the historic tunnels, still undergoing archaeological excavation, which linked several churches in the area to the Cabildo and the port. The original purpose of these tunnels is a source of speculation—were they used for defense or smuggling? ⊠ *Perú 272, at Av. Julio A. Roca (known as Diagonal Sur), Plaza de Mayo* ☎ *11/4342–6973* ▣ *Free* ⊙ *Weekdays 10–7, weekends 3–7* Ⓜ *A to Plaza de Mayo, D to Catedral, E to Bolívar.*

Museo de la Ciudad. To the south of La Manzana de las Luces, on Alsina, are the Basílica y Convento de San Francisco, the smaller San Roque Chapel, and the City Museum. It houses temporary exhibits both whimsical and probing on aspects of domestic and public life in Buenos Aires in times past. The Farmacia La Estrella (Star Pharmacy) is a quaint survivor from the 19th century. ⊠ *Alsina 412, Plaza de Mayo* ☎ *11/ 4331–9855 or 11/4343–2123* ⊙ *Weekdays 11–7, Sun. 3–7* Ⓜ *A to Plaza de Mayo, D to Catedral, E to Bolívar.*

Top Experience

Strolling the Avenue

When you've had your fill of Plaza de Mayo, wander along Avenida de Mayo, which stretches from the square's western side. Although it seems older, the avenue was created just over a century ago in 1894, when the whole right half of the Cabildo was lopped off to make room for it. Architects from Eastern Europe were called in to design the imposing buildings that line it. More time-travel is on offer by dipping down into one of the subway stations on Línea A. The city's oldest line has clanking wooden carriages and gloomy tiled stations that haven't changed much in the last 50 years.

Stave off lunch long enough to check out the ornate **Casa de Cultura,** topped by a torch-bearing statue of Athena. Look closely for the newspaper under the bronze goddess's arm: the building was once the headquarters of conservative newspaper *La Prensa,* but was requisitioned by Perón, fed up of their criticism of his government. It's now the property of the city which organizes regular classical concerts in its exquisite Versailles-inspired Salón Dorado, where writer Borges gave his first conference. ✉ *Av. de Mayo 575, Plaza de Mayo* ☎ *11/4323–9669* ☉ *Weekdays 8–8.*

There's plenty of fodder for bookworms in Avenida de Mayo's 700 block, where the heaving shelves of dusty cave-like shops such as **El Ventanal** are full of antiquarian finds, as well as movie posters from 1930s tango films. ✉ *Av. de Mayo 769, Plaza de Mayo.*

NEED A BREAK?

For a breather, try the favorite haunt of literary greats Jorge Luis Borges and Roberto Arlt, the **Café Tortoni** (✉ Av. de Mayo 829, Plaza de Mayo ☎ 11/4342-4328 ⊕ www.cafetortoni.com.ar). It dates from 1858, making it the town's oldest café. A lowlit, ornate interior—all old-world elegance—makes it the perfect place for a *café con leche con medialunas* (coffee and croissants). Evenings, things heat up with tango and jazz performances.

For a more filling lunch, consider the traditional Iberian offerings in the neighborhood's unofficial Spanish quarter, on the other side of Avenida 9 de Julio. Hearty paellas and stews are worth going a block south of Avenida de Mayo to parallel street Hipólito Irigoyen's intersection with Salta. One of the corner restaurants, El Imparcial, got its name because of its owners' neutral stance during the Spanish Civil War, when talking politics was forbidden within.

The ornate neo-Gothic **Palacio Barolo** is an architectural homage to Dante Alighieri. The palacio is 100 meters tall, one meter for each of the 100 cantos of the *Divine Comedy.* The floors are divided into hell, purgatory, and the cupola-ed heaven, which contains a 300,000-bulb beam once used to transmit the results of the Dempsey–Firpo boxing match to the Uruguayan coast. So Dante-obsessed was its architect Mario Palanti that he considered trying to bring the poet's ashes from Italy. ✉ *Av. de Mayo 1370, Plaza de Mayo.*

The Language of Protest

THE URBAN LANDSCAPE changed overnight on December 19, 2001, when the country's economy crashed. The state froze all private bank accounts, and ensuing demonstrations escalated into riots due to the violence of police response.The backdrop for the protests was Plaza de Mayo, and the soundtrack was the steady clanging of people hitting *cacerolas* (pots and pans) with spoons. This gave rise to the term *cacerolazo*, a pot-beating demonstration. In the days that followed, Argentina went through six presidents, and the peso devalued alarmingly.

The streets eventually calmed down, but poverty in Argentina skyrocketed, forcing people to live by their wits. Some began to sift through garbage looking for such recyclables as paper and *cartón* (cardboard), which prompted people to call them *cartoneros*. Today, after dark, cartoneros comb the streets in organized armies, packing their findings into rickety carts or trucks.

Another protest phenomenon are the *piqueteros*, whose name comes from the picket lines they create at strategic entry points to the city, blocking traffic until their demands are met. The piqueteros are a mix of the seriously impoverished with reasonable demands and rowdy trouble-makers in the pay of political parties. Like it or not, the crisis has expanded the city's vocabulary, and until times get better it seems piqueteros, cartoneros, and cacerolazos are here to stay.

Also Worth Some Time

Catedral Metropolitana. The Metropolitan Cathedral's columned neoclassical facade makes it seem more like a temple than a church, and its history follows the pattern of many structures in the Plaza de Mayo area. The first of six buildings on this site was a 16th-century adobe ranch house; the current structure dates from 1822 but has been added to several times. The embalmed remains of General José de San Martín, known as the Liberator of Argentina for his role in the War of Independence, rest here in a marble mausoleum lit by an eternal flame. Soldiers of the Grenadier Regiment, an elite troop created and trained by San Martín in 1811, permanently guard the tomb. Group tours in English are available, but you need to call ahead. ⊠ *Rivadavia and San Martín Plaza de Mayo* ☎ *11/4331–2845* ☒ *Free* ☉ *Weekdays 8–7, weekends 9–7:30* Ⓜ *A to Plaza de Mayo, D to Catedral, E to Bolívar.*

Cabildo. Once the home of the city council—now in the ornate building over Avenida de Mayo—the Cabildo dates from 1765 and is the only colonial building on Plaza de Mayo. The epicenter of the May Revolution of 1810, where patriotic citizens gathered to vote against Spanish rule, the hall is one of Argentina's national shrines. However, this hasn't stopped successive renovations to its detriment, including the demolition of the whole right end of the structure to make way for the new

Avenida de Mayo in 1894. Inside, a small museum exhibits artifacts and documents pertaining to the events of the May Revolution as well as a jail cell. Admission is 3 pesos. Thursday and Friday from 11 to 6, an artisan fair takes place on the Patio del Cabildo. You can participate in glassblowing and other crafts; musical performances are held from 1 to 3. ⊠*Bolívar 65, Plaza de Mayo* ☎*11/4334–1782* ⊠*3 pesos* ☉*Tues.–Fri. 10:30–5, Sun. 11:30–6* Ⓜ *Line A, Plaza de Mayo; Line D, Catedral; Line E, Bolívar.*

ALMAGRO

At the heart of this classic tango neighborhood is the subdistrict of Abasto, which centers on the massive Art Deco building at Corrientes and Agüero that was once the city's central market. The abandoned structure was completely overhauled and re-opened in 1998 as a major mall, spearheading the redevelopment of the area, which now has several top hotels and an increasing number of restaurants and tango venues. More urban renewal is taking place a few blocks away at Sarmiento and Jean Jaurés, where the Konex foundation is recycling an abandoned factory into what's set to become a cutting-edge cultural venue.

Timing & Precautions

A couple of hours is enough to see all things Carlos Gardel—tango's greatest hero—and get a feel for the district. Although Almagro is on the up, many streets near the Abasto shopping mall are still quite run-down with many of the old houses functioning as squats, so wander with caution. The mall gets busier than most on weekends because of the Museo de los Niños (Children's Museum), so come midweek for some space to move in.

Worth Some Time

Ⓒ **Museo de los Niños.** The real world is scaled down to kiddie-size at this commercially sponsored museum in the Abasto shopping mall. Children can play at doing things grown-ups do, from sending letters and going to a bank, to acting in a mini-TV studio or making a radio program. You need to speak Spanish to be able to participate in most of the activities properly, but the play areas and giant pipes re-creating the city's water system are internationally comprehensible. ⊠ *Abasto Shopping Center, Level 2, Av. Corrientes 3247, Almagro* ☎*11/4861–2325* ⊕*www. museoabasto.org.ar* ⊠ *9 pesos, 4-person family ticket 27 pesos* ☉ *Tues.–Sun. 1–8.*

Museo Casa Carlos Gardel. Hard-core tango fans shouldn't pass up a visit to the home of tango's greatest hero, Carlos Gardel. The crumbling *casa chorizo* (sausage house, that is a long, narrow house) has been restored with the aim of recreating as closely as possible the way the house would have looked when Gardel and his mother lived here, right up to the placement of bird cages on the patio. Concise but informative Spanish texts talk you through the rooms and Gardel paraphernalia, and there are lots tango souvenirs on offer in the shop. ⊠ *Jean Jaurés 735, Almagro* ☎ *11/4516–0943* ⊠ *3 pesos* ☉ *Weekdays 11–6.*

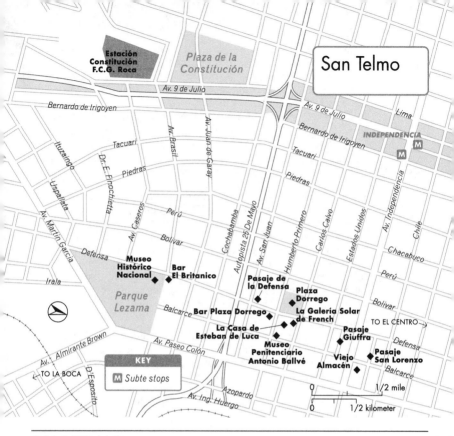

Estación
Constitución
F.C.G. Roca

Plaza de la
Constitución

San Telmo

Av. 9 de Julio

Bernardo de Irigoyen

Av. 9 de Julio

Lima

Bernardo de Irigoyen

INDEPENDENCIA

M

Tacuarí

Av. Juan de Garay

Av. Brasil

Dr. E. Finochietta

Piedras

Tacuarí

Av. Independencia

Iturraingo

Piedras

Chile

Uspallata

Av. Caseros

Perú

Cochabamba

Autopista 26 De Mayo

Av. San Juan

Humberto Primero

Carlos Calvo

Estados Unidos

Av. Martín García

Bolívar

Chacabuco

Perú

Defensa

Museo
Histórico
Nacional

Bar
El Britanico

Pasaje de
la Defensa

Plaza
Dorrego

Bolívar

Irala

Parque
Lezama

Balcarce

Bar Plaza Dorrego

La Galería Solar
de French

TO EL CENTRO →

Almirante Brown

Av. Paseo Colón

La Casa de
Esteban de Luca

Pasaje
Giuffra

Defensa

Av. Almirante Brown

Museo
Penitenciario
Antonio Ballvé

Viejo
Almacén

Pasaje
San Lorenzo

Av. Esposito

D'Esposito

KEY

M Subte stops

Balcarce

← TO LA BOCA

Azopardo

Av. Ing. Huergo

0   1/2 mile

0   1/2 kilometer

SAN TELMO

With soaring turn-of-the-century Italianate town houses, cobbled streets straight out of *Amélie*, and Spanish-style mansions whose patios are filled with antiques from all over the world, it seems appropriate that San Telmo is named after the wandering patron saint of seafarers. Midway between downtown and the port area of La Boca, San Telmo is top of the most-wanted list for foreigners investing in the city's pied-à-terres. They all want to ride the wave of urban renewal—the *reciclaj*e (recycling), as porteños call it—that's sweeping the area.

San Telmo was Buenos Aires's first suburb, inhabited by sailors and fishermen. It then became the domain of wealthy Spaniards, who, in turn, abandoned it with the outbreak of yellow fever in the late 1800s. The mansions they left were converted into tenements and occupied by immigrants. Thanks to government subsidies and urban renewal plans, the worn sidewalks and crumbling structures are being transformed into quaint streets lined with antiques shops, galleries, chic restaurants, and traditional tango halls. To reach San Telmo by subway, take Línea E to the Independencia station, and be prepared to walk nine blocks east along Avenida Independencia to Calle Defensa, the city's oldest street. Alternatively, take Línea E to Bolívar station or Línea D to Catedral station and walk eight blocks south along Bolívar.

Timing & Precautions

San Telmo thrives on Sunday, thanks to the art and antiques market in Plaza Dorrego. Crowds can get so thick that only judicious elbowing gets you close to the stalls on the squares; explore this neighborhood during the week for more relaxed strolling. A few hours will give you time to see the sights, though you could easily spend a full day wandering. San Telmo is one of the city's seedier districts, and you should exercise caution when walking here—especially at night. Violent crime is rare, but unemployment in the area, combined with the knowledge that it's popular with tourists, has led to instances of petty crime.

Top Sights

Museo Histórico Nacional. Enormous magnolia, palm, cedar, and elm trees shade the sloping hillside of Parque Lezama, site of the National History Museum. Bronze statues of Greek heroes, stone urns, and an imposing fountain shipped from Paris are part of the landscaping. Patchy grass, cracked paths, and unpainted benches suggest that San Telmo's wave of renovation hasn't made it south yet. The onion-shaped domes of the Catedral Santísima Trinidad Iglesia Ortodoxa Rusa (Holy Trinity Russian Orthodox Church) overlook the park, which was immortalized by Argentine writer Ernesto Sabato in his novel *Sobre Heroes y Tumbas* (*Of Heroes and Tombs*). The park is said to be the site on which the city was first founded by Pedro de Mendoza, who is celebrated in a monument at its northwestern corner. In the 1700s the Company of Guinea operated its slave trade from here.

Entrepreneur and horticulturalist Gregorio Lezama purchased the large tract of land and the chestnut-and-white Italianate mansion on it in 1858. The building was subsequently used as a refuge from both the cholera and yellow-fever epidemics. It was extensively remodeled prior to opening as this museum in 1897.

The mansion houses artifacts and paintings spanning the 16th through 20th centuries, organized chronologically. Although most items have inventively translated English labels, there are no explanations of their significance, so unless you have a detailed knowledge of Argentine history many exhibits will be meaningless. Nonetheless, an hour perusing maps, clothing, and personal effects is enough to get an idea of what life in Buenos Aires used to be like. Scuffed walls, lighting in need of replacement, and dry displays are partly made up for by endearingly enthusiastic staff. The once-weekly tours in Spanish are often given by the museum's director.

Highlight: The first Argentine flag, designed by General Manuel Belgrano and flown by him in 1813 during the War of Independence against Spain. Belgrano lost his battles, but the flag was hidden by a priest sympathetic to the cause behind a painting in his parish church at Macha, Bolivia, where it remained forgotten until accidental discovery in 1896.

✉ *Calle Defensa 1600, San Telmo* ☎ *11/4307–4457* 💳 *2 pesos* ☉ *Feb.–Dec., Tues.–Fri and Sun. 11–5.*

Bar El Británico, on the northwest corner of Parque Lezama, is a vintage neigh-borhood bar favored by bohemian students and old men. Perk up with a *cortado* (espresso "cut" with a dash of milk) or imitate the old-timers and unwind with a *ginebra* (gin-like spirit). ⊠ *Brazil 399, at Defensa* ☎ *11/4300–6894.*

★ **Plaza Dorrego.** Stately trees shade outdoor tables in the city's second old-est square. The surrounding architecture provides an overview of the influences—Spanish colonial, French classical, and ornate Italian ma-sonry—that shaped the city in the 19th and 20th centuries. On Sunday from 10 to 5 the square comes alive with the Feria de San Pedro Telmo (San Pedro Telmo Fair) and its vendors and tango dancers. Shop for tango memorabilia, leather goods, antique silver, brass, jewelry, crystal, and turn-of-the-20th-century Argentine and European curios. Prices are high at stalls on the square and astronomical in the shops surrounding it, and don't expect to bargain.

Feria Must-Have: Antique (or just plain old) glass soda siphons that used to adorn every bar top in Buenos Aires. Classic colors are bottle green or turquoise; prices start at around 20 pesos.

Top Experience

Walk of Ages

On weekdays, a leisurely half-hour walk through the quiet cobbled streets around Plaza Dorrego affords a glimpse of what the city looked like in centuries past. The colonial building at Number 1179 Calle De-fensa, a block south of Plaza Dorrego, is known as a *casa chorizo* (sausage house) because of its long, narrow structure. The internal Roman-style courtyards are referred to as **Pasaje de la Defensa** (Defence Alley). Once the home of the well-to-do Ezeiza family, it became a *con-ventillo* (tenement house) and is now a picturesque spot for antiques and curio shopping. The stores here are open daily 10 to 6. North of Plaza Dorrego, at Defensa 1066, is **La Galería del Solar de French,** a neoclas-sical mansion built on the site where Domingo French, a hero of the War of Independence, once lived. **La Casa de Esteban de Luca** (⊠ Calle De-fensa 1000 ☎ 11/4361–4338), on the corner of Defensa and Carlos Calvo, was once the home of the distinguished poet and soldier who wrote the country's first national anthem and was a hero of the May Revolution of 1810. It's now a quaint, if somewhat touristy, restaurant serving in-ternational and local cuisine; Antonio Banderas dined here during the filming of *Evita.*

Off Defensa to the right is the short alley known as **Pasaje Giuffra,** home to the exclusive Universidad del Cine, a top local film school.

Although a stretch of **Calle Balcarce** is known for its touristy tango spots, the 900 and 1000 blocks have some unique Spanish colonial ar-chitecture, such as Number 1016, the former home of painter Juan Car-los Castagnino. Stroll down this street to reach one of the first of the quickly vanishing conventillos of the past, on the corner of Humberto I. **Viejo Almacén** (⊠ Balcarce 786, San Telmo ☎ 11/4307–6689 or 11/

4300–3388 ⊕ www.viejo-almacen.com.ar) is both a hot spot for tango and a fine example of colonial architecture. Built in 1798 as a general store, it served as the British Hospital in the 1840s, and then as a customhouse. Tango artist Edmundo Rivero purchased it in 1969. It's only open for dinner and shows. Off Calle Balcarce, **Pasaje San Lorenzo** is a typical and charming colonial alley. At Number 380 stand the ruins of the city's thinnest building—about 8 feet wide. It once belonged to a freed slave.

NEED A BREAK? Original wood-panelling, dust-festooned bottles, peanut shells underfoot, and gloomy lighting pull both ancient regulars and laptopped trendies to **Bar Plaza Dorrego**, San Telmo's best-known café. Look out over the square as you sip your *cafecito* (espresso) or icy beer. ⊠ *Defensa 1096, on Plaza Dorrego* ☎ 11/4361–0141.

Also Worth Some Time

Museo Penitenciario Antonio Ballvé (Antonio Ballvé Penitentiary Museum). Exhibiting artifacts from early-20th-century prison life, this modest museum, once a women's hospice, includes a genuine striped uniform and jail cell. Behind its large courtyard stands Nuestra Señora del Carmen chapel, named after the patron saint of the federal penitentiary service. The chapel dates from the Jesuit period. ⊠ *Humberto Primero 378, San Telmo* ☎ 11/4362–0099 ☜ *1 peso* ⊙ *Wed.–Fri. 3–7, Sun. 3–7.*

LA BOCA

WELCOME TO THE REPUBLIC OF LA BOCA proclaims a sign on the neighborhood's northern edge. It's a reference to a group of striking Genovese port workers who tried, in 1882, to declare their Buenos Aires neighborhood independent. The petition was unsuccessful, but the idea lives on in a strong barrio identity that makes the inhabitants feel they're a nation apart. La Boca sits on the fiercely polluted Riachuelo River, where rusting ships and warehouses, watched over by the hulking Avellaneda Bridge, remind you that this was once the city's main port. Thousands of European immigrants arrived here at the end of the 19th century. Many settled in the area, building their houses from the corrugated metal and brightly colored paint left over from the shipyards. Cafés, pubs, and general stores that once catered to passing sailors are now tourist traps dotting a renovated port. Although the Caminito area may seem dolled-up, most of La Boca is still very working class.

Timing & Precautions

A couple of hours should give you enough time to explore La Boca. Expect crowds on weekends, when the market is in full swing. Although the nightlife here is singular, it's best not to wander about after dark. Stay in the area of the Caminito and avoid straying into surrounding areas. Note that the subte does not go to La Boca, and the surrounding neighborhoods are rough; taxi travel is a good bet.

Top Sight

Calle Museo Caminito. Cobblestones, tango dancers, and haphazardly constructed, vividly painted conventillos have made Calle Museo Caminito the darling of Buenos Aires's postcard manufacturers since this pedestrian street and open-air museum/art market opened in 1959. The name Caminito comes from a tango by Juan de Dios Filiberto, who is said to have composed it while thinking of a girl leaning from the balcony of a ramshackle house like the ones here.

Artists fill the block-long street with works depicting port life and tango, which is said to have been born in La Boca. Although the conventillos still make Caminito a must-see, too long at the top of the tourist list has made the street more commercial than cultural. *Tangueros* and their sultry partners, dressed to the nines in split skirts and fishnets, spend more time trying to entice you into photo ops than actually dancing. The quality of the art on sale varies considerably, too. If nothing tempts you check out the small mosaics set into the walls behind the stalls, such as Luis Perlotti's *Santos Vega*. They, at least, hint of days when El Caminito was less about the sell and more about the art.

1

The market spills over into the square on the other side of Olivarría, which crosses the end of Caminito. Expect to be canvassed by rival restaurant owners here and along every other side street: the best tactic to get by them is to accept their menu leaflets with a serene smile and *"gracias."* Disused train tracks run along Garibaldi, the first street to the left. The presence of the river has shaped even the sidewalks in La Boca, which are often up to a foot high to prevent flooding; this street has some uneven examples. The forest green and tomato red house that is Number 1429 is the Museo Conventillo de Marjan Grum, a one-time tenement recycled by its artist owner into a gallery and cultural center. Opening hours are erratic but the facade, painted with brightly colored scroll-work known as *fileteado* is worth a look. Turning left into Magallanes takes you back to the start of Caminito, past more converted conventillos festooned with more fileteado signs and stocked with the tackiest of souvenirs.

The plastic Che Guevaras and dancing couples make the shops in the **Centro Cultural de los Artistas** (⊠ Magallanes 861 ⊘ Mon.–Sat. 10:30–6) as forgettable as all the others on the street, but the uneven stairs and wrought-iron balcony give an idea of what a conventillo interior would have been like.

⊠ *Caminito, between Av. Pedro de Mendoza (La Vuelta de Rocha promenade) and Olivarría, La Boca* ▨ *Free* ⊘ *Daily 10–6.*

Top Experience

Get Your Kicks

Tens of thousands of ecstatic fans jump up and down in unison, roaring modified cumbia classics to the beat of carnival drums; crazed supporters sway atop 10-foot fences between the stands and the field as they drape the barbed wire with their team's flags; showers of confetti and sulfurous smoke from colored flares fill the air. The occasion? Just another day's *futbol* (soccer) match in Argentina—and all this before the game even begins.

For most Argentines soccer is a fervent passion. The national team is one of the world's best, and the World Cup can bring the country to a standstill as workers gather in cafés and bars to live out the nation's fate via satellite. Feelings run high during the biannual local championships— families have often supported the same team for generations, and rivalry between *hinchas* (fans) gets heated. In a country where people joke that if soccer great Diego Maradona were to run for president he'd win hands down, futbol is the source of endless debate, fiery dispute, suicidal despair, love, and hate.

Matches are held year-round and are as exciting as they are dangerous. You're safest in the *platea* (preferred seating area), which costs around 20 to 60 pesos, rather than in the chaotic 10-peso *popular* (standing room) section. Be careful what you wear—fans carry their colors with pride, and not just on flags and team shirts. Expect to see painted faces, hundreds of tattoos, and even women's underwear with the colors of the best-known teams: Boca Juniors (blue and gold) and their arch rivals River Plate (red and white), as well as Independiente (red), Racing (light blue and white), and San Lorenzo (red and blue). The no-man's-land that separates each team's part of the stadium, the drum-banging antics of hooligan mafias known as the *barra brava,* and the heavy police presence at matches are a reminder of how seriously the game is taken.

That said, the sheer level of passion and pageantry surrounding Argentineans' obsession with soccer has to be seen to be believed, and no self-respecting sports fan should pass up the chance to attend a game. You can buy tickets at long lines at the soccer stadiums up to four days before matches; through **Ticketek** (☏ 11/4323–7200); or from the teams' official Web sites.

★ Walls exploding with huge, vibrant murals of insurgent workers, famous inhabitants of La Boca, and futbol greats splashed in blue and gold let you know that the **Estadio Boca Juniors** is at hand. The stadium that's also known as La Bombonera (meaning candy box, supposedly because the fans' singing reverberates as it would inside a candy tin) is the home of Argentina's most popular futbol club and is also used as a concert venue. Boca Juniors' history is completely tied to the port neighborhood. The nickname, *xeneizes,* is a mangling of *genovés* (Genovese), reflecting the origins of most immigrants to the Boca area. The blue and gold that decks the stadium's fiercely banked seating—and just about everything else in the area—was inspired by a Swedish ship's flag.

Inside the stadium is **El Museo de la Pasión Boquense** (The Museum of Boca Passion), a large-scale celebration of the club. Pricey admission and slick displays are testament to the club's affluence under the guidance of dollar-savvy businessman and wannabe-politician Mauricio Macri. The modern, two-floor space chronicles Boca's rise from neighborhood club in 1905 to its current position as one of the world's best teams. Among the innovative exhibits is a giant football containing 360-degree footage of screaming fans and players, creating all the passion of a match for those too faint-hearted to attend the real thing. Trophies, videos, shirts, match histories, and a hall of fame make up the rest of the circuit, together with a huge mural of Maradona, Boca's most beloved player. Also on display is the specially commissioned blue and gold guitar Lenny Kravitz used to close his 2005 concerts in the stadium. Everything you need to Boca up your life—from team shirts to bed linen, school folders to G-strings—is available in the gift shop. Cheaper copies are available in shops and stalls outside the stadium.

If you fancy treading the same ground as futbol gods Batistuta and El Diego, then the extensive stadium tour is worth the extra money. Light-hearted guides take you all over the stands as well as to press boxes, locker rooms, underground tunnels, and the emerald grass of the field itself. ✉ *Brandsen 805, at del Valle Iberlucea, La Boca* ☏ *11/4309–4700 stadium, 11/4362–1100 museum* ⊕ *www.bocasistemas.com.ar, www. musoboquense.com* 🎟 *Museum: 7.90 pesos. Stadium: 7.90 pesos. Museum and stadium: 12.90 pesos* ☉ *Museum daily 10–6 except when Boca*

CLOSE UP

The Top Three: Evita, Maradona & El Che   1

ARGENTINES ARE PROUD of their famous sons and daughters, none more so than the local holy trinity of Evita Perón, Diego Maradona, and Ernesto "Che" Guevara. Like 'em or loathe 'em, these three figures are permanent engravings—metaphorically speaking on the Argentine imagination and literally speaking on billboards, T-shirts, and tattoos.

Known by her supporters as the mother of the nation, Eva Duarte de Perón was revered as a saint in Argentina long before West End musicals and Hollywood films made her internationally famous. Despite her humble origins, she became half of the most famous presidential couple in Argentina's history, until her untimely death from cancer at age 33. Evita is a contradictory figure: despite her famed designer frocks and perfect blonde chignon, her politics were extremely radical, to the horror of the conservative oligarchy of the time. Her tireless activism championed the poor, the working class, and marginalized groups like single mothers, and brought her millions of fanatical followers, who still campaign for her to be made Santa Evita.

Ask any local soccer fan what nationality God is, and his or her answer will be "Argentine," in clear reference to football prodigy Diego Armando Maradona. He grew up in one of Buenos Aires's shantytowns, but started playing professionally at the age of 10. He shot to fame in the early '80s with Boca Juniors and then the Italian team Napoli, before his 1986 goal against England won Argentina the World Cup and immortality for him. Too much time at the top took its toll, though: after retiring, Maradona's cocaine addiction bloomed and his weight skyrocketed. For a while it looked like the hero was on his way out. In 2005, however, the nation wept tears of joy as the man known as El 10 (Number 10), El Diego de la Gente (Diego of the People), La Mano de Dios (The Hand of God), and countless other hyperbolic epithets returned to Argentina slimmed-down and drug-free to host a TV show.

If Maradona is Argentina's god, then the bearded icon tattooed on his left forearm is Argentina's messiah: Ernesto Guevara de la Serna, known as El Che. Born in Rosario, the middle-class medical student's life was changed forever by the trip up South America immortalized in his book *Mi primer Gran Viaje*, taken to the big screen by Walter Salles as *The Motorcycle Diaries*. His horror at the plight of peasants and workers led to his participation in the Cuban revolution, for which he is best known, as well as the attempt to start a guerrilla uprising in Bolivia, where he was assassinated in 1967. He remains the figurehead of many left-wing student movements as well as a pop icon adorning T-shirts across Latin America.

plays at home; stadium tours hourly 11–5 (English usually available, call ahead to check).

Argentina's international soccer matches take place at the River Plate stadium, **Estadio Antonio Vespucio Liberti** (✉ Av. Pte. Figueroa Alcorta 7597, Núñez ☎ 11/4788–1200 ⊕ www.cariverplate.com.ar), better known as the Monumental, for its size. The stadium is far out in the northwest of the city; you can get there by suburban train from Retiro (get off at Nuñez station) or by Línea D to Congreso de Tucumán and then taking a taxi.

⌐ NEED A
  BREAK?

With an excellent view of the port activity, the century-old, wood-paneled **La Perla** café is a traditional spot for a *licuado* (milk shake), an inexpensive *cortado* (coffee "cut" with a drop of milk), or a tostada. ✉ *Av. Pedro de Mendoza 1899, La Boca* ☎ *11/4301–2985.*

Also Worth Some Time

Fundación Proa (Prow Foundation). This thoroughly modern art museum is a refreshing addition to the traditional neighborhood—a classic 19th-century Italian housefront belies Proa's clean, contemporary interior lines. The luminous main gallery retains the building's original Corinthian-style steel columns but has sparkling white walls and polished concrete floors. Choice international exhibits, concerts, and events take place year-round. After you're done looking at the artwork, you can watch the sun set over the river from the terrace. There's also a reading room and trestle-table bookstore of quirky local fiction and art books. English versions of all exhibition information are available. ✉ *Av. Pedro de Mendoza 1929, La Boca* ☎ *11/4303–0909* ⊕ *www.proa.org* 💲 *3 pesos* ☉ *Tues.–Sun. 11–7.*

Museo de Bellas Artes de La Boca de Artistas Argentinos (La Boca Fine Arts Museum of Argentine Artists). Artist and philanthropist Benito Quinquela Martín, one of La Boca's most famous sons, donated this huge building to the state to create a cultural center in 1936. Don't be surprised to have to jostle your way through kids filing into class: downstairs is an elementary school, something that the galleries' bland institutional architecture doesn't let you forget. Quinquela Martín set out to fill the second floor with Argentine art—on the condition that works were figurative and didn't belong to any 'ism.' Badly lit rooms and lack of any visible organization make it hard to enjoy the minor paintings by Berni, Sívori, Soldi, and other local masters. The smaller third floor contains only Quinquela Martín's own work, namely the vibrant port scenes that first put La Boca on the map. Outside is a huge sculpture terrace with great views of the river and old port buildings on one side; and the Boca Juniors stadium and low-rise downtown skyline on the other. Signs about the history of the museum are translated into English, but nothing else is. ✉ *Av. Pedro de Mendoza 1835, La Boca* ☎ *11/4301–1080* 💲 *3 pesos* ☉ *Tues.–Fri. 10–5, weekends 11–5.*

PUERTO MADERO

The port was originally constructed in 1890 as the European gateway to Argentina but spent most of the 20th century abandoned thanks to a new port, Puerto Nuevo. The city has been busy reviving the area (construction is still underway), transforming its redbrick warehouses and grain mills into the city's most expensive office and living spaces, university buildings, a cinema complex, luxury hotels, and a string of swank restaurants. It was recently designated the 47th and newest barrio of Buenos Aires, a tribute to its significant overhaul.

You can reach the area, five blocks east of Florida, from the Leandro Alem subte station on Línea A; once you leave the station, walk down Avenida Corrientes toward the river. On your right you'll see the majestic Correo Central (Central Post Office); on your left is Luna Park, where many sporting events and concerts are held. Crossing Avenida Eduardo Madero, you'll reach Avenida Alicia M. de Justo, which runs the length of the port area. Cross over any bridge and keep going and you'll reach the city's largest green space, the Reserva Ecológica.

Timing & Precautions

Walking the 15-block boardwalk should take you no more than an hour or two. In the morning it's a lovely place to jog or to sip coffee at a waterfront café. Suits flood in at lunchtime; in the evenings a fashionable crowd gathers for dinner. Although tony Puerto Madero is well patrolled by private security and the port police, you should avoid strolling far from the boardwalk at night.

Worth Some Time

Buque Museo Corbeta Uruguay (*Uruguay* Corvette Ship Museum). The oldest of the Argentine fleet, bought from England in 1874, the ship has been round the world several times and was used in the nation's Antarctic campaigns at the turn of the 20th century. ⊠ *Dique 4, at J. M. Gorriti and Machacha Güemes, Puerto Madero* 🕾 *11/4314–1090* 🎫 *1 peso* ☉ *Daily 9–8.*

Buque Museo Fragata A.R.A. Presidente Sarmiento (*President Sarmiento* Frigate Museum). The navy commissioned this frigate from England in 1898 to be used as an open-sea training vessel. It has completed 39 voyages across the world's oceans. ⊠ *Dique 3, at J.M. Gorriti and Puente de la Mujer, Puerto Madero* 🕾 *11/4334–9386* 🎫 *2 pesos* ☉ *Daily 9–8.*

Museo de la Inmigración. The Hotel de Inmigrantes that houses the modest Immigration Museum was the first stop for many of the millions of Europeans who arrived in Argentina between 1880 and 1930. Inside the imposing building, their lives and times are told through photos, personal effects, and film footage, with Spanish-only explanations. ⊠ *Antiguo Hotel de Inmigrantes, Av. Antárdida Argentina 1355* 🕾 *11/ 4317–0285* ⊕ *www.mininterior.gov.ar/migraciones/museo/* 🎫 *1 peso suggested donation* ☉ *Weekdays 10–5, weekends 11–6.*

Puente de la Mujer. Tango dancers inspired the sweeping asymmetrical lines of Valencian architect Santiago Calatrava's design for the pedestrian-only Bridge of the Woman. Puerto Madero's street names pay homage to famous Argentine women, hence the bridge's name. (Ironically its most visible part—a soaring 39-meter arm—represents the man of a couple in mid-tango.) The $6-million structure was made in Spain and paid for by local businessmen Alberto L. González, one of the brains behind Puerto Madero's redevelopment; he also built the Hilton Hotel here. Twenty engines rotate the bridge to allow ships to pass through. ⊠ *Dique 3, C. Lornzini, at Alicia M. de Justo, Puerto Madero.*

NEED A BREAK?

If you're homesick for some deli action, relief is on hand at **iFresh Market,** which does perfect berry smoothies, caffè lattes, and snacks. True to Puerto Madero's "first world" approach, the menu was overseen by Dean and Deluca's Roberto Sablay Rolles. ⊠ *Azucena Villaflores at Olga Cossentini, Puerto Madero* ☎ *11/ 5775-0330* ⊕ *www.ifreshmarket.com.ar.*

Reserva Ecológica. The 900-acre Ecological Reserve was built over a landfill and is home to more than 500 species of bird and a variety of flora and fauna. On weekends thousands of porteños vie for a spot on the grass, so come midweek if you want to birdwatch and sunbathe in peace or use the jogging and cycling tracks. A monthly guided "Walking under the Full Moon" tour begins at 8:30 PM; otherwise avoid the area at night. It's just a short walk across any bridge from Puerto Madero. ⊠ *Av. Tristán Achával Rodríguez 1550, Puerto Madero* ☎ *11/ 4315–1320, 11/4893–1588 tours* ☑ *Donation suggested* ☉ *Apr.–Oct., Tues.–Sun. 8–6; Nov.–Mar., Tues.–Sun. 8–7.*

LA RECOLETA

Open green spaces border this elegant residential and shopping district. It's named for the barefoot Franciscan Recoleto friars who settled here in the early 1700s; it later became home to brothels. The outbreak of yellow fever in 1871 in the south of the city caused the elite to swarm here, laying the foundations for a concentration of intellectual and cultural activity.

Stately mansions, the highbrow Jockey Club, private apartments, and the graceful embassies of France and Brazil frame Plazoleta Carlos Pellegrini, a square that's now primarily used for parking. To the west elegant Avenida Alvear is lined with French-style structures, haute couture boutiques, and the exquisite Alvear Palace Hotel. Two blocks farther along, a staired sidewalk on the left (called R. M. Ortiz) leads past a gargantuan rubber tree and a string of slightly cheesy cafés, pubs, and eateries. Just beyond, some of Argentina's most illustrious citizens found their final resting places in the Cementerio de La Recoleta.

Though a number of buses run through here, a taxi ride is your best bet. No subte route directly serves La Recoleta; the closest station is eight blocks away at Estación Pueyrredón.

Timing & Precautions

You can explore La Recoleta in half a day, though you could easily spend a full morning or afternoon in the cemetery or cultural centers alone. This area is relatively safe day and night, but always be aware of your surroundings.

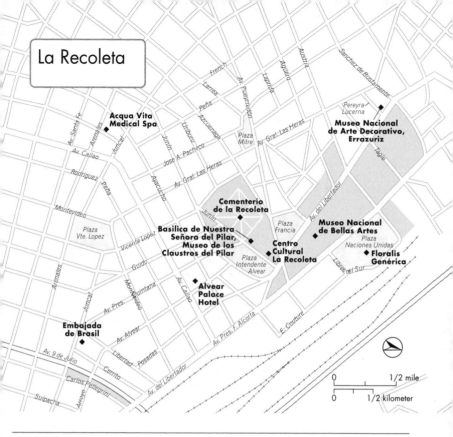

Top Sights

Basílica de Nuestra Señora del Pilar. This basilica beside the famous Cementerio de la Recoleta on Junín is where Buenos Aires's elite families hold weddings and other ceremonies. It was built by the Franciscan Recoleto friars in 1732 and is considered a national treasure for its six German baroque-style altars, the central one overlaid with Peruvian engraved silver, and relics sent by Spain's King Carlos III. In the church cloisters, which date from 1716, is the **Museo de los Claustros del Pilar,** a small museum of religious artifacts as well as pictures and photographs documenting the Recoleta area's evolution. There are excellent views of the cemetery from the small upstairs windows. More of the church's former cloisters and internal patios of the Franciscan monks have been converted into **Centro Cultural La Recoleta** (✉ Junín1930 ☎ 11/4803–1040 ⊕ www.centroculturalrecoleta.org ⊙ Tues.–Fri. 2–9, Weekends 10–9), a dynamic cultural center with exhibits, performances, and workshops. Kids love the minimuseum inside it, whose name, Prohibido No Tocar (Not Touching Is Forbidden), says it all. On weekends the entire area around the basilica and cemetery teems with artisans and street performers in one of the city's largest artisan fairs, known as **La Feria de Plaza Francia.** At the end of a *veredita* (little sidewalk), you'll find the Paseo del Pilar lined with expensive places to eat and the Buenos Aires Design Center.

Fodor'sChoice   **Cementerio de la Recoleta.** The ominous gates, Doric-columned portico, and labyrinthine paths of the oldest cemetery in Buenos Aires (1822) may leave you with a sense of foreboding. The final resting place for the nation's most illustrious figures is a virtual city of the dead covering 13½ acres that are rumored to be the most expensive real estate in town. The cemetery has more than 6,400 elaborate vaulted tombs and majestic mausoleums, 70 of which have been declared historic monuments. The mausoleums resemble chapels, Greek temples, pyramids, and miniature mansions. The administrative offices at the entrance provide a free map, and caretakers throughout the grounds can help you locate the more intriguing tombs.

Highlights: The embalmed remains of Eva Perón, who made it here after 17 years of posthumous wandering; the brutal *caudillo* (dictator) Facundo Quiroga, buried standing—a sign of valor—at his request; and prominent landowner Dorrego Ortíz Basualdo, in the most monumental sepulcher, complete with chandelier.

Spooky Stories: One of the cemetery's inhabitants, Rufina Cambaceres, is known as the girl who died twice. She was thought dead after suffering a cataleptic attack and was entombed on her 19th birthday in 1902. Rufina awoke inside her casket and managed to claw the top open but died of a heart attack before she could be rescued. When Alfredo Gath—one of the founders of the now-defunct store Gath & Chaves—heard of Rufina's story he was appalled and commissioned a special mechanical coffin with an opening device and alarm bell. Gath successfully tested the coffin in situ 12 times, but on the 13th the mechanism failed and he died inside. ⊠ *Junín 1760, La Recoleta* ☎ *11/4803–1594* 🖃 *Free* ⊙ *Daily 8–5:30.*

★   **Museo Nacional de Bellas Artes.** At the National Museum of Fine Arts, some 11,000 works—from drawings and paintings to statues and tapestries—are displayed in a huge golden-colored stone building whose elegant columned front belies the fact that it used to be the city's waterworks. The ground-floor European collection has 24 rooms of dimly lit galleries arranged chronologically. Information about the works is in Spanish only; it's also lengthy and overly academic, so if you don't speak Spanish you're not missing much. The wing at the left has medieval religious paintings and minor works by El Greco, Goya, Rubens, Tiepolo, Titian, and Zurbarán. The circuit leads you back behind the entrance hall to some of the museum's many Rodin sculptures. The right wing contains 19th- and 20th-century French art, including paintings by Manet, Degas, Monet, Pisarro, Gaugin, and Toulouse-Lautrec. Look also for works by Klee, Kandinsky, Modigliani, Chagall, and Picasso.

Truth be told, though, it's the world's biggest collection of 19th- and 20th-century Argentine art that's the draw here. You're much better off heading straight to the first floor galleries, while you're still feeling fresh. Leave the European collection for later.

The beautifully curated Argentine circuit starts in Room 102 with works from colonial times through the 19th century. Overviews on the wall are clear and interesting but in Spanish only. Don't miss the María Luisa Bemberg Room, tucked away off to the right, with pieces by artists from the River Plate area. Follow the galleries around to the right, where early 20th-century works include 1920s salon art and scenes of port life in La Boca. The huge final gallery down the ramp shows the involvement of Argentine artists in European avant-garde movements before adopting homegrown ideas. Works here include geometric sculptures and the so-called *informalismo* (informalism) of the '60s, marked by its innovative use of collage. Psychedelic paintings, op art, and kinetic works follow. The circuit finishes with contemporary Argentine artists. Be sure to check out the corner covering 30 years of conceptual art.

Highlights of the Argentine Collection: Battle paintings by Cándido López, who learned to paint with his left hand after losing his right arm in the War of the Triple Alliance of the 1870s (his work spearheaded contemporary primitive painting); landscapes by local master Eduardo Sívori; turn-of-the-century gaucho portraits by Cesáreo Bernaldo de Quirós; the highly colored depiction of port laborers in *Elevadores a Pleno Sol* by Benito Quinquela Martín, La Boca's unofficial painter laureate; Emilio Pettorutti's *El Improvisador* (1937), which combines cubist techniques with a Renaissance sense of space; Lino Enea Spilimbergo's *Terracita* (1932), an enigmatic urban landscape; the early figurative paintings and latter-day collages of Antonio Berni, *enfant terrible* turned grand old man of Argentine painting; autodidact and '60s cultural guru Jorge de la Vega's huge abstract canvases.

Multitasking security staff in the entrance hall are too rushed to deal with questions, and although the themed guided tours are excellent, they're only offered in Spanish. If you only speak English, check into the MP3 audio guides (15 pesos) in the scant gift shop at the bottom of the stairs. ⊠ *Av. del Libertador 1473, La Recoleta* ☎ *11/4803–0802 tours (in Spanish)* ⊕ *www.mnba.org.ar* ⊠ *Free* ☉ *Tues.–Fri. 12:30–7:30, weekends 9:30–7:30.*

Also Worth Some Time

Floralis Genérica. The gleaming steel and aluminum petals of this giant flower look very space age, perhaps because they were commissioned from the Lockheed airplane factory by architect Eduardo Catalano, who designed and paid for the monument. The 20-meter-high structure begins to open at dawn and closes at dusk, when the setting sun turns its mirrored surfaces a glowing pink. Local opinions are divided on the flower, but it counts cutting-edge Argentine artist Guillermo Kuitca among its fans. The flower stands in the Plaza Naciones Unidas (behind El Museo Nacional de Bellas Artes over Avenida Figueroa Alcorta), which was remodeled to accommodate it. The small square is refreshingly free of dog

Day Spa Escape: Acqua Vita

CLOSE UP

THE SCENT OF aromatherapy oils and the sound of water tempt you up the stairs from La Recoleta's busy streets into a world of calm. Clean white walls, warm lighting, and turquoise Venetian-tiled rooms are the backdrop to the many treatments (for men and women) offered by the small, decidedly urban Acqua Vita Medical Spa. There's an emphasis on health as well as beauty. All the employees are trained therapists, not just estheticians, and very used to treating foreign clients. If you want to take things to the next level, the spa's founder, Dr. Rubén Mühlberger, runs a top esthetic surgery clinic on an upper floor. The spa serves delicious Brazilian teas but no food.

Services: Aromatherapy, shiatzu, lymphatic drainage, deep-tissue,

reflexology, hot-stone, anti-cellulite, and Reiki massage; hydrotherapy; Scottish and Vichy spring showers; full-body clay treatment; seaweed wrap; full-body exfoliation; permanent hair removal; facials; manicures; pedicures.

Package Picks: Anti-Stress Day (five hours; full-body exfoliation, a body wrap, hydrotherapy, Scottish shower, aromatherapy steam bath, deep-tissue massage, foot reflexology, and a shiatsu facial for 385 pesos). Aqua Luna (two hours; full-body exfoliation, hydrotherapy, and massage for 198 pesos).

General Info: ⊠ Arenales 1965, La Recoleta ☎ 11/4812-5989 ⊕ www.acquavitamedicalspa.com ⊙ Mon.-Sat. 9-9 ⊟ MC, V

mess and thus a great place for a picnic or for kids to roll on the grass. ⊠ *Plaza Naciones Unidas, at Av. Figueroa Alcorta and J. A. Biblioni, La Recoleta* ⊙ *Dawn-dusk.*

Museo Nacional de Arte Decorativo. The harmonious, French neoclassic mansion that houses the National Museum of Decorative Art is as much a reason to visit as the period furnishings, porcelain, and silver within it. Ornate wooden paneling in the Regency ballroom, the imposing Louis XIV red-and-black marble dining room, and a lofty Renaissance-style great hall are some of the highlights of the only house of its kind open to the public in Buenos Aires. There are excellent English descriptions of each room, and they include gossipy details about the house's original inhabitants, the well-to-do Errazuriz family. The museum also contains some Chinese art. Guided tours include the Zubov collection of miniatures from Imperial Russia and one of the family bedrooms, otherwise off-limits to visitors. ⊠ *Av. del Libertador 1902, La Recoleta* ☎ *11/4801-8248* ⊕ *www.mnad.org* ☜ *2 pesos, free Tues.* ⊙ *Tues.-Sun. 2-7; free guided tours in English Sun. at 5:30.*

NEED A BREAK? The afternoon sun catches the outside tables of **Errazuriz** (⊠ Av. Libertador 1902 ☎ 11/4806-8639), an elegant café in the courtyard of the Museo Nacional des Arte Decorativo. Rest your museum feet with a coffee or a glass of Malbec as you gaze at the mansion's Parisian-style stone facade to the tune of the bubbling stone fountain beside you.

PALERMO

Trendy shops, bold dining, elegant embassies, and acres of parks—Palermo really does have it all. The city's largest barrio is subdivided into various unofficial districts, each with its own distinct flavor.

Spanish-style town houses beautifully recycled into luminous boutiques, minimal lofts, endless bars, and the most fun and daring restaurants in town have made Palermo Viejo the epicenter of Buenos Aires's design revolution. Originally the whole area south of Avenida Santa Fe, the district is now subdivided into Palermo SoHo and Palermo Hollywood, respectively east and west of Avenida Juan B. Justo. The majority of shops and eateries—not to mention desirable properties—in Palermo Viejo fill the cobbled streets around Plazoleta Cortázar, at Honduras and Serrano, nine blocks south of Plaza Italia. In Palermo Hollywood, quiet barrio houses and the rambling flea market at Dorrego and Niceto Vega sit alongside sharp tapas bars filled with media types from the TV production centers that give the neighborhood its name.

The patchwork of parks north of Avenida del Libertador are known collectively as Los Bosques de Palermo (The Palermo Woods) and provide a peaceful escape from the rush of downtown. Reach them by walking about six blocks from Plaza Italia (on subte Línea D), at the intersection of Avenidas Sarmiento, Santa Fe, and Las Heras, where the zoo and botanical gardens are.

Plastic surgery and imported everything are the norm in Palermo Chico (between Avenidas Santa Fe and Libertador), whose Parisian-style mansions are shared out between embassies and rich local stars like diva Susana Giménez. The new kid on the block is the gleaming MALBA (Museum of Latin American Art of Buenos Aires), whose clean stone lines stand out on Avenida Figueroa Alcorta.

Timing

An even-paced ramble through Los Bosques de Palermo should take no more than two hours, though you could easily spend an entire afternoon at the zoo, Japanese Garden, and Botanical Garden. Dedicated shoppers could spend their whole trip in Palermo Viejo, and there are also the Alto Palermo shopping center (at the Bulnes stop on Línea D) and the shops and boutiques along Avenida Santa Fe. As subte stops are often far from where you want to go, taxis are a good option for Palermo.

Top Sights

★ **Museo Evita.** Eva Duarte de Perón, known universally as Evita, was the wife of populist president Juan Domingo Perón and one of the most important and controversial figures of recent Argentine history. She unfailingly caused extreme reactions and was both revered as a saint by her working-class followers, and despised by the anglophile oligarchy of the time. The excellent Museo Evita tries to get away from images of Madonna belting out "Don't Cry For Me Argentina" and convey as many facts about Evita's life and works as possible.

The solid, gray-stone mansion that houses the museum was built in 1909 by the Carabaza family. In 1948 the building was purchased by the Fun-

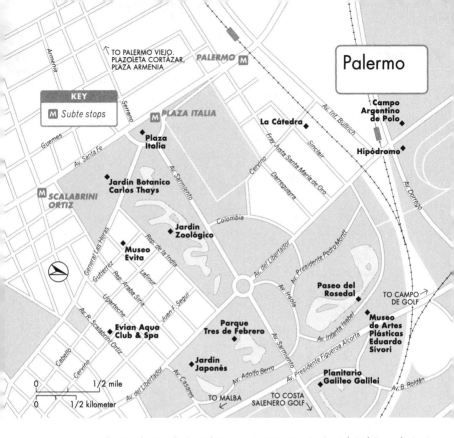

dación de Ayuda Social Eva Perón (Eva Perón Social Aid Foundation) and converted into a transitory home for single mothers, to the horror of the rich, conservative families living nearby. With the fall of Perón's government in 1955 the house was requisitioned as an administrative building until mid-2002, when the museum opened.

The main entrance leads into a columned medieval-style hall watched over by portraits of Evita and General Perón. To the right, a darkened room screening intense footage of thousands of mourners queuing to see Evita's body begins the well-labeled route through the collection. Evita's humble origins and life as a B-list actress before meeting Perón are documented on the ground floor.

Upstairs, shining parquet, heavy wood doors, and ornamental stone molding surround videos and artifacts that tell the tale of Evita's political career, particularly the social aid programs she instituted and her key role in getting women the vote. Evita's reputation as national fashion-plate is reflected in the many designer outfits on display. The final rooms follow Evita's withdrawal from political life and her death from cancer at age 33. Downstairs are a temporary exhibition space, a small gift shop, and a quiet café with a sunny patio. Laminated cards with English translations of the exhibits are available in each room and at the ticket booth. Knowledgeable, friendly staffers answer questions enthusiastically. Excellent guided visits are available in Spanish or English but must be arranged by phone in advance.

Highlights: English-subtitled footage of Evita's incendiary speeches to screaming crowds. The Patio Andaluz (Andalucian Patio), used as a play area by the children once housed here and decorated with hand-painted Spanish tiles with ultramarine and gold designs.

Strangest Detail: The posthumous fate of Evita's cadaver, which was embalmed by Perón, stolen by political opponents, and moved and hidden for 17 years before being returned to Argentina, where it now rests in the Recoleta Cemetery.

On the Menu: A creamy slice of *torta de ricotta* (ricotta cheesecake) and a *café con leche* (coffee with frothy milk) at one of the museum café's outside tables, shaded by classy black umbrellas.

✉ *Lafinur 2988,1 block north of Av. Las Heras, Palermo* ☎ *11/ 4807-9433* ⊕ *www.museoevita.org* 💲 *5 pesos* ☉ *Tues.–Sun. 1–7* Ⓜ *D to Plaza Italia.*

FodorsChoice **Museo de Arte de Latinoamericano de Buenos Aires** (MALBA; Museum of
★ Latin American Art of Buenos Aires). The fabulous MALBA is one of the cornerstones of the city's cultural life. Córdoba-based studio AFT Arquitectos beat other architects in the competition to design the building, and their distinctive triangular construction in creamy stone and steel is one of the museum's draws. The main galleries run along the left of a stunning four-story atrium, flooded in natural light from a wall of windows—local artists often create installations.

Businessman and founder Eduardo Constantini's collection of more than 220 works of 19th- and 20th-century Latin-American art—one of the world's largest and the museum's centerpiece—is on the first floor. It includes paintings by Diego Rivera, Tarsila do Amaral, Xul Solar, Roberto Matta, and Joaquín Torres García, who brought their experiences in the European avant-garde to bear on Latin American realities. Geometric paintings and sculptures from the 1940s represent movements such as Arte Concreto, Constructivism, and Arte Madí, all born in Latin America. There's also a solid collection of optical and kinetic sculptures. The main gallery has works by the likes of Frida Kahlo and Fernando Botero, and concludes with abstract, psychedelic, and conceptual pieces from the late 20th century. All labels are in English, though not all the excellent gallery introductions are. Young, enthusiastic guides give great tours in Spanish; you can call ahead to arrange group English-language tours.

World-class temporary exhibitions are held on the second floor three or four times a year, and two small basement galleries show art by cutting-edge locals. You can give your feet—and eyes—a rest on the first floor sculpture deck, with views over Belgrano and Barrio Norte. MALBA also has by far the best art cinema in town, it shows restored copies of classics, never-released features, and silent films with live music, as well as local films of note. Be sure to leave yourself time to browse the art books and funky design objects of the museum's excellent gift shop.

Highlights of the Constantini Collection: The iconic shapes and tropical colors of *Abaporu* (1928) by Tarsila do Amaral, a Brazilian involved in the "cannibalistic" Movimento Antropofágico (rather than eating white Europeans, proponents of the movement proposed devouring European culture and digesting it into something new); autodidact Xul Solar's watercolors, which fuse Latin American symbols with kabbalistic ideas; Antonio Berni's poptastic collage *The Great Temptation* (1962) and the bizarre sculpture *Voracity or Ramona's Nightmare* (1964), both featuring the eccentric prostitute Ramona, a character Berni created in this series of works that criticize consumer society.

Kids Love: Hands on kinetic works like Julio Le Parc's *Seven Unexpected Movements,* a wall-mounted sculpture with gleaming parts that move at the press of a button.

Argentine Artists of the Moment: Liliana Porter, Marta Minujín, Guillermo Kuitca, and Alejandro Kuropatwa.

Don't Leave Without Buying: A one-of-a-kind book from offbeat publishing house Eloisa Cartonera—the covers are handpainted on cardboard bought from *cartoneros* (people who sift through garbage looking for such recyclables as paper and cardboard), and the texts are provided by quirky local writers like Fabián Casas or Washington Cucurto (6 pesos); old-style wooden toys and spinning tops by Trompos (35 pesos and up); one of Roman Vitali's purses or lamps made entirely from individually wired jewel-colored beads (200 pesos and up).

On the Menu: The sleek split-level **Malba Restaurant** (☎ 11/4801–3386 🕑 Sun.–Wed. 9–9, Thurs.–Sat. 9–1 AM) is itself a reason to visit the museum. Wait for the collections to open over a *submarino* (steamed milk with dark chocolate melted into it) and *rogel Mendocino* (mille-feuille pastry with dulce de leche), or linger between closing time and a film in the cinema for a dinner of *cordero con milhojas de papa* (lamb shank with layered potatoes) and the not-to-be-missed chocolate mousse. Alternatively, catch up on your wine tasting with the excellent selection of local wines available by the glass.

✉ *Av. Presidente Figueroa Alcorta 3415, Palermo* ☎ *11/4808–6500* ⊕ *www.malba.org.ar* 🎫 *7 pesos, free on Wed.* 🕑 *Thurs.—Mon. noon–8, Wed. noon–9.*

★ 🄲 **Parque Tres de Febrero** has nearly 200 acres of lawns, copses, lakes, and trails, but is really a crazy-quilt of smaller parks known locally as Los Bosques de Palermo. Rich grass and shady trees make this an urban oasis, although the busy roads and horn-honking drivers that crisscross the park never quite let you forget what city you're in. South of Avenida Figueroa Alcorta you can take part in organized tai chi and exercise classes or impromptu soccer matches; you can also jog, bike, in-line skate, or take a boat out on the small lake.

If you're looking for a sedate activity, try the **Museo de Artes Plásticas Eduardo Sívori** (Eduardo Sívori Art Museum; ✉ Av. Infanta Isabel 555,

Palermo ☎ 11/4774–9452 ⊕ www.museosivori.org ✉ 3 pesos, Wed. free ☉ Tues.–Fri. noon–6, weekends 10–6), exhibiting 19th- and 20th-century Argentine art. The 4,000-works-strong collection includes sculptures, engravings, and paintings by local masters like Lino Eneo Spilimbergo and the museum's namesake Sívori, as well as handmade textiles and weavings from all over the country.

Close to the Museo de Artes Plásticas Eduardo Sívori is the **Paseo del Rosedal** (Rose Garden; ✉ Avs. Infanta Isabel and Iraola), where approximately 15,000 rosebushes, representing more than 1,000 different species, bloom seasonally. A stroll along the clay paths takes you through the Jardín de los Poetas (Poets' Garden), dotted with statues of literary figures, and to the enchanting Patio Andaluz (Andalusian Patio) whose majolica tiles and Spanish mosaics sit under a vine-covered pergola.

The sci-fi exterior of the landmark **Planetario Galileo Galilei** (Galileo Galilei Planetarium; ✉ Avs. Sarmiento and Belisario Roldán ☎ 11/4771–6629 ✉ Free ☉ Weekdays 9–5, weekends 3–8) holds more appeal than its flimsy content. This great orb positioned on a massive concrete tripod looks like something out of *Close Encounters of the Third Kind,* and it seems as though small green men in foil suits could descend from its central staircase at any moment. A highlight is the authentic asteroid at the entrance; the pond with swans, geese, and ducks is a favorite with children.

Arched wooden bridges and walkways traverse still waters in the **Jardín Japonés** (Japanese Garden) (✉ Avs. Casares and Adolfo Berro ☎ 11/4804–4922 ⊕ www.jardinjapones.com.ar ✉ 3 pesos ☉ Daily 10–6). A variety of shrubs and flowers frame the ponds, which brim with friendly koi carp that let you pet them should you feel inclined. The traditional teahouse, where you can enjoy adzuki-bean sweets and tea, overlooks a zen garden.

On sunny weekends, Los Bosques de Palermo get crowded and garbage-strewn, as this is where families come for strolls or picnics. Street vendors sell refreshments and *choripan* (chorizo sausage in a bread roll) within the park, and there are also many posh cafés lining the Paseo de la Infanta (running from Libertador toward Sarmiento in the park). ✉ *Bounded by Avs. del Libertador, Sarmiento, Leopoldo Lugones, and Dorrego, Palermo.*

Top Experiences

The Palermo Phenomenon

Ask any porteño which barrio is *fashion* (inventive local-speak for "trendy"), and the answer will be Palermo Viejo. Home to all things hip since the economic crisis, the area blends boho style with truly hedonistic pleasures. Instead of museums and monuments, it's window- and people-watching that are top activities here. Young fashion and homeware designers strive for boutiques in the revamped town houses near **Plazoleta Cortázar** (✉ (better known as Plaza Serrano) Intersection of Honduras and Serrano, Palermo). The shady cobbled streets are ideal for all-day shopping safaris. When your energy or your credit cards run

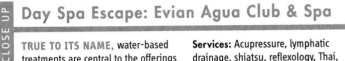

CLOSE UP

Day Spa Escape: Evian Agua Club & Spa

TRUE TO ITS NAME, water-based treatments are central to the offerings at this French-run spa. High-society porteños come here as much for the exclusive atmosphere as the top-notch treatments. One locally inspired hit is the 2-by-4 massage, named for the beat of the tango music that plays throughout the session and for the four hands of the two therapists that dance your body into a state of utter relaxation. The naturally lit reading room is a great place to while away more relaxing hours, and there's a natural-food bistro offering snacks that won't make you feel guilty. If it all sounds too indulgent, you can compensate by doing time in the fitness center which offers classes as well as weights and aerobic machines.

Services: Acupressure, lymphatic drainage, shiatsu, reflexology, Thai, Tui-Na, Ayurvedic, and double-handed massage; hydrotherapy; Turkish bath; Scottish shower; Finnish bath; Jacuzzi; facials; exfoliation; body wraps.

Package Picks: Any one of the many massage and water-treatment combos, such as Agadir (a massage followed by an invigorating Scottish shower and a Turkish bath for 130 pesos). Ad Hoc (lunch and four treatments for 290 pesos).

General Info: ⊠ Cerviño 3626, Palermo ☎ 11/4807–4688 ⊕ www. aguaclubspa.com 🗀 AE, MC, V

low, restaurants and bars offering a perfect mix of gourmet and glam surround the area. Outside tables at cafés on nearby **Plaza Armenia** (⊠ Armenia, between Nicaragua and Costa Rica, Palermo) are a great place to watch alluring *palermitaños*—many arty rock- and film-stars live here—and see what's hot this season.

Horsing Around

It's said that the mighty Argentine Thoroughbreds contributed greatly to the British victory in the South African Boer War. Argentines import select stock for breeding swift horses, prized throughout the world. Although the past 40 years of economic instability has handicapped the industry, Argentine horses still win their share of races worldwide. Catch the Thoroughbreds in action at the **Hipódromo Argentino de Palermo** (⊠ Av. del Libertador 4101, Palermo ☎ 11/4777–9009). In Argentina's golden days the 100,000-capacity grandstand was always full and even now major races pull a crowd. The 1878 belle-époque architecture and gardens give an elegant touch to the sport. Check the *Buenos Aires Herald* for schedules.

Major polo tournaments take place at the **Campo Argentino de Polo** (Argentine Polo Field; ⊠ Av. del Libertador 4000 at Dorrego, Palermo). The stunning athletic showmanship displayed at these events is a source of national pride—indeed, the top-ranked polo players in the world are all Argentine. Admission to autumn (March–May) and spring (September–December) matches is free. The much-heralded Campeonato Argentino Abierto (Argentine Open Championship) takes place in November; admission runs 15 to 200 pesos. You can by tickets in advance by phone through **Ticketek** (☎ 11/4323–7200) or at the polo field on the day of the event. For polo match information contact the **Asociación Argentina de Polo** (☎ 11/4331–4646 ⊕ www.aapolo.com).

Keeping it Green

Golf isn't just an experience for the countryside, especially when you have a neighborhood as lush as Palermo within the city limits. The 18-hole municipal course, **Campo de Golf de la Ciudad de Buenos Aires** (⊠ Tornquist 6397, Palermo ☎ 11/4772–7261), is between Palermo and Belgrano. It's open Tuesday through Sunday from 7:30 to 5 for a 20-peso greens fee on weekdays, and a 30-peso fee on weekends. If you want a range with a view, **Costa Salguero Golf** (⊠ Av. Costanera Rafael Obligado at y Jerónimo Salguero ☎ 11/4805–4734 ⊕ www.costasalguerogolf.com.ar) is right on the river and includes a pitch 'n' putt as well as club and ball hire. Access to the greens costs 11 pesos, and the course is open Monday from noon to 9:30, other weekdays from 8:30 to 9:30, and weekends from 8 to 8:30. For information on golf in the area, contact the **Asociación Argentina de Golf** (Argentine Golf Association; ☎ 11/4394–2743 ⊕ www.aag.com.ar).

Also Worth Some Time

Jardín Botánico Carlos Thays. With 18 acres of gardens and 5,500 varieties of exotic and local flora, the Charles Thays Botanical Garden is an unexpected green haven wedged between three busy Palermo streets. Different sections re-create the environments of Asia, Africa, Oceania, Europe, and the Americas. Among the treasures is the Chinese "tree of gold," purportedly the only one of its kind. Winding paths lead to hidden statues, a brook, and past the resident cats and dragonflies. The central area contains a beautiful greenhouse, brought from France in 1900, and the exposed-brick botanical school and library. ⊠ *Av. Santa Fe 3951, Palermo* ☎ *11/4832–1552* ✍ *Free* ☉ *Sept.–Mar., daily 8–8; Apr.–Aug., daily 9–6.*

NEED A BREAK? **Near the Botanical Garden and steps away from the Palermo Polo field is La Cátedra** (⊠ Cerviño and Sinclair, Palermo ☎ 11/4777–4601), a perfect spot for lunch or a drink outdoors.

☝ **Jardín Zoológico.** You enter through the quasi-Roman triumphal arch into the architecturally eclectic, 45-acre city zoo. The pens, mews, statuary, and fountains themselves—many dating from the zoo's opening in 1874—are well worth a look. Jorge Luis Borges said the recurring presence of tigers in his work was inspired by time spent here. Among the expected zoo community are a few surprises: a rare albino tiger; indigenous monkeys, known to perform lewd acts for their audiences; and llamas (watch out—they spit). Some smaller animals roam freely, and there are play areas for children, a petting farm, and a seal show. *Mateos* (traditional, decorated horse-drawn carriages) stand poised at the entrance to whisk you around. ⊠ *Avs. General Las Heras and Sarmiento, Palermo* ☎ *11/4806–7412* ⊕ *www.zoobuenosaires.com.ar* ✍ *8 pesos* ☉ *Tues.–Sun. 10–5:30.*

Paper Tiger

LEGEND HAS IT that Argentina's greatest writer, Jorge Luis Borges, first read that greatest of Spanish works, Don Quixote, in English, and when faced with the Spanish original thought it inferior. For although Borges was a magician with the Spanish language, the first language he learned to read in was English, thanks to his English grandmother. The trickery of words fascinated him, and as a writer he examined time and again the artifice of language and literature.

Borges was born in 1899 and claimed all his life to belong far more to the 19th century than the 20th. A lifelong Anglophile and extreme conservative, his politics earned him the passionate hatred of many Argentine intellectuals, although lots of them were sufficiently overcome by his literary brilliance to forgive him. He produced a massive amount of poems, stories, and essays—though never novels—throughout his 86 years, despite going blind in his 50s.

Although Borges is best known for the self-referential, metafictional short stories that appeared in collections such as The Aleph, Fictions, and Dr. Brodie's Report, his first book was a collection of poetry. Entitled Fervor de

Buenos Aires, it clearly indicates Borges's fixation with his city of birth. He wrote, in his poem The Mythical Foundation of Buenos Aires, that he found it hard to believe that city had been created, for "I judge her as eternal as the water and the air."

At once recognizable but fantastical, Borges's Buenos Aires revolves around the micro rather than the macro. He describes specific barrios, blocks, and street corners rather than grandiose visions of a unified metropolis. Perhaps the most famous of these is "The even block that persists in my barrio / Guatemala, Serrano, Paraguay, Gurruchaga," which consecrates the four Palermo streets that surrounded one of his childhood homes. Today, only a plaque remains to mark its location. A part of Serrano has been renamed J. L. Borges in his honor, despite the fact that he once said that he didn't want a street named for him, but would rather "that Borges be forgotten." Other important Borgean locations include the Buenos Aires Zoo, where he is reputed to have first seen the tigers that reappear in his poems, and the Fundación Jorge Luis Borges, the international center for the study of his works, which is at Anchorena 1660.

WHERE TO EAT

By Robin S. Goldstein

Buenos Aires isn't just the most cutting-edge food town in Argentina—it's the most cutting-edge food town in the southern hemisphere. Here, more than in any other Latin American capital, three things have come together to create a truly modern cuisine: diverse cultural influences, high culinary aspirations, and a relentless devotion to aesthetics, from the design of a banquette to the artistic plating of a dessert.

And yet, at their core, even the most modern, international restaurants in Buenos Aires are fundamentally porteño, deeply informed by this city's aristocratic appreciation of the pleasure of a good bottle of wine, shared with friends and family, over a long and languid meal. People may eat dinner at 10 or 10:30 all over Argentina, but only in Buenos Aires are you likely to see a family, toddlers in tow, strolling into their local *parrilla* (steakhouse) at midnight.

Three areas—Palermo Soho, Palermo Hollywood, and Las Cañitas—have emerged as the epicenters of Argentina's modern food movement. In these neighborhoods, sushi is all the rage, and you'll find Patagonian lamb, trout, and king crab rubbing elbows with Asian curries and northern Argentine *locros* (stews). And much of it is excellent. So committed to good food are Buenos Aires restaurants, that it's easier to find fresh *centolla* (Patagonian king or spider crab) here, where it's often flown in on ice, than it is in Patagonia, where the norm is the frozen version.

Still, much of the old guard stands strong. Most porteños have Italian ancestry, which is evident in the proliferation of pizzerias all over the city, from the simple and ubiquitous Ugi's chain to the trendy pizza-and-champagne joints, some of whose pies are seared in brick ovens just as elaborate as those in Italy. But don't miss the chance to try the deeper-dish Argentine-style pizza, the most classic of which is the *muzzarella* (cheese and tomato pizza) and the immortal combination of *jamón* (ham), *morrón* (roasted red pepper), and *aceitunas* (olives). Typical, too, is the *fugazza* (tomato-less pizza covered with onion and cheese).

Cafés are also a big part of Buenos Aires culture: open long hours, they constantly brim with locals knocking back a quick *cafecito* (espresso) or taking their time over a *café con leche* (coffee with milk) served with *medialunas* (croissants), most popular for breakfast or during the late afternoon *merienda* hour. And finally, as elsewhere in Argentina, there are the delicious *heladerías* (ice-cream shops) to finish it all off.

WHAT IT COSTS In Argentine Pesos				
$$$$	**$$$**	**$$**	**$**	**¢**
AT DINNER over 32	25–32	17–24	9–16	under 9

Restaurant prices are for one main course at dinner.

El Centro & Environs

Restaurants here specialize more in lunch than dinner; you can expect crowds of office workers at midday. You can also expect much more traditional Argentine fare than the modern fusion cuisine that characterizes hipper neighborhoods.

Cafés

¢–$ ✕ **Confitería La Ideal.** Part of the charm of this spacious 1918 coffeeshop-milonga is its sense of nostalgia: think fleur-de-lis motifs, time-worn European furnishings, and stained glass. No wonder they chose to film the 1998 movie *The Tango Lesson* here. La Ideal is famous for its *palmeritas* (glazed cookies) and tea service. Tango lessons are offered Monday through Thursday from noon to 3, with a full-blown tango ball Wednes-

What's Your Pleasure?

- AGE-OLD ARGENTINE: **Club Eros,** Palermo Soho, ¢–$. **El Globo,** El Centro & Environs, $–$$. **El Sanjuanino,** La Recoleta, ¢–$$. **Ña Serapia,** Palermo, ¢. **Sabot,** El Centro & Environs, $–$$$$.

- BELOVED: **Abril,** San Telmo, $–$$. **Da Da,** Retiro, $–$$$. **El Encanto,** Palermo Hollywood, ¢–$. **Gran Bar Danzón,** Retiro, $$–$$$. **La Caballeriza,** Puerto Madero, $–$$. **Sabot,** El Centro & Environs, $–$$$$. **Sushi Club,** Las Cañitas, $–$$$$.

- BRUNCH: **Mark's,** Palermo Soho, ¢–$. **Novecento,** Las Cañitas, $–$$$. **Ølsen,** Palermo Hollywood, $$.

- CUTTING-EDGE CUISINE: **Bar Uriarte,** Palermo Soho, $$–$$$$. **Casa Cruz,** Palermo Soho, $$$$. **Nectarine,** La Recoleta, $$$$. **Ølsen,** Palermo Hollywood, $$$. **Restó,** El Centro & Environs, $$$$. **Sucre,** Belgrano, $$–$$$$. **Thymus,** Villa Crespo, $$$$.

- DEALS & STEALS: **Club Eros,** Palermo Soho, ¢–$. **El Encanto,** Palermo Hollywood, ¢–$. **La Farmacia, Ña Serapia,** Palermo, ¢. **La Parolaccia,** El Centro & Environs, $–$$. **El Sanjuanino,** La Recoleta, ¢–$$. **Social Paraíso,** Palermo Soho, $–$$.

- FODOR'S CHOICE: **La Brigada,** San Telmo, $–$$$. **Casa Cruz,** Palermo Soho, $$$$. **Restó,** El Centro & Environs, $$$$. **Tancat,** Retiro $–$$$$.

- LEGENDARY: **Bar Dorrego,** San Telmo, ¢–$. **El Cuartito,** El Centro & Environs, ¢–$. **Gran Café Tortoni,** El Centro & Environs, ¢–$. **El Imparcial,** El Centro & Environs, $–$$. **Pippo** La Recoleta, ¢–$.

- MAMA MIA: **Las Cuartetas,** El Centro & Environs, ¢–$. **El Cuartito,** El Centro & Environs, ¢–$. **Filo,** Retiro, ¢–$$. **La Parolaccia,** El Centro & Environs, $–$$. **Piola,** Retiro, ¢–$$$. **San Babila,** La Recoleta, $$$–$$$$.

- MEATY: **La Brigada,** San Telmo, $–$$$. **La Caballeriza,** Puerto Madero, $–$$. **Don Julio,** Palermo Soho, ¢–$$$. **El Estanciero,** Las Cañitas, $–$$. **Juana M,** La Recoleta, ¢–$. **El Obrero,** La Boca, $–$$.

- OFFBEAT: **Lelé de Troya,** Palermo Soho, $–$$. **Te Mataré, Ramírez,** Palermo Soho, $$–$$$.

- ROMANCE: **Casa Cruz,** Palermo Soho, $$$$. **Central,** Palermo Hollywood, $$. **Desde El Alma,** Palermo Soho, $$–$$$. **Oviedo,** El Centro & Environs, $$$–$$$$. **Tancat,** Retiro, $–$$$$. **Tomo I,** El Centro & Environs, $$$$.

- TANGO SPIN: **Confiterí La Ideal,** El Centro & Environs, ¢–$. **Gran Café Tortoni,** El Centro & Environs, ¢–$. **Lelé de Troya,** Palermo Soho, $–$$. **Malevo,** Almagro, $–$$.

- VEGETARIAN FRIENDLY: **Bar Uriarte,** Palermo Soho, $$–$$$$. **Filo,** Retiro, ¢–$$. **Freud y Fahler,** Palermo Soho, ¢–$$. **Lotus Neo Thai,** Las Cañitas, $$–$$$$. **Piola,** Retiro, ¢–$$$. **Sarkis,** Villa Crespo, ¢–$. **San Babila,** La Recoleta, $$$–$$$$. **Social Paraíso,** Palermo Soho, $–$$.

Feeling small at Perito Moreno Glacier, Parque Nacional Los Glaciares, Patagonia.

(top) Gaucho festival. (bottom) Iguazú Falls.

(top) Magellanic penguins, Reserva Faunistica Punta Tombo, Patagonia. (bottom) Typical architecture in Ushuaia, Tierra del Fuego, Patagonia.

La Boca district, Buenos Aires.

(top) Llamas. (bottom) Tango dancers in La Boca, Buenos Aires.

(top left) El Diego de la Gente (Diego of the People): soccer legend Diego Maradona. (top right) Straight up in Parque Nacional Talampaya, the northwest. (bottom) 18th-century Iglesia San Francisco, Salta.

(top) Evita's tomb, Cementerio de la Recoleta, Buenos Aires. (bottom) Malbec harvest, Bodega Terrazas de los Andes, Mendoza.

Along a road less traveled, Jujuy Province.

day and Saturday from 3 to 8. The waitstaff seem to be caught up in their own dreams—service is listless. ⊠ *Suipacha 384, at Av. Corrientes, El Centro* ☎ *11/4326–0521* ▭ *No credit cards* ☾ *No breakfast weekends* Ⓜ *C to C. Pellegrini, D to 9 de Julio.*

★ ¢–$ ✕ **Gran Café Tortoni.** In the city's first confitería (confectionery), established in 1858, art nouveau decor and high ceilings transport you back in time. Carlos Gardel, one of Argentina's most famous tango stars; writer Jorge Luis Borges; local and visiting dignitaries; and intellectuals have all eaten and sipped coffee here. Don't miss the *chocolate con churros* (thick hot chocolate with baton-shaped donuts for dipping). You must reserve ahead of time for the nightly tango shows, for which you'll pay a 20-peso cover. ⊠ *Av. de Mayo 825, Plaza de Mayo* ☎ *11/4342–4328* ⊕ *www.cafetortoni.com.ar* ▭ *AE, MC, V* Ⓜ *A to Perú.*

Italian

$–$$ ✕ **La Parolaccia.** A polite waitstaff serves decent Italian food in a warm, relaxing environment. Lasagna and other pasta dishes are well executed. The real reason to go, though, is for the amazing-value three-course set lunch—including a complimentary lemon digestif—which will set you back 12 whole pesos or so. It's enough to make you wonder why you live in such an overpriced country—whatever country that might be. ⊠ *Riobamba 146, El Centro* ☎ *11/4812–1053* ▭ *AE, MC, V* Ⓜ *C to Congreso, B to Callao.*

Japanese

★ $$–$$$$ ✕ **Yuki.** Once you find your way through the unmarked door, you'll quickly notice the real Japanese clientele—no Palermo hipsters here. Even more impressive is the flopping-fresh fish, which transcends the city's ubiquitous salmon norm with interesting local white fishes like *lisi, reza,* and *pejerrey.* Fried fish is great, too; the *teishoku* dinners are interesting prix-fixe tasting menus, but if you just want raw fish, stick to a sushi combination platter or order à la carte. ⊠ *Pasco 740 between Independencia and Chile, San Cristóbal* ☎ *11/4942–7510* ▭ *AE, MC, V* Ⓜ *E to Pichincha.*

New Argentine

$$$$ ✕ **Restó.** Reserve at least a week in advance. Seriously. After training with
Fodor'sChoice two of the world's most renowned chefs—Spain's Ferran Adriá and
★ France's Michel Bras—chef-owner María Barrutia came back to Buenos Aires and made a very big splash in this very small space, hidden deep inside the Society of Architects. Her menu is short, sweet, and reasonably priced. Three set-price menus pair exotic ingredients like *codorniz* (quail) with Argentina's more traditional foods like *zapallo* (squash). They're all honored with classic European treatments, including expertly reduced sauces. The molten chocolate cake, adapted from Bras, is unforgettable. ⊠ *Montevideo 938, El Centro* ☎ *11/4816–6711* ▭ *No credit cards* Ⓜ *D to Callao* ☾ *Closed Sat.–Sun. No dinner Mon.–Wed.* ◿ *Reservations essential.*

★ $$$$ ✕ **Tomo I.** The famed Concaro sisters have made this restaurant, on the mezzanine of the Hotel Panamericano, a household name. The French-inspired menu has excellent fried, breaded calf brains, and a chocolate

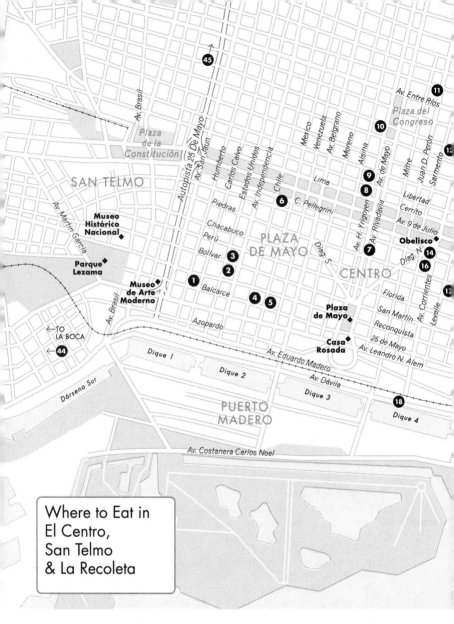

Where to Eat in El Centro, San Telmo & La Recoleta

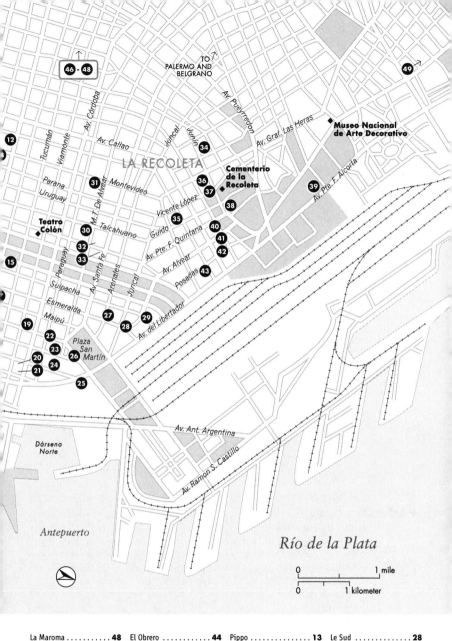

tart that oozes warm, dark ganache. White linen–covered tables are set far apart, in the romantic red room, making quiet conversation easy. Service is arguably tops in the city. ⊠ *Carlos Pellegrini 521, El Centro* ☎ *11/4326–6698* ✍ *Reservations recommended* ▭ *AE, DC, MC, V* ☾ *Closed Sun. No lunch Sat.* Ⓜ *B to Carlos Pellegrini, D to 9 de Julio.*

Peruvian

$–$$ ✕ **Status.** It's got the best Peruvian food in town, and the warm but simple dining room feels like home except for one thing: staffers can be aloof, so you have to be assertive. Go for the *ceviche de pescado* (raw marinated fish) rather than the mixed-seafood version; the fish is impeccably fresh. Good, too, are the *criollo* rice dishes, and potatoes any which way. ⊠ *Virrey Cevallos 178, Congreso* ☎ *11/4382–8531* ⊕ *www. restaurantstatus.com.ar* ▭ *AE, MC, V* Ⓜ *A to Sáenz Peña.*

Pizza

☾ **¢–$** ✕ **Las Cuartetas.** The huge, flavor-packed deep-dish pizzas are a challenge to finish. If you want, you can walk up to the bar and order just a slice; the simplest version—*muzzarella*—is usually the freshest. They also do a good *fugazza* (onions, but no tomatoes). Las Cuartetas is a good place for a quick solo lunch—among the mobs at the Formica-top tables you'll see not just older men but also women eating alone, a rarity in Buenos Aires. ⊠ *Corrientes 838, El Centro* ☎ *11/4326–0171* ▭ *No credit cards* ☾ *No lunch Sun.* Ⓜ *B to C. Pellegrini, C to Diagonal Norte, D to Estación 9 de Julio.*

¢–$ ✕ **El Cuartito.** This porteño classic has been making pizza and empanadas since 1934, and the surroundings have changed little in the last 40 years. The brusque waitstaff is part of the charm. Drop in for a slice at the *mostrador* (counter) or make yourself comfortable under the portraits of Argentine sporting greats for fantastic, no-nonsense food. Try a slice of *fainá* (like a chickpea-flour flatbread), one of the traditional Argentine variations on pizza, and don't miss out on their flan with dulce de leche. ⊠ *Talcahuano 937, El Centro* ☎ *11/4816–4331* ▭ *No credit cards* Ⓜ *D to Tribunales.*

Spanish

★ **$$$–$$$$** ✕ **Oviedo.** First and foremost there's the dreamy ambience—dim lamps that illuminate the room like meditative orbs, walls lined with tantalizing wine bottles, and irreproachable service. And then there's the Spanish food, which makes virtuoso use of luxurious ingredients in preparations like foie gras ravioli and tenderly seared sea scallops. You'll pay dearly (by Buenos Aires's standards, anyway) for the experience, but there's little chance that you won't leave completely satisfied. ⊠ *Beruti 2602 and Ecuador, El Centro* ☎ *11/4821–3741* ✍ *Reservations recommended* ▭ *AE, DC, MC, V* Ⓜ *D to Pueyrredón.*

$–$$ ✕ **El Globo.** Much like the neighborhood in which it resides, El Globo is touristy but good. Hearty *pucheros* (mixed boiled meat dinners), roast suckling pig, squid, and other Spanish-Argentine fare are served in a large dining area, as they have been since the restaurant opened in 1908. The *cazuela de mariscos* (seafood stew) is another specialty. ⊠ *Hipólito Yrigoyen 1199, Plaza de Mayo* ☎ *11/4381–3926* ▭ *AE, DC, MC, V* Ⓜ *C to Av. de Mayo, A to Lima.*

$-$$ ✕ **El Imparcial.** Founded in 1860, the oldest restaurant in town owes its name (meaning impartial) to its neutrality in the face of the warring political factions of Buenos Aires's Spanish immigrants. Hand-painted tiles, heavy wooden furniture, and paintings of Spain are all strong reminders of the restaurant's origins, as are the polite, elderly waiters, many of whom are from the old country. Talking politics is no longer banned within, good news for today's Argentines, who keep coming to El Imparcial for the renowned puchero as well as seafood specialties like paella. ⊠ *Hipólito Yrigoyen 1201, Plaza de Mayo* ☎ *11/4383–2919* 🖃 *AE, DC, MC, V* Ⓜ *C to Av. de Mayo, A to Lima.*

Traditional Argentine

★ **$-$$$$** ✕ **Sabot.** You might consider Sabot a find if you're a tourist—but this dignified, timeless lunch room is part of daily life to the scores of downtown businesspeople who have been coming here for ages. For more than three decades, they've been doing the same things, day after (week)day. This means absolutely impeccable service, fresh centolla, and a puchero that gets at the very essence of what boiled meat is all about. ⊠ *25 de Mayo 756, between Cordoba and Viamonte, El Centro* ☎ *11/4313–6587* 🖃 *AE, DC, MC, V* Ⓜ *B to L. N. Alem* ⊘ *Closed Sat.–Sun. No dinner* ⌓ *Reservations essential.*

$$-$$$ ✕ **La Pérgola.** On the third floor of the Sheraton Libertador hotel, this weekday, lunch-only restaurant caters to a local business crowd, serving an all-you-can-eat appetizer buffet that includes dozens of salads, and then a fairly standard Euro-Argentine menu of meats and fishes. Ask for the daily specials. ⊠ *Sheraton Libertador, Av. Córdoba 680, El Centro* ☎ *11/4321–0000* ⊘ *Closed Sat.–Sun. No dinner* 🖃 *AE, DC, MC, V* Ⓜ *C to Lavalle.*

¢-$$ ✕ **El Palacio de la Papa Frita.** This longtime standby is popular for its fanciful old-world atmosphere and hearty traditional meals—succulent steaks, homemade pastas, and fresh salads. The *papas soufflé* (inflated french fries) reign supreme; try them *a la provençal* (sprinkled with garlic and parsley) along with the classic *bife a medio caballo* (steak topped with a fried egg). ⊠ *Lavalle 735, El Centro* ☎ *11/4393–5849* Ⓜ *C to Lavalle* ⊠ *Av. Corrientes 1612, El Centro* ☎ *11/4374–8063* Ⓜ *B to Callao* 🖃 *AE, DC, MC, V.*

¢-$ ✕ **Pippo.** Historic Pippo, open since 1942, is a porteño classic known for its simplicity and down-to-earth cooking. Pastas like *tallarines* and ravioli are the most popular choices, but try also the *estofado* (beef stew), or *lomo* (sirloin) with fries. For dessert, flan is topped off with cream or dulce de leche. It's in the heart of the Corrientes theater district; as such, don't expect particularly attentive service. ⊠ *Paraná 356, El Centro* ☎ *11/4374–6365* Ⓜ *B to Uruguay* ⊠ *Av. Callao 1077, La Recoleta* ☎ *11/4812–4323* 🖃 *No credit cards.*

Almagro

Almagro is one of Buenos Aires's traditional tango neighborhoods. It's now increasingly trendy, with many bars, nightclubs, restaurants, and fringe theaters complementing the long-established tango spots.

Indian

$–$$ ✕ **Katmandú.** Step over rose petals into an Indian oasis—Katmandu may be off the beaten path, but the serenity and hospitality more than compensate. Chefs create spicy vindaloos and curries in full view. Consider sharing the tandoori or Indian sampling platter for two; then indulge in milky desserts. An international crowd gathers here. Upstairs you can purchase Indian furnishings. ⊠ *Córdoba 3547, Almagro* ☎ *11/ 4963–1122* ⊟ *AE, DC, MC, V* ⊘ *Closed Sun. No lunch.*

New Argentine

$–$$ ✕ **Malevo.** Named for the villain of the tango, Malevo was the first eatery to bring sleek modern dining to the city's classic tango district. The old corner building has large plate-glass windows and an intimate slate and aubergine interior where lights are low and white linen abounds. The house's excellent wine selection is on display behind a polished wooden bar—savor a bottle with your *Rebelión en la Granja* (pork with braised fennel and tapenade) or homemade goat-cheese ravioli with sun-dried tomatoes and almonds. ⊠ *Mario Bravo 908 at Tucumán, Almagro* ☎ *11/4861–1008* ⊟ *AE, D, MC, V* ⊘ *Closed Sun. No lunch Sat.* Ⓜ *B to Carlos Gardel.*

Traditional Argentine

¢–$ ✕ **La Maroma.** The specials in this chaotic *bodegón* (tavern-style restaurant) are erratically scrawled on bits of paper stuck on the walls under hams hanging from the ceiling, strings of garlic, and demijohns of wine. The homemade pastas are excellent, especially the lasagna, and so are the *milanesas* (breaded meat cutlets). Portions are large—don't be surprised if you can't finish your order. ⊠ *Mario Bravo 598 at Humahuaca, Almagro* ☎ *11/4862–9308* ⊟ *AE, V* Ⓜ *B to Carlos Gardel.*

Puerto Madero

This strip of docks along a canal east of El Centro is home to many large, new hotels. In terms of dining it's a bit of a minefield. Some establishments cater to young locals and become hopping pubs later in the evening; others cater almost exclusively to tourists. You can eat well here, but you can also pay a lot for mediocre food.

Parrilla

★ **$–$$** ✕ **La Caballeriza.** People flock from all over the world to empty their wallets at touristy Cabaña Las Lilas next door, but locals in the know come instead to this big, lively, informal steakhouse, where you'll pay much more reasonable prices for grilled meat that's arguably better. Sip champagne at the friendly bar while you wait for a table. The parrilla is wood-fired, Uruguayan style, and the *asado de tira* (rack of beef short ribs) is a highlight, but you also can't go wrong with the classic *bife de chorizo* (bone-in sirloin or rump steak). There's another branch by the Recoleta mall next to the cemetery, but this one is superior. ⊠ *A. M. de Justo 580, Puerto Madero* ☎ *11/4514–4444* ⊟ *AE, DC, MC, V* Ⓜ *B to L. N. Alem.*

All of the Cow but the Moo

CLOSE UP

ARGENTINA IS THE WORLD'S capital of beef, and Buenos Aires the capital of Argentina. So does Buenos Aires have the world's best steak?

It's hard to say no after your first bite into a tender morsel of deeply flavored, grass-fed beef, carefully charred by an open fire. Indeed, aside from the *estancias* (ranches) on the Pampas grasslands themselves, Buenos Aires is probably the best place to eat in a *parrilla* (steakhouse). That said, it can be difficult, upon a first glance at the bewildering menu of a parrilla, to know where to begin. Merely speaking Spanish isn't enough: entire books have been written attempting to pin down which cuts of meat in Argentina correspond to which ones in the United States and Europe. There's much disagreement. The juicy *bife de chorizo*, for example, the king of Argentine steaks, is translated by some as a bone-in sirloin, by others as a rump steak—and it's not as if "sirloin steak" is well defined to begin with.

Don't worry about definitions. If you order a *parrillada*—everything but the kitchen sink—a sizzling platter will be brought to you. Don't be timid about trying the more unfamiliar pieces. The platter will usually include a salty, juicy link or two of *chorizo* (a large, spicy sausage), and a collection of *achuras* (innards), which some first-timers struggle with. King among them is the gently spicy and oozingly delicious *morcilla* (blood sausage—like the British black pudding or the French *boudin noir*); give it a chance. Even more challenging are the chewy *chinchulines* (coils of small intestine),

which are best when crisped on the outside, and the strongly flavored *riñones* (kidneys). Although *mollejas* (sweetbreads) aren't usually part of a parrillada spread (they're more expensive), don't miss their unforgettable taste and fatty, meltingly rich texture, like a meatier version of foie gras. You'll also want to try the rich *provoleta* (grilled provolone cheese sprinkled with olive oil and oregano) and garlic-soaked grilled red peppers.

You can also skip the ready-made parrillada and instead order à la carte, as the locals often do. You might try the *vacio* (flank steak, roughly translated), a common cut that is flavorful but can also be tough, especially if overcooked. You may instead be seduced by the *lomo* (tenderloin or filet mignon), the softest and priciest cut, and like the immortal *bife de chorizo*, always a safe bet. Both of those steaks are better when requested rare (*"vuelta y vuelta"*), or, at the least, medium-rare (*"jugoso"*).

But the true local favorite, is the inimitable *asado de tira,* a rack of beef short ribs often cooked on a skewer over an open fire. Done properly, the asado brandishes the meatiest grass-fed flavor of all. As for accompaniments, the classics are a mix-and-match salad and/or french fries. And don't forget that delicious Argentine red wine; Malbecs and Cabernets both pair well with the deeply flavored meat. And with the amount of food that you're likely to consume over the course of the evening, you won't have to worry much about getting too drunk.

San Telmo

San Telmo is a good place to drink and wander, but it's not Buenos Aires's best dining neighborhood. Plaza Dorrego is full of touristy dinner-show joints with eminently forgettable food. Aside from the listed establishments, your best bets are the basic parrillas, throwbacks to a simpler Buenos Aires.

Cafés

★ ¢–$ ✕ **Bar Dorrego.** It probably hasn't changed much for the last 100 years or so. Dark wood and politely aloof waiters set the stage; good coffee, *tragos* (alcoholic drinks), sangria, and snacks complete the scene. On nice days you can sit out on Plaza Dorrego and take in one of San Telmo's most classic hubs of activity, most lively during the Sunday festival. ⊠ *Defensa 1098 and Humberto I, on Plaza Dorrego, San Telmo* ☎ *11/ 4361–0141* ▤ *No credit cards* Ⓜ *C or E to Independencia.*

New Argentine

$–$$ ✕ **Abril.** Sometimes atmosphere completely carries a restaurant. Such is the case with Abril, a bright, quirky space that it's impossible not to be enchanted by, even if the food isn't as captivating. An unusual assortment of memorabilia—some Argentine, some American—is the backdrop for the quick and friendly service, which caters largely to a business lunch crowd (there's a good 14-peso prix fixe). Dishes have everything from Mexican to Asian preparations. Presentations are uniformly beautiful, though the pastas, such as salmon ravioli, are the best choices. ⊠ *Balcarce 722, between Chile and Pasaje S. Lorenzo, San Telmo* ☎ *11/ 4342–8000* ▤ *No credit cards.*

$–$$ ✕ **La Farmacia.** Mismatched tables and chairs, comfy leather sofas, and poptastic colors fill this cute, century-old corner house that used to be a traditional pharmacy. Generous breakfasts and afternoon teas are served on the cozy ground floor, lunch and dinner are in the first-floor dining room, and you can have late-night drinks on the bright-yellow roof terrace. Arts and dance workshops are run upstairs, and the building has two boutiques selling local designers' work. The modern Argentine dishes are simple but well done, and the fixed-price lunch and dinner menus get you a lot for a little. ⊠ *Bolívar 898, San Telmo* ☎ *11/4300–6151* ▤ *No credit cards* ⊘ *Closed Mon.* Ⓜ *C or E to Independencia.*

Parrilla

$–$$$ ✕ **La Brigada.** You'd be hard-pressed to do better for Argentine steaks,
Fodor'sChoice   anytime, anyplace. Amid elaborate decor, including scores of soccer memementos, a courtly staff will treat you to unimpeachable *mollejas* (sweet-
★   breads) and *chinchulines de chivito* (kid intestines), plus a brilliant array of grilled steaks. The baby beef is tender enough to cut with a spoon. Skip the sister restaurant in Barrio Norte, which isn't up to the same standard. ⊠ *Estados Unidos 465, between Bolívar and Defensa, San Telmo* ☎ *11/4361–5557* ⌖ *Reservations recommended* ▤ *AE, DC, MC, V* ⊘ *Closed Mon.* Ⓜ *C or E to Independencia.*

Spanish

$–$$$$ ✕ **Taberna Baska.** Old-world decor and efficient service are hallmarks of this busy, no-nonsense Spanish restaurant. Try such typical dishes as *chiripones en su tinta* (a variety of squid in ink) or *fideua de chipirones* (a saffron dish with baby squid that's like a noodle version of paella). Meals come served with four different Basque sauces. ✉ *Chile 980, San Telmo* ☎ *11/4334–0903* ⊟ *AE, DC, MC, V* ☺ *Closed Mon. No dinner Sun.* Ⓜ *C to Independencia.*

★ **$–$$** ✕ **Burzako.** Classic Basque dishes reinvented for a young Argentine public keep Burzako's tables busy. Dishes such as *rabo de buey* (a rich oxtail-and-wine stew) and seasonally changing fish use only the best and freshest local ingredients, and the huge portions leave you loathe to move. Recover from the meal over another bottle from their savvy, well-priced wine list. Despite the rustic tavern furnishings, Burzako draws a funky crowd, and on weekends the basement becomes a bar where local bands often play. ✉ *México 345, San Telmo* ☎ *11/4334–0721* ⊟ *AE, DC, MC, V* ☺ *Closed Sun.*

La Boca

Touristy La Boca is one of the worst areas for restaurants. Make a special effort to avoid the mediocre places along Caminito, where shills irritatingly badger passersby. Since there's so much competition, prices are relatively low, but so is the quality.

Parrilla

$–$$$ ✕ **El Obrero.** When the rock band U2 played Buenos Aires and asked to be taken to a traditional Argentine restaurant, they were brought to this legendary hole-in-the-wall. For 50 years El Obrero has served juicy grilled steaks, sweetbreads, sausages, and chicken. The extensive blackboard menu includes *rabas* (fried calamari) and puchero. Try the *budín de pan* (Argentine version of bread pudding). This spot is popular with tourists and local workmen alike, so expect a short wait. La Boca is sketchy at night, so lunch is preferable; in any case, take a taxi. ✉ *Augustín R. Caffarena 64, La Boca* ☎ *11/4363–9912* ⊟ *No credit cards* ☺ *Closed Sun.*

Retiro

Retiro is a busy neighborhood near many top hotels and office buildings. Thanks to the abundance of internationals that visit this zone, its restaurants are fairly cosmopolitan, if not as cutting-edge as those in Palermo. The prices, like those in nearby Recoleta, are high (by Buenos Aires standards).

Eclectic

$$–$$$ ✕ **Bengal.** Bengal serves a mixture of Italian and Indian fare in quiet wood-paneled surroundings with dark colors. If you're anxious for some heat, try the *jhing masala* (prawn curry). Those with tender tastebuds should go for one of the delicious homemade pasta dishes. Their commitment to wine is serious, with a detailed list, decanters, and artistic glasses. ✉ *Arenales 837, Retiro* ☎ *11/4394–8557* ⊟ *AE* ☺ *Closed Sun. No lunch Sat.* Ⓜ *C to San Martín.*

$–$$ ✕ **Gran Bar Danzón.** Expansive wine lists have become all the rage in 21st-century Buenos Aires, but it will take more than just a rage to topple this king of wine bars from its lofty throne. The room is dark, loud, cramped, and filled with beautiful people; the menu is versatile, sometimes too much so—there's a king crab risotto on one end, sushi on the other. But skip the raw fish and focus on the simple small plates that serve as good accompaniments to one of the thousands of excellent red wines on offer. If you can't find it here, then you can probably only find it at private auction. ☒ *Libertad 1161, Retiro* ☏ *11/4811–1108* ⌕ *Reservations essential* ▭ *AE, DC, MC, V* ☉ *No lunch* Ⓜ *C to San Martín.*

French

$$$–$$$$ ✕ **Plaza Grill.** Wrought-iron lamps and fans hang from the high ceilings, and delft tiles decorate the walls at this favorite spot of executives and politicians. Visiting dignitaries have been dining here since the turn of the 20th century. The feeling, as you might expect, is formal, the wine list is extensive, and the European-centric menu includes excellent steak, salmon with basil and red wine, and pheasant with foie gras. Prices are stratospheric by local standards. ☒ *Marriott Plaza Hotel, Florida 1005, Retiro* ☏ *11/4590–8974* ⌕ *Reservations essential* ▭ *AE, DC, MC, V* Ⓜ *C to San Martín.*

★ $$$–$$$$ ✕ **Le Sud.** The Sofitel's flagship eatery blows away every other French restaurant in Buenos Aires—and that's really saying something. Chef Thierry Pszonka, the recipient of numerous culinary accolades in his native France, came over a few years ago to contribute his own brand of *nouvelle cuisine* to the Argentine dining landscape in this careful and elegant dining room. The results have been nothing less than spectacular, from an *amuse-bouche* of soothing chicken liver mousse to a dish of sensationally tender braised sweetbreads glazed with a silky brown sauce. ☒ *Hotel Sofitel, Arroyo 841–849, Retiro* ☏ *11/4831–0131* ⌕ *Reservations essential* ☉ *Closed Sun.* ▭ *AE, DC, MC, V* Ⓜ *C to San Martín.*

Irish

$–$$ ✕ **Matías.** Wash down a savory lamb stew or a chicken potpie with a brew at this cheery Irish pub. The steaks are excellent—try the *lomo relleno* (wrapped in bacon and served with plums) or the *lomo al bosque* (in a wild mushroom sauce). By night, the place becomes quite a scene, especially for foreigners and expats. ☒ *Reconquista 701, Centro* ☏ *11/4311–0327* ▭ *AE, DC, MC, V* ☉ *Closed Sun.* Ⓜ *C to San Martín.*

New Argentine

$$$–$$$$ ✕ **Crystal Garden.** There's one, and only one, reason to come to the overpriced restaurant of the Hotel Park Tower: to take in the evening views across Retiro from the glass-covered dining room. Everybody needs that gleaming-modern-city feeling now and then. The best time to come is during the 7 PM–10 PM happy hour; drinks and apps are free for hotel guests, but visitors, too, can crash the party, buy drinks, and partake of the extensive free buffet, which could easily become your dinner if you don't watch out. (The real dinner menu, however, is overpriced.) ☒ *Hotel Park Tower, Leandro N. Alem 1193, Retiro* ☏ *11/4318–9211* ▭ *AE, DC, MC, V* Ⓜ *C to San Martín.*

★ $–$$$ ✕ **Da Dá.** Eclectic porteño '60s pop culture characterizes one of the city's best-kept secrets, where murals inspired by Dalí, Miró, Lichtenstein, and Mondrian are splashed across the walls and jazz fills the small, intimate space. Seasonal specials are chalked up behind the cluttered bar. The short but inventive menu showcases local produce, with relentlessly modern flavor combinations, and the bar is a scene at night. ✉ *San Martín 941, Retiro* ☎ *11/4314–4787* ▭ *AE, MC, V* ⊙ *Closed Sun.* Ⓜ *C to San Martín.*

Pizza

★ ¢–$$$ ✕ **Piola.** The first Piola opened in Treviso, Italy in 1986; this was the second. Although there are now replicas in Brazil, Chile, Miami, and New York, this branch has become a well-loved landmark, and for good reason: beneath the trendy, funky veneer—modern art, modern music, and a palm-shaded garden—the imposing oven turns out the best pizza in town. Crusts are perfectly seared, and sauce and toppings are judiciously applied for an uncanny replica of the real Italian thing. Don't miss the pizza with *mozzarella di bufala* (buffalo-milk mozzarella), which must be the most authentic in South America. ✉ *Libertad 1078, Retiro* ☎ *11/4812–0690* ▭ *AE, DC, MC, V* Ⓜ *C to San Martín* ⊙ *Closed Sun. No lunch Sat.*

★ $–$$ ✕ **Filo.** Come here for the hip, lively atmosphere, but be prepared for crowds at all hours. The excellent individual-size pizzas are flat, in the Italian style; the bubbly crust is wonderfully charred by the enormous brick oven in the open kitchen. Toppings and sauce are remarkably authentic—you can tell that the ownership is Italian. Embrace the city's chic pizza-and-champagne aesthetic and wash your meal down with a 30-peso bottle of bubbly. Even the rock music is great; on your way to the restroom, check out the art space in the basement. ✉ *San Martín 975, between Alvear and Paraguay, Retiro* ☎ *11/4311–0312* ▭ *AE, MC, V* Ⓜ *C to San Martín.*

Spanish

$–$$$$ ✕ **Tancat.** Who would have thought that this calm Catalan tapas restau-
Fodor'sChoice rant in a calm part of downtown could be such a showstopper? Tan-
★ cat's romantic, warmly lit room has a mellow vibe, just the right balance of bustle, music, and noise; here, awkward moments just don't seem possible. The food, meanwhile, couldn't be more authentic if this were Barcelona. Begin with *pan con tomate* (grilled bread rubbed with garlic, olive oil, and tomato) paired with buttery Spanish ham. A deep, rich stew of *callos* (tripe) and *gambas al ajillo* (garlic shrimp) enjoy equal success. Even the price is right. ✉ *Paraguay 645, Retiro* ☎ *11/4312–5442* ▭ *AE, DC, MC, V* Ⓜ *C to San Martín* ⊙ *Closed Sun.*

La Recoleta

Touristy La Recoleta is full of designer boutiques and malls and home to the famous cemetery. On the one hand, there are lots of fast-food and higher-end chains as well as expense-account restaurants that offer some of the worst value for the money in town. On the other hand, there are some of the city's top restaurants—expensive but worth every penny. Choose carefully.

American

¢–$ ✕ **Buller Brewing Company.** The city's first microbrewery (the name is pronounced in the American way, not the Spanish double-L way) is more notable for its beer and its lively atmosphere than for its American-influenced brewpub food. But the brews really are impressive, and they're all made in a careful, German-inspired style. Don't miss the India Pale Ale or the unique honey beer. In a Recoleta that's full of cookie-cutter Irish pubs, this is a nice break. ⊠ *RM Ortiz 1827, La Recoleta* ☎ *11/ 4808–9061* ⊟ *AE, DC, MC, V.*

Cafés

¢–$$ ✕ **La Biela.** Porteños linger at this quintessential sidewalk café opposite the Recoleta Cemetery, sipping espressos, discussing politics, and people-watching—all of which are best done at a table beneath the shade of an ancient rubber tree. ⊠ *Quintana 600, at Junín, La Recoleta* ☎ *11/4804–0449* ⊟ *V.*

¢–$ ✕ **Modena Design Café.** This spacious Internet café has an ultramodern techno feel and showcases Ferraris—not surprisingly, it attracts porteño trendsetters. Log on while snacking on sushi, or nurse a *lagrima* (milk with a teardrop of coffee) while you sit back in an oversize chair. It's behind the Museo Nacional de Bellas Artes. ⊠ *Av. Figueroa Alcorta 2270, La Recoleta* ☎ *11/4809–0122* ⊟ *AE, V.*

French

★ $$$$ ✕ **La Bourgogne.** White tablecloths and fresh roses emphasize the restaurant's innate elegance. A sophisticated waitstaff brings you complimentary hors d'oeuvres as you choose from chef Jean-Paul Bondoux's creations, which include foie gras, rabbit, escargots, chateaubriand, *côte de veau* (veal steak), and wild boar cooked in cassis. The fixed-price menu is more affordable than à la carte selections. Sit in the wine cellar for a more intimate experience. ⊠ *Alvear Palace Hotel, Ayacucho 2027, La Recoleta* ☎ *11/4805–3857 or 11/4808–2100* ⊛ *Reservations essential* 🏛 *Jacket and tie* ⊟ *AE, DC, MC, V* ⊗ *Closed Sun. No lunch Sat.*

$$$$ ✕ **Nectarine.** This high-flying temple to *nouvelle* French cuisine has an eight-course tasting menu costing (at last check) 140 pesos. Every dish on the menu is delicious, though ambitious, and the wine list is extraordinary. Set aside an entire evening for this gustatory trip. The feeling in the second-floor room is formal, except for the open kitchen—a concession, perhaps, to the trends of modern high-concept dining. ⊠ *Pasaje del Correo, Vicente López 1661, Local 15, 1er piso, La Recoleta* ☎ *11/4813–6993* ⊛ *Reservations essential* ⊟ *AE, DC, MC, V* ⊗ *Closed Sun. No lunch Sat.*

German

$–$$$ ✕ **Munich Recoleta.** Jam-packed Munich Recoleta has been a favorite gathering spot for half a century, and the menu has barely changed since its 1956 opening. Premium cuts of meat, milanesas, creamed spinach, shoestring potatoes, and *chucrut* (cabbage) are served quickly and in generous portions. The reasonably priced wine list is enormous but well-chosen. The lively atmosphere attracts young and old alike, despite the often cantankerous waiters. Arrive early to avoid a wait. ⊠ *R. M. Ortíz 1879, La Recoleta* ☎ *11/4804–3981* ⊛ *Reservations not accepted after 9 PM* ⊟ *AE, V* ⊗ *Closed Tues.*

Italian

$$$–$$$$ ✕ **San Babila.** This trattoria is known for its excellent handmade pastas and classic Italian dishes, created from the century-old recipes of the chef's grandmother. *Cappelletti di formaggio* (cheese-filled round pasta) and *risotto alla milanese* are good bets. Prices are high, but there are fixed-price menus to choose from and a friendly English-speaking staff. The outdoor terrace is a treat. ⊠ *R. M. Ortíz 1815, La Recoleta* ☎ *11/4804–1214* ▤ *AE, DC, MC, V* ⊗ *No lunch Mon.*

Mediterranean

★ **$$$–$$$$** ✕ **Le Mistral.** The superb dining room at the Four Seasons is warm, inviting, and, well, Mediterranean—without any of the bright, antiseptic, or stuffy qualities of competing hotel restaurants. Lobster is treated with loving care, and the flavors on the menu are as often refreshingly subtle and delicate as they are bold. Even the north African side of the Mediterranean isn't overlooked with such dishes as the Tunisian-inspired *brik a l'oeuf.* ⊠ *Four Seasons Hotel, Posadas 1086, La Recoleta* ☎ *11/4321–1730* ⌔ *Reservations recommended* ▤ *AE, DC, MC, V.*

Middle Eastern

$–$$$ ✕ **Club Sirio.** You walk up a curved double staircase to the lobby bar of this breathtaking second-floor Syrian restaurant. Expect hummus, stuffed grape leaves, and lamb in the superb Middle Eastern buffet. Belly dancers entertain Wednesday through Saturday, and coffee-ground readers predict fortunes. You can order a *narguilah* (large water-filtered tobacco pipe) to finish things off in Syrian style. ⊠ *Pacheco de Melo 1902, La Recoleta* ☎ *11/4806–5764* ⊕ *www.chefabdala.com.ar* ▤ *AE, V* ⊗ *Closed Sun. No lunch.*

Parrilla

$ ✕ **Juana M.** The minimalist chic decor of this basement restaurant stands in stark contrast to the menu: down-to-earth parrilla fare at good prices. Catch a glimpse of meats sizzling on the grill behind the salmon-color bar—the only swath of color—then head to your table to devour your steak and *chorizo* (fat, spicy sausage). The homemade pastas aren't bad, either. The staff is young and friendly. ⊠ *Carlos Pellegrini 1535, La Recoleta* ☎ *11/4326–0462* ⊗ *No lunch Sat.* Ⓜ *C to San Martín.*

Traditional Argentine

¢–$$ ✕ **El Sanjuanino.** Northern Argentine fare is served at this long-established, if touristy, spot. El Sanjuanino is known city-wide for its tamales, *humitas* (steamed corn cakes wrapped in husks), and especially its empanadas, which crowds of people line up to take out for a picnic in the park (they're 20% cheaper to go). But they also make good *locro, pollo a la piedra* (chicken pressed flat by stones), venison, and antelope stew; skip the boring, hamlike *lomito de cerdo* (pork steak). The decor in the cozy space borders on cheesy, with hanging hams and a stuffed deer head, but the feeling is still fun. ⊠ *Posadas 1515 at Callao, La Recoleta* ☎ *11/4805–2683* ▤ *AE, MC, V.*

Palermo

This designation encompasses only the more generic areas of Palermo. There aren't as many restaurants as in Palermo Viejo and Las Cañitas, but there are worthwhile spots here and there.

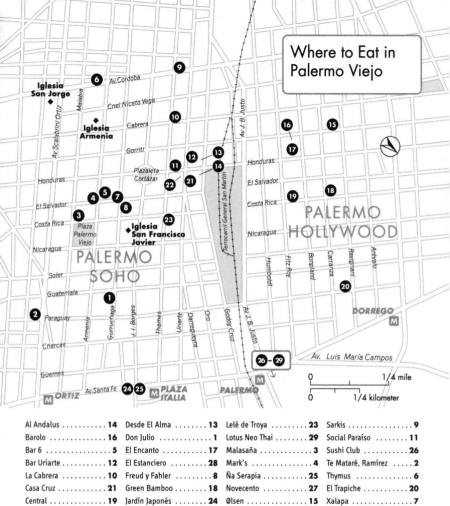

Where to Eat in Palermo Viejo

Japanese

$$–$$$$ ✕ **Jardín Japonés.** Easily the most impressive setting for sushi in Buenos Aires is inside the Japanese Garden on the northern edge of Palermo. Come for lunch, before or after touring the garden, or come for a romantic dinner. The sushi and sashimi are fresh, especially the salmon, although the hot dishes, such as pork with mushrooms, won't necessarily blow you away. Taxis tend to have trouble finding the place; tell them you're going to the garden. ✉ *Av. Casares 2966, Jardín Japonés, Bosques de Palermo* ☎ *11/4800–1322* ☾ *Closed Tues.*

Traditional Argentine

¢ ✕ **Ña Serapia.** Ña Serapia, across from Parque Las Heras, is well known for its hearty, authentic northern Argentine food. Creamy, steamed *humitas,* made from cornmeal and fresh corn, are excellent, as are cheese and onion empanadas. Carafes of wine, like everything else, are an unbelievable bargain. This is strictly no-frills—it's nothing but a basic room with a few little tables—but the food is consistently good. Don't miss the quirky wall art, which includes a portrait of the owner stabbed in the heart. ✉ *Av. Las Heras 3357, Palermo* ☎ *11/4801–5307* ▭ *No credit cards.*

Palermo Soho

If Palermo Viejo is the nerve center of the modern Buenos Aires food scene, then Palermo Soho is its mitochondrion. Restaurants are especially thick on the streets surrounding Plaza Serrano (known informally as Placita Serrano). Restaurants have relentlessly international cuisine, emphasizing fusion; they're often flooded with expats; and their style ranges from the merely hip to the super-hip. Quiet, cobblestoned streets mean you can enjoy eating outside.

Delicatessen

¢–$ ✕ **Mark's.** The first deli to arrive in Palermo Viejo, Mark's big sandwiches and salads have been steadily drawing crowds for all-day munching (it's open 10:30 AM–8:30 PM). It's also become something of a scene for twentysomethings with New York fetishes—and perhaps unsurprisingly, also a top choice for brunch. Ingredients are top quality, combinations inventive, and the large variety of breads—the house specialty—is baked on premise. Tastefully mismatched tables, chairs, and sofas are available if you want to eat in; there's also a small patio if you want some sun. The cheesecake in itself is an excuse for a visit. ✉ *El Salvador 4701, Palermo Soho* ☎ *11/4832–6244* ▭ *No credit cards.*

Eclectic

$$–$$$ ✕ **Te Mataré, Ramírez.** Te Mataré Ramírez, which translates as "I Will Kill You, Ramirez," is as unusual as it sounds. This self-styled "erotic restaurant" seduces with such dishes as "With Two Women" (caramelized chicken in a sherry, ginger, and grapefruit sauce) and desserts such as "Premature Palpitations of Pleasure" (warm white-chocolate cake). Thursday the temperature rises with a tastefully done "erotic theater" show and Wednesday night brings live jazz. From behind the red velvet bar comes all variety of cocktails to sip as you peruse the illustrated menu or gaze at the restaurant's erotic art collection. ✉ *Paraguay 4062,*

Palermo Soho ☎ *11/4831–9156* Ⓜ *D to Scalabrini Ortíz* ✉ *Primera Junta 702, San Isidro* ☎ *11/4747–8618* ▭ *AE, DC, MC, V* ☺ *Closed Mon. No lunch.*

$–$$ ✗ **Lelé de Troya.** This is one of the most spectacularly unusual spaces in the city. Each room of this converted old house is drenched in a different color—from the walls to the chairs and plates—and the food is just as bold. The kitchen is on view from the vine-covered lemon-yellow patio, and you can watch as loaf after loaf of the restaurant's homemade bread is drawn from the clay oven. Follow dishes like salmon ravioli or mollejas in cognac with one of Lelé's many Middle Eastern and Italian desserts. The restaurant holds tango classes on Monday nights and has a changing art space. ✉ *Costa Rica 4901, Palermo Soho* ☎ *11/ 4832–2726* ▭ *AE, MC, V.*

Mexican

¢–$$ ✗ **Xalapa.** Don't expect regional Mexican authenticity here, but by all means come when you get a margarita craving. This tangerine-color corner restaurant serves up mostly Tex-Mex versions of tacos, burritos, and enchiladas, as well as more ambitious dishes such as chicken *con mole* (a rich, spicy, chocolaty sauce), all at excellent prices, which appeal to the youthful crowd that floods the place on weekends. Dishes can be spiced up on request. ✉ *El Salvador 4800, Palermo Soho* ☎ *11/ 4833–6102* ▭ *No credit cards* ☺ *Closed Tues. No lunch except Sat.*

Middle Eastern

¢–$ ✗ **Sarkis.** Full to bursting with cane tables and chairs, this chaotic family-style restaurant does great Middle Eastern food. You could easily fill yourself up on several dishes from the large selection of mezes, which are the restaurant's best work. Be sure to leave room for a few baklava and other dripping, nut-filled pastries on offer. The place is technically in Villa Crespo, but it's only about a block from Palermo Soho, across Avenida Córdoba. ✉ *Thames 1101 at Jufré, Villa Crespo* ☎ *11/ 4772–4911* ▭ *AE, MC, V.*

New Argentine

$$$$ ✗ **Casa Cruz.** Trendsetters come and go, but there are few whose food
Fodor'sChoice is truly sublime. Casa Cruz plays up to the hipsters; with its unmarked
★ entrance, dim lighting, expanses of mahogany, and cozy banquettes, you'd have to be a bumbling fool not to impress your date. And yet it is chef Germán Martitegui's kitchen that will really blow your mind, working rabbit medallions into a state of melting tenderness, pairing delicately crisped *morcilla* (blood sausage) with jammy fruit. Is this the single best restaurant in Buenos Aires? Believe the hype. ✉ *Uriarte 1656, Palermo Soho* ☎ *11/4833–1112* ▭ *AE, DC, MC, V* ☺ *Closed Sun. No lunch* ✎ *Reservations essential.*

★ **$$–$$$$** ✗ **Bar Uriarte.** There is perhaps no place that better represents Palermo Viejo's dining revolution than the bustling kitchen of Bar Uriarte, which is enticingly set in the front of the restaurant, exposed to the street. Inside lies a sophisticated bar with two intimate dining spaces. You can even take your meal while lounging on a sofa. Chef Paula de Felipe's dishes are as sleek as the surroundings. Best are the pizzas and other dishes that come out of the prominent wood-fired mud oven. For lunch, there's a ridiculously cheap prix-fixe. Discrete live DJs warm things up on the weekend. ⊠ *Uriarte 1572, Palermo Soho* ☎ *11/4834–6004* ⊟ *AE, DC, MC, V.*

$$–$$$$ ✕ **Thymus.** Just over the border of Palermo Viejo into Villa Crespo, Thymus (the name of the gland from which sweetbreads are derived) is one of the more ambitious restaurants in this ambitious culinary neighborhood. Even if the minimalist decor with its sparse stone artwork cries out New York City, 1992, the feel is soothing and upscale. One of the best features here is the tasting menu, which allows each guest to sample small portions of two starters, two mains, and two desserts. Not everything on the ultramodern fusion menu works, but it's always interesting, and they have a particular way with duck breast. ⊠ *Lerma 525 at Malabia, Villa Crespo* ☎ *11/4772–1936* ⊟ *AE, DC, MC, V* ☉ *Closed Sun.–Mon. No lunch.*

$$–$$$ ✕ **Desde El Alma.** It would be hard to create a cuter restaurant than this cozy little gem, which is nestled just to the Palermo Soho side of the train tracks. In front, you can sit around an intimate fireplace, while the back room feels like an old Argentine family *comedor* (dining room). The menu is relatively short and simple; dishes like leek quiche and sesame-crusted salmon are tasty and thoughtful without overreaching. ⊠ *Honduras 5298, Palermo Soho* ☎ *11/4831–5812* ⊟ *No credit cards* ☉ *Closed Sun. No lunch* ⪪ *Reservations recommended.*

$$–$$$ ✕ **Malasaña.** You'll feel like you're eating inside a gigantic wine cellar in this dizzying architectural jumble of glass, stone, and creative spot lighting. (Okay, maybe a wine cellar from *Star Trek*.) The menu is varied and ambitious, and often good (try the mushroom risotto with duck confit, if available), but the atmosphere is more the point than the food. It's equally, if not more, worthwhile to come just for a cocktail or a bottle of wine and to experience the cutting edge of Palermo Soho ridiculousness. ⊠ *Honduras 5298, Palermo Soho* ☎ *11/4831–5812* ⊟ *No credit cards* ☉ *Closed Sun. No lunch.*

$–$$ ✕ **Bar 6.** The seasonally changing menu ambitious—sometimes too ambitious—cycling through a universe of ingredients and preparations, from breakfast to Asian stir-fry to polenta to grilled seafood. Past highlights have included marinated salmon with cilantro, and goat-cheese ice cream with candied tomatoes. The waiters are usually too busy being beautiful to attend to you in a hurry. Even if the service lags and the kitchen can be inconsistent, it's worth stopping by for a drink and to admire this dramatic stone, wood, and glass space—simultaneously modern and down to earth. ⊠ *Armenia 1676, Palermo Soho* ☎ *11/ 4833–6807* ⊟ *AE, MC, V* ☉ *Closed Sun.*

$–$$ ✕ **Social Paraíso.** Simple, airy, friendly, elegant—this Med-Argentine bistro has just the vibe for a lunch or dinner stop after a cheery round of shopping. Pastas such as ravioli are best; vegetarians will also be happy here, with inventive entreés that feature meaty vegetables like eggplant. Social Paraiso has also refreshingly kept its prices low even as its fame has grown, and the two-course lunch for (at last check) 12 pesos is a gift. ⊠ *Honduras 5182, Palermo Soho* ☎ *4831–4556* ⊟ *AE, MC, V* ☉ *Closed Mon. No dinner Sun.*

¢–$$ ✕ **Freud y Fahler.** Red walls, colored pane-glass screens, and vintage chandeliers give warmth to this glassed-in corner restaurant along a peaceful cobblestoned street. The menu is short but imaginative; try the braised lamb, if available, perhaps followed by spiced white-chocolate cake with plum ice cream and orange sauce. The young, well-informed staff gives friendly advice on food and wine. The lunch menus, which are more vegetable-oriented, are an excellent value. It's also a popular stop for an afternoon drink or a coffee. ⊠ *Gurruchaga 1750, Palermo Soho* ☎ *11/4833–2153* 🖃 *AE, V* ✆ *Closed Sun.*

Parrilla

¢–$$ ✕ **Don Julio.** In a neighborhood where it's becoming increasingly hard to find a parrilla, this is an aberration, and a good one. As a result, it's almost always packed with locals, who come to sample the work of the distinguished *parrillero*, who can be seen from the sidewalk, tending to the glowing embers. The room is simple and pleasant, with exposed brick walls, and the service is extremely polite. The creamy, spicy morcilla is a knockout. ⊠ *Guatemala 4691 and Gurruchaga, Palermo Soho* ☎ *11/4831–9564* 🖃 *AE, MC, V.*

Spanish

$–$$ ✕ **Al Andalus.** At this Andalusian restaurant, you'll have trouble choosing between the lamb *tagine* (a rich, dark stew cooked with plums and almonds), the *Pastel Andalusí* (a sweet-and-sour filo packed with lamb and chicken), or the goat cheese, saffron, and wild mushroom risotto. The *torta antigua* (chocolate cake) is not to be missed. You can eat in a tented dining room, under the ceramic lights of the quieter rust-red bar, or stretched out on sofas draped with Moroccan rugs beside a tiled fountain in the plant-filled courtyard. ⊠ *Godoy Cruz 1823, Palermo* ☎ *11/4832–9286* 🖃 *AE, MC, V* ✆ *Closed Sun.*

Traditional Argentine

¢–$ ✕ **Club Eros.** A basic dining room attached to an old soccer club, Club Eros has developed a cult following for its downscale charm. The excellent renditions of classic *criolla* fare at rock-bottom prices have begun to draw young Palermo trendies as well as older customers who have been loyal to the club for decades. There's no menu, but you can confidently order a crispy milanesa, or, if available, a bife de chorizo and fries. Pasta sauces fall flat, but the flan con dulce de leche is one of the best (and biggest) in town. ⊠ *Uriarte 1609, Palermo Soho* ☎ *11/4832–1313* 🖃 *No credit cards.*

Palermo Hollywood

Palermo Hollywood is more sparsely furnished than Palermo Soho, but it's also newer, and in some ways even hipper and more artsy. As such, this neighborhood has an assortment of over-the-top trendy restaurants, especially around the Plaza Palermo Viejo. A few parrillas and the like hark back to a time when this was a run-down part of town.

New Argentine

$$–$$$ ✕ **Barolo.** Its opening in 1998 helped to spark Palermo Hollywood's emergence as a dining mecca. It's on a quiet street in an old town house

done up in bright green and mauve. Don't miss the Patagonian lamb or the risotto with cognac-sautéed sweetbreads, spinach, Gruyère cheese, and Chardonnay. Wines of the month are chalked up on a blackboard over the bar. ⊠ *Bonpland 1612, Palermo Hollywood* ☎ *11/4772–0841* ⊟ *AE, V* ⊗ *Closed Sun. No lunch Sat.*

$$ ✕ **Central.** This candlelit space wins you over with its looks; so do the servers, who are uniformly sexy, whether male or female. You can chill out at the bar or eat side-by-side on low-slung couches. Don't expect fireworks from the menu, but the cocktails are well thought out and they do an unusually good job with *rollos de pollo* (chicken rolled with ham and cheese). In keeping with the spirit of the neighborhood, there are also plenty of lighter and vegetarian options (how else would everyone here be so thin?). ⊠ *Costa Rica 5644, Palermo Hollywood* ☎ *11/4776–7370* ⊟ *AE, DC, MC, V.*

Parrilla

$–$$$ ✕ **El Trapiche.** The enormous *matambre de cerdo,* a thin grilled pork steak, is the juicy highlight at this busy parrilla. High ceilings hung with hams and walls stacked with wine contain a pleasant racket. Share a selection of barbecued meats, as most do, or have the *sorrentinos de calabaza al scarparo* (squash-filled fresh pasta in a spicy cream sauce) all to yourself. If you have room, finish with a fruit-filled crepe, flambéed at your table. The wine list is great. ⊠ *Paraguay 5599, Palermo Hollywood* ☎ *11/4772–7343* ⊟ *AE, DC, MC, V* Ⓜ *Line D, Estación Palermo.*

★ **$–$$** ✕ **La Cabrera.** Palermo's best parrilla is on the quiet corner of Cabrera and Thames. Fun ancient paraphernalia hangs everywhere, giving the feel of an old grocery store. La Cabrera is particularly known for its excellent *provoleta de queso de cabra* (grilled goat cheese) and its *chinchulines de cordero* (small intestines of lamb). Try also the *cuadril vuelta y vuelta* (rare rump steak) and the mollejas, which are also top-notch. ⊠ *Cabrera 5099, Palermo Hollywood* ☎ *11/4831–7002* ⊗ *No lunch Mon.*

★ **¢–$** ✕ **El Encanto.** The hardest thing about eating in this soccer-memorabilia-packed space is getting a seat. Come early or come late; otherwise, it will be packed with locals taking advantage of the staggeringly low prices. Don't expect tip-top service; do expect perfectly good grilled meat and a certain chaos that makes for a fun evening—if you're in the mood for chaos, that is. ⊠ *Bonpland 1690, Palermo Hollywood* ☎ *No phone* ⊟ *No credit cards.*

Scandinavian

$$ ✕ **Ølsen.** Ølsen is a showcase for Nordic flavors *and* contemporary Scandinavian design. Past the walled sculpture garden and white lounge chairs is a cavern of exposed-brick walls. Lime-green furniture and cowhide barstools lend a '70s feel. Best are the *smørrebrød* (open sandwiches) with different vodka shots (the vodka selection is impressive here); other starters like gravlax and *rösti* (crispy sautéed potatoes) are better than the often dry and underseasoned meat entrées. This is *the* place for Sunday brunch. ⊠ *Gorriti 5870, Palermo Hollywood* ☎ *11/4776–7677* ⊟ *AE, V* ⊗ *Closed Mon.*

Vietnamese

$$–$$$ ✕ **Green Bamboo.** At Buenos Aires's first Vietnamese restaurant, the walls are black, the waiters slick, and the olive-green vinyl chairs usually occupied by thirtysomething actors and producers. And those chairs are usually *all* occupied. The food is reasonably authentic; take your time over it and then move on to one of the fantastic *maracuyá* (passion fruit) daiquiris once Green Bamboo's bar begins to warm up. ✉ *Costa Rica 5802, Palermo Hollywood* ☎ *11/4775–7050* ⊟ *AE, V* ⊘ *Closed Sun. No lunch.*

Las Cañitas

The food in this hip little neighborhood doesn't always match the hype, but interesting cuisine abounds. The area is good for a night out with the locals; most of the foreigners are over in Palermo Soho and Palermo Hollywood.

Japanese

$–$$$$ ✕ **Sushi Club.** The restaurants in this mini-chain beat the competition with an ever-present atmosphere of young, cutting-edge luxury. If there's a wait for a table in the dim, lively room—and there often is—you can expect to be served an aperitif while you wait. Sushi menus don't vary much in this city, and these joints are no exception; choose from dozens of variations on salmon, which is what they do best. The two Las Cañitas branches are strangely right near each other; the third is in Puerto Madero. ✉ *Ortega y Gasset 1812, Las Cañitas* ☎ *810/2227–8744* Ⓜ *D to Ministro Carranza* ✉ *Báez 268, Las Cañitas* ☎ *810/2227–8744* Ⓜ *D to Ministro Carranza* ✉ *Alicia M. de Justo 286, Puerto Madero* ☎ *810/2227–8744* Ⓜ *B to L. N. Alem* ⊟ *AE, DC, MC, V.*

New Argentine

$$–$$$ ✕ **Novecento.** This bistro, which has branches in New York and Miami Beach, is going for a *newyorquino* feel, and as such, it's become a magnet for young, highbrow porteños. Snug, candlelit tables offer intimacy. The menu is eclectic, but it drifts toward Italian. Try the pyramid of green salad, steak, and fries, or shrimp with bacon. Crème brûlée and "Chocolate Delight" are tempting desserts. The Sunday brunch is notable, and in summer you can dine outdoors. ✉ *Báez 199, Las Cañitas* ☎ *11/4778–1900* ⊕ *www.bistronovecento.com* ⊟ *AE, MC* Ⓜ *D to Ministro Carranza.*

Parrilla

$–$$ ✕ **El Estanciero.** It perfectly captures the vibrancy of Las Cañitas; even on weekdays, you'll see groups casually ambling in to dine as late as midnight. They come for the juicy steaks and *achuras* (innards), all of which are grilled over an open fire in full view of the restaurant. Grab one of the tables on the open second floor and you'll get an even better view of the parrilla. Ask for your steak *vuelta y vuelta* (rare) for best results. ✉ *Báez 202 and Argüibel, Las Cañitas* ☎ *11/4899–0951* ⊟ *AE, DC, MC, V* Ⓜ *D to Ministro Carranza.*

Thai

$$–$$$$ ✕ **Lotus Neo Thai.** The only Thai restaurant in Buenos Aires at this writing charms with its homely, hippie-ish space that inhabits a re-done apartment. Enormous flower decorations and trippy music seem straight out of *Alice in Wonderland,* and if you want, you can dine sitting on pillows on the floor. Tropical frozen cocktails hit the spot; among main courses, curries are best. Although the Thai food doesn't excel by international standards, it's a spicy break from the city's norm, and it's a good choice for vegetarians. ⊠ *Ortega y Gasset 1782, Las Cañitas* ☏ *11/4771–4449* ⊕ *www.restaurantelotus.com.ar* ⊟ *AE, DC, MC, V* ⊘ *Closed Sun. No lunch* Ⓜ *D to Ministro Carranza.*

Belgrano

Belgrano is an affluent, laid-back residential zone northwest of El Centro, past Palermo and Las Cañitas. It's not as packed with places to eat as other areas, but it has several upscale restaurants that make it worth the trip.

Mexican

$$–$$$ ✕ **María Félix.** This Mexican restaurant represents the best of Belgrano: a laid-back, friendly environment, good service, and good comfort food. There's the requisite sombrero-and-folk-art theme, but in this airy space, which is often full of families, it's casually charming, not overbearing. A well-balanced margarita and a satisfying *queso fundido* (Mexican cheese fondue) are a good way to get going; enchiladas and shrimp dishes are authentic and tasty. ⊠ *Soldado de la Independencia 1150, Belgrano* ☏ *11/ 4775–0380* Ⓜ *D to José Hernandez* ⊠ *Dardo Rocha 1680, Martínez* ☏ *11/4717–1864* ⊕ *www.mariafelix.com.ar* ⊟ *AE, DC, MC, V.*

New Argentine

★ **$$–$$$$** ✕ **Sucre.** Though it's in something of a no-man's land at the northern tip of a neighborhood known as Belgrano Chico, Sucre has become synonymous with high-concept dining. The visual impact is immediate, from the open kitchen that stretches the length of the airy, warehouse-like space to a catwalk that's suspended next to the dramatic floor-to-ceiling wall of illuminated liquors. The menu is original and inspired, drawing in elements from Asia with dishes like a spectacular citrus-and-soy-laced *tiradito de pescado* (like a fusion ceviche). Equally impressive are the duck ravioli and the beautifully designed desserts. ⊠ *Sucre 676, Belgrano* ☏ *11/ 4782–9082* ⊕ *www.sucrerestaurant.com.ar* ⊟ *AE, MC, V.*

WHERE TO STAY

By Brian Byrnes

Buenos Aires is experiencing a tourism boom unlike any in its history. The cheap peso has made it one of the planet's most affordable cities, and dollar- and euro-wielding visitors are arriving in record numbers. How is this good news in terms of where to stay? Well, lots of new hotels have been built, and many existing ones have been renovated, so you have more (and better) choices than ever, regardless of preferences and price limits.

What to Expect

Smaller hotels have a family-run feel, with all the charming quirks that entails. Rooms in medium-price hotels may be smaller than expected, but the facilities and service are usually of high quality. Posh properties obviously provide world-class comforts. In general, hotels have bidets (a nod to the Continent) and Internet and/or e-mail access (a nod to going global) but not, say, ice makers or vending machines (a nod to the fact that South Americans have different ideas about creature comforts from their neighbors to the north). As a rule, check-in is after 3 PM, check-out before noon; smaller hotels tend to be more flexible.

Rates

Prices include breakfast. Though some small Argentine-owned hotels advertise their rates in pesos, most places cite them in dollars. That said, always confirm which currency is being quoted. If a hotel staffer tries to take a peso room rate and slap a dollar or euro sign on it, politely remind him or her that price gouging is a no-no. Unless there's a clearly advertised special for Argentine citizens, prices are the same for all visitors, regardless of nationality. The lodging tax is 21%; this may or may not be included in a rate, so always ask about it.

WHAT IT COSTS In Argentine Pesos				
	$$$$	**$$$**	**$$**	**$**	**¢**
HOTELS	over 550	401–550	251–400	100–250	under 100

Hotel prices are for two people in a standard double room in high season.

El Centro

$$$$ 🏨 **Marriott Plaza Hotel.** This Buenos Aires landmark brims with old-school
Fodor'sChoice   style. Built in 1909 and renovated in 2003, the hotel sits at the top of
★   pedestrian-only Florida Street and overlooks the leafy Plaza San Martín. The elegant lobby, crystal chandeliers, and swanky cigar bar evoke Argentina's opulent, if distant, past. Rooms are comfortable and clean, if not particularly spacious. The hotel is next to both the Kavanagh Building, a 1930's art deco masterpiece that was once South America's tallest, and the Basilica Santísimo Sacramento, where renowned Argentines of all stripes, like Diego Maradona, have tied the knot. Exploring the myriad nooks and crannies of this grand old hotel is part of its timeless appeal. ⊠ *Florida 1005, El Centro, 1005* 🕾 *11/4318–3000, 800/228–9290 in U.S.* ⊕ *www.marriott.com* 🛏 *313 rooms, 12 suites* ♨ *2 restaurants, coffee shop, room service, IDD phones, in-room safes, minibars, cable TV with movies, in-room data ports, pool, gym, health club, hair salon, hot tub, sauna, bar, laundry service, concierge, DSL Internet, Wi-Fi in lobby, business services, meeting rooms* ☰ *AE, DC, MC, V* ⏅ *BP* Ⓜ *C to San Martín.*

★ **$$$**   🏨 **Buenos Aires cE Design Hotel.** It drips with coolness. The lobby's glass floor looks down to a small pool, just one example of the transparency theme that runs throughout. Floor-to-ceiling windows afford amazing views, and mirrors are placed for maximum effect. Rooms feel like pimped-out Tribeca lofts, with rotating flat-screen TVs that let you watch from bed or one of the leather recliners. Mattresses are high and mighty and covered in shades of brown and orange. Kudos go to the architect, Ernesto Goransky, who also did the Design Suites next door.

Location, Location, Location

1

- **Best for international luxury:** El Centro, La Recoleta.

- **All about boutique hotels:** Palermo, San Telmo.

- **Best place to "live" like a local:** Palermo.

- **Great for shoppers:** Palermo (young Argentine designers, trendy shops); El Centro, La Recoleta (international names, great malls).

- **Tops for tango:** San Telmo, Almagro, La Recoleta.

- **Great for food—morning, noon, and night:** Palermo, La Recoleta.

- **Best for fresh air and green spaces:** Puerto Madero, Palermo.

⊠ *Marcelo T. Alvear 1695, El Centro, 1060* ☎ *11/5237–3100* ⊕ *www. designce.com* ⬅ *28 rooms* ⌂ *In-room safes, hot tub, kitchenettes, cable TV, in-room data ports, pool, gym, bar, laundry service, DSL Internet, Wi-Fi in lobby, meeting room, travel services* ═ *AE, DC, MC, V* Ⓜ *D to Callao.*

$$$ ▥ **Claridge.** Long white columns front the entrance, beyond which is the high-ceilinged lobby and a traditional British café and piano bar. The redbrick building dates from 1946 and was built with an Anglo-Argentine clientele in mind; that feeling lingers in the spacious, elegant rooms with their bright floral patterns and wood paneling. Bathrooms are on the small side. The pool and spa are ideal for chilling out after a long Porteño night. ⊠ *Tucumán 535, El Centro, 1049* ☎ *11/4314–7700, 800/ 223–5652 in U.S.* ⊕ *www.claridge.com.ar* ⬅ *155 rooms, 6 suites* ⌂ *Restaurant, room service, IDD phones, in-room safes, minibars, cable TV, in-room data ports, pool, gym, health club, massage, spa, bar, laundry service, concierge, DSL Internet, business services, meeting room, airport shuttle, no-smoking floors* ═ *AE, DC, MC, V* ℺ *BP* Ⓜ *C to San Martín.*

$$$ ▥ **Inter-Continental.** The hotel is lovely, but the location is lousy. After the office workers head home, the area is desolate; it's also on the fringe of some sketchy streets where it's ill-advised to venture at night. Taxis are the way to go. By day, though, you can readily explore the quaint antique shops, restaurants, and tango halls of nearby San Telmo. Rooms are modern, spacious, and equipped with sleeper chairs. The lobby bar is a great place for a drink; if the weather's right, sit in the courtyard, where you'll forget you're in a concrete jungle. ⊠ *Moreno 809, El Centro, 1091* ☎ *11/4340–7100* ⊕ *www.ichotelsgroup.com* ⬅ *310 rooms, 10 suites* ⌂ *2 restaurants, café, room service, DSL Internet, Wi-Fi in lobby, IDD phones, in-room safes, cable TV, in-room data ports, indoor pool, gym, hot tub, massage, sauna, Turkish bath, bar, babysitting, laundry service, concierge, business services, meeting room, parking (fee), no-smoking floors* ═ *AE, DC, MC, V* ℺ *BP* Ⓜ *E to Belgrano.*

★ **$$$** ▥ **NH City.** This enormous art deco hotel is a throwback to an earlier era. It would be the perfect image for a cover of Ayn Rand's *The Fountainhead*. Inside molded pillars support a stained-glass ceiling, which filters sunlight onto white marble floors. Upstairs the contemporary rooms have dark wood floors and color schemes that include bold oranges, reds, and black. The rooftop pool and patio are beloved by TV-commercial producers, thanks to the view of the cupolas in nearby San Telmo. ⊠ *Bolívar 160, El Centro, 1066* ☎ *11/4121–6464* ⊕ *www.nh-hotels. com* 🛏 *297 rooms, 6 suites* ⚐ *Restaurant, café, room service, IDD phones, in-room safes, minibars, cable TV, in-room data ports, pool, gym, sauna, bar, laundry service, concierge, DSL Internet, Wi-Fi in lobby, business services, meeting rooms* ⊟ *AE, DC, MC, V* ¡◎¡ *BP* Ⓜ *A to Perú, E to Bolívar.*

$$$ 🏨 **Panamericano.** The popular, upscale Panamericano is near the famed Teatro Colón and the landmark Obelisco. The lobby's checked-marble floors lead to large salons, a snazzy café, and an Irish pub. Rooms are spacious and elegant, with dark wooden headboards and smart furnishings. Don't miss a chance to dine in the outstanding Tomo I restaurant or at what must be the nation's highest sushi bar, Kasuga, on the 23rd floor. The top-floor pool and spa afford amazing views. Visit in the late afternoon to watch the soft pastels of a smoggy sunset give way to the neon glow on the world's widest avenue, Av. 9 de Julio. ⊠ *Carlos Pellegrini 551, 1009* ☎ *11/4348–5000* ⊕ *www.panamericanobuenosaires.com* 🛏 *345 rooms* ⚐ *3 restaurants, coffee shop, room service, IDD phones, in-room safes, mini-bars, cable TV, pool, gym, health club, sauna, bar, laundry service, concierge, DSL Internet, Wi-Fi in rooms, business services, meeting rooms, parking (fee)* ⊟ *AE, DC, MC, V* Ⓜ *B to C. Pellegrini.*

$$$ 🏨 **Sheraton Buenos Aires Hotel.** What it lacks in charm, it makes up for in practicality, professionalism, and energy. There's always something happening here: a visiting dignitary, an international conference. Rooms are standard, clean, and well equipped, all of which explain the hotel's popularity among American businesspeople. The luxurious Park Tower Hotel, next door, has large, lavish rooms with round-the-clock butler service. When Latin heartthrobs like Luis Miguel or Ricky Martin are in town, they stay in the penthouse suite; scores of ecstatic Argentine females can usually be found holding vigils outside. ⊠ *San Martín 1225, El Centro, 1104* ☎*11/4318–9000, 800/325–3535 in U.S.* ⊕*www. sheraton.com* 🛏*713 rooms, 29 suites* ⚐*2 restaurants, coffee shop, room service, IDD phones, in-room fax, in-room safes, minibars, cable TV with movies, in-room data ports, 2 tennis courts, 2 pools, fitness classes, gym, health club, hair salon, massage, sauna, bar, lobby lounge, babysitting, laundry service, concierge, DSL Internet, Wi-Fi in lobby, business services, convention center, meeting rooms, car rental, travel services, parking (fee), no-smoking rooms* ⊟ *AE, DC, MC, V* ¡◎¡ *BP* Ⓜ *C to Retiro.*

$$$ 🏨 **Sheraton Libertador.** It's on chaotic Avenida Córdoba, so you're better off choosing it if you're here in town on business or if you're looking for American-style service and nothing more. Rooms are clean, comfortable, and look like any other chain-hotel rooms in the world; for a little peace, request one facing away from the avenue. The street-level lobby café is one of the best places in the city to gawk inconspicuously at gorgeous Argentine passersby. ⊠ *Av. Córdoba 690, El Centro, 1054* ☎ *11/4321–0000* ⊕ *www.sheraton.com* 🛏 *193 rooms, 6 suites*

 ♧ *Restaurant, room service, IDD phones, in-room fax, in-room safes, some kitchenettes, minibars, cable TV with movies, in-room data ports, indoor-outdoor pool, gym, health club, hot tub, massage, sauna, bar, babysitting, laundry service, concierge, DSL Internet, Wi-Fi in lobby, business services, meeting rooms, no-smoking rooms = AE, DC, MC, V* ➡❘ *BP* Ⓜ *C to Lavalle.*

$$ ☐ **Design Suites.** It can be hard to find a well-located, modern, minimalist hotel that's also reasonably priced. This is it. The futuristic lobby cranks chill house music and has a slim little swimming pool that's often used for photo shoots with equally slim models. Sleek rooms have wooden floors, chrome furniture, and kitchenettes with espresso machines. You're close to excellent shopping on Avenida Santa Fe and in the stately Palacio Pizzurno. ✉ *M. T. de Alvear 1683, El Centro, 1060* ☎ *11/4814–8700* ⍥ *www.designsuites.com* ➜ *40 rooms* ♧ *Restaurant, room service, in-room safes, some in-room hot tubs, some kitchenettes, cable TV, in-room data ports, pool, gym, bar, laundry service, DSL Internet, meeting room* = *AE, DC, MC, V* Ⓜ *D to Callao.*

$$ ☐ **NH Florida.** Shiny parquet wood floors, extra fluffy pillows, and smiling young staffers are among the reasons to stay. The hotel sits in the shadow of the massive Harrod's Building; the famed British department store was once *the* place for porteños to shop, but it has been sitting dark and abandoned on Florida Street for years. A few blocks away, the NH Latino has similar decor and services to the NH Florida. ✉ *San Martín 839, El Centro, 1004* ☎ *11/4321–9850* ⍥ *www.nh-hoteles.com* ➜ *148 rooms* ♧ *Restaurant, IDD phones, in-room safes, minibars, cable TV, in-room data ports, bar, laundry service, DSL Internet, business services, free parking* = *AE, DC, MC, V* ➡❘ *BP* Ⓜ *C to San Martín.*

$$ ☐ **NH Jousten.** The historic Jousten Building on crazy Avenida Corrientes has some of the most luxurious rooms in the NH chain and has hosted the likes of Evita Peron over the years. Rooms have big, bouncy beds and handsome wood desks; the small bathrooms disappoint, though. The lobby café sits a half-story above the sidewalk and offers grand views of the chaos below. Suites have private terraces overlooking the city and the River Plate. ✉ *Corrientes 280, El Centro, 1043* ☎ *11/4321–6750* ⍥ *www.nh-hoteles.com* ➜ *80 rooms, 5 suites* ♧ *Restaurant, room service, IDD phones, in-room safes, minibars, cable TV, in-room data ports, lobby lounge, babysitting, dry cleaning, laundry service, concierge, DSL Internet, Wi-Fi in lobby, business services, travel services* = *AE, DC, MC, V* ➡❘ *BP* Ⓜ *B to L. N. Alem.*

$$ ☐ **Posta Carretas.** The interior feels like an Andean ski lodge, with bedrooms that recall those at your Aunt Martha's house: slightly musty and definitely not redecorated since your cousin Jeffrey moved out to train for the 1960 Winter Olympics. Even the menu looks like it was brought down from the mountains: *ciervo* (deer) and *jabalí* (boar) are served at breakfast. The lobby bar overlooks an indoor pool, and there's a small garden where you can relax after a long day of hiking, er, shopping. ✉ *Esmeralda 726, El Centro, 1007* ☎ *11/4322–8567* ⍥ *www.postacarretas.com.ar* ➜ *90 rooms, 26 suites* ♧ *Coffee shop, room service, IDD phones, in-room safes, some in-room hot tubs, minibars, cable TV, in-room data ports, indoor pool, gym, sauna, bar, dry cleaning, laundry*

service, Internet, business services, meeting room, parking (fee) ⊟ *AE, DC, MC, V* |O| *BP* Ⓜ *C to San Martín.*

$ ▦ **Castelar Hotel.** This 1929 hotel is a European potpourri: Spanish architecture, French interior design, Italian marble. Revolving doors lead to the impressive lobby bar–restaurant, whose shiny floor and bold bronze ornamentation are throwbacks to the days when Buenos Aires earned its reputation as the so-called Paris of Latin America. The charm stops there, though: rooms have sparse old furnishings, and beds and bathrooms are tired. ⊠ *Av. de Mayo 1152, El Centro, 1085* ☎ *11/4383–5000* ⊕ *www. castelarhotel.com.ar* ⤴ *153 rooms, 7 suites* ♿ *Restaurant, coffee shop, room service, IDD phones, in-room safes, minibars, health club, hair salon, massage, sauna, spa, Turkish bath, laundry service, Internet, business services, meeting room, parking (fee)* ⊟ *AE, MC, V* |O| *BP* Ⓜ *A to Lima.*

$ ▦ **Hotel Facon Grande.** Named after a famous Argentine cowboy, this place takes the gaucho motif to the max, filling common areas with wood and leather furniture plucked directly from the cattle ranches outside Buenos Aires. In guest rooms, hints of the Pampas disappear; expect small, clean spaces equipped with tiny TVs. The bar and restaurant attract local business folks for lunch; the hotel appeals to Brazilians and provincial Argentines. ⊠ *Reconquista 645, El Centro, 1003* ☎ *11/4312–6360* ⊕ *www.hotelfacongrande.com* ⤴ *97 rooms, 3 suites* ♿ *Restaurant, room service, IDD phones, in-room safes, minibars, cable TV, bar, laundry service, Internet, meeting room, parking (fee)* ⊟ *AE, DC, MC, V* |O| *CP* Ⓜ *B to Alem.*

$ ▦ **Lancaster.** The friendly staff at this 60-year-old hotel takes real pride in the building's past. Rumor has it that many shady political deals were sealed over pints inside the White Rose, an adjoining British pub popular with the after-work crowd. Long, red-carpeted hallways conjure up images of *The Shining*, and rooms don't look like they've been refurbished since the 1970's. The style is classic indeed: wood parquet floors, old aristocratic artwork, and simple white-tiled bathrooms. At this writing, an international hotel group has just taken over. Plans for renovation are on the table; let's hope they call for modernizing without sacrificing charm. ⊠ *Av. Córdoba 405, El Centro, 1054* ☎ *11/4311–3021* ⊕ *www.lancasterhotel-page.com* ⤴ *72 rooms, 18 suites* ♿ *Room service, IDD phones, in-room safes, minibars, cable TV, in-room data ports, pool, gym, hair salon, sauna, spa, squash, pub, dry cleaning, laundry service, concierge, Internet, business services, meeting room, travel services* ⊟ *AE, DC, MC, V* |O| *CP* Ⓜ *C to San Martín.*

$ ▦ **Principado.** It was built for the 1978 World Cup, which Argentina hosted and won, and it doesn't look like it's had much of a touch-up since. All the same, the price is right, the staff is helpful, and the rooms are cozy. If you get one on the street side, even the double plated windows aren't likely to drown out the noise of the motorbike mail couriers zipping by. Ask for a room at the back. The restaurant serves up tasty, affordable dishes. ⊠ *Paraguay 481, El Centro, 1057* ☎ *11/4313–3022* ⊕ *www.principado.com.ar* ⤴ *88 rooms* ♿ *Restaurant, coffee shop, room service, IDD phones, in-room safes, minibars, cable TV, in-room data ports, bar, dry cleaning, laundry service, Internet, business services, parking (fee)* ⊟ *AE, DC, MC, V* |O| *CP* Ⓜ *C to San Martín.*

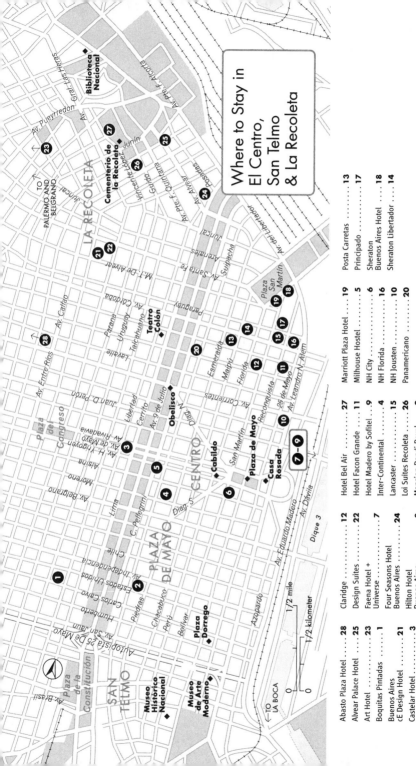

Where to Stay in El Centro, San Telmo & La Recoleta

Abasto Plaza Hotel **28**
Alvear Palace Hotel **25**
Art Hotel **23**
Boquitas Pintadas **1**
Buenos Aires
cE Design Hotel **21**
Castelar Hotel **3**

Claridge **12**
Design Suites **22**
Faena Hotel +
Universe **7**
Four Seasons Hotel
Buenos Aires **24**
Hilton Hotel
Buenos Aires **8**

Hotel Bel Air **27**
Hotel Facon Grande ...**11**
Hotel Madero by Sofitel ..**9**
Inter-Continental **4**
Lancaster **15**
Loi Suites Recoleta **26**
Mansion Dandi Royal ...**2**

Marriott Plaza Hotel ...**19**
Milhouse Hostel **5**
NH City **6**
NH Florida **16**
NH Jousten **10**
Panamericano **20**

Posta Carretas **13**
Principado **17**
Sheraton
Buenos Aires Hotel ...**18**
Sheraton Libertador ...**14**

¢ 🏨 **Milhouse Hostel.** This lovely and lively hostel goes the extra mile to make backpackers feel welcome. The house, which dates from the late 1800s, has been tricked out with funky artwork and accessories. Its three floors overlook a beautiful tiled patio and all lead out to a sunny terrace, which the hostel skillfully uses to entertain guests, regardless of their interests. Morning yoga classes may well be followed by rowdy beer-swilling *asados* (barbecues). The dorm rooms are clean and big, and most have private bathrooms. ⊠ *Hipólito Irigoyen 959, El Centro, 1086* ☎ *11/4345–9604 or 11/4343–5038* ⊕ *www.milhousehostel. com* 🛏 *13 private rooms, 150 beds total* ⚒ *Restaurant, fans, Ping-Pong, bar, library, laundry facilities, DSL Internet, travel services, parking (fee); no a/c, no room phones, no room TVs* ⊟ *No credit cards* ⏛ *CP* Ⓜ *A to Piedras, C to Av. de Mayo.*

Almagro

★ **$$$$** 🏨 **Abasto Plaza Hotel.** This place is *all* about the tango. Photos and paintings of famous musicians line the walls that surround the checked-marble dance floor, which is next to a boutique where you can buy sequined skirts, stilettos, and fishnet stockings. Suites each have their own dance floor for private lessons, or you can join other guests for nightly tango lessons and a live show. Rooms are large and elegant with—surprise, surprise—a tango theme. The hotel is two blocks from an alleyway and theater dedicated to the godfather of tango, Carlos Gardel. The enormous Abasto Shopping Center is across the street. ⊠ *Av. Corrientes 3190, Almagro, 1193* ☎ *11/6311–4466* ⊕ *www.abastoplaza.com* 🛏 *120 rooms, 6 suites* ⚒ *Restaurant, snack bar, room service, IDD phones, minibars, cable TV, in-room data ports, pool, gym, health club, bar, lobby lounge, DSL Internet, Wi-Fi in all rooms, business services, 7 meeting rooms* ⊟ *AE, DC, MC, V* ⏛ *BP* Ⓜ *B to Carlos Gardel.*

San Telmo

$$$$ 🏨 **Mansion Dandi Royal.** For a glimpse into early-20th-century high society, look no farther than this hotel. Owner and tango legend Hector Villalba painstakingly transformed this 100-year-old mansion into both a hotel and a tango academy. The 15 exquisite rooms are decorated with classic wood furnishings and period murals. A stunning chandelier, a sweeping staircase, and original artwork lend still more authenticity. Tango lessons take place daily in the gorgeous dance hall, and every evening the staff accompanies dancers to milongas, all-night tango parties that take place all over town. ⊠ *Piedras 922, San Telmo, 1070* ☎ *11/4307–7623* ⊕ *www.mansiondandiroyal.com* 🛏 *15 rooms* ⚒ *Room service, IDD phones, in-room safes, pool, gym, spa, hair salon, cable TV, bar, library, laundry service, DSL Internet, meeting room, airport shuttle, parking (fee)* ⊟ *AE, DC, MC, V* Ⓜ *C to San Juan.*

Fodor'sChoice
★

$ 🏨 **Boquitas Pintadas.** The whimsically named "Little Painted Mouths" (a tribute to Manuel Puig's novel of the same name) is a self-proclaimed "pop hotel," and the German owner, Heike Thelen, goes out of her way to keep things weird and wild. World-famous "nude" photographer, Spencer Tunick, staged a shoot here in 2002 and ended up spending the night. Local artists, inspired by an array of provocative themes, redecorate the six rooms every two months. The restaurant serves dishes not found often in the city, including goulash. DJs spin tunes until dawn. The hotel is in the Constitucion neighborhood, west of San Telmo, across Avenida 9 de Julio. Use caution at night; the surrounding area is dodgy. ⊠ *Estados Unidos 1393, Constitución, 1101* ☎ *11/4381–6064* ⊕ *www.boquitas-pintadas.com.ar* 🖙 *5 rooms, 1 suite* ♿ *Restaurant, room service, cable TV, bar, library, nightclub, dry cleaning, laundry service, Wi-Fi Internet, business services, travel services* 🗖 *No credit cards* Ⓜ *E to San José.*

Puerto Madero

$$$$ 🏨 **Faena Hotel + Universe.** Lenny Kravitz and his entourage stayed here,
Fodor'sChoice   and actor Owen Wilson said it was, "one of the coolest hotels I've ever
★   been to in my life." If a rock god and the Butterscotch Stallion can dig this creation of Argentine fashion impresario Alan Faena and famed French architect Philippe Starck, then chances are you can, too. Rooms are feng shui perfect with rich reds and crisp whites. Velvet curtains and Venetian blinds open electronically to river and city views; marble floors fill expansive baths; velvet couches, leather armchairs, flat-screen TVs, and surround-sound stereos lend still more luxury. The so-called Experience Managers are basically personal assistants, making reservations and tending to every whim. Other highlights are two excellent restaurants and an elaborate spa with a Turkish bath. In El Cabaret, a blood-red music box dotted with red leather couches, you can swig champagne and watch sensual flamenco shows or the even sexier El Rebenque Revue, which starts well after midnight. ⊠ *Martha Salotti 445, Puerto Madero, 1107* ☎ *11/4010–9000* ⊕ *www.faenahotelanduniverse.com* 🖙 *105 rooms* ♿ *2 restaurants, room service, 24-hour butler service, flexible check-in, IDD phones, in-room safes, minibars, cable TV, DVD player, in-room data ports, pool, gym, health club, massage, sauna, Turkish baths, 2 bars, lounge, babysitting, laundry service, DSL Internet, Wi-Fi in all rooms, concierge, business services, meeting rooms, parking (fee), no-smoking rooms* 🗖 *AE, DC, MC, V.*

$$$ 🏨 **Hilton Hotel Buenos Aires.** This massive glass-and-steel structure puts you close to downtown *and* the restaurants and fresh air of Puerto Madero. In the atrium lobby, exposed glass elevators and wraparound hallways are unique and dizzying at times. Rooms have big beds, walk-in closets, and large desks with stationery and magazines. Turn-down service always includes delicious little chocolates. The rooftop pool is a great place to sip a fruit smoothie, stare at the skyline, and chat with the many flight attendants who stay here. ⊠ *Macacha Guemes 351, Puerto Madero, 1106* ☎ *11/4891–0000, 800/774–1500 in U.S.* ⊕ *www.hilton.com* 🖙 *418 rooms, 13 suites* ♿ *Restaurant, room service, IDD phones, in-room safes, minibars, cable TV, in-room data ports, pool, gym, health club, hair salon, massage, 2 bars, lounge, babysitting, laundry service, DSL Internet, Wi-Fi in lobby, concierge, business services, meeting rooms, parking (fee), no-smoking rooms* 🗖 *AE, DC, MC, V* ⊚ *BP.*

$$ ⊞ **Hotel Madero by Sofitel.** This slick, affordable hotel is within walking distance of downtown as well as the riverside ecological reserve. The big, bright, modern rooms have wood accents and white color schemes. Many rooms also have fantastic views of the docks and city skyline. The restaurant, Red, serves great Argentine–French fusion cuisine in an intimate setting. The breakfast buffet features tons of exotic fresh fruits and Argentine baked goods. ⊠ *Rosario Vera Penaloza 360, Dique 2, Puerto Madero, 1007* ☎ *11/5776–7777* ⊕ *www.hotelmadero.com* ➝ *165 rooms, 28 suites* ⚖ *Restaurant, bar, 24-hour room service, in-room safes, cable TV, in-room data ports, pool, gym, bar, laundry service, DSL Internet, meeting room* ▭ *AE, DC, MC, V.*

La Recoleta

★ **$$$$** ⊞ **Alvear Palace Hotel.** If James Bond was in town, this is where he'd hang his hat. In fact, Sean Connery *has* stayed here, because when it comes to sophistication, the Alvear Palace is the best bet in Buenos Aires. It's hosted scores of dignitaries since opening its doors in 1932, and although new and more affordable hotels are making it something of a gray ghost, the Alvear is still stately and swanky. It's all about world-class service and thoughtful touches: butler service, fresh flowers, feather beds with Egyptian-cotton linens. The lunch buffet is out of this world, and the super-chic French restaurant, La Bourgogne, is one of the city's best. ⊠ *Av. Alvear 1891, La Recoleta, 1129* ☎ *11/4808–2100, 11/4804–7777, 800/448–8355 in U.S.* ⊕ *www.alvearpalace.com* ➝ *100 rooms, 100 suites* ⚖ *2 restaurants, coffee shop, room service, IDD phones, in-room safes, some in-room hot tubs, minibars, in-room data ports, indoor pool, gym, health club, sauna, bar, laundry service, concierge, DSL Internet, Wi-Fi in all rooms, business services, meeting room, no-smoking rooms* ▭ *AE, DC, MC, V* ⦿ *BP.*

★ **$$$$** ⊞ **Four Seasons Hotel Buenos Aires.** This exquisite hotel envelops you in a pampering atmosphere that screams turn-of-the-19th-century Paris. In fact, the gorgeous French embassy is just up the block. The hotel's 13-floor marble tower has an impressive art collection and large, luxurious rooms. The neighboring hotel mansion draws some of the world's most famous folks: Madonna (who stayed while filming *Evita*), the Rolling Stones, Jennifer Lopez, and Robbie Williams, to name a few. ⊠ *Posadas 1086, La Recoleta, 1011* ☎ *11/4321–1200* ⊕ *www.fourseasons.com/buenosaires* ➝ *138 rooms, 27 suites* ⚖ *Restaurant, room service, IDD phones, in-room fax, in-room safes, minibars, cable TV, in-room data ports, pool, fitness classes, gym, health club, massage, sauna, bar, lobby lounge, babysitting, dry cleaning, laundry service, concierge, DSL Internet, Wi-Fi in all rooms, business services, meeting rooms, airport shuttle, travel services, parking (fee), no-smoking rooms* ▭ *AE, DC, MC, V* ⦿ *BP.*

$$$$ ⊞ **Loi Suites Recoleta.** A white marble lobby leads to a garden area where you can enjoy breakfast or an afternoon drink in a poolside chair. Sleek guest rooms have white and gray color schemes complemented by black and white photos on the walls. Executive Suites have whirlpool baths and amazing views of a place that high-society Argentines have been dying to get into for years: Recoleta Cemetery. Loi Suites also operate two smaller apart-hotels downtown. ⊠ *Vicente López 1955, La Recoleta, 1128* ☎ *11/5777–8950* ⊕ *www.loisuites.com.ar* 🛏 *88 rooms, 24 suites* ◊ *Restaurant, room service, IDD phones, in-room safes, minibars, microwaves, cable TV, in-room data ports, indoor-outdoor pool, gym, sauna, bar, dry cleaning, laundry service, DSL Internet, Wi-Fi in lobby, business services, meeting rooms, parking (fee)* ▬ *AE, DC, MC, V* ⦿| *CP.*

★ **$$** 🏨 **Hotel Bel Air.** Given the fancy French-style facade, you could mistake the Bel Air for a neighborhood hotel somewhere in Paris. Inside, a more modern feel takes over, with a round wood-paneled lobby bar and a snazzy café that looks onto exclusive Arenales Street. Rooms have handsome wooden floors and simple but stylish desks and couches. ⊠ *Arenales 1462, La Recoleta, 1062* ☎ *11/4021–4000* ⊕ *www.hotelbelair.com.ar* 🛏 *77 rooms* ◊ *Restaurant, café, room service, IDD phones, in-room safes, minibars, cable TV, in-room data ports, gym, bar, dry cleaning, laundry service, Internet, business services, meeting rooms, airport shuttle, travel services, no-smoking rooms* ▬ *AE, DC, MC, V* ⦿| *BP.*

$ 🏨 **Art Hotel.** The aptly named Art Hotel has an impressive ground-floor gallery where exhibits of paintings, photographs, and sculptures by acclaimed Argentine artists change monthly. You might even run into some fabulous art aficionados sipping Chardonnay and admiring the creations. Rooms are classified as "small and cozy," "queen," or "king" and many have wrought-iron bed frames with white canopies. The building's 100-year-old elevator will take you to the rooftop patio, where there's a hot tub and plenty of room to soak up some sun. ⊠ *Azcuenaga 1268, 1115* ☎ *11/4821–4744* ⊕ *www.arthotel.com.ar* 🛏 *36 rooms* ◊ *Café, IDD phones, in-room safes, mini-bar, cable TV, bar, laundry service, DSL Internet, travel services* ▬ *AE, MC, V* Ⓜ *D to Pueyrredón.*

Palermo

$$ 🏨 **1555 Malabia House.** Behind the unassuming white facade of this 100-year-old Palermo Soho town house is what the proprietors have dubbed Argentina's "first designer B&B." Common areas have bold, colorful paintings and fanciful sculptures. Rooms, only some of which have en suite baths, are all about pale-wood floors and furnishings and simple white bedding and curtains. Both sides of the narrow hallways are lined with rooms, eliminating any sense of privacy but the bustling Palermo location is hard to beat. The young staff can steer you toward the neighborhood's newest restaurants and nightspots. ⊠ *Malabia 1555, Palermo Soho, 1414* ☎ *11/4832–3345 or 11/4833–2410* ⊕ *www.malabiahouse. com.ar* 🛏 *11 rooms, 4 suites* ◊ *Room service, IDD phones, fans, in-room safes, minibars, cable TV, bar, library, laundry service, concierge, DSL Internet, meeting room, airport shuttle, parking (fee)* ▬ *AE, DC, MC, V* ⦿| *CP* Ⓜ *D to Scalabrini Ortiz.*

★ **$$** 🏨 **Home Buenos Aires.** It's run by Argentine Patricia O'Shea and her British husband, Tom Rixton, a well-known music producer, and it oozes cool-ness and class. Each distinct room is decorated with vintage French wall-paper and has a stereo, a laptop friendly safe, and either a bathtub or a wet room. On site there's a vast garden; a barbecue area; an infinity

KEY

Ⓜ Subte stops

Where to Stay in Palermo Viejo

0   1/4 mile
0   1/4 kilometer

PALERMO SOHO

PALERMO HOLLYWOOD

PALERMO

pool; a holistic spa; and a funky lounge bar where you can sip a cocktail and listen to mood music created especially for the hotel by famed record producer Flood (U2, Smashing Pumpkins, Nine Inch Nails), one of the hotel's investors. ⊠ *Honduras 5860, Palermo Hollywood, 1414* ☎ *11/4778–1008* ⊕ *www.homebuenosaires.com* ↩ *14 rooms, 4 suites* ᐃ *Restaurant, room service, bar, IDD phones, in-room safes, minibars, cable TV, stereo, spa, pool, library, DSL Internet, Wi-Fi in all rooms, travel services* ⊟ *AE, MC, V* Ⓜ *D to Ministro Carranza.*

$$ 🏨 **Bo-Bo.** Quaint, quirky Bo-Bo shrewdly combines the bourgeois with the bohemian. In fact, the hotel's name is a play on David Brooks' 2000 book, *Bobos in Paradise,* which you can find in the lobby library. Each room has a different motif—art deco, minimalist, techno. The largest and most luxurious, the Argentina Suite, is decorated in bright colors and has a small outdoor patio and hot tub. All rooms have such creature comforts as soft robes and such technological comforts as Wi-Fi access and DVD players. The downstairs restaurant-café is a nice place to relax after pounding Palermo's pavement all day. ⊠ *Guatemala 4882, Palermo Soho, 1425* ☎ *11/4774–0505* ⊕ *www.bobohotel.com* ↩ *7 rooms* ᐃ *Restaurant, room service, IDD phones, in-room safes, cable TV, bar, library, laundry service, DSL Internet, Wi-Fi in rooms, parking (fee)* ⊟ *AE, MC, V* Ⓜ *D to Plaza Italia.*

$ ▦ **Hotel Alpino.** This simple neighborhood hotel is decorated in dark browns and has wood paneling. Rooms are clean and comfortable, although they could definitely use a touching up. The location is good, though: close to the Parque Zoológico and the Jardín Botánico as well as the nightlife and restaurants in Palermo Soho. ⊠ *Cabello 3318, Palermo, 1425* ☎ *11/4802–5151* ⊕ *www.geocities.com/alpinohotel* ⇋ *35 rooms* ⚹ *Room service, IDD phones, in-room safes, minibars, cable TV, in-room data ports, DSL Internet, laundry service, meeting rooms, parking (fee)* ⊟ *AE, DC, MC, V* ⏃⏐ *CP* Ⓜ *D to Plaza Italia.*

¢–$ ▦ **Giramondo Hostel.** The funky Giramondo has all that a hostel needs: plenty of beds and bathrooms, a kitchen, a TV and computer lounge, and a patio, where backpackers from around the world grill up slabs of Argentine beef. The dark, dank underground bar serves up cheap drinks; it also has a small wine cellar. Giramondo is two blocks from buses and the subte on Avenida Santa Fe—an ideal locale for taking part in Palermo's pulsing nightlife while also being close to downtown. ⊠ *Guemes 4802, Palermo Soho, 1425* ☎ *11/4772–6740* ⊕ *www.hostelgiramondo. com.ar* ⚹ *Kitchen, fans, bar, library, TV/DVD room, safety boxes, laundry facilities, DSL Internet, travel services; no a/c, no room phones, no room TVs* ⊟ *No credit cards* Ⓜ *D to Palermo.*

NIGHTLIFE

By Brian Byrnes

Porteños *love* to party. Many don't think twice about dancing until 6 AM and heading to work at 8 AM. And alcohol doesn't play a vital role in whether people enjoy themselves or not; porteños could have fun at an insurance convention, provided the conversation and music were good and everyone looked marvelous. Indeed, for many, it's better to *look* good than to *feel* good.

Being stylish is just one factor for a successful night on the town. Another is knowing that when we say this is a late-night town, we mean it. Clubs, which generally attract crowds in the 18–35 age range, don't begin to fill up until 2 or 3 AM. Theater performances start at 9 PM or 9:30 PM, and the last movie begins after midnight. That said, the subte closes at 10 PM, so going out late means taking a taxi home or waiting until 5 AM for trains to resume running.

The Palermo, La Recoleta, and Costanera areas have the most diverse nightlife, and places are fairly close to one another. El Centro and San Telmo have equally good options, but things are more spread out; for your well-being and that of your feet, take a taxi.

El Centro

Downtown is chaotic by day during the week and quiet at night and on weekends. It still has lots of great nightspots though, including several dance clubs and a bevy of traditional Irish pubs.

Bars

La Cigale. Sip cocktails at a large turquoise bar while smooth sounds and heavy cigarette smoke spin around you. Tuesday is French Soirée Night,

CLOSE UP

What's Up Buenos Aires?

What's Up Buenos Aires (⊕ www. whatsupbuenosaires.com) is much more than just a Web site with club listings. It's an innovative bilingual (English and Spanish) site dedicated to spreading the word about Buenos Aires's burgeoning cultural scene, providing vital insider information about nightlife, theater, art exhibits, conferences, restaurants, and more.

The site was created and operated by Grant Dull, a native of San Antonio, Texas, who has lived in Buenos Aires for the better part of the past seven years. Says Dull, "Buenos Aires amazes me, it moves me, and I feel like I am a part of it. Sharing this emerging cultural scene with the rest of the world just needs to be done."

The site has a daily updated events calendar, a community forum, music by local musicians, and a tourism unit that arranges housing for foreigners and conducts guided nightlife tours. If you want to know what's up in Buenos Aires, visit this site.

–Brian Byrnes

and things get lively with techno and trance music mixed with sounds straight from Gay Paree. ⊠ *25 de Mayo 722, El Centro* ☎ *11/4312–8275* Ⓜ *C to San Martín.*

The Kilkenny. It serves surprisingly good Irish food and has Guinness on draft. Celtic or rock bands play every night, entertaining the after-work crowd from nearby government and commercial buildings. ⊠ *Marcelo T. De Alvear 399, El Centro* ☎ *11/4312–7291* Ⓜ *C to San Martín.*

★ **Milión.** At this beautiful mansion you can enjoy a cold Cosmopolitan or a nice Malbec at the upstairs bar while sophisticates chat around you. Be sure to explore all the hidden corners, including the back garden salon, which is lit with candles and soft colored lights. ⊠ *Paraná 1048, El Centro* ☎ *11/4815–9925* Ⓜ *D to Callao.*

Plaza Bar. A refined crowd gathers for Scotch and cigars at the Marriott's elegant downstairs bar. It's old-school Argentina at its finest, all dizzying Persian rugs and black-leather trim. ⊠ *Florida 1005, El Centro* ☎ *11/ 4318–3000* Ⓜ *C to San Martín.*

Dance Clubs

Fodor'sChoice **Bahrein.** Chic (some might say "sheik") and super-stylish, this party palace
★ is in a 100-year-old former bank. Upstairs is a fantastic restaurant, Crizia. In the main floor's Funky Room, young women in tight denim and even tighter halter tops groove to pop, rock, and funk. The downstairs Excess Room has a heady mix of electronic beats and dizzying wall visuals. Five-hundred pesos gets you locked inside the steel vault, where you can guzzle champagne all night with other beautiful (and bewildered) people—an entirely new kind of VIP experience. ⊠ *Lavalle 345, El Centro* ☎ *11/4315–2403* Ⓜ *B to Alem.*

Cocoliche. Cocoliche enjoys cult-like status in both the straight and gay community for its diverse artistic and musical offerings. Upstairs it's all about culture, with a gallery of art by young locals. Downstairs it's all about anonymous anarchy, with house music motivating the masses to move on one of the city's darkest dance floors. ⊠ *Rivadavia 878, El Centro* ☎ *11/4331–6413* Ⓜ *A to Piedras.*

Gay & Lesbian Clubs

Angels. Angels has several dance floors that play electronica, pop, and Latin music. It attracts a primarily gay male and transvestite clientele, but heterosexuals are welcome, too. ⊠ *Viamonte 2168, El Centro* ☎ *No phone* Ⓜ *D to Facultad de Medicina.*

Contramano. It's been around since 1984, when it was the city's most popular and pioneering gay disco, but today it operates more as a laid-back bar with an older, male-only clientele. Occasionally there's live music and male strippers. ⊠ *Rodríguez Peña 1082, El Centro* ☎ *No phone* Ⓜ *D to Callao.*

Palacio. This massive downtown club attracts a mixed-age crowd of gays and lesbians on Friday and Sunday nights for electronic music and pop tunes. On Saturday, the club goes straight and changes its name to Big One for a night of hard-core techno. ⊠ *Alsina 940, El Centro* ☎ *11/ 4331–1277* Ⓜ *A to Piedras.*

Jazz Joints

Clásica y Moderna. An older, artsy crowd gathers here for drinks, philosophy, and live jazz. ⊠ *Callao 892, El Centro* ☎ *11/4812–8707* Ⓜ *D to Callao.*

Gran Café Tortoni. A Buenos Aires institution, this classic café is perhaps the best example of what life was like for aristocratic Argentines some 150 years ago. Look for live jazz and tango shows on weekends. ⊠ *Av. de Mayo 825, El Centro* ☎ *11/4342–4328* Ⓜ *A to Piedras.*

Notorious. It's a jazz bar, restaurant, and record shop rolled into one. Some of the area's best jazz musicians, like Ricardo Cavalli and Adrian Iaies, play here often. You can also listen to the club's extensive music collection on the CD players at each table. ⊠ *Av. Callao 966, El Centro* ☎ *11/4815–8473* Ⓜ *D to Callao.*

San Telmo

The city's oldest and most bohemian neighborhood holds the promise of very late, very wild nights. Some streets are sketchy; take taxis, and don't walk alone.

Dance Clubs

Club Museum. It's an enormous, multilevel love den that packs in college kids looking to party like its 1995. From the second- and third-floor balconies overlooking the gigantic dance floor, some flirtatious souls have tried (unsuccessfully) to introduce Mardi Gras–like behavior to the mix. But flashing is entirely unnecessary; this place gets wild enough on its own. ⊠ *Perú 535, San Telmo* ☎ *11/4654–1774* Ⓜ *C to San Juan.*

Rey Castro. Just because this Cuban restaurant-bar gets jumping and jiving on weekends, doesn't mean things get out of hand: the bad-ass bouncers look like they could play in the NBA. This place is popular

CLOSE UP

Tango 1: The Dances

TANGO IS MUCH MORE than just a spectator sport, and if you want to take to the floor yourself there are plenty of neighborhood *milongas* (dance halls) to choose from. It's a complex cultural scene and not for the fainthearted. Dancers of all ages sit at tables that edge the floor, and men invite women to dance through subtle eye contact and head-nodding, known as *cabeceo*—a hard art to master. Women sitting with male partners won't be asked to the floor by other men, so couples wanting variety should sit apart.

Dances come in sets of three, four, or five, broken by an obvious divider of non-tango music, and it's common to stay with the same partner for a set. Being discarded in the middle is a sign that you're not up to scratch. Staying for more than two sets with the same partner could be interpreted as a come on. Although clement dancing kings and queens may take pity on left-footed beginners, getting a partner can be hard at first. Many milongas start with chaotic group classes and practice sessions, but if you want to be taken seriously, take some private lessons. Good teachers will also give you clued-in advice for making the most of the milonga.

Behind the unmarked doors of **La Catedral** (⊠ Sarmiento 4006, Almagro ☎ No phone) is a hip club

where the tango is very rock, somehow—the milonga is casual, and it's a cool night out even if you're not planning to dance. Watch locals in action in the open air at **Glorieta Barrancas de Belgrano** (⊠ 11 de Septiembre at Echeverría, Belgrano), which takes place in a park every Sunday evening. On Monday afternoon, golden oldies cut a rug on the first floor of **La Ideal** (⊠ Suipacha 384, Plaza de Mayo ☎ 11/4601-8234), an old-world tearoom, and a great place to learn from their experience.

The gay milonga of the week is held on Wednesday at **La Marshall** (⊠ Yatay 961, Almagro ☎ 11/4912-9043). The Wednesday-night milonga at **El Nacional** (⊠ Alsina 1465, Congreso ☎ 11/4307-0146) is a mid-week favorite with locals. Belle-époque-style **El Niño Bien** (⊠ Humberto I 1462, Constitución ☎ 11/4147-8687) is the place to go late on Thursday night. On Monday and Friday nights, head for **Salón Canning** (⊠ Av. Scalabrini Ortíz 1331, Palermo ☎ 11/4832-6753), a serious milonga, where the action goes on into the small hours. A young crowd gathers on weekends at chaotic club **La Viruta-La Estrella** (⊠ Armenia 1366, Palermo ☎ 11/4774-6357), which mixes tango with rock, salsa, and cumbia.

—Victoria Patience

for birthday parties and serves great mojitos. After the nightly live dance show, DJs crank up the Cuban rhythms. You'll definitely learn some sexy new dance moves here. ⊠ *Perú 342, San Telmo* ☎ *11/4342-9998* Ⓜ *C to San Juan.*

Music Club

La Trastienda. A San Telmo institution, La Trastienda brings in respected artists from all over to play its intimate stage. Some shows are seated affairs; others pack 1,000-plus into the small space to listen and dance to jazz, blues, tango, salsa, reggae, or rock. World-renowned musicians like Maceo Parker, Café Tacuba, Jorge Drexler, and Kevin Johansen have played here, but the club takes pains to promote local artists as well. ⊠ *Balcarce 460, San Telmo* ☎ *11/4342–7650* Ⓜ *A to Bolívar.*

Puerto Madero

Many of the area's restaurants have bars where you can nurse a post-dinner drink. This is the most rapidly developing part of the city, though, so we expect more nightspots to open in the years to come.

Bar

Asia de Cuba. Once *the* spot to be seen sipping champagne and eating sushi, Asia de Cuba still draws local celebrities, even though it's lost some of its white-hot luster. The red-and-black Asian decor and candlelight set the mood for an exotic (by local standards) evening. Sometimes there's live music. ⊠ *Pierina Dealesi 750, Puerto Madero* ☎ *11/4894–1329.*

Dance Club

Opera Bay. Pinstripes, pumps, and hormones collide at this huge Puerto Madero nightspot every Wednesday for the city's largest after-work party, complete with a cacophony of pop, rock, and techno tunes. The three dance floors hop on weekends, too. This place is impossible to miss; it looks like a miniature version of the Sydney Opera House. ⊠ *Cecilia Grierson 225, Puerto Madero* ☎ *11/4315–8666.*

La Recoleta

Nightlife in La Recoleta is diverse, with everything from swanky supper clubs to neighborhood watering holes. The area surrounding Recoleta Cemetery is packed with American-style bars as well as "gentlemen's" clubs that are frequented by prostitutes and male tourists from around the world.

Bars

Buller Brew Pub. The city's only brewpub has six tasty homemade choices on tap, including Honey Beer and India Pale Ale. Locals and tourists mingle here over pints, peanuts, and pop music. ⊠ *R. M. Ortíz 1827, La Recoleta* ☎ *11/4808–9061.*

Deep Blue. It draws a steady stream of foreign students and the Argentines who are anxious to woo them. The billiards tables attract some serious pool sharks. The coolest thing about this place is that each plush blue booth has its own self-service beer tap, which doesn't seem to excite the alcohol-apathetic Argentines but can prove devastatingly dangerous for American and European visitors. ⊠ *Ayacucho 1240, La Recoleta* ☎ *11/4827–4415* Ⓜ *D to Pueyrredón.*

Dance Club

Shamrock. This rowdy place is owned by a couple of Irish guys and is one of the city's most popular expat hangouts. You can drink a Guinness and yap away in English, easily forgetting that you're in South America. Follow the techno beats to the smoky downstairs dance club, where the enormous disco ball reminds you (1) that you're in Buenos Aires and

Tango 2: The Shows

FOR MANY the tango experience begins and ends with the flashy *cena-shows* in expensive clubs. These usually include drinks and a three-course dinner. Expect sequined costumes, gelled hairdos, and high-kicking moves, known as *tango de fantasía*. The shows might not be so fancy, but the dancing at more traditional, lower-key venues is just as skilled.

Musicians and dancers perform at **Bar Sur** (⊠ Estados Unidos 299, San Telmo ☎ 11/4362-6086 ⊕ www.bar-sur.com.ar), a traditional bar. **La Esquina de Homero Manzi** (⊠ San Juan 3601, Boedo ☎ 11/4957-8488 ⊕ www.esquinahomeromanzi.com.ar) has reasonably priced shows in an opulent café. An evening at **Madero Tango** (⊠ Alicia Moreau de Justo at Brasil, Puerto Madero ☎ 11/4314-6688 ⊕ www.maderotango.

com) may break the bank, but the chef is a local legend, and the dancing is fantastic.

Consistently well-attended performances are held at the classic café **El Querandí** (⊠ Perú 302, at Moreno, San Telmo ☎ 11/4342-1760 ⊕ www.querandi.com.ar). The daily shows at glitzy **Señor Tango** (⊠ Vieytes 1655, Barracas ☎ 11/4303-0231 ⊕ www.senortango.com.ar) are aimed at tourists. The fancy show at **Taconeando** (⊠ Balcarce 725, San Telmo ☎ 11/4307-6696 ⊕ www.taconeando.com) is popular with foreigners. A traditional show takes place at **Viejo Almacén** (⊠ Balcarce 786, at Independencia, San Telmo ☎ 11/4307-6689 ⊕ www.viejo-almacen.com.ar).

–Victoria Patience

(2) why you came in the first place. ⊠ *Rodríguez Peña 1220, La Recoleta* ☎ *11/4812–3584* Ⓜ *D to Callao.*

Gay & Lesbian Club
Glam. Young, hip and buff men come for smooth cruising in a classy setting: a fashionably restored home. Lesbians and straight women come for the festive atmosphere and raucous music. ⊠ *Cabrera 3046, La Recoleta* ☎ *11/4963–2521* Ⓜ *D to Pueyrredón.*

Wine Bar
Gran Bar Danzon. If Carrie, Samantha, Charlotte, and Miranda lived in Buenos Aires, they'd probably frequent this first-floor hot spot where local business sharks and chic internationals sip wine and eat sushi by candlelight. It's extremely popular for happy hour, but people stick around for dinner and the occasional live jazz shows, too. The wine list and the appetizers are superb. ⊠ *Libertad 1161* ☎ *11/4811–1108* Ⓜ *C to Retiro.*

Palermo

The undisputed hub of porteño nightlife has something for everyone. Palermo Soho is the area closer to downtown; Palermo Hollywood begins after you cross Avenida Juan B. Justo.

Bars

★ **Congo.** A fashionable post-dinner, pre-club crowd—in faded fitted jeans, hipster sneakers, and leather jackets—frequents this hangout. The back garden can get lively enough on warm nights to cause many would-be clubgoers to stick around for another gin and tonic. ⊠ *Honduras 5329, Palermo Soho* ☎ *11/4833—5857.*

Mundo Bizarro. It has one of the city's most extensive cocktails lists, including such concoctions as MintSake (mint, lime, apple juice, ginger, and sake) and The Sinner (Jack Daniels, peach schnapps, pastis, and orange juice). Day-glow artwork, random B-movie images, and red lighting lend an underground and (sometimes) uneasy feel. ⊠ *Guatemala 4802, Palermo Soho* ☎ *11/4773–1967.*

Spell Café. All three levels of this massive place offer something different: dining downstairs, drinks at mid-level, and DJs upstairs. Another location in Puerto Madero offers a more American speakeasy atmosphere with beer and burger options. ⊠ *Malabia 1738, Palermo Soho* ☎ *11/4832–3389.*

Único. There's nothing really special about this corner bar-restaurant *except* for its location at the epicenter of Palermo Hollywood, close to TV studios and an array of great restaurants. A funky mix of rock, rap, and electronic music pumps up the hard-core clubbers who stop to whet their whistles on large Heineken drafts before a night of debauchery. ⊠ *Honduras 5604, Palermo Hollywood* ☎ *11/4775–6693.*

Dance Clubs

Club Aráoz. It may be intimate, but it attracts a serious party crowd. Thursday night is hip-hop night; Friday and Saturday see DJs from Asia, Europe, or the Middle East. ⊠ *Aráoz 2424, Palermo* ☎ *11/4833–7775.*

Niceto. Although its ever-changing lineup of artists represents the whole spectrum of local music, Niceto is best known for Club 69, a raucous Thursday night party that combines cocktails and campy bravado. The main room has a balcony with the best views of the dance floor. A chillout room in the back always has great projected visuals on the walls. ⊠ *Cnel. Niceto Vega 5510, Palermo Hollywood* ☎ *11/4779–9396.*

Podestá Super Club de Copas. It's like the 1969 Altamont Raceway concert in this place, except the Hells Angels and hippies get along a lot better. The dark ground-floor room plays rock and serves stiff drinks. Upstairs dance-friendly music is pumped into a psychedelic setting. ⊠ *Armenia 1742, Palermo Soho* ☎ *11/4832–2776.*

The Roxy. The cream of the Argentine rock-and-roll scene hangs out at this large club, so black leather jackets and long locks are the norm most nights. It hosts a '70s disco party and other events, often with scantily clad dancers. Order a Quilmes beer and take in the scene. ⊠ *Arcos del Sol, between Casares and Sarmiento, Palermo* ☎ *11/4899–0313.*

Gay Club

Kim y Novak Bar. On the edge of Palermo Soho, Kim y Novak is a kitschy cocktail bar that attracts both gay and straight lounge lizards. Upstairs, you can enjoy a mixed drink seated on vintage couches or in

Tango 3: The Music

THE AVERAGE PORTEÑO is much more likely to go to see tango musicians than tango dancers. Offerings range from orchestras churning out tunes as was done in Gardel's day to sexy, bluesy vocals from divas like Adriana Varela to pared-down revisitings of the tango underworld by young groups like 34 Puñaladas. If you want tango that packs a punch, look out for the electronic fusion of groups like Gotan Project and Bajofondo Tango Club.

Young musicians perform hip sets at **Centro Cultural Torcuato Tasso** (⊠ Defensa 1575, San Telmo ☎ 11/ 4307–6506), which also holds milongas at weekends. Celebrated old-guard tango musicians Salgán and De Lío frequently perform in the intimate surroundings of the **Club del Vino** (⊠ Cabrera 4737, Palermo ☎ 11/ 4833–0050). The classic **Gran Café Tortoni** (⊠ Av. de Mayo 829, Plaza de Mayo ☎ 11/4342–4328) is one of the best places to listen to tango music. Small, recycled theater **ND Ateneo** (⊠ Paraguay 918, Microcentro ☎ 11/ 4328–2888) has become a showcase for live music performances.

–Victoria Patience

booths. Downstairs it's about predominantly gay men dancing to heavy electronic beats. ⊠ *Guemes 4900, Palermo Soho* ☎ *11/4773–7521.*

Jazz Joints

★ **Club Del Vino.** Wine and choice live jazz, tango, and other music come together at this intimate theater-café packed with small tables and eclectic art. Wash down a *picada* (a plate of cheese, meat, bread, and olives) with a fantastic Argentine blend, straight from the impressive wine cellar. ⊠ *Cabrera 4737, Palermo Soho* ☎ *11/4833–0050* Ⓜ *D to Scalabrini Ortiz.*

Thelonious Bar. The best porteño jazz bands (and occasional foreign imports) play at this intimate, upscale spot. Arrive early for a good seat; not all the tables have decent sight lines. ⊠ *Salguero 1884, Palermo* ☎ *11/ 4829–1562.*

Music Clubs

★ **La Peña del Colorado.** There's nothing pretentious about this place. Laidback groups gather to enjoy traditional Argentine folk music and delicious empanadas and tamales. Exposed brick walls are adorned with rustic memorabilia, including guitars that you're welcome to play if so inspired. ⊠ *Guemes 3657, Palermo* ☎ *11/4822–1038.*

Lo de Pueyrredón. Top-notch Argentine folk musicians play at this cozy bar–restaurant. Even though it's in the heart of super-urban Palermo Soho, inside it feels like a traditional *pulpería,* where gauchos go to blow off some steam. Come early for a typical northern Argentine dinner and then stick around for the music. ⊠ *Armenia 1378, Palermo Soho* ☎ *11/ 4773–7790.*

Las Cañitas

Impossibly hip Las Cañitas draws crowds every night of the week, but dinner, drinks, and people-watching here on a Thursday night is an absolute must. The neighborhood is a vaguely defined area behind the National Polo Fields in Palermo. Báez is the main drag, although you'll find some surprises by wandering a few blocks in any direction. Boutiques, bars, and restaurants are opening all the time.

Bars

Beat House. It's the perfect spot to chill out in a bean bag upstairs and watch tragically chic porteños jockey for position at the various eateries below. Cool trance and techno music fills the air, and there's also a small music boutique downstairs. ⊠ *Báez 211, Las Cañitas* ☎ *11/ 4775–5616.*

Soul Café. One of the neighborhood's first nightspots has some of the city's sexiest female bartenders as well as its tastiest caipirinhas. A sleek red room lined with tables on one side leads to a large back room, where rock and hip-hop tunes fire up the crowd for a long night of partying. ⊠ *Báez 246, Las Cañitas* ☎ *11/4778–3115.*

Van Koning. This Dutch-theme pub got a PR boost in 2002 when an Argentine woman married the Netherlands's crown prince and secured her spot as the future queen of Holland. The walls are now covered with photos of the hopelessly blonde Willem and Maxima and other Dutch memorabilia. Folks flock here to sip cold Heinekens, eat salty peanuts, and chat in wooden booths. Upstairs a rowdy patio cranks out rock music. ⊠ *Báez 325, Las Cañitas* ☎ *11/4772–9909.*

Wine Bar

Arguibel. You can sip Syrah and soak up the art and the attitude, at this wine-bar-cum-art gallery-slash-restaurant. Arguibel is porteño pretentiousness to the max; the service and food are fair, but the building is impressive: a three-story converted warehouse with an industrial, Chelsea-loft feel. ⊠ *Arguibel 2826* ☎ *11/4899–0070.*

Costanera

Hit the coast for the country's most famed and fabulous dance clubs. Most are within a mile of each other, tucked up against the Río de la Plata and underneath the buzz of the nearby domestic airport. Taxis are the only way to get here.

Dance Clubs

La Diosa. Twenty- to thirtysomethings let off steam at this relaxed bar, where anything from live bands to strippers fills the stage. Be prepared to deal with large, loud groups. This is a popular place for people celebrating a birthday or other event. ⊠ *Av. Costanera Rafael Obligado 3731 at Salguero, Costanera* ☎ *11/4806–1079.*

★ **Jet.** The speedboats, yachts, and pastel neon set such a "Miami Vice" tone at this superfashionable, riverfront club that you feel as if Crockett and Tubbs could walk through the door at any minute. Gangs of gorgeous people come here for sushi and cocktails before heading down

The Other Side of Buenos Aires

TO SEE A SEEDIER, sexier and often sadder side of Buenos Aires, contact **Tour Experience** (☎ 11/4383-0717 Ext. 36 ⊕ www.tourexperience.com.ar), the city's first "reality tour" company. The brainchild of 33-year-old Argentine artist and musician Martin Roisi, the tours offer glimpses into aspects of Argentine society that most people never see.

"I think these are important experiences for any traveler. I want tourists to see the reality of Argentina, not just the pretty parts," says Roisi.

The most popular excursion is the Villa Tour, which takes you into the city's largest *villa miseria* (shantytown) where thousands live in tin-roof-shack squalor, often without heat or running water. Argentina's recent economic woes have caused scores of shantytowns to pop up around the city's perimeter, just a few minutes and miles from the opulence of the Paris of Latin America. The villas are populated by provincial Argentines who come to the city seeking work; thousands of immigrants from neighboring countries like Paraguay, Bolivia, and Peru live in them, too. On the tour, you'll meet poor but proud residents, visit a children's community center and art gallery, and partake of a typical Argentine *asado* at a roadside grill. All tour profits go to the people of the villa.

The Cumbia Tour introduces you to the music that was born in the villas. A hybrid of salsa, tropical, reggae, and rap, *cumbia* music is extremely popular throughout Latin America. The outing will introduce you to its musicians, and after hearing their stories, you'll spend an evening in a local cumbia club, dancing under fluorescent lights to the sounds of such favorite local bands as Damas Gratis, La Base, and Los Pibes Chorros.

The most unusual tour involves examining a unique phenomenon: the acceptance of transvestites in everyday Argentine society. Buenos Aires is very sexually liberated, and homosexuals don't generally suffer discrimination here. In 2003, this was the first Latin American city to grant civil unions to same-sex couples. On the heels of this landmark decision, transvestites began seeking more acceptance, and these days it's downright en vogue to be seen with a drag queen. Transvestite performer Florencia de la V is one of the country's most sought-after actresses, appearing on top-rated TV sitcoms, in Las Vegas-style reviews as a *vedette* (show girl), and on the cover of the Argentine edition of *Rolling Stone* magazine. Tour Experience takes you into the homes of transvestites to learn about their lives and their struggles and drives through various red light districts, where a majority of the transvestites toil as sex workers.

All the tours include door-to-door car service and are accompanied by local security. The tours cost around 200 pesos per person.

—Brian Byrnes

the road to the all-night dance parties at Mint and Pachá. ✉ *Av. Costanera Rafael Obligado 4801, Costanera* ☎ *11/4782–5599.*

Mint. You'll pound Red Bull and champagne alongside trendy college kids and wealthy twentysomethings at this happening riverfront electronica club. It's essentially one cavernous room, with a dance floor surrounded by elevated VIP areas and an outside terrace. Stick around to watch the sun rise over the Río de la Plata, a rite of passage for any respectable porteño nightcrawler. ✉ *Punta Carrasco, Av. Costanera Rafael Obligado and Av. Sarmiento, Costanera* ☎ *11/4771–5870.*

Fodor'sChoice **Pachá.** This pink, multilevel, riverbank behemoth is the mecca of the
★ Buenos Aires dance-music scene. Look for raucous raves hosted by such top DJs as Hernán Cattáneo and Fatboy Slim. It can be ruthlessly hot and crowded, but for most people, total sensory overload is the point. ✉ *Av. Costanera Rafael Obligado and La Pampa, Costanera* ☎ *11/ 4788–4280.*

Rumi. Rumi gets packed with rich suburban socialites and the occasional fashion model or two who come for the less intense setting (compared with other Costanera clubs) and the electronica and pop music. Two large bars surround the dance floor and elevated booths readily allow for the most favorite of all Argentine pastimes: checking people out. ✉ *Av. Figueroa Alcorta 6442, Costanera* ☎ *11/4782–1307.*

Tequila. Unless you're a member of the Australian National Rugby team or Lenny Kravitz (both previous visitors), you might have to work the bouncers hard to get into this small coastal club. A magnificent mix of actors, models, and fashionistas comes here for pre-game cocktails. Make an early dinner reservation for one of the plush booths, and you'll not only avoid velvet-rope rejection, but you'll also get a bird's-eye view of porteño pick-up artists in action. ✉ *Av. Costanera Rafael Obligado and La Pampa, Costanera* ☎ *11/4781–6555.*

SHOPPING

By Victoria
Patience

Fashion-obsessed porteños head to Avenida Alvear and Calle Quintana in La Recoleta for haute couture; Avenida Cabildo (from the 1600 block to the 2200 block) in Belgrano and Avenida Santa Fe (800 to 1500) in El Centro for ready-to-wear, vintage, and club clothing; Calle Florida, also in El Centro, for leather goods; and Avenida Córdoba (4400 to 5000) in Palermo for discount goods. Malls, *galerías* (arcades), and chain stores, many of them local, abound. So do boutiques and open-air markets.

With the devaluation of the peso, your money will go a long way, here, whether you have dollars, euros, or pounds sterling. But just because you have a favorable foreign-exchange rate, doesn't mean you have to shop like a foreigner. Here's how to navigate the shopping scene with local savvy.

Getting the Goods

Porteños take shopping seriously, and they dress for the occasion. You should, too. Sloppily dressed customers usually get sloppy service. That said, unless you're petite, plan to pack appropriate attire for shopping (or any other activity): sizes here attest to the fact that porteños are, on average, smaller than Europeans and North Americans. Chic women's boutiques often don't have any clothes in sizes larger than a U.S. 8. (Though a law has been passed requiring stores to carry larger sizes—just one step toward attempting to curb an anorexia epidemic—at this writing, stores had yet to comply.)

To make matters for big and tall women worse, bare midriffs are the thing, so pants are cut in the very low, hipster style and tops are navel-skimming. It doesn't get any better for men: a porteño men's "large" will seem more like a "small" to many foreigners, and trousers come in very few different lengths. Shoes in larger sizes for either sex are also hard to come by.

So what can you buy if the apparel here is too small?

Leather belts, bags, and other accessories are good bets. Items are cut from cowhide, antelope, kidskin, pigskin, sheepskin, lizard, snake, and porcupine in an array of colors and styles. A local specialty is the soft, speckled leather of the *carpincho* (capybara)—the world's largest rodent.

Handicrafts are also good buys. Look for traditional ponchos, mate kits, *boleadoras* (gaucho lassos), wood carvings, and alpaca products. Silver jewelry, Brazilian emeralds, and semiprecious Argentine *rodocrosita,* "rose of the Inca" stones—which range in color from pink to red—should also make your list.

Locked shop doors are standard anti-theft practice. Don't be surprised (or intimidated by) by having to ring a doorbell and be buzzed in. "Refund" seems to be a dirty word in Argentina, so always try before you buy.

Quality & Pricing

There are lots of good-value local brands on offer, and many items—particularly leather goods—are cheaper here than abroad. Just be mindful that the quality may match the price. Pay particular attention to seams and hems; local stitching isn't always superlative. This is true even with international-brand items, which are nearly always locally made.

Open-air markets are the best places for deals on souvenir-quality crafts and jewelry. For top-quality items, though, head to specialty stores. Prices may be higher, but the quality is more reliable.

Stores in tourist areas (such as Calle Florida) may try to charge you in dollars or euros what they charge Argentines in pesos. Always confirm which currency you're dealing with up front. Bargaining is accepted only in some leather-goods shops on Calle Florida. Elsewhere—even in markets—prices are fixed.

Keep your receipts: the 21% VAT tax, included in the sales price, is entirely refundable for purchases exceeding $200 at stores displaying a duty-free sign. When you depart, allow time to visit the return desk at the airport to obtain your refund.

El Centro & Environs

Calle Florida is a pedestrian-only street where high-quality chains sit cheek by jowl with easy-come easy-go boutiques. Leather clothing is the draw,

Best Buys

CLOSE UP

1

- **Mate for Two.** Even if you don't see yourself drinking mate (tea made from a South American shrub) every day, the drink's paraphernalia make unusual souvenirs. You could fork over hundreds of dollars for one of Juan Carlos Pallarols's ornate silver kits (a drinking vessel and metal straw), but the kid-size sets at Recursos Infantiles or La Pescadería go for 40 pesos, include a mini kettle and thermos and are easier to pack. Although the best boxy leather mate bags (for carrying thermos and vessel) sell at La Feria de Mataderos, another market, for 70 pesos and up, at La Feria de la Recoleta, simple vessels made from gourds start at 5 pesos. Supermarkets sell mate; Rosamonte, one of many brands, costs 4 pesos.

- **Dressing to Match.** You've come to Argentina, you've been to the fútbol stadium, and you've seen a match—what's left to do? Buy a T-shirt. Go neutral with the pale-blue and white national team shirt, or choose a local team's colors. **Código Fútbol** (✉ Juncal 1502 La Recoleta) sells a great range of shirts; prices start at 75 pesos.

- **Football at Your Fingertips.** The chances of seeing the nation's soccer hero, Diego Armando Maradona, in action are slim, but get your hands—or thumbs, rather—on his greatest moment with the photo flipbook *El Gol del Siglo*. It shows his famous goal against England in the 1986 World Cup, and sells for 19 pesos at the MALBA book shop and Prometeo.

- **Comic Relief.** It may be unfamiliar to you, but the classic '60s cartoon strip "Mafalda" is close to the heart of all Argentines. The idealistic little girl it stars is an icon, and most downtown *kioscos de diarios* (newsstands) sell the flimsy Ediciones de la Flor collections of the strip for around 15 pesos. Alternatively, Prometeo often stocks pricier English translations.

Sweet Stuff. It's brown, goopy, and sickly sweet . . . but you know you want more *dulce de leche* (a spread made from sweetened condensed milk). All supermarkets stock such popular brands as La Serenísima (3 pesos), or go to one of the many Havanna café-shops (they proliferate the city like Starbucks branches in Seattle) for a posh glass jar (10 pesos). Havanna's *alfajores* (chocolate-covered dulce-de-leche–filled cookies) are also sure to earn you fans back home (16 pesos for 12).

The Best Cuts. Sneaking a bloody steak in your suitcase won't work. A more packable souvenir of is the traditional *asado* knife. Practical wood- or horn-handled knives are available at most markets starting at around 50 pesos, depending on blade quality (surgical steel is best if you intend to actually use the knife). Silver and alpaca are often used to decorate the hilt and sheath of the more elaborate knives sold for much heftier prices at silversmiths like Platería Parodi.

Wine-ing Away the Hours. Argentina is the world's fifth-largest wine producing country. Although a bottle of award-winning red stuff like Catena Zapata might stretch to hundreds of dollars, other excellent wines include Trapiche's Fond de Cave Malbec Reserva, available for around 25 pesos from Ligier as well as most major supermarkets.

and armies of salesman are strategically positioned outside shops with unfailing radars identifying tourists, aka potential customers. If you find the crowds and traffic of Florida and its environs overwhelming, browse through the big-name local stores inside the Galerías Pacífico mall, which fills a whole block at Florida's intersection with Avenida Córdoba. At the very least, schedule a refueling stop here—crazily narrow side streets, clouds of exhaust fumes, and constant hustling can cause rapid retail burnout. In the swankier district north of Avenida Santa Fe, art galleries line quiet Calle Arroyo; entrance is free and browsing welcomed.

The retail highlight of the Almagro district, just a few subte stops from downtown, is the Abasto mall. On its east side, the block-long pedestrian-only Calle Gardel is a good place to pick up fridge magnets and postcards, though there should be prizes for the person who can find these souvenirs without tango dancers on them.

Malls

Abasto. The soaring art deco architecture of what was once the city's central market is as much a reason to come as the three levels of shops. Although Abasto has many top local chains, it's not as exclusive as other malls, so you can find bargains. Shops like Ver, Yagmour, and Comma do cheap 'n' cheerful clothes for chicks to flop around the house in. Those same chicks can also dress up at Ayres, Paula Cahen D'anvers, Akiabara, or the Spanish chain Zara. Levi's, Quiksilver, Puma, and Adidas are among the casual international offerings; for something smarter, there's Dior. Men can hit such trendy shops as Bensimon and Mancini or go for the *estanciero* (estate owner) look with Legacy chinos and polos. Take a break in the fourth-floor food court beneath the glass panes and steel supports of the building's original roof. ☒ *Av. Corrientes 3247, Almagro* ☎ *11/4959–3400* ⊕ *www.abasto-shopping.com.ar* Ⓜ *B to Carlos Gardel.*

Galerías Pacífico. Upscale shops line the three levels of this building, which designed during the city's turn-of-the-20th-century golden age. Stores are organized along four glass-roofed passages which branch out in a cross from the central stairwell, whose cupola is decorated by several Argentine greats, including Antonio Berni. Many of the stores at the top-end of Florida have branches here. The mall is particularly strong on leather clothing. It also has a basement food court, a cinema, and the Centro Cultural Borges, whose small international art exhibitions have featured Andy Warhol, Salvador Dalí, and Henri Cartier-Bresson. ☒ *Calle Florida 753, at Av. Córdoba, Microcentro* ☎ *11/4319–5100* ⊕ *www.galeriaspacificos.com.ar* Ⓜ *B to Florida.*

Specialty Shops

ART & ANTIQUES **Galería Ruth Benzacar.** This private gallery has been showcasing modern Argentine art for almost 50 years and remains one of the city's best. Ask to see the vast collection of paintings in the basement. ☒ *Florida 1000, Microcentro* ☎ *11/4313–8480* ⊕ *www.ruthbenzacar.com* Ⓜ *C to San Martín.*

CLOTHING **La Martina.** With branches in Saratoga Springs and London, it's clear
★ that the clothing line of polo team La Martina is targeted at the horsing jet set—and with prices to match. But it's not just about boots and jodhpurs; there are also corduroy pants and cashmere sweaters for

lounging around your country house in style. Screen-printed tees—including the Argentine national polo-team shirt—are somewhat cheaper options. ⊠ *Paraguay 661, El Centro* ☎ *11/4311–5963* ⊕ *www.lamartina.com* Ⓜ *C to San Martín.*

CRAFTS **Platería Parodi.** This über-traditional store is chock-a-block with everything a gaucho about town needs to accessorize with, all in top-quality silver. There are belt buckles and knives for the boys, and the no-nonsense Pampa-style women's jewelry would go great with Gap and Ralph Lauren alike. ⊠ *Av. de Mayo 720, Plaza de Mayo* ☎ *11/4342–2207* Ⓜ *A to Piedras.*

Fodor'sChoice ★ **Tierra Adentro.** Beautiful indigenous crafts come with a clean conscience at Tierra Adentro, which insists on trading fairly with the native Argentine craftsmen whose work they stock. Fine weavings are the shop's hallmark, but wide silver bracelets and gobstopper-size turquoise beads are other tempting offers. Mapuche earrings, cut entirely out of a sheet of silver hammered flat, are a bold accessory. ⊠ *Arroyo 946* ☎ *11/4393–8552* ⊕ *www.tierraadentro.info* Ⓜ *C to San Martín.*

HOUSEWARES **30quarenta.** Magazine ads from the 1930s and '40s are the inspiration behind the poptastic furniture at 30quarenta. Kitsch up your living room with an ornate loveseat stripped of its paint and reupholstered in original prints or candy-cane stripes. Divide and conquer with an old steel street ad transformed into a folding screen. Carlos Gardel's face beams from painted bowling pins, just some of a few items that fall on the wrong side of the offbeat–tasteless dividing line. ⊠ *Arroyo 890* ☎ *11/4326–1065* Ⓜ *C to San Martín.*

JEWELRY **Cousiño.** Veined pinky-red rhodochrosite, Argentina's national stone, comes both in classic settings and as diminutive sculptures at this shop specializing in the unusual stone. Cousiño's sculptures of birds in flight are also exhibited in the National Museum of Decorative Arts. ⊠ *Sheraton Buenos Aires Hotel, San Martín 1225, El Centro* ☎ *11/4318–9000* ⊕ *www.cousinojewels.com* Ⓜ *C to Retiro.*

Fodor'sChoice ★ **Plata Nativa.** This tiny shop tucked away in an arcade is filled with delights for both boho chicks and collectors of singular ethnic jewelry. Complex, chunky necklaces with turquoise, amber, and malachite—all based on original Araucanian (ethnic Argentine) pieces—and Mapuche-style silver earrings and brooches are some of the offerings. Sharon Stone and Liv Ullman have fallen for Florencia Bernales's knitted silver necklaces; other happy customers include Pedro Almodóvar and the Textile Museum in Washington, D.C. Weavings and religious wooden statues complete the finds. ⊠ *Unit 4, Galería del Sol, Florida 860* ☎ *11/4312–1398* ⊕ *www.platanativa.com* Ⓜ *C to San Martín.*

LEATHER **Arandú.** For sheepskin jackets, head to Arandú, which also sells fur-lined saddles, boots, and other leather goods for that Marlboro-man look, Argentine-style. If you find the supple canvas and leather sports bags too conventional, check out such novelties as leather rifle-cases. ⊠ *Paraguay 1259, El Centro* ☎ *11/4816–6191* ⊕ *www.tal-arandu.com* Ⓜ *D to Tribunales.*

Carpincho. This shop specializes in the stippled leather of the carpincho (cabybara—the world's largest rodent, native to Argentina), which has super-soft skin. The real draw, though, are the gloves, which come in

The Chain Gang

IF YOU SCAN any Buenos Aires mall plan most of the stores will be unfamiliar—foreign labels in Argentina are mainly limited to sportswear and designer gear. Here's an overview of the homegrown chains.

Akiabara (⊕ www.akiabara.com). Slick jeans, pants, and suits pull sharp twenty- and thirtysomething chicks to Akiabara like metal to a magnet. The slinky tops and soft, asymmetric knits come unadorned—no prints, no embroidery, just plain lines and good draping.

Ayres (⊕ www.ayres.com.ar). Fine, strappy tops in bold colors like cherry and tangerine tell you that women who shop at Ayres don't mind standing out at the bar. For sweeter wallflowers there are ultra-soft cache-coeurs (wraparound cardigans), suits in powder-blue drill or rose-patterned-burgundy velvet—pretty but cool at the same time. The jeans are beginning to rival Rapsodia's at the top of the most-wanted list.

Bensimon (⊕ www.bensimon.com. ar). Imagine the lovechild of Paul Smith and Laura Ashley—Bensimon is it. It's the first local menswear brand to prove that even macho porteños can wear pink, and its retro-print tees and floral shirts have become some of the most-imitated items on the market. Add to this the brand's jeans and its thinned-down Scandinavian-look sweaters and corduroy jackets, and you have the place David

Beckham would shop were he on a budget. Bright turquoise walls with hand-painted cherry blossoms offset heavy mahogany-look cabinets whose open drawers are filled with stripy socks and colorful boxers that just ache to be taken home.

Caro Cuore (⊕ www.carocuore.com. ar). Argentina's favorite underwear brand does cute cotton panty and bra sets in bright colors as well as sexier fare. Although the stuff sold here is fun for flopping on the couch or spending the day in bed, don't come looking for support, be it structural or from the sales staff. Assistants look on unsympathetic to the fact that the bras have no cup size and the Calvin-clone men's boxers have a very limited size range.

Giesso (⊕ www.giesso.com.ar). A classic gents' tailor for nearly a century, Giesso is now pulling a Thomas Pink by adding jewel-colored ties and shirts to its range of timeless suits. Plain and pin-striped button downs are still on offer, though, as are cufflinks. A new women's-wear line includes sober suits and cashmere overcoats.

Kosiuko (⊕ www.kosiuko.com.ar). Branches of Kosiuko, the ultimate local teen brand, are always packed with trendy adolescents served by hip-wiggling staff not much older than they are. The girls come for the improbably small, low-cut pants, the guys for budding metrosexual-wear.

both carpincho and kidskin and in many colors, from classic chocolate brown to tangerine and lime. ⊠ *Esmeralda 775* ☎ *11/4322–9919* ⊕ *www.carpinchonet.com.ar* Ⓜ *C to Lavalle.*
Casa López. Don't let Casa López's drab store-front put you off: you're as likely to find a trouser suit in flower-print suede as a handbag for grandma. It's a store in two parts: the right-hand shop (Number 658)

Kosiuko's fragrances and deodorant are a favorite with the population's most-perspiring age-group.

Ona Saez (⊕ www.onasaez.com). The ultra-fitted jeans at Ona Saez are designed to be worn with sky-high heels and slinky tops for a sexy night out. The menswear is equally slick, mixing dressed-down denim with cool cotton shirts and tees.

Paula Cahen d'Anvers (⊕ www.paulacahendanvers.com.ar). This store's founder hails from a local dynasty and her choice of logo—a little embroidered crown—lets you know that that her clothes are for urban princesses. Her take on preppy is tongue-in-cheek, mixing blazers and straight-leg pants with puffed-sleeve shirts and ties, or floral tees. The candy-striped onesies and bright corduroy dresses of the kids' line, teamed with patent Mary Janes, are enough to make even the biggest girls' hearts melt.

Portsaid (⊕ www.portsaid.com.ar). Professional women who want a feminine touch to their work clothes shop at Portsaid, where satin-ribbon ties and discreet beadwork soften otherwise practical garments. Simply-cut suits and twin-sets come in colors like baby pink and aqua to make you stand out in a drab office; woolen winter coats are always a bargain both in terms of quality and style, be they classic cuts or fuller '60s-influenced designs.

Prüne (⊕ www.prune.com.ar). It's definitely favored by smart working chicks. Prüne does handbags that are chic but practical, with thoughtful compartments and enough room for all your bits 'n' bobs. Colors tend to be rich and dark and leathers are ultra-supple. Details like steel rings linking bags to straps lend urban touches. Leather jackets, belts, and shoes are also on offer.

Rapsodia (⊕ www.rapsodia.com.ar). The most sought-after jeans in town come from Rapsodia—look for the ocher wing design on local girls' back pockets. The shop is also the temple of Buenos Aires' boho princesses, who can't get enough of owner and model Sol Acuña's floaty, embroidered Indian tops. She's also a big Stones fan, as many of the thin rock-print T-shirts testify.

Yagmour (⊕ www.yagmour.com). Although Austin Powers fans delight in this shop's name—pronounced "Shag more"—they might find the clothes a bit low-key. Argentina's answer to the Gap does basic knock-around gear for women and girls. Stock up on practical khakis and candy-color crewnecks to wear to death on excursions out of town; or go for prettier corduroy skirts, cute Capri pants, and appliqué tops from the slightly pricier Et Vous line.

has totes and soft-sided suitcases in chestnut- and chocolate-colored leather that looks good enough to eat; there are also classic jackets. More un-usual fare—fur sacks with natural wool fringes, black cowhide baguettes, aubergine leather clutches—are next door at Number 640. ⊠ *M. T. de Alvear 640 and 658, Palermo* ☎ *11/4311–3044* ⊕ *www.casalopez. com.ar* Ⓜ *C to San Martín.*

WINE **Ligier.** Ligier has a string of shops across town and lots of experience guiding bewildered shoppers through their impressive selection. Although they stock some boutique-vineyard wines, they truly specialize in the big names like Rutini and Luigi Bosca. Their leather wine carrying cases make a great picnic accessory. ⊠ *Av. Santa Fe 800* ☎ *11/4515–0126* ⊕ *www.ligier.com.ar* Ⓜ *C to San Martín.*

San Telmo

It's entirely appropriate that San Telmo, with its colonial architecture, is the place to shop for timeless collectibles and curios. Stores on dozens of small streets—such as Pasaje de la Defensa—deal entirely in antiques or forgetabilia. The blocks of Defensa near Plaza Dorrego are lined with a mind-boggling number of shops. The more upscale places are used to dealing with foreign customers; most can arrange shipping. Although things may be cheaper than back home, San Telmo isn't a bargain basement: expect to pay top dollar for top goods. Plaza Dorrego itself hosts the open-air Feria de San Pedro Telmo, with street vendors, performers, and antiques, every Sunday from 10 to 5.

Specialty Shops

ART & ANTIQUES **Arte y Diseño de la Pampa.** An artist-and-architect duo is behind these original works, which are inspired by native Argentine art. They use an unusual papier-mâché technique to create boxes, frames, wall-hangings, and freestanding sculptures. The primitive-looking pieces, a vision of rich rusts and earthy browns, make highly original gifts. ⊠ *Defensa 917, San Telmo* ☎ *11/4362–6406* ⊕ *www.artepampa.com.*

La Candelaria. A light-filled Spanish-style house is the site of several choice shops. One is filled with enough miniature wooden furniture to fill several dollhouses; another sells golden-age Argentine cinema posters. Wind-up monkeys, brass fittings, and old leather suitcases ready to be packed are other possible finds. ⊠ *Defensa 1170* ☎ *No phone.*

Churrinche. Hidden in the dusty chaos are old train sets and nests of silver-topped walking sticks. Glasses are another forte: there are 20-piece sets—many in two-tone cut glass—in the appropriate shapes for wine, water, brandy, sherry, and just about anything else. If you need to fix a chandelier, a rack of replacement glass baubles fills the window—mounted on wire hooks, they'd also make innovative earrings. ⊠ *Defensa 1031, San Telmo* ☎ *11/4362–7612* ⊕ *www.churrinche.com.ar.*

Gabriel del Campo. There doesn't seem to be much logic behind the selection of curios in this boudoir-red shop. Who cares though, when 50-year-old Louis Vuitton trunks sit beside scale-model ships, complete with canvas sails and all? Church-statues in the window look ready to go for a spin in the motorized toy racing Bugatti that makes an arresting storefront display. ⊠ *Defensa 990, San Telmo* ☎ *11/4361–2061.*

Gil Antigüedades. Sequined flapper dresses, dashing white linen suits, and creamy lace wedding veils are some of the things you might find in this pink casa chorizo. Cabinets of period accessories include Castilian hair combs and lacey fans that beg you to bat your eyelashes from behind them. ⊠ *Humberto I 412, San Telmo* ☎ *11/4361–5019* ⊕ *www.gilantiguedades.com.ar.*

Dance Gear

SERIOUS DANCERS and listeners should take advantage of the range of tango music, shoes, and clothing on offer in Buenos Aires. Some of the best tango shoes in town, including classic spats, 1920s T-bar designs, as well as glitzier numbers are all made to measure at **Flabella** (✉ Suipacha 263, Microcentro ☎ 11/4322–6036).

Tango Brujo (✉ Esmeralda 754, Microcentro ☎ 11/4326–8264 ⊕ www.tangobrujo.com.ar) is a one-stop tango shop selling shoes, clothes, and how-to videos. Recordings by just about every tango musician under the sun can be found at **Zivals** (✉ Av. Callao 395 El Centro ☎ 11/4371–7500 ⊕ www.zivals.com).

HB Anticuario. Step in for an eyeful of the exquisite art deco furniture that's the specialty here. White-leather trefoil chairs and gleaming walnut side tables with black-lacquer details are among the items that will send you to Charleston heaven. Equally collectable and much more packable are the Clarice Cliff dinner services, though they don't come cheap. ✉ *Defensa 1016/18, San Telmo* ☎ *11/4361–3325* ⊕ *www.hbantiques.com.ar.*

★ **Juan Carlos Pallarols Orfebre.** Argentina's legendary silversmith has made pieces for a mile-long list of celebrities that includes Frank Sinatra, Sharon Stone, Jacqueline Bisset, Bill Clinton, Nelson Mandela, the king and queen of Spain, and Princess Máxima Zorrequieta—Argentina's export to the Dutch royal family. He's designed everything from tableware and trays to papal chalices; a set of his ornate silver-handled steak knives is the perfect way to celebrate cow country, though you'll part with a few grand for the pleasure. The less pragmatic can make like Antonio Banderas and Maradona: commission a silver rose (thorns and all) for their true love. ✉ *Defensa 1039, San Telmo* ☎ *11/4362–0641* ⊕ *www.pallarols.com.ar.*

Pallarols Anticuarios. Two things eclipse all others here: chandeliers and mirrors. For the most part, mirrors have gold-painted with baroque-style designs. The chandeliers that reflect in them include elegant fin-de-siècle cascades as well as boxier 1920s designs. ✉ *Defensa 1015, San Telmo* ☎ *11/4362–5438.*

★ **Silvia Petroccia.** Despite being crammed with furniture, this corner store manages to look extravagant rather than chaotic. It's probably due to the alluring collectibles, which range from Louis XV–style chairs reupholstered in buttercup-yellow silk to packable gilt-wood church candles. Gold-framed mirrors and a host of chandeliers round out the luxuries. ✉ *Defensa 1002, San Telmo* ☎ *11/4362–0156.*

CLOTHING **La Pescadería.** This small store wears its nostalgic heart on its sleeve—all its products are tongue-in-cheek celebrations of what Argentine childhood used to be about. For wistful sports fans there are cotton piqué football shirts that imitate club jerseys of the 1950s and replica old-style leather football shoes—studs 'n' all. Cool kids wear includes little tees with the faces of Gardel and Che Guevara—revolutionary gifts. ✉ *Carlos Calvo 467, San Telmo* ☎ *11/4361–6287.*

Un Lugar En El Mundo. The barrio's hippest shop showcases young designers, whose men's and women's clothing is both wearable and affordable. Un Lugar en el Mundo is also one of the few places in town to get a bag by Bolsas de Viaje, whose vinyl and canvas creations evoke the golden age of air travel. Mir's satchels and totes in heavily stitched chestnut leather make you want to go back to school, and Paz Portnoi's cowhide heels are perfect for dressing up. ⊠ *Defensa 891, San Telmo* ☎ *11/4362–3836.*

JEWELRY **Abraxas.** "Yes" is guaranteed if you propose with one of the period engagement rings—emerald, ruby, sapphire, or diamond—that dazzle in the window of this antique jewelers. If you're not planning on an "I do" anytime soon, how about some art deco earrings with the tiniest diamonds or a gossamer-fine bracelet? ⊠ *Defensa 1092, San Telmo* ☎ *11/4361–7512.*

Midas Antigüedades. Everything a gentleman needs to accessorize like a lord is arrayed in the minimalist storefront. Watches are the specialty: a 1940s Longine with a snakeskin strap is one debonair option, though the 20th-century pocket watches may make you give up wrist wear for good. Jeweled tie-pins, cufflinks, and antique fountain pens round out the stock. ⊠ *Defensa 1088, San Telmo* ☎ *11/4300–6615.*

La Recoleta

If you forget you're in Latin America on a stroll along Avenida Alvear, you could almost be forgiven. Perfectly maintained Parisian-style town houses surround the street's most important landmark, the Alvear Palace Hotel, a gorgeous golden-stone mansion, where the likes of the Spanish royal family stay when in town. La Recoleta's shopping scene complements its aristocratic residents: along quiet sidewalks, store windows discreetly announce names like Christian Dior, Armani, and Versace. Such darlings of Argentine style as Pablo Ramírez, Martín Churba, and Jessica Trosman also have their boutiques here—on Avenidas Alvear, Quintana, and Rodríguez Peña and in the Patio Bullrich mall. Look for humbler offerings at the Feria Artesanal de Recoleta, a weekend arts-and-crafts market. The Buenos Aires Design Center, a housewares mini-mall, overlooks the market. La Recoleta isn't as accessible by subte as other places, but you'll need a taxi for all those bags, anyway.

Malls

Buenos Aires Design. This fledgling mall alongside the Recoleta Cemetery mainly sells housewares—most of them imported and no less expensive than stuff back home. There are, however, a few shops with noteworthy suitcase-size bits and pieces. Two-level Morph does all manner of quirky colorful household items (think Philippe Starck on a budget). Rival OKKO is all Indian appliqué and heavy rustic furniture. The must-see, though, is one-stop **Puro Diseño Argentino** (☎ 11/5777–6104 ⊕ www.purodiseno.com.ar), where Argentine designers show off their crafts, jewelry, clothing, accessories, furniture, and household items. This is one of the few places to pick up a one-of-a-kind Manto Abrigo coat, hand woven in luminous colors in the north of Argentina. Other stylish options include leather-bound notebooks, acid-green cow-

Life Before Malls

NO SHOPPING TRIP is complete without whisking yourself back in time by browsing one of the city's many *galerías*. These quirky shopping arcades are the precursors of malls and were mostly built in the 1960s and '70s. Their boxy architecture often includes gloriously kitsch touches, and the unpredictable retail offerings of the small stores inside each could include designer gear, no-name brands, used books, sex toys, cigars and pipes, tattoos, imported vinyl records, and other wonders. Though many galerís have closed down, they're still thick on the ground along Avenida Santa Fe (800 to 1500) and Avenida Cabildo (1500 to 2200).

A favorite with teenagers and clubbers alike is **Galería Bond Street** (✉ Av. Santa Fe 1607, La Recoleta ☎ no phone). Downstairs stores sell club wear, punky T-shirts, and band pins. The top floor has the classier pickings of local designers who aren't big enough to move to Palermo yet.

Vintage vultures should swing by the **Galería Quinta Avenida** (✉ Av. Santa Fe 1270, La Recoleta ☎ no phone), which has a host of dusty boutiques ideal for a couple of hours of rack-roaming. There's a particularly good selection of leather jackets, as well as accessories like specs from the 1950s and '60s.

skin rugs, and cute geometric purses by Dara. The mall's open-air terrace has several cafés and restaurants with views of Avenida del Libertador. ✉ *Pueyrredón 2501, La Recoleta* ☎ *11/5777–6000* ⊕ *www.purodiseno.com.ar.*

Patio Bullrich. The city's most upscale mall was once the headquarters for the Bullrich family's meat-auction house. Inside stone cow heads mounted on pillars still watch over the clientele. A colonnaded front, a domed glass ceiling, and curlicued steel supports are other reminders of another age. Top local stores that usually occupy prime mall space are relegated to the lowest level, making way for the likes of Lacroix, Cacharel, and Maxmara. Urban leather-ware brand Uma has a shop here, as does Palermo fashion princess Jessica Trosman, whose spare women's clothes are decorated with unusual heavy beadwork. The enfant terrible of Argentine footwear, Ricky Sarkany, sells dangerously pointed stilettos in colors that walk the line between exciting and kitsch. Edgy but elegant menswear line Etiqueta Negra has its first store outside the snooty northern suburbs here. When the gloriously huge bags these shops pack your purchases into begin to weigh you down, stop for a calorie-oozing cake at Nucha, on the Avenida del Libertador side of the building. ✉ *Enter at Posadas 1245 or Av. del Libertador 750, La Recoleta* ☎ *11/4815–3501* ⊕ *www.shoppingbullrich.com.ar* Ⓜ *C to Retiro (walk 7 blocks up Av. del Libertador).*

Specialty Shops

CLOTHING

FodorsChoice

★

Cat Ballou. As the name suggests, golden-age Hollywood glamour is the order of the day at Cat Ballou. Everything in this tiny corner boutique breathes delicacy, from bias-cut satin dresses with whispery tulle details to llama-wool felt jackets with berry-colored belts. The shop's housewares, including pink velvet loveseats and antique chandeliers, are the icing on this slice of urban luxury. ⊠ *Av. Alvear 1702, La Recoleta* ☎ *11/4811–9792.*

★ **La Dolfina Polo Lifestyle.** Being the world's best polo player wasn't enough for Adolfo Cambiaso—he founded his own team in 1995, and then started a clothing line for which he does the modeling. And if you think polo is all about knee-high boots and preppy chinos think again: Cambiaso sells some of the best urban menswear in town. The Italian-cotton shirts, sharp leather jackets, and to-die-for totes from the After Polo collection are perfect for after just about anything. ⊠ *Av. Alvear 1315, La Recoleta* ☎ *11/4815–2698* ⊕ *www.ladolfina.com.*

Fahoma. This small split-level boutique has enough accessories to make the rest of your outfit a mere formality. Berry-size beads go into chunky but affordable necklaces, and all manner of handbags—from fluffy totes to sleek clutches—hang on the back wall. ⊠ *Libertad 1169, La Recoleta* ☎ *11/4813–5103* ⊕ *www.fahoma.com.*

Locos X El Fútbol. The merchandising section of Locos X El Fútbol has everything a serious football fan needs to dress like the best. You can get jerseys for local, national, and international teams. ⊠ *Inside Village Recoleta complex, Vicente López at Uriburú, La Recoleta* ☎ *11/4807–3777* ⊕ *www.codigofutbol.com.ar.*

★ **Pablo Ramírez.** The simple but spacey dresses of porteño fashion god Pablo Ramírez were once only available by hard-won appointment, but the opening of this Recoleta store means even non-celebrities can have a masterpiece. Pablo's couture doesn't come cheap, but given the peso prices, his dressy numbers are a (relative) bargain. Black is the color he favors both for women's wear and slick gent's suits, though a few other shades are beginning to creep in. ⊠ *Callao 1315, La Recoleta* ☎ *11/4815–5147* ⊕ *www.pabloramirez.com.ar.*

Fodor'sChoice **Tramando, Martín Churba.** Martín Churba, the undisputed leader of local
★ textile design, is one of Argentina's few designers to have gone international with boutiques in New York and Tokyo. Unique evening tops made of layers of sheer fabric adorned with geometric slashes and perfectly circular beads look like something an urban mermaid would wear. Sheer microfiber bustiers, screen-printed tees, and even vases are some of the other woven wonders in the hushed town house store. ⊠ *Rodríguez Peña 1973, La Recoleta* ☎ *11/4811–0465* ⊕ *www.tramando.com.*

CRAFTS **Aire del Sur.** Alpaca, carved deer bone, onyx, and leather are some of the
★ materials that might be combined into perfectly crafted trays, candelabras, or photo frames at Aire del Sur. The winning mix of these traditional materials with contemporary designs has won the hearts of stores like Barneys in New York and Paul Smith in London. You can cut out all those middlemen, though, on a visit to this Recoleta showroom. ⊠ *Arenales 1618, 9th floor, La Recoleta* ☎ *11/5811–3640* ⊕ *www.airedelsur.com.*

[handwritten: now not the address]

JEWELRY **Homero.** Shiny, colorful acrylic discs offset diamonds and white gold in Homero's innovative necklaces, which go to show that luxury jewelry can be funky, too. Other rock-star pieces include cross-shape pendants and silver rings with acid-color stones. ⊠ *Posadas 1399, La Recoleta* ☎ *11/4812–9881* ⊕ *www.homero-joyas.com.ar.*

[handwritten: Perez Sanz - Sculptor/leather]

Santino. Delicate curlicued diamond rings are Santino's signature and a favorite accessory at top local fashion shoots. Contemporary art-deco style brooches share space in the small wine-red shop with the real antique McCoy, or you can step out in style with a silver-topped walking stick. ⊠ *Av. Callao 1702, La Recoleta* ☎ *11/4806–0120* ⊕ *www.santinoba.com.*

Zanotti. This store's location at the front of the ultra-luxurious Alvear Palace Hotel lets you know that only the serious stone-wearer need enter. Among the classic diamond and pearl pieces are refreshing numbers like necklaces made of knitted gossamer-fine silver chains and dripping pendant earrings. Silver gaucho-style knives make for designer souvenirs. ⊠ *Av. Alvear 1883, La Recoleta* ☎ *11/4804–7212.*

LEATHER **Cardon.** Pine floors, pine walls, and pine cabinets—it's all very country down at Cardon. The estancia crowd comes here for reasonably priced, no-nonsense sheepskin jackets, cashmere sweaters, and riding boots. Items from the line of *talabartería* (traditional gaucho-style leather items), including cowboy hats, make great gifts. ⊠ *Av. Alvear 1847, La Recoleta* ☎ *11/4804–8424* ⊕ *www.cardon.com.ar.*

Mayorano. If Katharine Hepburn had dressed in leather, Mayorano would have been just up her alley. The selection is small, but the ultra-simple tan suits and trench coats in flawless calfskin are more than enough to justify a visit. ⊠ *Av. Alvear 1824, La Recoleta* ☎ *11/4804–2398.*

Rossi y Caruso. Top-quality workmanship and classic cuts are what bring distinguished customers like King Juan Carlos of Spain to Rossi y Caruso. The shop specializes in riding gear (think Marlborough foxhunt rather than Marlboro man) but also sells conservative handbags, leather jackets, and shoes. And should you need a saddle during your trip, those sold here are the best in town. ⊠ *Posadas 1387, La Recoleta* ☎ *11/4811–1538* ⊕ *www.rossicaruso.com.*

SHOES **Guido.** In Argentina, loafers means Guido, whose retro-looking logo has been the hallmark of quality footwear since 1952. The old-world mahogany interior is the perfect place to try on timeless handmade Oxfords and brogues. There are also fun items (e.g., raspberry cow-skin handbags) on offer. ⊠ *Av. Quintana 333, La Recoleta* ☎ *11/4811–4567* ⊕ *www.guidomocasines.com.ar.*

Lonte. There's something naughty-but-oh-so-nice about Lonte's shoes. Chunky gold peep-toe heels are a retro-queen's dream, and the outré animal print numbers are a favorite of local diva Susana Giménez. For more discreet feet there are tweed boots or classic heels in straightforward colors. ⊠ *Av. Alvear 1814, La Recoleta* ☎ *11/4804–9270* ⊕ *www.lonteweb.com.*

Zapatos de María. María Conorti was one of the first young designers to set up shop in the area, and she's going strong. Wedge heels, satin ankle-ties, and abundant use of patent leather are the trademark touches of her quirky designs. Knee-high suede pirate boots come in colors like ochre and lavender. ⊠ *Libertad 1661, La Recoleta* ☎ *11/4815–5001* ⊕ *www.zapatosdemaria.com.ar.*

WINE **Grand Cru.** Don't let the small shop-front put you off: as with all the
Fodor'sChoice best wine shops, the action is underground. Grand Cru's peerless selec-
★ tion includes wines from Patagonian vineyard Noemia, one of the coun-

Good Marketing Skills

THE ARRAY OF OPEN-AIR *ferias* (markets) in Buenos Aires testifies to the esteem in which Argentina holds its craftspeople, both traditional and contemporary. Browsing the stands you'll find unique items while enjoying wonderful street performances. The selections include not only crafts but also art, antiques, curios, clothing, jewelry, and housewares, and stalls are often attended by the artists themselves. Bargaining is not the norm, although you may get a small discount for buying lots of items. Opening times vary, though most markets take place on weekends from 10 to 5.

The town's busiest market is the classic **Feria de San Pedro Telmo**, which packs a small San Telmo square every Sunday. Elbow your way through the crowds to pick through antiques and curios of varying vintages as well as tango memorabilia, or watch dolled-up professional tango dancers perform on the surrounding cobbled streets. As it gets dark, the square turns into a *milonga*, where quickstepping locals show you how it's done. ⊠ *Plaza Dorrego, Humberto I y Defensa, San Telmo* ☎ *11/4331-9855* ⊕ *www. feriadesantelmo.com* ⊙ *Sun. 10–5* Ⓜ *E to Independencia (then walk 9 blocks east along Independencia to Defensa). Alternatively, A to Plaza de Mayo, D to Catedral, E to Bolívar (then walk 8 blocks south on Bolívar).*

In the heart of colorful La Boca, **Vuelta de Rocha Handicrafts Market (Caminito)** showcases local artists all week long. You can find attractive port-scenes in watercolors, as well as stylish photographs of the neighborhood's old houses, though don't expect any budding Picassos. The market expands at weekends with stalls selling handicrafts and tacky souvenirs. As shoppers here are almost exclusively tourists, prices tend to be overambitious—sometimes irritatingly so. ⊠ *Av. Pedro de Mendoza and Caminito, La Boca* ⊙ *Art market daily 10–6; craft market weekends 10–6.*

The largest crafts market in town is the **Feria Artesanal de la Recoleta**, which winds its way through several linked squares outside the Recoleta Cemetery. Artisans sell handmade clothes, jewelry, and housewares as well as more traditional crafts here. ⊠ *Avs. Libertador and Pueyrredón, La Recoleta* ☎ *11/4343-0309* ⊙ *Weekends 10–6.*

The business conducted in hip Palermo Viejo's **Feria de Plaza Serrano** rivals that done in the neighborhood's trendy boutiques. In a small square—which is actually round—artisans sell wooden toys, ceramics, and funky jewelry made of stained glass or vintage buttons. This is also a great place to buy art: the railings around the playground act as an open air gallery for Palermo artists, and organizers control the quality of art on display. The feria continues unofficially at many nearby bars, which push their tables and chairs aside to make room for clothing and accessory designers: expect to find anything from cute cotton underwear and one-off T-shirts to clubbing dresses and silver necklaces. ✉ *Plazoleta Cortázar (Plaza Serrano), at Honduras and Serrano, Palermo Viejo* ⊘ *Weekends 11–5.*

Far from the tourist trail, the sheltered **Mercado de las Pulgas** (Flea Market) is packed with furniture on its second (or third or fourth) time round. You won't come across any Louis XV in the warren of stalls, but original pieces from the 1940s, '50s, and '60s may turn out to be bargain investments. Lighting up your life is also a cinch: choose from the many Venetian-glass chandeliers, or go for a chrome-and-acrylic mushroom lamp. If your taste is more rustic, there's also a sizeable selection of hefty farmhouse-style tables and cabinets in oak and pine. Don't be deceived by the stalls' precarious-looking set-up: vendors are used to dealing with big-name local customers and can often arrange overseas shipping. ✉ *Niceto Vega 200 block, between Dorrego and Concepcion Arenales, Palermo Hollywood* ⊘ *Daily 10–5.*

On weekends upscale craftsmen transform a posh Belgrano square into the **Feria de Artesanías de Belgrano.** Alpaca is a popular material here, both for jewelry and for adorning items like divided boxes for storing tea-bags. Other offerings include leather sandals and clogs, knitted ponchos, and wooden toys. If you're in town near Christmas this is a great place to buy nativity scenes and tree ornaments. ✉ *Juramento and Av. Cuba, Belgrano* ⊘ *Weekends 10–5.*

One of the last surviving European-style indoor food markets in town, the **Feria Modelo de Belgrano** is a gourmet's dream. The building has stood more or less unchanged since 1891, and its 30 stalls are the ideal place to ogle top national produce like Patagonian trout and lamb, porcini mushrooms, and stuffed meats. The cheese stalls sell creamy ricotta by the kilo and chunky wheels of *queso Mar del Plata*, an eminently snackable Gouda-style cheese. ✉ *Juramento 2527, at Ciudad de la Paz, Belgrano* ⊘ *Mon.–Sat. 8–1 and 5–8:30, Sun. 8–1.*

The best handicrafts in town and an authentic gaucho atmosphere make the trek west to the traditional **Feria de Mataderos** well worth it. As well as stalls selling great-value mates, *asado* knives, *boleadoras* (gaucho lassos), and leather goods, there are usually traditional dance performances. Look out for real-life gauchos wearing woolen berets, scarves, and baggy pants wandering round with a horse or two in tow. Part of the experience is chomping through a *vaciopan* (dripping steak sandwich) from the immense barbecue; wash it down with a plastic beaker of *vino patero* (semi-sweet red wine). The subte doesn't go to Mataderos; take Bus 126 from outside the Retiro train station, or take a taxi (about 15 pesos from downtown). ✉ *Lisandro de la Torre at Avenida de los Corrales, Mataderos* ⊘ *Sun. 10–5.*

try's best and exclusive to the shop. The Pulenta Gran Corte 2003, from Mendoza, is highly recommended. Incredibly savvy staffers will guide you, and should you buy more than your suitcase can hold, they can FedEx up to 12 bottles anywhere in the world. ⊠ *Av. Alvear 1718, La Recoleta* ☎ *11/4816–3975* ⊕ *www.grandcru.com.ar.*

WOOL   **Claudia Giuliano.** The chunky-knit sweaters and cardigans rival Donna Karan's and at a fraction of the cost. If you fancy something more local, try the llama wool wraps or heavy woven ponchos in colors like coffee and chocolate—as warm as the beverages they evoke. The northern-Argentine *copla* music that plays lets you know where all this natural goodness originates. ⊠ *Ayacucho 1885, La Recoleta* ☎ *11/ 4804–2991.*

Palermo

Porteño fashionistas have turned their gaze from foreign brands to those from home. They prowl the cobbled streets of Palermo Viejo in search of that slinky little number no one else has yet. This is also a neighborhood for cool housewares: contemporary Argentine designers are showcased at Calma Chicha and Spoon, and Newton and Gropius sell great retro furniture. Competition for a dinky shop-front in one of the barrio's Spanish-style town houses is fierce. Parallel streets Honduras and El Salvador are full of such darlings of the vanguard clothing scene as Trosman, Cora Groppo, Nadine Zlotogora, and los Hermanos Estebecorena.

Take your time shopping—the whole point of Palermo is to wander and be seduced—then sit back and admire your finds at a café. School yourself in the latest Palermo trends with the free and funky *Mapas de Buenos Aires*, whose Palermo editions are divided into three: *indumentaria* (clothing and accessories), *equipamiento* (housewares), and *gastronomía* (eating and drinking). The maps are updated quarterly and are available in most Palermo boutiques.

Mall

★ **Alto Palermo.** A prime Palermo location, choice shops, and a pushy marketing campaign have made Alto Palermo popular. Giggly teenage hordes are seduced by its long, winding layout. Ladies who lunch sip espresso in the cafés of its top-level food hall. The 154 shops are particularly strong on local street-wear brands like Bensimon and Bowen for the boys and Akiabara, Ona Saez, and Rapsodia for the girls. Surf and skate store Cristobal Colón does as storming trade in board shorts and All-Stars; locally made versions of Puma and Adidas streamlined footwear disappear fast despite high price tags. Other international names include the ubiquitous Levi's as well as Spanish megabrand Zara, famous for its cut-price versions of catwalk looks that go on sale almost before the models are off the runway. The mall also has a cinema; if you prefer live entertainment, the Avenida Santa Fe atrium has a Ticketek booth. ⊠ *Av. Santa Fe 3251, at Av. Colonel Díaz, Palermo* ☎ *11/ 5777–8000* ⊕ *www.altopalermo.com.ar* Ⓜ *D to Bulnes.*

Specialty Shops

ACCESSORIES &   **Etnia.** Upscale hippy chicks love Etnia's classier take on the dangly earrings and big necklaces that fill Buenos Aires's street markets—and so
JEWELRY

does Saks Fifth Avenue, which stocks their jewelry. Unique to the shop are Maremagnum's colorful blown-glass beads, which look like strings of candies ready to pop into your mouth. ☒ *El Salvador 4792, Palermo Viejo* ☎ *11/4831–9003* ⊕ *www.etniaccessories.com.*

Exelens. Fallout bunker meets spaceship in this eyewear store's minimal interior. The absolute cream of local specs is arranged along backlit concrete shelves—wide rectangular numbers are the most favored. ☒ *Armenia 1636, Palermo Viejo* ☎ *11/4832–0373* ⊕ *www.exelens.com.*

★ **Infinit.** Infinit's signature thick acrylic frames are favored by graphic designers and models alike. If the classic black rectangular versions are too severe for you, the same shape comes in a range of candy colors and two-tones. Bug-eye shades with lenses in shades of 1970s brown are perfect ray-stoppers. ☒ *Thames 1602, Palermo Viejo* ☎ *11/4831–7070* ⊕ *www.infinitnet.com.*

María Medici. Industrial-looking brushed silver rings and necklaces knitted from fine stainless steel cables are some of the attractions at this tiny shop. María Medici also combines silver with primary-colored resin to make solid, unusual-looking rings. ☒ *Niceto Vega 4619, Palermo Viejo* ☎ *11/4773–2283.*

La Mercería. This sumptuous haberdashery is a shrine luxury. You can count on losing yourself in its low-lit depths amid piles of floaty Indian scarves or fur-lined leather gloves: everything here begs to be touched. Even more hands-on are the reels of lace trims and sequined edging that line the walls, and the jewel-tone silk flowers are perfect enough to adorn just about anything. ☒ *Armenia 1609, Palermo Viejo* ☎ *11/4831–8558.*

Positivo. Among the kitsch offerings at Positivo are the metallic mate vessels and thermos-flasks that come in enough garish colors for you to match them to any outfit. Satin handbags covered in little buttons are also winners. ☒ *Honduras 4820 Palermo Viejo* ☎ *11/4831–2451* ⊕ *www.positivodesign.com.ar.*

Salsipuedes Condimentos. Frothy bead and fishing-line necklaces and plastic bangles from the 1960s are some of the fun but cheap accessories here. The selection of shoes and slippers changes constantly—you may find brocade Mary Janes or leather flip-flops—and fabric purses complete the offerings. ☒ *Honduras 4874, Palermo Viejo* ☎ *11/4833–9403.*

ART & ANTIQUES **Braga Menéndez.** Owner Florencia Braga Menéndez has created a world-class space where a core group of 30 artists is fast becoming popular with independent collectors. Curious browsers get a warm welcome, and serious buyers get highly professional guidance as well as assistance with the complicated business of exporting purchases. ☒ *Humboldt 1574, Palermo Hollywood* ☎ *11/4775–5577* ⊕ *www.galeriabm.com.*

Daniel Maman Fine Art. This gallery is severe, but try to let the art do the talking. Expect avant-garde artists like the Mondongo collective, whose wacky collages mix resin-encased *fiambres* (cold cuts) with textiles and X-rated photos. London's Tate Modern and New York's MoMA both snapped up a work for their permanent collections. Follow in their footsteps and trust Daniel Maman's unfailing nose for talent. ☒ *Av. del Libertador 2475, Palermo* ☎ *11/4804–3700* ⊕ *www.danielmaman.com.*

Oda (Objetos de Artistas). Making beauty a necessity and necessity beautiful is the philosophy at Oda, where the artist-designed clothes, bags, and trinkets are wearable and collectable. The exquisitely heavy blown-glass paperweights could spice up even the dullest desk. ⊠ *Costa Rica 4670, Palermo Viejo* ☎ *11/4831–7403.*

BEAUTY **Sabater Hermanos.** Third-generation Spanish soap makers are behind this small simple shop that sells nothing but—let's come clean about it—soap. There's no choice but to get into a lather over the trays of no-nonsense rectangles that come in heavenly sandalwood, chocolate, old lavender, and tea-rose, to name a few. You can also buy your soap in brightly colored petals, ideal for bath-tub sprinkling. ⊠ *Gurruchaga 1821, Palermo Viejo* ☎ *11/4833–3004* ⊕ *www.shnos.com.ar.*

BOOKS **Prometeo.** It's a low-key corner store frequented by trendy design types and bearded literature students alike. Non-Spanish speakers need not despair: this is the place to pick up diminutive flipbooks by Cine de Dedo, which poke good-natured fun at such icons of Argentine culture as tango and steaks. The larger *Gol del Siglo* flipbook depicts Maradona's celebrated goal against England in the 1986 World Cup. ⊠ *Honduras 4912, Palermo Viejo* ☎ *11/4832–0466* ⊕ *www.prometeolibros.com.ar.*

CLOTHING: MEN'S **Bolivia.** Porteño dandies know that Bolivia is *the* place for metrosexual fashion relief. Floral prints feature big: expect them on shirts, leather belts, and Filofaxes. Aged denim, top-quality silk-screen T-shirts, vintage military jackets, and even hand-knit slippers are among the items that fill this converted Palermo townhouse almost to bursting. ⊠ *Gurruchaga 1581 Palermo Viejo* ☎ *11/4832–6284* ⊕ *www.boliviaonline. com.ar.*

★ **Félix.** Waxed floorboards covered with worn rugs, exposed brick, and aging cabinets are the backdrop to the shop's very cool clothes. Beat-up denim, crisp shirts, and knits that look like a loving granny whipped them up are among the metrosexual delights. ⊠ *Gurruchaga 1670, Palermo Viejo* ☎ *11/4832–2994* ⊕ *www.felixba.com.ar.*

Hermanos Estebecorena. The approach to design at this trendy streetwear store is 100% practical. All the flat-front shirts, pants, and rain jackets have pockets, seams, and buttons positioned for maximum utility. Everything looks pretty good, too, and the range of products, which includes footwear and underwear, makes this a one-stop guy shop. ⊠ *El Salvador 5960, Palermo Viejo* ☎ *11/4772–2145* ⊕ *www. hermanosestebecorena.com.*

Kristobelga. Lovers of Carhartt-style utility wear will find plenty of heavy-duty clothing at Kristobelga. As well as standard khakis and grays, the store also has carpenter trousers, tees in more upbeat colors, and hard-wearing canvas anoraks. ⊠ *Gurruchaga 1677, Palermo Viejo* ☎ *11/4831–6677* ⊕ *www.kristobelga.com.*

CLOTHING: MEN'S **Adidas Originals.** This is one of the few Adidas shops in the world to & WOMEN'S stock limited-edition items, though there may only ever be one in the shop at a time. If you're less fussy about other people being able to own the same clothes as you, Adidas's retro jogging jackets are still as cool as it comes. The "I heart" Buenos Aires T-shirt is a local gem. ⊠ *Malabia 1720, Palermo Viejo* ☎ *11/4831–0090* ⊕ *www.adidas.com/orginals.*

Antique Denim. Burberry meets Diesel at Antique Denim, where smart, dark jeans are worn with colored tweed jackets with leather elbow patches. The denim cuts are sharp and tailored, made for cruising the

1

town rather than crashing at home. ☒ *Gurruchaga 1692, Palermo Viejo* ☎ *11/4834–6829.*

A.Y. Not Dead. Rainbow vinyl, pearly fake snakeskin, and truck loads of nylon: it's all very synthetic at A.Y. Not Dead. Seen anywhere other than under a strobe, the clothes may be hard to take, but if you want to carve a space for yourself on a heaving club floor, shopping here could be the way forward. ☒ *Soler 4193, Palermo Viejo* ☎ *11/4866–4855* ⊕ *www.aynotdead.com.ar.*

Besteedo. If you like your clothes with a message, check out the T-shirts and hoodies at Besteedo, which has some of the quirkiest prints in town. It also sells a great line of retro items like funnel-neck coats and bowling shirts. ☒ *Costa Rica 4865, Palermo Viejo* ☎ *11/4833–1536.*

Mercer. There's no sign outside Mercer, but you can't miss the huge shop front covered with a crazy-quilt of colorful '70s tiles. Inside are reasonable priced Levi's-style jeans, which you can match with slick leather jackets, shirts, and screen-printed tees. ☒ *Gurruchaga 1686, Palermo Viejo* ☎ *11/4833–4587.*

Nadine Zlotogora. Bring your sense of humor to Nadine Zlotogora: her way-out designs are meant to be playful, though they're also exquisitely put together with prices to match. Sheer fabrics are heavily embroidered with organic-looking designs, then worn alone or over thin cotton. Even the menswear gets the tulle treatment: military-look shirts come with a transparent top-layer. ☒ *El Salvador 4638, Palermo Viejo* ☎ *11/ 4831–4203* ⊕ *www.nadinez.com.*

Nike Soho. You may know Nike inside-out and backwards, but the Palermo shop is unique: the recycled rooms of an old town house are the unlikely backdrop for the brand's more exclusive lines. Ultra-tech women's tees and flexible yoga shoes contrast with riotous floral wallpaper and mauve lace curtains. Battered paint-stripped walls behind a layer of chicken wire offset swoosh wear for the boys. ☒ *Gurruchaga 1615, Palermo Viejo* ☎ *11/4832–3555.*

Retro. The queen of this multibrand boutique is Lupe Posse, whose bright '80s-inspired T-shirt dresses are all about draping and plunging necklines. The Furtado label is lower key, centering on cute ultrafine cotton tees. For dedicated followers of *Flashdance* there are some unusual horizontal knits in glitter-specked wool, perfect for pairing with legwarmers. ☒ *Malabia 1583, Palermo Viejo* ☎ *11/4831–4141.*

Salamanca. Only the hippest pre-loved togs get a place in this sunny-yellow store, though the downside is that price-tags might seem hard to swallow for second-hand gear. ☒ *Pasaje Santa Rosa 5038, Palermo Viejo* ☎ *11/4832–3666.*

Seco. Singing in the rain is encouraged at Seco, where all the clothes are designed to get wet. See-through plastic macs come with matching southwesters worth risking a soaking for. Cutesy shoulder capes are probably more suitable for a light drizzle. For puddle-jumping bliss, how about some red vinyl Wellingtons? ☒ *Armenia 1646, Palermo Viejo* ☎ *11/ 4833–1166* ⊕ *www.secorainwear.com.*

★ **Varanasi.** The structural perfection of Varanasi's clothes is a clue that the brains behind them originally trained as architects. Equally telling is the minimal, cavernous shop, fronted by acres of plate-glass. Inside, pleated shot silk and unadorned bias cuts are some of the night-out joys that local celebs shop for—indeed, few others can afford to. ⊠ *El Salvador 4761, Palermo Viejo* ☎ *11/4833–5147* ⊕ *www.varanasi-online. com.*

CLOTHING: **Adorhada Guillermina.** Local cinema and graphic design students love
WOMEN'S Adorhada Guillermina's '80s-feel clothes. Box-pleated denim skirts are edgy but practical. More unusual materials such as metallic plush are also on hand. Dress things up or down with one of a hundred tops in fine, bias-cut T-shirt fabric. ⊠ *El Salvador 4723, Palermo Viejo* ☎ *11/ 4831–2553* ⊕ *www.adorhadaguillermina.com.ar.*

La Aurora. At La Aurora it's clear that work clothes don't have to be drab. Details like geometric embroidery or satin trims spice up the clean lines and natural fabrics of Birkin's shirts and skirts. Even the most basic of trench coats stands out here in emerald green. Glass-topped cabinets display Mariana Arbusti's beautiful cotton underwear with contrasting lace trims. ⊠ *Honduras 4838, Palermo Viejo* ☎ *11/4833–4965.*

Cora Groppo. One of the queens of porteño haute-couture, Cora Groppo made her name designing flirty cocktail dresses with lots of cleavage and swooping skirts. Her small prêt-à-porter Palermo store sells lower-key clothing, though the whisper-thin cotton jersey most things are made of doesn't do much for those without catwalk figures. ⊠ *El Salvador 4696, Palermo Viejo* ☎ *11/4832–5877* ⊕ *www.coragroppo.com.*

Fortunata Alegría. The sparse, all-white interior of this Palermo stalwart make it easy to appreciate the fresh colors of the clothes it sells. Many of the A-line skirts and deep-V tops are adorned with simple geometric line-and-ball designs. Winter sees bright knits come with huge buttons and collars ideal for snuggling down into. ⊠ *Gurruchaga 1739, Palermo Viejo* ☎ *11/4831–8197* ⊕ *www.fortunataalegria.com.ar.*

Marcelo Senra. Irregular natural linen, heavy hand-knit sweaters, cow-hair boots around—it's all about texture at Marcelo Senra. At the front of an old town house, beige walls and a fountain set the tone for the clean, low-profile but elegant designs. Natural leather accessories complement the clothes' earthy palette. ⊠ *Gurruchaga 1519, Palermo Viejo* ☎ *11/4833–6230* ⊕ *www.marcelosenra.com.*

María Alló. Trashy but nice is the best way to describe María Allo's full-on designs. Although the black-gingham skirt suit with blood-red lace trim might be hard to wear to work, less outré possibilities include pearl leather cowboy boots, ideal for glamming up your jeans. ⊠ *Armenia 1637, Palermo Viejo* ☎ *11/4831–3733.*

María Cher. Let the yards of racks draw you into this lanky shop, where simple cuts and natural fabrics make urban working clothes feel just a tad Jedi-like. The earthy, deconstructed look of the linen cache-coeurs and printed canvas skirts is also due to details like unfinished hems or exposed seams. ⊠ *El Salvador 4714, Palermo Viejo* ☎ *11/4833–4736* ⊕ *www.maria-cher.com.ar.*

María Marta Facchinelli. The designs of this Palermo goddess are feminine without being girly. Shirts and jackets are close-fitting but not vampish and come in pastels. Evening dresses follow the same lines: those done in fabrics like heavily-draped rose satin are glamorous but not flashy. ⊠ *El Salvador 4741, Palermo Viejo* ☎ *11/4831–8424* ⊕ *www.facchinelli.com.*

Objeto. Creative use of fabrics and quirky crafting make the everyday clothes Objeto sells something special. Their feminine T-shirts are textile collages combining silk screening and appliqué techniques; their skirts and jackets often mix new materials with original '60s offcuts. If you like to make a splash on rainy days, check out the waterproof jackets cut from gingham-print tablecloths complete with photos of food. ⊠ *Gurruchaga 1649, Palermo Viejo* ☎ *11/4834–6866.*

Pesqueira. Big girls and little girls can thrill together at the quirky but feminine silk-screen T-shirts that are Pesqueira's signature garments. Most have beautifully transferred photos of objects like an old Pentax that looks like it's hung round your neck. Simple casual clothes in pastels—a blush-colored denim sailor jacket, for instance—are here to combine with the tees. ⊠ *Armenia 1493, Palermo Viejo* ☎ *11/4833–7218.*

Salsipuedes. Carrie Bradshaw would have loved the cocktail dresses of Aida Sirinian, one of several designers showcased in this party-frock boutique. Geometrically embroidered turquoise satin with tulle underskirts and 1930s-style bias-cut velvet are worth organizing a ball for. Salsipuedes also sells hard-to-find Manto Abrigo woolen coats—one-off, hand-made designs from the north of Argentina. ⊠ *Honduras 4814, Palermo Viejo* ☎ *11/4831–8467.*

Tienda Tres. Three designers, three styles; hence the *tres* of this shop's name. What the chic clothes of Verónica Alfie, María Lombardi, and Flavia Martini have in common, though, are excellent cuts and a feminine feel. Dress up any of their outfits with satin-beribboned fur clutches that are strokeable enough to become your new pet. ⊠ *Armenia 1655, Palermo Viejo* ☎ *11/4831–4193.*

★ **Trosman.** Highly unusual beadwork is the only adornment on designer Jessica Trosman's simple clothes. There's nothing small and sparkling at hand, though: her beads are smooth, inch-wide acrylic orbs, that, when grouped together, look futuristic but organic at the same time. A toned-down palette, soft natural fabrics, and draped necklines are taking Trosman international: look for stores in Paris and Tokyo. ⊠ *Armenia 1998, Palermo Viejo* ☎ *11/4833–3085* ⊕ *www.trosman.com.*

HOUSEWARES **Arte Étnico Argentino.** Rich, naturally dyed weavings and hand-hewn
★ wooden basins are some of the things made by indigenous craftsmen at this shop-cum-gallery. Owner Ricardo Paz handpicks items like exquisite woolen rugs, the most transportable of the shop's temptations. ⊠ *El Salvador 4600, Palermo Viejo* ☎ *11/4833–6661* ⊕ *www.arteetnicoargentino.com.*

★ **Calma Chicha.** Calma Chicha's simple but fun approach to household items is flourishing in this warehouse-like shop. Signature pear-shaped bean bags—covered in denim, bright canvas, or leather—are ideal for living-room chilling. Complete the scene with folding butterfly chairs in matching fabrics. Quirky local bits and bobs are arrayed on trestle tables. Unusual gifty items include an oh-so-retro *pingüino* (penguin-shaped wine jug). ⊠ *Honduras 4925, Palermo Viejo* ☎ *11/4831–1818* ⊕ *www.calmachicha.com.*

★ **Gropius 1920–2000.** Always hankered after furnishings by the likes of Mies van de Rohe, Charles and Ray Eames, Arne Jacobsen, or Pensi but never been able to afford them? Retro relief is on hand at Gropius, which

CLOSE UP

Big Spenders

IF YOU'RE A SHOPPER who just isn't satisfied by small-fry spending, why not splash out on something a little more extravagant, like, say . . . a house? It may sound funny, but Buenos Aires's latest shopping trend is led by a horde of foreigners who are acquiring porteño pied-à-terres, either as second homes or as investments. Although tango-obsessed visitors spearheaded the tendency, now more and more outsiders who simply love the Buenos Aires lifestyle are getting in on the action.

Most buyers look for a classic apartment from the 1920s, '30s, or '40s, with 10-foot ceilings, crafted wooden doors and windows, and acres of gleaming floorboards. The most desirable districts are San Telmo, Palermo, and Recoleta, though there's been a surge in the sales of glitzy new Puerto Madero apartments. Prices vary considerably from district to district. Expect to pay from $900 per square meter (10.7 square feet) in San Telmo and about twice that in La Recoleta; equally attractive properties in lesser-known areas cost a lot less.

According to Reynolds Homes, a well-established real estate agency catering to foreigners, those who buy apartments over the Internet sight-unseen tend to go for cheaper

properties at around the $70,000 mark. Buyers who pound the pavement, end up being tempted into spending more: $150,000 on average. Paying cash in dollars can get you a hefty discount, though bringing cash into the country incurs a massive 1.5% levy. Although there are few restrictions imposed on non-Argentines buying property, the process can be a headache so it's best to deal with an agency that can smooth out all the bumps.

Years of experience have made **Reynolds Propiedades** a failsafe option for foreign buyers. Reynolds works with other estate agents to increase the number of properties it can offer, and then guides you through the paperwork. Staffers can even help you furnish your house when you're done. ✉ *Junin 1655 3rd floor, La Recoleta* ☎ *11/4801–9291* ⊕ *www.argentinahomes.com.*

If you feel guilty about taking the property out of the hands of locals, you can go easy on your conscience at **Ojo Propiedades,** where all profits go to the Red Cross. This hip outfit deals primarily with Palermo properties and has lots of foreign customers. ✉ *Serrano 1503, Palermo Viejo* ☎ *11/4832–4040* ⊕ *www. ojopropiedades.com.*

---

sells practically perfect replicas of the 20th century's greatest designers at relatively affordable prices. Its gravel-floor warehouse down the road has the real thing in mint condition; prices soar. ✉ *Honduras 5851, Palermo Hollywood* ☎ *11/4774–1535* ✉ *Honduras 6027, Palermo Hollywood* ☎ *11/4774–2094* ⊕ *www.gropiusdesign-1920-2000.com.*
Milagros. All the ingredients for a tea party are available at Milagros's huge trackside warehouse, which is stuffed to bursting with the girliest housewares in town. Patchwork and chintz dominate the quilts, crochet bedcovers, and velvet cushions in colors like baby blue, lilac, and—of course—pale pink. Larger-scale items, which the store can ship to you,

include ironwork bedsteads and glass chandeliers. ✉ *Gorriti 5417, Palermo Viejo* ☎ *11/4899–0991* ⊕ *www.milagrosresta.com.ar.*

Newton. Fans of designers like Ray and Charles Eames or Le Corbusier will be in chair heaven at Newton. Gleaming white acrylic and chrome creations are piled to the ceiling, and although things here don't come cheap, it's all still a bargain compared to what you'd find back home. Indeed, the store is no stranger to foreign design-vultures and can ship furniture. ✉ *Honduras 5360, Palermo Viejo* ☎ *11/4833–4007* ⊕ *www. newtonba.com.ar.*

Reina Batata. Many of Palermo's trendiest restaurants commission their tableware from Reina Batata, where simple white china has such patterns as retro flowers or good fairies. The slice-shaped pizza plates are a stylish way to serve Argentina's favorite fast food. ✉ *Gurruchaga 1785, Palermo Viejo* ☎ *11/4831–7572* ⊕ *www.reinabatata.com.ar.*

Spoon. A variety of established local designers sell their sleek, Ron Arad–style items through Spoon. Although a boxy leather chaise-longue may be too big to take away, dinner services decorated with motifs like ants and dragonflies will fit in a suitcase. ✉ *Honduras 4876, Palermo Viejo* ☎ *11/4831–3786* ⊕ *www.spoon.com.ar.*

LEATHER **Devacas.** "From the cows" is roughly how this corner store's name translates. It's apt: everything is made from Argentine cow skin and leather. In addition to your straightforward attaché cases, the store sells beautifully crafted chocolate-color mate carrying cases and novel cow-skin covered cocktail shakers. ✉ *Gurruchaga 1660, Palermo Viejo* ☎ *11/4831–6570.*

Fodor'sChoice **Humawaca.** After years of operating from a showroom for a privileged
★ few, the city's trendiest leather brand finally has its own shop. Mere mortals can now delight in the signature circular leather handbags, cowhide clogs, and butterfly-shaped backpacks. Price tags may make you gulp. ✉ *El Salvador 4692, Palermo Viejo* ☎ *11/4832–2662* ⊕ *www. humawaca.com.*

★ **Uma.** Light, butter-soft leather takes very modern forms here, with geometric stitching the only adornment on jackets and asymmetric bags that might come in rich violet in winter and aqua-blue in summer. The top-quality footwear includes teetering heels and ultra-simple boots and sandals with, mercifully, next to no elevation. ✉ *Honduras 5225, Palermo Viejo* ☎ *11/4832–2122* ⊕ *www.umacuero.com.*

LINGERIE **Amor Latino.** Amor Latino does stylish and oh-so-hot underwear and negligées—sexy rather than sturdy. There are even high-heeled slippers for tripping from the sofa to the bed. Look for sets in all manner of fun, tactile materials—whisper-light Lycra, gleaming satin, violet plush. The 1940s-inspired figure-hugging satin nightgowns are pure bedroom glamour. ✉ *Gorriti 4925, Palermo Viejo* ☎ *11/4831–6787* ⊕ *www.amorlatino.com.ar.*

Bendita Tu Eres. The name translates as "Blessed among Women," and its colorful cotton knickers edged with lace are divine for every day. When you want to make an impression, there are funkier sets in gold lamé or animal-print tulle with red lace trim. The rose smell that fills the air comes from the bath salts and body creams at the back of the store. ✉ *Thames 1555, Palermo Viejo* ☎ *11/4834–6123.*

Victoria Cossy. Flaunting it is the order of the day at Victoria Cossy, whose lingerie comes only in sheer materials. Her white tulle *culottes,* edged with lace and a dash of sequins, is a cross between girly briefs and a sexy string. Printed mesh panties, bras, and crop tops are comfortable and playful. ⊠ *Armenia 1499, Palermo Viejo* ☎ *11/4831–5565.*

PAPER & **Papelera Palermo.** Piles of handmade paper, leather-bound diaries, and
STATIONERY vintage notebooks are arrayed on simple trestle tables. Writing implements range from old-world dipping pens to chunky pencils, and the soft leather artists' rolls are a luxurious way to carry them around. The store often showcases work by top engravers and graphic artists, who return the favor by designing the covers of sketchbooks. ⊠ *Honduras 4945 Palermo Viejo* ☎ *11/4833–3081* ⊕ *www.papelerapalermo.com.ar.*

SHOES **Josefina Ferroni.** Points that taper out way beyond the norm and thickly wedged heels are some of the trademarks. For stepping out in a crowd try the high heels in metallic leather with a contrasting trim or the slick black boots with a detail down the back that looks like leather ticker-tape. ⊠ *Armenia 1471, Palermo Viejo* ☎ *11/4831–4033* ⊕ *www.josefinaferroni.com.ar.*

Mandarine. High-heeled spats and brightly colored cowboy boots are some of the fun shoes here. Sturdy, top-quality leather, careful crafting, and reasonable prices ensure good value for the money. If your size is out of stock, ask whether the branch around the corner on Gurruchaga has it. ⊠ *Honduras 4940, Palermo Viejo* ☎ *11/4833–0094.*

Mariano Toledo. There's something very Vivienne Westwood about the arching high-heel brogues at Mariano Toledo, only a good few inches lower. Draping is his other forte: affordable party dresses hang in semi-sheer, toga-like folds; colors like aubergine and lime are arresting. ⊠ *Armenia 1564, Palermo Viejo* ☎ *11/4831–4861* ⊕ *www.marianotoledo.com.ar.*

Mishka. At this long-time Palermo favorite your feet can be sexy in high-heel lace-ups or brash in metallic pirate boots. The footwear comes in leather as well as in fabrics like brocade. Most styles are very narrow—truly flattering to some, merely painful to others. ⊠ *El Salvador 4673, Palermo Viejo* ☎ *11/4833–6566.*

Mourelos. The only adornments at this hole-in-the-wall boutique are elegant, understated leather shoes. Men can dress up with mildly gleaming chestnut city shoes or play it cool in camper-ish trainers. Although many of the women's shoes have extremely pointed toes, there's nothing punishing about the heels. ⊠ *Armenia 1693, Palermo Viejo* ☎ *11/4833–6222* ⊕ *www.mourelos.com.ar.*

TOYS **Recursos Infantiles.** Everything is designed with li'l ones in mind, right up to the small tables and kid-centered menu at the in-store café. Beautifully illustrated picture-books delight even non-Spanish speakers, and wood is the material du jour in the wonderful yesteryear toys. The small-scale mate sets by D'ak—complete with mini kettle and thermos flask—come ready for action in a colorful bag. ⊠ *J. L. Borges 1766, Palermo Viejo* ☎ *11/4834–6177.*

Sopa de Príncipe. Sopa de Príncipe does funky fabric toys. Heavy stitching on cotton and flannel gives their dolls an appealingly punky look, ideal for kids who don't like their toys too saccharine. Crates down one wall are filled with an ark-worthy selection of calico animals—great, easy-to-pack gifts. ✉ *Thames 1719, Palermo Viejo* ☎ *11/4831–8505* ⊕ *www.sopadeprincipe.com.ar.*

WINE **La Finca.** Great value finds, including unusual wines from boutique vine-
★ yards are the specialty. Like their stock, the staff hails from Mendoza, capital of Argentine oenology, and they're a friendly, knowledgeable crew. Past the rustic shelving piled high with bottles are a few tables where you can sample the produce of vineyards like Carmelo Patti or Bramare, accompanied by a light *picada* (snack) of goat cheese and black olives, also from Mendoza. ✉ *Honduras 5147, Palermo Viejo* ☎ *11/4832–3004.*

Terroir. A wine-lovers heaven is tucked away in this white stone Palermo town house. Expert staffers are on hand to help you make sense of the massive selection of Argentine wine, which includes collector's gems like the 1999 Angélica Zapata Cabernet Sauvignon. Terroir ships all over the world. ✉ *Buschiazzo 3040, Palermo* ☎ *11/4778–3443* ⊕ *www.terroir.com.ar.*

WOOL **María Aversa.** There's a touch of gypsy in María Aversa's colorful knitwear, and the two-story town house that houses the store gives you plenty of room to roam, too. In addition to large-gauge knits, look for more unusual offerings, such as a velvet jacket with crocheted sleeves. ✉ *El Salvador 4580, Palermo Viejo* ☎ *11/4833–0073* ⊕ *www.mariaaversa.com.ar.*

Ñann. Although the woolen clothes at this store are fit to hang on the wall as a craft-piece, you'll have more fun wearing them. You can face the winter in a full-length woven coat with unfinished hems or greet spring with an Edwardian-style shoulder cape. Super-soft llama-wool kiddie ponchos in acid colors are enviable playground-wear. ✉ *Serrano 1523, Palermo Viejo* ☎ *11/4831–8835* ⊕ *www.nannargentina.com.*

Priscia. Heavy, rustic cardigans are this store's forte, but there are also more unusual knits, such as bright wool scarves with colored fur strips woven into them. ✉ *Honduras 4847, Palermo Viejo* ☎ *11/4832–3179* ⊕ *www.priscia.com.ar.*

BUENOS AIRES ESSENTIALS

Transportation

By Brian
Byrnes

BY AIR

International flights arrive at and depart from Aeropuerto Internacional Ministro Pistarini de Ezeiza, known simply as Ezeiza (EZE), 47 km (29 mi) west of downtown Buenos Aires. Ezeiza is served by foreign carriers as well as domestic lines with international routes. Upon leaving the country you must pay an $18 departure tax inside the airport after checking in for your flight; cash (pesos, dollars, or euros) and major credit or debit cards are accepted.

Flights within Argentina and those to and from Uruguay generally depart from Aeroparque Jorge Newbery (AEP), known as Aeroparque, about

15 minutes north of downtown. The departure tax for flights to Uruguay is $8, which is paid at the airport after check-in.

🛈 **Aeroparque Jorge Newbery (AEP)** ☎ 11/5480-6111 ⊕ www.aa2000.com.ar. **Aeropuerto Internacional Ministro Pistarini de Ezeiza (EZE)** ☎ 11/5480-6111 ⊕ www. aa2000.com.ar.

AIRPORT Information counters within the airports can help you choose among
TRANSFERS the various licensed transport services that run between the airports and into town. Generally, *colectivos* (city buses) are cheapest, but you're only allowed two bags. You can catch the buses outside Terminal B at Ezeiza (2 pesos; two hours to downtown) and directly outside Aeroparque's main entrance (80 ¢; 15 minutes to downtown)

Private bus or van service, with scheduled departures, costs about 25 pesos per person to downtown from Ezeiza and about 10 pesos from Aeroparque to downtown. Manuel Tienda Leon provides comfortable, reliable bus service from Ezeiza every 30 minutes to various spots downtown. *Remises* (unmarked cars with drivers that work with prearranged fixed prices) run around 60 pesos from Ezeiza and 15 pesos from Aeroparque; they're limited to four passengers. Metered taxis, available at the sidewalk outside the terminals, can be steeper depending on traffic.

The main highway connecting Ezeiza with the city is the Autopista Ricchieri, which you can reach by taking either Autopista 25 de Mayo out of the city or the Avenida General Paz, which circles the entire city. The trip from downtown to Ezeiza takes around 45 minutes. Note that most flights to the United States depart Buenos Aires in the evening, so plan to offset afternoon traffic snarls with at least an hour of travel time to Ezeiza.

There are several routes to Aeroparque from downtown—about a 15-minute trip. The easiest way is to take Avenida Libertador north to Avenida Sarmiento, and then take a right and follow it until Costanera Rafael Obligado. The airport will be on your left. Traffic isn't usually an issue. A private car will cost around 20 pesos, van service about 10 pesos.

Allow 45 minutes for travel between the two airports. Aeroparque is near Avenida General Paz, which circles the entire city and can connect you with the Autopista Ricchieri toward Ezeiza. A private car will cost around 50 pesos; a van will cost roughtly 25 pesos.

🛈 **Bus Info Manuel Tienda León** ☎ 11/4383-4454 or 0810/888-5366 ⊕ www.tiendaleon. com.ar.

BY BOAT

Vessels crossing the Río de la Plata between Buenos Aires and Uruguay often sell out, particularly on summer weekends. Book a few days ahead at ticket sales offices or with a credit card via phone. Buquebus has twice-daily service for passengers and vehicles between Buenos Aires and Colonia and Montevideo, with continuing bus service to Piriápolis, Punta del Este, and other spots on the Uruguayan coast. The three-hour journey to Colonia costs 100 pesos round trip. The voyage to more distant Montevideo still only takes three hours (the boat's faster) and costs 310 pesos round trip. FerryLineas's twice-daily one-hour hydrofoil trips to Colonia cost 180 pesos round trip. Both companies operate at the same Puerto Madero dock.

🚢 **Buquebus** ✉ Av. Antartida Argentina 821, Puerto Madero ✉ Patio Bullrich Shopping Mall, Av. Libertador 750, La Recoleta ☎ 11/4316-6550 ⊕ www.buquebus.com. **FerryLineas Argentina** ✉ Av. Antartida Argentina 821, Puerto Madero ☎ 11/4314-2300 ⊕ www.ferrylineas.com.uy.

BY BUS

ARRIVING & DEPARTING Most long-distance and international buses use the Estación Terminal de Omnibus in Retiro. The terminal houses more than 60 companies, arranged by destinations served, not by name. Rates vary according to distance, services, and season; compare prices before purchasing.

🚌 **Estación Terminal de Omnibus** ✉ Av. Ramos Mejía 1680, Retiro ☎ 11/4310-0700.

GETTING AROUND Colectivos connect the city's barrios and greater Buenos Aires. You're assured a seat on a *diferencial* bus (indicated by a sign on the front); they run less frequently than colectivos and are more expensive. Stops are every other block (200 meters [656 feet] apart) and are marked by small, easy-to-miss metal signs citing number of the bus line. Buses, which are generally safe, run 24 hours a day, although service is less frequent at night.

Hail your bus and let the driver know your destination; then insert your coins in the machine (exact change isn't necessary, but coins are), which will print your ticket. Fares are 80¢ within the city, 1.25 to 1.65 pesos outside the city; diferencials cost 2 pesos. There are no daily or weekly discount passes.

Once on board, head for the back, which is where you exit. A small bell on the grab bar lets you signal for a stop. Don't depend on drivers for much assistance; they're busy navigating traffic. You can purchase a *Guia T,* an essential guide to the routes, at any news kiosk, or visit the Spanish-language colectivo Web site for info.

🚌 **Colectivo** ⊕ www.loscolectivos.com.ar.

BY CAR

Avenida General Paz completely encircles Buenos Aires. If you're driving into the city, you'll know you're in Buenos Aires proper once you cross this road. If you're entering from the north, chances are you will be on the Ruta Panamericana, which has wide lanes and good lighting. The quickest way from downtown to Ezeiza Airport is Autopista 25 de Mayo to Autopista Ricchieri. The R2 (Ruta 2) takes you to the Atlantic beach resorts in and around Mar del Plata.

Porteños drive with verve and a disdain for the rules. Having a car in Buenos Aires is really more hassle than it's worth; there are ample taxis and public transportation options. If you're up to the challenge, however, drive defensively. And be cautious when approaching or exiting overpasses; there have been incidences of *ladrillazo* (brick throwing) for the purpose of theft. Daily rental rates range from around 75 pesos to 200 pesos, depending on the type of car and the distance you plan to travel.

A more convenient option than driving yourself is to have your travel agent or hotel arrange for a *remis* (car and driver), especially for a day's tour of the suburbs or nearby pampas. This service costs about 30–40 pesos per hour, sometimes with a three-hour minimum and an additional charge per kilometer (½ mi) if you drive outside the city limits. Remises usually end up being cheaper than cabs, especially during peak hours. If your driver is helpful and friendly, a 10% tip is appropriate.

PARKING Parking can be a problem in the city, though there are several underground municipal parking garages and numerous private ones. Look for a blue sign with an E (for *estacionamiento* [parking]). The cost is about 3–4 pesos for the first hour and 1–1.50 pesos for each additional half hour. Most malls have garages, which are usually free or give you a reduced rate with a purchase.

RULES OF THE ROAD Most driving rules in the United States apply here, but keep in mind the following: right turns on red are not allowed; never park on the left side of the street, where there's a yellow line on the curb, or near a bus stop; and left turns are seldom allowed, unless indicated. Where there are no traffic lights, intersections are a free-for-all, though vehicles coming from your right theoretically have right-of-way. During the week, Microcentro, the bustling commercial district bounded by Carlos Pellegrini, Avenida Córdoba, Avenida Leandro Alem, and Avenida de Mayo, is off-limits to all but public transit vehicles.

🚗Local Rental Agencies **Annie Millet** ⊠Av. Santa Fe 883, fl. 1, El Centro ☎11/6777-7777 ⊕ www.amillet.com.ar. **Gracia** ⊠ Paraguay 658, El Centro ☎ 11/4313-4844.

GVS ⊠ Leandro N. Alem 699, El Centro ☎ 11/4315-0777. **Localiza** ⊠ Av. Rivadavia 1126, El Centro ☎ 0800/999-2999 or 11/4382-9267 ⊕ www.localiza.com.ar. **Rent-a-Sol** ⊠ Av. Libertador 6553, Belgrano ☎ 11/4787-2140 or 11/4787-1414 ⊕ www.rent-a-sol. com.ar.

🚗 Remises **Annie Millet Transfers** ⊠ Av. Santa Fe 883, fl. 1, El Centro ☎ 11/6777-7777. **Remises Full-Time** ⊠ Paraguay 4552, Palermo Soho ☎ 11/4775-9596 or 11/4775-1011. **Remises REB** ⊠ Billinghurst 68, Palermo ☎ 11/4863-1226 or 11/4862-6271. **Remises Rioja** ⊠ Rioja 3023, Olivos ☎ 11/4794-4677. **Remises Universal** ⊠ 25 de Mayo 611, fl. 4, El Centro ☎ 11/4315-6555.

BY SUBTE

Single-ride tickets cost 70¢ to anywhere in the city; you can buy passes in stations for 1, 2, 5, or 10 trips or a rechargeable card. The subte shuts down around 11 PM and reopens at 5 AM.

Línea A travels beneath Avenida Rivadavía from Plaza de Mayo to Primera Junta and is serviced by handsome antique wooden cars. Línea B begins at Leandro Alem Station, in the financial district, and runs under Avenida Corrientes to Federico Lacroze Station. Línea C, under Avenida 9 de Julio, connects the two major train stations, Retiro and Constitución, making stops along the way in El Centro. Línea D runs from Catedral Station on Plaza de Mayo to Congreso de Túcuman in Belgrano. Línea E takes you from Bolívar Station, at Plaza de Mayo, to Plaza de los Virreyes, in the neighborhood of Chacabuco.

The subte is generally safe and pleasant. During morning and evening commuter hours, cars do get crowded, though. The stations are well-patrolled by police and many are decorated with artworks, including murals by Argentine artists. You'll likely hear musicians and see actors performing on trains and in the stations.

Metrovías ⊕ www.metrovias.com.ar.

BY TAXI

All taxis in Buenos Aires city are black and have yellow tops. An unoccupied one will have a small, red LIBRE sign on the lefthand side of its windshield. When hailing a taxi on the street make sure it says RADIO TAXI and that you see a CB antenna attached to the hood. Radio taxis are part of licensed fleets and are in constant contact with dispatchers; nonlicensed cabs are occasionally driven by unscrupulous men looking to rip off tourists; avoid them. If you telephone for a taxi, you'll have to wait a few minutes, but you can be sure of its origin and safety. Legally, all taxis are supposed to have working seatbelts, but this isn't always the case.

Meters start at 1.98 pesos and charge 22¢ per ¼ km (⅛ mi); you'll also end up paying for standing time spent at a light or in a traffic jam. From the central downtown area, it will cost you around 6 pesos to Recoleta, 5 pesos to San Telmo, 9 pesos to Palermo, and 11 pesos to Belgrano. Drivers don't expect tips; if you round up to the next peso and pay that fare, most drivers will be thrilled.

Taxi Companies Blue Way Taxi ☎ 11/4777-8888. **Cirtax Taxi** ☎ 11/4504-8440. **City Taxi** ☎ 11/4585-5544. **Su Taxi** ☎ 11/4635-2500.

BY TRAIN

Commuter rail lines provide extensive service throughout the city proper and the suburbs for a great price. A network of lines operated by six companies—Ferrobaires, Ferrovías, Metropolitano, Metrovías, Trenes de Buenos Aires, Tren de la Costa—spreads out from five central stations in Buenos Aires.

Most trains leave at regular 7- to 20-minute intervals, though there may be less frequent service for trains traveling long distances. Fares range from 35¢ to 1.50 pesos. Purchase tickets before boarding the train at ticket windows or through coin-operated machines at the stations. Hold on to your ticket until you reach the end of the line. If an official asks for your ticket and you don't have it, you'll have to pay a 3.50–6.50 pesos on-the-spot fine.

Estación Buenos Aires, in the city of Temperley, connects lines in the southern part of greater Buenos Aires; Metropolitano operates out of here. Two rail companies operate out of Estación Constitución. The Metropolitano rail line serves the southern part of greater Buenos Aires and extends to the city of La Plata. Ferrobaires serves the Atlantic coastal resorts, such as Mar del Plata, Pinamar, and Miramar.

Estación Federico Lacroze, in Belgrano, provides train service to the northeastern part of the city and greater Buenos Aires through the Metrovías rail company. Estación Once, in the city center, serves the western part of the city and greater Buenos Aires through Trenes de Buenos Aires. Ferrobaires provides train service to some cities in the provinces of Buenos Aires and La Pampa.

Trains running out of Estación Retiro, across from Plaza San Martín, serve the northern part of the city and greater Buenos Aires. Several rail companies operate from here: Ferrovías, Metropolitano, Trenes de Buenos Aires, and Tren de la Costa.

🚆 Commuter Lines **Ferrobaires** ☎ 11/4553-1295. **Ferrovías** ☎ 11/4511-8833. **Metropolitano** ☎ 0800/666-358-736 ⊕ www.tms.com.ar. **Metrovías** ☎ 11/4959-6800 or 0800/555-1616 ⊕ www.metrovias.com.ar. **Tren de la Costa** ☎ 11/4002-6000 ⊕ www.trendelacosta.com.ar. **Trenes de Buenos Aires** (TBA) ☎ 11/4317-4400 or 0800/ 3333-822 ⊕ www.tbanet.com.ar.

🚆 Commuter Stations **Estación Buenos Aires** ✉ Padre Mugica 426, Temperley ☎ 11/4244-2668. **Estación Constitución** ✉ Av. General Hornos 11, near San Telmo, Constitución ☎ 11/4304-0028. **Estación Federico Lacroze** ✉ Federico Lacroze 4181, Belgrano ☎ 11/4553-1916. **Estación Once** ✉ Av. Pueyrredón and Bartolomé Mitre, Balvanera ☎ 11/4861-0043. **Estación Retiro** ✉ Av. Ramos Mejía 1430, Retiro ☎ 11/4317-4400.

Contacts & Resources

BANKS & EXCHANGE SERVICES

Ever since the Argentine peso was devalued in 2002, U.S. dollars haven't been widely accepted, so you need pesos. In the Ezeiza airport you can exchange money at Casa Piano and Banco Nación in Terminal A on the ground level. You can also hit the ATM in Terminal A, extracting pesos at a decent exchange rate. If you're taking licensed transportation into town, you can pay in dollars or euros at the stands next to the arrival gates.

Of course, while conducting any financial transaction, be aware of your surroundings and don't flash cash on the street. Staffers at exchange houses will require a passport or ID card to conduct transactions. An easier option is to ask your hotel to change your money; most now offer better rates, rivaling those at exchange houses.

ATMS You can find ATMs throughout the city. Those that are part of the Banelco network are the most prevalent. They're identified by a burgundy sign, and you'll find them in banks, service stations, and malls.

🏧 **American Express** ✉ Arenales 707, El Centro ☎ 11/4310-3000. **Banco Piano** ✉ San Martín 345, El Centro ☎ 11/4394-2463. **BankBoston** ✉ Florida 99, El Centro ☎ 11/4820-2000. **Cambio America** ✉ Sarmiento 501, El Centro ☎ 11/4393-0054. **Citibank** ✉ Florida 199, El Centro ☎ 11/4329-1000. **Forex Cambio** ✉ M. T. de Alvear 540, El Centro ☎ 11/4010-2000. **HSBC Republic** ✉ Florida 201, El Centro ☎ 11/4320-2800. **Western Union** ✉ J. L. Borges 2472, Palermo ☎ 11/4777-1940.

EMERGENCIES

There's a pharmacy–indicated by a green cross—on nearly every block. Your hotel will be able to guide you to the nearest one. *Farmacias de turno* rotate 24-hour shifts or remain open 24 hours and will deliver to hotels in their area.

🚑 Emergency Services **Ambulance** ☎ 107. **Fire** ☎ 100. **Police** ☎ 101 or 11/4346-5770.

🏥 Hospitals **British Hospital** ✉ Pedriel 74, Barracas ☎ 11/4304-2052, 11/4334-9000 emergencies. **German Hospital** ✉ Av. Pueyrredon 1640, La Recoleta ☎ 11/4821-1700.

▪️ 24-Hour Pharmacies **Farmacia Cabildo** ✉ Av. Cabildo 1971, Belgrano ☎ 11/4781-8788. **Farmacia DeMaria** ✉ F. J. Sta. Maria de Oro 2927, Palermo ☎ 11/4778-7311. **Farmacia Luciani** ✉ Av. Las Heras 2002, La Recoleta ☎ 11/4803-6111. **Farmacity** ✉ Florida 474, El Centro ☎ 11/4322-7777. **Farmacity** ✉ Alicia M. de Justo 350, Puerto Madero ☎ 11/4313-0986.

INTERNET, MAIL & SHIPPING

Many places in Argentina have high-speed Internet access. Nearly every hotel in Buenos Aires has the Internet on computers in the lobby or business center that are available for free or for a fee. All the international hotels offer in-room connections. Wi-Fi isn't widely available, and service can be shaky. There are scores of Internet cafés, known as *locutorios*, throughout the city. Most have high-speed access and charge around 3 pesos an hour.

You can mail cards and packages from various convenience-type stores throughout town; pharmacies, phone centers, and malls also provide mail services, in addition to the post offices. Several local and international private couriers compete with the Correo Argentino (Argentine Post) with such services, as overnight mail, packaging, arranging money wires and telegrams, and tracking certified letters.

▪️ Internet Cafés ✉ H.Yrigoyen 971, El Centro ☎ 11/4331-0338. ✉ Av. 25 de Mayo 843, El Centro ☎ 11/4343-2726. ✉ Lima 7, El Centro ☎ 11/5093-4135. ✉ Godoy Cruz 2767, Palermo ☎ 11/5237-5710. ✉ F. J. Sta. Maria de Oro 2744, Palermo ☎ 11/6775-1706.

▪️ Courier Services **DHL** ✉ Moreno 927, El Centro ☎ 0810/2222-345. **Federal Express** ✉ 25 de Mayo 386, El Centro ☎ 11/4630-0300. **UPS** ✉ Pte. Luis Saenz Peña 1351, Constitución ☎ 11/4339-2877 or 0800/222-2877.

▪️ Post Offices **Belgrano** ✉ Av. Cabildo 2349 ☎ 11/4784-2590 ⊘ Weekdays 8-8. **El Centro** ✉ Sarmiento 151 ☎ 11/4316-3000 ⊕ www.correoargentino.com.ar. **La Recoleta** ✉ Av. Las Heras 2863 ☎ 11/4802-4598.

Excursions from Buenos Aires

Trips to Uruguay, Buenos Aires Province, the Coast & Iguazú Falls

WORD OF MOUTH

"If you like to be in a quiet place and experience life like it was years back, then the area around Colonia—even Colonia itself—will do."
—Graziella5b

". . . Our travel photos from Iguazú don't do it justice. Its beauty is breathtaking."
—IgorVodov

"We spent one afternoon in San Antonio de Areco, which is an extremely nice small town with interesting museums. I recommend the experience."
—lilla

"Mar del Plata is a very nice city, but Pinamar and Cariló are smaller, cuter towns."
—hellagirl

Revised by
Victoria
Patience

To hear porteños talk of Buenos Aires, you'd think Argentina stops where the city ends. Not far beyond Buenos Aires, however, the skies open up and the huge grasslands of the pampas begin, stretching far beyond the horizon. When European settlers arrived in Argentina, they flocked to these rich, fertile soils to start their farms; these days the plains are still dotted with small towns where gaucho traditions are alive and well.

Ranchland gives way to watery wonders to the north of Buenos Aires, where a network of rivers and tributaries form the delta of the Paraná river, lined with luscious tropical vegetation and accessible only by boat. If you like your natural wonders supersized, take a short flight to Iguazú's hundreds of roaring falls—a spectacle that caused Eleanor Roosevelt to exclaim "Poor Niagara!"

The sand and sea of the Atlantic coast begin just a few hours south from the capital. It might not be the Caribbean, but there's something charmingly retro about resorts like Mar del Plata and Pinamar. In the summer months, when temperatures in Buenos Aires soar, hordes of porteños seek relief here, and the capital's music and theater scene decamps with them, making these *the* places to see and be seen.

One of South America's most beautiful towns, Colonia del Sacramento, Uruguay, juts out on a small peninsula into the Río de la Plata and is only an hour away from Buenos Aires. Here, sleepy cobbled streets and colonial buildings are a reminder of days gone by.

ORIENTATION & PLANNING

Orientation

Argentina's famous pampas begin in Buenos Aires province—an unending sea of grass, occasionally interrupted by winding streams and low hills. Nearly one-quarter of the country's landscapes are pampas, including the provinces of La Pampa and southern Córdoba and Santa Fé, in addition to Buenos Aires Province. In the province it's possible to travel from town to town by train and bus. However, deserted beaches in between towns can only be reached by car.

All along the region's Atlantic coastline are *balnearios* (small beach clubs), where you can rent tents and umbrellas and find casual meals. The season begins in December, really springs to life in January and February, and tails off in late March. Some cities, such as Mar del Plata and Pinamar, are known for their nightlife, party attitude, and sophisticated crowds, not to mention crowded sands. Others, such as Villa Gesell, are family oriented—a more low-key beach getaway.

Colonia del Sacramento, Uruguay is best reached from Buenos Aires by hydrofoil ferry. Roughly 1,360 km (840 mi) northeast of Buenos Aires and readily accessible by plane are the famous Cataratas del Iguazú. At a bend in the Río Iguazú, the falls extend for almost 3 km (2 mi) in a 270-degree arch that runs between the Argentine province of Misiones and Brazil.

Top Reasons to Visit

The Wall of Water The Cataratas del Iguazú (Iguazú Falls) are among the wildest wonders of the world, with nature on the rampage in a unique show of sound and fury.

Cowboy Culture A visit to the Pampas region isn't complete without a stay at an *estancia:* a sprawling, secluded, country mansion complete with gaucho guides who will lead you through the grasslands.

Colonial Days The cobblestone lanes and well-preserved buildings in romantic Colonia del Sacramento, Uruguay, let you step back in time.

Delta Dreaming The network of rivers and islands that makes up the Paraná delta is bursting with lush vegetation, making for a very tropical escape just an hour from Buenos Aires.

Life's a Beach Rolling dunes and coastal pine woods make the windy beaches of the Atlantic coast a peaceful place for some sea air in the low season, while in the summer it's Argentina's top party spot.

Colonia del Sacramento, Uruguay

It's hard not to fall in love with Colonia. The picturesque town has a six-by-six-block old city with wonderfully preserved architecture, rough cobblestone streets, and an easy grace. Tranquillity reigns here—there are more bicycles in town than cars.

Tigre

Just north of Buenos Aires is Tigre, a great base for exploring the beautiful delta of the Paraná River. Rivers replace streets as the best way to get to luxury lodges and shoreline restaurants far from the bustle of the city. Tropical vegetation and a huge variety of birds are some of the natural attractions here.

Buenos Aires Province

Some of the province's best sights are within an hour's drive of Buenos Aires. La Plata is notable as a fully planned city; in fact, what's best about the place is the architecture. Northwest from the capital are Luján, an important Catholic pilgrimage site, and San Antonio de Areco, the Pampean town that most lives up to the gaucho tradition.

The Atlantic Coast

During the last few decades, increased tourism has transformed the Atlantic coastal towns of Buenos Aires Province into summer vacation hotspots. Argentines flood the shore (most notably Mar del Plata) in January and February. Don't expect sugary sand or crystal-clear waters here, but the area is a good break from the city stifle.

Iguazú Falls

The grandeur of this vast sheet of white water cascading in constant cymbal-banging cacophony makes Niagara Falls and Victoria Falls seem sedate. Allow at least two full days to take in this magnificent sight, and be sure to see it from both the Argentine and Brazilian sides.

Planning

Peak season is summer (January–March). During this time it can be difficult to get a table at a restaurant or a room in a hotel, so be sure to make reservations well in advance. Winter (June–September) has a different feel, but beaches get cold and windy. Many hotels in Buenos Aires province require partial payment to secure a reservation during high season. Only the most expensive hotels have air-conditioning.

Be In the Know

In most of the beach towns, hotels are the best places to get information. Even if you're not a guest, almost every hotel will give you a map and point you in the right direction.

Tourist Offices Cariló ⊠ Av. Bunge 654 ☎ 2254/491-680 ⊗ Mar.–Nov., daily 9–7; Dec.–Feb., 8 AM–10 PM. **Cataratas del Iguazú** ⊠ Visitor center at park entrance ☎ 3757/420-180 ⊗ Daily 7 AM–8 PM. **Colonia del Sacramento** ⊠ General Flores and Rivera, Colonia del Sacramento ☎ 598/522-6141 ⊕ www.guiacolonia.com.uy ⊗ Weekdays 8 AM–7 PM; weekends 10 AM–6 PM. **Foz do Iguaçu** ⊠ Av. Jorge Schimmelpfeng and Rua Benjamin Constant, Foz do Iguaçu, Brazil ☎ 5545/574-2196 ⊕ www.fozdoiguacu.pr.gov.br ⊗ 7 AM–11 PM. **La Plata** ⊠ Palacio Campodónico, Diagonal 79 between calles 5 and 56 La Plata ⊕ www.laplata.gov.ar ☎ 221/422-9764 ⊗ Weekdays 10–6. **Luján** ⊠ Casa de la Cúpula, Luján ☎ 2323/420-453 ⊕ www.lujan.gov.ar ⊗ Weekdays 8–2.

Mar de las Pampas ⊠ Avenida 3 at intersection with Rotunda, Mar de las Pampas ☎ 225/470-324 ⊕ www.mardelaspampas.info ⊗ Dec.–Mar. **Mar del Plata** ⊠ Bv. Marítimo 2270, Local 51, Mar del Plata ☎ 223/495-1777 ⊕ www.mardelplata.gov.ar ⊗ Mar.–Nov., daily 8–8; Dec.–Feb., daily 8 AM–10 PM. **Pinamar** ⊠ Av. Bunge 654, Pinamar ☎ 2254/491-680 ⊕ www.pinamar.gov.ar ⊗ Daily 8 AM–10 PM. **Puerto Iguazú** ⊠ Av. Victoria Aguirre 311, Puerto Iguazú ☎ 3757/420-800 ⊗ Daily 7-1 and 2-9. **San Antonio de Areco** ⊠ Boulevard Zervoni and Arrellano, San Antonio de Areco ☎ 2326/453-165 ⊕ www.arecoturismo.com.ar ⊗ Weekdays 8–7, weekends 8–8. **Tigre** ⊠ Estación Fluvial, Mitre 305, Tigre ☎ 11/4512-4497 ⊕ www.tigre.gov.ar ⊗ Daily 9–5. **Villa Gesell** ⊠ Av. 3 820, Villa Gesell ☎ 2255/458-596 ⊕ www.gesell.com.ar ⊗ Daily 8–3 and 5 PM–12 AM.

Border Crossings

U.S., Canadian, and British citizens need only a valid passport for stays of up to 90 days in Uruguay. Border procedure for crossing into Brazil at Iguazú is inconsistent. In theory, Brazil operates a reciprocal visa policy, which means that it requires visas of citizens of countries who require them of Brazilians, usually at the same price. So, technically speaking, Canadian and American citizens crossing into Brazil to visit the falls need a visa, while British visitors don't. In practice, however, authorities rarely stamp visitors in and out, especially if you are with an organized tour, but sometimes just note down your name and passport number. Opinions are divided on whether it's worth the hassle (and cost) of getting a visa when you probably won't be asked for one. If you want to be on the safe side, allow a couple of days for processing. In Puerto Iguazú, the Brazilian consulate is open weekdays 8–12:30, and in Buenos Aires from 10–1 PM.

Brazilian Consulates In Puerto Iguazú ⊠ Av. Córdoba 264 Puerto Iguazú ☎ 3757/421-348. **In Buenos Aires** ⊠ Carlos Pellegrini 1363, 5th fl., Buenos Aires ☎ 11/4515-6500 ⊕ www.conbrasil.org.ar.

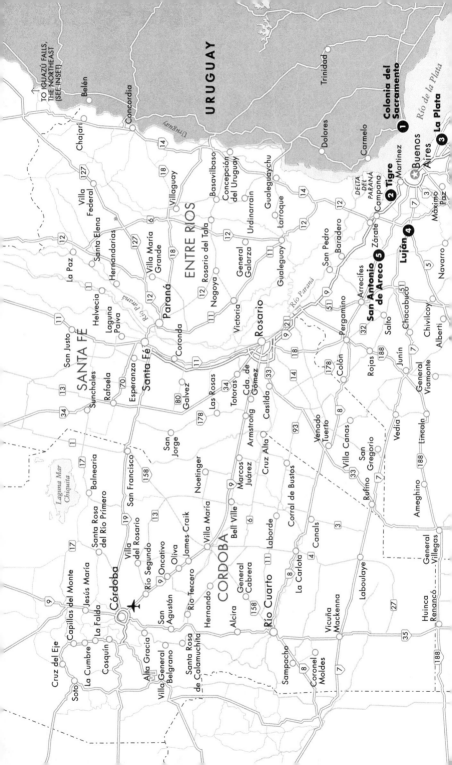

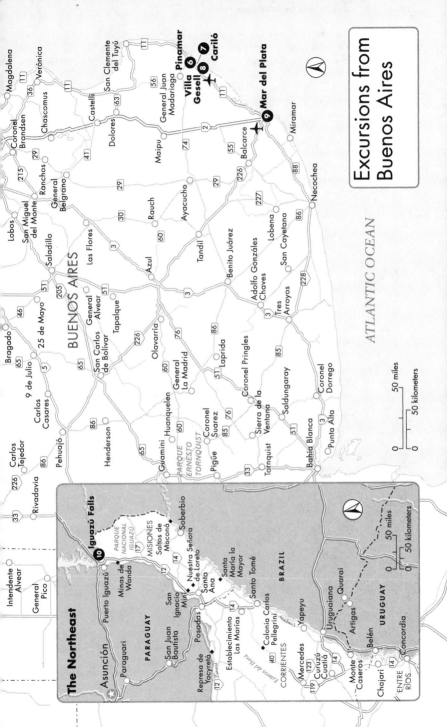

Excursions from Buenos Aires

6 Pinamar
7 Cariló
8 Villa Gesell
9 Mar del Plata
10 Iguazú Falls

ATLANTIC OCEAN

BUENOS AIRES

The Northeast

PARAGUAY

BRAZIL

URUGUAY

CORRIENTES

ENTRE RÍOS

MISIONES

PARQUE NACIONAL IGUAZÚ

PARQUE ERNESTO TORNQUIST

Magdalena
Verónica
Coronel Brandsen
Chascomus
Ranchos
Lobos
San Miguel del Monte
General Belgrano
Saladillo
Las Flores
General Alvear
25 de Mayo
9 de Julio
Bragado
Carlos Tejedor
Carlos Casares
Pehuajó
Henderson
Rivadavia
San Clemente del Tuyú
Castelli
Dolores
General Juan Madariaga
Maipu
Balcarce
Miramar
Necochea
Ayacucho
Rauch
Tandil
Benito Juárez
Adolfo Gonzáles Chaves
Lobena
San Cayetano
Tres Arroyos
Coronel Pringles
Laprida
Olavarría
General La Madrid
Coronel Suárez
Sierra de la Ventana
Saldungaray
Coronel Dorrego
Pigüe
Tornquist
Bahía Blanca
Punta Alta
Guamini
Huanquelen
San Carlos de Bolívar
Tapalque
Azul
San Carlos de Bolívar

Asunción
Paraguari
Puerto Iguazú
Minas de Wanda
San Ignacio Mini
San Juan Bautista
Represa de Yacyretá
Posadas
Establecimiento Las Marías
Santa Ana
Santa María la Mayor
Nuestra Señora de Loreto
Soberbio
Saltos de Moconó
Santo Tomé
Colonia Carlos Pellegrini
Mercedes
Curuzú Cuatiá
Monte Caseros
Chajari
Concordia
Belén
Yapeyu
Uruguaiana
Arrigas
Quarai

50 miles
50 kilometers

Intendente Alvear
General Pico

OTHER
PRACTICALITIES
To call Uruguay from Argentina, dial the country code of 598, and then the area code without the initial zero. To call locally, dial the digits of the numbers (Colonia's numbers have five digits) without any prefix (such as an area, which would be 052 in Colonia). The country code for Brazil is 55; the area code for Foz do Iguaçu is 45. When dialing a Brazilian number from Argentina, drop the initial zero from the local area code. With the privatization of the Brazilian telecommunications network, there's a wide choice of long-distance companies. Hence, to make direct-dial long-distance calls, you must find out which companies serve the area from which you're calling and then get their access codes—the staff at your hotel can help. For long-distance calls within Brazil, dial 0 + the access code + the area code and number.

Uruguayan bills come in denominations of $5, $10, $20, $50, 100, $200, $500, and $1,000 pesos uruguayos. Coins are available in 50 centavo pieces (half a peso), $1, and $2. Brazil's unit of currency is the real (R$; plural: *reais*, though it's sometimes seen as *reals*). One real is 100 centavos (cents). There are notes worth 1, 5, 10, 20, 50, and 100 reais, together with coins worth 1, 5, 10, 25, and 50 centavos and 1 real.

Iguazú Info

If tropical heat and humidity hamper your style, plan to visit Iguazú Falls between April and October. Note that though the falls are thrilling year-round, five upstream Brazilian barrages (mini-dams) on the Iguazú River cast a man-made unreliability on the natural wonder: depending on the river's flow and seasonal rains, barrages may affect the water volume in the falls anywhere from 1,500 cubic meters per second up to 8,000 or more (usually dam operators are careful not to shut down the falls on weekends or holidays).

Besides staying in the town of Puerto Iguazú, you can also stay in the Parque Nacional Iguazú at the Sheraton Internacional Iguazú; the Garganta del Diablo, one of the best restaurants in the area, is in the hotel. Competition from cheaper hotels in Foz do Iguaçu, on the Brazilian side, forces hotels in Puerto Iguazú to keep rates down. During low season (late September–early November and February–May, excluding Easter), rooms are discounted up to 50%. The town's restaurants are far from spectacular; generally, the best eating is found in the nicer hotels.

Many travel agencies offer packages from Buenos Aires that include flights, transfers, accommodation, and visits to the falls (and surrounding areas, depending on the length of your stay). Local travel agencies and tour operators also offer trips that will take you to both sides. Be sure to book a deal that includes a boat trip, an unmissable—though drenching—experience which gets you almost under the falls. More elaborate packages take in the San Ignacio mission ruins in Argentina, or a helicopter ride on the Brazilian side of the falls (note that helicopters are illegal on the Argentinean side due to their effect on wildlife). Tour operators that cover both sides of the falls will help with border formalities, though those that only work on the Argentine side have a reputation for complicating the issue to get you to do all your tourism on their side of the falls. If you want to set your own pace, you can tour the Argentine side and then take a taxi or one of the regularly scheduled buses across the International Bridge, officially called the Ponte Presidente Tancredo Neves, to Brazil.

Three of the most reliable agencies are Aguas Grandes, Sol Iguazú, and the popular Iguazú Jungle Explorer, which has four trips to the jungle and falls. The best of these is the Gran Aventura trip, which includes a truck ride through the forest and a boat ride to San Martín, Bossetti, and the Salto Tres Mosqueteros (be ready to get soaked). Another tour takes you to Garganta del Diablo. Park ranger Daniel Somay organizes personalized Jeep tours with an ecological focus through his Explorador Expediciones in Puerto Iguazú. Bring binoculars to see the birds.

Helisul operates short helicopter rides over the falls, which leave opposite the Tropical das Cataratas hotel, on the Brazilian side. Though they offer a fabulous view, you should be aware that they have a seriously detrimental effect on local wildlife, hence Argentina's ban on their side.

🗂 Tour Companies **Aguas Grandes** ✉ Mariano Moreno 58, Puerto Iguazú ☎ 3757/421-140 ⊕ www.aguasgrandes.com. **Explorador Expediciones** ✉ Shop 16, Sheraton International Iguazú, Puerto Iguazú ☎ 3757/421-632 ⊕ www.hotelguia.com/turismo/explorador-expediciones. **Helisul** ✉ Rodavia das Cataratas, Km. 16.5, Foz do Iguaçu, 85863-000, Brazil ☎ 5545/529-7474 ⊕ www.helisul.com. **Iguazú Jungle Explorer** ✉ Sheraton Internacional Iguazú Hotel, Puerto Iguazú ☎ 3757/421-600 ⊕ www.iguazujungleexporer.com. **Sol Iguazú Turismo** ✉ Av. Victoria Aguirre 316 ☎ 3757/421-008 ⊕ www.soliguazu.com.ar.

Price It Right

WHAT IT COSTS In Argentina Pesos					
	$$$$	$$$	$$	$	¢
RESTAURANTS	over 35	25–35	15–25	8–15	under 8
HOTELS	over 300	220–300	140–220	80–140	under 80

Restaurant prices are for one main course at dinner. Hotel prices are for two people in a standard double room in high season.

Life on the Fringe

One side of the highway between Buenos Aires and La Plata has mile after sobering mile of some of the nation's worst shantytowns. It's an especially jarring sight if you're coming straight from the hip, modern capital. These illegal settlements, called *villas emergencias* (emergency towns)—or, as they're known to most Argentines, *villas miserias* (towns of misery)—are conglomerations of shacks slapped together with corrugated tin and even cardboard, carcasses of old automobiles, and piles of deteriorating rubber tires. Some villas miserias have electricity or running water, but many don't. Often you'll see a makeshift soccer field somewhere in the village.

Cityfolk will warn you not to enter a villa miseria, and you should heed their advice—tourists are immediate targets for muggings and kidnappings. In fact, not even the police deign to go in; the result is an underworld that exists completely off the radar of Argentina's government and economy. It's not quite lawlessness, rather a makeshift system of community policing enforces a rather different system of norms—a code of conduct driven by the constant and relentless need merely to survive, whatever it takes.

COLONIA DEL SACRAMENTO

❶ The peaceful cobbled streets of Colonia are just over the river Plate from Buenos Aires, but they seem a world away. Founded in 1680, the city was subject to a long series of wars and pacts between Spain and Portugal, which eventually gave up its claim. Its many small museums are dedicated to the story of its tumultuous history. The best sightseeing activity in Colonia, however, is simply walking through its *Barrio Histórico* (Old Town).

Begin your tour at the reconstructed **Portón de Campo** or city gate, where remnants of the old bastion walls lead to the river. A block farther is **Calle de los Suspiros,** the aptly named Street of Sighs, a cobblestone stretch of one-story colonial homes that can rival any street in Latin America for sheer romantic effect. Clusters of bougainvillea flow over the walls, from which hang old lanterns. Art galleries and antiques shops line the street, which opens out to **Plaza Mayor,** a lovely square filled with Spanish moss, palm, and spiky, flowering *palo borracho* trees. The many cafés around the square are an ideal place to take it all in.

Three of the city's principal museums are on Plaza Mayor. The one that's worth a visit is **Museo Portugués** (⊠ Corner of Plaza Mayor and Calle de los Suspiros 🎟 10 pesos ⊙ Daily 11–4:30), which documents the city's ties to Portugal. It's most notable for its collection of old map reproductions based on Portuguese naval expeditions. A small selection of period furnishings, clothes, and jewelry from Colonia's days as a Portuguese colony complete the offerings. Exhibits are well-labeled, but in Spanish only. Next door is the Museo Municipal, which has a collection of sundry objects related to the city's history housed in another early Portuguese settlement. Also near the plaza are the San Francisco convent ruins, dating from 1683 but destroyed by Spanish bombardment not long after. Towering above these surviving walls is the *faro* or lighthouse, built in 1857. You can climb to the top for a view of the old city. A block away up Calle San Antonio is the Plaza de Armas Manoel Lobo, overlooked by the simple white facade of the oldest church in Uruguay, the Iglesia Matriz. The square itself is crisscrossed with wooden catwalks over the ruins of a house dating to the founding of the town. The tables from the square's small eateries spill from the sidewalk right onto the cobblestones.

Where to Stay & Eat

$$ ✕ **El Drugstore.** The outside tables at this quirky corner restaurant sit on the cobblestones of the Plaza de Armas, with a great view of the Iglesia Matriz. While away the wait for the ferry with a beer and a selection of Spanish-style tapas, or take a break from steak with their seasonally changing à la carte menu, which might include sushi or a fish curry. ⊠ *Vasconcellos 179* 🕾 *052/25241* ▭ *AE, MC, V.*

2

$$ ✕ **El Mesón de la Plaza.** Simple dishes—many steak-based—made with top-quality ingredients have made this small restaurant a favorite with porteño visitors to Colonia. The comprehensive wine list showcases Uruguayan vineyards hard to sample anywhere outside of the country. Try to get one of the outside tables which sit right on the peaceful Plaza de Armas. ⊠ *Vasconcellos 153* ☏ *052/24807* ▭ *MC, V.*

$ ✕ **La Bodeguita.** This hip restaurant with backyard tables overlooking the river serves incredibly delicious, crispy pizza, sliced into bite-size rectangles. ⊠ *Calle del Comercio 167* ☏ *052/25329* ▭ *MC, V.*

$$$$ ✕▣ **Four Seasons Carmelo.** Serenity pervades this harmoniously decorated resort an hour west of Colonia del Sacramento, reachable by car, boat, or a 15-minute flight from Buenos Aires. Everything is done in a fusion of Asian styles—from tai chi classes at the incense-scented and bamboo-screen health club to bungalows (considered "standard rooms") with private Japanese gardens (and marvelous outdoor showers). In the evening torches illuminate the paths, which meander through sand dunes. The hotel also offers free sunset cruises on the Río de la Plata. If you can't lodge here, try dining at one of the wonderful restaurants. ⊠ *Ruta 21, km 262, Carmelo* ☏ *598/542–9000* ⊕ *www.fourseasons.com/carmelo* ⤳ *24 duplexes, 20 bungalows* ⚙ *2 restaurants, room service, in-room safes, minibars, IDD phones, cable TV, in-room VCRs, 18-hole golf course, 2 tennis courts, pool, health club, massage, sauna, spa, boating, bicycles, horseback riding, Ping-Pong, bar, casino, lobby lounge, video game room, babysitting, children's programs (ages 5–12), laundry service, Internet, business services, meeting rooms, airport shuttle* ▭ *AE, DC, MC, V.*

FodorsChoice ★

$ ▣ **Hotel Plaza Mayor.** This lovely hotel with an impeccable location in the middle of the *Barrio Históricó* dates from 1840. The simple rooms, many with high ceilings and beveled-glass doors, overlook a peaceful garden with a trickling fountain. Ask for one of the upstairs rooms, which have views of the river. ⊠ *Calle del Comercio 111* ☏ *052/23193* ⊕ *www.hotelplazamayor.com.uy* ⤳ *8 rooms* ⚙ *Coffee shop, room service, minibars, hot tub, laundry service* ▭ *AE, DC, MC, V.*

★ ¢ ▣ **Posada de la Flor.** This colonial-style hotel, which opened in early 2003, is on a quiet, dead-end street, and is arranged around a verdant courtyard. Second-floor rooms cost a few dollars more, but come with air-conditioners and cheery quilts. All the rooms are named after flowers: ask for the most spacious, called "Nomeolvides," or "Forget-me-not." A lovely third-floor terrace shaded with bamboo looks out over the river. The posada is a pleasant five-minute walk to Plaza Mayor. If you arrive via the Buquebus ferry landing, the English-speaking owner, Roberto, will pick you up. ⊠ *Calle Ituzaingó 268* ☏ *052/30794* ⤳ *10 rooms* ⚙ *Café, cable TV, in-room safe, babysitting, laundry service; no a/c in some rooms* ⊕ *www.guiacolonia.com.uy/posadadelaflor* ▭ *AE, DC, MC, V* ❙❑❙ *CP.*

TIGRE & THE PARANÁ DELTA

A coastal train ride or a drive through the shady riverside suburbs of Buenos Aires takes you to the river port town of Tigre, the embarkation point for boats that ply the Delta del Paraná. The delta is a vast maze of canals, tributaries, and river expanding out like the veins of a leaf. Heavy vegetation and rich birdlife (as well as clouds of mosquitoes) make the network of rivers feel very tropical. The delta's many islands hide peaceful luxury getaways and cozy riverside restaurants accessible only by boat.

Tigre

❷ *30 km (19 mi) northwest of Buenos Aires on the Ruta Panamericana, 35 km (22 mi) northwest of Buenos Aires on Avenida Libertador.*

The focus of the action at Tigre is the picturesque **Puerto de Frutos** market, in the central part of the port area. It's a good place to find handicrafts at excellent prices and is particularly busy on weekends, the best time to visit it. The most comfortable—though most touristy—way to travel the delta's waterways is aboard the two-story catamarans that leave from here. **Río Tur** (⊠ Sarmiento at Buenos Aires ☎ 11/4731–0280 ⊕ www.rioturcatamaranes.com.ar) does two-hour round trips. For an especially memorable ride, take a sunset cruise.

A cheaper, more authentic way to explore the delta's waterways are the low-slung wooden *lanchas colectivas* (boat buses), which locals use to get from the port to their houses on the delta. These leave from the Estación Fluvial (Boat Station), on the other side of the roundabout from Tigre Station. **Líneas Delta Argentino** (⊠ Stand 6, Estación Fluvial ☎ 11/4731–1236 ⊕ www.lineasdelta.com.ar) does one- and three-hour trips. As the boats leave the delta, they pass the magnificent turn-of-the-century buildings of Tigre's heyday, like the ornate Club Canottieri Italiani (Italian Rowing Club). Farther along the way you'll see colorfully painted houses built on stilts to protect them from floods.

☺ Aside from the river, the main attraction is the **Tren de la Costa** (Coastal Train), originally built in 1895 as a passenger train and refurbished in 1990. Along its way from Estación Retiro in Buenos Aires to Tigre, the train meanders through some of Buenos Aires's most fashionable northern suburbs, stopping at 11 stations.

☺ At the end of the Tren de la Costa is **Parque de la Costa** (Coastal Park), one of Argentina's largest, most modern amusement parks. If you want to combine a visit here with sightseeing, take the ferryboat trip for a half-hour ride on the river delta. There's also an IMAX theater and restaurants with surprisingly good Argentine fare.

Where to Stay & Eat

$ ✕ **TBC.** An expansive wooden veranda with a great view of the river is the main attraction at TBC. Cool breezes sweep the tables, and skiff after wooden skiff from the local rowing clubs scoot by below you. The menu has a good range of standards like *milanesas,* pasta dishes, and the inevitable steak which, though nothing to write home about, does the trick. ⊠ *Paseo Victorica 156* ☎ *11/4731–0196.*

¢ ✕ **Chapaleo.** Don't be put off by the rough-and-ready tables of this riverside parilla: the *lomo, vacío,* and other barbecue beef cuts are excellent. The wisecracking waiters are both fast and friendly. ⊠ *Paseo Victorica 874* ☎ *11/4749–1901* ▭ *No credit cards.*

$ ⌂ **Casona La Ruchi.** This family-run bed-and-breakfast looks over the Río Tigre, just across from the boat station. Rooms in the mock-Tudor house are spacious, with iron bedsteads and crisp white sheets. Behind the house is a well-kept garden, complete with swimming pool and barbecue area. The Escauriza family's ultra-friendly reception means that Casona La Ruchi is often full of returning porteños, so try to book in advance. ⊠ *Lavalle 557, 1648* ☎ *11/4749–2499* ⊕ *www.casonalaruchi. com.ar* ⌷ *5 rooms with shared bath* ⌂ *Dining room, BBQ, pool; no room TVs, no room phones* ⊟ *No credit cards* ⫶⊙⫶ *CP.*

The Paraná Delta

The network of waterways and close-packed islands that stretch northwest of Tigre are the most accessible part of the 14,000 square kilometers (5,400 square miles) that make up the Paraná delta, where roads are replaced by rivers. Churning brown waters and heavy vegetation are reminiscent of Southeast Asia, though the chi-chi houses and manicured gardens that line the rivers of the *Primera Sección* (the First Section, closest to Tigre) are a far cry from Mekong River settlements. If you want to take in more of the delta than a short boat trip allows, do as the porteños do and combine it with a day's wining and dining at an island restaurant or a weekend at one of the luxury tropical lodges a little farther afield. Many offer private transport; otherwise inquire about which boat services take you there and the timetables. The delta gets very hot and humid in the summer, and the mosquitoes are ferocious, so be sure to take plenty of insect repellent.

Where to Stay & Eat

$$$ ✕ **El Gato Blanco.** It's easy to make a day out of lunch at El Gato Blanco, which is about a half hour from Tigre by boat—take any service going to the Río Capitán. House specialties like *lenguado à la citron vert* (flatfish in a lime and champagne sauce) are served at tables arranged on huge wooden verandas, which have great views of the river. Weekends the place is incredibly popular with porteños and elbow-room becomes scarce. After lunch, kids can play in the sweeping parkland behind the restaurant, while you relax in a riverside deckchair. ⊠ *Río Capitán no. 80* ☎ *11/4728–0390* ⌂ *Reservations essential on weekends* ⊟ *AE, MC, V* ⊙ *No dinner Sun.–Fri.*

$$$ ✕⌂ **Alpenhaus.** Steeply sloping roofs and ornate wooden balconies are part of the Alpine theme at this little slice of Germany, delta-style. Though the complex's exterior is slightly kitsch, the tiled floors and wooden furnishings of the self-contained bungalows are unassuming. Alpenhaus is on a small river, meaning you can enjoy the large lawns and swimming pool without the noise of too many boats. Everything served at the small restaurant-cum–beer garden from the fondues to the silky sachertortes (dark chocolate–and-nut cakes) is entirely homemade—this is *the* place for a German food fix. To get here, take an Interisleña boat from Estación Fluvial going to Rama Negra. ⊠ *Arroyo Rama Negra, ³⁄₁₀ mi from Río Capitán, 1648* ☎ *11/4728–0422* ⊕ *www. alpenhaus.com.ar* ⌷ *1 room, 3 bungalows* ⌂ *Restaurant, IDD phones, in-room hot-tubs, refrigerators, cable TV, pool, gym, kayaking, beer garden* ⊟ *No credit cards* ⫶⊙⫶ *CP.*

$$$$ 🏨 **La Pascuala Delta Lodge.** Wooden walkways connect the luxurious bun-

Fodor'sChoice   galows—each with a private riverside deck—at this hideaway. Natural

★   materials pervade the rooms, all of which have hardwood walls, jute rugs, and feather pillows in thick cotton cases. Comfort has been carefully thought out here: rooms have CD players, mosquito netting on the balconies, and reading lights over the bathtubs. You can get in touch with the delta by exploring in boats or kayaks, or simply soak up the jungle atmosphere by the lagoonlike pool. As well as a dining room and a grill, nighttime entertainment options include a red living-room-style bar serving top cocktails and a well-stocked library. The lodge is a bit out-of-the-way to justify a night's visit: inquire about their two- and three-day all-inclusive packages. ☒ *Arroyo las Cañas, 1648* 🕾 *11/4728–1253* ⊕ *www.lapascuala.com.ar* ⊲ *15 bungalows* ⚒ *2 restaurants, fans, pool, outdoor hot tubs, boating, waterskiing, fishing, bar, library; no room phones, no room TVs, no kids under 16* ☰ *AE, MC, V* ⏀*All inclusive.*

$ 🏨 **Bonanza Deltaventura.** Thick vegetation surrounds the tomato-red 19th-century country house that is the center of the eco-action at Bonanza Deltaventura. The idea behind the establishment is to share the natural wonders of the area with visitors through organized nature walks, kayak expeditions, and horseback rides. Ten-foot ceilings, rustic furniture, and nothing but green outside the huge windows are some of the simple pleasures awaiting at the end of the day. Hearty barbecues and drawn-out *mateadas* (mate tea and cake) are also highlights. Day packages are offered. ☒ *Río Carapachay, 1648* 🕾 *11/4806–6119* ⊕ *www. deltaventura.com* ⊲ *4 rooms, 3 guesthouses* ⚒ *Dining room, BBQ, pool, boating, horseback riding; no room phones, no room TVs* ☰ *No credit cards* ⏀ *All-inclusive.*

BUENOS AIRES PROVINCE

Flat plains fan out where the city of Buenos Aires ends: this is the beginning of the pampas, the flat grasslands deeply infused in the Argentine identity. Their name derives from the native Quéchua word for "flat field"—the pampas' famous fertile earth is home to the horses and cattle that make up the mainstay of Argentina's economy. All over are signs of active ranch life, from the cattle grazing to the modern-day gauchos working the wide-open spaces. The region is also noted for its crops; throughout are extensive farms dotted with alfalfa, sunflowers, wheat, corn, and soy.

In 1880, during the Campaign of the Desert undertaken by General Julio A. Roca, the pampas were "cleared" of indigenous tribes, making extensive agriculture and cattle breeding possible. By the latter half of the 19th century, the region became known as the grain supplier for the world. From 1850 to 1950 more than 400 important estancias were built in Buenos Aires Province alone. Some of these have been modified for use as guest ranches and provide the best glimpse of the fabled Pampean lifestyle.

La Plata

🌀 *50 km (31 mi) southeast of Buenos Aires via R1 and R14.*

At the famous 1889 Paris Exposition (think Eiffel Tower), Jules Verne honored La Plata with a gold medal, citing the newly built city as a symbol of resplendent modernity. Accepting the medal was Dardo Rocha, the Buenos Aires governor who a few years prior assembled a team of architects and planners and created the provincial capital from the dust of semi-arid desert.

La Plata succeeds today from that creative genesis, a beautiful city of palatial estates on an ordered grid intersected by wide, diagonal boulevards and a rational scheme of parks and plazas every six blocks. The core of the city's planning is the "monumental axis" between 51st and 53rd streets, which contains most of the attractive churches, and government and cultural buildings. Streets have numbers instead of names, and though the city's perfect geometry makes it seem like a cinch to get your bearings, the diagonals can be quite disorienting, so keep your map at hand.

The geographic center of the city is **Plaza Moreno,** where the Piedra Fundacional (La Plata's Founding Stone) was laid in 1882.

The graceful, pink-brick **Catedral de la Inmaculada Concepción** stands at the south end of Plaza Moreno's tiled walkway, and is a jewel of late-19th-century architecture. The neo-Gothic structure, inspired by cathedrals in Amiens and Cologne, was originally inaugurated in 1932 but lacked the long double spires. During the past decade of restoration, the monumental stained-glass window was completed and a museum documenting the church's history was added in the crypt. Construction wasn't complete until November 19, 2000—118 years to the day after the city's foundation stone was laid. A carillon with 25 bronze bells enlivens the western (51st Street) tower; the eastern (53rd Street) tower has an elevator that rises to a lookout with the city's best views. ⊠ *Calle 14 between Calles 51 and 53* ☏ *221/427–3504, 221/422–5026 guided tours* ⊙ *Museum daily 9–8.*

At the north end of Plaza Moreno is the 1883 German neoclassical **Palacio Municipal,** which is recognizable by its central clock tower. The sumptuous interior is worthy of exploration, especially the Salón Dorado (Golden Salon), with its marble staircase, painted ceilings, and mosaic tile floors. ⊠ *Plaza Moreno s/n* ⊙ *Daily 10–6.*

The equestrian statue of South American liberator José de San Martín stands in the center of **Plaza San Martín.** On the north side of the square is the black slate roof of the French neoclassic Legislatura (provincial legislature) building.

The cultural epicenter of La Plata is the **Pasaje Dardo Rocha,** housed in a massive Parisian-style building on the northwest side of Plaza San Martín. Once the city's main train station, it's now home to a small art-house theatre, temporary exhibition and performance spaces, and several small art museums including the MACLA (Museum of Contemporary Latin American Art). ⊠ *Calle 50 between calles 6 and 7* ☎ *221/425–1990* ⊗ *Tues.–Fri. 10–8, weekends 2–10.*

One of La Plata's architectural highlights is the **Casa Curutchet,** the only building designed by Le Corbusier in Latin America. The ultra-geometric structure embodies all the modernist architectural principals the French master was famous for. ⊠ *Bvd. 53 no. 320* ☎ *221/482–2631* ⊠ *Free* ⊗ *Mon., Wed., Fri. 8–1.*

In the northern portion of the city, the eucalyptus-shaded forest promenade, **Paseo del Bosque,** is La Plata's biggest green space and a good place to relax. Recreational options include a small zoo, lake with paddle-boat rentals, an outdoor amphitheater, botanical gardens, observatory, and an equestrian center.In the middle of the Paseo del Bosque is the **Museo de Ciencias Naturales,** Argentina's only natural history museum and the apple of La Plata's eye. Both the museum and the rambling building housing it date to 1889, and despite an ongoing renovation procedure the museum still seems eccentrically Edwardian. On the ground floor, dusty glass cases display a host of bones, including a substantial dinosaur collection, while upstairs are Latin American archaeology exhibits. ⊠ *Paseo del Bosque* ☎ *221/425–7744* ⊕ *www.fcnym. unlp.edu.ar/museo* ⊠ *12 pesos* ⊗ *Tues.–Sun. 10–6; guided tours (in Spanish) weekends on the half-hour.*

Where to Stay & Eat

★ ¢–$ ✕ **Cervecería Modelo.** This alehouse restaurant opened its doors in 1892—just 10 years after the city was founded. The most interesting tradition is tossing peanut shells to the floor. Pigeons, who have cleverly found a way inside, peck at the jettisoned shells. But this spot isn't just about established quirkiness—it has what may be the largest menu in the country, which an exceptionally friendly and fast waitstaff guides you through. The homemade pasta is a good bet; you'll have a choice of 25 sauces. The restaurant stays open late: until 2 AM weekdays and 3 AM weekends. ⊠ *Calle 5 at Calle 54* ☎ *221/421–1321* ⊟ *AE, DC, MC, V.*

¢ ▥ **Benevento Hotel.** This comfortable hotel resulted from the complete restoration of a circa 1890 home, which revealed sumptuous, long-hidden details. The elegant, bright white building has round corner bays on the upper three of its four floors and low, black iron rails on the balconies. Rooms—which have 15-foot ceilings, wood floors, and new bathrooms—vary in design, so you might want to look at a few before committing to one. The corner rooms are magnificent. ⊠ *Calle 2 645, 1900* ☎☎ *221/489–1078 or 221/437–7721* ⊕ *www.hotelbenevento.com. ar* ⤴ *20 rooms, 1 suite* ⭢ *Restaurant, room service, in-room safes, bar, laundry service* ⊟ *AE, MC, V* ⭢| *BP.*

Nightlife

La Plata is a university town and nightlife tends to be student-centered, revolving around long nights at coffee shops and boisterous bars. There is also a thriving music scene, and rock and jazz bands often play intimate venues. Diagonal 74 between calles 56 and 59 is the center of the action.

Old movie posters line the walls at laid-back student haunt **El Copetín** (✉ Diagonal 74 no. 2290, at Calle 59 ☎ 221/453–9221). You could make a dinner out of their bar snacks: pizza, *picadas* (cold-cuts), and sandwiches filled to bursting, then settle in as the lights dim and the rock 'n' roll gets going.

Luján

❹ *60 km (40 mi) west of Buenos Aires via R7.*

In 1630 a mule train, originating in Portugal, made its way out of Buenos Aires. Among the items being carried were two terra-cotta statues of the Virgin Mary. After the caravan stopped for a break along the banks of the Río Luján, one ox pulling the statues refused to budge. Finally, the leaders of the caravan realized that a statue of the Virgin had fallen out and was blocking the way. They took this as a sign that this is where the Virgin wanted to stay and built a basilica on the spot where the caravan stopped.

Every year at least 5 million people make the pilgrimage to Luján to pray to the Virgin at the imposing **Basílica de la Virgen de Luján.** The towering pinkish spires of the structure are more interesting than beautiful, but the Basílica is worth a visit to witness the extent of the cult following the Virgin, including the endless products adorned with her figure sold on stalls outside the precinct. ✉ *Calle San Martín and Calle Padre Salvaire* ☎ *232/342–1070* ☉ *Daily 7:30 AM–9 PM.*

Where to Eat

$$ ✕ **L'eau vive.** The Basílica is not the only place in Luján that warrants a pilgrimage—the town's most famous restaurant is run by Cordon-Bleu–trained nuns. However, there's nothing puritan about the rich French classics they serve, which might include frogs' legs or trout in a prawn, cider, and cream sauce. L'eau vive is routinely packed with savvy porteños, who aren't put off by the restaurant's location 15 blocks from Luján's main square or by the drab textured wallpaper and dull green linens; the consistently heavenly food is what keeps them coming back. ✉ *Constitución 2112* ☎ *2323/421–774* ▭ No *credit cards* ☉ *Closed Mon. No dinner Sun.*

San Antonio de Areco

❺ *110 km (68 mi) west of Buenos Aires.*

At this small town off R8 you'll find the most authentic scenes of traditional life in the pampas. During the early 1700s the town was a regular stop on the route to Peru. Buenos Aires was still a part of the viceroyalty of Peru, and San Antonio de Areco was the last Spanish-populated settlement on the border of the native inhabitants' territory. The town has come to represent gaucho life, most notably at the gaucho museum, and many of its inhabitants still maintain the gaucho lifestyle. Across the street from the museum entrance is a typical *parrilla* (restaurant specializing in grilled meats), run by a local family, where traditional gaucho songs are sung.

The Legend of the Gaucho

THE GAUCHO—the rugged Argentine cowboy—is, for the most part, just a legend now, a whisper from the days when cowboys wandered unhindered across the pampas. Gauchos made a living from the cows that they herded, roaming from one dusty watering hole to the next, free—for a time—from the influence of any individual estancia and its wealthy foreign landowners. The image is unmistakable: the huge chest, the leathery hands, the *bombacha* (baggy pants), the small *facón* (knife), the scarf and narrow-brimmed hat, and the *chifle* (bull horn, used for drinking water on long trips).

In the late 19th century, landowners increasingly saw gauchos as an untapped labor source, and set out to co-opt their skills. A law was pushed through, barring men without jobs from traveling around the pampas. This law forced many to take jobs at estancias, stripping them of their independence—and with it, much of the romantic ideal. It is the free-roaming gaucho, rather than the estancia ranch hand, that is most idealized in Argentine lore.

The writer Ricardo Güiraldes (1886-1927) is credited with making that figure of the gaucho a profound part of the collective consciousness of Argentina. His 1926 novel *Don Segundo Sombra*, inspired by a man Güiraldes had met at La Porteña, his father's estancia in San Antonio de Areco, introduced the gaucho persona to the world. The book was, in the words of Waldo Frank, "the story of a boy who, like boys the world over, learns to become a man by taking life humbly and bravely." Indeed, Güiraldes's protagonist was not just the Marlboro man of the 1800s—a rugged, wandering, romantic hero who was never portrayed without a cigarette in one hand—but rather an Everyman, a symbol of human struggle. Güiraldes writes: "The gaucho, within his limited means, is a complete type of man. He has moral principles. 'A gaucho of law,' he admits that there exists an 'individual law,' a sort of destiny that takes every man down a special road. [the gaucho is] someone who has died according to what he was destined for."

Still, the sex appeal of the gaucho was undeniable. "He has dances of extraordinary charm and gallantry," writes Güiraldes, "little love relations," and "a particular style of movement that involves aesthetics, education, and respect of one's own attitude." Certainly this romantic gaucho is the image most associated with the pampas, and it continues to be part of the draw of its estancias. Indeed, if you stay at an estancia, your horseback riding guide will likely be in the full gaucho get-up. All this might seem contrived, and perhaps it is; even if he does herd cattle, he probably makes most of his living leading tourists around on horses. But give your gaucho a chance. He may come closer than you think to conforming to Güiraldes' stereotype. He will lead you around with an open smile, and most importantly, he will assure your safety on horseback. But you might well notice him, in deference to his predecessors, with one eye on the distant horizon of the impossibly wide grasslands that are the pampas.

—By Robin S. Goldstein

In summer the Río Areco (Areco River), which runs through town, is teeming with swimmers—especially near the center of town, at the Puente Viejo (Old Bridge), which is overlooked over by the open-air tables of various riverside parillas. The sleepy downtown itself is made up of a couple of cobblestone shopping streets lined with Italianate houses typical of small-town Buenos Aires province. During the week surrounding November 10th, the *Día de la Tradición* (Day of Tradition), the town transforms into one long gaucho party, including shows, community barbecues, riding competitions, and a huge crafts fair. To really complete the gaucho experience, consider spending a day or two at one of the many *estancias* (ranches) around the town (⇨ Go to the Gauchos box, *below*).

The **Museo Gauchesco Ricardo Güiraldes** (Gaucho Museum) conjures up the gaucho life of the past by letting you explore traditional estancia grounds just outside of town, including a 150-year-old *pulpería* (an old country store from gaucho times) tavern with wax figures, a replica of an 18th-century hacienda, an old chapel, and lots of gaucho paraphernalia. The museum also documents the life and work of Ricardo Güiraldes (1886–1927), whose gaucho novels captured the popular imagination of the Argentine people. Güiraldes is buried in town. ⊠ *Camino Ricardo Güiraldes* ☎ *2326/456–201* 🎫 *5 pesos* ⊗ *Wed.–Mon. 11–5.*

Centro Cultural y Taller Draghi. San Antonio is famed for its silversmiths, and Juan José Draghi is the best in town. This small museum adjoining his workshop showcases the emergence and evolution of the Argentine silverwork style known as *platería criolla.* The pieces are mostly gaucho-related: spurs, belt buckles, knives, stirrups, and the ubiquitous mates, some dating to the 18th century. Also on display is the incredibly ornate work of Juan JoséDraghi himself, which you can take home from the shop. ⊠ *Lavalle 387* ☎ *2326/454–219* 🎫 *2 pesos* ⊗ *Daily 9–1 and 3:30–9:30.*

Where to Stay & Eat

¢–$ ✕ **Almacen de Ramos Generales.** This old general store is airy and charming, with remnants stowed away in every corner. The food here is simply outstanding, and the small-town setting makes this all the more remarkable. The *picada* begins with salami, pork, cheese, eggplant *en escabeche* (pickled), and wondrous french fries with basil. The *bife de chorizo* (sirloin steak), meanwhile, is one of the best anywhere, perfectly juicy, tender, and flavorful. The atmosphere, too, is just right: it's country-store-meets-elegant-restaurant. Pleasant hues of light pour in from the plate-glass windows while you enjoy the impeccable service and memorable food. ⊠ *Zapiola 143, between Lavalle and Sdo. Sombra* ☎ *2326/456–376* ⊕ *www.ramosgeneralesareco.com.ar* ⊟ *No credit cards.*

FodorśChoice ★

$ 🛏 **El Hostal de Areco.** Pink might not be the most gaucho of colors, but the colonial building housing this small hotel is painted unrepentantly deep rose. Things are more traditional inside, where the shady rooms have solid hardwood furniture and plain white walls, and a huge log fireplace roars in the reception area during winter. During the Día de la

CLOSE UP

Go to the Gauchos

IN THE LATE 19TH CENTURY, well-to-do European families bought huge blocks of land in the pampas. Here they built their *estancias* (ranches), often with luxurious houses reminiscent of the old country. The advent of industrial agriculture put most of these crop or beef farms out of business. Today many are luxurious bed-and-breakfasts or tourist attractions. The gauchos and *peones* (ranch hands) who once kept the cows and worked the land are now putting on riding shows or preparing large-scale *asados* (wood barbecues). But the estancia can be a jarringly real experience of old-time feudalism. *Mate* is sipped at afternoon tea, when the *estanciero* (ranch owner) sits down with his ranch hands in a gesture of communion.

You can do a day trip from Buenos Aires to an estancia, which is typically spent enjoying an *asado*, barbecue accompanied by empanadas and red wine, while watching a demonstration of gaucho skill and dexterity. These day-packages are known as a *día de campo*, and include transport, meals, and activities. Alternatively, you can stay overnight or for a weekend. Accommodations, food, and activities vary greatly at each estancia, but for the real experience try to opt for one still run by a family, rather than by a hotel chain. You can count on comfortable lodgings with equal parts rusticity and European flair. Horseback riding may or may not be an option. And, no, you won't be asked to do chores.

All of the estancias listed below are within a few hours drive from Buenos Aires, and many will arrange private transport. Although some are close to

towns or villages, it's rare to leave the estancia during a stay. San Antonio de Areco is one town with many estancias nearby.

✕⊞ **La Bamba.** The main house, owned by the venerable Aldao family, dates from around 1832 and is done in traditional Argentine style with beautiful, roofed verandas and an interior courtyard with a well. Inside, heavy mismatched furniture, chintz curtains, and handmade quilts ooze aristocratic country splendor. There are lovely views of the surrounding plains and all kinds of ranch activities. ⊠ *Ruta 31, Cuartel IV, San Antonio de Areco 1609* ☎🖶 *11/4314–0394 Buenos Aires reservations; 2326/456–293 estancia* ⊕ *www.la-bamba.com.ar* ⇌ *8 rooms, 2 cabins* ⚎ *Dining room, pool, massage, fishing, horseback riding, volleyball, laundry service* ▭ *AE, MC, V* ⦿| *All-inclusive* $$$$.

✕⊞ **Estancia Cabaña Los Dos Hermanos.** Horses are the focus of the action at this low-key estancia; there are no fancy shows here, just lots of riding. The owners, Ana and Pancho Peña, welcome guests personally. If you're not up for the cowboy act, they have a carriage in which to tour the land in style. Rustic cabins have heavy wood furniture and lots of horse-related decorations on the walls. Meals are homey, revolving round lots of beef. ⊠ *Ruta 193, Km 10.5 Escalada 2800* ☎🖶 *11/4765–4320* ⊕ *www.estancialosdoshermanos.com* ⇌ *3 rooms, 5 cabins* ⚎ *Dining room, cable TV, pool, croquet, horseback riding, Ping-Pong, volleyball, laundry service.* ▭ *No credit cards* ⦿| *All-inclusive* $$$$.

✕⊞ **Juan Gerónimo.** South of La Plata in the tiny village of Veronica, this estancia, which is said to have once belonged to a shipwrecked English bandit, makes a perfect weekend getaway. The early 1920s ranch is set on a mammoth plot of land. Day visits can be arranged. Horse enthusiasts love the grounds—there are 150 horses to choose from, and it's said that you can ride around the estancia for three days without covering the same terrain. ⊠ *In Veronica, 100 km (63 mi) south of La Plata, 165 km (103 mi) south of Buenos Aires* ⌖ *Arroyo 873, Buenos Aires 1007* 🕾 *11/4937–4326 Buenos Aires reservations, 2221/481–414 estancia* ⊕ *www.juangeronimo.com.ar* ⇆ *11 rooms* ⚷ *Dining room, pool, fishing, hiking, horseback riding, laundry service* ▭ *AE, MC, V* ¶⊙¶ *All-inclusive* $$$$.

✕⊡ **El Rosario de Areco.** The same family has owned this ochre-colored estancia since 1892, and though it's now a slick outfit it retains a family feel. Rooms are in renovated stable buildings and a former barn houses the dining room and living area. The estancia runs a polo school; it offers single lessons as well as week-long polo packages. ⊠ *Ruta 41, San Antonio de Areco 2760* 🕾 *2326/451–000* ⊕ *www.rosariodeareco.com.ar* ⇆ *16 rooms* ⚷ *Dining room, pool, horseback riding, polo, volleyball, lounge, Internet, meeting rooms* ▭ *No credit cards* ¶⊙¶ *All-inclusive* $$$$.

★✕⊡ **Santa Rita.** A path shaded by gum trees and ombúes leads up to the rose-colored main house, which dates to 1790, making Santa Rita one of the oldest estancias in Argentina. A huge open-plan living room has exposed brick walls and a sunken seating area ideal for curling up with a book. Up the majestic main staircase are spacious, wooden-floored rooms lit by chandeliers and kept warm by log fires; some even have four-poster beds. ⊠ *Antonio Carboni, Lobos 7240* 🕾 *2227/495–026* ⊕ *www.santa-rita.com.ar* ⇆ *13 rooms* ⚷ *Din-*

ing room, IDD phones, pool, bicycles, horseback riding ▭ *No credit cards* ¶⊙¶ *All-inclusive* $$$$.

★✕⊡ **Villa Maria.** This incredible Norman-Tudor mansion on 110 acres of countryside is evocative of the estates of English landed gentry. The expansive estate was bought in the 1890s by one of Argentina's wealthiest families. The crops were planted then, but the mansion itself—designed by Argentine architect Alejandro Bustillo—wasn't built until 1923. Whether wandering amidst the grounds, designed by Carlos Thays (of Buenos Aires botanical gardens fame), horseback riding, or sitting down to a formal, family-style lunch in the colonial dining room, you can live out your aristocratic Argentine fantasies here. ⊠ *R205, Km 47, Máximo Paz, 1814* 🕾 *2274/450–909 Estancia, 11/4322–7785 Buenos Aires reservations* ⊕ *www.estanciavillamaria.com* ⇆ *15 rooms* ⚷ *Dining room, tennis court, pool, bicycles, horseback riding, laundry service* ▭ *No credit cards* ¶⊙¶ *FAP* $$$$.

Tradición celebrations this is one of the most sought-after hotels in town, as the friendly but reserved staff and simple furnishings are much in keeping with the gaucho style. ⊠ *Zapiola 25, 2760* ☎ *2326/456–118* ⊕ *www.hostaldeareco.com.ar* ↩ *7 rooms* ⌂ *Dining room, no room phones.* ⊟ *AE, MC, V* ¶◯¶ *CP.*

Nightlife

One of the coolest watering holes in the entire region, **Las Ganas** (⊠ Vietyes and Pellegrini ☎No phone) has the requisite dim lighting, live music, boisterous local crowd, and an unbelievable collection of bottles lining the walls. **La Ochava de Cocota** (⊠ Alsina and Alem ☎ 2326/452–176) is a dim haunt, with old wooden tables and chairs and creatively modern lamps that swing from the ceiling. In addition to being a laid-back place to down a couple of drinks, it makes great empanadas.

Shopping

San Antonio de Areco is an excellent place to pick up handicrafts and gifts, especially traditional silverware and leather goods. Workshops that double as shops fill the old houses lining the streets leading off the main square.

The handwoven belts and ponchos **Cristina Giordano** (⊠ Sarmiento 112 ☎ 2326/452–829) created in soft, naturally-dyed fibers are fit to hang on the wall as art, and have justifiably made her San Antonio's best-known exponent of the traditional craft of weaving.

It's not surprising that the smell of leather hits you even before you go into **El Ombú** (⊠ Alsina and San Martín ☎ 2326/455–443), as everything in this beautiful corner shop is made of the stuff.

Gustavo Stagnaro (⊠ Arellano and Matheu ☎ 2326/454–801 ⊕ www.stagnaro.com.ar) is a big name in San Antonio silversmithing. His majestic corner store sells gaucho knives, no-nonsense silver jewelry, and mate paraphernalia.

All the gaucho accessories you can think of—including knives, belt buckles, and kerchief rings—are exquisitely made in silver at **Platería del Campo** (⊠ Sdo. Sombra 526 ☎ 2326/455–020).

THE ATLANTIC COAST

Southern Buenos Aires Province is synonymous with one thing—*la playa* (the beach). Every summer Argentines flock to the beaches at resort towns along the coast, many of which were originally large estates converted in the same way: with a *peatonal* (a pedestrians-only street) and a central plaza with a church. Nowadays it can be hard to see the sand in the summer months, when the towns are packed with porteños desperate to escape the city. However, by walking (or driving) a little farther, you can get some beach action in more agreeable surroundings even in peak season. Off-peak, the beaches tend to be deserted, and luxury accommodations are half the price. Though the weather can get chilly, walks along the windswept sands—when followed by an evening in front of a warm log fire—can be very romantic.

Mar del Plata is the capital of the beach towns, a sprawling city with a retro vibe that harks back to its 1970s heyday. Nevertheless, much of Buenos Aires' nightlife transports itself here for January and February, making this the center of hip summer action. Pinamar and Cariló have made their names as more exclusive (and thus expensive) destinations, whereas low-key Villa Gesell and Mar de las Pampas are more family- and backpacker-oriented.

Pinamar

6 *112 km (69 mi) south of San Clemente del Tuyú on Rte. 11, 342 km (212 mi) southeast of Buenos Aires via R2.*

The chic resort town of Pinamar attracts the Argentinian jet set, including film and television stars, models, and politicians (those who haven't gone to the even snootier Punta del Este in Uruguay). Top local-brand boutiques compete for space with family-run shops along the main street, Avenida Bunge, which is usually packed with browsing teens during peak season. The beach has pale sands, though to get a view of the dunes Pinamar was once famous for you need to go much farther north or south of the main drag. The best beaches in the area are in Ostende, a small town which is officially 8 km (5 mi) south of Pinamar, but effectively one of its suburbs.

Where to Stay & Eat

$$ ✕ **Tante.** Though this restaurant's huge menu offers food from all over the world, it's the signature German dishes that keep Pinamar residents coming back for more. At lunch or dinner, there's classic Alpine fare like fondues (meat, cheese, and chocolate), smoked pork ribs, or goulash, all artfully presented. Alternatively, come for an afternoon tea of Tante's calorie-filled homemade cakes, strudels, and pastries, as you watch the world pass on Avenida Bunge through the restaurant's big windows. ⊠ *De las Artes 35* ☎ *2254/482–735* ▤ *MC, V.*

$$ ✕ **El Viejo Lobo.** This classic joint has long been serving the best seafood in town. The airy open-plan dining room doesn't offer intimacy, but the checkered tablecloths are as cheery as the waitstaff. Deliciously garlicky chili prawns are the must-have starter; follow them with a more unusual fish dish like *pez lenguado con alcaparras* (flatfish in a browned butter and caper sauce). ⊠ *Av. del Mar and Av. Bunge* ☎ *2254/483–218* ▤ *MC, V.*

$ ✕ **Cantina Tulemei.** The mounted fishing rods and artistically draped nets adorning the wooden walls of Cantina Tulemei let you know that seafood is the focus here. The house specialty is squid, which could come in a sky-high pile of calamari, or in a red and green capsicum sauce. Wash away any lingering flavors with a *Don Pedro*: vanilla ice cream doused in scotch and scattered with nuts. ⊠ *Av. Bunge 64* ☎ *2254/488–696* ▤ *No credit cards.*

$$$$ ✕▥ **Hotel del Bosque.** Rolling parkland surrounds this hotel, which is an oasis of calm after the bustle of the beach. The all-white rooms are simple, but not stark, with fluffy pillows and flower arrangements. Ask for one with a view over the gardens. The outdoor pool is shaded by huge trees, and the indoor pool has a windowed wall overlooking the park, so you don't have to renounce the outdoors entirely when the wind kicks up. On cold days, one of the living room's sofas is a great place to curl up in front of a glowing fireplace. The hotel's restaurant is one of the best in town, serving modern Mediterranean dishes that showcase seasonal ingredients; seafood is a sure bet. During the high season, top local jazz musicians croon you through your meal. ⊠ *Av. Bunge 1550, 7167* ☎ *2254/482–480* ⍦ *Restaurant, café, room service, IDD phones, cable TV, 2 tennis courts, indoor pool, pool, gym, health club, hot tub, massage, sauna, racquetball, volleyball, bar, casino, recreation room, children's programs (ages 4–16; summer only), laundry service, convention center, free parking* ⊟ *AE, D, MC, V* ⦿| *CP.*

$$$ ✕⌂ **Viejo Hotel Ostende.** Belle Epoque charm oozes from this old-world hotel, which dates to 1913, when the Ostende resort first opened. Guests treading its black-and-white tiled corridors once included authors Silvina Ocampo and Adolfo Bioy Casares, as well as Antoine de St. Éxupery, of Little Prince fame. Though the grand reception area and cozy buttercup-yellow restaurant are luxurious, rooms are simple, with unadorned walls and the most understated wooden furniture, much of which is as old as the hotel. The hotel's restaurant does some of the best food in Ostende, centering on simple Argentine fare made with the best ingredients and served with great gravitas. ⊠ *Biarritz and Cairo, Ostende, 7364* ☎☎ *2254/486–081* ⊕ *www.hotelostende.com.ar* ⇌ *82 rooms* ⍦ *Restaurant, room service, no room TVs, pool, beach, lobby lounge, children's programs (ages 5–15; summer only)* ⊟ *MC, V* ⦿| *MAP.*

$$–$$$ ⌂ **Hotel las Calas.** This self-proclaimed boutique hotel is made up of units that are a cross between rooms and apartments. Outside, they've tried to make things very zen, with a gravel and bamboo patio and earthy stucco walls. Plain white walls and drab linens mean that the rooms verge on the basic, though the bathrooms with their big bowl-style sinks are more of a step in the right direction. Off-season the hotel is sometimes closed weekdays, so call ahead to check. ⊠ *Bunge 560, 7167* ☎ *2254/ 482–447* ⊕ *www.lascalashotel.com.ar* ⇌ *16 suites* ⍦ *Restaurant, room service, minibars, cable TV, in-room data ports, in-room safe, gym, massage, wine bar, meeting rooms* ⊟ *AE, MC, V* ⦿| *CP.*

$–$$ ⌂ **Los Pájaros.** Units here are spacious, with separate bedrooms and dining/living rooms. The look is Argentine country, with exposed brick walls and heavy wooden furniture. Prices double in high season, when rooms are rented out only by the week. ⊠ *Del Tuyú 919, 7167* ☎ *2254/490– 618* ⊕ *www.lospajaros.com.ar* ⇌ *30 units* ⍦ *Restaurant, kitchenettes, pool, gym, bar* ⊟ *AE, DC, MC, V.*

Nightlife

Most of Pinamar's nightlife centers on the cafés and ice cream parlors on Avenida Bunge and the streets branching off it. As in other beach towns, going to the movies is an immensely popular nighttime activity; buy your tickets early at **Cine Bahía** (⊠ Av. Bunge 74 ☎ 2254/481–012).

Dancers groove atop speakers at Pinamar's most popular nightclub, **Ku** (⊠ Bartolome Mitre 28 ☎ 2254/49–3198), which draws a young crowd who don't seem to mind the wide variety of music—from rock, house, salsa, and cumbia—played on any given night. Some of the best cocktails in town are at trendy beachfront bar **UFO Point** (⊠ Av. del Mar y Tobís ☎ 2254/488–511), which gets clubby later on.

Cariló

❼ *8 km (5 mi) south of Pinamar.*

Cariló, the new darling of the summer resorts, represents an entirely new concept in Argentine beach tourism. Rather than a built-up town with a central square, a business center, and a bustling beach scene, Cariló is more like an exclusive seaside forest—a protected community with bungalows, hotels, and condos hidden in strategic places along a network of winding dirt roads. As a result, the beaches are pristine, the air is clean and quiet, and the beach experience is more intimate, but the experience is not steeped in Argentine history or culture. It's especially good for groups or families looking for a bucolic getaway. There is an 18-hole golf course just outside the town, and many companies offer outdoor activities like horseback riding and trekking—inquire at your hotel.

Where to Stay & Eat

$$$ ╳ **Camelia Sensi.** A modern take on traditional Swiss fare is the inspiration behind the menu at chic Camelia Sensi. If you're feeling adventurous, go for the house specialty, *lomo à la pierrade*: a chef brings a hot slab of marble to your table and cooks the thinly sliced beef and vegetables on it, right under your nose. The fondues are also good. ⊠ *Boyero and Avellano* ☎ *2254/470–369* ▤ *AE, MC, V.*

$$ ╳ **Via Vittoria.** The delicate dishes at Via Vittoria are a far cry from the stodgy pastas that are usually the mainstay of Italian restaurants in Argentina. After antipasti, consider the risotto trio: three delicious mounds flavored with squid ink, Milanese, and wild mushrooms. The excellent wine list includes both local and Italian vintages, with most available by the glass. Regular live music performances reach their peak in the summer, when tenors from the Colón theater put on two shows. ⊠ *Divisadero between Cerezo and Avellano* ☎ *2254/470–386* ⚶ *Reservations essential* ▤ *AE, MC, V.*

$–$$ ╳ **La Pulpería.** Rustic tables and chairs, cast-iron grills, and big steaks might sound a bit too gaucho for Cariló's posh crowd, but this traditional parilla is a firm local favorite. As well as the usual beef cuts, La Pulpería does great barbecued pork, chicken, and *achuras* (sweetbreads). ⊠ *Divisadero at Avellano* ☎ *2254/470–296* ⚶ *Reservations essential* ▤ *MC, V.*

$$$ ╳▣ **Hostería Cariló.** This small hotel has put a lot of effort into creating an artsy vibe: the background music in the lobby is classic jazz, and there is a substantial video library from which you can borrow both classics and new releases. Downstairs is the Fellini "microcinema," which shows an arthouse flick nightly—guests vote on the pick. Rooms are spacious and comfortable, though the peach-colored walls and non-matching bedspreads aren't very inspiring. The hotel's restaurant, Tiramisu, is filled with rustic wooden tables; at night the lights are lowered and crisp white linen emerges. Great cocktails come from behind the cluttered bar, decorated with Tiffany-style lamps and old photos. The hotel has a range of spa treatments, and often offers all-inclusive packages. ⊠ *Avutarda and Jacarandá, 7167* ☎ *2254/470–703* ⊕ *www. hosteriacarilo.com.ar* ⤳ *16 suites, 4 duplexes, 12 apartments* ♻ *Restaurant, room service, IDD phones, cable TV, in-room VCRs, indoor pool, pool, gym, hot tub, massage, bicycles, bar, cinema, recreation room, playground* ⊟ *AE, MC, V* |◎| *CP, MAP.*

$$–$$$ 🖼 **Hotel Talara.** The second-oldest hotel in Cariló, this fresh, airy establishment a few steps from the beach has comfortable rooms with pleasant balconies, some with spectacular water views. The lobby and upstairs lounge brim with plant life, and the bar and restaurant downstairs are equally stylish. There's a big breakfast spread and a helpful staff. The hotel combines the familiarity and charm of a smaller hotel with the comfort level of a bigger one. ⊠ *Laurel and Costanera, 7167* ☎ *2254/ 47–0304* ⊕ *www.talarahotel.com.ar* ⤳ *28 rooms* ♻ *Restaurant, room service, minibars, indoor pool, gym, massage, sauna, beach, horseback riding, bar, lobby lounge* ⊟ *MC, V* |◎| *CP.*

Villa Gesell, Mar de las Pampas & Mar Azul

❽ *16 km (10 mi) south of Pinamar.*

Villa Gesell was settled in 1931 by the German businessman Carlos Gesell, who experimented with forestation techniques to stabilize the vast tracts of dunes. Within a decade, Gesell had created a paradise of pine trees and forest. The town became a nature preserve and vacation spot. Once the most bohemian beach on the coast, it's now the haunt of middle-class Argentine families, who come for the tranquility, the dunes, and the alpine architecture. It has also become very popular in recent years with young people, who fill the town's many campsites and budget units in summer.

Mar de las Pampas, Mar Azul, and Las Gaviotas are three handkerchief-size beach towns 5 km–10 km (3 mi–6 mi) south of Villa Gesell down the Ruta Interbalnearia. They function like distant suburbs and maintain the peaceful back-to-nature vibe that Villa Gesell once had.

At the **Casa de la Cultura** (Culture House) you can see displays of local crafts. It's also the site of yearly arts festivals, including the Villa Gesell song festival in February. ⊠ *Av. 3 between Paseos 108 and 109* 🖃 *Free* ☉ *Mon.–Sat. 10–6.*

Picturesque **Faro Querandí** (Querandí Lighthouse), about 30 km (18 mi) south of Villa Gesell, is surrounded by forest and sand dunes and can only be reached by four-wheel-drive vehicle or quad-bike, both of which can be rented in town. The lighthouse itself is not open to the public. ⊠ *On Rte. 11* ☎ *No phone.*

Where to Stay and Eat

Villa Gesell has over ten different campsites, which the tourist office can direct you to. Be warned that during the summer most campsites are packed to bursting with noisy teenagers.

2

★ **$-$$** ✕ **Cartajena D'Indias.** The waiters know all their local customers by name at this Spanish-style *bodegón* (tavern restaurant), but they give an equally enthusiastic welcome to out-of-towners. Terra-cotta roof-tiles cover the outside tables; inside white stucco walls are chaotically hung with aging keepsakes and the odd farming instrument. You might be tempted to make a meal of the many appetizers, but resist doing so— you must try the *lomo a las tres pimientas* (beef in a three-pepper sauce) or the mozzarella, shallot, and nut-filled *agnolottis* (extra-large ravioli) in a creamy spinach sauce. If you've still got room, there are towering ice-cream sundaes for dessert. ⊠ *Av. 3 No. 215, at Paseo 103* ☎ *2255/ 462–858* ▭ *No credit cards.*

$-$$ ✕ **Viejos Tiempos.** Tea houses abound in Villa Gesell and Mar de las Pampas, but none have more tranquil surroundings than Viejos Tiempos, which sits in a beautifully kept garden. In summer, hummingbirds hover over the flowers, while tea and cakes are served at heavy wood tables set with floral-patterned china and crisp tablecloths. An open fireplace keeps things toasty in winter. After years of making some of the best cakes in town, Viejos Tiempos has added (bizarrely) Mexican dishes to their menu, but it's the sweets that remain the main draw here. ⊠ *Leoncio Paina at Cruz del Sur, Mar de las Pampas* ☎ *2255/479–524* ▭ *No credit cards.*

¢-$ ✕ **Windy.** No-nonsense hamburgers, steaks, and big plates of fries make Windy the perfect low-key refueling stop after (or during) a long day of sun and sand. Its tables spill out onto the beach, and the owners have gone for the pirate vibe, with dark-wood paneling and the odd skull and crossbones on the walls. If you're in town off-season, their specialty coffees are great winter warmers. ⊠ *Paseo 104 at the beach* ☎ *2255/460– 430* ▭ *No credit cards.*

★ **$$** ✕▣ **Heiwa.** Sea breezes ruffle the cotton drapes at this beachfront hotel in quiet Las Gaviotas. The low-key, white-walled, simply furnished rooms are often booked up months in advance by returning devotees, but even if you can't stay, don't miss eating at the restaurant, which has the best food in town. Mismatched crockery, paper lampshades, and sandy floors provide the backdrop for platters of homemade sushi and sashimi, as well as other options like casseroles and fish kebabs. The dessert *de rigueur* is the orange and ginger spring rolls. If you just want a drink, Heiwa makes delicious juices and cocktails under the white canvas awnings of their beach bar, which is lit with flaming torches after dark. ⊠ *Calle 34 at the beachfront, Las Gaviotas* ☎ *2255/453–674* ⊕ *www. lasgaviotas.com.ar/heiwa* ⤶ *5 apartments* ⚐ *Restaurant, refrigerators, beach, bar* ▭ *No credit cards* ⊘ *Closed weekdays Apr.–June and Aug.–Nov.* ⦿ *CP, MAP.*

$$$$ ▣ **Miradores del Bosque.** Just a block from the beach, the white clapboard cabins and open parkland of this family-oriented spot make for a peaceful stay. Furnishings are simple, but the fully stocked kitchens, hot tubs, and CD players in each room make the cabins homes away from home. In summer, the complex organizes excursions to the nearby Querandí Lighthouse. ⊠ *Julio A. Roca, at Hudson, Mar de las Pampas 7165* ☎ *2255/452–147* ⊕ *www.miradoresdelbosque.com* ⤶ *2 studios, 11 apartments* ⚐ *BBQs, IDD phones, fans, in-room safes, in-room* *hot tubs, kitchens, microwaves, refrigerators, cable TV, pool, gym, hot tub, massage, sauna, beach, Ping-Pong, bar, recreation room, playground, free parking* ⊟ *AE, MC, V* ⦿ *CP.*

$$ ⊡ **Abedul.** Solid stone walls, oak fixtures, and hand-woven drapes make the split-level cabins at Abedul very earthy. Outside each is a wooden deck with its own barbecue, and you can arrange for your breakfast to be brought here at the hour of your choice. The bedrooms look out over Mar de las Pampas' unspoiled woods, and the beach is only three blocks away. ⊠ *Santa María, between El Lucero and El Ceibo, 7165* ☎ *2255/ 455–819* ⦿ *www.mardelaspampas.com.ar/abedul/* ⮡ *7 cabins* ⬠ *BBQs, no room phones, kitchenettes, microwaves, refrigerators, cable TV, bicycles, free parking* ⊟ *AE, MC, V* ⦿ *CP.*

¢ ⊡ **Residencial Viya.** Budget accommodations aren't hard to come by in Villa Gesell, but this family-run hotel is one of the best options. The simple rooms have plain wooden furniture and shared bathrooms, but are kept incredibly clean. In the well-kept garden, there's an outside seating area shaded by trees. ⊠ *Av. 5 No. 582, 7165, Villa Gesell* ☎ *2255/ 462–757* ⦿ *www.gesell.com.ar/viya* ⮡ *8 rooms* ⬠ *Restaurant, laundry service; no room TVs* ⊟ *No credit cards* ⦿ *CP.*

Mar del Plata

❾ *123 km (77 mi) southeast of Villa Gesell on Rte. 11, 400 km (248 mi) south of Buenos Aires via R2.*

Come summer, Argentina becomes obsessed with Mar del Plata. The city of 600,000 residents is the most popular beach resort in the country— and at least five times as big as any runners-up. Beaches are comically crowded in January and February, when there's a carnival-like atmosphere day and night (no one seems to notice that the sun goes down). Dull gray sand and chilly water may not make for the best beach experience, but in Mar del Plata activities like people-watching, eating, shopping, and clubbing are just as important. The tourist infrastructure hums, with more than 700 hotels, countless eateries, and an array of theme parks, theaters, and specialized museums. It's not the most tranquil location, but it's a definite summertime experience. Off-season, the windy sands and almost deserted boulevards feel cinematic, though it can get a bit lonely. The city has several beaches in the downtown area; the summertime action revolves around Playa Bristol. The trendiest strip of sand in Mar del Plata is south of the lighthouse, but you need a car to get there comfortably.

All roads in Mar del Plata now lead to the **Rambla Casino** (⊠ Av. Marítimo 2100 ☎ 223/495–7011), in an attractive 1930s brick-and-limestone building with black mansard roof. Next door is an identical building that housed the city's first beachfront hotel, the Hotel Provincial. The Casino is the centerpiece of city nightlife, open daily 3–3. It is not, however, properly air-conditioned.

The port area, simply called **El Puerto,** is worth a visit for its restaurants, attractive boats, and a colony of *lobos marinos* (sea lions). (The frequently powerful stench along the jetty guides you to them.) Hundreds of sea lions lounge at your feet, cavort in the water, and sun themselves atop decaying, poetically half-sunken ships in an offshore area called the **Barranco de los Lobos.** From this breakwater you can watch the scores of bright orange fishing boats heading back to the port at sunset. ✉ *2 km (1 mi) west of the casino on Av. Marítimo.*

Museo del Mar is an attractive, modern showcase for a collection of more than 30,000 seashells. The four-story complex has numerous large fish tanks, a multilevel cyber-café, an art exhibition space, a library, and a gift shop. The rooftop Mirador del Faro (Lighthouse Lookout) provides panoramic views of the city. ✉ *Av. Colón 1114* ☎ *223/451-3553* ⊕ *www. museodelmar.com* 🔳 *3 pesos* ⊙ *Jan.–Feb., daily 8 AM–2 AM; Mar.–Dec., Mon.–Thurs. 8 AM–9 PM, Fri. and Sat. 8 AM–midnight, Sun. 9–9.*

Punta Mogotes, a few miles west of Barranco de los Lobos, is a wide area of 24 side-by-side beach clubs. Each has colorful cabanas, snack shops, restaurants, and activities like volleyball and water sports. ✉ *Off Av. Martítima, 2 km (1 mi) west past the port.*

More of a sea-theme amusement park than a true aquarium, ☼ **Mar del Plata Aquarium** has performing dolphins and sea lions, waterskiing shows, and a 3-D movie. The aquarium also has a beach with beach chairs, umbrellas, and a bar. It's south of Punta Mogotes on R11. ✉ *Av. Martinez de Hoz 5600* ☎ *223/467-0700* ⊕ *www.mdpaquarium.com.ar* 🔳 *20 pesos* ⊙ *Jan. and Feb., daily 10 AM–11 PM; last ticket sold at 9.*

Where to Stay & Eat

$–$$$ ✕ **Torreón del Monje.** This multilevel castle structure has some of the best views in town, overlooking the entire beach, bay, and cityscape of Mar del Plata. Crowds of beachgoers and local folks spread out over a series of terraces shaded by scores of umbrellas. The fare is predictable—an overambitious mix of fish, meat, pasta, and Argentine pizza (which isn't bad)—but the fried calamari and a large bottle of Quilmes served up in an ice bucket really hit the spot on a sunny afternoon. ✉ *Paseo Jesús de Galíndez* ☎ *223/451-5575* 🍴 *AE, DC, MC, V.*

★ ¢–$$$ ✕ **Trenque Laquen.** Impostors abound in Mar del Plata, but this place is the original Trenque Laquen; they've been preparing some of the best steak in the region since 1956. The heavily local, middle-age clientele seems to know this well, which is why they routinely make the trek to this somewhat unlikely residential neighborhood (it's within easy walking distance of downtown, though). The plate of *mollejas* (grilled sweetbreads) is a revelation, an impossibly tender, crispy, creamy delight that melts in your mouth. The *bife de chorizo,* a boneless sirloin steak served on its own wooden cutting board, is juicy and flavorful. The dining room is traditional, simple, and a bit too bright, but it's supremely appropriate for a steak house. The oceanfront branch is nearly as good as the original. ✉ *Mitre 2807 at Garay* ☎ *223/493-7149* ✉ *Trenque Lauquen de la Costa* ✉ *Blvd. Marítimo 4099* ☎ *223/514-269* 🍴 *AE, DC, MC, V.*

★ $$ ✕ **Viento en Popa.** Word of mouth is the only advertising this restaurant seems to need: it doesn't even have a sign outside yet its tables are always full. Owner Nieco Gioffi is a pioneer of so-called South Atlantic cuisine, aiming to show off the quality of the local fish and seafood, rather than bathe them in sauces. Dishes such as the *Burriqueta en oliva* (burriqueta fish in olive oil and tarragon served with asparagus) are testament to the success of his formula. ⊠ *Blvd. Martínez de Hoz 163, El Puerto* ☎ *223/489–0220* ⊛ *Reservations essential* ☰ *AE, MC, V* ⊙ *Closed Mon.–Wed. Apr.–Nov.*

$–$$ ✕ **Pepe Nero.** Three generations of Italian chefs are behind the menu at this restaurant. The old building has exposed brick walls, offsetting the traditional white tablecloths and gleaming cutlery. You'll certainly be happy with the fantastic homemade pastas, but the rabbit and seafood dishes are also good. ⊠ *Avellaneda and Córdoba* ☎ *223/494–9854* ☰ *AE, D, MC, V.*

$$$$ ▦ **Hotel Costa Galana.** All the rooms at this hotel have sea views, which means gorgeous sunrises if you get up early (or stay up late) enough. Rooms are richly decorated with thick wool carpets, mahogany furniture, and heavy drapes, which together with good sound-proofing, keep the noise of downtown far away. The hotel's top-notch restaurant, Le Frac, does an Argentine take on modern Mediterranean cuisine. Local seafood is shown off in dishes like *Salmón rosado con croustillade de hierbas* (pink salmon in a herb crust, served with avocado parfait and tomato relish). You can look over the bay from the restaurant's sea-view terrace. ⊠ *Blvd. Marítimo P. P. Ramos 5725, 7602* ☎ *223/486–0000* ⊕ *www.hotelcostagalana.com* ⇱ *186 rooms* ⚭ *2 restaurants, café, room service, IDD phones, in-room hot-tubs, in-room safes, minibar, cable TV, pool, gym, spa, sauna, piano bar, recreation room, babysitting, children's programs (ages 3–12), laundry service, concierge, Internet, business center, parking (fee).* ☰ *AE, D, MC, V* ⦿ *BP.*

$$$$ ▦ **Sheraton Mar del Plata.** You'll find peerless comforts within this soaring, modern building that sets the standard for luxury in Mar del Plata. Inside, the 11-story atrium defines the space, and a wide lobby gives way to second- and third-floor restaurants and cafés. Though it's rather removed from the city center and the shoreline, a sane distance may be a sign of wisdom in this party-frenzied city. Half of the rooms have views over a golf course to the naval base and the sea. Las Barcas restaurant is an elegant take on the parrilla. ⊠ *Av. Alem 4221, 7600* ☎ *223/499–9000* ⊕ *www. sheraton.com* ⇱ *160 rooms, 32 suites* ⚭ *Restaurant, coffee shop, snack bar, room service, in-room safes, minibars, IDD phones, in-room data ports, in-room hot-tubs, cable TV, golf privileges, indoor pool, pool, gym, hair salon, hot tub, sauna, spa, lobby bar, babysitting, laundry service, concierge, Internet, convention center, meeting rooms, car rental, travel services, parking (fee), no-smoking rooms.* ☰ *AE, DC, MC, V* ⦿ *BP.*

$ ▦ **El Hostal de Alem.** This 70-year-old stone house is in the quiet, residential neighborhood of Playa Grande. Beaches are within walking distance. Rooms have comfortable beds (with box springs—a bragging matter in small Argentine hotels) and new furnishings. The on-site restaurant is very good, and the overall experience is one of tranquillity and comfort. ⊠ *Rawson 233 at Av. Alem, 7600* ☎ *223/486–4008 or 223/486–2265* ⊕ *www.elhostaldealem.com.ar* ⇱ *28 rooms* ⚭ *Restaurant, tea shop, room service, minibars, IDD phones, in-room data ports, bar, babysitting, laundry service, Internet, meeting rooms* ☰ *AE, DC, MC, V* ⦿ *BP.*

Nightlife & the Arts

Especially in summer, Mar del Plata offers a dizzying selection as the Buenos Aires theater, clubbing, and music scenes decamp to the beach. The Hotel Provincial Tourist Office publishes a free monthly activity guide. In March, the city hosts an international film festival.

NIGHTLIFE   Ultra-cool **Avalon** (⊠ Güemes 2782 ☎ 223/486–0113) has everything you need for a complete night-out: a post-beach happy hour, restaurant, and all-night club. Airport-lounge style windows give you a great view of the beach as you groove all night to the beats of top DJs. There's a laid-back surfer vibe at **La Princesa** (⊠ Bernardo de Irigoyen 3820), which does great cocktails and bar snacks. The most popular night in town for Argentines in their twenties and thirties is at **Sobremonte** (⊠ Constitución 6690 ☎ 223/479–2600 ⊕ www.sobremonte.com.ar), a very modern complex of restaurants and dance clubs. The latter generally open after midnight and don't really get going until 3 AM. The most favored bar of Mar del Plata's gay community is **Xtasis** (⊠ Corrientes 2044 ☎ 223/492–0338).

THE ARTS   Mar del Plata's annual film festival, the **Festival de Cine de Mar del Plata** (⊕ www.mdpfilmfestival.com.ar), is held in March. It's Argentina's biggest, and attracts choice flicks and big names in international cinema. During January and February open-air stages are set up on the beach at **Punta Mogotes** (⊠ Off Av. Martítima, 2 km (1 mi) west past the port). Top local radio stations such as La Rock and Pop host the gigs, which feature big Argentine bands.

The **Centro Cultural General Pueyrredón** (⊠ 25 de Mayo 3108 ☎ 223/493–6767) is the largest theater venue, especially in summer. There are four screens at the movie theater **Cines del Paseo** (⊠ Diagonal Pueyrredón 3058 ☎ 223/496–1100). **Los Gallegos** (⊠ Rivadavía 3050 ☎ 223/492–3700) is a mall with the newest movie theater in town. Let the professional, English-speaking staff at the **tourist office** (⊠ Hotel Provincial, Av. Marítimo 2400 ☎ 223/495–1777) direct you to the hottest cultural events. It's open daily 8 AM–10 PM.

Sports & the Outdoors

BEACHES   Mar del Plata's main beach is a crescent that stretches out just below the entire length of the city center. Seriously packed all summer, it attracts young, old, and families alike until 6 or 7 PM, and it's dotted with places to get food or drink. There are lots of smaller beaches further out from the city center—south of the lighthouse are the most fashionable sand spots.

BIKING   **Cicloturismo** (⊠ Av. Alem 3655 ☎ 223/481–0082) organizes various biking tours (starting at 25 pesos, including lunch) that lead you around the city's green areas and incorporate city history.

BOATING &   **Turimar** (⊠ Banquina de Pescadores at El Puerto ☎ 223/489–7775) or-
FISHING   ganizes hour-long boat tours of the coast departing from the port daily every 40 minutes 10–6:30. Buy tickets (7 pesos) at the kiosk in the Centro Comercial del Puerto. Turimar also arranges five-hour deep-sea fishing expeditions for 75 pesos and up, including equipment.

Crucero Anamora (✉ Dársena B at El Puerto ☎ 223/489–0310) has a boat with a dance floor and bar. The hour-long port-to-casino trip departs four times a day in the summer.

The web-based company **Aquafish** (☎ 223/492–3007 ⊕ www.aquafish. com.ar) organize all-day fishing excursions that include rods, lines, baits, and meals as well as transport.

GOLF **Los Acantilados Golf Club** (✉ Paseo Costanero Sur 5 ☎ 223/467–2500) has a 27-hole course that's among the country's best. **Mar del Plata Golf Club** (✉ Aristóbulo del Valle 3940 ☎ 223/486–2329) has two 18-hole courses within the city limits.

HORSEBACK **Campo del Mar** (✉ Paseo Costanero Sur Presidente Illía, Playa los Lobos, RIDING 11 km (7 mi) from downtown ☎ 223/460–5448) organizes horseback riding on the beach a little way out of town.

IGUAZÚ FALLS

⑩ Iguazú consists of some 275 separate waterfalls—in the rainy season there are as many as 350—that send their white cascades plunging more than 200 feet onto the rocks below. Dense, lush jungle surrounds the falls: here the tropical sun and the omnipresent moisture make the jungle grow at a pace that produces a towering pine tree in two decades instead of the seven it takes in, say, Scandinavia. By the falls and along the roadside, rainbows and butterflies are set off against vast walls of red earth, which is so ubiquitous that eventually even peso bills in the area turn red from exposure to the stuff.

Puerto Iguazú, a town of 25,000 people 17 km (11 mi) west of the falls, is the best base. The town originated as a port for shipping wood from the region. It was in the early 20th century that Victoria Aguirre, a high-society porteña, funded the building of a road that extends to Cataratas del Iguazú to make it easier for people to visit the falls. You may find Puerto Iguazú preferable to its livelier Brazilian counterpart, Foz do Iguaçu—it's considerably more tranquil and safer (when you go to the Brazilian side, leave your valuables in the hotel and be on the alert; crime is more frequent there).

Exploring the Falls

The best way to immerse yourself in the falls is to wander the many access paths, which are a combination of bridges, ramps, stone staircases, and metal catwalks set in a forest of ferns, begonias, orchids, and tropical trees. The catwalks over the water put you right in the middle of the action, so be ready to get doused by the rising spray. (Be sure to bring rain gear.)

The Brazilians are blessed with the best panoramic view, an awesome vantage point that suffers only from the sound of the gnatlike helicopters that erupt out of the lawn of the Hotel das Cataratas right in front of the falls. (Unfortunately, most indigenous macaws and toucans have abandoned the area to escape the whine of the helicopters' engines.) The

TO ESTACIÓN
GARGANTA
DEL DIABLO
↓

Argentine side offers the better close-up experience of the falls, with excellent hiking paths, catwalks that approach the falls, a sandy beach to relax on, and places to bathe in the froth of the Río Iguazú.

The falls on the Argentine side are in the **Parque Nacional Iguazú** (Iguazú National Park), which was founded in 1934, declared a World Heritage Site in 1984, and refurbished by a private concession in 2001. There's a Visitor Center, called Yvyra Reta ("country of the trees" in Guaraní tongue) with excellent facilities, including a good explanation of the region's ecology and human history. From here you can catch the gas-propelled Tren de la Selva (Jungle Train), which departs every 20 minutes. It makes a stop at Estación Cataratas and then proceeds to Estación Garganta del Diablo (Devil's Throat Station), where a new wheelchair-accessible, metal catwalk leads to a platform right beside one of the most dizzying spots in the world. Here the Iguazú river plummets, with an awesome roar, more than 230 feet into a horseshoe-shape gorge, amid a perennial cloud of mist. Be sure to take a plastic bag to stash your camera in.

If a more relaxed stroll is preferred, take the well-marked, ½ km (.3 mi) **Sendero Verde** (Green Path) past Estación Cataratas and connect with **Circuito Superior** (Upper Circuit), which stretches along the top of the falls for 1 km (½ mi). With six sightseeing balconies, this easy walk of about an hour and a half provides great upper views of the falls Dos Hermanas, Ramírez, Bossetti, Méndez, and the most impressive, named after the *Libertador* (Liberator) San Martín. Near the falls look for *vencejos,* swallows that nest behind the curtains of water. Note that the paths beyond the San Martín have more than a few stairways and, therefore, are not wheelchair-accessible.

The **Circuito Inferior** (Lower Circuit) starts by a water-and-watch tower and is a 1.7-km-long (1.1-mi-long) loop that consists of a metal catwalk, lots of stairways, and protected promontories at the best spots. At the beginning of this walk, you'll pass the small Salto Alvar Núñez Cabeza de Vaca falls, named after the Spanish conquistador who stumbled onto the spectacle in the 16th century; the Peñón de Bella Vista (Rock of the Beautiful View); and the Salto Lanusse (Lanusse Falls). These are just preliminaries to get you warmed up for the main event. Halfway along this circuit you get a panoramic peek at what's to come—through the foliage you can see the gigantic curtain of water in the distance. The trail leads along the lower side of Brazo San Martín, a branch of the Iguazú river that makes a wide loop to the south before following the same vertical fate as the main branch, along a mile-long series of falls. The last part of the trail offers the most exciting views of the main falls, including Garganta del Diablo in the background. Allow about an hour and a half to walk this circuit. There's no way to get lost on the catwalk, but English-speaking guides, found at the visitor center, can be hired to provide detailed explanations of the falls.

From Circuito Inferior you can reach the pier where a free boat service crosses the river to **Isla San Martín** (San Martín Island). This service operates all day, except when the river is too high. On the island, after a steep climb up a rustic stairway, a circular trail opening presents three spectacular panoramas of Salto San Martín, Garganta del Diablo, and Salto Ventana (Window Falls). Few people make the effort to cross the river to Isla San Martín and do this climb, so you can often enjoy the show in solitary splendor.

The **Sendero Macuco** (Macuco Trail) extends 4 km (2½ mi) into the jungle, ending at the Salto Arrechea (Arrechea Falls) farther downriver from the main falls. The trail is very carefully marked, and descriptive signs in Spanish explain the jungle's flora and fauna. The closest you'll get to a wild animal is likely to be a paw print in the dirt, though you may be lucky enough to glimpse a monkey. The foliage is dense, so the most common surprises are the jungle sounds that seem to emerge out of nowhere. You can turn back at any point, or continue on to the refreshing view of the river and Salto Arrechea, where there is a swimming spot. The best time to hear animal calls and to avoid the heat is either early in the morning or just before sunset. The battalions of butterflies, also best seen in the early morning or late afternoon, can be marvelous, and the intricate glistening cobwebs crisscrossing the trail are a treat in the dawn light. Plan on spending about three hours for the whole trip. The **Centro de Investigaciones Ecológicas Subtropicales** (Center for Subtropical Ecological Investigation; ☎ 3757/421–222) maintains the trail.

Yerba Mate

This herbal infusion has long been an integral component of not only the northeast's diet but also its culture. The Guaraní introduced the herb to the Jesuit missionaries, who learned to cultivate it. Yerba mate here is much like tea in England; it often serves as the basis of social interaction: people drink it at almost any hour of the day, and it's often extended to strangers as a welcoming gesture. Typically, ground-up yerba mate leaves are placed in a carved-out gourd. Then hot water from a thermos is added, sometimes accompanied by a spoonful of sugar. You drink the infusion through a metal tube with a filter at the bottom. When the drink is finished, the gourd is refilled with hot water and is passed to the next person in line. In the provinces of Corrientes and Misiones, the nation's largest yerba mate–producing regions, it's not uncommon in public places to find an enormous kettle containing hot water with which to fill your thermos to make the drink.

On the Brazilian side, the falls, known in Portuguese as the Foz do Iguaçu, can be seen from the **Parque Nacional Foz do Iguaçu,** Brazil's national park. The park runs for 25 km (16 mi) along a paved highway southwest of downtown Foz do Iguaçu, the nearest town. Note that from November through February, Brazil is one hour ahead of Argentina. The **park entrance** (⊠ Km 17, Rodovia das Cataratas ☎ 005545/529–8383) is the best place to get information; it's open daily 8–5, and the entrance fee is roughly 20 reales. Much of the park's 457,000 acres is protected rain forest—off-limits to visitors and home to the last viable populations of panthers as well as rare flora such as bromeliads and orchids. The falls are 11 km (7 mi) from the park entrance. The luxurious, historic Hotel das Cataratas sits near the trailhead. Public parking is allowed on the highway shoulder and in a small lot near the hotel. The path to the falls is 2 km (1 mi) long, and its walkways, bridges, and stone staircases lead through the rain forest to concrete and wooden catwalks that take you to the falls. Highlights of the Brazilian side of the falls include first the Salto Santa Maria, from which catwalks branch off to the Salto Deodoro and Salto Floriano, where you'll be doused by the spray. The end of the catwalk puts you right in the heart of the spectacle at Garganta do Diablo ("Devil's Throat" in Portuguese), for a perspective different from the Argentine side. On the last section of the main trail is a building with facilities, including a panoramic elevator; it's open daily 8:30–6, and there's a small fee.

Where to Stay & Eat

Neither Puerto Iguazú nor Foz do Iguaçu are known for their restaurant scenes. While eateries in both places are generally cheap, quality is rarely anything to write home about and you may well be the only diner in the place. Most hotels and even hostels have their own restaurants, which are the best—and most convenient—options.

$ ✗ **El Charo.** This restaurant is in a shabby old house that looks like it could easily be blown down with a huff and a puff: all the paintings are tilted, the roof is sinking, and the cowhide on the seats is faded. Nevertheless, this is one of town's most popular restaurants because of its consistently delicious and inexpensive *parrilladas* (a sampling of grilled meat), as well as its pasta and grilled fish. Note that napkins come only by request. ⊠ *Av. Córdoba 106, Puerto Iguazú, Argentina* ☎ *3757/421–529* ▭ *No credit cards.*

$ ✗ **Jardín Iguazú.** At lunch and at odd hours, when everything else is closed, this restaurant serves a good fixed-price meal—for about $5 you get an empanada, a salad, a main dish with pasta and meat, and a beverage. The place is rather shiny, with highly polished stones on the floor and a stage (used for live music in the evenings) speckled with silver chips. Jardín Iguazú is close to the bus terminal and stays open until 2 AM. ⊠ *Avs. Misiones and Córdoba, Puerto Iguazú, Argentina* ☎ *3757/423–200.*

★ $$$$ ✗▥ **Hotel Cataratas.** Though this redbrick hotel with green window sills and white awnings isn't especially attractive from the outside, inside is a different story: the classy lobby and ample guest rooms are tastefully decorated with the finest materials and furnishings. Ask for a master double, which is the same price as the standard double, but slightly nicer. The hotel also has beautiful grounds and excellent facilities, including an enormous pool with landscaped waterfalls. The high-quality restaurant, serving international cuisine, has an à la carte menu and a fixed-price buffet (dinner only). ⊠ *R12, Km 4, Argentina 3370* ☎ *3757/421–100* ⇨ *112 rooms, 4 suites* ♤ *Restaurant, room service, in-room safes, minibars, tennis court, pool, gym, massage, sauna, volleyball, bar, business services, meeting room, travel services* ▭ *AE, DC, MC, V.*

★ $$$$ ✗▥ **Sheraton International Iguazú.** The building may be an eyesore, but it's just a short walk from the falls. Half of the rooms have direct views of them—be sure to reserve one of these well in advance (note that they're about 30% more expensive). Floor-to-ceiling windows reveal the inspiring scene to the lobby, restaurants, bars, and even the pool. The Garganta del Diablo ($$) restaurant is one of the area's finest; the trout in pastry and the surubí in banana leaves are exquisite. The restaurant is only open for dinner, which starts after the last bus to Puerto Iguazú leaves; if you're not a Sheraton guest, plan on laying out over 50 pesos for the taxi ride back to your hotel. ⊠ *Parque Nacional Iguazú, Argentina 3370* ☎ *3757/41800* ⊕ *www.sheraton.com* ⇨ *176 rooms, 4 suites* ♤ *2 restaurants, room service, IDD phones, in-room safes, minibars, cable TV, 3 tennis courts, pool, gym, sauna, bicycles, bars, lobby lounge, babysitting, laundry service, Internet, business services, convention center, airport shuttle, car rental, travel services, free parking, no-smoking rooms* ▭ *AE, DC, MC, V.*

★ $$$$ ✗▥ **Tropical das Cataratas.** Not only is this stately hotel within the national park on the Brazilian side just a stone's throw from the falls, but it provides many comforts—large rooms, terraces, even hammocks. Galleries and gardens surround this pink building, and its main section has been declared a Brazilian national heritage sight. The restaurant serves traditional Brazilian food. ⊠ *Km 25, Rodovia das Cataratas, Brazil*

85850-970 ☎ *5545/521–7000* ⊕ *www.tropicalhotel.com.br* 🛏 *200 rooms* ㊧ *2 restaurants, coffee shop, 2 tennis courts, pool, bar, shops, business services, meeting room* ☰ *AE, DC, MC, V.*

¢ ✕⊡ **Los Helechos.** This hotel is such a great bargain it doesn't have to discount its rooms during the off-season to draw travelers. It's also convenient to the center of town and two blocks from the bus terminal. Rooms are simple but clean and comfortable; half have air-conditioning and television (these cost 10 pesos more). Be sure to get up in time for the buffet breakfast, which includes platters of tropical fruit. ✉ *Paulino Amarante 76, Puerto Iguazú, Argentina 3370* ☎☎*3757/420–338* 🛏*25 rooms* ㊧ *Restaurant, pool, bar; no a/c in some rooms* ☰ *AE, DC, MC, V.*

★ ¢ ✕⊡ **Hostel-Inn Iguazú.** Don't be put off by the "hostel" in the name: as well as great-value dorm accommodations there are double rooms with private bathrooms. All rooms are spacious, with huge windows and lots of light. The Hostel Inn is on the road halfway between Puerto Iguazú and the falls, which makes getting to the park early much easier; the friendly staff can sort out excursions. At night the restaurant does simple fare like stuffed pork, and has an all-out asado once a week. A lovely outdoor pool, a bar, and a lounge area are three more reasons not to have to make the trek to town. ✉ *Ruta 12, Km. 5, 3370* ☎ *3757/421823* ⊕ *www.hostel-inn.com* 🛏 *36 rooms (206 beds)* ㊧ *Restaurant, pool, bar, Ping-Pong, laundry services, travel services.* ☰ *No credit cards* ⭐ *CP.*

EXCURSIONS ESSENTIALS

Transportation

BY AIR

The Aeropuerto Internacional Mar del Plata (on R2, about five minutes outside the city) is the beach region's main airport. There are numerous daily flights year-round to and from Buenos Aires on Aerolíneas Argentinas. Note that this is a coveted route in summer, so make reservations early. LADE flies to most major towns within the country, including Mar del Plata, but only once a week.

Aerolíneas Argentinas flies three times daily between Buenos Aires and the Argentine airport near Iguazú; the trip takes an hour and three quarters. LAN does the same trip twice daily. Southern Winds also flies daily to and from Buenos Aires and can be cheaper, especially if you book in advance. Normal rates are about 200 pesos each way, but promotional rates, called *bandas negativas,* are sometimes available if you reserve ahead. The Brazilian airline Varig has offices in Foz do Iguaçu and offers connecting flights all over Brazil.

Argentina and Brazil each have an airport at Iguazú. The Argentine airport is 20 km (12 mi) southeast of Puerto Iguazú, Argentina; the Brazilian airport is 11 km (7 mi) from Foz do Iguaçu and 17 km (11 mi) from the national park. The Colectivo Aeropuerto shuttle has service to hotels in Puerto Iguazú for 3 pesos. To get from the hotel to the airport, call two hours before your departure, and the shuttle will pick you up. Taxis to Puerto Iguazú cost 25 pesos.

Airlines Aerolíneas Argentinas ☎ 11/4320-2000 in Buenos Aires, 223/496-0101 in Mar del Plata, 3757/420-849 or 3757/420-168 in Puerto Iguazú ⊕ www.aerolineas.com. ar. **LADE** ☎ 11/4514-1524 in Buenos Aires, 223/493-8211 in Mar del Plata ⊕ www.lade. com.ar. **LAN** ☎ 1174378-2200 ⊕ www.lan.com. **Varig** ☎ 5545/523-2111 in Foz do Iguaçu, 11/4329-9211 in Buenos Aires.

Airports Aeropuerto Internacional Mar del Plata ✉ Ruta 2, Km 398, Mar del Plata ☎ 223/478-5811. **Aeropuerto Internacional de Puerto Iguazú** ✉ Ruta Provincial 101, Puerto Iguazú ☎ 3757/421-996. **Foz do Iguaçu Cataratas International Airport** ✉ BR 469, Km. 16, Foz do Iguaçu, Brazil ☎ 5545/574-1744.

BY BOAT

Hydrofoils and ferries cross the Río de la Plata between Buenos Aires and Uruguay several times a day. Boats often sell out quickly, particularly on summer weekends, so it's important to book tickets at least a few days in advance at the dock or ticket sales office or by phone. Buquebus provides two kinds of service for passengers and cars between Buenos Aires and Colonia, Montevideo, Piriápolis, and Punta del Este, Uruguay; and you can also book tickets on other ferry companies, such as Ferrylíneas, through their ticket office. The quickest crossing takes an hour on the hydrofoils or catamarans (90 pesos), although the ferry takes around 3 hours (52 pesos). Ask Buquebus about their packages, which include lunch, a city tour, and a night in a hotel.

The main transport company for the Tigre River delta is Interisleña, whose *lanchas colectivas* (boat-buses) serve all of the Primera Sección, the closest islands to the town.

Buquebus ✉ Av. Antartida Argentina 821, Puerto Madero ✉ Patio Bullrich Shopping Mall, Av. Libertador 750, La Recoleta ☎ 11/4316-6500 ⊕ www.buquebus.com. **Interisleña** ✉ Estación Fluvial, Mitre 305 ☎ 11/4749-0900.

BY BUS

Buses from Buenos Aires to just about every point in the country leave from Retiro bus station, where you can buy tickets. Traveling by bus to the beach from Buenos Aires is very common. Every beach town has at least a bus stop, and many have a bus station or a bus ticket office in the center of town. Cóndor, Flechabus, and la Estrella are recommended services from Buenos Aires to La Plata and Mar del Plata. The bus from Buenos Aires to La Plata costs about 7 pesos one-way and takes 1¼ hours. Buenos Aires to Mar del Plata takes about five hours and costs about 30 pesos. Each of the beach towns is connected by a local bus system. For Pampas towns such as San Antonio de Areco, bus service is available from several companies including Pullman General Belgrano and Chevallier.

Organized tours to Puerto Iguazú and the Cataratas del Iguazú can be arranged through most Buenos Aires travel agencies, though they're often not that much less expensive than traveling by plane. Via Bariloche has the quickest and most comfortable service between Puerto Iguazú and Buenos Aires; be sure to ask for the *coche cama* (sleeper) service. The trip takes 16 hours, costs about 90 pesos, and includes meals. Expreso

Singer takes 18 hours and costs 82 pesos. The Puerto Iguazú Terminal de Omnibus is in the center of town.

From Puerto Iguazú to the falls, take El Práctico from the terminal; buses leave every 45 minutes 7–7 and cost 6 pesos round-trip.

🚍 Bus Depots **Puerto Iguazú Terminal de Ómnibus** ✉ Avs. Córdoba and Misiones, Puerto Iguazú ☎ 3757/422-730. **Terminal de Ómnibus Retiro** ✉ Av. Antártida Argentina and Av. Ramos Mejía, Buenos Aires ☎ 11/4310-0700 ⊕ www.tebasa.com.ar.

🚍 Bus Lines **Agencia de Pasajes Noelia** ☎ 3757/422-722 in Puerto Iguazú. **Chevallier** ☎ 11/4311-0033 ⊕ www.nuevachevallier.com. **El Cóndor** ☎ 11/4313-3762. **El Práctico** ☎ 3757/422-722 in Puerto Iguazú. **Expreso Singer** ☎ 11/4313-3927. **Flechabus** ☎ 11/4315-2781 ⊕ www.flechabus.com.ar. **Pullman General Belgrano** ☎ 11/4315-6522 ⊕ www.gralbelgrano.com.ar. **Via Bariloche** ☎ 11/4315-3122 in Buenos Aires, 3757/420-854 in Puerto Iguazú ⊕ www.viabariloche.com.ar.

BY CAR

Driving is the best and most convenient option for getting to towns in Buenos Aires Province, including the coast. It's possible to rent cars in all the towns covered in this chapter, though bear in mind that car rental can be costly. Localiza and Hertz Annie Millet are two agencies with branches in most large towns and cities. Gas—known as *nafta*—isn't cheap, and if you plan to drive extensively, it's worth looking into hiring a vehicle running on natural gas (GNC) which will reduce fuel costs drastically. There are plenty of gas stations in cities and on major highways (though not all of these sell GNC, and huge queues can form at GNC stations on weekends). Stations can be few and far between on rural roads, so keep your tank full. A useful Web site when planning roadtrips is ⊕ www.ruta0.com, which calculates distances and tolls between two places and offers several route options.

The expressways that feed into Buenos Aires fan out in every direction from the city's ring road, General Paz, and are better suited to the quantities of traffic they carry. However, large quantities of porteños leave town for the weekend so expect heavy traffic out and in on Friday and Sunday evenings, respectively. Drivers weave alarmingly in and out of lanes at high speed, so be on your guard. Both these expressways and many inter-provincial routes tend to be privately owned, which means frequent tolls. There are nearly always alternative roads to use, but they are generally smaller, slower and have surfaces in poor condition. On main roads the speed limit is 80 kph (50 mph), while on highways it's 120 kph (75 mph), though Argentinean drivers rarely pay heed to this.

Luján lies 68 km (42 mi) northwest of Buenos Aires on RN-7, also known as the Acceso Oeste. To get to San Antonio de Areco, 113 km (70 mi) from Buenos Aires, either continue along RN-7 from Luján then go north on RP-41 (total tolls of 5.50 pesos) or leave Buenos Aires on RN-9, crossing to RN-8 when it intersects (total tolls of 4 pesos). The highway RN-2 connects Buenos Aires with La Plata (tolls of 4 pesos) and continues on to Mar del Plata (tolls of 11 pesos), though the drive is just one long straight highway and gets very busy in summer. A more interesting way to get to coastal towns is to continue out of La Plata on RP-36 for about 90 km (56 mi) where it joins with RP-11, also known as the Interbal-

neária, which connects the coastal towns (tolls 13 pesos to Pinamar).
Though this meandering coast road is a more pleasant drive, it does add
about 80 km (50 mi) to your journey.

BY TAXI

Taxis in major cities are generally inexpensive; the fare is based on the
number of blocks traveled. Taxis can be hailed, but if leaving from a
hotel or restaurant, it's generally easier to get them to call you one. In
smaller towns, numerous minicab firms (*remises*) replace taxis. These
can't be hailed on the street or called. In many touristy towns, you can
book remises to ferry you around for several days. With a group of three
or four, you may find this a more economical and convenient way to
get around.

🚹 **Remises Arena** ⊠ Villa Gesell 🕾 2255/422-444. **Remises San Antonio** ⊠ San Antonio de Areco 🕾 2326/456-320. **Remis Cariló** ⊠ Cariló 🕾 2254/570-808. **Remicoop** ⊠ Mar del Plata 🕾 223/475-1111. **Remises Iguazú** ⊠ Puerto Iguazú 🕾 3757/422-008. **Remises San Martín** ⊠ Luján 🕾 2323/425-910. **Taxis Colonia** ⊠ Colonia del Sacramento 🕾 598/522-2920. **Taxi-Com La Plata** ⊠ La Plata 🕾 221/453-3333. **Taxis Pinamar** ⊠ Pinamar 🕾 2254/482-369. **TeleTaxi Mar del Plata** ⊠ Mar del Plata 🕾 223/475-8888.

BY TRAIN

The cheapest way of getting to Tigre by train is on the suburban commuter train leaving from Retiro Station—there are about four departures an hour on the Línea Mitre, Ramal Tigre; a round-trip tickets costs
1.90 pesos. The slick, tourist-oriented Tren de la Costa is a more pleasant ride that runs along the riverbank. It starts halfway between Buenos
Aires and Tigre, so you'll have to first take Línea Mitre to Mitre Station, where you can change lines. A return fare costs 12 pesos.

Suburban trains run several times an hour from Buenos Aires' Constitución station to La Plata. The service is slower than traveling by bus,
and both the station and the ride itself can be dangerous, especially at
night when muggers hang out around the station. Ferrobaires runs several daily trains from Constitución to Mar del Plata (22 to 45 pesos),
the best option being the Super-Pullman service, which, unfortunately,
makes only one trip a week on Friday night. There is daily service to
Pinamar (22 to 29 pesos) Tickets can be bought at the train station or
booked by phone. Within the rest of Buenos Aires Province, train service is limited. Buses are generally more reliable.

🚹 Train Stations **Estación de Trenes de La Plata** ⊠ Corner of Calle 1 and Calle 44 🕾 221/423-2575. **Estacíon de Trenes Constitución** ⊠ General Hornos 11, Buenos Aires 🕾 11/4303-0023. **Estacíon de Trenes Retiro** ⊠ Av. Ramos Mejía 1508, Buenos Aires 🕾 11/4307-4407.

🚹 Train Lines **Ferrobaires** 🕾 11/4304-0028 in Buenos Aires, 223/451-2501 in Mar del Plata. **Trenes de Buenos Aires (Línea Mitre)** 🕾 11/4317-4400 ⊕ www.tbanet.com.ar. **Tren de la Costa** 🕾 11/4732-6000 ⊕ www.trendelacosta.com.ar.

Contacts & Resources

BANKS & EXCHANGE SERVICES

Local banks in all towns have 24-hour ATMs, recognizable by the
"Link" or "Banelco" signs.

As a general rule, most banks in Argentina are open from 10 AM to 3 PM, though those specializing in currency exchange may stay open longer. In Colonia, most restaurants and hotels accept Argentine pesos and many accept dollars—try to have a rough idea of the exchange rate to avoid being overcharged. You can also exchange currency at the ferry terminal, though the commission is often high. Dollars and pesos are used interchangeably in Puerto Iguazú; to exchange other currencies, but not traveler's checks, go to Argecam. For other banking needs in Puerto Iguazú, try Banco Macro, which has ATMs. You will need Brazilian currency, reais, on the Brazilian side: there are small exchange booths in the bus stations at Puerto Iguazú and Foz do Iguaçu, and the Banco do Brasil also changes currency.

Argecam ⊠ Av. Victoria Aguirre 562, Puerto Iguazú ☎ 3757/420-273 ⊘ Weekdays 8-7. **Banco de la Nación Argentina** ⊠ Calle 42 at Calle 21, La Plata ☎ 221/422-5509 ⊠ Av. Shaw 156, Pinamar ☎ 2254/481-880 ⊠ Alsina 250, San Antonio de Areco ☎ 2326/4259 ⊠ Av. 3 and Paseo 109, Villa Gesell ☎ 2255/463-562 ⊕ www.bna.com.ar. **Banco de la Provincia de Buenos Aires** ⊠ Av. Divisadero s/n, Cariló ☎ 2254/470-660 ⊕ www.bapro.com.ar.

Banco do Brasil ⊠ Av. Brasil 1377, Foz do Iguaçu, Brazil ☎ 55/45/3521-2525 ⊕ www.bb.com.br. **Banco Macro** ⊠ Av. Victoria Aguirre 330, Puerto Iguazú ☎ 3757/420-212 ⊘ Weekdays 8-1. **BBVA Banco Francés** ⊠ San Martín 198, Luján ☎ 2323/430-210 ⊕ www.bancofrances.com.ar. **Citibank** ⊠ Av. Luro 2983, Mar del Plata ☎ 223/499-0240 ⊕ www.citibank.com.ar.

EMERGENCIES

Emergency phone numbers are nationwide, and most major hospitals have some English-speaking doctors.

Emergency Services Ambulance ☎ 107. **Fire** ☎ 100. **Police** ☎ 101.

Hospitals Hospital de Luján ⊠ San Martín and Belgrano, Luján ☎ 2323/423-333. **Hospital de Pinamar** ⊠ Av. Shaw 255, Pinamar ☎ 2254/491-670. **Hospital Emilio Zerboni** ⊠ Moreno and Mitre, San Antonio de Areco ☎ 2326/452-759. **Hospital General de Agudos** ⊠ Av. 3 and Paseo 124, Villa Gesell ☎ 2254/462-618. **Hospital Interzonal Mar del Plata** ⊠ Juan B. Justo 6800, Mar del Plata ☎ 0223/477-0265. **Hospital Interzonal San Martín** ⊠ Calle 1 1791, La Plata ☎ 221/421-5665. **Hospital Samic** ⊠ Av. Victoria Aguirre 131, Puerto Iguazú ☎ 3757/420-288.

Late-Night Pharmacies Cariló ⊠ Farmacia Outóon, Centro Comercial Local 17 ☎ 2254/470-190. **La Plata** ⊠ Farmacia del Aguila, Calles 9 and 45 ☎ 221/421-0892. **Luján** ⊠ Farmacia San Martín, San Martín 238, Luján ☎ 2323/420-150. **Mar del Plata** ⊠ Av. Luro 4102 ☎ 223/472-1810. **Pinamar** ⊠ Farmacia Osvaldini, Av. Shaw 658 ☎ 2254/482-867. **Puerto Iguazú** ⊠ Farmacia Bravo, Av. Victoria Aguirre 423 ☎ 3757/420-479. **San Antonio de Areco** ⊠ Farmacia Botiquín Solís, San Martín 615 ☎ 2326/492-115. **Villa Gesell** ⊠ Farmacia Llanos, Av. 3 no.352 ☎ 2254/463-340.

Córdoba

WORD OF MOUTH

"Córdoba is the Argentine vacation province that tends to be overlooked by foreigners. Córdoba City is a beautiful old Jesuit city with the continent's first university and Argentina's oldest cathedral. We rented a car and drove about 30 minutes north to Villa Carlos Paz, where we stayed in a bungalow by the lake.

Next time, we'd stay in La Cumbre, which is a little farther from Córdoba City but very charming and less kitschy than Carlos Paz. We also drove south to Alta Gracia, where we toured the Jesuit estancia—probably the best museum we saw."

—Suyo

By Victoria Patience

A GLORIOUS MIX OF PAST AND PRESENT CHARACTERIZES CÓRDOBA Province, Argentina's geographical heart. The area is known as much for its rolling hills dotted with 400-year-old Jesuit estates and snooty golf courses as for its paragliding, UFO-spotting, and wild party goers. Both the province and its capital city played a vital role in Argentina's colonial history: before Buenos Aires became the hub, Córdoba served as an essential middle point between the Spanish in Peru and those in Spain. Gradually, Buenos Aires took over, but Córdoba remains a favorite vacation spot for many Argentines, second only to the Atlantic coast in popularity.

ORIENTATION & PLANNING

Orientation

Córdoba Province is the geographical center of Argentina, and its eponymous capital, 710 km (426 mi) northwest of Buenos Aires, is a chaotic, cosmopolitan hub filled with students and businesspeople. A meandering drive from the city through the mountain towns is a lovely way to spend a day or two—or an entire summer.

Córdoba City is served by daily flights from Buenos Aires as well as lots of long-distance bus companies, many of which have a comfortable *cama* (sleeper) service. Within the city, hiring a car isn't necessary (or even advisable, given the chaotic traffic): the center is compact, and official black-and-yellow taxis abound.

Córdoba City

The city's most interesting sights and hotels are in the 10 blocks around Plaza San Martín. Like most Spanish-founded cities, Córdoba is laid out on a rigid grid system, although north of Plaza San Martín some blocks are crisscrossed by smaller lanes. Both north–south and east–west streets change name at the *cabildo* (town hall) on Plaza San Martín.

A few blocks west of the center, the grids are cut by a wide concrete channel containing a small stream known as La Cañada. This is lined by leafy Avenida Marcelo T. de Alvear (changing to Avenida Figueroa Alcorta north of Dean Funes), one of the city's main roads. The main bus terminal, NETOC, is six blocks east of Plaza San Martín along Corrientes. Many cheaper hotels are in this section of town.

The epicenter of Córdoba's emerging restaurant scene is the Nueva Córdoba neighborhood, a few blocks south of the center. Avenida Hipólito Yrigoyen is its main thoroughfare. Southeast of the center, on the other side of Avenida Poeta Lugones, is the Parque Sarmiento, home to the zoo and fine arts museum.

The best way to enjoy Córdoba's colonial architecture and slower pace of life is on foot: most places of interest are within easy walking distance of Plaza San Martín. The bus system is complicated and drivers unhelpful, but there are plenty of taxis. These are also the best option at night, especially along La Cañada, which can get a bit lonely.

CLOSE UP

Top Reasons to Visit

The Second City. Although visitors often overlook its charms, Argentina's second-largest city has a beautifully preserved colonial downtown, a great restaurant scene, and hopping nightlife.

Jesuit Estancias. Grandiose stone buildings and stark colonial churches take you back to the times when the Jesuits had huge landholdings. Some of their estates are tucked away in the mountains, others are in the centers of hill towns not far from Córdoba City.

Golfing and Gliding. In sporting terms, Córdoba is synonymous with two things: golf and paragliding. Many courses have fantastic hill

views, as do the parapets that form natural launching spots for the gliders.

Climb Every Mountain. Within a short drive of Córdoba city are small hill towns surrounded by a plethora of easily hikable peaks whose summits are circled by condors and eagles. Horseback treks are also an option.

Naturally Delicious. Hearty, homemade food focusing on local ingredients is the big attraction at many family-run restaurants, hotels, and estancias. The province is also known for its jams, beers, and *alfajores* (cookies).

Around Córdoba

North and south of Córdoba City are strings of mountain towns: choose one for a day-trip, or take two or three days to drive through each region at your leisure. The northern region—especially the towns on Highway RN8, such as La Cumbre and Capilla del Monte—is known as the Valle de la Punilla. Here rugged landscapes include huge red rock formations and ancient cave paintings. In the northeastern part of the province, Jesuit estates are scattered off Highway RN9, known informally as El Camino de la Historia (The History Trail).

Milder, more European scenery lies to the south, in the Valle de Calamuchita, where German and Austrian immigrants built Alpine-looking mountain villages in the first half of the 20th century. The well-marked slopes around towns like Santa Rosa de Calamuchita and La Cumbrecita have some of the country's best hikes.

Planning

Córdoba is at its best in the spring and autumn, before the summer sun parches the mountains. Even in the summer, though, nights can be chilly in the mountain towns, so pack a warm jacket. Walking boots are also a good idea if you plan to do much hiking. During the summer holidays (January and February), *porteños* (as the citizens of Buenos Aires are called) fill the mountain resorts, which means inflated prices and less peace and quiet. Temperatures rarely go below freezing in winter, and the snowcapped sierras are lovely.

You only need a day or two to see the sights in Córdoba City, and although you can easily visit most of the nearby towns on day trips, try to spend a night or two in the sierras to really breathe in the mountain air. Regional bus companies connect the city with the hill towns north and south, but limited service can mean hours of hanging around. Renting a car is a better option, especially for overnight stays. If you don't fancy being behind the wheel or are tight on time, consider hiring a car with a driver or going on an all-inclusive excursion. The main routes connecting major towns have reasonably maintained Tarmac surfaces but only one or two lanes in each direction. Farther afield, dirt roads are the norm, especially to reach Jesuit estates, but you can visit all the places mentioned in this chapter without a four-wheel drive.

Tour at Your Leisure

The Cabildo Tourist Office organizes free walking tours of downtown Córdoba, and also arranges smaller personalized tours (prices depend on the visit and number of people). It also has a basic selection of maps and brochures. English-language tours leave at 9:30 AM and 4:30 PM daily (more often in high season); if possible, let staffers know in advance that you're coming. ☒ *Cabildo, Deán Funes 15* ☏ *351/428–5856.*

Latitud Sur specializes in adventure tourism, including trekking, rock climbing, paragliding, skydiving, mountain biking, and horseback riding. As well as all-inclusive day excursions, they regularly organize longer camping trips. ☒ *Fructuoso Rivera 70* ☏ *351/462–723* ⊕ *www.latitudsurtrek. com.ar.*

Nativo Viajes runs guided city tours and themed day trips into the province with English-speaking guides. If you're up for something more active, the Semana de la Aventura (Adventure Week) package includes horseback riding, mountain biking, climbing, and trekking; you can do the whole lot or dip in for the bits you fancy. Nativo also arranges vehicle hire, transfers, and accommodations. ☒ *27 de Abril 11* ☏ *351/424–5341* ⊕ *www.cordobanativoviajes.com.ar* ☒ *4-hour city tours 55 pesos; all-day excursions 60 pesos–100 pesos (transport and meals included).*

Stylo Viajes has English-language van tours that take you to various sights in the sierras, including Jesuit ruins and the rock paintings at Cerro Colorado. Higher-adrenaline offerings include lake-diving, paragliding, and hangliding, as well as trekking on foot and horseback. Stylo also organizes the **Córdoba City Tour** (☉ Mon., Tues., and Thurs. 5 PM; Fri. and Sat. 11 AM and 5 PM; Sun. 11 AM ☒ 12 pesos), a double-decker bus jaunt that covers a good portion of the city, including Sarmiento Park, La Cañada, and downtown. Call ahead to inquire about tours in English. ☒ *Av. Chacabuco 325* ☏ *351/424–6605* ⊕ *www.stylocordoba.com. ar* ☒ *Private city tours 30 pesos; all-day excursions 50 pesos–100 pesos.*

Where the Money Goes

When Argentines vacation in Córdoba, their friends at home expect just one thing on return: a box of *alfajores,* the national cookie. The *alfajores cordobés,* the Córdoban variety, has soft dough and comes filled with homemade jam or dulce de leche and dipped in a thin white frosting. There are hundreds of varieties to choose from: many vendors will let you sample their goods. Other homemade foods are also high on the list of must-haves: organic honey, jams from every fruit under the sun, cheeses and salamis, and extra-virgin olive oil. A variety of handicrafts is also made by provincial artisans. Rustic housewares, including hand-carved wooden spoons and chopping boards, are easy to find, as are decorated *mate* (tea) vessels.

	$$$$	$$$	$$	$	¢
WHAT IT COSTS In Argentina Pesos					
RESTAURANTS	over 35	25–35	15–24	8–14	under 8
HOTELS	over 300	220–300	140–219	80–139	under 80

Restaurant prices are for one main course at dinner. Hotel prices are for two people in a standard double room in high season.

CÓRDOBA

Stone buildings dating from the 17th and 18th centuries line the cobbled streets around shady Plaza San Martín in Córdoba's compact Centro Histórico, which has the highest concentration of colonial buildings in Argentina. The city's history stretches back to 1573, when Geronimo Luís de Cabrera first set foot here. His family was from Córdoba, Spain, and he named the town accordingly.

The tolling bells and cross-topped towers of downtown's 10 churches are evidence of the role the Jesuits played here. This was the center of their missionary work, from their arrival in 1599 until their expulsion from Argentina in 1767. Other architectural reminders of their presence abound, most notably at the Manzana Jesuítica (Jesuit Block), a block-long conglomeration of 17th-century buildings that has been declared a UNESCO World Heritage Site. For more than two centuries the city was Argentina's cultural and intellectual hub. Its national university, established in 1613, earned the city its nickname—La Docta, or the Learned. Today this provincial capital is the country's second-largest city (population 1.3 million).

Exploring

★ The heart of Córdoba has always been **Plaza San Martín**. The square is crossed by diagonal walkways, which from dawn to dusk are filled with busy-looking office workers and residents out for a stroll. Of the many native trees shading it, the most spectacular are the bulging, thorn-covered *palo borracho* (literally, drunken stick) and the jacaranda, which blazes with violet blossoms in spring. In the middle of the square, an exuberant equestrian statue of General San Martín faces west, toward Pasaje Santa Catalina between the cathedral and the old city hall.

Córdoban poet Luís Roberto Altamira called the **Catedral de Córdoba** (⌧ Calle Independencia 64, at Plaza San Martín ☉ Daily 8–noon and 4:30–8), on the west side of Plaza San Martín, a "stone flower in the heart of the homeland." Construction began in 1577, though it wasn't until 1784 that the church was completed—which left a trail of disparate styles. Note the musical angels on the baroque front towers. They were sculpted by indigenous peoples in 1776, and they bear the faces of their sculptors.

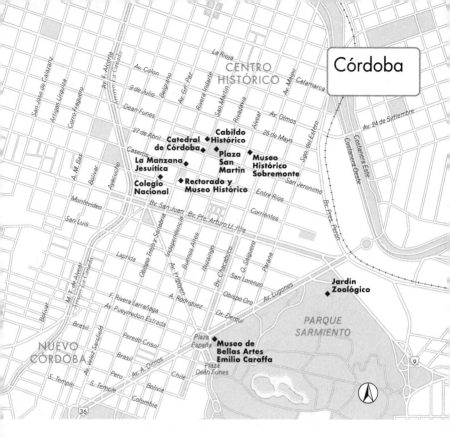

Córdoba

Next to the cathedral on Plaza San Martín's western side the **Cabildo Histórico** (✉ Calle Independencia at Plaza San Martín ☎ 351/428–5856 ⊙ Weekdays 9–9, weekends 9–8) now functions as a cultural center. Construction of the long, two-story, arcaded structure began in 1588 (excavated cells—including what was probably a prison—date from as early as the 17th century) but wasn't completed until the late 18th century; the facade dates from this time. For more than 300 years, wealthy residents gathered here to discuss town affairs. The upstairs Salón Rojo (Red Salon) is still used for official receptions. The main floor houses an exhibition space, a café, a library, a tourist office, and a souvenir shop. In the summer, tango dances are held in the Patio de Tango late on Friday nights. A plaque in the Pasaje Santa Catalina alludes to a darker time in the building's history. It reads, THE CABILDO FUNCTIONED, BEGINNING IN 1976 DURING THE MILITARY DICTATORSHIP, AS A CLANDESTINE CENTER OF DETENTION, TORTURE, AND DEATH.

★ A block east of Plaza San Martín is the **Museo Histórico Provincial Marqués de Sobremonte,** former home of the Marquis de Sobremonte, a Córdoban governor of the late 18th century. This is Córdoba's oldest private residence, and one of the country's best examples of colonial architecture. Five courtyards, a chapel, and 26 rooms are distributed over two floors; the latter are furnished with period pieces, costumes, old photographs and oil paintings of the Cusqueña school, a 17th- to 18th-century movement of artists based in Cuzco, Perú. Their baroque-style paintings are usually heavily gilded and depict religious figures, often with indigenous features. A tour of the home's labyrinthine corridors can lead your imagination back in time. ⊠ *Rosario de Santa Fé 218, at Ituzaingó* ☎ *351/433–1661* 🖘 *2 pesos* ⊘ *Tues.–Fri. 10–4, Sat. 8–2.*

Fodor'sChoice A decade after the foundation of Córdoba, **La Manzana Jesuítica**, a whole
★ city block, was given to the Society of Jesus, testament to the order's political and social clout in the Americas at the time. From here, the Jesuits held sway over the religious, educational, and cultural activities of the city and surrounding lands. Their church, the **Templo de la Compañía de Jesús** (Temple of the Society of Jesus) (⊠ Obispo Trejo at Av. Caseros ⊘ Tues.–Sat. 10–11:30 and 5–7) is along the block's northern flank, facing onto the diminutive Plazoleta Rafael García. It was begun between 1640 and 1650 (stones with different dates adorn the front, and historians are undecided) and consecrated in 1671 and is—regardless of the date controversy—Argentina's oldest church. Both the stone facade and the soaring nave are soberingly simple. Inside a dome made of Paraguayan cedar resembles an inverted ship's keel: Felipe Lemaire, the Jesuit brother who oversaw the work, was a Belgian ship maker. From the Calle Caseros side of the church, you can enter the Capilla Doméstica—a stunning chapel with a wood ceiling decorated with primitively painted rawhide. On the walls are copies of European paintings done in the 17th century by members of the Peruvian Cusqueña school.

South of the Manzana Jesuítica is the creamy facade of the **Rectorado y Museo Histórico de la Universidad Nacional de Córdoba** (⊠ Obispo Trejo 242, between Av. Caseros and Av. Duarte Quirós ☎351/433–2075). This two-story building is the formal administrative center of a sprawling campus whose educational standards rivaled those of any European university in its heyday. Early graduates of Latin America's second-oldest university became the doctors and lawyers who ran the fledging nation; some are even Catholic saints. Inside is a Jesuit library that includes such rarities as a 1645 Bible written in seven languages, as well as a spectacular collection of maps, religious works, and historical documents such as the first draft of the Argentine Civil Code. The interior patio contains a statue of Fray Fernando Trejo, who donated the money to build the university for Jesuit education in 1613. Admission to the library is free; it's open weekdays 8 AM–9 PM and Saturday 8 AM–noon.

Next door to the Universidad Nacional de Córdoba, the **Colegio Nacional de Nuestra Señora de Montserrat** (⊠ Obispo Trejo at Duarte Quirós) is a humanities-oriented high school that was first opened in 1687 at a nearby site. It was moved here in 1782, and the classrooms occupy what were once the Jesuits' living quarters. Despite the fiercely traditional atmosphere—note the small wooden desks the students use, and the beautiful majolica tiles of the entrance hall—in the late 1990s girls were finally admitted to the school. Guided tours of the Manzana Jesuítica, including the university and the high school, leave from the Museo Histórico de la Universidad. ⊠ *City block flanked by calles Casero, Obispo Trejo, Duarte Quirós, and Avenida Vélez Sarsfield, en-*

The Jesuit Missionaries

OVER MORE THAN 150 YEARS, Spanish Jesuits established 30 missions in the area that now encompasses parts of present-day Argentina, Paraguay, and Brazil. They created a society that's still of great interest to scholars and social theorists.

In 1534 a Catholic priest named San Ignacio de Loyola founded the Jesuits, who were officially approved by Pope Paul III in 1540. With the objective of "seeking the greater glory of God and salvation of souls," they concentrated their efforts on spreading Catholicism. In the mid-16th century the first Jesuits arrived in South America, in what is today Peru and Brazil. In 1607 the Jesuit Diego Torres went to Asunción and established the Jesuit province of Paraguay.

The first missions were created in 1610 in the region of Guayrá in present-day Brazil. The Franciscans had previously entered these territories but failed to convert the indigenous Guaraní. The Jesuits were almost immediately successful. Their tactic was to send in a few Jesuits, who bestowed presents on the tribal chiefs, befriended them, and thenlived among the community, learning the culture and language before spreading their teachings. The Guaraní helped the Jesuits construct missions. At their apogee, the largest missions had more than 4,000 Guaraní inhabitants, generally along with two or three missionaries.

At the outset the missions were constantly raided by Portuguese slave traders. For this reason, the missions of the Guayrá region relocated in 1631 to the banks of the Paraná and Uruguay rivers. Nevertheless, the attacks continued. In 1640 the royal crown of Spain granted the missions the right to use firearms and to raise armies. Jesuits and Guaranís fought side by side and defeated the slave traders in the Battle of Mbororé.

The missionaries became economically self-sufficient through cattle ranching and the cultivation of crops such as corn, manioc, sugar, tobacco, rice, and yerba mate. They also produced honey and made highly detailed metal works, leather goods, and cloth. The missions had an effective communication system, and nearly all had the same physical layout: an enormous central plaza, surrounded by living quarters, a church, a school, workshops, and a cemetery.

Culturally, too, the missions were quite advanced. Musical instruments were crafted, and each mission had its own chorus and orchestra. At Nuestra Señora de Loreto, a printing press was built. Works such as the Bible were printed in Guaraní and Spanish. And an architectural and artistic style, Baroque-Guaraní, was developed.

But in 1767, when the missions were at their economic and cultural peak, King Carlos III of Spain expelled the Jesuits. The prevailing theory as to why is that the king feared that the missions had gained too much power. After the Jesuits departed, governmental mismanagement led to large-scale migration of the Guaraní to the large cities or back to the jungle. And most who remained behind at the old missions were killed by Paraguayan troops fighting for territorial expansion.

trance at Obispo Trejo 242 ☎ 351/423–9196 ☜ 3 pesos ⊙ Daily 9–1 and 4–8; guided tours at 10, 11, 5, and 6.

★ **Córdoba Subterranea** (Underground Córdoba) is a fascinating series of spooky subterranean constructions, including old jail cells, dating from 1588. You can only visit by guided tours, which leave from the cabildo (you can purchase the 8-peso tickets at the cabildo or Obispo Mercadillo tourist offices) and last a couple of hours.

In Nuevo Córdoba, the southern part of the city center, is the splendid
Ⓒ **Parque Sarmiento.** It was designed by French landscape architect Charles Thays and has a zoo, a lake skirted by palms and cypress where you can rent rowboats, an outdoor swimming complex, an amusement park, vast landscaped zones, wide lawns, and cafés. ☒ Av. Poeta Lugones and Av. Amado Sabattini (Ruta 9 Sur).

On Parque Sarmiento's western corner, opposite Plaza España, is the city's leading visual art space, the **Museo de Bellas Artes Emilio Caraffa.** The austere 1916 neoclassical facade is deceptive: inside, simple white-painted rooms exhibit a spry collection of 19th- and 20th-century paintings, engravings, and sculpture. Most of the artists represented are Argentine—including Córdobans Genaro Páez, Emilio Caraffa, and Fernando Fader. ☒ Av. Hipólito Hirigoyen 651 ☎ 351/433–3412 ☜ Free ⊙ Tues.–Sun. 11–7.

Where to Stay & Eat

$–$$$ ✕ **Alcorta Carnes y Vinos.** Alcorta is a great choice for a long, indulgent, and impeccable meal. The meat, including the bife de chorizo (sirloin), is simply excellent. Ask for it rare and it really comes rare, which is a welcome aberration in Argentina. The voluminous wine list has offerings from all over the country, including some hard-to-find reds. The service is attentive and deferential without ever seeming in the way. The wide-open, airy interior is modern, elegant, and refined. ☒ Alcorta 330 at Cañada and Santa Rosa ☎ 351/424–7916 ☖ Reservations essential ⊕ www.alcortacarnes.com.ar ▭ AE, DC, MC, V.

★ **$$** ✕ **La Nieta'e La Pancha.** You won't be disappointed by anything on the menu, which is written in the Córdoban dialect rather than straight Spanish. Local specialties done with flair include cabrito (roast kid) in cream sauce, peppers, and sweet potatoes or matambre (roast pork) served with a "tower" of eggplant, onions, and cheese. Most memorable is the river trout, from the nearby Rio Ceballos, with sautéed peppers and carrots in olive oil. The warm, rustic decor, soothing live guitar music, and the friendly owners all come together perfectly. ☒ Belgrano 783 ☎ 351/ 468–1920 ▭ AE, MC, V.

$–$$ ✕ **Al Malek.** Tony Raphael, a Lebanese-American, runs this stylish, colorful restaurant a block from the Museo Caraffa in Parque Sarmiento. Picada Árabe for two has hummus, eggplant, tabbouleh, empanadas, and stuffed grape leaves. The 20% discount for takeout orders makes Al Malek an appealing option for picnics in the park. ☒ Derqui 255, Nueva Córdoba ☎ 351/468–1279 ▭ No credit cards ⊙ No lunch Mon. No dinner Sun.

$–$$ ✕ **El Paso.** It's an upscale place that does fantastic parrilla fare—and, yes, in endless quantities. The owner runs the show, ensuring friendly service despite the hordes of demanding Córdoba trendies. For 22 pesos there's as much sizzling beef as you can eat, as well as cabrito, salads, grilled vegetables, and even an empanada as a starter. The restaurant is northwest of downtown in Argüello district, but don't be put off: it's only a 10-minute taxi ride. ✉ *Av. Rafael Núñez 5652, Argüello* ☎ *3543/ 420–394* ⚜ *Reservations essential* ☰ *No credit cards.*

★ **$–$$** ✕ **La Yaya.** The secret to this parrilla is that most of the ingredients come from its own farm. And if you thought beef and chicken are the only things Argentines barbecue, think again: at La Yaya lamb, pork, and even rabbit might be on the grill. Although the country vibe abounds thanks to chunky wooden tables and rough-hewn carving boards, there's nothing bumpkinny about the staff. Friendly and quick, they often even rattle out a tune on the restaurant's piano while the proud owner looks on. ✉ *Independencia 468, Nueva Córdoba* ☎ *351/411–5487* ⚜ *Reservations essential* ☰ *AE, DC, MC, V* ☾ *No dinner Sun.*

$ ✕ **Giovannino.** Unusual pasta dishes and divinely crisp wood-oven-cooked pizzas take this trattoria beyond most Argentine-Italian restaurants. Beef comes as mini-steaks in a creamy cress sauce. The *spaghettini con frutti de mare* (angel hair with shrimp, mussels, and salmon) or *cappelletti al forno* (pork-and-ricotta-filled pasta in a Parma ham sauce) are also good. Light from the huge plate-glass windows floods the spacious, open-plan dining room at lunchtime, when the three-course prix-fixe menu attracts visitors and businesspeople alike. ✉ *Av. Sabatini 2050* ☎ *351/455–5659* ☰ *AE, DC, MC, V.*

$$$–$$$$ ▨ **Sheraton Córdoba Hotel.** The Sheraton rockets 16 floors of glass sleekness into Córdoba's skyline. It's popular with business travelers, thanks to its high level of service and many amenities, but it's a 15-minute walk (or 5-peso taxi) from historic downtown. Views over the city from windows in rooms on the upper floors are stunning. ✉ *Duarte Quirós 1300, 5000* ☎ *351/526–9000, 0800/888–3535 toll-free* ⊕ *www.sheraton. com* ⇝ *183 rooms, 5 suites* ⚭ *Restaurant, room service, IDD phones, in-room data ports, in-room safes, in-room hot tubs, minibars, cable TV, golf privileges, tennis court, pool, gym, hair salon, massage, 2 saunas, lobby lounge, babysitting, laundry service, concierge, Internet, business services, convention center, car rental, free parking, no-smoking rooms* ☰ *AE, DC, MC, V* ⵌ *BP.*

★ **$$** ▨ **NH Panorama.** The beds are huge and so are the breakfasts at NH Panorama, which has world-class rooms at very local prices. Although all that bed acreage doesn't leave space for much else, the gleaming parquet, rich cotton sheets, and eminently covetable bathrobes more than make up for it. Another winning detail is the early-risers' breakfast, which comes in handy if you're doing day trips out of town. There are fabulous views of the Centro Histórico from the rooftop pool, hence the hotel's name. The hotel's restaurant, Tipuana, is in a glass-domed space between the two towers that house the rooms: go for the classic Córdoban dish *cabrito* (roast goat) if you stay in for dinner. ✉ *Marcelo T. de Alvear 251, 5000* ☎ *351/410–3900* ⊕ *www.nh-hotels.com* ⇝ *137 rooms, 3 suites* ⚭ *Restaurant, coffee shop, room service, IDD phones, in-room* *data ports, minibars, cable TV, pool, hot tubs, sauna, babysitting, dry cleaning, laundry service, business services, convention center, car rental, free parking* ▭ *AE, DC, MC, V* ⦿ *BP.*

$ 🏨 **Ducal Suites Hotel.** All basic but tasteful rooms at the Ducal include a kitchenette and small lounge area. Extras, like a lobby Internet connection, are appreciated. The location is also a pull: Plaza San Martín and the Manzana Jesuítica are just three blocks away. ✉ *Corrientes 207, 5000* ☎ *351/570–8888* ⊕ *www.hotelducal.com.ar* 🛏 *82 suites* 🍴 *Restaurant, room service, in-room safes, kitchenettes, cable TV, pool, gym, hot tubs, sauna, bar, laundry service, business services, meeting rooms, free parking* ▭ *AE, DC, MC, V* ⦿ *CP.*

$ 🏨 **Hotel Victoria.** This aging hotel has a great location in the pedestrian shopping area, three blocks from Plaza San Martín. The communal kitchen is a great cost-cutter, but if you'd rather have someone else do the cooking, you'll need to go out: the simple dining room only serves breakfast and lunch. The hotel has the dubious honor of having been the first in Córdoba to have running water and en suite bathrooms (Carlos Gardel had a little suite here way back when). Although its heyday is past, its rooms are clean, and it hasn't given up on such classic perks as free newspapers with breakfast. ✉ *25 de Mayo 240, 5000* ☎ *351/429–0898* ⊕ *www.hotelvictoriacord.com.ar* 🛏 *110* 🍴 *Dining room, no a/c in some rooms, cable TV, Internet, parking (fee)* ▭ *No credit cards* ⦿ *CP.*

¢ 🏨 **Córdoba Hostel.** Dorm beds aren't the only option at this friendly hostel: there are several doubles and triples, all with en suite bathrooms. Rooms are basic but filled with light and very clean, even if you do have to put your own bedsheets on. There's even a pool, which though tiny, is a welcome relief in the summer. The action round the bar each night means you don't really need to go out at all. It's in Nueva Córdoba—a good 10 blocks from the Centro Histórico, but right in the heart of the city's culinary scene. There are stunning views over nearby Parque Sarmiento from the roof terrace. ✉ *Ituzaingó 1070, 5000* ☎ *351/468–7359* ⊕ *www.cordobahostel.com.ar* 🛏 *38 beds* 🍴 *Picnic area, barbecues, bar, pool, Ping-Pong, recreation room, laundry service, Internet, travel services* ▭ *No credit cards.*

Nightlife

Córdoba is a round-the-clock city. For low-key nights on the town, there are traditional *confiterías* (cafés) on practically every downtown street corner. Many stay open well into the wee hours, and serve alcoholic drinks, coffee, and sandwiches. The hub for trendier bars and cafés is the Nueva Córdoba district, just south of the center.

Bars

Café Novecento (✉ Cabildo, Deán Funes 33 ☎ 351/460–5299) is a café and wine bar so cutting edge that it has a branch in New York City. It's still Argentine, in spite of the Euro–new-age music and North American styling. A good daily selection of wines by the glass is scrawled across a chalkboard. The place couldn't be more central. **Galileo** (✉ Gauss 5700, Villa Belgrano ☎ 3543/444–090) is the arty café of choice. Rub shoulders with young trendies and well-to-do intellectuals who come here as much for the drinks and sublime cakes as for the live music.

Mandarina (✉ Obispo Trejo 171 ☎ 351/426–4090) is actually a restaurant—you can watch the meals being made in the open-plan kitchen—but the live music and cultural goings-on make it seem more like a café–bar. It's laid back, with simple rustic furniture. It's also open for breakfast. **Villa Agur** (✉ Tristán Malbrán 4335, at José Roque Funes, Cerro las Rosas ☎ 351/481–7520) is an ultra-cool bar with low leather sofas and frequent live music shows. It also has a small restaurant and an open-air terrace.

Dinner Show

El Arrabal (✉ Belgrano 899 ☎ 351/460–2990 ⊕ www.elarrabal.com.ar) is a restaurant and café with tango shows at midnight Thursday–Sunday. The cost is 8 pesos, and reservations are a must.

Nightclubs

Córdoba is known for nightclubs where the action doesn't get going until 2 or 3 AM and continues well past dawn. Electronic music is big here, and international DJs play frequently, as do touring rock bands. The most popular drink in the province is *Fernet con coca,* also known as a "Fernando," a mixture of the sticky Italian apéritif Fernet Branca with Coca-Cola. The resulting witches' brew has brown froth and is sold by the bucket-sized glass. Most of the hotspots are north of the center, in the exclusive Chateau Carreras and Cerro de las Rosas neighborhoods or slightly lower-key Villa Belgrano and El Abasto. Travel by taxi.

Classy electronic music fills **Factory** (✉ Av. Rafael Núñez 3964, Cerro de las Rosas ☎ 351/1555–6106 ☉ Fri.–Sun. 1 AM onward), one of the most popular clubs in town. The building is small, so expect packed dance floors. **Hangar/18** (✉ Bvd. Las Heras 116, El Abasto ☉ Thurs.–Sun. midnight onward) is Córdoba's most popular gay disco and often has live shows in between DJs. It's in a big warehouse-like space, just north of the center. **Shark** (✉ Av. Laplace 5675, Villa Belgrano ☎ 03543/440–012) is a trendy place for drinking, relaxed dancing, and music Thursday through Saturday. The crowd is mostly thirtysomethings.

Shopping

Córdoba's main shopping area is the pedestrian-only street San Martín, which runs north from Plaza San Martín. Stores are shaded by awnings and bougainvillea, which provide a welcome relief from the sun in the summer. The street is particularly strong on surf- and mountain-wear, testament to the outdoors offerings just outside town.

Alfajores

Perhaps the most famous alfajores in town are made by **Chammas** (✉ Rivadavía 77 ☎ 351/426–5693), a long-running establishment whose cookies go by the dozen.

Antiques & Crafts

A small collection of stalls selling genuine antiques and plain old stuff form the **Feria de Antigüedades** (✉ Pasaje Revol and Belgrano ☉ Fri.–Sun. 6 PM–11 PM). There doesn't seem to be any rule governing prices here, so shop around. Late on weekend afternoons, stalls fill a winding cobbled space near La Cañada to create the **Feria Paseo de las Artes** (✉ Achával Rodríguez at La Cañada ⊙ Fri.–Sun. 5 PM–11 PM), the city's best crafts market. Bargaining isn't common practice, though you can expect a small discount if you buy in quantity.

Malls

Big, brash, **Nuevocentro Shopping** (✉ Duarte Quirós 1400 ☎ 351/488–8800 ⊕ www.nuevocentro.com.ar) is slightly west of the center, opposite the Sheraton hotel. As well as good range of clothes shops and a cinema, it has a big supermarket and a branch of Brazilian department store Falabella. Posh **Patio Olmos** (✉ Av. San Juan and Bv. Vélez Sarsfield ☎ 351/570–4100 ⊕ www.patioolmos.com) is behind a sweeping stone facade that once belonged to an exclusive school. The mall is in the middle of downtown and has a cinema multiplex and mostly Argentine-brand shops.

NORTH OF CÓRDOBA CITY

The highway from Córdoba City to the Jesuit country around the town of Ascochinga passes so many centuries-old estancias that it's been dubbed El Camino de la Historia (The History Trail). Farther afield, another 100 km (62 mi) north of Ascochinga, is Cerro Colorado and its pre-Hispanic petroglyphs.

Northwest of the city is the Valle de la Punilla and its many villages. In high season, the southernmost places—Villa Carlos Paz, Cosquín, and La Falda—are flooded by vacationing porteños. A little farther north are less hectic La Cumbre and Capilla del Monte. Here rolling hills are interspersed with strange formations of rich red sandstone at the Cerro Uritorco and Parque Natural Ongamira. The weird and wonderful shapes make it easy to see why this is Argentina's favorite UFO spot. Trekking both on foot and on horseback, golf, and extreme sports like paragliding are other popular activities.

Ascochinga

58 km (36 mi) north of Córdoba on RN53.

The bracing air of Ascochinga's rolling hills and woods made the town a logical choice for a tuberculosis sanatorium. These days, it's a sleepy vacation spot within easy access of the estancias at Jesús María, Caroya, and Santa Catalina. Ascochinga is also synonymous with golf: its 18-hole course has incredible views of the Sierras Chicas.

The farming town of **Jesús María**, 20 km (13 mi) west of Ascochinga on E66, was once a native Argentine settlement. It changed radically in 1688 when the Jesuits bought over 100 square kilometers (37 square miles) of land here. They planted more than 48,000 vines from which came Lagrimilla, the first New World wine to be presented at the Spanish court (it's still produced). In the first fortnight of January the town comes to life with the Festival Nacional de La Doma y el Folklore (National Rodeo and Folklore Festival), which is more about heavy drinking than cowboy activities.

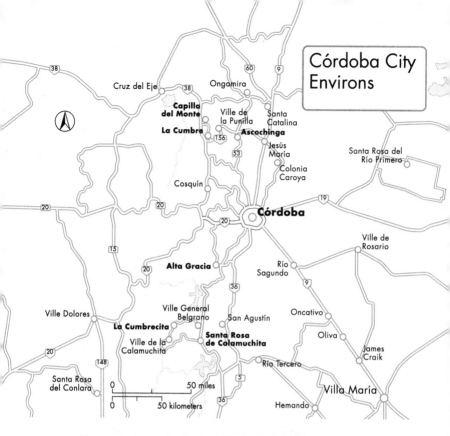

The stately three-wing **Estancia San Isidro Labrador** was once the nerve-center of the Jesuits' vast holdings in Jesús María. Two stories of arched galleries range around three sides of the main courtyard; behind them lie the priests' living quarters and communal rooms. The estancia's single-nave church is a beautiful example of the Jesuits' no-nonsense building style: the only adornment is the relief-work of the copula, which is thought to have been created by native Argentine artisans. Inside the estancia is the Museo Jesuítico Nacional (National Jesuit Museum), which has a 10,000-piece-strong collection that includes religious artifacts, colonial art and furnishings, and agricultural and wine-making paraphernalia. ⊠ *Pedro de Oñate s/n* ☎ *3525/420–126* ☒ *2 pesos* ☽ *Apr.–Sept., weekdays 8–7, weekends 10–noon and 2–6; Oct.–Mar., weekdays 8–7, weekends 10–noon and 3–7.*

Five kilometers (3 mi) southwest of Jesús María—via the RN9 and the E156—is the village of **Colonia Caroya**. Its name means "leather face" in Quechua, the Andean language spoken here prior to the arrival of the Jesuits, and its famous for two things: fabulous homemade salami (the town is home to descendents of Italian immigrants) and Argentina's oldest Jesuit estate. The **Estancia Jesuítica de Caroya** was founded in 1616 and evolved over the centuries: the ascetic stone chapel dates from its founding, while the patio, cloisters, and outbuildings were added during the 18th and 19th centuries. During the wars of independence, the building had the brief but dubious honor of being Argentina's first knife and sword factory; later it became a sort of summer camp for the students of Códoba's prestigious Colegio de Nuestra Señora de Montserrat. Heavy rustic furniture and religious paintings from the Cuzqueña school fill the 10 rooms that were once the priests' cells, while more weapons—this time 18th-century rifles—fill the gallery. The patio is shaded by elms, orange trees, and palms—all rustled by cool breezes. ☒ West side of Caroya ☎ 3525/426–701 ☑ 2 pesos ☉ Apr.–Sept., daily 9–1 and 2–6; Oct.–Mar., daily 9–1 and 3–6.

★ A heavily wooded dirt trail leads from Ascochinga 11 km (7 mi) north to the **Estancia Jesuítica de Santa Catalina,** once the Jesuits' largest estate. When the Jesuits acquired it in 1622, the first thing they did was construct a massive underground irrigation system to water the dry lands. There area remains a massive agricultural center. The jewel in the estancia's crown is the **Iglesia de Santa Catalina** (Saint Catherine's Church), whose twin belfries tower over the estate. It took the Jesuits almost 100 years and more than three architects to complete the structure, which was finally consecrated in 1726. The stone they used—the local *piedra de sapo* (literally, toad stone)—is porous, and the church's baroque facade is regularly whitewashed to protect it from the elements: you may find it dazzling white or beautifully weather-stained, depending on when it was last painted. Inside, a spartan nave leads up to the building's only decoration, a gleaming gilded retable with a portrait of Saint Catherine. The estancia's arched galleries stretch off on either side of the church, giving way to several shady courtyards with fountains. ☎ 3525/421–600 ⊕ www.santacatalina.info ☑ 2 pesos ☉ Apr.–Sept., 10–1 and 2–6; Oct.–Mar., 10–1 and 3–7:30. Guided tours available except Jan.–Feb. and Holy Week.

OFF THE
BEATEN
PATH

★ **PARQUE ARQUEOLÓGICO Y NATURAL CERRO COLORADO –** This small reserve well north of Ascochinga is one of Argentina's most important pre-Hispanic sites, with over 30,000 petroglyphs painted on red rock formations. The oldest date to roughly AD 800 and include pictures of llamas, condors, *yaguaretés* (a local alligator species), and human hunters, though most of the paintings remain uninterpreted. Later works represent mounted figures, a unique indigenous record of the arrival of the conquistadores. To visit the paintings, you must take one of the four daily guided walks that leave from the hut at the entrance to tiny Cerro Colorado village. Two fords cross the dirt road into the village, so drive carefully. ⊹ 110 km (75 mi) north of Jesús María on RN9, then 10 km (6 mi) west on a dirt road just north of Santa Elena ☑ 2 pesos ☉ Daily 9–6.

Where to Stay & Eat

$–$$ ✕ **La Ranchería.** Top-quality handicrafts surround you at this colorful restaurant-cum-shop, which has been owned by the same family since the late 18th century. Snack your way to a meal with a *picada* (platter of cold-cuts) of locally cured ham and homemade cheeses washed down with some ice-cold beer—ask what *cervezas artesanales* (local microbrewery beers) are available. Hearty parrilla fare is also on offer if you need something more filling. ✉ *Next to Estancia Santa Catalina, Santa Catalina* ☎ *3525/422–073* ▤ *No credit cards* ☉ *No dinner Sun.*

★ $ ✗ **El Faro.** Local opinion is unanimous: this is the best parrilla in the north of Córdoba, and the perfect place to break up a day of estancia-seeing. All over the province, restaurants have begun to imitate El Faro's unusual serving style: *asadores* (barbecuers) carve slices from the sizzling beef sides on the grill and return time and again with dripping portions on wooden boards. They also do fantastic *chivito* (goat). ✉ *Juan Bautista Alberdi 245, Caroya* ☎ *No phone* ▤ *No credit cards.*

$$$$ ✗▥ **Estancia La Paz.** Colonnaded galleries run round the outside of Estancia La Paz, which belonged to Argentine president Julio Roca at the end of the 19th century. The false wardrobe connecting his bedroom with that of his lover isn't the only reminder of the estancia's past: the owners' choice of antique furniture, period ornaments, and heavy silk drapes all take you back in time. Ducks swim serenely on the huge lake behind the estancia, whose manicured grounds were designed by landscaper Carlos Thays and make for perfect picnic territory. When you sit down for dinner ($$$$) at the long, damask-clothed dining table, expect some surprises: as well as top-notch classic Argentine fare, chef Bruno Glaudo also prepares exotic national dishes that feature llama, deer, wild boar, capybara, and even *yacaré* (a local alligator). ✉ *Ruta E66, Km 14, Ascochinga 5117* ☎ *3525/492–073* ⊕ *www.estancialapaz.com.ar* ⤶ *23 rooms* ♨ *Dining room, room service, IDD phones, no in-room TVs, golf privileges, tennis court, pool, lake, spa, boating, fishing, horseback riding, lounge, library, laundry service, travel services, free parking* ▤ *AE, DC, MC, V* ⟊ *All-inclusive.*

Fodor'sChoice ★

★ $$ ✗▥ **Posada Camino Real.** A long and winding dirt track leads to the family-run Posada Camino Real, whose grounds were once part of the Jesuits' holdings at Santa Catalina. Outside, the stucco buildings are a harmonious dusky rose; inside rich chestnuts and ochers abound in rooms furnished with hefty iron bedsteads and chunky wooden furniture. Although the rooms and living area—complete with a huge hearth—are lovely, you'd be mad to stay indoors: the countryside is teaming with wildlife, and the hotel organizes excursions on foot and horseback. Top chefs come regularly to train the kitchen staff, which produces modern takes on traditional Argentine fare; much of the produce they use is grown in the estancia's own gardens. Meals aren't only held inside: beef and whole goats are roasted over coals in the barbecue. ✉ *10 km (6 mi) north of Santa Catalina on road from Ascochinga, Santa Catalina* ☎ *351/552–5215* ▤ *351/613–4287* ⊕ *www.posadacaminoreal.com.ar* ⤶ *12 rooms* ♨ *Dining room, picnic area, IDD phones, refrigerators, cable TV, 3-hole golf course, pool, spa, bicycles, croquet, horseback riding, bar, laundry service, free parking* ▤ *No credit cards* ⟊ *All-inclusive.*

Golf

Ascochinga Golf Club (✉ Zona Urbana Círculo Fuerza Aerea, Ascochinga ☎ 3525/492–015 ⊕ www.ascochingagolf.com.ar 🖃 Greens fees for non members: 35 pesos Sat., 30 pesos other days) is a 72-par, 18-hole golf course that looks over the rolling hills around Ascochinga.

La Cumbre

96 km (60 mi) north of Córdoba on RN38.

Once part of a massive Spanish hacienda, by the first half of the 20th century, La Cumbre had become a mini British colony, filled with the summer houses of those involved with construction of the railway. Though their legacy remains in the mock-Tudor buildings at the town's snooty golf course, nowadays La Cumbre is synonymous with adventure tourism, notably paragliding. Although there isn't much to do in the town itself, there are lots of hotels and restaurants, making it a great base for exploring La Punilla.

El Paraíso, a museum that was once the home of writer Manuel Mujica Láinez, is nestled in the posh hilltop neighborhood of Cruz Chica, overlooking La Cumbre. Displays consist of his personal effects, including a 15,000-strong library and objects collected from his extensive travels. But you should stop by just to soak up the atmosphere in its rooms and its gorgeous gardens, which were designed by Carlos Thays. ⊠ *Cruz Chica, 2 km (1.6 mi) north of La Cumbre* ☎ *3548/491–596* 🖃 *3 pesos* ⊙ *Daily 9:30–12:30 and 5–7:30.*

Cuchi Corral, in the hills west of La Cumbre, is a vast natural balcony with views over the Río Pinto valley. Once used by native Argentines for spiritual rituals, it now sees another kind of natural high: paragliding. With a drop of 402 meters (1,320 feet), Cuchi Corral is Argentina's top spot for the sport, and international championships are held here every March. Even if you can't take the leap, stop by for the views. About 1.5 km (1 mi) from the viewpoint, back towards La Cumbre, are the ruins of **Estancia Cuchi Corral,** an 18th-century adobe house. ⊠ *8 km (5 mi) east of La Cumbre on RN38.*

Where to Stay & Eat

$–$$ ✕ **La Casona del Toboso.** The little cottage that houses La Cumbre's best-known restaurant looks a bit fairy tale from the outside, though the sunny beer garden lessens the effect somewhat. The hard chairs and dubious artwork inside do nothing to put locals off: the food outweighs any complaints. The specialty is trout, fished locally and served baked, grilled, or as brochettes. Great grills and pastas are also on offer. ⊠ *Belgrano 349* ☎ *3548/451–436* 🖃 *AE, DC, MC, V.*

$$$ ✕🖻 **Hotel Victoria.** Although this chalet-style hotel is on the links of La Cumbre's renowned golf course, guests are as likely to be foodies as they are golfers: the restaurant ($$–$$$) is unmatched in the area. Local produce is the backbone of the menu, which includes dishes like lamb in a pear and garlic confit, artichoke ravioli, or salmon lasagna. If you can, go for an all-inclusive plan so as to munch your way through the hotel's four delicious meals of the day, one of which is afternoon tea. The checkered floor tiles and leaded windows in the reception and lounge areas feel old worldly; on cold nights there's a log fire in the downstairs living room. ⊠ *Posadas at Moreno, 5178* ☎ *3548/451–412* ⊕ *www.hotelvictoria.com.ar* 🖘 *7 rooms, 5 apartments* ⚭ *Restaurant, picnic area, IDD phones, cable TV, pool, bar, library, lounge, babysitting, laundry service, free parking* 🖃 *AE, MC, V* ⭘ *CP, MAP, FAP.*

$$ ☐ **Posada Los Cedros.** Rooms in the century-old main house of this family style hotel look over sweeping lawns; in the apartments you open your curtains onto the sierras. The flowery chintz and heavy wooden furnishings may feel a bit old-ladyish, but the place is very clean and well organized. Be sure to get up in time for breakfast, which includes mouthwatering homemade jams and is served on a veranda bathed in sunlight. ☒ *Avenida Argentina 837, La Cumbre 5178* ☎ *3548/451–028* 🖷 *3548/452–524* ⊕ *www.posadaloscedros.com* ⇥ *12 rooms* 🖒 *Dining room, room service, IDD phones, cable TV, pool, lounge, recreation room, laundry service, free parking* ⊟ *No credit cards* ⦿ *CP.*

Shopping

For local crafts and produce, drive along the winding Camino de los Artesanos (Craftsmen's Road), which is lined by more than a dozen workshop-cum-shops, each selling its own craft specialty. It runs parallel to RN38 between La Cumbre and Villa Giardino to the south.

See the world through purple-tinted spectacles at **Domaine de Puberclair** (☒ RN38, Km 68.5 ☎ 3548/451–639), a lavender plantation that distills the plant and sells its own soaps, perfumes, and creams.

Of the shops selling local produce, by far the best is **Jardines de Yaya** (☒ Camino de los Artesanos ☎ 3548/1563–7215), a biodynamic farm with hundreds of different homemade jams, preserves, and liqueurs. It does a sideline in textiles and hand-carved housewares. The **Estancia del Rosario** (☒ 5 km [3 mi] from La Cumbre on ruta E66 toward Ascochinga ☎ 3548/451–257) is an organic farm that has been making alfajores, jams, and home made liqueurs for over 80 years.

Sports & the Outdoors

GOLF   The pride of town, the 18-hole course of **La Cumbre Golf Club** (☒ Belgrano 1095 ☎ 3548/452–283 ⊕ www.lacumbregolf.com.ar 🖂 Greens fees for non members: 35 pesos), was built in 1924 by British railway families: the almost excessively English-looking Tudor-style clubhouse is vivid proof.

HORSEBACK RIDING   **La Chacra** (☒ Pasaje Beiró s/n ☎ 3548/451–703) is a riding and polo school that also runs horseback trips; the specialty is moonlit night rides. **La Granja del Gringo** (☒ RN38, just north of La Cumbre ☎ 3548/1557–4317) is a farm just out of town where you can saddle up for excursions that stretch from an hour to several days.

PARAGLIDING   **Escuela de Parapente Carlos Vega** (☒ RN38 at the turn-off to Cuchi Corral ☎ 3548/491–941) is run by an internationally qualified paraglider and arranges jumps from different lofty spots. **Pablo Kuniss and Guillermo Olmos** (☒ RN38, Km 65 ☎ 3548/422–587 ⊕ www.cordobaserrana.com.ar/parapente.htm) offer one-off *vuelos de bautismo* (baptism flights) in tandem with an instructor for beginners as well as longer courses.

Capilla del Monte

14 km (9 mi) north of La Cumbre on RN38.

Shop windows filled with New Age books and T-shirts proclaiming close encounters of the third kind let you know that Capilla del Monte is synonymous with the out-of-this-world activity at nearby Cerro Uritorco, Argentina's number one UFO-spotting location. Locals are also proud of the *calle techada* (roofed street), which is just what it sounds like: in the 1970s the residents found themselves without a gallery for an upcoming photography exhibition, so they built a roof over part of the main drag. It was such a hit that it's never been dismantled. On one end of the street is a square where a small craft market is held on weekends. Unusual area rock formations and several national parks make hiking one of the main activities here.

You may not see flying saucers, but you probably will catch stunning views over the valley to the west from the craggy top of **Cerro Uritorco.** The 6 km (4 mi) climb up takes about three hours, following a well-signed path that starts on the other side of a small bridge near the Balneario La Toma on the Calabalumba river, north of Plaza San Martín. There's a small ticket booth (☒ 1 peso) at the trailhead, which is on private land. Although guides tabound, it's a straightforward ascent. Take plenty of water and avoid walking in the midday sun.

Over the last 180 million years, air and water have eroded soft red sandstone to form the huge, bizarrely shaped formations in the park of **Los Terrones.** Although you can drive through the arid landscape, it's worth leaving your car at the entrance: the two-hour trail makes for a fascinating walk that culminates in great views of the Cerro Pajarillo and the valleys surrounding Capilla del Monte. Watch for condors, eagles, and falcons, which are often seen from the top. ☒ *18 km (11.5 mi) north of Capilla del Monte on RN38 then east on RP17* ⊕ *www.losterrones. com* ☒ *5 pesos* ☉ *Daily 9–dusk.*

The countryside surrounding **Ongamira,** a small town 1,408 meters (4,620 feet) above sea level, is one of the few places in the Punilla where you can see remains of the indigenous cultures that lived in the area before the Jesuits' arrival decimated their population. The valley of Ongamira was formed 130 million years ago, and over time the elements have carved its dusky sandstone into all manner of caves and grottos, known as **Grutas de Ongamira.** The people who eventually formed the Comechingón nation arrived here around AD 200, although other tribes lived here as much as 8,000 years ago. Their only legacy is rock paintings of animals and human figures. Follow the signs to the special viewpoint to see these pre-Hispanic works.

The Comechingones held out for a long time against the "civilizing" impulses of the Spanish invaders in what is now the privately owned **Parque Natural Ongamira** (☒ Entrance on RP17 ☒ 2 pesos ☉ Daily 9–dusk). Legend has it that the last point of resistance was the Cerro Colchequí, from which the defeated people flung themselves in 1574, preferring death to slavery. The park has views of both this hill and Cerros Pajarillo and Aspero, which inspired the likes of Chilean poet and Nobel prize–winner Pablo Neruda, who once stayed here. A 3-km (2-mi) trail leads to the peak of Cerro Colchequí. 25 km (15.5 mi) from Capilla del Monte (8 km north on RN38 then 17 km east on RP17).

Where to Stay & Eat

Capilla del Monte's main street, the Calle Techada, is lined with restaurants all offering variations on the same parrilla fare. This is one of the few towns where vegetarianism isn't considered an inhuman concept, so ask for veggie alternatives to the cow cuts with confidence.

$–$$ ✕**La Tramontana.** If you like your meals with a view then it's worth making the 5 km (3 mi) trip out of town for lunch at La Tramontana. The low pastel-colored buildings blend into the landscape and house a small restaurant and a trout farm: no prizes for guessing what the specialty is. The whitewashed dining room walls are hung with farming instruments; the floors are a patchwork of colored cement. ⊠ *RN38, Km 89.5* ☎ *3548/1563–5049* ▤ *No credit cards.*

$$ ✕▦**La Guarida.** Individuality reigns at this small complex. The cabins and suites are all decorated differently with a name to match: for example, the ocher-painted Mexicana cabin is surrounded by agave plants, and its exposed-stone walls are hung with Mexican artwork. The king-size beds in each suite face large hearths; private decks are the perfect places to devour the contents of the daily breakfast basket, complete with bread still warm from the oven. The freshest local produce is at the center of the nightly three-course meal (there are also à la carte options and vegetarians are well cared for), which may feature goat, venison, or even guinea pigs. If you stay in a cabin you can arrange for the chef to come and cook in situ. ⊠ *Los Terrones 1008, Capilla del Monte 5184* ☎ *3548/1563–2283* ⊕ *www.laguarida.com.ar* ⇨ *4 suites, 3 cabins* ♿ *Restaurant, picnic area, room service, BBQs, fans, in-room safes, in-room hot-tubs, refrigerators, cable TV, pool, massage, volleyball, lounge, laundry service, travel services, free parking; no room phones* ▤ *No credit cards* ⎪○⎪ *CP or MAP.*

$$$$ ▦**Estancia Dos Lunas.** Shady verandas circle the pale-yellow buildings of this century-old estancia, which was built by an English family. The owners have brought modern comforts like a sparkling deck-edged pool, but the old world remains intact inside. In the bedrooms thick cotton sheets clothe chunky iron bedsteads, and bathrooms have footed bathtubs and majolica tiles. At night, log fires keep things warm. The estancia leads treks—on foot or on horseback—into the nearby Parque Natural Ongamira, whose hills provide Dos Lunas' spectacular backdrop. ⊠ *Altos de Ongamira, turn-off just east of Ongamira on RP17, Ongamira* ☎ *3525/424–847* ⊕ *www.doslunas.com.ar* ⇨ *8 rooms* ♿ *Dining room, pool, massages, bicycles, horseback riding, 2 lounges, laundry service* ▤ *No credit cards* ⎪○⎪ *BP.*

Hiking & Horseback Riding

Agua de los Palos (⊠ Pueyrredón at Av. Las Gemelas ☎ 351/521–1109) is a complex just out of town that organizes trekking and horseback riding excursions in the area. **Fabio Cepeda** (⊠ Belgrano 211 ☎ 3548/489–702) is a reliable local guide who can organize excursions to all the trekking spots around Capilla del Monte.

LA VALLE DE CALAMUCHITA

Small streams crisscross the pine-covered hills that form the Calamuchita Valley, which runs between the Sierras Chicas to the west and the Sierras Grandes and Comechingones to the east. In the first half of the 20th century German and Austrian immigrants made this their home, and among the chalet-style hotels and torte-filled tearooms, you'd be forgiven for thinking yourself in the Alps. Myriad paths wind around the slopes of this part of Córdoba—trekking and viewpoint-climbing are the main attractions here (tearooms and Oktoberfest aside).

Highway RP5 winds south from Córdoba city through Jesuit town Alta Gracia and ultra-touristy Villa General Belgrano before petering out not far south of Santa Rosa de Calamuchita, the last stop on the highway. The unnumbered and partly unpaved road that runs from RP5 to La Cumbrecita is one of the pleasantest drives in the province, providing great views of the tranquil countryside.

Alta Gracia

38 km (24 mi) south of Córdoba on RP5.

The gateway to the Calamuchita Valley grew up around a Jesuit estancia whose ruins are, in turn, clustered around Plaza Solares, in what is now the town center. The bracing air that sweeps over the low hills outside town made it a popular destination for rest cures in the early part of the 20th century; one of the town's most famous residents, Ernesto "Che" Guevara, was brought by his parents to live here in the hope that the mountain air would cure his asthma. Today many people come to hike, horseback ride, and fish in nearby rivers, which also make great swimming spots in summer. There are also two great golf courses here.

The massive stone walls of the main estancia buildings dominate one side of Plaza Solares. After the Jesuits' expulsion from Argentina, the buildings' most illustrious resident was Viceroy Santiago de Liniers, famous for defending Buenos Aires against invading British forces. Liniers lived here briefly in 1810, before his pro-Spanish sympathies cost him his life when Argentina became independent. Despite its name, the ★ **Museo Casa del Virrey Liniers,** a well-organized museum, isn't just about Liniers, but also documents life on the estancia and includes some exhibits about the native Comechingón people who inhabited the area prior to the Europeans' arrival.

You enter the building through a crumbling baroque gate, which gives way to the main courtyard. Overlooking this are the priests' cells, which house period furniture, religious art, and Liniers's personal effects. Deeper within the building are the original kitchens, the forge, and the euphemistic *areas comunes* (common areas), the Jesuits' toilets. These were discovered by archaeologists in the 1970s, mysteriously filled with porcelainware. Adjoining the museum to the south is the **Iglesia Parroquial Nuestra Señora de la Merced,** finished only a few years before the Jesuits' expulsion. Unlike the museum, the church hasn't been well maintained or restored. North of the main building, and outside its confines, is the **Tajamar** (Breakwater), built by the Jesuits in 1643 to create a reservoir for their estate. ✉ *Padre Domingo Viero and Solares* ☎ *3547/421–303* ⊕ *www.museoliniers.org.ar* ☉ *Apr.–Sept., Tues.–Fri. 9–1 and 3–7, weekends 9:30–12:30 and 3:30–6:30; Oct.–Mar., Tues.–Fri. 9–8, weekends 9:30–8. Guided tours in English at 10, noon, 5, and 7; call ahead to arrange.*

A few blocks north of the square in the Carlos Pellegrini neighborhood is the **Museo Casa de Ernesto "Che" Guevara,** in one of several houses rented by the future revolutionary's family during his youth. Thoughtful exhibits fill 10 rooms and include photographs and such personal possessions as school reports and the contents of his bookshelf—testaments to a precocious intellect. Although the museum is touching in its devotion to the figure it celebrates, it provides little historical context, which may be meaningless if you don't know much about Che's life. ✉ *Avellaneda 501* ☎ *3547/428–579* 🎫 *2 pesos* ☉ *Daily 9–7.*

Where to Stay & Eat

$$ ✕ **Morena.** Hearty Cordoban dishes like *cazuela de conejo* (rabbit stew) are great winter warmers, while the trout—best appreciated garnished with only a little herbed butter—is fished locally. If you're looking for something more elaborate, don't miss the *ravioles Morena*, squid-ink black pasta filled with pink prawn, leek, and ricotta mousse—as delicious as it is visually striking. The friendly young staff are happy to talk you through your options. ✉ *Av. Sarmiento 413* ☎ *3547/426–365* ⚶ *Reservations essential* ▭ *AE, MC, V* ☉ *Closed Mon.*

$$ 🏨 **El Potrerillo de Larreta.** The heavy-set main building of this hotel-cum–country club was once part of the Jesuit's holdings. The grounds are now Alta Gracia's prestigious golf club—you can wake up and step right out onto the green. The simple white-walled rooms certainly feel very colonial, with big brass bedsteads, floral curtains, and hardwood floors. Modern installations like air-conditioning assure that old doesn't mean uncomfortable. The downstairs dining room, which has huge windows looking over the greens, serves such traditional Argentine dishes as *medallón de lomo a la pimienta* (black pepper steak) and hearty gnocchi. ✉ *Camino a los Paredones, Km 3, 5186* ☎ *3547/423–804* ⊕ *www. potrerillodelarreta.com* 🛏 *3 rooms, 4 suites* ⚹ *Restaurant, 18-hole golf course, outdoor pool, horseback riding, bicycles, travel services, free parking; no room phones, no room TVs* ▭ *AE, DC, MC, V* ⦿ *CP and MAP.*

Sports & the Outdoors

Alta Gracia Golf Club (✉ Av. Carlos Pellegrini 1000 ☎ 3547/422–922 ⊕ www.aggc.com.ar 🎫 Greens fees for non-members: 15 pesos weekdays, 28 pesos Sat., 18 pesos Sun.) is known as much for its 18-hole course as for its fantastic restaurant. And, oh, yeah: Che Guevara played here. **El Potrerillo de Larreta** (✉ Camino a los Paredones, Km 3 ☎ 3547/ 425–987 ⊕ www.potrerillodelarreta.com 🎫 Greens fees for non-members: 40 pesos Sat., 22 pesos other days) is said to be Córdoba's best 18-hole course. There are at least four (sometimes five) tee-offs per hole, benefiting women and high-handicap players.

Santa Rosa de Calamuchita

60 km (37 mi) south of Alta Gracia on RN5.

In the heart of the valley that bears its name, this mountain resort is extremely popular with porteños. In summer several nearby rivers provide welcome relief from the heat. Things can get rowdy during the Oktoberfest and the more unusual local Strudel festival, which takes place on or around Easter weekend. The rest of the year Santa Rosa is fairly sleepy, visited mainly by outdoors types: climbing and hiking are the main activities, but horseback riding, fishing, kayaking, and paragliding are also popular. Tucked into a bend in the Santa Rosa River, the town doesn't have a central square; Calle Libertad is the main drag, with most restaurants and hotels either on it or an intersecting street.

All that remains of Santa Rosa's Jesuit estancia is the **Capilla Vieja** (Old Chapel) at the northern end of Libertad. The original 1784 building was made of adobe, which fell into disrepair and was largely reconstructed in 1877. The chapel has been lovingly restored and is a peaceful haven during the town's bustling high season. Inside the chapel is the **Museo de Arte Religioso** (⊠ 2 pesos ☉ Daily 10–noon and 3–6), which includes some unusual articulated statues of saints and a 16th-century wooden Christ. ⊠ *Libertad beween Pasaje Centenario and Juana de Fernández.*

Cerro Champaquí rises to 2,901 meters (9,517 feet), due west of Santa Rosa. The easiest way to reach the peak is via the sleepy hamlet of Villa Yacanto, 30 km (19 mi) west of Santa Rosa de Calamuchita. From here, a dirt road takes you most of the way up: if the road is in good condition you can park your car and walk the last half hour to the summit. The breathtaking views take in Conlara Valley to the west and San Javier to the east; condors are a common sight.

Where to Stay & Eat

★ **$–$$** ✕ **La Pulpería de los Ferreyra.** Plan on loosening your belt after dinner at this family-run *pulpería* (tavern). Good bets include *locro* (a meat and corn stew), trout, and barbecued meat. You'd be mad not to try the house specialty, *la facón de la pulpería,* a meat and vegetable brochette cooked and served dramatically speared on a stiletto knife. The restaurant also has a shop selling its own wines and preserves both sweet and savory: try the *vizcacha en escabeche* (lean vizcacha, a llama relative) for something truly different. ⊠ *Libertad 578* ☎ *3546/421–769* ⌀ *Reservations essential during summer* ☰ *AE, DC, MC, V.*

$ ⊞ **Hotel Yporá.** Undulating wooded grounds crossed by small streams stretch for 24 acres around this hotel just outside of town. The main building is strangely curved, meaning that the smallish rooms often have unusual shapes. Simple wooden furniture and modern bathrooms aren't anything special. The staff is well-informed about area activities. ⊠ *RN5 Km 90, 5196* ☎☎ *3546/421–223* ⊕ *www.hotelypora.com* ⤵ *27 rooms* ⌂ *Restaurant, café, room service, IDD phones, room safes, cable TV, pool, tennis court, volleyball, playground, meeting room, Internet, free parking* ☰ *AE, MC, V* ⦿I *CP.*

Nightlife
Sheik (✉ Cerro de Oro s/n ☎ 3546/421–500) is the most popular club in town: don't head here until late, though.

Shopping
Craftspeople gather to sell wooden housewares, endless mates, ceramics, and jams and cookies at the **Feria de Artesanos** (Craft Fair) (✉ Córdoba and Av. J. Cárcano ☉ Jan.–Feb., daily; Mar.–Dec., weekends).

Trekking
Calamuchita Four Trax (✉ Av. Costanera P. Roasenda 1100 ☎ 3546/420–340) rents four-wheel-drive vehicles, which are useful for exploring outside Santa Rosa if the weather's been bad or for reaching the top of Cerro Champaquí without having to hike. **Eduardo Medina** (✉ Independencia 323 ☎ 3546/1565–1162), a local mountainbike champion, rents bikes by the hour or day, and also leads excursions. **Naturaleza y Aventura** (☎ 3546/464–144 ⊕ naturaleza@calamuchitanet.com.ar) organizes trekking and 4WD safaris in the mountains around Santa Rosa. There's no office; just call ahead to discuss your options.

La Cumbrecita

84 km (52 mi) southwest of Alta Gracia: 50 km (31 mi) south on RN5 to Villa General Belgrano, then 34 km (21 mi) west on an unnumbered provincial road.

Immigrants from Switzerland and Austria built this village in the 1930s, and its wooden chalets wouldn't look out of place in the Alps. La Cumbrecita is surrounded by tree-filled slopes, and well-marked trails lace the area. The peace extends right into La Cumbrecita, which is a car-free zone in the daytime (many residents use golf carts to get around). Two clean rivers, the Almbach and the Río del Medio, run close to the village; both have small cascades and *balnearios* (bathing spots). The village has a mild microclimate, with warm but not roasting summers; snow is a frequent sight in winter, which puts the finishing touches to La Cumbrecita's alpine look. The village has no main square and isn't laid out on a grid. Instead, two roads run through it, European-style; the lower Paseo Bajo has several restaurants and hotels along it.

North of town on Paseo Bajo, water from the peaks has created the small pools known as **Almbachsee**, also called La Olla. They're over 8 meters (26 feet) deep, and even in summer the water temperature never exceeds 15°C (59°F), making this the perfect place to cool off on hot days. The rock face behind the pools is a favorite with local rock climbers. In winter, hot drinks and rich German-style cakes await at Confitería Tante Liesbeth, on the other side of the stream beyond the pools.

From the Almbachsee, a path continues up to the top of **Cerro Wank,** one of the most popular walks in La Cumbrecita. The peak is at 1,728 meters (5,670 feet) above sea level. The walk up takes about an hour, with fantastic views from the top over the Calamuchita Valley. A brisk half-hour walk along the winding path that starts at the Hostería Kuhstall takes you through pine woods to **La Cascada,** a 14-meter-tall (46-foot-tall) waterfall on the Almbach. You can swim in the pool it forms.

Where to Stay & Eat

$–$$ ✕ **Bar Suizo.** Consistently excellent Swiss–German fare makes this small woodclad restaurant the best of the Alpine eateries that line the Paseo Bajo. Pork dishes feature heavily on the menu, but the *raclette* (a relative of cheese fondue), trout in herb butter, and ravioli with wild mushroom sauce are other winning options. At tea time, berry cakes and apple strudel accompany Viennese *Eiskaffee* (iced coffee topped with whipped cream). ☒ *Las Truchas s/n* ☎ *3546/481–067* ☐ *No credit cards.*

★ **$** ✕ **Confitería Tante Liesbeth.** The founder of La Cumbrecita's most famous teahouse was Liesbeth Mehnert, one of the original immigrants to arrive here. She passed her secrets on to her daughter-in-law, who continues to turn out the best confections in town. ☒ *North end of Paseo Bajo, crossing the Almbach River* ☎ *3546/481–079* ☐ *No credit cards.*

$$$ ✕▢ **Hotel La Cumbrecita.** The massive chalet is a local style icon, synonymous with the image of La Cumbrecita. This was the first hotel to be built in the valley, and a pioneer of the village's transition to popular resort. Although its scale is still impressive, its heavy hardwood furniture, floral bedspreads, and rather dim lighting feel old-fashioned. All meals are served in the wooden-clad dining room: unsurprisingly, German and Austrian fare is the basis of the menu. ☒, *5194* ☎ *3546/481–052* ⊕ *www.hotelcumbrecita.com.ar* ↩ *33 rooms, 3 bungalows* ♨ *Restaurant, room service, cable TV, tennis court, pool, gym, fishing, horseback riding, Ping-Pong, library, recreation room, meeting room, travel services* ☐ *AE, DC, MC, V* ▢⃝ *All-inclusive.*

$$ ▢ **La Colina.** Pine-filled hills are the first thing you see each morning at this small apart-hotel on a natural balcony over town. You can even bathe with a view: the stone-clad hot tubs are surrounded by massive plateglass windows. The spacious suites all have bouncy king-size beds with rich cotton linens in soft colors like taupe and camel; the irregular wooden swathes that line the walls are a modern take on alpine style. You can also get an eyeful of the view from the hotel's restaurant, where owner-chef Ricardo Nogueira does excellent nightly set menus of Central European dishes like pork ribs and sauerkraut. His son, Juan Pablo, organizes rappelling, rock-climbing, horseback riding, and 4WD excursions. ☒ *Calle Pública s/n, 5194* ☎ *3546/481–063* ⊕ *www.suitesdelacolina.com* ↩ *6 suites* ♨ *Restaurant, room service, in-room hot tubs, minibars, cable TV, fishing, bicycles, laundry service, travel services; no smoking* ☐ *No credit cards* ▢⃝ *CP.*

CÓRDOBA ESSENTIALS

Transportation

BY AIR

The Aeropuerto Internacional Ingeniero Aeronáutico Ambrosio Taravella (phew!) is 13 km (8 mi) north of Córdoba City. Although it's technically an international airport, it primarily handles domestic flights. Aerolíneas Argentinas runs more than 10 daily flights between Buenos Aires and

Córdoba. The two other airlines operating between the two cities are LAN (three to four daily flights) and Southern Winds (one or two flights daily). The flight takes just over an hour and round-trip fares start at around 200 pesos, but can vary greatly depending on how far in advance you book and whether or not you're a foreigner or an Argentine. You can take a private shuttle and the local bus to the city center.

Aerolíneas Argentinas ☎ 11/4320-2000 in Buenos Aires, 351/410-7676 in Córdoba ⊕ www.aerolineas.com.ar. **Aeropuerto Internacional Ingeniero Aeronáutico Ambrosio Taravella** ✉ Camino a Pajas Blancas, Km 11, Córdoba ☎ 351/475-0871. **LAN** ☎ 11/4378-2200 in Buenos Aires, 351/425-3030 in Córdoba ⊕ www.lan.com. **Southern Winds** ☎ 810/777-7979 ⊕ www.fly-sw.com.

BY BUS

There are dozens of daily buses to Córdoba from Buenos Aires's Retiro bus station. Companies like Chevallier and General Urquiza run *semi-cama* services (standard with reclining seats, air-conditioning and sometimes video entertainment) as well as highly comfortable sleeper services (known as *cama* or *ejecutivo*) with fully reclinable seats, refreshments, videos, and shorter journey times. Generally these are only 10 or 20 pesos more expensive than semi-camas, which start at around 50 pesos one-way. Daily Chevallier buses travel directly from Buenos Aires to Alta Gracia and Santa Rosa de Calamuchita; General Urquiza goes several times daily from Buenos Aires to Capilla del Monte and La Cumbre and once daily to Ascochinga. All buses pass through Córdoba City.

From Córdoba, local bus companies can connect you with nearly every mountain town. Buses leave once or twice an hour from the central bus station, Nueva Estacion Terminal de Omnibus de Córdoba (NETOC), to La Cumbre (2 hours) and Capilla del Monte (3 hours), with slightly less frequent departures to Alta Gracia (1 hour), Ascochinga (2 hours), and Santa Rosa de Calamuchita (2 hours). Sarmiento is a reliable company serving all these destinations; Ciudad de Córdoba does the north of the province, and Sierras de Calamuchita covers the south. Pájaro Blanco is a mini-bus company that makes several daily trips from Córdoba via Villa General Belgrano to both Santa Rosa de Calamuchita and La Cumbrecita.

Bus travel is largely unnecessary within the Córdoba City as most sights and hotels are within walking distance. This is a relief as routes are messy, there are no maps, and drivers are unhelpful. If, however, you decide to brave the system, electric trolley buses run 24 hours a day throughout the city. You need to buy an 80¢ *cospel* (token) or *tarjeta magnética* (multi-journey pass) from a *kiosco* (drugstore) before getting on.

Bus Depot NETOC ✉ Bv. Perón 380, Córdoba ☎ 351/434-1692 ⊕ www.terminalcordoba.com. **Bus Lines Ciudad de Córdoba** ☎ 351/424-0048 in Córdoba. **General Urquiza** ☎ 11/4000-5222 in Buenos Aires, 351/421-0711 in Córdoba ⊕ www.generalurquiza.com.ar. **Nueva Chevallier** ☎ 11/4000-5200 in Buenos Aires, 351/422-0936 in Córdoba ⊕ www.nuevachevallier.com. **Pájaro Blanco** ☎ 351/425-2854 in Córdoba, 3546/46-1709 in Villa General Belgrano, 3546/42-0234 in Santa Rosa de Calamuchita, 3546/48-1096 in La Cumbrecita. **Sarmiento** ☎ 351/433-2161 in Córdoba. **Sierras de Calamuchita** ☎ 351/422-6080 in Córdoba.

BY CAR

Two roads act as the main north–south axes just outside Córdoba City. Running along the province's northeastern side is RN9, which takes you to Ascochinga, as does the winding E53 (also known as RN53), a more scenic, but longer route. To the northwest, the RN38 passes through the Valle de la Punilla. The RP17 crosses the north of the region, along a dusty road that takes you past Ongamira. Farther south is RN156, which meanders through the mountains between Jesús María and La Cumbre. Highway RP5 is the main access for Calamuchita, south of Córdoba City.

BY TAXI

Taxis are a relatively cheap and convenient way of getting around Córdoba City. Official black-and-yellow cabs are everywhere, and all run on a meter, which includes luggage and all passengers. Most Córdobans hail taxis on streets—those with a light on the top are usually considered more reliable, though no one will be able to tell you why. Most restaurants and hotels are happy to call a taxi for you. Given the meter system, hiring a cab for the day is expensive so arranging a chauffeur-driven car is probably a better idea. As well as reasonable prices, they have a lot of experience with the routes most visitors like to take (which is sometimes a problem for local taxi drivers).

In smaller towns there are no official taxis; instead car services—known as *remises*—do the job, which means you have to phone for one or go to an agency. Some remises may be prepared to do longer trips or be at your disposition for a whole day, in which case fares are arranged in advance with the agency.

🚖 Taxi Companies **Remises Centro** ✉ Rivadavia 411, Capilla del Monte ☎ 3548/481-844. **Remises La Terminal** ✉ Av. Carraffa 217, La Cumbre ☎ 3548/451-500. **Remises La Unión** ✉ Saavedra 145, Santa Rosa de Calamuchita ☎ 3546/421-257. **Taxi-Run** ✉ Malvinas Argentinas 236, Alta Gracia ☎ 3547/420-555. **Transmitaxis** ✉ Mariano Fragueiro 3401, Córdoba ☎ 351/470-0000.

Contacts & Resources

BANKS & EXCHANGE SERVICES

There are ATMs all over Córdoba City (identifiable by a sign saying LINK or BANELCO), and in some hill towns. Although hotels in the towns outside Córdoba may accept U.S. dollars, it's safer to change any currency in the city: Citibank is a good bet. As in the rest of Argentina, banking hours are 10 AM to 3 PM weekdays. Note that neither La Cumbrecita nor Ascochinga have banks.

🏦 **Banco de la Nación Argentina** ✉ Av. Belgrano 115, Alta Gracia ☎ 3547/422-344 ✉ Av. Pueyrredón 438, Capilla del Monte ☎ 3548/481-012 ✉ 25 de Mayo 255, La Cumbre ☎ 3548/451-351 ⊕ www.bna.com.ar. **Banco de la Provincia de Córdoba** ✉ Libertad 599, Santa Rosa de Calamuchita ☎ 3546/420-255 ⊕ www.bancor.com.ar. **Citibank** ✉ Rivadavía 104, Córdoba ⊕ www.citibank.com.ar

EMERGENCIES

🚨 Emergency Services **Ambulance** ☎ 107. **Fire** ☎ 100. **Police** ☎ 101.
🏥 Hospitals **Clínica Regional** ✉ Libertad 330 Santa Rosa de Calamuchita ☎ 3546/420-198. **Hospital Alta Gracia** ✉ Av. Del Libertador 1450, Alta Gracia ☎ 3547/429-

282. **Hospital Municipal** ⊠ López y Planes 83, La Cumbre ☎ 3548/451-100. **Hospital Municipal Dr. Oscar Américo Luqui** ⊠ Sarmiento 486, Capilla del Monte ☎ 3548/481-082. **Hospital Privado de Córdoba** ⊠ Av. Chacabuco 4545, Córdoba ☎ 223/499-0000.

VISITOR INFORMATION

🔃 **Alta Gracia** ⊠ Av. del Tajamar at Calle del Molino ☎ 3547/428-128 ⊕ www.altagracia.gov.ar. **Capilla del Monte** Ex-Estación de Ferrocarril, ⊠ Av. Pueyrredón at Diagonal Buenos Aires ☎ 3548/481-878 ⊕ www.capilladelmonte.com.ar. **Córdoba** ⊠ Cabildo, Deán Funes 15 ☎ 351/428-5856 ⊠ Centro Obispo Mercadillo, Rosario de Santa Fe 39 ☎ 351/428-5600 Ext. 9159 ⊠ Airport ☎ 351/434-8390 ⊠ Bus Terminal, Ground Floor ☎ 351/433-1982. **La Cumbre** ⊠ Ex-Estación de Ferrocarril, Av. Caraffa 300 ☎ 3548/452-966 ⊕ www.lacumbre.gov.ar. **La Cumbrecita** ⊠ At village entrance, in the first block after the car park ☎ 3546/481-088 ⊕ www.lacumbrecita.gov.ar. **Santa Rosa de Calamuchita** ⊠ Güemes 13 ☎ 3546/429-654 ⊕ www.vallecalamuchita.com.

The Northwest

WORD OF MOUTH

"We enjoyed the dry, breezy days and cool nights of this region. We found the best prices and selection of textiles and ceramics here. We also thought the Salta/Jujuy region offered the best food, with more flavor and spices than the other regions."

—Nicci

"Salta is fantastic—and so beautiful. So is Jujuy. If you can travel during Easter you'll catch some of the traditional festivities and eat some of the best empanadas. . . ."

—miss_saigon

Updated by
Brian Byrnes

NEIGHBORING BOLIVIA calls the high-altitude Andean desert of this region by its Spanish name, the *altiplano,* but Argentina prefers the ancient Quechua term for the region, the Puna. The desert covers an area of 90,000 square km (34,750 square mi) from Catamarca north across the Andes into Bolivia, Peru, and Chile. Alpaca, guanaco, llama, and vicuña are the only animals you'll see; dry grasses and thorny shrubs with deep roots searching for moisture the only plants. The wind is relentless. Who could live here? Just as you've asked yourself this question, the colorful red poncho of a *coya* (native woman of this region) momentarily brightens the barren landscape as she appears out of nowhere, herding llamas into an unseen ravine. Many people can't breathe at this altitude, let alone walk or sleep: luckily, ordinary mortals can experience a taste of the Puna from El Tren a las Nubes (The Train to the Clouds) in Salta, or by car driving north from Humahuaca to La Quiaca on the Bolivian border.

Down in the valleys, the colonial villages of Cafayate and Cachi bask in the warm, sunny Calchaquíes Valley on the border of Tucumán and Salta provinces. The soaring cliffs of the Talampaya Canyon in La Rioja, the Quebrada de Las Conchas between Salta and Cafayate, and the Quebrada de Humahuaca in Jujuy Province all impress with their peculiar rock formations.

The history of Argentina began in the Northwest, in the provinces of Jujuy, Salta, and Tucumán, along the ancient road of the Incas. In the late 1400s, the Incan people traveled southward from Peru along this route to conquer the tribes of northern Argentina and Chile. Half a century later the Spaniards traveled the same route in search of gold and silver. By 1535 the Royal Road of the Inca had become a well-established trade route between the mines in the north and the agricultural riches of Argentina to the south. Examples of the pre-Hispanic and colonial cultures remain in the architecture, music, language, dress, and craftsmanship found in small villages throughout the region. Churches built by the Jesuits in the 17th century dot the landscape; Incan ruins lie half-buried in remote valleys and high plateaus; and pre-Inca mummies continue to be discovered in the highest peaks of the Andes near Salta.

ORIENTATION & PLANNING

Orientation

The landscape in Argentina's northwestern reaches is incredibly varied—from 22,000-foot-high Andean peaks to the high, barren plateau known as the Puna, subtropical jungles, deserts with multicolor mountains, and narrow sandstone gorges cut by raging brown rivers. Much of the area is desert, cut and eroded by rivers that wash away everything in sight during summer rains, leaving deep red-rock canyons (*quebradas*) with strange rock formations and polychromatic mountainsides, resembling parts of the American Southwest. Snowcapped peaks, some higher than 18,000 feet, in the Aconquija range in Tucumán, form a startling backdrop to the lush green subtropical jungle that climbs the slopes of the pre-cordilleras (foothills).

Top Reasons to Visit

Colonial Architecture Salta and its neighboring towns are quickly earning a reputation worldwide among lovers of colonial architecture and rural charm. Various cathedrals, *casas*, and churches in the vicinity offer interesting glimpses into the region's past. In Cafayate, you can learn about wine making, shop for local crafts, and visit colonial spots. San Fernando del Valle de Catamarca, meanwhile, has a lovely unhurried colonial spirit of its own. Though most of La Rioja's colonial buildings were destroyed in an 1894 earthquake, the town's church (built in 1623) survived and is the oldest building in Argentina.

Wine Though they usually takes a back seat to wines from the central Mendoza province, the wines of the north, especially in the Cafayate region of Salta, are quickly earning a reputation both in Argentina and beyond for their high-altitude excellence. There are vineyards scattered throughout the Northwest where you can taste the goods and learn more about the Argentine wine-making traditions. **Bodega Colomé**, southwest of Salta city in the Calchaquí Valley, dates back to 1831 and claims to be the oldest working vineyard in Argentina. Colomé is also home to a magnificent estancia boutique hotel (⊕ www.bodegacolome.com).

The Quebrada A craggy, vast, splashed-with-color landscape awaits lovers of the great outdoors here, with the possibility of hiking, horseback riding, and biking. Route 9 curves its way past many small, willow-tree-shaded villages. Walking among waterfalls near Tilcara, driving outside Purmamarca, and catching your breath to stare at the stars or at the otherworldly carved walls of the gorge are among the reasons to visit this awesome terrain.

Sports & the Outdoors Mountains, valleys, lakes, and streams are all a part of this diverse region of the country, making it an ideal spot for all kinds of sports from golf and tennis to rafting and fishing to off-road wheeling and hang-gliding. There are plenty of places to hike and camp; rock-climbing is also popular in The Quebrada.

Folk Music The Northwest is the unofficial home of Argentina's folkloric music scene, with Salta being the hot spot of the region. Some of the country's top folk musicians, like traditionalists Ricardo Vilca and Fortunato Ramos and the more modern Los Nocheros, hail from this region and have earned both national and international audiences. Wind instruments, diverse percussion, and soaring harmonies define the high-Andean sound that provides this region with its special soundtrack.

Salta & Jujuy

The northern frontier of Argentina's sprawling landscape is occupied by the provinces of Salta and Jujuy. In this misty corner of Argentina, you'll come across Spanish-colonial plazas with hand-painted signs, cloud-shrouded river valleys, arid salt flats with craggy red rocks, train tracks into the clouds, Andean pan flute music, and locals munching on coca leaves—available at any corner store in the region, they're the ultimate antidote for altitude sickness.

The youthful city of Salta is quickly becoming a northern Argentine favorite for its fabulous colonial architecture, while outlying towns (including Cachi, San Lorenzo, Quilmes, and Cafayate) take country charm and off-the-beaten-path traveling to a new level. In the provincial capital of Jujuy, you can sample delicious authentic Northwestern cuisine after a day of exploring the outlying canyons, mountains, and high Puna, which is a sublime spot for both horseback riding and hiking.

Quebrada de Humahuaca

This massive, exploding-with-color gorge can be reached by following Route 9 north from Jujuy. Inexhaustible stretches of craggy landscape define this area, peppered here and there with charming towns, such as Purmamarca (where you can eat some of the best Andean food the region has to offer at El Manantial del Silencio), Tilcara (which has a fort and several museums), Humahuaca (whose memorable town hall merits a visit), and the small towns on the Bolivian border called La Quiaca and Yavi.

Tucumán, Catamarca & La Rioja

Tucumán may be the smallest province in the country, but it is among the richest (it is the largest producer of lemons in the world). Its provincial capital, San Miguel de Tucumán, is Argentina's fourth-largest city; here you can stroll amongst college students down wide avenues shaded by leafy trees, stopping to rest at lush plazas or outdoor cafés. Traffic and crowds may define this city when you're pounding the pavement, but an interesting history and plenty of good eats await the curious.

Planning

To fully appreciate the historical significance and the scenic and cultural diversity of the Andean Northwest, you must visit not only the major cities of Salta and San Miguel de Tucumán but also the high plateaus, deep canyons, and colonial villages wherein lie the stories of pre-Hispanic civilizations, conquering Spaniards, and the determining forces of nature.

Timing It Right

The best times to visit are spring (October–December) and early autumn (April and May), when the weather is most pleasant. Winter (June–September) is brisk and downright cold on the Andean Puna but is actually the Northwest's peak tourist season. Rooms in better hotels may fill up at this time as well as during Semana Santa (Holy Week) and fiestas, so reserve ahead. Summer (January–March) is hot and rainy, and those rains frequently cause landslides that block mountain roads. (The Tucumán–Tafí del Valle route is notorious in that regard.) Most facilities do remain open year-round, but the region's famed Tren a las Nubes rail excursion from Salta does not operate at all in summer.

Delicious Eats & Sleeps

The Northwest's indigenous heritage has influenced the unique cuisine: corn and potatoes are common ingredients in many of the region's

Folklore & Festivals

SEVERAL LOCAL FESTIVALS in the Northwest's high mountain villages and colonial cities celebrate Argentina's rich history. The parades, performances, costumes, music, and dancing of these festivals draw on 2,000-year-old Inca rituals, Catholic beliefs, political history, gaucho tradition, agricultural practices, local handicrafts, and regional food. Inti Raymi (Festival of the Sun), celebrated since Inca times on June 21 (winter solstice), marks the end of one year's planting and the beginning of the next. The indigenous residents, many of them dressed in traditional costumes handed down through generations, come from nearby villages to sing, dance, play music, and pay tribute to Pachamama (Mother Earth), and to pray to Inti, the Sun, for a good harvest. Festivities begin the night before in Huacalera on the tropic of Capricorn (105 km [65 mi] north of San Salvador de Jujuy in the Humahuaca Valley).

The Virgen de la Candelaria (the patron saint of Humahuaca) is honored on February 2 in Humahuaca. During the event, *sikuris* (bands of young men playing Andean flutes) parade through the cobblestone streets accompanied by dancers and musicians. The Fiesta del

Poncho (Gaucho Festival), a parade held on June 17 in Salta, is an impressive display of the power of the legendary gauchos and their fine horses. Pre-Lenten Carnaval is celebrated in towns and villages throughout the Northwest. In Salta, a parade of floats depicting historic events accompanies dancing characters wearing feathered and mirrored masks—some of them caricaturing local dignitaries. Beware of *bombas de agua* (water balloons) dropping from balconies.

El Éxodo Jujueño (Jujuy Exodus), also known as the Semana de Jujuy (Week of Jujuy), is a historic festival held August 23–24 to commemorate General Belgrano's successful evacuation of the city in August 1812, before Spanish troops arrived. Salta celebrates the Fiesta del Milagro (Festival of the Miracle) September 6–15 in thanks for being spared damage from nine days of earth tremors in 1692. Figures of Christ and the Virgin Mary, credited with protecting the city, are paraded through the streets. In Tucumán, the cradle of Argentina's freedom, Independence Day is celebrated with special fervor on July 9 and the battle of Tucumán on September 24.

dishes. Some dishes worth trying include *locro,* a soup of corn, beans, and red peppers, which becomes a stew when meat is added; *tamales,* ground corn baked with potatoes and meat and tied up in a corn husk; and *humitas,* grated corn with melted cheese cooked in a corn husk. Grilled *cabrito* (goat) is a specialty of the region. For dessert, you may come across *cayote,* an interesting concoction of green-squash marmalade served with nuts and local cheese.

Hotels in the Northwest's major cities tend to be modern and comfortable. Most accept credit cards, though several offer discounts if you pay in cash. Many *estancias* (ranches) in the foothills accept guests and are listed with local tourist offices. ACA (Automóvil Club Argentino) maintains good campgrounds with numerous amenities. Note that as you travel farther north into smaller towns, English is rarely spoken at hotels.

WHAT IT COSTS In Argentina Pesos					
	$$$$	$$$	$$	$	¢
RESTAURANTS	over 35	25–35	15–25	8–15	under 8
HOTELS	over 300	220–300	140–220	80–140	under 80

Restaurant prices are for one main course at dinner. Hotel prices are for two people in a standard double room in high season.

Transportation 101

To decide the best way to explore the Northwest, first take a look at how much independence and flexibility you want, and how much spontaneity you feel comfortable exercising. Bus service is reliable and affordable, but you may not be able to follow your every whim on the road; car rental is significantly more expensive, but you will be able to explore beckoning side roads and rural towns.

AIR TRAVEL   All flights between Buenos Aires and the Northwest use Aeroparque Jorge Newbery, the capital's domestic airport. A variety of domestic carriers offer flights to Catamarca, La Rioja, Salta, San Salvador de Jujuy, and Tucumán.

BUS TRAVEL   Taking the bus to and through the Northwest is relatively easy; just be prepared for a long ride from most other areas of the country. Planning ahead and doing some research pays off (some companies offer roadside pick-up; others have luxury double-decker buses offering overnight services).

CAR TRAVEL   Considering the many miles you'll need to cross to get to the Northwest from most other regions of Argentina, car rental can be expensive when you include insurance, drop-off fees, extra mileage, and gas expenses. However, driving is a terrific way to go if you want to shape your own journey. Consider flying to the Northwest from the capital and renting a car there. With some research, you can find reasonable car-rental agencies in Salta, San Salvador de Jujuy, and Catamarca. After that's taken care of, then only the winding and colorful mountain roads await you.

Visitor Information

The Northwest's five provincial tourist offices are helpful, friendly sources of solid information. You'll see a lot of INFORMACIÓN TURÍSTICA signs around, but these are often storefront travel agencies interested in selling their own tours rather than providing general information.

The Catamarca tourism office is open weekdays 7–1 and 4–9 and weekends 9–1 and 5–9. It's difficult to find, so taking a taxi is recommended. La Rioja's tourism office is open weekdays 8–1 and 4–9 and on Saturday 8–noon. English is spoken at the tourism office in Salta, which is open weekdays 8:30 AM–9 PM and weekends 9–8. English is also spoken at San Salvador de Jujuy's tourism office, which stays open daily 8 AM–9 PM. The Tucumán tourism office is open weekdays 8–8 and weekends 9–9.

🛈 **Catamarca** ✉ General Roca and Mota Botello ☎ 383/343-7791 ⊕ www. turismocatamarca.gov.ar. **La Rioja** ✉ Pelagio B. Luna 345 ☎ 382/242-6384 ⊕ www. larioja.gov.ar/turismo. **Salta** ✉ Buenos Aires 93 ☎ 387/431-0950 ⊕ www.turismosalta. gov.ar. **San Salvador de Jujuy** ✉ Gorriti 295 ☎ 388/422-1343 ⊕ www.turismo.jujuy. gov.ar. **Tucumán** ✉ 24 de Septiembre 484 ☎ 381/422-2199 ⊕ www.tucuman.gov.ar.

SALTA & JUJUY

The provinces of Salta and Jujuy make up the northern frontier of the vast Argentine territory. The farther north you progress, the more things start to feel Northern Andean, more evocative of Bolivia and Peru than of the modern industrialized capitals of central Argentina. Indeed, many travelers wind up in these provinces by way of the Chilean Andes and the Puna, or one of the notorious border crossings from Bolivia and Paraguay.

Salta—the unofficial capital of the Argentine North and a growing hotspot for international tourism—is known throughout the country for its colonial architecture and its unassuming provincial appeal. The circuit south of Salta, including the smaller towns of San Lorenzo, Cachi, Cafayate, and Quilmes, has even more rural charm, although the roads connecting these villages are often unpaved. Progressing north from Salta, though, roads become yet narrower, prices get lower, and faces turn more indigenous as backpacker havens give way to rural villages so off-the-beaten-path, even the backpackers haven't discovered them yet. After the big provincial capital of Jujuy, towns get progressively smaller and wilder as you follow the R9 road, which snakes along the valley of the spectacular gorge, La Quebrada de Humahuaca. After passing the adobe villages of Purmamarca and Tilcara, Humahuaca is the most northerly destination featuring much in the way of modern amenities; north or west of that, you'll want a four-wheel-drive vehicle and an enterprising spirit. The intrepid will eventually arrive at the frontier outposts of Yavi and La Quiaca on the Bolivian border.

Salta

2 hrs from Buenos Aires by plane; 311 km (193 mi) north of Tucumán on R9 or 420 km (260 mi) north of Tucumán on R68 via Tafí del Valle, 92 km (57 mi) south of San Salvador de Jujuy on R9 or 311 km (193 mi) south of San Salvador de Jujuy on R34 (La Cornisa Rd.).

It's not just "Salta" to most Argentines, but "Salta la Linda" (Salta the Beautiful). That nickname is actually redundant—"Salta" already comes from an indigenous Aymara word meaning "beautiful"—but for the country's finest colonial city, it's worth stating twice. Walking among its well-preserved 18th- and 19th-century buildings, single-story houses, wooden balconies, and narrow streets, you could easily forget that this is a city of 500,000 people. But the ever-increasing traffic, the youthful population, and the growing contingent of international itinerants also give the

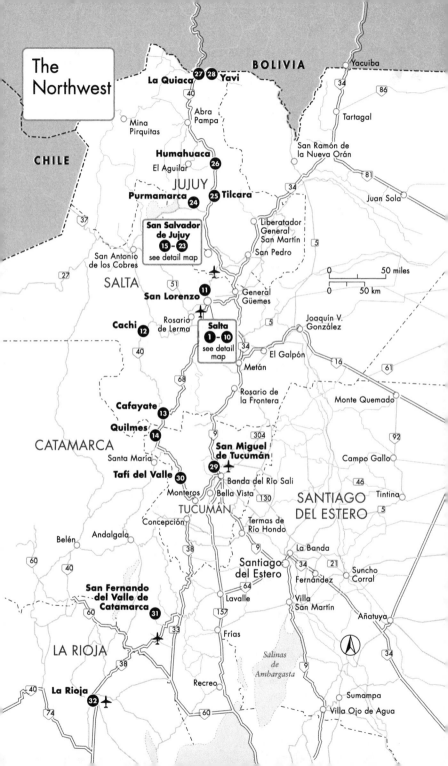

city an irresistible cosmopolitan edge. All in all, it's a hard place to leave. Salta is also the best base for a thorough exploration of the Northwest.

Timing

If you don't linger at the sights, you can do this walk in less than two hours, but spending more time inside the buildings adds perspective. Note that many places close for three or four hours in the afternoon. So either resign yourself to getting a very early start or split the walk in two. Weekdays are best; most places don't reopen on weekend afternoons.

What to See

❻ Cabildo (Town Hall). This whitewashed building, first constructed in 1582 and rebuilt many times since, houses Salta's municipal government. The **Museo Histórico del Norte** (History Museum of the North) occupies two floors of the Cabildo with an eclectic mix of exhibits about the pre-Hispanic, colonial, and religious history of city of Salta and the surrounding province. The museum also highlights the works of regional artists in temporary exhibits. ⊠ *Caseros 549* ☎ *387/421–5340* 🗐 *2 pesos* ⊘ *Tues.–Fri. 9:30–1:30 and 3:30–8:30, Sat. 9:30–1:30 and 3:30–8, Sun. 9:30–1* ⊕ *www.museonor.gov.ar.*

❺ Casa de Hernández (Hernández House). Inside an 1870 neocolonial house is the **Museo de la Ciudad.** The first floor displays an exceptional collection of musical instruments. Rooms upstairs document the history of Salta through paintings and photographs. ⊠ *La Florida 97* ☎ *387/437–3352* 🗐 *1 peso* ⊘ *Weekdays 9–1 and 4–8:30.*

❷ Catedral de Salta (Salta Cathedral). The city's 1882 neoclassical cathedral fronts the central plaza and is notable for the enormous frescoes on the portico around the altar, which portray the four gospel writers. On either side of the altar, small chapels hold the icons of the Señor y Virgen del Milagro, the patrons of Salta. Tradition credits these statues of Christ and the Virgin Mary with minimizing the damage of nine days of earth tremors in 1692. Inside the entrance is the Panteón de las Glorias del Norte, enclosing the tombs of General Martín Miguel de Güemes and other heroes from the War of Independence. ⊠ *España 537* 🗐 *Free* ⊘ *Mon.–Sat. 6:30–12:30 and 4:30–8:15, Sun. 6:30–12:30 and 5:30–8:15.*

❾ Convento de San Bernardo (Convent of St. Bernard). The oldest religious building in Salta served as a chapel first, then a hospital. Today a cloistered order of Carmelite nuns lives here, so the convent is closed to the public. The wooden rococo-style door, hand-carved by indigenous craftsmen in 1762, contrasts markedly with the otherwise stark exterior of the 1625 structure. ⊠ *Caseros 73.*

❽ Iglesia San Francisco (St. Francis Church). Every Salteño's heart and soul belong to the town's landmark church, with its white pillars and bright terra-cotta-and-gold facade. The first temple and convent were built in 1625; the second, erected in 1674, was destroyed by fire; the present church was completed in 1882. The 173-foot-high belfry, with five independent sections piled on top of each other, houses the Campaña de la Patria, a bell made from the bronze cannons used in the War of Independence, which rings with an atonal, strangely hypnotic rhythm,

Fodor'sChoice
★

for more than 20 minutes, each afternoon at 5:30. In the sacristy, the **Museo Convento San Francisco** displays religious art and furniture from the colonial period. ✉ *Córdoba 33* ☎ *387/432–1445* 🖃 *Church free, museum 1 peso* ☉ *Church daily 7–noon and 5–9; museum daily 9–noon and 5–8.*

❸ **Museo de Arqueología de Alta Montaña** (Museum of High Mountain Archaeology). This museum exhibits the mummified remains of six children from a pre-Inca civilization and assorted funerary objects discovered at the summit of the 22,058-foot Volcán Llullaillaco, on the Argentine-Chilean border. The children are presumed to have been part of a ritual sacrifice; the burial site is thought to be the world's highest tomb. ✉ *Mitre 77* ☎ *387/437–0499* 🌐 *www.maam.org.ar* 🖃 *10 pesos, free Wed.* ☉ *Tues.–Sun. 9–1 and 4–9.*

❹ **Museo de Bellas Artes** (Fine Arts Museum). The 18th-century home of General Félix Árias Rengel now holds Salta's principal art museum. Its collection of colonial-era religious art includes figures from Argentina's Jesuit missions as well as Cuzco-style paintings from Peru and Bolivia. Another hall of the museum highlights 20th-century works by Salteño artists. ✉ *La Florida 20* ☎ *387/421–4714* 🖃 *1 peso* ☉ *Mon.–Sat. 9–1 and 4–8.*

❼ Museo Presidente José Evaristo Uriburu (President José Evaristo Uriburu Museum). Fine examples of late-colonial architecture—an interior courtyard, thick adobe walls, a reed-and-tile roof—abound in this simple building, the 19th- and 20th-century home of the Uriburu family, which gave Argentina two presidents. Furniture, costumes, paintings, and family documents are on display in six rooms. ⊠ *Caseros 417* ☎ *387/421–5310* 🎫 *1 peso* ☉ *Tues.–Sun. 9:30–1:30 and 3:30–8:30.*

❾ Plaza 9 de Julio (July 9 Square). The heart of Salta is quintessential Latin America: a leafy, bustling central plaza named for the date of Argentina's independence. Arcaded buildings, many housing sidewalk cafés, line the streets surrounding the square, providing perfect spots to while away a warm afternoon.

NEED A BREAK?

Van Gogh. This Parisian-style café, with reproductions of works of its namesake master, is one of the best coffee shops lining Plaza 9 de Julio. Come here to enjoy great coffee and cakes while writing postcards to folks back home. ⊠ *España 502* ☎ *387/431–4659* 🖃 *AE, MC, V.*

❿ Teleférico a Cerro San Bernardo (Cable Car to San Bernardo Hill). The Cerro San Bernardo looms east of downtown Salta, a cool 880 feet higher than the city center. A cable car takes you from a station across from Parque San Martín to the top of San Bernardo in less than 10 minutes. Views of the entire Lerma Valley reward you at the top. ⊠ *San Martín and H. Yrigoyen* ☎ *387/431–0641* 🎫 *4 pesos one-way* ☉ *Daily 9–6:45.*

Fodor's Choice ★   **Tren a las Nubes** (Train to the Clouds). A 14-hour round-trip train excursion takes you to the high, desolate Puna and back. The trip begins at 4,336 feet as the train climbs out of the Lerma Valley into the mountains. As the train rattles over steel bridges that span wild rivers, it winds ever upward through many turns and tunnels and passes over the 210-foot-high Viaducto La Polvorilla, until it reaches the top at 13,770 feet, just beyond San Antonio de los Cobres. At this point you can disembark to test the thin air and visit a train-side market set up by locals. When the train returns the short distance to San Antonio de Los Cobres, it makes a second stop, and the market reappears. The only town of its size in the Puna, San Antonio de Los Cobres is an important customs and trucking stop on the road (R40) to Chile. For 160 pesos you get a guide, lunch in the dining car, a first-aid car equipped with oxygen for altitude sickness, and the experience of a lifetime. Reservations are essential; they can be made at most local tourism agencies, which are ubiquitous downtown. *In Salta* ⊠ *Caseros 431* ☎ *387/431–4984* ⊠ *In Buenos Aires* ⊠ *Esmeralda 1008* ☎🖷 *11/4311–4282* ⊕ *www.trenubes.com.ar* ☉ *Apr.–June and Aug.–Nov., most Sat. at 7 AM; July, Tues. and weekends at 7 AM; occasionally runs Sun. in June, Aug., and Sept.*

Where to Stay & Eat

¢–$$$ ✕ **La Posta.** Red, gold, and green—the colors of the mountains—and funny gaucho pictures on the walls give a nice local ambience to this bright, cavernous downtown eatery. Start with the appetizer-salad bar and perhaps one of the outstanding cheese empanadas, and then move on to *cabrito al asador* (goat grilled over an open fire), a luscious, salty indulgence—pair it with a local Cabernet. And for dessert, don't miss the unique *dulce de cayote,* a molasseslike marmalade served with walnuts atop local goat cheese. ⊠ *España 456* ☎ *387/421–7091* ⊟ *AE, DC, MC, V.*

$–$$ ✕ **Doña Salta.** This warm, festive, family-friendly locale serves dishes quite typical of Salta and the Northwest, with furnishings to match. You'll dine amidst wine jugs and old wooden implements; it's a room steeped in local tradition, so not surprisingly, it's also a great spot to try classics like *humitas* (steamed corn husks filled with cheese) or one of the local stews, like *cazuela* or *locro.* Empanadas and meats are also reliable; the pastas are unremarkable, though. The location, across from Iglesia San Francisco, couldn't be more central. ⊠ *Cordoba 46* ☎ *387/ 432–1921* ⊕ *www.donasalta.com.ar* ⊟ *AE, DC, MC, V.*

★ **$–$$** ✕ **El Solar del Convento.** Beams of native wood support the thatched roof of this spacious restaurant, the "Sun Room of the Convent." Animal masks decorate walls washed with ocher paint, and an enormous *tapero* (a patchwork of handwoven saddle blankets) dominates the room. Innovative adaptations of local foods are featured, but they're outdone by the giant grill at the entrance, which sizzles with meat at lunch and dinner. Don't miss the chance to match red meat with the full-bodied San Pedro de Yocochuya, an absolute whopper of a Malbec-Cabernet hybrid red wine from the hills above Salta. ⊠ *Caseros 444* ☎ *387/421– 5124* ⊟ *AE, DC, MC, V.*

$ ✕ **Jovi Dos.** This is an eclectic, expansive, great-value restaurant in a quiet corner of downtown. The big, high-ceilinged room, with wood beams and big plate windows, is crammed with local businesspeople at lunchtime, but it retains a light, airy feel despite the lively crowd. The meal starts with the best marinated eggplant appetizer in town; baked meat empanadas are another good way to start. Grilled meats, seafood, pizza, and pasta have equal billing on the ridiculously long menu. Dishes such as the *ravioles mixtas* (ravioli filled with spinach and cheese and topped with a creamy pink sauce) are big enough for two people. There's elegant, attentive service and a solid wine list to boot. ⊠ *Balcarce 601* ☎ *387/ 432–9438* ⊟ *AE, DC, MC, V.*

¢ ✕ **New Time Café.** One of the trendier places in town, this modern *confitería* on the main plaza, has a slew of outdoor tables, which make for great people-watching as boisterous crowds of schoolchildren, families, and businesspeople buzz about central Salta in the afternoon. Inside, the mood is no less jovial, as swarms of couples and college students stop in for a snack or a drink. And for good reason: the coffee is great, and the medialunas are warm, buttery delights—the best in town. ⊠ *Corner of Mitre and Caseros* ⊟ *AE, DC, MC, V.*

$$$$ ▢ **Sheraton Salta Hotel.** This high-end international property opened in late 2005 and is already changing the tourism game in Salta. The clean, modern structure was built against a mountainside overlooking downtown in one of Salta's swankiest neighborhoods. The rooms are sleek and chic, decorated in white, gray, and orange prints. The pool patio offers stunning panoramic views of the city, the Lerma Valley, and the Andes—it's a great place to sip a drink and watch the sun go down. Do not miss the hotel's fantastic gourmet restaurant, Terracotta, which features unusual and delicious takes on duck, rabbit, and risotto. ⊠ *Av. Ejército del Norte 330, 4406* ☎ *387/432–3000* ⊕ *www.sheraton.com/ salta* ⤺ *145 rooms* ⚑ *Restaurant, in-room safes, minibars, pool, gym, sauna, bar, meeting room, dial-up Internet, business center* ▤ *AE, DC, MC, V.*

$$$
Fodor'sChoice
★
Hotel El Lagar. The wrought-iron door is always locked, and there's barely any sign to indicate there's a hotel here on this quiet street a few blocks north of the city center. But inside you'll find Salta's most exclusive—though not at all stuffy—bed-and-breakfast. Cusqueño religious art decorates the walls, and plush upholstered furniture and a cozy fireplace decorate the living room. Rooms all have private baths and canopy beds. This place is magnificent. Reservations are required. ⊠ *20 de Febrero 875, 4400* ☎ *387/431–9439* ✉ *ellagar@arnet.com.ar* ⤺ *10 rooms* ⚑ *Minibars, pool* ▤ *No credit cards.*

★ **$$$**
Hotel Salta. Antique furniture and a view of the plaza, the church steeple, or the surrounding mountains make every room attractive at this hotel in a handsome neocolonial building in the heart of the city. You'll also find wooden balconies, blue-and-white tiling, sitting rooms on every floor, and a poolside bar-restaurant with an area set aside for barbecues. Local master Ernesto Scotti painted the frescoes in the dining room. The staff speaks English, and rates include a buffet breakfast. ⊠ *Buenos Aires 1, 4400* ☎ *387/431–0740* ⊕ *www.hotelsalta.com* ⤺ *97 rooms* ⚑ *Restaurant, tea shop, pool, bar, dry cleaning, laundry service* ▤ *AE, DC, MC, V.*

★ **$$$**
Hotel Solar de la Plaza. A welcome retreat from the bustle of downtown Salta, this beautiful old house (once an aristocratic family residence) conceals well the wondrous modern comforts that lie within. The elegant lobby leads to a beautifully appointed sitting room and light, airy courtyard spaces and an expensive restaurant. An outdoor pool on the roof has great views of the city. The slightly pricier superior rooms have balconies overlooking a quiet plaza; the suites have private Jacuzzis. ⊠ *Leguizamón 669, 4400* ☎ *387/431–5111* ⊕ *www.solardelaplaza. com.ar* ⤺ *28 rooms, 2 suites* ⚑ *Restaurant, minibars, pool, gym, sauna, bar, DSL Internet in business center* ▤ *AE, DC, MC, V.*

$$
Gran Hotel Presidente. The black-and-white lobby with its red velvet curtains and faux-leopard-skin upholstered furniture is a bit much, but the soft-pastel rooms in this business-class hotel are, mercifully, much more subdued and easier on the eyes. Rates include a big buffet breakfast. It's a few blocks from the central plaza. ⊠ *Belgrano 353, 4400* ☎ *387/431–2022* ⊕ *www.grhotelpresidente.com.ar* ⤺ *96 rooms* ⚑ *Restaurant, in-room safes, minibars, pool, gym, sauna, bar, meeting room, dial-up Internet, business center* ▤ *AE, DC, MC, V.*

$
Hotel del Antiguo Convento. This charming property is built in a former convent and run by a cheerful and attentive young staff. The rooms are clean, bright, and well-priced. You can opt for a more private, apartment-style suite in the back that comes equipped with its own parrilla. The hotel is just a few blocks from many downtown attractions on one of the city's liveliest streets. ⊠ *Caseros 113, 4400* ☎ *387/422–7267* ⊕ *www.hoteldelconvento.com.ar* ⤺ *10 rooms* ⚑ *Snack bar, pool, laundry service, business center, parking (fee)* ▤ *No credit cards.*

$ ▣ **Hotel Marilián.** The deceptively narrow, modern front of this friendly hotel opens into a cheerful reception area and extends wide and deep as you walk inside. The bright rooms, some with a small patio, have white-tile floors and tan or blue fabrics. Rates include a buffet breakfast. You can get a 10% discount if you pay in cash. ⊠ *Buenos Aires 176, 4400* ☏☏ *387/421–6700* ⊕ *www.hotelmarilian.com.ar* ⇆ *49 rooms* ⟳ *Restaurant, pool, gym, laundry service, free parking* ⊟ *AE, DC, MC, V.*

Nightlife & the Arts
El Rastro Peña (⊠ Av. San Martín 2555 ☏ 387/434–2987) is a big auditoriumlike dining hall—that is, until the lights dim and the beat of a drum, the whine of *quenas* (bamboo pipes), and the strumming of a guitar begin. National folk groups appear regularly. Shows begin at 10:30 PM, and reservations are advised.

Just north of downtown Salta's main square, **Balcarce Street** is a hotbed of nocturnal activity, with a variety of happening nightspots, including several *Peñas*, traditional dance and music celebrations where locals and tourists alike gather to listen to regional folk bands give it their all on small, cramped stages. Adding to the rowdy, dinner-theater atmosphere are the local gaucho dancers who entice (and often entrap) foreign tourists into strutting their stuff on stage; it's always a good laugh, no matter what language you speak. A top spot for this type of party is **La Vieja Estacion** (⊠ Balcarce 885 ☏ 387/421–7727). Balcarce Street also has several hip restaurants and bars that attract a twentysomething crowd, like **Macondo** (⊠ Balcarce 980 ☏ 387/431–7191), a raucous and smoky pub where blues and beer are always on tap and you're just as likely to meet some backpacking Aussies as some local university law students.

Sports & the Outdoors
Turismo de Estancia provides the opportunity to stay on a working farm or ranch where you can you ride horses, hike, and get to know the countryside. At some estancias in the Calchaquíes and Lerma valleys, you can also participate in wine- and cheese-making. The **tourist office** (⊠ Buenos Aires 93 ☏ 387/431–0950) in Salta has a list of farms and ranches.

Loquacious local guide **Guillermo Smith** is a first-generation Argentine of British descent who speaks flawless English. Smith is an absolute expert on the history of the region and runs daily van tours throughout Salta and Jujuy. (☏ 387/439–5389)

Shopping
You could spend hours inside the 1882 Jesuit monastery that holds the **Mercado Artesanal** (⊠ Av. San Martín 2555 ☏ 387/434–2808) and at the open stalls across the street. Goods range from red-and-black Salteño ponchos, alpaca knitwear and weavings, and leather goods to wood masks of animals and fine silver. It's open daily 9–9.

EN ROUTE If you're in the mood for a scenic drive north of Salta, you can even take the more rural **Route 9** between Salta and Jujuy, which is actually more direct than the highway, but will take a bit longer. Unless you're squeamish about narrow, winding roads, the extra time and wear and tear on your tires is worth it. Be sure to leave with a full tank of gas before embarking on this isolated, one-lane road, which winds through pine forests and hills. Keep your headlights on and honk before each of the many hairpin turns. Be sure to stop along the way at one or two sleepy little towns, such as **El Carmen**, about 27 km (17 mi) south of Jujuy; it has a shady little colonial plaza that time has left behind. There's a police checkpoint right along Route 9 about 5 km (3 mi) before El Carmen, where approximately one in three cars is stopped. If you look like a tourist, chances are you'll be the one in three. You might be asked outright for a small fee of 5 pesos or so; if not, you may want to tactfully take the initiative by saying something along the lines of "Will it help to pay a fee?" Be polite and *don't* refer to the "fee" as a "colaboración" (bribe) which might offend and get you into hotter water.

San Lorenzo

⑪ *10 km (6 mi) northwest of Salta.*

Salta is hardly an urban jungle, but some visitors opt to stay in the quieter hillside suburb of San Lorenzo a few miles away and a cooler 980 feet higher. It's a great place to stay if you have a car or can adhere to the every-30-minute bus service to and from Salta.

Where to Stay & Eat

¢–$ ✕**Lo de Andrés.** Folks from Salta favor this bright, airy semi-enclosed brick-and-glass building with a vaulted ceiling for weekend dining. Andrés grills a lightly spiced Argentine-style parrillada, but if you're not up for such a feast, there are empanadas and *milanesas* (breaded steak) as well. ☒ *Juan Carlos Dávalos and Gorriti* ☎ *387/492–1600* ⊟ *AE, DC, MC, V* ☺ *No lunch Mon.*

$$–$$$ ▦**Eaton Place.** Despite appearances, this elegant Georgian-style mansion and its beautiful gardens are only a dozen years old. The bright and airy rooms in the main house and guesthouse have huge windows, hardwood floors, and period furniture. And you've likely never seen accommodations as huge as the dark-wood-paneled penthouse suite, complete with a vaulted ceiling. Rooms in the back guesthouse are smaller but still regal, in a more subdued way. Two of the guesthouse double rooms share a sitting room, making them ideal for a family or group. Rates include a huge breakfast. ☒ *San Martín, 4401* ☎☎ *387/492–1347* ⊕ *www.eatonplace. com.ar* ⌘ *8 rooms, 1 suite* ⌂ *Pool* ⊟ *No credit cards.*

$ ▦**Hostal Selva Montana.** A friendly German couple has created a quiet oasis in their hillside stucco house near the center of town. The white rooms, some with balcony, all have light-wood trim, pleasant pastel bedspreads and drapes, and stupendous views. The grounds extend down to a pool and tennis court, and even farther down into the Quebrada San Lorenzo. Rates include a huge breakfast, and there's a 10% discount if you pay with cash. ☒ *Alfonsina Storni 2315, 4401* ☎ *387/492–1184* 🖷 *387/ 492–1433* ⊕ *www.iruya.com/ent/selvamontana* ⌘ *28 rooms* ⌂ *Tennis court, pool, horseback riding, meeting room* ⊟ *AE, DC, MC, V.*

Driving south toward Cafayate on R68 through the **Quebrada de Las Conchas** (Canyon of the Shells), you'll see red-sandstone cliffs, sculpted by eons of wind and water into strange yet recognizable rock formations. Many formations have imaginative names such as Los Castillos (The Castles), El Anfiteatro (The Amphitheater), and La Garganta del Diablo (The Devil's Throat).

Cachi

12 *157 km (97 mi) southwest of Salta.*

The long route to Cayafate follows a narrow gravel road through the Calchaquíes Valley. Along its river are a few colonial hamlets, untouched and little changed over the years. Cachi, on the site of a pre-Hispanic settlement of the indigenous Chicoana community, is the most interesting of these. Its charming **Iglesia San José**, with a cactus-wood altar, sits on the palm-and-orange–tree-lined central plaza. Watching over it all is the 20,800-foot Nevado del Cachi, a few miles away.

Cafayate

13 *185 km (115 mi) southwest of Salta via R68, 340 km (211 mi) southwest of Salta via R40, 230 km (143 mi) northwest of San Miguel de Tucumán.*

Basking in the sunny Calchaquíes Valley, Cafayate deserves much more than a day to absorb its colonial charm, see its fine museums, shop for authentic handicrafts, and visit some of the surrounding vineyards for which it's known. Street-side cafés, shaded by flowering quebracho trees, face the plaza, where a burro is likely to be tied up next to a car. Look for the five naves of the cathedral on the plaza.

For 66 years, Rodolfo Bravo collected and catalogued funerary and religious objects from local excavations. These objects, made out of clay, ceramic, metal, and textiles, are on display at the **Museo Regional y Arqueológico Rodolfo Bravo** (Rudolfo Bravo Regional and Archaeological Museum). Artifacts from the Incas (15th century) and Diaguitas of the Calchaquíes Valley are also part of the collection. ⊠ *Colón 191* ☎ *3868/ 421054* 🎫 *1 peso* ⊗ *By appointment only.*

Learn about wine making at the **Museo de la Vid y del Vino** (Museum of Grapevines and Wine), which is in a building dating back to 1881. Machinery, agricultural implements, and old photographs tell the history of wine making in this area. ⊠ *R40, Av. General Güemes* ☎ *3868/421– 125* 🎫 *1 peso* ⊗ *Daily 8–8.*

For a sample of Cafayate's Torrontés white wine, head to **Etchart Bodega** (⊠ *Finca La Florida*), south of town on R40 and within walking distance. **Michel Torino Bodega** (⊠ *Finca La Rosa*), on R68 northeast of town, offers tours and wine samples to familiarize you with Cafayate's most celebrated product.

Where to Stay & Eat

¢–$ ✕**Juanita.** Everything is freshly made on the spot, and served in the front room of this family house—it's the closest thing to home cooking among local restaurants. ✉ *Camino Quintana de Niño 60* ☎ *No phone* ▤ *No credit cards.*

¢–$ ✕ **La Casona de Don Luis.** Come here to feast on humitas and locro and drink local Torrontés wine while listening to a guitarist playing gaucho laments. The interior, vine-covered patio is especially pleasant on a sunny afternoon. ✉ *Salta and Almagro* ☎ *3868/421–249* ▤ *No credit cards.*

$$$$ 🏨 **Patios de Cafayate Hotel & Spa.** This new luxury hotel, part of the Starwood chain, is likely to bring even more international visitors to the undisturbed Calchaquí Valley of Argentina. The rustic rooms are decorated in rich red and green tones and overlook the nearby vineyards. The hotel's creature comforts and gourmet restaurant make this a top choice in Cafayate. Be sure to spend an afternoon at the Wine Spa, a first-of-its-kind in Argentina, where local blends are used for wine-based treatments that are sure to replenish your skin and soul. ✉ *Ruta Nacional 40 at Ruta Nacional 68, 4427* ☎ *3868/421–201* ⊕ *www.starwoodhotels.com* ⇗ *30 rooms* ⌂ *Restaurant, wine bar, in-room safes, minibars, pool, gym, meeting room, Wi-Fi, free parking* ▤ *AE, DC, MC, V.*

¢ 🏨 **Hotel Gran Real.** The swimming pool, patio, barbecue area, and quiet rooms with basic furnishings more than make up for the torn plastic furniture in the lobby. Rates include an ample breakfast. ✉ *Av. General Güemes 128, 4427* ☎ *3868/421–231* ⇗ *34 rooms* ⌂ *Café, pool, bar* ▤ *MC, V.*

¢ 🏨 **Hotel Tikunaku.** This small *residencial* (pension) with carpeted rooms is clean and comfortable and has an attentive staff. Note that there's a 10% discount if you pay with cash. ✉ *Diego de Almagro 12, 4427* ☎ *3868/421–148* ⇗ *7 rooms* ⌂ *Café* ▤ *V.*

Sports & the Outdoors

The town is flat, so bicycles are a common means of transportation. The tourist office on the plaza can suggest nearby destinations for hiking or biking. If you're ambitious, take a long ride along the Río Calchaquí on R40 (Argentina's longest highway paralleling one of its longest rivers); along the way you'll pass through quiet colonial hamlets and ever-changing scenery. Bicycles and camping and fishing equipment can be rented at **Rudy** (✉ Av. General Güemes 175). Horses are available from **La Florida** (✉ at the Etchart Bodega), 2 km (1 mi) south of town on R40.

Quilmes

⓮ *50 km (31 mi) south of Cafayate.*

South of Cafayate, just over the border into Tucumán Province, lie Argentina's most well preserved ruins, home to a community of indigenous Quilmes between the 11th and 17th centuries. Some 5,000 people lived within this walled city at its peak (late 1600s). The Quilmes valiantly resisted the arrival of the Spaniards but were eventually subjugated and deported from the region. A small **museum** documents the history of the 75-acre site. ✉ *Off R40* ☎ *3892/421–075* 🎟 *2 pesos* ☉ *Daily 9–dusk.*

San Salvador de Jujuy

1,643 km (1,020 mi) northwest of Buenos Aires, 97 km (60 mi) north of Salta, 459 km (285 mi) north of Tucumán.

San Salvador de Jujuy (simply Jujuy to most Argentines, and s. s. DE JUJUY on signs) is the capital of the province of Jujuy (pronounced "hoo-*hoo*-wee"). Founded by Spaniards in 1593, it was the northernmost town on the military and trade route between the Spanish garrisons in Peru and the northern cities of Argentina.

History has not been kind to the city: war and earthquakes over the centuries have taken their toll. San Salvador de Jujuy today is modern, with a large indigenous population and a few monuments to its proud past. The city lacks nearby Salta's colonial dreaminess, as well as its southern neighbor's wide selection of accommodations. That said, it has a pleasant downtown and unadulterated local culture with a bit of frontier-town charm; there's less tourist-oriented development here than in Salta, and it's a great base from which to explore the Puna region.

🔟 The whitewashed 1867 **Cabildo** (City Hall) houses the **Museo Histórico Policial** (Police-History Museum), a small collection of historical police uniforms and weapons. You may want to skip the gruesome second-floor exhibit of preserved body parts and fetuses. ⊠ *North side of Plaza General Belgrano* ☎ *388/423–7715* 🖼 *Free* ⊙ *Mon.–Sat. 8–1 and 4–9.*

㉓ The austere 1777 **Capilla de Santa Bárbara** (Chapel of St. Barbara) houses a collection of paintings brought from Cuzco, one of which depicts the church's patron, St. Barbara. You can see the inside during Sunday mass at 8 and 10 AM; the building is locked the rest of the week (thefts have been a problem), but if you call ahead you can probably convince the key-bearers to let you in for a look around. A few pesos tip is appropriate. ⊠ *San Martín and La Madrid* ☎ *388/422–3009* 🖼 *Free* ⊙ *Weekdays 10–noon and 5–10, weekends 7–noon and 5–10.*

🔞 The 1907 **Casa de Gobierno** (Government House) fronts the Plaza General Belgrano on San Martín and contains the offices of Jujuy's provincial government. A second-floor hall, the Salón de la Bandera, displays the original Argentine flag donated by General Belgrano in 1813, a gift to the city after its famed exodus during the War of Independence. You'll have to ask a guard to let you into the hall, which is always locked. ⊠ *San Martín 450* ☎ *388/423–9400* 🖼 *Free* ⊙ *Weekdays 9–1 and 3–8.*

🔟 **Catedral de Jujuy** dates to 1763 but has been augmented and remodeled so many times that it's now a hodgepodge of architectural styles. The impressive interior contains the city's most stunning work of art, an ornately carved, gold-plated pulpit, said to be the finest in South America. A close look at the pulpit reveals an intricate population of carved figures, biblical and otherwise. It was inspired by the Cusqueña school of art from Cuzco, Peru, as were the building's ornate doors and confessionals. ⊠ *West side of Plaza General Belgrano* ☎ *388/423–5333* 🖼 *Free* ⊙ *Weekdays 10–noon and 5–10, weekends 7–noon and 5–10.*

San Salvador
de Jujuy

Harking back to the Northwest's rail heyday is the pink art-nouveau **Estación de Ferrocarril,** a former train station built in 1901.

The centerpiece of the **Iglesia de San Francisco** (Church of St. Francis), two blocks west of Plaza General Belgrano, is an ornate 18th-century wooden pulpit with dozens of figures of monks. There's some debate about who carved the pulpit: it may have been local artisans, or the pulpit may have been transported from Bolivia. Despite the colonial appearance of the church and bell tower, the present structure dates only to 1930. ⊠ *Belgrano and Lavalle* 🎫 *Free* 🕐 *Daily 10–1 and 5–9.*

The **Museo Arqueológico Provincial** (Provincial Archaeological Museum) contains archaeological treasures such as a 2,600-year-old ceramic goddess and a mummy of a two-year-old child dating back 1,000 years. Ceramic pots painted with geometric designs from Yavi and Humahuaca are constantly being added to the collection, and a diorama shows what life was like here 9,000 years ago. ⊠ *Lavalle 434* 🕿 *388/422–1315* 🎫 *1 peso* 🕐 *Daily 9–noon and 3–9.*

Arms, trophies, and memorabilia from military campaigns collected from the 25 years of fighting for independence are on display at the **Museo Histórico Provincial Juan Lavalle** (Juan Lavalle Provincial History Museum).

In this adobe building, General Juan Lavalle, a hero of the wars of independence and an enemy of the dictator Juan Manuel de Rosas, was assassinated. A replica of the door through which Lavalle was shot in 1746 is part of the exhibit. ✉ *Lavalle 256* ☎ *388/422–1355* 💵 *1 peso* 🕐 *Mon.–Sat. 8–noon and 4–8.*

OFF THE BEATEN PATH

PARQUE SAN MARTÍN – An oasis of fountains and tree-shaded relaxation, this park will delight young children with horse rides, a miniature train, and a little amusement park. Young families flood the park on Sundays. It's within easy walking distance of downtown—just head west on Alvear or Güemes. ✉ *Bounded by General Paz, Avenida España, and Avenida Córdoba.*

⓱ Orange trees and various vendors populate the city's central square, **Plaza General Belgrano**, which is lined with beautiful colonial buildings—including the imposing government palace—but strangely empty most of the time. ✉ *Bounded by Belgrano, San Martín, Sarmiento, and Gorriti.*

Where to Stay & Eat

$ ✗ **Carena Resto Bar.** Probably the hippest spot in the entire Jujuy province, this restaurant-bar goes straight for New York chic, and in the process creates an exciting brand of Jujeña cuisine that's utterly unique in the region. Try the liver pâté with brioche and mango chutney or pork tenderloin with caramelized onions and brown sugar. Even the basics, like a dressed *lomito* sandwich, are well executed and even inexpensive. The lighting is appropriately muted, and the big plate-glass windows and slick furniture only add to the 1980s-bond-trader effect; the clientele here is clearly the local bourgeoisie. ✉ *Belgrano and Balcarce* ☎ *388/422–2529* 💳 *DC, MC, V.*

$ ✗ **Madre Tierra.** A vegetarian island in Argentina's sea of steak and empanadas, "Mother Earth" serves a meat-free fixed-price menu that rotates daily. A fairly bland salad, soup, juice, dessert, and whole-grain breads from the popular bakery accompany the main course, which could be spinach lasagna or stuffed eggplant. Don't expect culinary fireworks, but at least it's something different. Try to be seated in back, where you'll be lulled into the proper nature-loving mood by the view of a backyard garden. ✉ *Otero and Belgrano* ☎ *388/422–9578* 💳 *No credit cards* 🕐 *Closed Sun. No dinner.*

¢–$ ✗ **Altos de la Viña.** High on a hill overlooking the city sits this simple country-style restaurant and inn, with flowery curtains and red-checkered tablecloths. The fare is the usual pastas, meat, fish, and fowl served with fresh vegetables—hearty and healthful. It also functions as a relaxing, if rustic, place to stay in the countryside, renting out a few rooms by night. ✉ *R56, Km 4, Pasquini López 50* ☎ *388/426–2626* 💳 *AE, DC, MC, V.*

¢–$ ✗ **Manos Jujeñas.** This is one of the best places in the entire region to try authentic Northwestern cooking. Ponchos on the walls, old paintings, native artifacts, stucco archways, and muted lighting are complemented by the piped-in Andean music. This is *the* place to try *locro*: maize, white beans, pork, chorizo, pancetta, and a wonderful red pepper oil glaze come together in a menage of savory, flowery, and starchy flavors

Fodor'sChoice ★

that take this dish—which costs only 4.50 pesos—to another level. ⊠ *Senador Pérez 222* ☎ *388/422–2366* ☰ *DC, MC, V* ⊘ *No lunch Sun. No dinner Mon.*

¢ ✕ **Royal Restaurant/Pub.** With bustling tables both inside and out on the sidewalk, this is a deservedly popular local *confiteria* right in the thick of things downtown. It's a pleasant choice any time of day, whether just for a *cortado* (coffee with milk; here it's served in a tall glass), *medialuna* (croissant), and a morning newspaper or a quick lunch of a *lomito completo* (meat sandwich with ham, cheese, egg, lettuce, tomato, and mayonnaise). ⊠ *Av. Bolivia 1501* ☎ *388/423–5121* ☰ *MC, V.*

$$ ▥ **Jujuy Palace Hotel.** Large rooms with impeccable facilities and balconies overlooking the street, a rooftop gym, a gated parking lot, and a formal second-floor dining room with first-class service add to the comforts of this exceptional hotel. Views from the top floors are outstanding, spanning the cloud-covered hills and Spanish colonial domes of the city center. You receive a 20% discount if you pay with cash. ⊠ *Belgrano 1060, 4600* ☎☎ *388/423–0433* ⊕ *www.imagine.com.ar/jujuy. palace/* ⇒ *54 rooms, 5 suites* ⌂ *Restaurant, gym, sauna, bar, meeting room, parking (fee)* ☰ *AE, DC, MC, V.*

$$ ▥ **Termas de Reyes.** This countryside complex is perched on the edge of a spectacular river valley. Life here focuses on the virtues of relaxation and panoramic views. The centerpiece is the natural thermal baths, indoor and out, bubbling up from underground hot springs. Rooms are clean and comfortable. It's located 19 km (12 mi) outside Jujuy on a road that's paved for all but 5 km (3 mi). ⊠ *Ruta 4, Km 19* ☎☎ *388/492–2522* ⊕ *www.termasdereyes.com* ⇒ *60 rooms* ⌂ *Restaurant, pool, spa, bar* ☰ *AE, DC, MC, V.*

¢ ▥ **Gran Hotel Panorama.** The modern Panorama, one of the nicer hotels in town, sits on a quiet corner a couple of blocks removed from the hubbub of Avenida Belgrano. It serves mostly businesspeople. Soft earth tones decorate the dark-wood-paneled rooms, which are a bit on the plain side. You get a 20% discount if you pay with cash. ⊠ *Belgrano 1295, 4600* ☎☎ *388/423–2533* ✉ *hotelpanorama@mail.com.ar* ⇒ *64 rooms, 3 suites* ⌂ *Café, pool, bar, laundry service, meeting room* ☰ *AE, DC, MC, V.*

Nightlife & the Arts

The hip, modern hot spot **Carena Resto Bar** (⊠ Belgrano and Balcarce ☎ 388/422–2529) is the place, pre- and post-dinner, to sip imported scotch and discuss politics. If it's a musical evening you're after, though, you can hear local bands on Friday and Saturday at **Royal Restaurant–Pub** (⊠ Av. Bolivia 1501 ☎ 388/423–5121).

For something more elaborate and traditional, head for the amusingly named **Chung King** (⊠ Alvear 627 ☎ 388/422–2982), a restaurant that turns into an upscale dinner-entertainment venue with a good *peña* (folkloric music performance) on weekends.

Sports & the Outdoors

With its incredible canyons, painted mountains, wild rivers, and high Puna, the area around Jujuy is great for hiking and horseback riding. Miles of wild, open terrain separate the most interesting places, making driving a necessity. The tourist office can help you organize trips. Another solution is to stay at **Alojamiento El Refugio** (☒ R9, Km 14, Yala ☎☎ 388/490–9344), 15 km (9 mi) from town on the Río Yala; it has cabins and campsites, along with a pool and children's playground, and organizes hikes and horseback rides.

QUEBRADA DE HUMAHUACA

Fodor'sChoice ★ North of Jujuy, the inimitable Route 9 continues into the **Quebrada de Humahuaca** (Humahuaca Gorge), an explosion of color stretched across over long stretches of craggy, bare rock, and one of Argentina's most distinctive landscapes. Variegated tones of pink, red, and gray color the canyon walls like giant swaths of paint. As the gorge deepens and narrows approaching Humahuaca on its northern tip, the colors become more vibrant, and mustard and green are added to the hues. Bright-green alamo and willow trees surround villages, contrasting with the deep red tones in the background. In summer and fall, torrential rains mixed with mud and melting snow from the high mountains rush down the mountainsides, carving deep ravines before pouring into the chalky gray Río Grande. Often this flow of water washes out the road, leaving it in constant need of repair.

Along the way, the R9 winds past the dusty villages of Purmamarca, Tilcara, Humahuaca, Tres Cruces, and ultimately La Quiaca and Yavi on the Bolivian border. The 65 km (40 mi) stretch between Jujuy and Purmamarca is half gravel, half pavement, and laden with detours for the ongoing construction of a fully paved thoroughfare. When workers hold a flag up above their heads, it means to stop your car; a waving flag means to go on. Another option is to take Route 9 as far as Purmamarca, and then turn off onto Route 52 and continue on to Route 16 to undertake a harrowing drive that will take away your breath— literally: it goes across the Andes and the Jama Pass to Chile's San Pedro de Atacama, an adobe oasis town and backpackers' haven on the eastern edge of the driest desert on Earth. The R9, meanwhile, is fully paved between Purmamarca and Humahuaca, an easy 1½-hour drive through spectacular scenery.

Purmamarca

㉔ *65 km (40 mi) north of San Salvador de Jujuy.*

Nestled spectacularly in the shadow of craggy rocks and multicolored, cactus-studded hills with the occasional low-flying cloud happening by, the colonial village of Purmamarca (altitude 7,200 feet) is a great stopover along the Quebrada—with a great hotel to boot. Here, blazing red adobe replaces the white stucco architecture you may be used to, and the simple, square buildings play off the matching red rock to create a memorable effect. The village is reached by a clearly marked 3-km (2-mi) detour off R9 onto R52. It's nothing more than a one-horse town with a few basic stores, places to eat, and artisans selling their wares in the pleasant, tree-shaded plaza. But Purmamarca's beauty is striking, and its few lights and dry air make it one of the best places in the region for star gazing.

The most notable item downtown on the central plaza is the landmark 1648 **Iglesia de Santa Rosa de Lima,** which was constructed from adobe and thistlewood. Looming above Purmamarca is the **Cerro de Siete Colores,** Hill of Seven Colors, with its lavenders, oranges, and yellows. Look closely and see if you can find all seven—most people can only pick out four. The best way to see the hill is by driving a 3-km (2-mi) loop called the ★ **Paseo de Siete Colores**; there's a turn-off just before the entrance to Purmamarca off R52. This spectacular gravel road winds precariously through bizarre, humanlike formations of bright, craggy, red rock, then opens up onto a series of stark, sweeping, Mars-like vistas with patches of verdant trees along the river valley. The road then passes a few family farms and ends with a striking view of the Cerro itself. The one-lane road can be traversed with most any car, though the ride is a bit bumpy. Better yet is to walk the Paseo; you'll see more, and it's an easy one-hour hike, start to finish. The loop ends up right back in the center of Purmamarca.

Where to Stay & Eat

$$ ×🍴 **El Manantial del Silencio.** It's like a song, the blend of verdant weeping willows, cornfields, red rocks, and chirping birds in the gardens of this spectacular stucco mansion, a tranquil retreat that's hemmed in on every side by the craggy Quebrada in utter calmness. The colonial-style splendor is balanced harmoniously with local artifacts and character; warm and spacious common areas are decked out in adobe colors. Service is first-rate, and there's a restaurant with fascinating local cooking—haute Andean, if you will—including a great llama steak. ⊠ *RN52, 3 km (2 mi) from RN9* ☎ *388/490–8080* ⊕ *www.hotelmanantial.com.* ⫟ 🛏 *18 rooms* ⚭ *Restaurant, pool, bar* ⊟ *AE, DC, MC, V.*

Fodor'sChoice
★

Tilcara

㉕ *18 km (11 mi) north of Purmamarca, 83 km (51 mi) north of San Salvador de Jujuy via R9.*

The town of Tilcara (altitude 8,100 feet), founded in 1600, is on the eastern side of the Río Grande at its confluence with the Río Huasamayo. Many battles during the War of Independence were fought in and around Tilcara, as indicated on a monolith by the gas station. Purveyors of local artisanry crowd around the main plaza, and two museums on the town's main Plaza Alvarez Prado are worth visiting.

At the **Museo Arqueológico,** an archaeology museum run by the University of Buenos Aires, you can see pre-Hispanic tools and artifacts found in the nearby *pucará* (an indigenous fort). ⊠ *Belgrano 445* 🎫 *3 pesos* ⊙ *Daily 9–6.*

The **Museo Regional de Pintura José Antonio Terry** (José Antonio Terry Regional Museum of Painting), in an 1880 house, displays works by painter José Antonio Terry, who primarily focused on the scenery, people, and events in Tilcara. ⊠ *Rivadavía 459 at the Plaza de Tilcara* 🎫 *2 pesos* ⊙ *Tues.–Sat. 9–7, Sun. 9–noon and 2–6.*

On a hill above the left bank of the Río Grande, about a mile from town, sit the remains of the **Pucará de Tilcara** (Tilcara Fort). This fortified, pre-Inca settlement was part of a chain throughout the Quebrada de Humahuaca.

Seven kilometers (4 mi) west of town is **La Garganta del Diablo** (The Devil's Throat), a narrow red-rock gorge where you can walk to many waterfalls. The tourist office in San Salvador de Jujuy can recommend guides and excursions to this area.

The cemetery of **Maimará** is a striking apparition in the middle of the Quebrada, right aside the R9 road. Crosses, shrines, and tombs are scattered haphazardly all across a barren hillside, making for a spooky, jarring sight in the shadow of a bigger, more colorful hill called La Paleta del Pintor (the Painter's Palette). ⊠ *R9, south of Tilcara, toward Purmamarca.*

Humahuaca

❷❻ *126 km (78 mi) north of San Salvador de Jujuy.*

The narrow stone streets of the village of Humahuaca, enclosed by solid whitewashed walls, hark back to pre-Hispanic civilizations, when the first aboriginal tribes fought the Incas who came marauding from the north. Their struggle for survival continued into the 16th century, when the Spanish arrived and Jesuit missionaries built unpretentious little churches in villages throughout the valley. At 9,700 feet, Humahuaca is at the threshold of the Puna. Because of its choice location, Humahuaca has recently become a bit touristy, flooded with vendors hawking artisan wares and some jarring yuppie-style coffee joints. But it's also a fantastic place to buy handicrafts such as Andean weavings at low prices.

You can easily visit the town and nearby gorge as a day trip from San Salvador de Jujuy or Salta, either with a car or with a tour group. The town has a few extremely basic lodging options and one self-proclaimed luxury hotel (which really isn't, despite its high prices).

Humahuaca's picturesque **Cabildo** (town hall), on the main square, is the most striking building in the village, with a beautifully colored and detailed clock tower. Each day at about noon, everyone crowds into the plaza to watch as a life-size statue of San Francisco Solano pops out of the tower—it's kitschy fun. The interior can't be visited, but you can peer into the courtyard. ⊠ *Central plaza.*

The 1641 **Iglesia de la Candelaria** contains fine examples of Cusqueño art, most notably paintings depicting elongated figures of Old Testament prophets by 18th-century artist Marcos Sapaca. ⊠ *Calle Buenos Aires, west side of central plaza.*

OFF THE BEATEN PATH

IRUYA – Those brave enough to endure the harrowing five-hour, 50-km (31-mi) drive east from Humahuaca on an unpaved cliffside road are rewarded with one of Argentina's most stunning settings. This cobblestoned town precariously clings to the edge of a valley on a rainbow of sheer rock, and the community's remoteness has truly frozen it in time. Take the bus from Humahuaca rather than attempting to drive your own rental car to Iruya; one must know the road, as the bus drivers do, to negotiate it safely. There are some good hikes from Iruya, and a few basic places to stay and eat.

Where to Eat

$$$$ ✕ **Hostel El Portillo.** This restaurant-café-inn, which also rents out some nice little rooms, is representative of the tourist culture that has sprung up in Humahuaca, catering to the Quebrada- or Puna-bound travelers passing through town. However, this place retains a rustic, local feel despite its tourist clientele. Friendly service puts customers at ease, and a cute little adobe courtyard allows for a lazy lunch in the midday sun. You can get a llama steak or a hearty version of the classic regional dish, *locro* (here it's made with yellow squash, pureed beans and corn, and various types of pork). There's even a short wine list. ⊠ *Tucumán 69* ☎ *3887/421–288* ▭ *No credit cards.*

La Quiaca

❷❼ *163 km (101 mi) north of Humahuaca, 289 km (179 mi) north of San Salvador de Jujuy on R9.*

On the Bolivian border, the frontier and former railroad town of La Quiaca, at 11,400 feet, is cold, windy, and not on most people's itinerary. The town, however, is the base for exploring the **Laguna de los Pozuelos,** the largest body of water in the Puna and home to more than 50,000 birds, mostly Andean flamingos. Travel agencies in San Salvador de Jujuy can help arrange tours.

Yavi

❷❽ *15 km (9 mi) east of La Quiaca.*

Beginning in 1667, Yavi (altitude 11,600 feet) was occupied by noble Spanish families and was the seat of the marquis de Campero, a feudal lord with considerable property. The train tracks running along the side of the river once connected Argentina with Bolivia and Peru: those who remember this route (including Paul Theroux in his travel book *The Old Patagonian Express*) would like to see it rebuilt. In the town chapel, slabs of alabaster used in the windows cast a golden light on the gilded carvings of the altar and pulpit.

TUCUMÁN, CATAMARCA & LA RIOJA

Although Tucumán Province is the smallest in Argentina, it's one of the richest in industry, commerce, culture, and history. Sugar cane, tobacco, livestock, and citrus fruits all come from the region—in fact, Tucumán is the largest producer of lemons in the world. The high and dry plains in the eastern portion of the province contrast with green forests in the pre-cordillera, which rises to the snow-packed 8,000-foot Aconquija mountain range. Copious amounts of rainfall and the variety of climates have earned Tucumán the title "Garden of the Nation."

Catamarca Province has the most dramatic changes of altitude of any region in the country. The barren north has miles of *salinas grandes* (salt flats) at 1,300 feet. In the west, the Aconquija range has some of the highest mountains in the Andes, including the world's highest volcano, Ojos del Salado, at 22,869 feet. Fortified towns occupied first by the Diaguitas and later by the Incas are visible in the foothills.

San Miguel de Tucumán

29 *1,310 km (812 mi) northwest of Buenos Aires, 597 km (370 mi) north of Córdoba, 243 km (151 mi) north of Catamarca via R38, 311 km (193 mi) south of Salta via R9.*

In the center of Tucumán Province sits the bustling provincial capital and Argentina's fourth-largest city, San Miguel de Tucumán, or just Tucumán in local parlance. Local university students, combined with the constant flow of commercial activity, make the streets of this town crowded, and the traffic intense. The city is full of grand colonial architecture, broad avenues, and enormous, leafy plazas, all of which are overwhelmed with schoolchildren in uniform midday and early evening. Although the center of Tucumán is not quite beautiful by conventional standards, its youthful joie de vivre is infectious: it bursts with good restaurants, bars, outdoor cafés, and nightlife.

Tucumán is beloved by Argentines as the cradle of their independence. On July 9, 1816, congressmen from all over the country gathered in what is now called the **Casa Histórica de la Independencia** (Historical House of Independence) to draft Argentina's Declaration of Independence from Spain. Most of what you see here is a faithful reconstruction, not the original house, but the exterior is authentic, built from 1761 to 1780. A nightly sound-and-light show at 8:30 reenacts the arrival of these representatives and the historic signing; it's quite moving if you understand Spanish. ⊠ *Congreso 151* ☎ *381/431–0826* 🖃 *2 pesos* ☉ *Wed.–Mon. 9–1 and 3:30–7.*

The monumental 1912 art-nouveau **Casa de Gobierno,** with fantastical onion-bulb cupolas almost evocative of Eastern Europe, housing Tucumán's provincial government, sits on one side of the central **Plaza Independencia.** Across the street are the cheery, bright-yellow Iglesia de San Francisco (St. Francis Church) and the more somber cathedral. Behind the government house and the church are two pedestrian-only shopping streets.

An escape to the **Parque 9 de Julio**—with its artificial lake for boating, tennis courts, and lovely gardens—provides a peaceful interlude, much in the spirit of New York's Central Park (without actually being centrally located). ⊠ *6 blocks east of the plaza, past Av. Soldati.*

Where to Stay & Eat

¢–$$ ✕ **La Corzuela.** Prices are a tiny bit higher here than elsewhere and the restaurant is a bit off the beaten path, but both things are justified by the fine fare on offer at this eclectic Argentine restaurant. Perhaps it's because Tucumán attracts so few tourists that this place is able to tack up all manner of regional artifacts, from weavings to horse paraphernalia, and pipe in regional music, and yet still not feel touristy, with a devoted crowd of older locals. You can't go wrong with anything on the menu, which features, in equal measures, regional specialties, grilled meats (the parrilla is king here, as elsewhere), seafood dishes (including trout and paella), and pasta. Even simple dishes such as *milanesa alla napoletana* (breaded, fried veal with mozzarella, ham, and tomato sauce) are satisfying. ⊠ *L'Aprida 866* ☎ *381/421–6402* ▤ *AE, DC, MC, V.*

$ ✕ **El Fondo.** Generally acknowledged as the most distinguished place in town for grilled meat, El Fondo lives up to its billing with an impressive *parrilla* spread. A self-service salad bar and good wine list enhance the meal. The room and service are rather formal, but in an enjoyable way—you'll feel like you're in a huge, old Spanish colonial dining hall, and that's part of the experience here. Meat is cooked on the well-done side, so adjust your order accordingly. For a wine to accompany the meat, try the soft, round Montchenot, a Cabernet-Malbec-Merlot blend that's aged at least 12 years before its release. It's a unique Argentine red. ⊠ *Av. San Martín 848* ☎ *381/422–2161* ▤ *AE, DC, MC, V.*

★ **$** ✕ **La Leñita.** This wonderful, lively parrillada also happens to be a great spot for some Argentine folk music, as each night around 11 PM, the waiters drop everything and break into song. The restaurant is rustic but welcoming, with red bricks, high ceilings, a country-lodge feel, and friendly service to boot. The *bife de chorizo* (sirloin steak) is juicy and tender, but the sublimely creamy grilled *mollejas* (sweetbreads), a parrilla appetizer, steal the show. There are also pasta and fish, and a salad bar. For dessert, the sweet, rich *panqueque* (crepe) with *dulce de leche* is glazed with burnt sugar for an unusual taste combination. ⊠ *Av. 25 de Mayo 377* ☎ *381/422–9241* ▤ *AE, DC, MC, V.*

¢–$ ✕ **Restaurant Paquito.** If you're longing for good grilled beef, chicken, french fries, and fresh salad, this is the place for you. Pastas, pizzas, and regional specialties round out the menu. ⊠ *Av. San Martín 1165* ☎ *381/ 422–2898* ▤ *AE, DC, MC, V.*

★ **$** ✕▥ **Hotel Carlos V.** Just steps off Tucumán's busiest street, this supremely central place is infinitely popular with Argentines, due in no small part to the fact that it's a spectacularly good value—book well in advance. The Carlos V has a bustling lobby and street-side café under an arched brick facade, along with a full-service restaurant that's good in its own right. Cream-color walls, dark wood, and well-appointed bathrooms make rooms feel more like an escape than just a place to drop your bags. Pay in cash for a 10% discount. ⊠ *25 de Mayo 330, 4000* ☎ *381/422–1972* ⊕ *www.redcarlosv.com.ar* ⤳ *70 rooms* ♨ *Restaurant, café, minibars, bar, DSL Internet, meeting room* ▤ *AE, DC, MC, V.*

$$ ▥ **Swiss Hotel Metropol.** The comfort-conscious Swiss owners have decreased the quantity of rooms and increased the quality by making the remaining ones bigger. Modernity and taste pervade, and pastel colors decorate the bright and airy rooms. The friendly, English-speaking personnel and the hearty breakfasts add to the appeal of this hotel, only one block from the plaza. ⊠ *24 de Septiembre 524, 4000* ☎ *381/431– 1180* ⊕ *www.swisshotelmetropol.com.ar* ⤳ *75 rooms, 10 suites*

🛍 *Snack bar, room service, pool, piano bar, DSL Internet, meeting room, car rental, travel services, laundry service* ⊟ *AE, DC, MC, V.*

$ 🏨 **Hotel del Sol.** Most of the rooms and the spacious, second-floor bar and buffet restaurant of this modern hotel look out over a leafy canopy of trees covering the main plaza. Polished granite floors, little nooks, and wood-paneled walls lend a distinctive air. A gallery lines the first-floor corridors, with displays by local artists. ✉ *Laprida 35, 4000* ☎ *381/431–1755* 🖂 *hotel_delsol@arnet.com.ar* 🛏 *88 rooms, 12 suites* 🛍 *Restaurant, pool, bar, meeting room* ⊟ *AE, MC, V.*

Nightlife & the Arts

With so many students and businesspeople in town, there's plenty of nightlife—-mostly in the form of late-night cafés, bars, and dance clubs. One of the most interesting bars in town is the **Plaza de Almas** (✉ Maipú 791, at Santa Fe), a remarkable art-nouveau bar (that also serves food) with warm lighting and multiple levels, nooks, crannies, and romantic courtyards that will keep you guessing—happily. Several other bars cluster around Plaza de Almas and even more are crammed into a four-block stretch of Avenida 25 de Mayo between Santiago del Estero and San Martín. Notable among those is **Club 25** (✉ 25 de Mayo 464 ☎ 381/422–9785), a postmodern Internet café–bar–restaurant with crazy lighting, a hyper-cool vibe, and a raging scene on weekends. It's open just about all night, even weekdays, when it's much more relaxed; don't miss the romantic garden out back.

For the university crowd, though, weekends really get going in another area of town. Head out of the center on Avenida Mate de Luna, a continuation of 24 de Septiembre, and you'll eventually find yourself on Aconquija, which will lead you, after about a 15-minute drive, to a neighborhood called Yerba Buena. There, along Aconquija, you'll find an unparalleled proliferation of modern restaurants, musical peñas, bars, and nightclubs filled with young locals.

Shopping

Mendoza and **Muñecas** (which turns into Buenos Aires), two *peatonales* (pedestrians-only streets) that intersect one block west and one block north of the plaza, are good for shopping. The **Gran Vía** (✉ Entrance on Av. San Martín at Muñeca) shopping center is an immense, air-conditioned labyrinth of shops and restaurants. The clothing shops resemble those in Buenos Aires—stylish menswear, sportswear, and women's clothing oriented mainly toward teenagers.

Tafí del Valle

🟢 *143 km (89 mi) southwest of Tucumán via R38 and R307.*

This ancient valley was inhabited by the Diaguita people around 400 BC, later visited by the Incas, and settled by Jesuits in 1700 (until they were expelled in 1767). It remained isolated from the rest of the country until 1943, when a road was built from the town of Tucumán. The Sierra de Aconquija to the west and the Cumbres de Calchaquíes to the north enclose the high (6,600-foot) oval-shape valley and its artificial lake, Lago

Angostura. You can best appreciate the size of this often fog-shrouded valley from El Pinar de los Ciervos (The Pinegrove of the Deer), just above the actual town of Tafí del Valle. Cerro Pelado (Bald Mountain) rises from the side of the lake to 8,844 feet. The main street of the town, Calle Golero, has several simple restaurants. This region is famous for its cheeses, ponchos, blankets, and leather, all sold in the shops around the main plaza.

Scattered about the landscape of the **Parque de los Menhires** (Menhirs Park) are stone monoliths said to be more than 2,000 years old. It's a good walk to the top of the hill, where you can see the reservoir from whose depths many menhirs were rescued and relocated when the dam was built. These ancient dolmens can still be found in the surrounding country, although many have been brought to the park in recent years. Some are 6 feet tall and carved with primitive cat or human motifs. The drive out of the valley on R307 toward the Calchaquíes Valley over a 10,000-foot pass gives you a glimpse of stone ruins, isolated menhirs, and then nothing but cactus as you leave the huge sweep of green valley and enter the desert landscape of the Puna. ⊠ *Park entrance 5 km (3 mi) from R307 into village of El Mollar.*

Where to Stay & Eat

¢–$ ✕ **El Portal del Tafí.** Come to this café-restaurant for sandwiches and local specialties such as locro, humitas, and tamales, as well as fish from the region. ⊠ *Av. Diego de Rojas* ☎ *No phone* ⊟ *No credit cards.*

$$ ⊡ **Hotel Mirador del Tafí.** Large urns filled with native plants, stone, and wood adorn this hotel overlooking the lake and valley. Rooms, done in soft desert pastels, with tile floors and wrought-iron lamps, open out onto a garden and a view of the valley. In winter, fireplaces in the lobby and the open-beam dining room keep out the cold. A string of horses for rent are tied to a hitching post at the entrance. ⊠ *Off R307, Km 61.2, 4137* ☎☎ *3867/421–219* ⊕ *www.miradordeltafi.com.ar* ⇆ *32 rooms* ⟋ *Restaurant, room service, café, meeting rooms, free parking, horseback riding* ⊟ *AE, MC, V.*

Sports & the Outdoors

You can fish for trout or *pejerrey* (a narrow, silver fish, similar to a trout), sail, windsurf, water-ski, or row on **Lago Angostura**. Rentals, guided tours, and campground information are available in the nearby village of El Mollar, off R307. Horses can be rented December–March from **Otto Paz** (☎ 3867/421–272); the tourist office or your hotel can also provide information.

San Fernando del Valle de Catamarca

31 *1,150 km (713 mi) northwest of Buenos Aires, 440 km (273 mi) northwest of Córdoba, 243 km (151 mi) south of Tucumán via R38.*

San Fernando del Valle de Catamarca is the capital of the Catamarca Province. Known by locals as Catamarca, the town was founded by the governor of Tucumán in 1683 (the fertile valley in which it sits used to be part of Tucumán Province). The valley has a mild climate year-round, and the agreeable colonial city has a nice unhurried feel. The pride of the town is the central **Plaza 25 de Mayo**, on which sits the bright, terra-cotta-color cathedral. Shops in town sell jewelry and other items made from local, semiprecious rose quartz as well as carvings out of teasel wood, ponchos, carpets, textiles, and blankets woven from alpaca, wool, and vicuña.

The **Museo Arqueológico Adán Quiroga** (Adán Quiroga Archaeological Museum), three blocks north of the plaza, has exhibits ranging from 10,000-year-old stone objects found in the nearby mountains to items from the Spanish conquest. You can also see stone and ceramic ceremonial pipes and offerings from the tombs of ancient cultures dating to the 3rd century. ⊠ *Sarmiento 446* ☎ *3833/437–413* 🎟 *1 peso* 🕙 *Weekdays 7–1 and 2:30–8:30, Sat. 9—noon.*

Where to Stay & Eat

¢–$$ ✕ **Valmont.** Conservative pinks and grays lend this restaurant, in an old building on the plaza, a genteel, old-club feel. The food is truly international: French, Russian, Swiss, and Italian. At lunchtime, you may only have room for the appetizer buffet. ⊠ *Sarmiento 683* ☎ *3833/450–494* ☱ *DC, MC, V.*

¢–$ ✕ **Viejo Bueno.** Good food and soccer on TV make this a local favorite. The grilled meats and chicken come in half and quarter portions. ⊠ *Esquiú 480* ☎ *3833/424–224* ☱ *DC, MC, V.*

$ 🏨 **Hotel Ancasti.** Good taste and attention to detail prevail throughout this ultramodern hotel, designed by the owner's architect son—from the sandstone walls covered with fine art (for sale) to the carpeted lobby to the custom-designed furniture. Rooms are sleek and spacious, with mostly built-in furniture. ⊠ *Sarmiento 520, 4700* ☎ *3833/435–951* ⊕ *www.ancastihotel.com.ar* ⤵ *85 rooms, 5 suites* ⬩ *Restaurant, room service, gym, sauna, bar, meeting room* ☱ *AE, DC, MC, V.*

¢ 🏨 **Hotel Leo III.** The regal crest of Leo III at the top of the brick-color tower of this modern hotel can be seen from almost every corner in Catamarca. The entrance is in a shopping arcade, which has a communications office with telephone, fax, and Internet service. From each of the nine floors, and the roof garden, you can see the Aconquija mountains. ⊠ *Sarmiento 727, 4700* ☎ *3833/432–080* ⤵ *37 rooms* ⬩ *Restaurant, café, pool, bar, meeting room* ☱ *AE, DC, MC, V.*

Sports & the Outdoors

Catamarca has just recently awakened to its potential for recreational tourism. The sparsely populated foothills and mountains west of town are ideal for mountain climbing, hiking, and horseback riding, and decent fishing can be found in the Calacaste and Punilla rivers to the northwest. For information, maps, and guides, contact the **tourism office** (⊠ General Roca and Mota Botello ☎ 3833/437–791).

La Rioja

32 *1,167 km (724 mi) northwest of Buenos Aires, 460 km (285 mi) northwest of Córdoba, 388 km (241 mi) southwest of Tucumán via R38, 155 km (96 mi) southwest of Catamarca via R38.*

In this province of red earth, deep canyons, and Argentina's former president Carlos Menem is the eponymous provincial capital of La Rioja.

The town was founded in 1591 by Juan Ramírez de Velasco, a Spanish conqueror of noble lineage who named the city after his birthplace in Spain. Surrounding the town are high red mountains with many interesting shapes eroded into form by wind and water, and green valleys of vineyards and olive trees.

The central **Plaza 25 de Mayo** is named for the date the town was established. An earthquake in 1894 destroyed most of the town's colonial buildings, save the 1623 **Convento de Santo Domingo** church, which is the oldest building in Argentina (it's one block from the plaza).

The main attraction in the region is the **Parque Nacional Talampaya** (Talampaya National Park), which is 230 km (143 mi) from La Rioja (take R38 south to Patquía, head west on R150, and then northwest on R26). The 220-million-year-old gorge here is one of Argentina's most spectacular natural wonders; in one place it narrows to 262 feet between walls of solid rock 480 feet high. Pictographs and petroglyphs by pre-Hispanic cultures are preserved on canyon walls. Wind and erosion have produced strange columns and formations, providing nesting spots for condors. Tours by four-wheel-drive vehicles to the park can be arranged in La Rioja at the **Agencia Provincial de Turismo** (⊠ Palagio B. Luna 345 ☎ 3822/426–384), which can also help you arrange hiking (guided or unguided) trips and camping. The nearest town with accommodations is Villa Unión, 55 km (34 mi) away from the park.

Where to Stay & Eat

¢–$ ✕ **Il Gatto.** Part of a chain based in Córdoba, this trattoria-style restaurant across the street from the plaza makes good pastas and fancy salads. ⊠ *Pelagio B. Luna* ☎ *3822/421–899* ☰ *MC, V.*

¢–$ ✕ **La Vieja Casona.** This big old house with wooden floors and a frontier character is a good place to try regional specialties, grilled meats, and pasta. ⊠ *Rivadavía 427* ☎ *3822/425–996* ☰ *DC, MC, V.*

$ ⊡ **Hotel Plaza.** On Saturday nights, the whole town seems to circle the plaza—by foot, motorcycle, bicycle, or car. The hotel's café, which faces the square, is the perfect spot to watch this Riojano ritual. Although the exterior is a bland, whitewashed structure, inside everything looks new and polished, and rooms are carpeted, quiet, and simply furnished. Drinks and snacks (excellent olives!) are served in the reception area, the small bar, and the restaurant-café. ⊠ *San Nicolás de Bari and 9 de Julio, 5300* ☎ *3822/425–215* ⇄ *60 rooms, 3 suites* ⌂ *Restaurant, café, pool, bar* ☰ *AE, DC, MC, V.*

Shopping

The locally produced olives (*aceitunas aimugasta*) are outstanding, as are the dates and the date liqueur; these can be purchased in shops around the main plaza. A **crafts market** (⊠ Pelagio B. Luna 790) takes place Tuesday–Friday 9–noon and 3–8, weekends 9–noon. **Regionales El Changuito** (⊠ B. Mitre 315), on the plaza, sells antique spurs, knives, leather belts, old coins, *mate* (green tea–like beverage) gourds, and *bombillas* (the straw you drink mate through).

THE NORTHWEST ESSENTIALS

Transportation

BY AIR

Aerolíneas Argentinas/Austral has direct flights from Buenos Aires to Catamarca, La Rioja, Salta, San Salvador de Jujuy, and Tucumán. The only connecting flight is between La Rioja and Catamarca. LAN and Southern Winds both fly from Buenos Aires to Salta. All flights between Buenos Aires and the Northwest use the capital's Aeroparque Jorge Newbery domestic airport.

🛫 Airlines **Aerolíneas Argentinas** ☎ 3833/424–460 in Catamarca, 3822/426–307 in La Rioja, 387/431-1331 in Salta, 3833/422–5414 in San Salvador de Jujuy, 381/431-1030 in Tucumán ⊕ www.aerolineas.com.ar. **LAN** ☎ 0810/999–9526 throughout Argentina. ⊕ www.lan.com. **Southern Winds** ☎ 351/4775-0808 in Córdoba. 387/421-0808 in Salta, 381/422-5554 in Tucumán ⊕ www.fly-sw.com.ar.

🛫 Airports **Aeropuerto Benjamín Matienzo** ⊠ 13 km (8 mi) east of Tucumán ☎ 381/426-4906. **Aeropuerto Dr. Horacio Guzmán** ⊠ 30 km (19 mi) southeast of San Salvador de Jujuy ☎ 388/491-1109. **Aeropuerto El Aybal** ⊠ 10 km (6 mi) southwest of Salta ☎ 387/437-5113. **Aeropuerto Felipe Varela** ⊠ 22 km (14 mi) south of Catamarca ☎ 3833/437-582. **Aeropuerto Vicente Almandos Almonacid** ⊠ 7 km (4 mi) east of La Rioja ☎ 3822/427-239.

BY BUS

Buses from all the major cities in Argentina have service to cities in the Northwest. Buses will even pick you up along the road when prearranged. All terminals are no more than a short taxi ride from downtown.

Buses in the Northwest are frequent, dependable, and convenient. Local tourist offices can advise which companies go where, or you can look up "Transportes" in the yellow pages. It's a good idea to buy tickets a day or two in advance; all bus companies have offices at town bus terminals.

Aconquija links Tucumán to Tafí del Valle and Cafayate; to continue on to Salta you must change to El Indio.

Andesmar and La Estrella run from Catamarca to Tucumán and San Salvador de Jujuy and from La Rioja to Catamarca, San Salvador de Jujuy, and Tucumán. Andesmar also runs from San Salvador de Jujuy to Salta, Tucumán, Catamarca, La Rioja, and Mendoza (20 hours).

Atahualpa buses travel from Salta to San Salvador de Jujuy and La Quiaca. Balut wins accolades from most locals for its efficient, punctual service. Buses connect Salta to San Salvador de Jujuy, Humahuaca, and Tucumán. El Tucumano has bus service between Tucumán and Salta and San Salvador de Jujuy. Mercobus has luxury double-decker buses for the overnight trip between Tucumán and Córdoba. Panamericano links San Salvador de Jujuy to Salta, Humahuaca, and La Quiaca.

🚌 Catamarca Bus Information **Andesmar** ☎ 3833/423-777. **La Estrella** ☎ 3833/430-921. **Terminal de Omnibus** ⊠ Güemes 850 ☎ 3883/437-578.

🚌 La Rioja Bus Information **Andesmar** ☎ 3822/422-430. **La Estrella** ☎ 3822/465-114. **Terminal de Omnibus** ✉ Artigas and España ☎ 3822/425-453.
🚌 Salta Bus Information **Atahualpa** ☎ 387/426-1926. **Balut** ☎ 387/432-0608. **El Indio** ☎ 387/421-9519. **Terminal de Omnibus** ✉ Av. Hipólito ☎ 387/401-1143.
🚌 San Salvador de Jujuy Bus Information **Andesmar** ☎ 388/422-4888. **Balut** ☎ 388/422-2134. **Panamericano** ☎388/423-7330. **Terminal de Omnibus** ✉Dorrego and Iguazú.
🚌 Tucumán Bus Information **Aconquija** ✉ Lavalle 395 ☎ 381/433-0205 in town, 381/422-7620 at terminal. **Andesmar** ☎ 381/422-5702. **Balut** ☎ 381/430-7153. **Mercobus** ☎ 381/424-5717. **Terminal de Omnibus** ✉ Brígido Terán 250 ☎ 381/430-4696.

BY CAR

A long, monotonous drive on Route 9 across central Argentina to Córdoba or Santiago del Estero brings you within striking range of the Northwest. North on R9, the ancient road of the Incas, takes you to Tucumán, Salta, San Salvador de Jujuy, and on to Bolivia. Southwest on R64 lie Catamarca and La Rioja. Another option is to fly to a major city in the Northwest (for instance, Salta) and then rent a car. The roads in the region are good and not very crowded. Before you set out, it's a good idea to visit an Automóvil Club Argentino (ACA) office for maps and road information, especially during the January–March summer season when heavy rains can cause landslides on mountain roads.

Traveling outside of the Northwest's cities is easiest by car, as some villages, canyons, parks, and archaeological sites are neither on a bus route nor included in tours. For some short trips, like going from Tucumán to Tafí del Valle or Salta to Cafayate, it might be worth it to hire a *remis* (taxi), especially if you have companions with whom to split the fare.

Most downtown hotels have enclosed garages, which is where you should leave your car. Renting a car can be expensive, especially because agencies generally charge extra for miles, drop-off fees, and tax. But when you've come so far, the investment is probably worthwhile. You'll want a car with at least a 1.6-liter engine, such as a Volkswagen Gol (about 120 pesos per day), as the mountain roads can be demanding. Better yet is a 4x4, if you don't mind spending about 250 pesos per day. Salta Rent a Truck, which will allow dropoffs in Tucumán for an extra fee, is a good option for either the Gol or a 4x4, and offers good travel tips and advice. Stay away from the flimsy Ford Ka around here. Smaller local outfits can sometimes offer better deals and better cars than the big chains, but check the paperwork in the glove compartment (expiration dates of insurance and so on) before leaving.

🚗 **Localiza** ☎ 0800/999-2999 central reservations ✉ Esquiú 789 and at the airport, Catamarca ☎3833/435-838 ✉Salta ☎387/431-4045 ✉San Juan 935, Tucumán ☎381/421-5334. **Salta Rent a Truck** ✉ Buenos Aires 1, Salta ☎ 387/431-2097.

BY TAXI

Remises (taxis) can be found at airports, bus stations, and usually on the corner of the main plaza—or your hotel can call one for you.

Contacts & Resources

BANKS & EXCHANGE SERVICES

It's not as easy to change dollars in this region as it is in Buenos Aires. Banks are generally open weekdays 7–1 and 4–8. Banco de Galicia and Banco de la Nación in Catamarca, Banco de Galicia in La Rioja, and Banco de la Nación in Salta all have ATMs. Banco de la Provincia in San Salvador de Jujuy changes dollars and will give you cash on your MasterCard only. Cambio Dinar and Horus in San Salvador de Jujuy change cash. Maguitur in Tucumán charges 2% to change money.

Tucumán and Catamarca provinces issue their own 2-, 5-, 10-, and 20-peso *bonos* (bonds), which circulate as currency within their respective jurisdictions along with pesos. They are worthless once you leave each province. Check your change carefully and spend the bonos quickly if you are about to leave. Luckily, they are easy to identify—there's mostly text on the back.

For ATMs, look for the maroon BANELCO sign of Argentina's largest ATM network. You can use your Plus or Cirrus card to withdraw pesos. Traveler's checks are not recommended in the Northwest. Few places accept them, and with ATMs so easy to find, there's little need for them.

CURRENCY EXCHANGE 🏧 In Catamarca **Banco de Galicia** ✉ Rivadavía 554. **Banco de la Nación** ✉ San Martín 626.
🏧 In La Rioja **Banco de Galicia** ✉ S. Nicolás de Bari and Buenos Aires.
🏧 In Salta **Banco de la Nación** ✉ Mitre 151 at Belgrano. **Cambio Dinar** ✉ Mitre 101 on Plaza 9 de Julio.
🏧 In San Salvador de Jujuy **Banco de la Provincia** ✉ Lamadrid. **Cambio Dinar** ✉ Belgrano 731. **Horus** ✉ Belgrano 722. **Scotiabank Quilmes** ✉ Belgrano 904.
🏧 In Tucumán **Maguitur** ✉ San Martín 765.

EMERGENCIES

🚑 Emergency Services **Ambulance/Medical Assistance** ☎ 107. **Fire** ☎ 100. **Police** ☎ 101.
🏥 Hospitals **Hospital Angel C. Padilla** ✉ Alberdi 550, Tucumán ☎ 381/424–0848. **Hospital Pablo Soria** ✉ Av. General Güemes 1345, San Salvador de Jujuy ☎ 388/422–1228 or 388/422–1256. **Hospital Presidente Plaza** ✉ Av. San Nicolás de Bari Este 97, La Rioja ☎ 3822/427–814. **Hospital San Juan Bautista** ✉ Av. Illia and Mariano Moreno, Catamarca ☎ 3833/423–964. **Hospital San Bernardo** ✉ Tobís 69, Salta ☎ 387/431–0241.
💊 Pharmacies **Farmacia Belgrano** ✉ Belgrano 700, Salta ☎ 387/431–1331. **Farmacia Centro** ✉ San Martín 1051, Tucumán ☎ 381/421–5494. **Farmacia Minerva** ✉ Sarmiento 599, Catamarca ☎ 3833/422–415. **Farmacia Rivadavía** ✉ Rivadavía 740, Catamarca ☎ 3833/423–126. **Farmacia Americana** ✉ San Martín 334, La Rioja ☎ 3822/427–009.

HEALTH

Soroche, or altitude sickness, which results in shortness of breath and headaches, can be a problem when you visit the Puna. To remedy any discomfort, walk slowly, eat carbohydrates, take aspirin beforehand, and drink plenty of fluids (but avoid alcohol). Locals have another solution that they swear by: *coqueando,* which means sucking on coca leaves (available in plastic bags at most little corner groceries in the region, and from street vendors in the smaller towns). Tear off the end of the stems, and then stuff a wad full of leaves into one side of your mouth, in the space between your teeth and cheek; leave them in for an hour or more, neither chewing nor spitting, but swallowing when you salivate. If symptoms don't subside, descend to a lower elevation immediately. If you have high blood pressure or a history of heart trouble, check with your doctor before traveling to high Andes elevations.

INTERNET, MAIL & SHIPPING
Because most people in the region don't have their own computers, there is no shortage of *locutorios,* phone and Internet centers, in any city.

Correo Argentino provides reasonably efficient mail service. Letters sent from Salta or Tucumán take about a week to reach North America and two weeks to reach Europe. Add several days if you post from a smaller city in the Northwest.

FedEx and Western Union services are available in San Salvador de Jujuy at J. Storni & Associates.

🔲 **Post Offices Catamarca** ⊠ San Martín 753. **La Rioja** ⊠ Av. Perón 764. **Salta** ⊠ Dean Funes 160. **San Salvador de Jujuy** ⊠ La Madrid and Independencia. **Tucumán** ⊠ 25 de Mayo and Córdoba.

🔲 **Overnight Services** J. **Storni & Associates** ⊠ Av. Senador Pérez 197 P.A., San Salvador de Jujuy 🖁🖁 388/423-0103.

SIGHTSEEING TOURS
Tours of Catamarca can be arranged through the Yocavil company. In La Rioja, Velasco Tur arranges tours to the Parque Provincial Talampaya.

In Salta, La Veloz runs city tours on its own fleet of buses. It also organizes trips to San Antonio de Los Cobres (by car or by the Tren a las Nubes), to Cafayate and the Calchaquíes Valley, and to San Salvador de Jujuy and the Quebrada de Humahuaca.

San Salvador de Jujuy has NASA, a family-owned and -operated travel office with two generations of experience. The company arranges airport pickups, city guides, and excursions for individuals or groups in and around San Salvador de Jujuy; English is spoken.

In Tucumán, Duport Turismo runs four-hour city tours and three- to four-day excursions to Tafí del Valle and other nearby areas of interest and makes local, national, and international reservations.

🔲 **Duport Turismo** ⊠ Mendoza 720, Galerí Rosario, Loc. 3, Tucumán ☎ 381/422-0000. **NASA** ⊠ Av. Senador Pérez 154, San Salvador de Jujuy 🖁🖁 388/422-3938. **Velasco Tur** ⊠ Buenos Aires 253, La Rioja ☎ 3822/427-474. **La Veloz** ⊠ Caseros 402, Salta ☎ 387/431-1010 🖷 387/431-1114 ⊠ Esmeralda 320, fl. 4, Buenos Aires ☎ 11/4326-0126 🖷 11/4326-0852. **Yocavil** ⊠ Rivadavía 916, Loc. 14-15, Catamarca ☎ 833/430-066.

Wine Regions

Mendoza & San Juan: The Heart of Wine Country

WORD OF MOUTH

"If you can, do lunch at one of the wineries. My wife and I ate a wonderful three-course meal outdoors with a spectacular view of the Andes, and the winemaker gave us an impromptu wine appreciation course. It doesn't get any better than this!"

—Jason01

"If you are planning to visit wineries on your own rather than taking an organized tour, try to make appointments before you leave."

—lovesprada

Updated by
Eddy Ancinas

WHEN YOU THINK ABOUT WINE COUNTRY, France, Italy, and Napa, California, immediately come to mind—but South America? Flying under the radar, Argentina is the world's fifth-largest wine producer; more than 200,000 hectares (494,200 acres) of vineyards bask in the hot Argentine sun. Melting Andean snow and underground aquifers provide ample water, and the wall of peaks protects the grapes from the Pacific's humid winds.

Mendoza and San Juan, by far the most important wine-producing provinces, are about the same distance from the equator as the best vineyards in France, Italy, and California. The region is often referred to as the Cuyo—a name passed down from the early indigenous Huarpe people who called it Cuyum Mapu (Land of Sand). Canals built by the Huarpes and improved upon by the conquering Incas and Spaniards, as well as by modern engineers, continue to capture the flow of the region's great rivers, transforming the Cuyo into the nation's largest irrigated area.

From Mendoza City south through the Valle de Uco (Uco Valley) to San Rafael, 500 wineries produce 70% of the nation's wine at an altitude of 2,000 to 5,000 feet. During summer's long hot days, the sun's rays ripen the grapes slowly, and cool nights maintain acidity for long lasting taste. Since this semidesert climate receives little rain, and irrigation of the mineral-rich snowmelt is controlled, pests are minimal. Many vineyards could be classified as organic, since chemicals are seldom used or needed. San Juan produces a wide range of varietals planted mostly in hot dry valleys where the sun shines 300 days a year. Syrah and fruity whites thrive, and many wineries produce sparkling wines, known as Spumante in Argentina.

Each area has its own unique *caminos del vino* (wine routes). San Juan wineries have pooled their resources to print a booklet, *Ruta del Vino,* with maps, photos, and information in Spanish. Member wineries guarantee certain standards for their guest facilities. San Rafael has a more casual approach; you can pick up information in your hotel or at the tourist office. Mendoza's caminos are featured on several maps; look for the **WINEMAP,** a publication consisting of four maps at bookstores and wineries.

ORIENTATION & PLANNING

Orientation

An Argentine province and its largest city usually have the same name. Each province is divided into departments, and each department contains a large town or city of the same name. The departments are also further divided into districts.

The city of Mendoza and its surrounding departments are in Mendoza Province's northern portion, 1,040 km (646 mi) from Buenos Aires and only 360 km (223 mi) from Santiago, Chile. The east–west Route 7 (RN7 Pan Americano) crosses the Andes from Mendoza to Chile and links Ar-

CLOSE UP

Top Reasons to Visit

Scenic Wonders. Wherever you go, the sight of those towering white Andean peaks rising into a clear blue sky never ceases to amaze. Even when you can't see them, you feel their presence. Snow-capped Tupungato Volcano (6,809 meters [22,340 feet]) stands sentinel over the grand sweep of green vineyards and pink orchards that blanket the Valle de Uco. Country roads, lined with stately alamos (a type of cottonwood tree), lead to towns and villages whose backstreets run through tunnels of weeping willows.

Fun in the Sun. From the top of the Andes to the deep river canyons of Mendoza, San Juan, and San Rafael, there are outdoor activities galore.

Whether you pedal a bike along the flat vineyard roads, ride a horse along trails through the Andes to Chile, or hike, ski, or rent a car and explore the byways on your own, the region will surprise and delight you.

Generation to Generation. Don't be surprised if the polite, young English-speaking man or woman escorting you through the winery is also the owner—many places are in the capable hands of a family's third and fourth generations. Their forefathers survived the whims of Argentine politics and economics, and this generation has shifted the focus of the wine industry from quantity to quality. The next generation's challenge will be navigating the huge export market.

gentina and neighboring southern cone countries (Brazil, Uruguay, Paraguay) with Pacific ports and the Asian market. Route 40 (RN40) runs north–south the length of the country, passing through San Juan and down to Mendoza, the Valle de Uco, and San Rafael.

Planning

The wine harvest ends in autumn (February and March) and is celebrated with weeks of festivities that culminate in the *vendimia* (wine festival), celebrated in Mendoza during the last days of February and first week of March. A parade of floats, beauty queens, and gauchos on horseback circles the Plaza Independencia and ends in the soccer stadium in San Martín Park with a grand finale of music, dancing, and religious ceremonies to ensure a good harvest. People shop and graze at sidewalk food stands in the parks and plazas.

Winter is time for pruning and tying vines. Ski season begins in June, though July has the best weather. It's also the month favored by Argentines and Brazilians for vacations on the slopes. August usually has plenty of snow, and September offers spring conditions. Weather in the Andes is unpredictable, though, so pack clothes for all conditions and get reports from ski areas before you arrive. Springtime in the Valle de Uco brings trees covered in pink and white blossoms and new life in the vineyards. The snowcapped Andes form a spectacular backdrop, so bring your wide-angle lens.

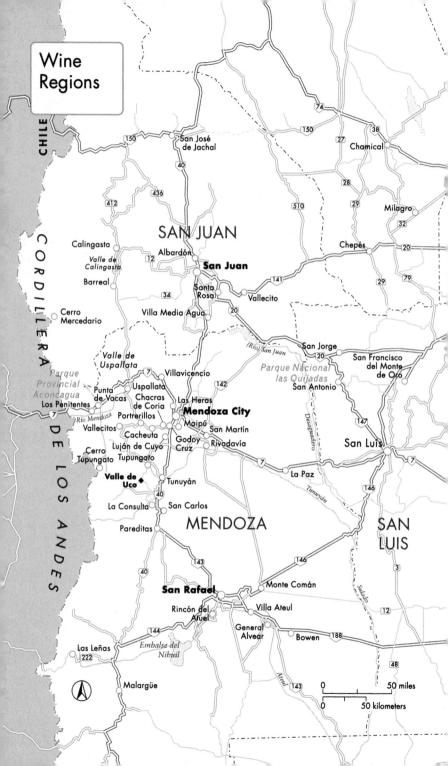

Wine
Regions

CHILE

CORDILLERA DE LOS ANDES

74

150
San José
de Jachal

150

27

38

Chamical

40

436

412

28

510

29

Milagro

32

SAN JUAN

Calingasta

Albardón

12

San Juan

Chepés

20

Valle de
Calingasta

Barreal

34

Santa
Rosa

141

29

79

Cerro
Mercedario

Villa Media Agua

20

Vallecito

(Río) San Juan

Valle de
Uspallata

San Jorge

20

San Francisco
del Monte
de Oro

Parque Provincial
Aconcagua

7

Villavicencio

142

Parque Nacional
las Quijadas

San Antonio

Los Penitentes

Punta
de Vacas

Uspallata
Chacras
de Coria

Las Heras

147

7

Río Mendoza

Portrerillos

Mendoza City

San Luis

Vallecitos

Cacheuta

Maipú

San Martín

Desaguadero

7

Cerro
Tupungato

Luján de Cuyo
Tupungato

Godoy
Cruz

Rivadavia

7

Valle de
Uco

Tunuyán

7

La Paz

146

Tunuyán

La Consulta

San Carlos

SAN
LUIS

40

Pareditas

MENDOZA

3

143

146

40

San Rafael

Monte Común

12

Rincón del
Atuel

Villa Ateul

144

General
Alvear

Bowen

188

Las Leñas

222

Embalse del
Nihuil

48

Salado

Atuel

143

0   50 miles

Malargüe

0   50 kilometers

Tour at Your Leisure

Mendoza City is a good place to begin your exploration. You can arrange tours to vineyards and other activities through your hotel or the tourist office in Mendoza before you arrive; this is particularly a good idea if you're traveling with a group and/or during the harvest. You can also hire a *remis* (hired car with driver) for an hour or a day and plan your own itinerary. Renting a car and hitting the road may end in frustration and wasted time, as signs outside of Mendoza are often misleading or invisible. Road construction, detours, and muddy roads during spring can add to the frustration or the spirit of adventure, depending on your temperament. If time isn't an issue and you have the patience, exploring on your own—stopping for photos, chatting with locals, and discovering new territory—has its rewards.

Buses between Mendoza, San Juan, San Rafael, and San Luís are frequent and comfortable. All four locations have local tourist offices, cheap taxis, and remis. If you're combining a ski vacation with wine tours, fly from Buenos Aires to San Rafael (or Malargüe, if you're on a tour), then travel north through the Valle de Uco to Mendoza.

Most wineries don't charge for tours or tastings but do request reservations; if you're visiting independently, call first. Don't be put off by such security precautions as a locked gate or a uniformed guard—the guards are friendly and helpful and will call the winery to announce your arrival.

Andesmar (⊠ Espejo 189, Mendoza ☎ 261/405–0800 ⊕ www. andesmar.com) is a large company with offices all over Argentina. They own the bus company of the same name and offer country-wide tours, outdoor excursions, and seven wine tours that visit three wineries per day in Mendoza.

Argentine Rafting Expeditions (⊠ Ruta Nacionál 7, Km 53, Potrerillos ☎ 262/482–037 ⊕ www.argentinarafting.com) offers rafting and kayak classes and day trips.

Atuel Travel (⊠ Buenos Aires 31, San Rafael ☎ 2627/429–282 ⊕ www. atueltravel.com.ar) in San Rafael can arrange wine and outdoor recreational tours.

★ **Aventura and Wine (Bacchus Tours)** (⊠ Grandaderos 1307 Mendoza ☎ 261/429–3014 ⊕ www.aventurawine.com) creates custom wine tours that allow you to tour the winery with the owner or winemaker. The company can also arrange anything from cooking classes to golf. Top hotels call on Aventura's multilingual staff as consultants for visiting VIPs.

Aymará Turismo (⊠ 9 de Julio 1023, Mendoza ☎ 261/420–2064 ⊕ www.aymara.com.ar) offers 4- to 11-day wine tours with an oenologist; longer tours cross the Andes to Chilean wineries. The vineyard tour on horseback is an original option. They also organize hikes, horseback trips, mountain climbing (including Mercederio, volcano treks, and a 19-day guided ascent of Aconcagua), white-water rafting, skiing, and mountain bike tours.

Badino (⊠ Paraguay 930, Buenos Aires ☎ 11/5238–2100 ⊕ www. badino.com.ar/patagonia/) organizes ski tours and handles Las Leñas hotel reservations.

Betancourt Rafting (⊠ Lavalle 36, Galería Independencia, Loc. No. 8, Mendoza 🖀🖥 261/429–9665 ⊕ www.betancourt.com.ar) has three small cabins and a lodge at the Cacheuta Hot Springs.

Cordon del Plata (⊠ Av. Las Heras 341 🖀 264/48303 ⊕ www. cordondelplata.com.ar) offers horseback rides from a day to a week, combination horse/trek/rafting trips, and mountain biking trips.

Dante Montes (⊠ Santa Fe 58 Galeria Estonell-Loc 31, San Juan 🖀 264/ 422–9019 ⊕ www.agenciamontes.com.ar) is a small, family-owned tour agency in San Juan with local and regional tours.

Ducher Viajes (⊠ Mendoza 322, San Juan 🖀🖥 264/427–5060 ⊕ www. ducherviajes.com.ar) is a full-service travel agency in San Juan with city and wine tours, plus trips to the mountains.

Fernando Grajales (⊠ 25 de Mayo 2985, Guaymallén 🖀🖥 261/429–3830) is an experienced guide and veteran of many Aconcagua summits.

Fortuna Viajes (⊠ Mariano Moreno s/n, Barreal 🖀 264/844–1004 ⊕ www.fortunaviajes.com.ar) offers a variety of horseback trips hiking, mountaineering, rafting, fishing, sand-surfing, and 4x4 excursions.

The Grapevine (⊠ Sarmiento 133, Gallería San Marcos, Loc. 12, Mendoza 🖀 261/429–7522 ⊕ www.thegrapevine-argentina.com) uses country inns as bases for touring the region. The five-day vendimia wine harvest tour is the best way to get to all the right events at the right time.

Hotel Club de la Nieve (⊠ San Martín 793, 14A, Buenos Aires 🖀🖥 11/ 4315–2067 ⊕ www.clubdelanieve.com) can arrange your hotel at Las Leñas and handle other ski-related reservations.

Huentata (⊠ Av. Las Heras 663, Mendoza 🖀🖥 261/425–3108 ⊕ www. huentata.com.ar) does trekking, biking, and horseback trips.

Inka Expeditions (⊠ Av. Juan B. Justo 345, Mendoza 🖀 261/425–0871 ⊕ www.inka.com.ar) has 10 years of experience leading tours to base camp at Aconcagua; they specialize in trekking and mountaineering.

Limité Zero (🖥 261/429–9165 in Mendoza, 11/5032–9932 in Buenos Aires ⊕ www.aventurarse.com) expertly handles guided horseback rides, trekking, mountain climbing, and ice climbing.

Mendoza Viajes (⊠ Paseo Sarmiento 129, Mendoza 🖀🖥 261/461–0210 ⊠ Hipólito Irigoyen 774, San Rafael 🖀🖥 2627/420–516 ⊕ www. mdzviajes.com.ar) is a full-service travel agency with day trips to wineries, city tours, and outdoor activities.

Money Tur (⊠ Santa Fe 202, San Juan 🖀 264/420–1010 ⊕ www.moneytur. com.ar) conducts city tours, wine tours, rural outings to inns in Barreal and Valle Fertíl, and high mountain trips.

★ **Postales de Plata** (⊠ 9 de Julio, 4th floor, Dpto 33, Mendoza 🖀 261/ 429–6210 ⊕ www.postalesdelplata.com) uses two lodges as a base for custom tours to nearby wineries. These trips can be combined with horseback rides, golf, a spa treatment, fishing, or skiing.

Raúl Labat (🖀🖥 261/429–7257) offers group horseback rides from his ranch, El Puesto, near Tupungato, into high rugged country.

Travesía (⊠ Montecaseros 699, Godoy Cruz 🖀 261/448–0289) conducts biking tours and provides maps for the foothills outside of Mendoza.

Be in the Know

Malargüe (⊠ Dirección de Turísmo, Ruta 40 Norte s/n 🖀 2627/471–659 ⊕ www.malargue.gov.ar). The large wooden building off the road in a park is a pleasant place to pick up information and directions.

CLOSE UP

Other Wine-Growing Regions

Though most of the country's wines come from the Mendoza and San Juan provinces, you'll find vineyards from Patagonia to Bolivia.

Catamarca: Sandwiched between the Salta and La Rioja provinces, Catamarca is just beginning to make the shift from table wines to more-refined vintages. This region benefits from high altitudes, sandy soil, and favorable temperatures.

La Rioja: North of Mendoza and San Juan, this area has low humidity, alluvial soil, and lots of sun. Torrontés and Barbera are the main varietals here, but vintners are also planting other grapes.

Neuquén: Between Mendoza and Patagonia, this is one of Argentina's

newer wine-growing regions. Winemakers are taking advantage of the good soil and favorable temperature fluctuations to grow Malbec, Merlot, and Pinot Noir.

Río Negro: Sémillon is the star in Argentina's southernmost wine-growing region, though Merlot, Pinot Noir, and other varietals are also grown. Ideal fall temperatures produce flavorful fruit.

Salta: You'll find some of the world's highest vineyards in Argentina's northwest corner. The focus is on Torrontés (though Cabernet Sauvignon, Chardonnay, and Malbec are also grown).

Mendoza (✉ San Martín 1143 and Garibaldi ☎ 261/420–1333 ⊕ www. turismo.mendoza.gov.ar). The provincial tourism office is inside the building, upstairs. Outside, on the corner of San Lorenzo, a street-side office has racks of brochures and general Mendoza information.

San Juan (✉ Sarmiento 24 Sur ☎ 264/421–0004 ⊕ www.sanjuan.gov. ar). A directory of lodging, restaurants, and tour agencies is available on request, along with information on wineries and tours to sights outside of the city.

San Luis (✉ Av. Presidente Illía and Av. Junín ☎ 2652/423–957 or 800/ 666–6176). Located in a colonial mansion, this office provides information on local tours, lodging, transportation and sports facilities.

San Rafael (✉ Av. H. Yrigoyen 745 ☎☎ 2627/424–217 ⊕ www. sanrafael.gov.ar). Friendly advice and stacks of brochures with maps are available across the street from the Tower Hotel.

Valle de Uco (✉ Av. Belgrano 348 ☎ 2622/488–007 ⊕ www.tupungato. Mendoza.gov.ar). This is a good place to pick up a detailed area map and information on lodging, outdoor activities, wineries, and ranch stays.

Eat Well

Most of the region follows national culinary trends—beef, lamb, chicken, and pork—*a la parrilla* (grilled). Second- and third-generation Italian restaurants serve family recipes enhanced with fresh ingredients like wild asparagus and mushrooms. Olive oil, garlic, melons (ripe February–March), and many other fruits and vegetables are grown locally. Hearty Spanish soups, stews, and casseroles are a connection to the region's past, as is *clérico*, a white-wine version of sangria. You may also have the opportunity to attend an *asado* (a traditional outdoor barbecue) while you tour the Wine Regions. Malargüe, southwest of San Rafael, is famous for its *chivito* (goat)—cooked *a la parrilla* or *asado*-style (skewered on a crossed metal bar stuck in the ground so that meat cooks slowly aslant a bed of hot coals).

Sleep Tight
Tourist offices can recommend all kinds of *hospedajes* (lodgings), apart-hotels (rooms with cooking facilities and sometimes a sitting area), *cabañas* (cabins), hostals, and *residenciales* (bed-and-breakfasts), all of which are generally well maintained and offer good bargains. In the countryside you'll find everything from campgrounds to *hosterías* (inns), and even a spa hotel. *Posadas* (country inns) can be cozy and old fashioned, sprawling and ranch-like, or sleek and modern. Some have first-rate restaurants and an extensive wine list. Afternoon tea, wine tastings and custom tours, horseback rides, and evening entertainment are all possible activities.

Mendoza City has a lively hostel, many medium-size hotels and apart-hotels, and the Hyatt for luxury. The smaller cities of San Luís, San Juan, and San Rafael have at least one nice, modern hotel (the rest are rather run of the mill). Los Alamos in San Rafael is a family-owned and operated country home with charm and history.

Price It Right

WHAT IT COSTS In Argentina Pesos				
$$$$	**$$$**	**$$**	**$**	**¢**
RESTAURANTS over 35	25–35	15–25	8–15	under 8
HOTELS over 300	220–300	140–220	80–140	under 80

Restaurant prices are for one main course at dinner. Hotel prices are for two people in a standard double room in high season.

MENDOZA PROVINCE

Mendoza is one of the world's wine capitals, and although this is certainly a major reason to visit, it's not the only one. You can also go rafting, soak in thermal baths, ski at Las Leñas and Penitentes, go horseback riding, and hike on Aconcagua—the western hemisphere's highest mountain. The Andean communities of Potrerillos and Uspallata, the Atuel Canyon near San Rafael, and Malargüe in the south are filled with wild rivers and majestic mountains.

The province has a population of 1,579,651 people, with 110,477 living in the city. The urban area known as Gran Mendoza (greater Mendoza) includes the city of Mendoza and the departments of Godoy Cruz, Guaymallén, Maipú, Junín, Luján de Cuyo, and Las Heras. These departments have grand shopping centers along the main highway, and small hotels, restaurants, wineries, and vineyards tucked back along country roads. Other wine-growing departments in Mendoza Province are the Valle de Uco and San Rafael.

Mendoza Musts

Los Mendocinos. Mendocinos are beautiful, fun-loving, and welcoming. They're proud of their wine and the land that produces it.

Food and Wine. Some of Argentina's premier chefs have left the grand resorts on the coast and the tony bistros of Buenos Aires for wine country inns and even wineries themselves—the perfect places to marry good food with good wine and innovate with fresh ingredients, local olive oil, and grass-fed beef.

Bed & Bodega. Country inns make wine touring a pure pleasure, with customized wine tours, gourmet meals, afternoon tastings, alternative activities, swimming pools, stunning scenery, and the camaraderie of fellow travelers in elegant and intimate settings.

5

The Wineries

The department of Maipú, south and slightly east of Mendoza City, has some 12 wineries in the districts of General Gutierrez, Coquimbito, and Cruz de Piedra. To the south, the department of Luján de Cuyo borders both sides of the Mendoza River and has 27 wineries in the districts of Agrelo, Carodilla, Chacras de Coria, Drummond, Perdriel, Ugarteche, and Vistalba. Aceso Sur (RN40), the main highway south, is the fastest way to get to the area.

Mendoza City

Located 1,040 km (600 mi) northwest of Buenos Aires, Mendoza is the main city in the Wine Regions. A cool canopy of poplars, elms, and sycamores shades its sidewalks, plazas, and low-rises. Water runs along the streets in *acéquias* (canals), disappears at intersections, then bursts from fountains in the city's 74 parks and squares. Many acéquias were built by the Huarpe Indians and improved upon by the Incas long before the city was founded in 1561 by Pedro del Castillo.

In 1861, an earthquake destroyed the city, killing 11,000 people. Mendoza was reconstructed on a grid, making it easy to explore on foot. Four smaller squares (Chile, San Martín, Italia, and España) radiate from the four corners of Plaza Independencia, the main square. Their Spanish tiles, exuberant fountains, shaded walkways, and myriad trees and flowers lend peace and beauty. Avenida San Martín, the town's major thoroughfare, runs north–south out into the southern departments and wine districts. Calle Sarmiento intersects San Martín at the tourist office and becomes a *peatonal* (pedestrian mall) bustling with outdoor cafés, shops, offices, and bars. It crosses the Plaza Independencia, stops in front of the Hyatt Plaza, then continues on the other side of the hotel. In winter, a *Bus Turístico* departs every two hours on a guided tour, letting you on and off at designated stops. Be sure to pick up the walking tour map "*Circuitos Peatonales*" in your hotel or at the city tourist office.

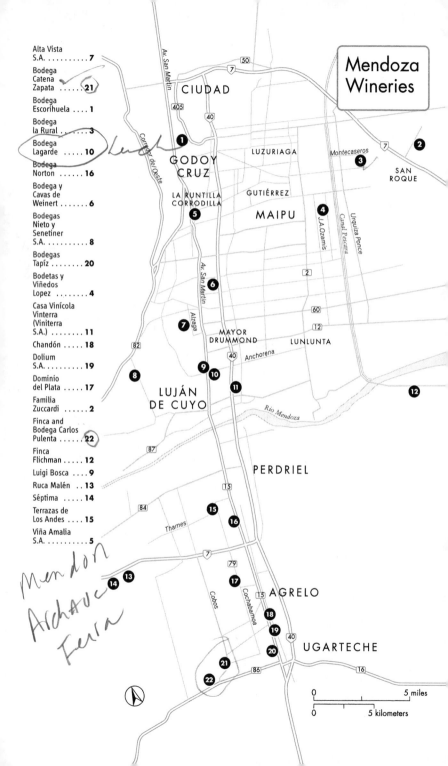

Mendoza Wineries

CIUDAD

Av. San Martín

LUZURIAGA

Montecaseros

SAN
ROQUE

Corridor del Oeste

GODOY
CRUZ

GUTIÉRREZ

LA RUNTILLA
CORRODILLA

MAIPU

J.A.Ozamis

Canal Pescara

Urquiza Ponce

Av. San Martín

Alzega

MAYOR
DRUMMOND

LUNLUNTA

Anchorena

LUJÁN
DE CUYO

Río Mendoza

PERDRIEL

Thames

AGRELO

Cobos

Cochabamoa

UGARTECHE

Mendoza
Archave
Feria

| 0 | | | 5 miles |

| 0 | | | 5 kilometers |

Wine Glossary

ARGENTINA WAS ONCE the world's fourth largest wine-consuming nation (behind France, Italy, and Spain) Unremarkable reds were either downed by beef-eating Argentines or exported in tankers to Europe. But in the 1980s, Dr. Nicolás Catena recognized his country's potential to compete in the world market by producing lower-yield, higher-quality grapes, and Argentine vintners began planting single varietals in ideal locations. They also improved irrigation and invested in new technology. Today you can find world-class Argentine wine in the U.S., Canada, Asia, and Europe.

Principal Wines produced in Argentina:

Whites:

Chardonnay: Rootstock from the U.S; golden to amber; fruit aromas of apple, pear, bananas.

Chenin Blanc: Ideal grape for hot areas; good acidity and flavor; compatible for blending. Argentina's grape of the future.

Torrontés: Argentine grape born in Spain of the Muscat grape. Pale gold; aromatic; citrusy with tropical fruits. Refreshing when very cold; similar to a dry Gewürztraminer.

Sauvignon Blanc: Recent arrival from France. Pale yellow; aromas of eucalyptus, grass, mango, apples.

Sémillon: Long history in Argentina; pale gold to straw; light citrus with aromas of peach, apricot.

Spumante: Argentina's sparkling wine. In the last few years, Argentine vintners and foreign investors have been making bubbles with a variety of grapes.

Viognier: French grape; new in Argentina and gaining popularity. Light gold; aromatic; melon, peaches, and slight white pepper.

Reds:

Bonarda: Intense red with violet hues; strong tannins; black fruit and plums; ages well.

Cabernet Sauvignon: Adapts well to all Argentine regions. Complex aromas of tobacco, black pepper, red fruits. Full-bodied and structured through aging.

Malbec: Argentina's signature grape; originally a blending grape from Cahors, France. Thrives in Argentina's loose, sandy soil, sun, and cold nights. Deep red color; plums, cherries, and red fruits; sweet tannins; aging potential.

Merlot: French variety; has adapted to cooler climates of Valle de Uco, Río Negro, and Neuquén provinces. Robust tannins; low yield; highest potential in cool zones.

Pinot Noir: French lineage; blended with Chardonnay for champagne (spumante in Argentina). Best potential in colder zones of Río Negro and Valle de Uco provinces; generous tannins; with aging, develops notes of coffee and tobacco.

Syrah: Originally from Persia (Shiraz in Iran); adapted well to warmer climates of San Juan and La Rioja provinces. Intense red; sweet, soft tannins; spicy flavors of ripe red fruit.

Tempranillo: From Spain; thrives in warm climates. Strong tannins; elegant red fruit; slightly dry.

5

WINERY CHART

Winery	Reservations	Restaurant	Hotel	Cabernet Franc	Cabernet Sauvignon	Gamay	Italian Varietals	Malbec	Merlot	Petit Verdot	Pinot Noir	Syrah	Tannat	Tempranillo
Mendoza				REDS										
7 Alta Vista S.A.					✔			✔	✔			✔		
21 Bodega Catena Zapata	✔	✕			✔			✔						
1 Bodega Escorihuela	✔				✔		✔	✔	✔			✔		
3 Bodega La Rural	✔				✔		✔	✔	✔		✔	✔	✔	
10 Bodega Lagarde				✔	✔			✔	✔	✔	✔	✔		✔
16 Bodega Norton	✔				✔		✔	✔	✔			✔		✔
6 Bodega y Cavas de Weinert					✔	✔		✔						
8 Bodegas Nieto y Senetiner S.A.	✔				✔			✔						
20 Bodegas Tapíz	✔	✕	🏨		✔			✔	✔			✔		
4 Bodegas y Viñedos López	✔				✔		✔	✔			✔	✔		
11 Casa Vinícola Viniterra	✔				✔			✔	✔			✔		
18 Chandón	✔				✔			✔	✔		✔	✔		
19 Dolium S.A.	✔				✔			✔						
17 Dominio del Plata	✔				✔		✔	✔				✔		
★ 2 Familia Zuccardi	✔	✕			✔		✔	✔	✔		✔	✔		✔
★ 22 Finca and Bodega Carlos Pulenta	✔	✕	🏨		✔		✔	✔	✔					
12 Finca Flichman					✔			✔				✔		
9 Luigi Bosca	✔				✔			✔	✔		✔	✔		✔
13 Ruca Malén	✔				✔			✔						
14 Séptima	✔				✔	✔	✔							✔
15 Terrazas de Los Andes	✔		🏨		✔			✔						
5 Viña Amalia	✔				✔			✔	✔	✔	✔	✔		

Rose	Chardonnay	Chenin Blanc	Gewurztraminer	Muscat	Pinot Grigio	Riesling	Sauvignon Blanc	Semillon	Tocai Friulano	Torrontes	Viognier	Labels
				WHITES								
	✔										✔	Alto, Grande Reserve, Finca Monte Lindo
	✔											Nicolás Catena Zapata, Catena, Catena Alta, Álamos
	✔						✔	✔			✔	Cavas San Julián, Pinar del Rio, Pont L'Eveque, Carcassonne, Gascón
	✔	✔	✔		✔							San Felipe, Trumpeter, Felipe Rutini
	✔			✔			✔	✔			✔	Henry, Lagarde, Altas Cumbres, Sémillon 1942
	✔						✔	✔		✔		Privada, Reserva, Barrel Select, Espumante Extra Brut
	✔	✔					✔					Weinert, Cavas de Weinert, Carrascal, Montfleury, Pedro del Castillo
	✔											Cadus, Don Nicanor, Santa Isabel, Reserva Nieto
	✔						✔					Tapíz, Zolo
	✔	✔					✔	✔				Montchenot, Chateaux Vieux, Rincón Famoso, López, Vasco Viejo, Traful
	✔				✔						✔	Viniterra, Terra, Omnium
	✔						✔	✔				Valmont, Latitud 33°, Beltour, Clos du Moulin, Castel, Insignia, O2, Dos Voces
✔							✔					Dolium, Andes Peak
		✔					✔					BenMarco, Susana Balbo, Crios de Susana Balbo
	✔						✔			✔	✔	Santa Julia, Vida Orgánica, Malamado, Zeta, "Q"
							✔					Corte A, Corte B, Corte C
	✔	✔				✔	✔					Dedicado, Caballero de la Cepa, Viña Plata, Paisaje de Tupungato, Paisaje de Barrancas
	✔		✔			✔	✔				✔	Reserva, Alta Gama, La Linda, Finca Los Nobles, Boheme
	✔											Kinien, Ruca Malén, Yauquén, Terruño
												Séptima
	✔											Terrazas, Afincado, Reserva
	✔						✔				✔	Viña Amalia, Carlos Basso, Villalobos, Villar, Cortés, Dos Fincas

WINERY CHART

Winery	Reservations	Restaurant	Hotel	Cabernet Franc	Cabernet Sauvignon	Gamay	Italian Varietals	Malbec	Merlot	Petit Verdot	Pinot Noir	Syrah	Tannat	Tempranillo
				REDS										
Valle de Uco														
㉔ Andeluna					✔				✔					
㉜ Bodega Aconquija	✔											✔		✔
㉓ Bodega Bombal	✔		🏨				✔	✔						
㉘ Bodega J&F Lurton	✔				✔		✔	✔				✔		
㉛ Bodega y Viñedos FAPES	✔							✔	✔			✔		✔
㉞ Bodega y Viñedos O. Fournier S.A.	✔							✔	✔			✔		✔
㉚ Bodega y Viñedos San Polo	✔							✔	✔			✔		✔
㉗ Bodegas & Viñedos Hinojosa	✔							✔	✔					
㉖ Bodegas Salentein	✔		🏨		✔			✔	✔		✔	✔		
★㉙ Clos de Los Siete	✔							✔						
㉝ Finca La Celia				✔	✔			✔	✔			✔		
㉕ La Azúl S.A.		✗						✔	✔					
San Rafael														
㊶ Balbi					✔			✔				✔		
㊲ Bodega Suter, S.A.					✔			✔	✔		✔			
㊵ Bodegas y Viñedos Valentín Bianchi	✔				✔			✔	✔		✔	✔		
㊷ Finca Viñas de Golf	✔		🏨		✔		✔	✔		✔				
★㊱ Goyenechea	✔				✔			✔	✔			✔		
㊳ Jean Rivier	✔				✔			✔						
㊴ Jorge Simonassi Lyon	✔				✔		✔	✔	✔			✔		
㉟ Lavaque	✔				✔			✔			✔			
San Juan														
㊹ Bodegas Santiago Graffigna S.A					✔		✔	✔	✔					
㊼ Bodegas y Viñas de Segisa					✔			✔			✔			
㊿ Callia	✔				✔		✔	✔						
㊸ Cavas de Zonda S.A					✔			✔	✔		✔			
㊾ Champañera Miguel Ángel Mas					✔						✔			
㊽ Fabril Alto Verde					✔			✔			✔			
㊻ Las Marianas					✔				✔		✔		✔	✔
㊺ Museo Antigua Bodega de San Juan					✔						✔			

Rosé	Chardonnay	Chenin Blanc	Gewürztraminer	Muscat	Pinot Grigio	Riesling	Sauvignon Blanc	Sémillon	Tocai Friulano	Torrontés	Viognier	Labels
				WHITES								
	✔											Andeluna
✔	✔											Aconquija, Alberto Furque, Furque
	✔					✔						Estancia Ancón, Bombal
✔	✔				✔					✔	✔	Lurton, Finca Las Higueras
												Don Enrique Fallardi, Primer Corte
												Acrux, Bcrux, Urban Uco
✔	✔											Auka, La Remonta, Piuquenes
						✔						Don Silvestre, Hinojosa
												Salentein, Primus, Finca El Portillo
	✔											Clos de Los Siete, Lindaflor, Petite Fleur, Festivo, Val de Flor
	✔				✔		✔	✔				Reserva, La Consulta, Furia, Magallanes, Angaro
												Azul, Reserva, Gran Vino
	✔											Calvet, Balbi
	✔	✔										Rojo, Etiqueta Marrón, Fritzwein
	✔	✔			✔	✔		✔	✔		✔	Famiglia Bianchi, Enzo Bianchi, Elsa, Elsa's Vineyard, 1887, Don Valentín Lacrado
												Viñas Del Golf
✔	✔					✔		✔				Marquez de Nevado, Vasconia, Centenario, Quinta Generación
✔		✔										Jean Rivier, Inti Valley
												Andrea's Cavas, Tempo, Finca Simonassi
		✔										Rincón Privado, Lavaque Roble
	✔				✔		✔				✔	Graffigna, Colón, Santa Silvia, Casa de Cubas, Centenario, Tío Paco
✔									✔			Premium, Fronda
												Magna, Alta, Signos
✔												Gran Cava
✔									✔			Miguel Mas, Maria Martín
✔												Buenas Ondas, Nuestra Escencia, Montgallard
												Fray Justo
✔							✔	✔				Viñas de Chirino, Ensamblache, Antigua Bodega 1929

Godoy Cruz

❶ Bodega Escorihuela. Founded in 1884 by Spaniard Miguel Escorihuela Gascón, this large winery features a 63,000-liter French barrel—the largest in the province. In 1993, a group of investors led by pioneer vintner Nicolás Catena bought the interests in the Bodega Escorihuela. Experimentation and innovation continue here with art exhibits and Francis Mallmanns' renowned restaurant, 1884. ☒ *Belgrano 1188, Godoy Cruz* ☏ *261/499–7044* ⊕ *www.escorihuela.com.ar* ⊘ *Weekdays 9:30–12:30 and 2:30–3:30; guided tours on the hour.*

Maipú

❸ Bodega la Rural. In 1855, Felipe Rutini left the hills of Italy to found a winery in the raw land of Coquimbito, Argentina. His descendants planted the first grapes (Chardonnay and Merlot) in the now-popular Tupungato District of the Valle de Uco. Today, Bodega la Rural is still family-owned and -operated. The winery's well-known San Felipe label was created by Alejandro Sirio, a famous Spanish artist. Inside the original adobe barns, the **Museo del Vino** (Wine Museum) has a fascinating collection of machinery; vintage carriages; 100-year-old leather, wood, and copper tools; and even an amazing mousetrap. ☒ *11 km (6.8 mi) from Mendoza, Montecaseros 2625, Coquimbito, Maipú* ☏ *261/ 497–2013* ⊕ *www.bodegalarural.com.ar* ⊘ *Tours every 30 min Mon.–Sat. 9–1 and 2–5; Sun. and holidays 10–1 with reservation.*

❹ Bodegas y Viñedos López. Wines up to 60 years old are stored in the main cellar of this traditional family winery, established in 1898. After a tour of the winery, tastings take place in the cave, where lunches can be arranged with a two-day notice. ☒ *Ozamis 375, Maipú, Mendoza, 13km/8mi/20 min from Mendoza* ☏ *261/497–2406* ⊕ *www.bodegaslopez.com.ar/* ⊘ *Mon.–Fri. hourly tours 9–5; Sat. and holidays hourly tours 9:30–10:30, and 12:30; Sun. by appt.*

❷ Familia Zuccardi. In 1950, Don Alberto Zuccardi, a civil engineer, developed a more modern system of irrigation for his vineyards in Maipú,

 Fodor'sChoice ★

and later in Santa Rosa. He and his team of 450 workers continue to discover new approaches to viniculture and wine tourism; their newest innovation, the *"Cava de Turísmo,"* is an air-conditioned cave where you can join tours of the bodega, often led by family members or an oenologist. A soft, soothing light glows on cobblestone floors, cement walls, and warm woodwork in the tasting room and gift shop. Outside, you can walk shoulder-to-shoulder with the neatly labeled vines to the garden restaurant for a wine-tasting lunch or tea. During harvest time (February to March), *Vení a Cosechar* (Come and Harvest) is a program for wannabe grape-pickers that includes an early-morning pickup at your hotel, breakfast, and a morning of hard work in the vineyards (guided by agronomists and oenologists). This is followed by a wine tasting and lunch. From June to August, a similar program teaches the art of pruning. Cooking classes, music, and art exhibits also take place here. ☒ *35 km (21.7 mi) from Mendoza, RP33, Km 7.5, Maipú, Mendoza* ☏ *261/ 441–0000* ⊕ *www.familiazuccardi.com* ⊘ *Mon.–Sat. 9–5:30; Sun. and holidays 10–5.*

⓬ Finca Flichman. In 1873, Don Sami Flichman, a Jewish immigrant, planted the first vines in the stony soil of a former riverbed in the *"bar-*

rancas" (ravines) next to the Mendoza River. His son Isaac acquired the property during the 1930s depression and had the foresight to produce only high-quality grapes. In 1983 the Wertheim family bought the winery, introduced new technology, and added another winery. Underground cellars—some ancient, some new—stainless steel tanks, and computerized temperature controls make this one of Argentina's most modern wineries. ⊠ *40 km (25 mi) from Mendoza, Munives 800, Barrancas/Maipú, Mendoza* ☎ *261/497–2039* ⊕ *www.flichman.com.ar* ⊙ *Wed.–Sun. 10–5.*

Luján de Cuyo

㉑ **Bodega Catena Zapata.** A faux Mayan pyramid rising from the vineyards fronts the towering snow-clad Andes at this landmark winery, where the architecture rivals the wine. Visitors descend from a crystal cupola through concentric spaces to the tasting room, which is surrounded by 400 oak barrels. Columbia University economics professor Nicolás Catena planted his vineyards at varying altitudes, then blended varietals from these different microclimates to create complex, distinctive wines. Special tastings with meals can be arranged for groups by prior notice. ⊠ *45 km (28 mi) from Mendoza, Calle J. Cobos s/n, Agrelo, Luján de Cuyo* ☎ *261/490–0214* ⊕ *www.catenawines.com.*

❿ **Bodega Lagarde.** Founded in 1897, Lagarde is one of the oldest and most traditional wineries in Mendoza. The third generation of the Pescarmona family remains committed to excellence in cultivating their grapes and producing limited quantities of quality wine, searching for ways to improve while avoiding fashionable trends. ⊠ *30 km (18 mi) from Mendoza, San Martín 1745, Mayor Drummond, Luján de Cuyo* ☎ *261/498–0011* ⊕ *www.lagarde.com.ar* ⊙ *Mon.–Fri. 10–5.*

⓰ **Bodega Norton.** In 1895, English engineer Sir Edmund Norton built the first winery in the valley south of the Mendoza River. Part of the old adobe house and a wing of the winery demonstrate the traditional construction of beamed ceilings with bamboo reeds under a zinc roof. In 1989 an Austrian businessman purchased the company, and his son continues to modernize and expand the 100-year-old vineyards. ⊠ *RP 15, Km 23.5, Perdriel, Luján de Cuyo, Mendoza* ☎ *261/490–9700* ⊕ *www.norton.com.ar* ⊙ *Hourly tours daily 9–12, 2–5.*

❽ **Bodegas Nieto y Senetiner S.A.** White adobe walls, tile roofs, colorful flowerbeds lining the walkways, and huge shade trees welcome you to this bodega, where groups of friends or families can harvest grapes right alongside the experts. From March 10 to mid-April, volunteer pickers arrive for breakfast, a brief explanation of harvest technique, and an introduction to their foreman. Then, with tools in hand, it's off to the vineyards with the agronomist until baskets are inspected to see who wins the prize for the best pick. From mid-August until the end of September, pruning (*podar*) takes place, and you can join the experts in cutting, tying, and modifying vines. Perhaps the most unusual tour is a 3-hour, 2-km (1.25-mi) horseback ride to a hilltop for a view of the mountains and vineyards. During a *maté* (a tealike beverage) and muffin break, an oenologist explains the varietals growing around you. All of these activities include lunch at the bodega, tasting, and a tour, and all require prior reservations. ☒ *Guaradia Viaje, between Ruta Panamericana and Rosque Sáenz Peña s/n, Vistalba, Luján de Cuyo, Mendoza* ☎ *261/498–0315* ⊕ *www.nietosenetiner.com* ⊗ *Summer: tours weekdays at 10, 11, 12:30, and 4; Other seasons: tours weekdays at 10, 11, 12:30, and 3.*

㉟ Bodegas Tapíz. When Kendall Jackson sold this modern bodega to the Ortiz family in 2003, CEO Patricia Ortiz, a medical doctor and mother of five, embarked on a slightly different approach to winemaking. Oenologist Fabián Valenzuela wants to make "happier wines" that are easier to drink and more food-friendly. Inside the bodega, walls of loose river rocks held in place by wire mesh contrast the slick granite walls and long corridors. In summer a two-horse carriage driven by a local gaucho takes guests on a learning tour of the vineyard. Club Tapiz, a seven-room inn with a spa, restaurant, and bicycles, is only 20 minutes away. ☒ *RP 15, Km 32, Agrelo, Luján de Cuyo* ☎ *261/490–0202* ⊕ *www.tapiz.com* ⊗ *Mon.–Fri. 9–5.*

⑱ Chandón. The president of Moët & Chandon was so impressed by the terroir and climate in Agrelo that he decided to build the first foreign branch of his family's company there. Today, the busy winery is producing wine and *vino spumante* (sparkling wine) in great quantities. In a one-hour class for groups of 2–15, an oenologist will guide you through the process of blending wine, and you can take your new private label home with you. During harvest (February, March, and April), an agronomist takes groups to work in the vineyard with modern equipment; lunch is included. Special workshops can be arranged for business groups, wine clubs, and wannabe winemakers. ☒ *40 km (25 mi) from Mendoza, Ruta 40, Km 29, Agrelo, Luján de Cuyo* ☎ *261/490–9968* ⊕ *www.chandon.com.ar* ⊗ *Hourly tours weekdays 10–1, 2–5; winter and holidays 11:30, 2, 3:30, and 5. Sat. with reservation.*

⑲ Dolium S.A. "Dolium" is the Latin word for the amphoras used by the Romans to store wine underground. Modern, innovative, and simple, the whole winemaking process occurs in what appears to be a small gray box set in the middle of a vineyard. Everything happens underground, but you can taste the wines upstairs in a glass-and-steel reception area that looks down into the wine works. ☒ *32 km (20 mi) from Mendoza, Ruta Provincial 15, Km 30, Agrelo, Luján de Cuyo* ☎ *261/490–0200* ⊕ *www.dolium.com* ⊗ *Weekdays 9–5, weekends by appointment.*

⑰ Dominio del Plata. Since 2001 Susana Balbo and her husband, viticulturalist Pedro Marchevsky, have combined their formidable skills with the newest technology and a passion for the care and cultivation of their land. Balbo, Argentina's first licensed female oenologist and an internationally known winemaking consultant, can look out her living room window across a sea of vineyards to the sparkling Cordón de Plata mountain range. From her dining room window, she can see the stainless steel tanks and pipes of the bodega she designed. ☒ *30 km (18.6 mi) from Mendoza, Cochebamba 7801, Agrelo, Luján de Cuyo* ☎ *261/498–6572* ⊗ *Weekdays 9–1, 3–5* ♦ *Reservations essential.*

㉒ Finca and Bodega Carlos Pulenta. Carlos Pulenta has been referred to as "the Robert Mondavi of Argentina." During his seven years as president of Salentein, a Dutch company with three bodegas, he increased the number of European varietals, installed the latest technology, and

FodorśChoice
★

put Salentein wine on the tables of the world. He left in 2004 and returned to his family's land in Vistalba, where he built his own bodega in the middle of the vineyard. The courtyard entrance frames a perfect view of the 4,900-meter (16,000-foot) Cordón de Plata mountain range. More than a bodega, the light stone and polished concrete complex houses an ultramodern 12-room inn, perhaps the best restaurant in the region (La Bourgogne), elegant meeting rooms, an underground salon for private parties, and a conference center. Inside the bodega, glass walls expose the tumbled rocks and dirt that Malbec thrives in. You'll find architectural surprises around every corner as you explore the cellars. Pulenta and his team of family advisors and oenologists have created three blends using Malbec, Cabernet, Merlot, and Bonarda, plus a delicate Sauvignon Blanc. ⊠ *Roque Saenz Peña 3531, Vistalba, Luján de Cuyo* ☎ *261/498–9400* ⊕ *www.carlospulentawines.com.*

❾ Luigi Bosca. Albereto, Raul, and Roberto Arizú—descendents of **Leoncio Arizú,** who brought the original vines from Spain in 1890—believe that a winemaker's job is to preserve what nature has delivered. Here, nature is on their side. Distinctive environments (*terroir*) produced by a variety of soils, climates, and vineyard locations have much to do with the unique character of Luigi Bosca's wine. This bodega is an architectural gem, with carved reliefs depicting the history of wine in Argentina, tile floors, inlaid wood ceilings, and painted arches. ⊠ *San Martín 2044, Drummond, Luján de Cuyo, Mendoza* ☎ *261/498–0437* ⊕ *www. luigibosca.com.ar* ⊘ *Daily tours at 10, 11, 12:30, and 4 (3 in winter).*

❸ Ruca Malén. Jon Pierre Thibaud brings 10 years of experience as president of neighboring Chandon vineyards to this modern, compact boutique winery situated just back from Route 7. Thibaud and his French partner, Jacques Louis de Montalembert, have dedicated their collective skill and passion to selecting the finest grapes for quality wines. Wine tours are led by an oenologist. With one day's notice, a gourmet lunch and wine tasting is available for 55 pesos per person. For reservations, contact Ruca Malén by phone or e-mail. ⊠ *RN7, Km 1059, Agrelo, Luján de Cuyo, Mendoza* ☎ *261/410–6214* ⊕ *bodegarucamalen.com* ⊘ *Weekdays 10–5, Sat. 10–1* ⋄ *Reservations essential.*

❹ Séptima. When the Spanish wine group Codorniú decided that Argentina would be their seventh great wine investment, they constructed their winery in the "pirca" style, in which natural stones are piled one atop the other. The Huarpe natives used this technique to build walls, dwellings, and sacred places. Inside the massive walls is a state-of-the-art winery with sleek wood and glass corridors. Visitors climb over hoses and machinery while they follow the grapes from vineyard to bottle in a natural working atmosphere. A rooftop terrace is available for private lunches, weddings, or sunset wine tastings. A rosé blend of Malbec and Pinot Noir is an interesting invention. ⊠ *RN 7, Km 6.5, Agrelo, Luján de Cuyo, Mendoza* ☎ *261/498–5164* ⊕ *www.bodegaseptima.com. ar* ⊘ *Weekdays 10–5* ⋄ *Reservations required.*

❺ Terrazas de Los Andes. Four vineyards situated at different heights (terraces)—Syrah at 800 meters (2,600 feet), Cabernet Sauvignon at 980 meters (3,200 feet), Malbec slightly higher, and Chardonnay at 1,200 meters (3,993 feet)—take advantage of different microclimates, allowing each varietal to develop to its maximum potential. Bare brick walls, high ceilings, and a labyrinth of soaring arches store premium wines in stainless steel tanks and oak barrels. Built in 1898 and restored in the mid-1990s, everything in the tasting room—from the bar to the tables to the leather chairs—is made with recycled barrels. A six-room guest house and a dining room are available for family or business gatherings. ⊠ *32 km (20mi) from Mendoza, Thames and Cochebamba, Perdriel, Luján de Cuyo, Mendoza* ☎ *261/448–0058* ⊕ *www. terrazasdelosandes.com* ⊙ *Weekdays 10–noon* ⌲ *required one day in advance by phone or e-mail.*

OTHER WINERIES **Alta Vista S.A.** ⊠ *Álzaga 3972, Chacras de Coria, Luján de Cuyo, Men-*
❼ *doza* ☎ *261/496–4684* ⊕ *www.altavistawines.com* ⊙ *Tues.–Sat. tours at 9:30, 11, 12:30, 3, and 4:30.*

❻ **Bodega y Cavas de Weinert.** ⊠ *San Martín 5923 Chacras de Coria, Luján de Cuyo, Mendoza* ☎*261/496–0409* ⊕*www.bodegaweinert.com* ⊙ *Weekday tours 9–1, 2–5; Sat. tours 9:30–4:30.*

⑪ **Casa Vinícola Viniterra (Viniterra S.A.).** ⊠ *Av. Acceso Sur, Km 17.5, Luján de Cuyo, Mendoza* ☎*261/498–5888 or 261/498–0073* ⊕*www.viniterra. com.ar* ⊙ *Weekdays 9–5 hourly, Sat. 9–noon, with reservations.*

❺ **Viña Amalia S.A.** ⊠ *San Martin 7440, Carrodilla, Luján de Cuyo, Mendoza* ☎ *261/436–0677* ⊕ *www.vinamalia.com.ar.*

Other Sights & Activities

In Mendoza

Museo del Area Fundacional. On the site of the original *cabildo* (town hall), the Foundation Museum explains the region's social and historical development. Of note is the display of a mummified child found on Aconcagua, with photos of his burial treasures—presumably an Inca or pre-Inca sacrifice. Underground excavations, made visible by a glass-covered viewing area, reveal layers of pre-Hispanic and Spanish remains. ⊠ *Beltrán and Videla Castillo* ☎ *261/425–6927* ⊡ *$1.50* ⊙ *Tues.–Sat. 8* AM–10 PM, *Sun. 3* PM–8 PM.

Museo Histórico de San Martín. The San Martín Historical Museum has a decent library and a token collection of artifacts from campaigns of the Great Liberator. ⊠ *Av. San Martín 1843* ☎ *261/425–7947* ⊡ *$1* ⊙ *Weekdays 8:30–1:30.*

Museo del Pasado Cuyano. Twice-Governor and Senator Emilio Civit's 26-bedroom 1873 mansion was the gathering place of the belle époque elite. Today it's the Museum of the Cuyo's Past, a gallery and archive with paintings, antiques, manuscripts, and newspapers. ⊠ *Montevideo 544* ☎ *261/423–6031* ⊡ *Donation* ⊙ *Weekdays 9–12:30.*

NEED A BREAK? Ice cream concoctions made with *dulce de leche* (sweet caramelized milk) and *granizado* (chocolate chips) will make you want to visit **Soppelsa** (⊠ Emilio Civit and Belgrano) daily.

Parque General San Martín. This grand public space has more than 50,000 trees from all over the world. Fifteen km (9 mi) of paths and walkways meander through the park, and the rose garden has about 500 varieties. You can observe nautical competitions from the rowing club's

Mendoza
City

Parque
Central

Parque
O'Higgins

Museo
del Area
Fundacional

Museo
Histórico
de San
Martín

Plaza Padre
del Castilla

Ayacucho

Maipu

Chacabuco

Beltran

Alberdi

Uroluza

Corrientes

Cordoba

San Luis

Entre Rios

Buenos Aires

Lavalle

Catamarca

Garibaldi

Av. Leandro N. Alem

P.B.Palacios

Montecaseros

Federico Moreno

Salta

Rioja

Bus
Station

Av. Jose Vicente Zapata

Rondeau

Parque
General
San Martín

Parana

Suipacha

A. del Ville

Juan de Dios Videla

Roque Sáenz Peña

J. V. Gonzalez

Av. Juan B. Justo

N.Avellaneda

A.Alvarez

Av. Emilio Civit

Aristi des Villanueva

Sobremonte

J.A.Maza

Coronel Plaza

Eusebio Blanco

Barcala

Godoy Cruz

General Paz

Av. Juan B. Justo

Av.las Heras

Necochea

Gutierrez

Espejo

Plaza
Independencia

Av. Sarmiento

Museo del
Pasado
Cuyano

Montevideo

San Lorenzo

Av. Colon

Av. Padro Molina

Barrio
Civico

Plaza
Chile

Plaza
Italia

Peatonal
Sarmiento

Rivadavia

Plaza
España

Plaza
San Martin

1. Ana Bistró
2. San Francisco Church

Tiburgio Benegas

Av. Boulogne Sur Mar

Belgrano

Martinez de Rosa

Paso de los Granaderos

Huarpes

J.Roca

M.Zapata

R.Ortega

25 de Mayo

Chile

Peru

Las Cubas

Av. Mitre

Patricias Mendocinas

España

9 de Julio

Av. San Martin

San Juan

KEY
🛈 Tourist information

balcony restaurant, visit the zoo, or play tennis or golf. Scenes of the 1817 Andes crossing by José de San Martín and his army during the campaign to liberate Argentina are depicted on a monument on top of *Cerro de la Gloria* (Glory Hill) in the park's center. The soccer stadium and Greek theater (capacity 22,500) attract thousands during vendimia, the annual wine harvest festival.

Plaza Independencia. In Mendoza's main square, you can sit on a bench in the shade of a sycamore tree and watch children playing in the fountains, browse the stands at a weekend fair, visit the Museo de Arte Moderno, or take a stroll after lunch at the historic Plaza Hotel (now a Hyatt) on your way to the shops and outdoor cafés on the pedestrian-only Calle Sarmiento, which bisects the square.

NIGHTLIFE **Avenida Arístedes Villanueva** is a hot spot of inexpensive bars and cafés. The area wakes up around 6 PM, when the bars, boutiques, wine shops, and sidewalk cafés open their doors, welcoming young Mendocinos, foreign tourists, and strolling couples. As the evening progresses, crowds get bigger, and the music—rock, tango, salsa—gets louder. The action peaks between 10 and midnight.

Inexpensive, casual **El Bar del José** (⊠Arístedes Villanueva 740 ☎No phone) was the first gathering place in the trendy Villanueva neighborhood.

Por Acá (⊠ Arístedes Villanueva 557) attracts a cosmopolitan crowd of locals and European travelers. Live rock music begins after 10 PM. The **Regency Casino** (⊠ 25 de Mayo and Sarmiento ☎ 261/441–2844) at the Park Hyatt Mendoza has black jack, stud poker, roulette tables, slot machines, and an exclusive bar.

SHOPPING Pick up leather goods, shoes, and clothing along the pedestrian part of Sarmiento, on Avenida Heras, and on side streets between. *Talabarterías* sell fine leather goods and everything equestrian, from saddles and hand made tack to hats, vests, and other gaucho-inspired gift items.

Mendocinos shop at **La Matera** (⊠ Villanueva 314 ☎ 261/425–3332) for boots, vests, belts, scarves, and riding equipment. On the Peatonal, **Cardón** (⊠ Sarmiento 224) carries gaucho clothing and accessories: bombachas (baggy, pleated pants), leather jackets and vests, boots, belts, scarves, ponchos, and silver knives. The 1884 **Mercado Central** (⊠ Av. Heras and Patricias Mendocinas) is the oldest market in Mendoza. Ponchos, Indian weavings, olive oil, fruit, and handcrafts are sold in open stalls daily from 9 to 1:30 and from 4:30 to 9. You'll find a huge selection of wine at **La Casa del Vino** (⊠ Villanueva 160 ☎ 261/423–5862). **Pura Cepa** (⊠ Peatonal Sarmiento 664) conducts in-store wine tastings. Before your picnic, grab a bottle of Malbec at **Juan Cedrón** (⊠ Peatonal Sarmiento 278). **Azafrán** is a wine bar, café, wine shop, and delicatessen with regional olive oil, jams, meats, and cheeses (⊠ Sarmiento 765 and Av. Villanueva 287 ☎ 261/429–4200). For all the things you forgot to pack, the indoor air-conditioned **Mendoza Plaza Shopping Center** (⊠ Lateral Accesso Este 3280, Guaymallén) has Falbella, an American-style department store (actually Chilean owned), plus shoe stores, cafés, and a bookstore (Yenny) with English titles. The children's indoor amusement park has a roller coaster, carousel, rides, and games. South of Mendoza, **Palmares Shopping Mall** (⊠ Panamericano 2650) has 10 movie theaters and many good shops and restaurants.

NEED A BREAK? For a cup of fresh-ground coffee or cappuccino, stop at **Bonafide Espresso** (⊠ *Peatonal Sarmiento 102* ☎ *261/423–7915*). Medialunas and alfajores (cookies with dulce de leche) add to the pleasure of a coffee break in this lively café, which is conveniently located on the busy corner of Sarmiento and 9 de Julio.

Elsewhere in the Region

Upsallata. This small town in the Uspallata River valley roughly 125 km (77 mi) west of Mendoza, between the foothills and the front range of the Andes, is ideally located at the crossroads of three important routes: R7 from Mendoza across the Andes to Chile, R57 from Mendoza via Villavicencio, and R39 from San Juan via Barreal in the Calingasta Valley. More than an overnight stopover, Uspallata is a good base for excursions into the mountains by 4x4 or on horseback to abandoned mines, a desert ghost town, and spectacular mountain scenery where the 1997 movie *Seven Years in Tibet* was filmed. Metals have been forged at **Las Bóvedas,** the pointed adobe cupolas a few miles north of town, since pre-Columbian time. Arms and canons for San Martín's army were made there.

★ **Camino del Año (Road of the Year).** From Mendoza traveling north on RP52, passing through Canota, you arrive at Villavicencio (47 km [29 mi]), the source of mineral water sold throughout Argentina. The nearby **Hostaria Villavicencio** serves lunch and dinner. Farther up the road, the Camino del Año begins its serpentine ascent around 365 turns to **El Balcón** on the top of the pass at **Cruz de Paramillo** (2,999 meters [9,840 feet]). Get out and look for the ruins of a Jesuit mine, the **Arucarias de Darwin** (petrified trees found by Darwin in 1835), and 1,000-year-old petroglyphs on **Tunderqueral Hill.** From the top of the pass you can see three of the highest mountains outside of Asia, all over 6,000 meters (20,000 feet): Aconcagua to the west, Tupungato south, and Mercederio north. At 67 km (41 mi), the road straightens out and descends into Uspallata, where you can continue west on RN7 to Chile or north on RN39 to **Barreal** in San Juan Province (108 km [67 mi]). The road to Barreal crosses a high desert valley, where the only sign of life is an occasional estancia partially hidden in a grove of alamos. At **Los Tambillos,** about 40 km (25 mi) from Uspallata, the Inca road that ran from Cusco, Peru, through Bolivia and into northern Argentina crosses the road. The site is surrounded by a fence that protects traces of the original road and remains of an Inca *tambo* (resting place). A map shows the route of the Incas. The mountains to the west, including Mercedario (6,768 meters [22,205 feet]), get higher and more spectacular as you approach Barreal. At the San Juan Province border, the road becomes R412 and is paved the remaining 50 km (31 mi) to Barreal.

Potrerillos. This little town in the Potrerillos Valley, 53 km (33 mi) west of Mendoza, is protected from the elements by the surrounding mountains. Its agreeable microclimate and the rushing Río Mendoza have made Potrerillos an ideal adventure sports center, and summer homes attract vacationing Mendocinos to the area. Rafting companies, mountain-bike rental shops, stables, and hiking and camping guides are headquartered here.

Fodor'sChoice **Parque Provincial Aconcagua.** This provincial park extends for 66,773
★ hectares (165,000 acres) over wild, high country with few trails other than those used by expeditions climbing the impressive Cerro Aconcagua (Aconcagua Mountain), the park's main attraction. At 6,957 meters (22,825 feet), it's the highest mountain in the Americas, and it towers over the Andes, its five gigantic glaciers gleaming in the sun. Although it seems amazingly accessible from the roadside, Aconcagua has claimed 37 climbers from the more than 400 expeditions that have attempted the summit. Nevertheless, every year hundreds of mountaineers try to conquer the "giant of America." A trail into the park begins at the ranger's cabin, follows the Río Horcones past a lagoon, and continues upward to the Plaza de Mulas base camp at 4,325 meters (14,190 feet), where there's a refugio (basic mountain cabin with bunk beds; ☎ 261/423–1571 in Mendoza for reservations).

Organized tours on horse or foot can be arranged in Mendoza or at the **Hostería Puente del Inca** (⇨ **Lodging, Parque Provincial Aconcagua,** below). The drive up the Uspallata Pass to the Parque Provincial Aconcagua is as spectacular as the mountain itself. Renting a car is worthwhile; there are many sights to stop and photograph along the way. You can make the 195 km (121 mi) trip from Mendoza in one long, all-day drive. Note that roads become icy in winter, and the altitude jumps from 762 meters (2,500 feet) in Mendoza to 3,184 meters (10,446 feet) at the top.

To reach the park, take the Camino del Año, or leave Mendoza heading south on Avenida San Martín to the Panamerican Highway (R7) and turn right. Green vineyards soon give way to barren hills and scrub brush as you follow the river for 30 km (19 mi) past the Termas Cacheuta. If you're still engulfed in fog and drizzle, don't despair: you'll likely find brilliant sunshine when you reach the Potrerillos Valley at 39 km (24 mi).

Beyond Uspallata, the last town before the Chilean frontier, the road goes through rolling hills into brooding black mountains. The Ríos Blanco and Tambillos rush down from the mountains into the Río Mendoza, and remnants of Inca tambos remind you that this was once an Inca route from Chile. At Punta de Vacas, corrals that once held herds of cattle on their way to Chile lie abandoned alongside now-defunct railway tracks. Two kilometers (1 mi) beyond the army barracks and customs office, three wide valleys converge. Looking south, the second-highest mountain in the region, Cerro Tupungato (6,798 meters [22,304 feet]), a white-capped volcano, reigns supreme above the Valle de Uco.

After passing the ski area at Los Penitentes (named for the rock formations on the southern horizon that resemble penitent monks), you arrive at Puente del Inca (2,700 meters [9,000 feet]), a natural bridge of red rocks encrusted with yellow sulphur that spans the river. The hot springs below are slippery to walk on but fine for soaking tired feet. A few miles farther west, after you pass the Chilean customs check, is the entrance to the park and the park ranger's cabin. About 15 km (9 mi) beyond the park entrance, the highway passes Las Cuevas, a settlement where the road forks right to Chile or left to the statue of Cristo Redentor (Christ the Redeemer) on the Chilean border (4,206 meters [13,800 feet]), commemorating the 1902 peace pact between the two countries.

SPORTS & THE OUTDOORS Along with local guides offering specific services, Mendoza also has several outfitters that do it all (⇨ **Tour at your Leisure,** above, for operators).

Hiking. November through March is the best time to take day hikes or weeklong treks along rivers and an Inca trail, through canyons and indigenous forests, or to the highest mountain peaks in the Andes.

Horseback Riding. *Cabalgatas* (horseback riding) is an enjoyable and natural way to explore the area. You can ride to the foot of Aconcagua or Tupungato, or follow the hoof prints of San Martín on a nine-day trip over the Andes.

Mountain Biking. Many of Mendoza's back roads lead through the suburbs and vineyards into the Andean foothills and upward to mountain villages—or all the way to Chile. Every February, La Vuelta Ciclísta de Mendoza, a bicycle race around Mendoza Province, attracts cycling enthusiasts.

Mountaineering. Mendoza offers challenging mountaineering adventures on Cordón de Plata, Tupungato, and Aconcagua. Permits for climbing Aconcagua can be obtained personally in Mendoza at **Centro de Visitantes** (⊠ Av. de Los Robles and Rotondo de Rosedal), in Parque San Martín near the entrance. The center is open weekdays 8–6 and weekends 9–1.

Skiing. Skiers bound for Las Leñas in Malargüe arrive from July through September and use Mendoza or San Rafael as their base. **Los Penitentes,** which has 20 runs and cross country skiing, is 153 km (95 mi) northwest of Mendoza on the Panamerican Highway. Despite the elevation (3,194 meters [10,479 feet]), the snow here is often thin, and the danger of avalanches can sometimes be severe. At the base of the ski area are hotels, restaurants, ski rentals, day care, a first-aid clinic, and a disco. In the hills rising up to the Cordón de Plata range, **Vallecitos,** only 80 km (49 mi) from Mendoza in Luján de Cuyo, attracts families with nearby vacation homes, as well as summer hikers and mountaineers who come to train for an assault on Aconcagua. For information, contact any of the tour agencies in Mendoza.

White-Water Rafting. Many adventure tour companies organize rafting or kayaking trips on the Río Mendoza. They can be combined with horseback treks and often include an asado.

Where to Stay & Eat

Mendoza

$$$$ ✕ **La Bourgogne.** "Cooking comes from regional traditions. My cuisine is tied to the land," says Jean Paul Bondoux, Argentina's only Relais Gourmand. He applies his French culinary skills to the best local produce, and every bite is fantastic in this casually elegant restaurant at Carlos Pulenta's winery. Lunch and cocktails are served on a porch overlooking the vineyards, Andean peaks looming in the distance. Guests are invited to cooking classes in the open kitchen. ⊠ *Roque Sáenz Peña 3531, Vistalba, Luján de Cuyo* ☎ *261/498–9400* ☉ *No dinner Sun. Closed Mon.* ⊕ *www.carlospulentawines.com* ✍ *Reservations essential* ☰ *AE, MC, V.*

$$$ ✕ **Terruño.** Light from a whimsical chandelier high in the timbered ceiling highlights the Malbec-colored walls and worn floors of this 1890 vintner's residence. Appetizers, such as Andean trout with mushrooms or a corn, tomato, and onion tart, are as good as the entrées. An experienced staff knows how to pair local wine with each course, including a unique dessert tasting course. ⊠ *Club Tapiz, Pedro Molina (RP60) s/n, Maipú* ☎ *261/496–4815* ✍ *Reservations essential* ⊕ *www.tapiz.com.*

★ **$$–$$$** ✕ **1884 Restaurante Francis Mallman.** The soft glow of candles on the patio under the prune trees at the 100-year-old Bodega Escorihuela sets the tone for Francis Mallman, who put Argentina on the map of international *alta cocina* (haute cuisine), to present his version of Patagonian cuisine. Empanadas are baked in mud ovens, a custom derived from the Incas. Students from his culinary school tend to guests with discreet enthusiasm, and the 36-page wine list has detailed information on grapes and bodegas. ⊠ *Belgrano 1188* ☎ *261/424–2698* ☰ *AE, DC, MC, V.*

$$ ✕ **La Tasca de Plaza España.** If the bright red walls with strange faces painted above the entrance and the eclectic array of art inside don't get your attention, the excellent tapas and Mediterranean dishes will. Seafood tapas, veal and artichoke stew, and a casserole of zucchini, onions, and peppers in a cheese sauce are a few of the tempting dishes served in this venerable—but irreverent—old house. ⊠ *Montevideo 117* ☎ *261/423–3466* ▤ *AE, MC, V.*

$–$$ ✕ **La Florencia.** Sidewalk tables invite strollers to stop and peruse the menu: grilled, baked, and broiled meats and fish; pastas; pizzas; game; and a variety of salads, along with a lengthy wine list. Step inside and admire the eclectic displays of antique weapons, telephones, and gaucho artifacts. The upstairs dining room has a breezy street view. ⊠ *Sarmiento and Perú* ☎ *261/429–1564* ▤ *AE, DC, MC, V.*

$ ✕ **La Marchigiana.** Homemade pasta has been served under the thatched roof and whirring fans of this cheerful Italo-Argentine eatery since 1950. Concoct your own salad and try a pitcher of sangria or clérico on hot summer afternoons. ⊠ *Patricias Mendocinas 1550* ☎ *261/423–071* ⊠ *Palmares Shopping Mall, Godoy Cruz* ☎ *261/439–1961* ▤ *AE, DC, MC, V.*

$ ✕ **El Mesón Español.** Stained-glass windows, bullfighting posters, reproductions of works by famous Spanish artists, and a worn tile floor transport you to Spain as you enter this old colonial house. Start with a cup of garlic soup, followed by paella or tapas, as Lucho, the blind pianist, plays blues, tango, swing, and Sinatra. ⊠ *Montevideo 244* ☎ *261/429–6175* ▤ *AE, DC, MC, V* ◷ *No lunch.*

★ **¢–$** ✕ **Azafrán.** Whether you view it as a gourmet grocery, wine shop, or restaurant, Azafrán (which means saffron) is a pleasant diversion. In the wine bar, an old wine press has been converted into a tasting table. Farther inside this 19th-century brick building, diners seated at small café tables enjoy cheeses, pâtés, and hot and cold tapas served on wooden platters. Shelves are stocked with Mendoza's finest: olive oils, smoked meats, dried herbs, mushrooms, olives, jams, and breads. ⊠ *Sarmiento 765* ☎ *261/429–4200* ⊠ *Villanueva 287* ▤ *MC, V* ◷ *Closed Sun.*

$$$$ 🏨 **Park Hyatt Mendoza.** Hyatt has preserved the landmark Plaza Hotel's 19th-century Spanish colonial facade: a grand pillared entrance and a wide veranda that extends to either side of the street. Lunch, afternoon tea, and dinner are served on this gracious terrace overlooking Mendoza's main square. A two-story wine wall separates the restaurant from the lobby. Minimalist bedrooms are softened by plump white pillows and duvets covering the simple ebony beds. Bathrooms have plenty of mirrors to compliment chrome and marble accents. ⊠ *Calle Chile 1124, 5500* ☎ *261/441–1234* ⊕ *mendoza.park.hyatt.com* ⤳ *171 rooms, 15 suites* ⚘ *Restaurant, café, dining room, pool, health club, spa, bar, casino, business services, meeting rooms, free parking* ▤ *AE, DC, MC, V* ⫢ *CP.*

★ **$$$** ✕🏨 **Chacras de Coria Lodge.** This casually elegant lodge, located in an upscale residential area 15 minutes from Mendoza, is ideal for visits to wineries in Maipú and Luján de Cuyo. Guests enjoy custom tours with oenologists and the intimate atmosphere of evening wine tastings, outdoor cooking classes, an outdoor asado, and candlelit dinners on the veranda. The manager can arrange privately catered meals as well as tours, golf, tennis, horseback riding, mountain biking—even tango lessons. ⊠ *Viamonte 4762, Chacras de Coria, Luján de Cuyo, M5528CCC* ☎ *261/496–1888* ⊕ *www.postalesdelplata.com* ↝ *6 rooms, 1 apt. with 2 rooms* ⌂ *Restaurant, bar, outdoor dining, swimming pool, Jacuzzi, Internet access, wine tours, outdoor activities arranged, wine tastings, cooking classes* ⊟ *AE, MC, V* ⓧ *CP.*

$$$$ ✕⊞ **La Posada Carlos Pulenta.** The enormous rooms on the second floor
Fodor'sChoice of this two story Tuscan terra-cotta building face east, where the sun
★ rises over the vineyards, or west, where it sets over the majestic Andes. Cream-colored tile floors, dark wicker furniture, and taupe and café-au-lait-covered furnishings are luxurious, but comfortable. Sumptuous chairs await you on the veranda for lunch, winetasting, or daydreaming. Breakfast and lunch or dinner are complementary, and meals can be served in your room. Equally appealing is the restaurant, La Borgogne, which has an open kitchen where guests can join a cooking class. Wine tours are also available. ⊠ *Roque Sáenz Peña 3531, Vitalba, Luján de Cuyo* ☎ *261/498–9400* ⊕ *www.carlospulentawines.com* ↝ *2 rooms* ⌂ *Restaurant, Wi-Fi, bar, lounge, business services, meeting rooms,* ⊟ *AE, MC, V* ⓧ *MA.*

★ **$$$** ✕⊞ **Club Tapiz.** This 1890 governor's mansion will feel like your own private villa. Stroll through the old winery, lounge on the enclosed patio, or gaze at the Andes from the outdoor pool or indoor Jacuzzi. Evening wine tastings in the reading room will whet your appetite for dinner in Terruña (Terroir). ⊠ *Pedro Molina (RP60) s/n, Maipú* ☎ *261/ 496–4815* ⊕ *www.tapiz.com* ↝ *7 rooms* ⌂ *Restaurant, bicycles, private rooftop dining room, bar, business center, library, spa, winery, winery tours* ⊟ *AE, MC, V.*

$$ ⊞ **Hotel Aconcagua.** You'll appreciate the efficient service at this modern hotel, which is on a quiet street near shops and restaurants. Serene tones of mauve and blue create a soothing atmosphere throughout the lobby and in meeting and guest rooms. Los Parrales, the restaurant, uses a mud oven and wood-fired grill to create typical Mendocino meals. ⊠ *San Lorenzo 545, M5500GFK* ☎ *261/520–0500* ⊕ *www.hotelaconcagua. com.ar* ↝ *159 rooms, 9 suites* ⌂ *Restaurant, pool, massage, sauna, business center, meeting rooms, travel services, free parking* ⊟ *AE, DC, MC, V* ⓧ *CP.*

$ ⊞ **Hotel Cervantes.** The simple rooms in this small, downtown owner-operated hotel are cheerfully decorated in floral prints. The front desk is knowledgeable, and a big-screen TV in the living room makes you feel at home. Sancho, the hotel's excellent restaurant and bar, is a popular lunch spot. ⊠ *Amigorena 65, 5500* ☎ *261/520–0400 or 261/520–0446* ⊕ *www.hotelcervantesmza.com.ar* ↝ *60 rooms, 5 suites* ⌂ *Restaurant, bar, business services, meeting rooms, travel services, free parking* ⊟ *AE, DC, MC, V* ⓧ *CP.*

$ ⊞ **Hotel Crillón.** The loyal clientele of this small hotel returns for the tranquil neighborhood—within walking distance of plazas, restaurants, museums, and shops. Small suites have separate work stations, and the helpful staff can plan excursions. ⊠ *Perú 1065, 5500* ☎ *261/429–8494* ⊕ *www. hcrillon.com.ar* ↝ *70 rooms, 6 suites* ⌂ *Café, pool, bar, meeting room* ⊟ *AE, DC, MC, V* ⓧ *CP.*

¢ ▦ **Damajuana.** The only property in Mendoza resembling a hostel has rooms for two, four, or six people, with lockers and shared baths. Guests feel at home inside or out: a bar, restaurant, fireplace, and TV are in the living room, and the spacious backyard has a grill and hammocks. The neighborhood—steps away from bars, boutiques, and cafés—is popular with young Mendocinos. ⊠ *Aristedes Villanueva 282, 5500* ☎ *261/ 425–5858* ⊕ *www.damajuanahostel.com.ar* ⇌ *8 rooms* ♻ *Restaurant, outdoor grill and firewood, pool, bar, Internet; no a/c.*

Uspallata

¢–$ ✕ **Lo de Pato.** This casual roadside grill and café serves cafeteria-style lunches and grilled meat and pasta dinners; get yourself a cold drink from the refrigerator. The souvenir shop sells candy bars, postcards, T-shirts, and other mementos. ⊠ *R7* ☎ *264/420–249* ▭ *AE, MC, V.*

$ ▦ **Hotel Uspallata.** Cavernous hallways, minimal decor, barren walls, and dim lighting are legacies of the Perón era, when the government built grand hotels for its employees and cronies. A facelift in 2004 improved the overall appearance somewhat, and the surrounding scenery compensates for the rather dull interior. The grounds and gardens are impressive, the dining room is grand, and the large rooms have closets for a month's stay. ⊠ *R7, Km 1149, 5500* ☎☎ *2624/420–066, Mendoza 261/ 420–4820* ⊕ *www.atahoteleria.com.ar* ⇌ *73 rooms* ♻ *Restaurant, café, pool, bar, bowling and Ping-Pong in the recreation room, travel services* ▭ *No credit cards* |○| *CP.*

$ ▦ **Hotel Valle Andino.** As you drive along R7, this brick building with a pitched tile roof and wood trim looks inviting. Inside you'll find an open, airy living room with places to sit around a woodstove. Outside, a large glass-enclosed swimming pool is surrounded by a lawn big enough for a soccer game. Rooms are modern; some have bunk beds, and all have brick walls and minimalist furniture. ⊠ *R7, 5500* ☎ *2624/420–033* ⊕ *www.hotelguia.com/hoteles/valleandino* ⇌ *26 rooms* ♻ *Restaurant, pool, bar, recreation room* ▭ *AE, MC, V* |○| *CP.*

Potrerillos

$–$$ ▦ **Hotel Potrerillos.** This Spanish-style, stucco- and tile-roofed building overlooks the foothills and is surrounded by lawns, gardens, and sports facilities. Originally built by the government, the public spaces were made to accommodate large groups, but tasteful wooden furnishings and woven rugs give it a more personal appeal. ⊠ *R7, Km 50 (from Mendoza), 5549* ☎ *2624/482–010* ♻ *Restaurant, café, tea shop, bar, pool, tennis, volleyball, meeting room.*

$$ ✕▦ **Hotel Termas Cacheuta.** Stop at this mountain spa for a sauna in a natural grotto, a volcanic mud bath, a hydromassage, and a soak in the large swimming pool filled with water from hot springs. Rooms overlook the lawn and swimming pool. The restaurant's healthy, natural cuisine features vegetables grown on site. Rates include three meals, two thermal baths, and one massage per day; hiking, river rafting, and mountain biking can be arranged. ⊠ *R7, Km 38, Cacheuta, 5500* ☎ *2624/482–082* ✉ *Reservations: Rodríguez Peña 1412, Godoy Cruz, 5501* ☎ *261/431–6085* ⇌ *16 rooms* ♻ *Restaurant, massage, sauna* ▭ *No credit cards* |○| *FAP.*

Parque Provincial Aconcagua

¢ ⊞ **Hostería Puente del Inca.** Vintage photos in the dining room reveal this hostel's history as a mountaineering outpost. Climbers still gear up here before attempting Aconcagua and afterward to relate their adventures. Guides and mules can be arranged. ✉ *R7, Km 175, Puente del Inca* ✉ *Turismo Aymara SRL, 9 de Julio 1023, Mendoza, 5500* ☎ *261/420–2064* ✆ *info@aymara.com.ar* ☞ *82 beds in doubles, 4- to 6-person dorms* ♨ *Dining room* ▤ MC.

VALLE DE UCO

The Valle de Uco extends southwest of Mendoza along the foothills of the Cordón de Plata and the Andes, whose two highest peaks, Tupungato Volcano and El Plata, rise over 580 meters (19,000 feet) on the western horizon. The Tunuyán river in the north and Las Tunas river in the south rush down from the mountains, bringing mineral-rich melted snow from the glaciers to the potato fields, apple and cherry orchards, olive groves, and vineyards planted across this immense valley. Old family ranches that once extended all the way to Chile are being sold off or converted to vineyards in what is now the fastest growing wine area in the country.

The most direct route from Mendoza to the Valle de Uco is south on RN40 to RP86, which branches southwest to San José and joins RP89 from Potrerillos. Driving south through fields of potatoes, almond and chestnut orchards, and vineyards, you arrive at Tupungato (43 km/27 mi), the westernmost town in the region. The wineries of Andeluna, La Azul, Estancia Ancón, and Salentein are along this route. Lurton, Clos de los Siete, and Doña Elvira are situated farther south and east of Tunuyán, in the districts of Los Sauces and Vista Flores. Tunuyán, a town twice the size of Tupungato, can be reached in an hour by driving south from Mendoza across the flat desert on RN40. Farther south, across the Tunuyán River in La Consulta and San Carlos, are more wineries, among them Bodega Aconquija, FAPES, and O'Fournier.

★ To make a grand entrance into the Valle de Uco, begin in the mountain resort town of **Potrerillos** and take RP89 south through the villages of Las Vegas and El Salto, where clusters of vacation cottages brim with flowers in summer and are covered with snow in winter. As the road climbs out of the canyon and over a pass, the great expanse of the Valle de Uco lies before you.

The Wineries

The Valle de Uco is one of the highest wine-growing regions in the world, with approximately 81,000 hectares (200,000 acres) planted at altitudes between 900 meters (3,000 feet) and 1,200 meters (3,900 feet). Cool nights and warm days cause an average temperature range of 14 degrees, allowing grapes to ripen slowly on the vine while developing excellent fruit flavor, good acidity in white wines, and the formation of strong tannins in reds.

Very Valle de Uco

Rustic Beauty. There are no large urban areas here—only the small towns of Tupungato, Tunuyán, and San Carlos. Small inns and ranches offer horseback rides, hiking, asados, wine tours, and the opportunity to interact with the locals.

Unique Terroir. All the big name wineries—Catena, Trapiche, Tapiz, Nieto Senetiner, Pulenta, Chandón, and many others—have planted vineyards in this high-altitude growing region, where grapes ripen slowly and all varieties show tremendous fruit flavors, making the wine from this region unique in character and quality.

Turísmo Rural. From Mendoza to Malargüe, many small ranches and country estates have made room for guests in their spare bedrooms and around their dining tables, where home-cooked (and often home-grown) food is enjoyed in a family atmosphere. Horseback rides on the property or into the mountains are a given, and the opportunity to view wildlife, hike, fish, explore pre-Columbian ruins, participate in ranch chores, or just sit back and enjoy the scenery is all part of the experience. About 10 of these ranches are listed with the tourist offices in Mendoza and Tunuyán.

Wineries in this region vary from traditional family-run operations to ultramodern facilities, and many names long-associated with Argentina's wine industry are building innovative ventures in this exciting region. Wineries tend to be scattered about in infrequently traveled areas, making reservations highly recommended. The easiest way to see the area is to take a tour or stay in a local lodge that offers tours. If you're on your own, be sure to get the **WINEMAP** at local wineries or before you leave Mendoza.

Tupungato

㉔ Andeluna. The collaboration of Ricardo Rutini, a member of one of Argentina's oldest wine-growing families, and international businessman H. Ward Lay, founder of Frito-Lay and former CEO of PepsiCo, is a partnership rich in business acumen and wine-growing tradition. Their vineyards climb the foothills of the Andes from 1,097 to 1,300 meters (3,600 to 4,265 feet), and their bodega utilizes the latest technology. ⊠ *Ruta 89 s/n, Tupungato, Valle de Uco* ⊕ *www.andeluna.com.*

㉓ Bodega Bombal. The first generation of Bombals arrived in Tupungato in 1760 and built their first bodega in 1914, where Lucila Barrionuevo de Bombal produced the family's first wines. Her son, Domingo, developed the vineyards and built a new bodega next to the Château d'Ancón, the family's summer home. Today, his daughter, Lucila Bombal, produces high quality wine and hosts the château's many visitors. ⊠*La Carrera s/n, Tupungato, Valle de Uco* ☎ *2622/488–245* ⊕ *www.estanciancon.com* ☻ *Tues., Thurs., and Fri. 11–5, weekends and holidays 11–6 with reservations.*

㉕ La Azul S.A. Exporters of wine as well as peaches, plums, cherries, and apples, this agro-wine complex's vineyard tours demonstrate the differ-

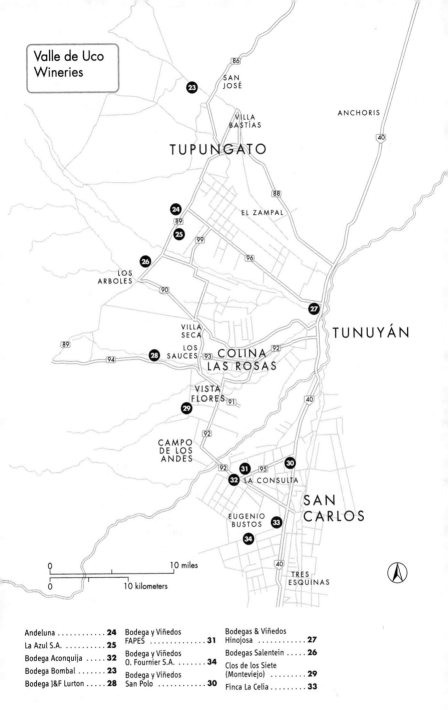

Valle de Uco
Wineries

86

SAN
JOSÉ

23

ANCHORIS

40

VILLA
BASTÍAS

TUPUNGATO

88

24

EL ZAMPAL

89

25

99

96

26

LOS
ARBOLES

90

27

TUNUYÁN

VILLA
SECA

89

LOS
SAUCES 93

COLINA
LAS ROSAS

92

28

94

VISTA
FLORES 91

40

29

92

CAMPO
DE LOS
ANDES

92 31 95

30

32 LA CONSULTA

SAN
CARLOS

EUGENIO
BUSTOS

33

34

0   10 miles

0   10 kilometers

40

TRES
ESQUINAS

ent vine-growing methods used over the centuries. ⊠ *Ruta 89 s/n, Agua Amarga, Tupungato, Valle de Uco* ☎ *2622/423–593* ⊕ *www. bodegalaazul.com* ☉ *Mon.–Fri. 9–5, by reservation only.*

Tunuyán

㉘ Bodega J&F Lurton. Jacques and François Lurton began searching for an Argentine vineyard in 1992. Three years later, they planted their grapes in Vista Flores, where low yields and wide temperature range would ensure premium wines with a defined varietal identity. The arched doorways of the wood and stucco colonial-style winery lead into three functional areas—one for winemaking, one for storage, and one for sales and tastings. Grapes are harvested by hand and carefully selected by experts—including Marco Toriano, who also leads wine tours and directs tastings. Horseback rides in the vineyards are an added attraction. ⊠ *Camino al Manzano, Ruta Provincial 94, Km 21, Vista Flores, Tunuyán, Valle de Uco* ☎ *2622/492–078, 261/424–8400 for tastings and lunch* ⊕ *www.bodegalurton.com* ☉ *Weekdays 10–5, res. only.*

㉗ Bodegas & Viñedos Hinojosa. Don Silvestre Hinojosa established the first winery in the Alto Valle de Uco (High Uco Valley) in 1960. Today, the third generation of his family is crafting wine in an area where wide temperature variations ensure big fruit concentration and deep color in their reds and fine acidity in their chardonnay. Award-winning Tempranillo is one of their many successes. ⊠ *San Martín 1942, Tunuyán, Valle de Uco* ☎ *2622/422–335, reservations: 2622/1566–6930* ⊕ *www. bodegahinojosa.com* ☉ *Weekdays 9–1, 3:30–6, weekends noon–3:30.*

㉖ Bodegas Salentein. Set on a knoll with the dramatic backdrop of the Andes, this ultra-modern winery is built in the shape of a cross. Each of its four arms operate as separate wineries with two divisions: one at ground level housing stainless steel tanks and one below ground where wine matures in oak barrels. These four wineries meet at a circular atrium where visitors are greeted and tastings, sales, and large events occur. Meanwhile, bottling and labeling take place underground. ⊠ *Ruta 89 y Videla, Tunuyán, Valle de Uco* ☎ *2622/429–000* ⊕ *www.bodegassalentein. com* ☉ *Daily 10–4.*

★ ㉙ Clos de los Siete. Seven partners share this Vistalba land in equal parts, each one choosing his grape variety. The grapes mature at different times because they're planted at different altitudes (this prolongs the harvest over five weeks). Of the three wineries here, only **Monteviejo** is open for public tours. Glass elevators transport visitors to the rooftop for a view of the white peaks of the Cordón de Plata and the vineyards, where you can take a 40-minute tour with an oenologist. The winery's glass walls reveal its inner workings. High-end wine tastings are charged by the bottle and can be shared. Wine books, the **WINEMAP,** and Michel Rolland's *Wines of Argentina* are sold in the wine shop. ⊠ *Clodomiro Silva s/n, Vista Flores, Tunuyán, Valle de Uco* ☎ *2622/ 422–054* ⊕ *www.monteviejo.com* ☉ *Weekdays 9–noon hourly, and at 2 and 5* PM *with 2 days prior res. by email.*

San Carlos

㉜ Bodega Aconquija. Handmade labels and dedication to quality characterize this boutique winery where only 80,000 bottles are produced annually. Aconquija means "snow near the moon"—an apt description, given the location of their vineyards. Blessed with sandy soil and wide temperature variation, grapes ripen slowly on the meticulously pruned 30-year-old vines. Their fruity Syrah and Rosé blend is interesting. ✉ *España 1094, La Consulta* ☎ *2622/470–379* ⊕ *www.aconquija. com* ⊗ *Weekdays 9–noon, 4–6 with reservations.*

⑪ Bodega & Viñedos FAPES. Since 1920, the same pioneer Argentine family has continued to improve this venerable winery's facilities. In 2004, one cave was reconstructed to receive visitors. Another was reopened to store wine for the FAPES Wine Club, whose members enjoy having their own bodega inside the bodega. ✉ *San Martín 701, La Consulta, San Carlos* ☎ *2622/470–262* ⊕ *fapes.com.ar* ⊗ *By reservation only.*

㉞ Bodega y Viñedos O. Fournier S.A. As you approach this winery on a lonely dirt road, it looks like a flying saucer has landed in the middle of a vineyard. Using modern technology and both local and international expertise, the Spanish Ortega Gil-Fournier family aims to produce the highest quality wines. Grapes are planted in rocky, sandy soil on three estates at 1,200 meters (3,950 feet) altitude, producing reds with intense color and strong tannins. Tours with an oenologist and lunch are available by appointment. There is a small charge for tasting. ✉ *Los Indios s/n, La Consulta, San Carlos* ☎ *2622/451–579* ⊕ *www.ofournier.com* ⊗ *By reservation only.*

㉚ Bodega y Viñedos San Polo. Juan Giol, Pascual Toso, and Bautista Gargantini were 19th-century Argentine wine pioneers. Giol acquired this bodega in 1915, and in the 1930s, his son and Eleanora Garantini renovated and planted vineyards on some of the best land in Mendoza. Four generations later, Juan Carlos Giol and Clotilde Toso continue this legacy of viniculture. Dedicated agriculturalists, they also grow cherries, peaches, apples, pears, plums, and garlic. ✉ *San Martín s/n, La Consulta, San Carlos* ☎ *2622/471–200* ⊕ *www.sanpolo.com.ar* ⊗ *By reservation only.*

㉝ Finca La Celia. Eugenio Bustos built this winery in 1890, and it flourished under his daughter Celia's leadership, producing an excellent Malbec. CCU, a Chilean company, now owns the winery and has invested in the latest technology and winemaking techniques. ✉ *Circunvalación s/n, San Carlos* ☎ *2622/451–012* ⊕ *www.fincalacelia.com.ar* ⊗ *By reservation only.*

Other Sights & Activities

Tupungato Volcano. The snow-covered cone of Tupungato Volcano (6,798 meters/22,304 feet) looms above the high peaks that march across the western horizon. Tour companies lead horseback rides and hikes into Tupungato Provincial Park, and mules can be hired to climb to South Glacier at 2,000 meters (6,560 feet).

Corredor Productivo (RP89) is the route from Mendoza to Tupungato that enters the valley from the north; it is lined with almond and chestnut trees, fields of potatoes, and vineyards. In spring (late September/October), cherry trees blossom across fields and along country roads.

Manzano Histórico, 40 km (25 mi) west of Tunuyán, is the site of an historic apple tree where General San Martín stayed on his return from liberating Chile in 1823. You can follow his hoof prints over the Andes with local outfitters.

Sports & the Outdoors

Horseback riding. Trips can be arranged into the high mountains above the valley or over the Andes to Chile through lodging facilities and ranches in the area, as well as tour companies in Mendoza. You can stay at **El Puesto R Labat** near Manzano Historico and ride to the foot of Tupugato or over the Andes to Chile with Raul Labat (☎ 261/496–0981). **Estancia Rancho'e Cuero,** near Tupungato, also offers ranch stays with riding, hiking, fishing, and excursions into the mountains to view condors and guanacos, as well as a trans-Andean horse/trek (☎ 261/496–4042 ⊕ ranchoecuero.com.ar). Also check out **Estancia San Pablo,** a family ranch that extends to the Chilean border. Cattle drives, fly-fishing on the premises, mountain biking, and day- or weeklong rides are some of the activities (☎🖶 2622/1567–1787 ⊕ www.estanciasanpablo.com.ar).

Where to Stay & Eat

Tunuyán

★ **$$** ✕ **Postales del Plata Valle de Uco Lodge.** Allow time for a long lunch or dinner at this country lodge, where you can enjoy local wines paired with fresh local ingredients expertly prepared in a mud oven or on a grill by the pool. On weekends, folklore groups, tango or local guitarists entertain guests. ✉ *Calle Tabanera, 400 meters (1,200 ft) from Corredor Productivo, Colonia de Las Rosas, Tunuyán* ☎ *2622/490–024* ⊕ *www.postalesdelplata.com* ⊟ *AE, MC, V.*

Tupungato

$$ ✕ **Restaurante Valle de Tupungato.** Traditional grilled meats, homemade pastas, and a table full of appetizers featuring locally made cold cuts are hearty fare at this friendly family-style restaurant. On Fridays, you can help yourself to steak, lamb, chicken, and goat at the open grill. Crowds of locals show up on weekends, overflowing onto the Astroturf lawn. ✉ *Belgrano 542* ☎ *2622/488–421* ⊟ *MC, V.*

$ ✕🖼 **Don Romulo.** Don Romulo is the president of the local Gaucho Association. His sons run this hotel and restaurant with warmth and enthusiasm and organize horseback rides, hikes, 4x4 excursions, and visits to wineries. Rooms are clean and basic, and the food is pure *criollo* (country cooking): empanadas, grilled meat, sausages, and salads. On weekends, lamb, goat, and beef are cooked out back on the *asador*. ✉ *Almirante Brown 1200* ☎🖶 *2622/489–020* ⊕ *www.donromulo.com. ar* ⮑ *10 rooms* ⌂ *Restaurant, travel services; no a/c, no room phones* ⊟ *No credit cards.*

$$$$ 🖼 **Château d'Ancón.** As you enter, curved oak doors open onto marble halls filled with antiques, statues, paintings, tapestries, and family photographs. You can taste estate-bottled wine in the English pub and dine in an exquisite room furnished with Bombal family antiques shipped from Europe in 1933. Lucy Bombal, the granddaughter of the original owners, entertains guests with stories of her family's history. This place isn't cheap, but the price includes all meals, tea, cocktails, a wine-tasting, a 4x4 vineyard tour, and a horseback ride. Children under 10 are not permitted. ✉ *R89, 2 km (1 mi) west of the village of San José and R86* ☎ *261/4235–8455 in Mendoza, 2622/488–245 in Tupungato*

⊕ *www.estanciancon.com* ➾ *6 rooms* ⚤ *Pool, horseback riding* ▭ *No credit cards* ◷ *Closed mid-May–mid-Oct.* ⫼⨀⫼ *FAP.*

$$$$ ✕⊞ **Postales del Plata/Valle de Uco Lodge.** If wine touring is all about good wine, good food, beautiful surroundings and sharing it all with like-minded people; this cozy lodge has it all. Located on a quiet country road, the low mission-style buildings look across vineyards to the lofty peaks of the Andes. Modern rooms have puffy white down comforters and soft beige walls. On the patio and around the pool, guests enjoy asados, evening folklore shows, and tasting local wine from the well-stocked cellar. Rivers to Reefs, the tour company that owns this hotel, can arrange custom wine tours with oenologists and other activities, including skiing at Las Leñas. ✉ *Calle Tabanera, 400 meters from Corredor Productivo, Colonia de Las Rosas, Tunuyán* ☎ *2622/490–024* ⊕ *www.postalesdelplata.com* ➾ *11 rooms* ⚤ *Restaurant, pool, bar, library/lounge, airport shuttle (fee)* ▭ *AE, MC, V* ⫼⨀⫼ *CP.*

$$$$ ⊞ **Posada Salentein.** Fifteen kilometers (9 mi) south of Tupungato on RN94, this posada is close to the ultra-modern Bodega Salentein and other wineries in the Valle de Uco. Formerly an adobe farm house, the inn is shaded by ancient chestnut trees and has pleasant pastel rooms that open onto a veranda overlooking the vineyards and the mountains. ✉ *Ruta 89, corner Elias Videla, Los Arboles, Tupungato* ☎ *2622/424722, reservations 261/423–8514* ⊕ *www.salenteintourism.com* ➾ *6 rooms, 1 cottage* ⚤ *Dining room, bicycles, horseback riding, pool* ▭ *AE, V* ⫼⨀⫼ *FAP.*

SAN RAFAEL

Southern Mendoza would be a vast territory of flat, arid plains, if it were not for the Atuel and Diamante rivers. Instead, numerous dams and acres of irrigated land have created vigorous agro-industrial oases in the departments of San Rafael (240 km [150 mi] south of Mendoza) and General Alvear (90 km [56 mi] southeast of San Rafael). In 1805, San Rafael was a fort, defending the early settlers from Indian raids—it wasn't until 1922 that it became a city. San Rafael is now the second-largest city in Mendoza Province, but its wide avenues lined with leafy sycamores and tall poplars fed by streetside canals give it a bucolic charm.

Avenida Hipólito Irigoyen crosses the downtown area north–south, dividing it into two sections: the east side around the Plaza San Martín is more traditional, the west side newer and more residential. Shops and restaurants are found in the center of town where Avenida Bartolomé Mitre meets Hipólito Yrigoyen at the intersection with Avenida San Martín. Note that siesta time lasts from lunch until 4:30.

The Wineries

San Rafael is one of the smallest regions in the country to claim a *Denominacióon de Origen* (D.O.C.). This is a point of pride for local vintners, but the quality of wine produced in this area can speak for itself. After the area was made safe from Indian raids in 1879, immigrants from Italy, Switzerland, and France brought their advanced viticultural skills

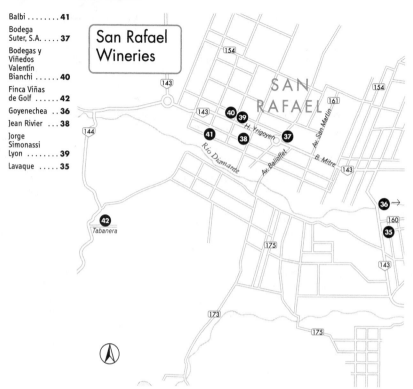

San Rafael
Wineries

and new grape varieties to this frontier region. When the railroad arrived in 1803, the fledgling wine industry was connected to Buenos Aires and the rest of the world.

San Rafael has a near perfect climate, low humidity, cold/dry winters, ample temperature variation, just enough rainfall, and plenty of water from the Diamante and Ateul rivers. But into every vineyard a little rain must fall—and when it comes in the form of hail (*granizo*), it can be devastating, destroying this year's crop and next year's tiny buds in one short shower. Most vineyards now protect their crops with expensive heavy netting that lets the water drip through and shades the grapes, aiding ripening.

Most of the wineries in this region are family-owned; consequently, the owners are busy in the vineyard, working in the bodega, testing wine with the oenologist, or tending to customers. Therefore, it is a courtesy to make an appointment. Signs are scarce, although the municipality is working to correct that. Pick up a **WINEMAP** from the airport, or get a copy at a wine shop, winery, or bookstore—this set of Mendoza Province maps has the best San Rafael city plan.

41 Balbi. Founded in 1930 by Juan Balbi and now owned by Allied Domecq, this winery has a reputation for making a French Bordeaux–style wine. Changes in winemaking techniques seem to be moving their wine toward a more readily drinkable style, as they blend grapes from the Valle de Uco and San Rafael. ⊠ *BA, Jensen & Sarmiento, Las Paredes, San Rafael* ☎ *2627/430–027* ☉ *By reservation only.*

37 Bodega Suter, S.A. In 1900 the Suter family journeyed to Argentina from Switzerland and planted the first Riesling variety in the country. Today, the fourth generation of the family continues to produce fine white wines, Malbec, Cabernet Sauvignon, and Spumante. A tour through this spotless showcase winery leads you through a labyrinth of underground caves filled with huge oak casks—used more to evoke atmosphere than to store wine. ⊠ *Hipólito Yrigoyen 2850, near the airport, El Toledano, San Rafael* ☎ *2627/421–076* ☉ *Mon.–Sat. 9–6.*

40 Bodegas y Viñedos Valentín Bianchi. Valentín Bianchi came to Argentina from Italy in 1910 and threw himself into a variety of endeavors until 1928, when he realized his dream of owning a winery and a vineyard. He struggled until 1934, when one of his fine wines won a gold medal in Mendoza and high praise in Buenos Aires. His legacy of hard work continues at this bodega, known as "La champañera" (the sparkling wine house). Built on a hilltop in the style of a Roman villa, its colonnaded entrance looks out over formal gardens, a reflecting pool, fountains, and the vineyards. ⊠ *Ruta 143 and Calle El Salto, Las Paredes, San Rafael* ☎ *2627/435–600* ⊕ *www.vbianchi.com* ☉ *Daily 9–12:30, 3–6.*

42 Finca Viñas de Golf. When Ricardo Jurado, son of famous Argentine golf pro José Jurado, was invited to San Rafael to consult on a golf course, he fell in love with the region and bought a small vineyard planted with Bonarda and Malbec. Over the years he has expanded and added more varietals. Today his son Ricky is president of this family enterprise, overseeing the wine production, wine tours, and the construction of a nine-room guest house. The 9-hole golf course, cooled by water canals and shady willows, looks out on the Sierra Pintada mountain range. ⊠ *Tabanera and Zanjón Los Inquilinos, Cuadro Benegas, San Rafael* ☎ *627/ 487–026* ⊕ *www.vinasdelgolf.com.ar.*

★ 36 Goyenechea. One of the country's oldest wineries, Goyenechea was founded in 1868 by a Basque immigrant family who had the foresight to build not only a solid brick winery, but also 60 houses for the working families, a school for their children, a repair shop, and a chapel. Today fifth-generation families live in the houses, and the school still rings with the laughter of their children. As you pass through the arched caves where wine ages in bottles, you can see the *piletas,* huge cement vats that held 8,976 gallons of wine when the industry was focused on quantity, not quality. English-speaking family members often lead tours, and visitors are sometimes invited for wine tastings and snacks next door on the family's patio. ⊠ *Sotero Arizú s/n, Villa Atuel* ☎ *2625/470–005* ⊕ *www.goyenechea. com* ☉ *Weekdays 8–noon, 3–6, weekends and holidays by reservation.*

38 Jean Rivier. The Swiss-French brothers who own this winery produce a limited quantity of quality wines from their own grapes. Tours of their spotless winery include crushing, fermentation, and tasting. ⊠ *Hilólito Yrigoyen 2385, Rama Caída, San Rafael* ☎ *2672/432–676* ⊕ *www. jeanrivier.com* ☉ *Mon.–Fri. 8–11, 3–6, Sat. 8–11.*

39 Jorge Simonassi Lyon. This small, old-fashioned bodega warmly guides visitors through the process of winemaking from grape to glass. A lovely house on the premises can occasionally be rented. Jorge's knowledge of growing grapes and blending wines was passed down to him from his Asti ancestors in northern Italy. ⊠ *Ruta Nacional 143, Km 657, Rama Caída, San Rafael* ☎ *2627/436–076* ⊕ *www.bodegasimonassi.com.ar.*

 Lavaque. The Italo-French Lavaque family planted their first vineyards in Cafayate, Salta in 1870. Their sons and grandsons carry on the tradition in San Rafael; their long white stucco and terra-cotta Spanish winery houses an aesthetically designed interior with Spanish tiles and adobe walls. ⊠ *Ruta 165, Cañada Seca, San Rafael* ☎☎ *2627/497–044* ⊕ *www.vinasdealtura.com* ☉ *Mon.–Fri. 7:30-4:30 by appointment only. Reservations by e-mail or fax only.*

Other Sights & Activities

Cañón del Atuel. The 160-km (102-mi) Atuel Canyon loop begins about 24 km (15 mi) from town on R173, where it enters a canyon and follows the Río Atuel as it descends between sandstone cliffs, creating natural swimming holes, sheltered picnic spots, and campsites. Along the way, small hotels, cottages, and campgrounds offer escape from the hot city, and shops rent rafting and kayaking equipment and arrange guided trips. The road continues up to Lago Valle Grande (Valle Grande Lake) and passes a series of dams before descending into a labyrinth of red, brown, and gray sandstone rock formations. Unfortunately, the river then disappears underground—sacrificed for hydroelectric power.

Malargüe. The small town of Malargüe was populated by the Pehuenche until the Spanish arrived in 1551. They were followed by ranchers, miners, and petroleum companies. In 1981 an airport was built to accommodate skiers headed for the nearby Las Leñas ski area, and since then Malargüe has made strides toward becoming a year-round adventure-tourism center. If you choose to drive to Malargüe, head south for 193 km (120 mi) on R40 from San Rafael and turn south on R101 at El Sosneado. A well-equipped and informative tourist office is on your right as you enter town.

Las Leñas. Located 70 km (43 mi) from Malargüe and 200 km (124 mi) south of San Rafael, Las Leñas is the largest ski area served by lifts in the western hemisphere—bigger than Whistler/Blackcomb in British Columbia, and larger than Vail and Snowbird combined. From the top (3,429 meters [11,250 feet]), a treeless lunar landscape of lonely white peaks extends in every direction. Numerous long runs (the longest is 8 km [5 mi]) extend over the 10,000 acres of skiable terrain. There are steep, scary, 610-meter (2,000-foot) vertical chutes for experts; machine-packed routes for beginners; and plenty of intermediate terrain in between. The area is ideal for off-piste (backcountry) skiing, and Fernando Passano, an expert ski mountaineer, has initiated a program called **Extreme Expedition.** With trained guides and avalanche experts, good intermediate skiers to experts can experience the thrill of skiing on untracked slopes.

The ski season runs from June through October. Most South Americans take their vacation in July, the month to avoid if you don't like crowds and higher prices, although the weather is generally more benign. August has the most reliable snow conditions, September the most varied. Prices for lifts and lodging are lowest from mid-June to early July and from mid-September to early October; rates are highest from mid- to late July.

The area has suffered bankruptcies, absentee owners (the banks), and several management teams. Accommodations range from dormy houses and apart-hotels—some in dismal states of disrepair—to super-deluxe hotels with indoor/outdoor pools, nice restaurants, bars, casinos, and a ski concierge. Unfortunately, the hotels are owned by tour operators, and you have to go through them to make a reservation. Travel offices in Buenos Aires, Mendoza, and San Rafael sell ski packages, which include lift tickets, equipment, and, in some cases, transportation—which may involve a combination of bus rides and charter flights. Commercial flights from San Rafael or Mendoza are another option. ⊠ *Las Leñas S.A. Cerrito 1186, fl. 8, Buenos Aires* 🕾 *11/4819–6000 in Buenos Aires* ⊕ *www.laslenas.com.*

Where to Stay & Eat

San Rafael

$–$$ ✕ **Cabaña Dos Amigos.** At this restaurant 6 km (4 mi) from town, the owner-chef greets you at the door and starts you off with bowls of appetizers, followed by salad, homemade prosciutto with melon, empanadas, grilled chorizo, and your choice of meat. ⊠ *Off R143* 🕾 *2627/ 441–017* ⊟ *No credit cards* ۞ *Closed Mon. No dinner Sun.*

$ ✕ **A Mi Manera.** Two tall doors open into this colonial-era building where the Spanish Club has met since 1910. With its 18-foot ceilings, soft gold tones, wood trim, and Spanish *escudos* (emblems of Spanish and Argentine provinces) on the walls, the restaurant is very traditional. So is the food: roasted and grilled meats, marinated vegetables, pasta, and paella. ⊠ *Comandante Salas 199 and Colonel Day* 🕾 *2627/423– 597* ⊟ *AE, DC, MC, V.*

¢–$ ✕ **Friends.** This popular local café is good for a coffee or a light lunch. Try the *barroluco* sandwich: steak, ham, cheese, and tomato pressed between thin slices of white bread. ⊠ *H. Yrigoyen and San Martín* 🕾 *No phone* ⊟ *No credit cards.*

$$$$ 🏨 **Finca los Alamos.** When this 150-year-old estancia was established by the great-grandparents of César and Camilo Aldao Bombal in 1830, San Rafael was still a fort. The ranch house is filled with an eclectic collection from around the world, and many of Argentina's foremost writers (including Jorge Luis Borges) and artists have stayed here; they left their paintings on walls and their poetry in books scattered around the premises. Here, guests dine with the owners, and a fireplace glows in every room on cool nights. Prices include all meals, plus tea on the veranda, an open bar, and wine from the family's 100-year-old vineyard. Horses are available for an extra charge. ⊠ *Bombal (R146), 10 km (6 mi) from town* 🕾 *Box 125, 5600* 🕾🕾 *2627/442–350* ➲ *7 rooms* ♿ *Dining room, pool, horseback riding, bar* ⊟ *No credit cards* ۩ *FAP* ⊕ *www. fincalosalamos.com.*

$$ 🏨 **Hotel Tower Inn and Suites.** This is the newest hotel in town, with spacious rooms that have plenty of shelves, big mirrors, picture windows, and views of distant mountains. In the summer, meals are served outside accompanied by live music. The hotel also arranges wine tours, and tour operator Mendoza Viajes has an office next door. ⊠ *H. Irigoyen 744, 5600* ☏ *2627/427–190* ⊕ *www.towersanrafael.com* ⌁ *89 rooms, 6 suites* ⌂ *Restaurant, pool, business center, meeting rooms, Wi-Fi in public areas, spa, gym, Jacuzzi, olive oil massage, bar* ☰ *AE, DC, MC, V.*

$$ ⊡ **Microtel Inn & Suites, Malargüe.** A large lobby with casual furniture, a fireplace, and a sitting room gives this small hotel a homey feel. The large restaurant's wine list is longer than the menu, and in summer, they have backyard barbecues. Modern rooms have cheery yellow walls and large windows. Don't forget to arrange for your 50% discount on lift tickets if you're skiing at Las Leñas. ⊠ *RN40 Norte, Malargüe 5613* ☏ *2627/472–300* ⊕ *www.microyel-malargue.com.ar* ⌁ *29 rooms, 4 suites* ⌂ *Restaurant, outdoor grill, garage, sauna, lobby bar, small glass-enclosed pool* ⍩⎮ *CP.*

$ ⊡ **Hotel San Rafael.** Just off busy Avenida San Martín, this basic hotel has views of the mountains and vineyards from the top floor, where it's quietest. The second floor pool and café are new additions, but the pedestrian decor and pictureless walls can make the adequate rooms seem a bit dreary. ⊠ *Colonel Day 30, 5600* ☏☏ *2627/430–125* ⊕ *www. sanrafaelhotel.com.ar* ⌁ *60 rooms* ⌂ *Café, minibars, free parking* ☰ *AE, DC, MC, V* ⍩⎮ *CP.*

Las Leñas

The village at the ski area has six full-service hotels, eight apart-hotels (condominium complexes), and four *dormy* houses with small rooms and kitchenettes. Shuttle buses run between lifts, hotels, restaurants, and shops. Hotels in Malargüe, 70 km (44 mi) from Las Leñas, offer 50% discounts on lift tickets, and the hot-springs resort town of Los Molles, 19 km (12 mi) away, offers less-expensive lodging options. Both towns offer bus service to and from the ski area. Day-trippers can lunch slope-side at the central El Brasero (cafeteria by day, grill at night), hotel restaurants, or the Pirámide shopping center. Hotel reservations must be made through tour operators.

$$$$ ⊡ **Aries.** This slope-side luxury hotel has plenty of diversions for stormy days: a space for children's games and activities; a piano bar in the lobby; a wine bar serving cheese and regional smoked meats; and a movie theater. Rooms are spacious and have large windows overlooking the slopes. Reservations must be made through **Hotel Club de la Nieve.** ⊠ *Las Leñas Ski Area* ☏ *Reservations: 11/4315–2067* ⌁ *72 rooms, 5 suites* ⌂ *2 restaurants, indoor pool, hot tub, massage, sauna, spa, ski shop, 2 bars, pub, cinema, recreation room, shop, children's programs (ages 1–12), travel services* ☰ *AE, DC, MC, V* ⍩⎮ *MAP.*

$$$$ ⊡ **Escorpio.** This small, intimate ski lodge is right on the slopes. Watch the action from the terrace while having lunch or taking a break, or hit the cozy piano bar for après-ski board games with tea or cocktails. A movie lounge for families is nearby. Many rooms have balconies and views of the mountains. Reservations must be made through **Badino.** ⊠ *Las Leñas ski area* ☏ *Reservations: 11/5238–2100* ⌁ *47 rooms, 1* *suite, 2 apartments ⚲ Restaurant, drugstore, kids' club, bar, movie lounge, ski-lift from slope to hotel ≡ AE, DC, MC, V* ⦿ *MAP.*

$$$$ ▦ **Piscis.** This deluxe hotel pampers its guests with spa services, ski equipment delivery, and a large indoor-outdoor pool. They have supervised indoor play activities for kids as well as ski instruction for all levels. Complimentary hot wine and hot chocolate are served in the afternoon. Reservations must be made through **Badino.** ⊠ *At Las Leñas ski resort* ☎ *Reservations: 11/5238–2100* ⬎ *90 rooms* ⚲ *2 restaurants, indoor-outdoor pool, gym, hair salon, hot tub, sauna, 3 bars, casino, recreation room, shop, babysitting, Internet, airport shuttle ≡ AE, DC, MC, V* ⦿ *MAP.*

SAN JUAN

In the Tulum Valley in the foothills of the Andes, the city of San Juan lies in an oasis of orchards and vineyards, surrounded by the Andes to the west and monotonous desert in every other direction. The shady streets and plazas of this easygoing agricultural town offer refuge, and the city is cooled by Spanish-built canals that still run beneath the streets. People work hard in the fields during the day, take long siestas in the afternoon, and head back to the fields until sundown. Be sure to venture north to the small villages of Barreal, Calingasta, Jachal—or head into the mountains on foot, horseback, or 4x4—where you'll be rewarded with huge valleys, mountains, and river gorges unspoiled by human presence.

Located 167 km (104 mi) northeast of Mendoza via R40, San Juan was founded in 1562 as part of the Chilean viceroyalty. On January 18, 1817, General José de San Martín gathered his army of 16,000 men in the town's plaza and set out on his historic 21-day march over the Andes to Chile, where he defeated the royalist army at the battles of Chacabuco and Maipú. A 1944 earthquake destroyed San Juan (but helped to establish Juan Perón as a national figure through his relief efforts, which won him much popularity). The low-rise buildings, tree-lined plazas, and pedestrian walkways you see today are the results of reconstruction.

The Wineries

San Juan has been producing wine since 1569, but wine tourism is a new concept. As a result, groups, tours, and individuals are often greeted by the owner or a member of the family. Friendly *San Juaninos* enjoy sharing their history and knowledge with visitors, and their wine tours are fresh and spontaneous. In 2004, the government tourist office and guide association formed a commission to evaluate wineries for membership in the *Ruta del Vino de San Juan*. Members guarantee knowledgeable personnel, tasting rooms, public restrooms, and reasonable hours of attendance. Eight wineries joined, and their helpful booklet with maps is available at the tourist office.

Graffigna and other major wineries first put down roots in San Juan in the 1890s. Production increased, and wineries began offering varieties other than the sweet white table wines, sherries, and ports that the area was known for. Then, two devastating earthquakes—one in 1944, one

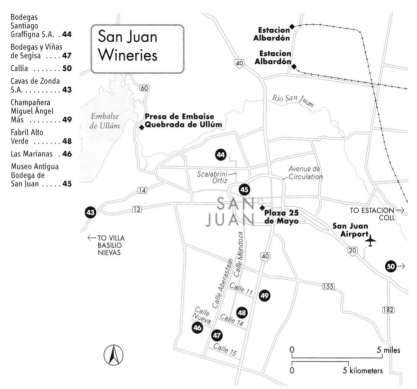

in 1977—destroyed the city, killing thousands, leveling homes, and ruining the wineries and their storage tanks.

It's hard to imagine this destruction if you visit the area today. Although San Juan wineries have been slower than the rest of the country to make the shift from quantity to quality, some 160 wineries have converted (or are converting) from producing bulk wine, and a new generation of oenologists and vintners is taking the lead. The province produces more wine than Napa and Sonoma combined, and you'll likely find the fine Cabernets, Bonardas, and Syrahs—as well as the whites and sparkling wines—of San Juan on the world's wine lists in short order.

The Ullum, Tullum, and Zonda valleys are the principal wine growing areas close to the city, and the San Juan River flows down from the mountains into 2,000 km (1,242 mi) of canals to irrigate about 120,000 acres of vineyards. Other wine-growing areas include El Perdenal, southeast near the Mendoza border, and Jachal, to the north.

🄴 **Bodegas Santiago Graffigna S.A.** Italian wine expert Don Santiago Graffigna founded this winery in 1870 and planted Tulum Valley's first vines. You can learn the history of his family and their vineyard in the excellent museum on the premises. Today, the company is owned by Allied Domecq, and grapes arrive at the winery from vineyards in many different valleys. An enormous barrel serves as a sitting area in the tasting room. ⊠ *Colón 1342 Norte, Desamparados, San Juan* ☎ *264/421–4227* ⊙ *Thurs.–Sat. 9–8, Sun. 10–8.*

㊼ Bodegas y Viñas de Segisa. The original stucco building constructed in 1906 was destroyed by earthquakes and abandoned. In 1995, the present owners resurrected what they could and built a new, anti-seismic facility, using the traditional high ceiling of bamboo canes held in place by crossed timbers, and thick brick walls and floors. Tours are conducted by the enthusiastic owners or the oenologist. ⊠ *Aberastain and Calle 15, La Rinconada, Pocito, San Juan* ☎ *264/492–2000* ⊕ *www.saxsegisa. com.ar* ⊙ *Daily 10–8.*

㊿ Callia. Located in a hot, dry, wide open valley with miles of new vineyards planted in every direction, this winery looks modern, but inside its superstructure is an old bodega with all new equipment. It is owned by Salentein, a Dutch company that also makes wine in the Valle de Uco. ⊠ *Pozo de los Algarrobos, Caucete, San Juan, 35 km (21 mi) from town* ☎ *264/423–6632* ⊕ *www.bodegascallia.com.*

㊸ Cavas de Zonda S.A. This winery is not on the "Caminos del Vino," but it should be; it is a temple. As you enter, a Gregorian chant echoes through the whitewashed chambers, creating a sense of drama. Storage, winemaking, bottling, and tasting all take place in a labyrinth of caves, allegedly carved out of the mountain by Yugoslav prisoners in 1932. Outside, a large park is an ideal place to enjoy a picnic lunch with a newly purchased bottle—a good idea, since the winery is farthest from town. ⊠ *Ruta Provincial 12, Km 15, Rivadavia, San Juan* ☎ *264/494–5144* ⊙ *Weekdays 9–5:30, weekends 11–5.*

㊾ Champañera Miguel Ángel Más. There's a lot going on at this small, unassuming little winery. There isn't a fancy tour, but workers will stop to show you how they make sparkling wine, turning the bottles slowly on the many racks. Everything is certified organic—from the wine to the garlic and tomatoes that grow out back. ⊠ *Calle 11 s/n, 300 meters east of RN40, Pocito San Juan* ☎ *264/422–5807* ⊙ *Daily 10–5.*

㊽ Fabril Alto Verde. Grapes from this spotless green winery are grown organically, and the wine and Spumante are stabilized without preservatives or additives. Internationally certified as organic, the wines are made in small quantities, and a great deal of care and control go into producing the best product. ⊠ *Ruta Nacional 40 between Calles 13 y 14, Pocito San Juan* ☎ *264/492–1905* ⊙ *Mon.–Sat. 9–6, Sun. 10–6.*

㊻ Las Marianas. Founded in 1922, this winery is a fusion of tradition and technology. Gold adobe walls, arched doorways, and wine casks filled with flowers give it an old Spanish air, but inside everything is state-of-the-art. Lots of personal care goes into irrigation, growing the grapes on *espalderas altos* (espaliers) or *parrales* (trellises), selecting grapes on the vine, hand harvesting, and hand crushing. The owner leads tours, and there's a small museum in the tasting room. ⊠ *Calle Nueva s/n, La Rinconada, Pocito, San Juan* ☎ *264/423–1191* ⊕ *bodegalasmarianas. com.ar* ⊙ *Daily 10–12:30, 4–8.*

㊺ Museo Antigua Bodega de San Juan. At this landmark bodega (founded in 1929), great cement wine storage tubs are exposed in a cavernous old building that survived three earthquakes and now functions as a winemaking museum. Another old building is a gallery displaying local artists' work, and there is a lovely garden in back. Wine and Spumante from the winery is served in the garden or at a wine bar in the front room. ✉ *Salta 782 Norte, Capital, San Juan* ☎ *264/421–6160* ⊙ *Daily 10–6.*

Other Sights & Activities

Casa Natal de Sarmiento. The Sarmiento Birthplace was home to Domingo Faustino Sarmiento (1811–88), known in Argentina as the Father of Education (he believed that public education was the right of every citizen). A prolific writer, Sarmiento was also a skilled diplomat and became senator of San Juan province in 1857, governor in 1862, and eventually president of the nation from 1869 to 1874. During this time, he passed laws establishing public education in Argentina. ✉ *Sarmiento 21 Sur* ☎ *264/421–0004* 🗈 *$1, Sun. free* ⊙ *Dec.–June, Tues.–Thurs. and Sun. 8–1 and 3–8, Mon. and Sat. 8–1; July–Nov., Tues.–Fri. and Sun. 9–7, Mon. and Sat. 9–2.*

Presa de Embalse Quebrada de Ullum. The Ullum Valley Dam Reservoir, 15 km (9 mi) from town, is a huge hydroelectric complex with grand views of the Río San Juan. Windsurfing, sailing, swimming, rowing, fishing, and diving keep San Juaninos cool on hot summer days. You can rent boating equipment at the Bahía Las Tablas sports complex, just beyond the dam, where there are a café and change cabins. There's a public beach at the Embarcadero turnoff. You can white-water raft and kayak in the San Juan, Los Patos, and Jachal rivers. Fishing in Las Hornillas River can be arranged through local tour companies.

Barreal. You'll encounter a landscape of high mountain ranges, wild rivers, and deep gorges on your way to the village of Barreal, whether you drive 136 km (84½ mi) west from San Juan on R12 or you head 133 km (82½ mi) north of Uspallata on R39. The narrow road from San Juan winds up 1,800 hairpin turns to dizzying precipices above the San Juan River gorge. Violent floods roaring down the barren mountainsides can do major damage to this road (and anyone on it). The road is open westbound to Calingasta Sunday to Friday 4 AM–1 PM and Saturday until 2:30 PM; you can travel eastbound to San Juan Sunday to Friday 4 PM–8 PM and Saturday 4:30 PM–8 PM. Check with police at either end for changes, fill your tank, and bring a picnic lunch. Be sure to consult the tourist office for an update on the plans to dam the river gorge.

Beyond the tunnel of trees that cover the streets of Barreal lie orchards, vineyards, and fields of mint, lavender, and anise. Using Barreal as your headquarters, you can mountain bike, horseback ride, hike, climb, or drive a 4x4 east into the Sierra Tontal, where at 3,999 meters (13,120 feet) you can see the highest range of the Andes, including Aconcagua (6,957 meters [22,825 feet]) and Mercedario (6,768 meters [22,205 feet]).

Reserva Natural El Leoncito. Twenty-two kilometers (13½ mi) south on R412 toward Uspallata, a dirt road turns off into the Little Lion Natural Reserve, a vast, rocky area with little vegetation. Follow this road for 17 km (10½ mi) to the observatory, known for its exceptional stargazing on dark and cloudless nights. Near the turnoff, on the western side of R412 at Pampa Leoncito, the sport of *carrovelismo* (sand-surfing) is practiced in wheeled sand cars called wind yachts that sail at 150 kph (93 mph) across a windy expanse of white sand.

Where to Stay & Eat

San Juan

$$ ✕ **Club Sirio Libanés.** Islamic tile walls mark the entrance to this popular eatery, and you must pass through a small mosque to enter the restaurant. Don't be dismayed by the bright lights and TV showing soccer games; just order a bottle of Malbec, head for the table of appetizers, and fill your plate with crab brochettes, pickled eggplant, fresh tomatoes, and sliced tongue. Entrées include pastas, chicken, and beef prepared with a Mediterranean touch. ⊠ *Entre Ríos 33* ☎ *264/422–9884* ⊟ *AE, V* ☯ *No dinner Sun.*

$$ ✕ **Remolacha.** A convenient location and sunny yellow décor, plus a variety of typical dishes—grilled goat, beef, chicken and vegetables, pasta, and crepes—draws locals off the streets and into this popular smoke-free restaurant. Lunch and dinner are served inside or out. *Tenedor libre* (free fork) means "all you can eat" for about 20 pesos. ⊠ *Av. J. I. de la Roza 199 Oeste, corner of Sarmiento* ☎ *264/422–7070* ⊟ *AE, DC, MC, V.*

$–$$ ✕ **Las Leñas.** This large, lively grill can serve up to 200 people under its high thatched roof and spinning fans. *Civita* (goat cooked asado style) is the specialty (it's available in March and April). Otherwise, enjoy the grilled meats, sausages, and chicken, which arrive sizzling at your table, accompanied by salad, pasta, pizza, and tasty appetizers. On Sunday afternoon, families fill the long tables. ⊠ *Av. San Martín 1670 Oeste* ☎ *264/423–2100* ⊟ *AE, DC, MC, V.*

$$ ✕▯ **Alkazar.** Polished granite floors, chrome, and glass lend this hotel's lobby a business-like air. There are plenty of gathering places on the main floor, including a small bar, street-side café, and restaurant. The modern rooms have views across the city to the mountains. ⊠ *Laprida 82 Este, 5400* ☎ *264/421–4965* ⊕ *www.alkazarhotel.com.ar* ▱ *104 rooms, 8 suites* ⟁ *Restaurant, café, in-room safes, minibars, pool, health club, sauna, bar, business center, airport shuttle, free parking* ⊟ *AE, DC, MC, V* ▯○▯ *CP.*

¢ ▯ **Capayán.** This hotel is located right off the main square and shopping street. It's working to upgrade its facilities by building a pool next to the café on the second floor. With a few more improvements, it'll lose its 1940s look. ⊠ *Mitre 31/41 Este, 5400* ☎ *264/421–4222* ▱ *35* ⟁ *Restaurant, 2nd-floor pool, poolside café, lobby bar, meeting rooms, garage* ⊟ *AE, DC, MC, V* ▯○▯ *CP.*

Barreal

$$$–$$$$ ▯ **Posada San Eduardo.** Former Formula One racer Ricardo Zunino inherited this 150-year-old estate from his family. A yellow adobe house with closed green shutters sits on a quiet corner under a canopy of trees. Inside, a classic colonial patio is surrounded by spacious rooms decorated with local weavings and rustic pine furniture. Lunch is served anytime on the lawn by the pool. ⊠ *Av. San Martín and Los Enamorados, 5500* ☎ *2648/441–046 in Barreal, 264/423–0192 in San Juan* ▱ *14 rooms* ⟁ *Restaurant, pool, horseback riding, paddle tennis, bar* ⊟ *V* ▯○▯ *CP.*

FodorsChoice
★

WINE REGION ESSENTIALS

Transportation

BY AIR

Mendoza's Aeropuerto Internacional Francisco Gabrielli is 6 km (4 mi)
from town on R40. Aerolíneas Argentinas has flights from Buenos Aires
to that airport and to San Rafael and San Juan. Lan Chile flies between
Mendoza and Santiago, Chile.

🛪 Airlines **Aerolíneas Argentinas** ☎ 261/420-4101 in Mendoza, 264/427-4444 in
Juan, 2627/425-0399 airport. San Rafael: 2627/438-808 in town, 2627/435-156 at the airport. **Lan Chile** ⊠ Rivadavia 135 ☎ 261/425-7900 in Mendoza, 0800/222-2424 elsewhere.
🛪 Airports **Aeropuerto Internacional de Mendoza (Francisco Gabrielli)** ⊠ Route
40, 6 km (4 mi) from Mendoza City ☎ 261/448-2603. **Aeropuerto San Rafael** ⊠ Route
143, Km 6.5 ☎ 2627/427-253. **Aeropuerto San Juan** ⊠ Route 20, Km 12 ☎ 264/425-
4133, 264/425-4134.

BY BUS

Mendoza's busy Terminal del Sol is in Guaymallén, a suburb east of downtown. From here, buses travel to every major Argentine city. Transport
companies include: Andesmar, with service to Bariloche, Salta–Jujuy, and
San Juan; Chevallier, with daily service to Buenos Aires; La Cumbre,
with daily service to San Juan and Córdoba along a scenic route; La Estrella, with buses via San Juan to La Rioja, Tucumán, and Jujuy, and to
Buenos Aires via San Luís; El Rápido, with daily buses to Buenos Aires
and Santiago, Chile, and three trips weekly to Lima, Peru; and T.A.C.,
with service to Bariloche, Buenos Aires, and Córdoba.

Both San Rafael and San Juan have service all over the country on the
same lines mentioned above. Long distance sleeper buses have fully reclining seats, serve meals, and are comfortable.

Every town has local buses, and if you can express where you want to
go and understand the reply, you can travel cheaply (but slowly). A number in brackets on the bus indicates the route. Almost every tour agency
runs minivans to local sights.

🚌 **Andesmar.** You can make reservations on their Web site. Buenos Aires is listed as
Retiro. ⊕ www.andesmar.com ☎ 261/438-0654 in Mendoza, 2627/427-720 in San
Rafael. **Chevallier** ☎ 261/431-0235. **La Cumbre** ☎ 261/431-9252. **La Estrella** ☎ 261/
431-1324. **El Rápido** ☎ 261/431-4094. **T.A.C** ☎ 261/431-1039, 2627/422-209 in San
Rafael. **Terminal de Ómnibus** ⊠ Av. Gobernador Videla and Av. Acceso Oeste, Men-
doza ☎ 261/448-0057 ⊠ **San Rafael** ⊠ Colonel Suarez and Avellaneda ⊠ **San
Juan** ⊠ Estados Unidos 492, between Santa Fe and España 985 ☎ 264/422-1604.

BY CAR

You can rent cars and 4x4s in all major cities, but it's a good idea to
make reservations in advance during peak season. Avis has a large fleet
at the Mendoza airport.

The trip from Buenos Aires to Mendoza is 1,060 km (664 mi) along lonely,
paved R7. From Santiago, Chile, it's 250 km (155 mi) east (the road is
sometimes closed in winter) on R7. Mendoza locals are known for their

cavalier attitude toward traffic rules. Outside the major cities, however, there's very little traffic. Mendoza to San Rafael is 232 km (144 mi), and it's 167 km (103 mi) to San Juan.

You can drive to most sights in the Wine Regions, but finding wineries on your own requires a good map and some knowledge of Spanish. Driving to the high Andean villages and the border with Chile is a remarkable experience, worth the expense of a rental car. If you fear getting lost or breaking down in remote areas, hire a *remis* (a car with a driver).

Pay attention to weather and road information. During winter, snow and avalanches close some roads. Torrential rainstorms can cause flash floods and obliterate seldom-used dirt roads. Good maps can be found in bookstores and at Automóvil Club Argentino.

Auto Club Contacts **Automóvil Club Argentino** (ACA) ✉ Av. del Libertador 1850, Buenos Aires ☎ 11/4808-4460 ✉ Gdor. Videla and Reconquista, Mendoza ☎ 261/431-4100 ✉ H. Yrigoyen and 9 de Julio, San Rafael ☎ 2627/424-288 ⏲ 24 hours ✉ 9 de Julio and Av. Rawson, San Juan ☎ 264/427-6433 ⊕ www.aca.org.ar. **Roadside Assistance** ☎ 0800/888-9888.

Rental Agencies **Hertz** has rental offices in the Mendoza and San Rafael airports. ✉ Espejo 415, Mendoza ☎ 2627/436-959 ✉ 25 de Mayo 450, San Rafael ☎ 261/423-0225 ⊕ www.milletrenyacar.com.ar. **Andina Rent A Car** ✉ Sarmiento 129, Mendoza ☎ 261/461-0210 ⊕ www.andinarentacar.com.ar. **Avis** ✉ Primitivo de la Reta 914, Mendoza ☎ 261/420-3178, 261/447-0150 airport ✉ Av. Lib. Gral. San Martín 685 oeste, San Juan ☎ 264/422-4622 ⊕ www.avis.com. **Localiza** ✉ Primitivo de la Reta 936, Loc. 4, Mendoza ☎ 261/4290-6800 ✉ Day and Castelli, San Rafael ☎ 2627/420-995 ⊕ www.localiza.com.ar ☎ 0800/999-2999.

BY TAXI

Metered taxis are inexpensive and plentiful in the Wine Regions. There's usually a taxi stand near the central plaza, and hotels and restaurants will call one for you. To tip, round the fare up. Drivers are generally honest, but for long trips it's a good idea to agree upon the fare before you go. Though more expensive, remises are good value for groups. They don't mind stopping for photos, meals, or shopping, and the drivers are often good guides. Arrangements can be made through your hotel or at the airport or bus station.

Class Remise ☎ 261/431-8238 local guided tours, 261/431-8244 airport transfers, 261/431-5810 business trips. **Imperio Remises** ✉ At the bus station, Loc. D23 ☎ 261/432-2222 or 0800/433-368. **La Veloz del Este** ✉ Alem 439 ☎ 261/423-9090.

Contacts & Resources

BANKS & EXCHANGE SERVICES

Banks in the region are generally open weekdays 10–4. ATMs are available everywhere (Banelco and LINK have ATMs in most cities). Hotels and some travel agencies will exchange dollars. Traveler's checks are inconvenient; you must go to a bank and pay a fee.

Mendoza Bank Information **Banelco** ✉ Av. San Martín 831 ✉ Sarmiento 29. **Banco de la Nación** ✉ Av. San Martín and Gutiérrez ☎ 261/423-4500 ✉ At bus terminal. **Citibank** ✉ Av. San Martín 1098 ☎ 261/420-4113. **Exprinter** ✉ Espejo 74 ☎ 261/429-1200.

🚻 San Juan Bank Information **Banco de Boston** ✉ Laprida and Mendoza ☎ 264/421-0708. **Banco de Galícia** ✉ General Acha and Rivadavía ☎ 264/421-2490. **Citibank** ✉ Av. J. I. de la Roza 211 Oeste ☎ 264/427-6999. **Lloyd's Bank** ✉ General Acha 127 Sur ☎ 264/420-6480.

🚻 San Rafael Bank Information **Banco de la Nación** (Link) ✉ El Libertador and Mitre ☎ 2627/422-265 ✉ H. Yrigoyen 113 ☎ 2627/43009. **Banco Boston**(Banelco) ✉ H. Yrigoyen 97 ✉ H. Yrigoyen 113. **Banco Galicia**(Banelco) ✉ H. Yrigoyen 28.

EMERGENCIES
🚻 **Ambulance-Medical Emergencies** ☎ 107. **Fire** ☎ 100. **Police** ☎ 101.

HOSPITALS & PHARMACIES

For national listings, ⊕ www.farmaciaesencia.com.

🚻 In Mendoza **Hospital Central** ✉ José F. Moreno and Alem, near the bus station ☎ 261/420-0600. **Farmacia del Puente (open 24 hrs)** ✉ Av. Las Heras 201 ☎ 261/425-9209.

🚻 In Luján de Cuyo **Farmacia Avenida** ✉ Saenz Peña 827 ☎ 261/498-2088.

🚻 In Tunuyán **Farmacia Galencia** ✉ San Martín 650 ☎ 2622/422-826.

🚻 In San Juan **Hospital Dr. G. Rawson** ✉ General Paz and E.E.U.U. ☎ 264/422-2272. **Farmacia Echague** ✉ Sarmiento 290 ☎ 264/427-6110 ⊙ Mon.-Sat. 8-1, 2-10 PM.

🚻 In San Rafael **Hospital Schestakow** ✉ Emilio Civit 151 and Corrientes ☎ 2627/424-290 or 2627/424-291. **Farmacia 16 Horas** ✉ Libertador 206 ☎ 2627/430-214 ⊙ Mon.-Sat. 8-midnight.

INTERNET, MAIL & SHIPPING
Modern hotels in Mendoza, San Rafael, and San Juan usually have Internet access in a dedicated room. San Rafael and Mendoza have top hotels with Wi-Fi in the lobby. Upscale inns in the Valle de Uco will let you check e-mail on their computers. Otherwise, look for a *locutorio* (long-distance telephone center), which will have Internet access and fax machines. Local calls can be made on public phones with tokens or phone cards available at kiosks. The cybercafé in San Rafael has few machines, but it does have good coffee and helpful, English-speaking attendants.

Post offices are generally open 8 AM to 8 PM, but it's best to ask at your hotel. UPS, DHL, and Federal Express have offices in Mendoza, San Rafael, and San Juan. American Service Pack is a private postal service in Guaymallén (in Mendoza).

🚻 Mendoza Cybercafés **Cyber Café** ✉ Av. San Martín and Garibaldi 7 ☎ 261/425-4020. **Arlink** ✉ Av. San Martín 928 ☎ 261/423-7195. **Telefónica** ✉ Av. San Martín 650.

🚻 San Juan Cybercafés **Casino Cyber Café** ✉ Rivadavía 12 Este ☎ 264/420-1397. **Interredes** ✉ Laprida 362 Este ☎ 264/427-5790. **Telefónica** ✉ Laprida 180 Oeste.

🚻 San Rafael Cybercafés **Cybercafé** ✉ In gallería on Av. San Martín 120. **Locutorio I** ✉ Avellaneda 76 ☎ 2627/43016. **Locutorio III** ✉ Terminal de Omnibus, Loc. No. 35 ☎ 2627/435-809. **Telefónica Argentina** ✉ San Lorenzo 131.

🚻 Shipping Contacts **American Service Pack** ✉ Casa Central, O'Brien 508 and San José, Mendoz ☎ 261/445-3178. **Mendoza Post Office** ✉ Av. San Martín and Colón ☎ 261/449-9500. **San Juan Post Office** ✉ Av. J. I. de la Roza 259 Este ☎ 264/422-4430. **San Rafael Post Office** ✉ San Lorenzo and Barcala ☎ 2627/421-119.

Patagonia

WORD OF MOUTH

"Although the towns of Villa La Angostura and San Martín de los Andes are smaller then Bariloche, we found them much more charming and unique—don't pass them up. And enjoy your trip! If we had the opportunity, we would do it all over again."
—MissMag

"Ushuaia is very special as the world's southernmost city, but its nature-related sites aren't as beautiful as in El Calafate. You can see the animals much closer near Puerto Madryn, which is definitely a 'happy' city. We talked to the locals, and they truly enjoy living there. Torres del Paine is an amazing place, and so is Peninsula Valdés, where we got very close to the penguins and seals."
—dudi

Revised by
Robin
Goldstein

PATAGONIA, THAT FABLED LAND of endless, empty, open space at the end of the world, has humbled the most fearless explorers. Many have described it as a cruel and lonely windswept place unfit for humans. Darwin called Patagonia "wretched and useless," yet he was deeply moved by its desolation and forever attracted to it. Today, the 800,000 square km (309,000 square mi) that make up Argentine Patagonia continue to challenge and fascinate explorers, mountaineers, nature lovers, sports enthusiasts, and curious visitors from around the world.

Although Patagonia—like all of Argentina—has become an increasingly trendy place for foreigners to speculate in land (Ted Turner, among others, has bought up enormous swaths), most of this vast territory, from the Río Colorado (Colorado River) in the north to Cape Horn, 2,000 km (1,200 mi) south, still seems monotonously devoid of life—uninhabited except by sheep, and inhospitable even to those creatures. Yet it is these very characteristics that make it one of the most amazing natural preserves on earth. Because the population in Patagonia is small relative to its land mass, a staggering variety of plants and wildlife exists in pristine habitats.

If the soundtrack to the Alps is Beethoven, the soundtrack to the peaks of Andean Patagonia is Stravinsky. These are not friendly snowcaps. They are tortured, writhing cones of white ice, disfigured by glaciers, studded with protrusions and amputations. The few blankets of smooth snow seem out of place, laid against sheer, threatening, dusty brown rock. It's as if the lakes beneath, placid pools of glacial turquoise, have been intimidated into pale submission by their unforgiving lords above.

Not so for Patagonia's cities, though: these defiant centers of commerce brandish modern airports and harbors, shipping goods and tourists in and out in ever-increasing numbers. Ushuaia, on the Canal Beagle (Beagle Channel) in Tierra del Fuego, prides itself on being the southernmost city in the world. Puerto Madryn, on the Atlantic coast in the province of Chubut, is the gateway to the Península Valdés and its unending show of marine life, while in the nearby towns of Gaiman and Trelew, a Welsh farming culture still thrives. And then there is fabled Bariloche, at the foot of the Andes in the northern lake district—by far the largest and most frequently visited city in Patagonia. While the city is undeniably picturesque, its true beauty, like most of Patagonia's, lies outside the city limits: on a mountain road, by a lake or stream, in the forest, or on the ski slopes in the surrounding mountains. There is the definite sense, at the end of the world, that man is still a humble servant of nature rather than a parasite upon it.

ORIENTATION & PLANNING

Orientation

Patagonia encompasses an enormous, diverse territory, virtually impossible to cover in one trip. The Lakes district, Argentina's renowned center of skiing and sportfishing, is becoming an increasingly important vacation spot among foreigners as well as Argentines, and it's nes-

Top Reasons to Visit

Trekking across a glacier. There's no better place than Patagonia to experience one of nature's most humbling phenomena. The most impressive—and beloved—glacier is Perito Moreno, in the Parque Nacional Los Glaciares near El Calafate. Here, even the little kids can don crampons and cross a stable portion of the behemoth—truly like a trip back to the Ice Age.

Wildlife. From the mountain aeries of the Andean east to the desolate Atlantic shoreline to the west, Patagonia provides a great chance to see animals in their natural habitats. At Península Valdés, countless species of marine life cavort in the sea and on land: sea lions breed in rookeries, followed by killer whales, which come to feed on elephant seals on the coast, and you can get a close-up viewing of thousands of right whales that come here to mate and give birth. In Punta Tombo, at the world's largest penguin rookery, over 300,000 Magellanic penguins waddle back and forth on "penguin highways."

Fun with snow. The Lakes district at the northern end of Argentine

Patagonia is famous for its great skiing. Tourists flock from Brazil and all over South America to hit the slopes at Cerro Catedral and Cerro Otto, near Bariloche, and Cerro Chapelco, near San Martín de los Andes. It may not be the most challenging terrain in the world, but the views are absolutely unbeatable—and travelers from the Northern Hemisphere get the unusual opportunity to ski in June, July, or August.

Tales from the end of the world. For many, the initial attraction to Patagonia comes from the romantic allure of its location at the "end of the world": closer to Antarctica than Buenos Aires, Ushuaia, Argentina is the southernmost city in the world and Chile's Puerto Williams the southernmost settlement. While travelers to Patagonia are invariably charmed by its incredible natural landscape, delicious food, and disarming hospitality, it's also hard to beat the chance to tell travel stories about reaching the end of the Pan-American highway in wild Tierra del Fuego, 17,848 km (11,090 mi) from where it begins in Alaska.

6

tled on the Argentine side of the Andes, an easy two-hour flight from the capital.

All the way across the cone, on the eastern edge of Patagonia, lies an area settled by Welsh farmers in the mid-1800s, and still populated by their descendants; and jutting out into the Atlantic is the Peninsula Valdés, which has the best wildlife viewing. This region, too, is best accessed by air from Buenos Aires; Comodoro Rivadavia and Trelew are the best-connected airports. Between cities lie hundreds of miles of windswept brush with more sheep than people.

Last but not least, there is the South: El Calafate and El Chaltén, gateways to the glaciers (and Puerto Natales and Parque Nacional Torres del Paine on the Chilean side of things) lie in the shadow of majestic peaks and fields of ice and starkly beautiful Tierra del Fuego, the island that marks land's end in South America. Tierra del Fuego, too, is generally accessed by air from Buenos Aires.

The Lakes

The bucolic Lakes region has long been the best-known part of Patagonia; Bariloche has been a boomtown for a few decades longer than its Patagonian counterparts to the east and south. Here lie the top ski resorts in Argentina—Cerros Catedral, Chapelco, and Otto—along with fabulous fishing, and some of the most luxurious hotels and restaurants in Argentina. Villa La Angostura is quickly catching up with Bariloche's preeminence as an affluent retreat, and its lake-and-mountain scenery is hard to beat, whether in summer or winter.

Atlantic Patagonia

Home to whales and Welsh settlers, this is the region of Patagonia least visited by foreign tourists, but not for want of things to see. You can relax amidst Welsh teahouses, visit the farms of rural Chubut, enjoy the burgeoning restaurant scene and nightlife of seaside Puerto Madryn, or head out to the Peninsula Valdés for some of the world's best whale-watching.

Southern Patagonia

Southern Patagonia is the glacier heartland of Argentina and Chile, home to the dazzling Perito Moreno glacier among many other icy natural wonders. It's a particular haven for hikers, who can base themselves in humble mountain refuges, spectacular all-inclusive luxury lodges, or anything in between. El Calafate, the heart of the region, now has a bevy of hip restaurants and bars to go along with its trekking options, and El Chaltén and Ushuaia are not far behind.

Planning

Patagonia's three nerve centers—the Lakes, Atlantic Patagonia, and Southern Patagonia—are not always internally well connected, so most people choose just one, or at most two, of these three areas on which to focus their travels. Even covering two regions can be difficult, but the introduction of direct flights from Bariloche to El Calafate, along with long-distance buses that connect Bariloche and El Bolsón to Trelew, make it much more possible. You should choose based on your interests—for skiing, fishing, or a luxurious, scenic waterfront retreat, head to the Lakes. For adventures with glaciers and penguins, head to the south. Or for whale-viewing and a taste of Welsh culture, choose the Atlantic side.

Timing It Right

January and February are the peak summer months in Patagonia, and for good reason: the wind dies down and long, warm days (the sun sets at 10 PM) ensure plenty of time to enjoy a multitude of activities. Hotel and restaurant reservations are necessary in popular destinations, and campgrounds get crowded. March and April are still good months to visit, although rainy, cloudy days and cold nights might curtail some activities. The rewards, however, are fewer crowds and the great colors of fall. Some hotels in remote areas close from May through September, as few want to brave the knock-down winds, rain, sleet, and snow of Patagonian winters.

In Bariloche and the northern lake district, ski season begins in June. The snow-covered mountains reflected in the blue lakes are spectacular, and the weather is typical of any alpine region—tremendous snowstorms, rain, and fog punctuated by days of brilliant sunshine. August and September are the best months for skiing. In July, the slopes are crowded with vacationing schoolkids and their families, and Bariloche becomes one big high-school discotheque.

December is spring in Patagonia. The weather might be cool, breezy, overcast, or rainy, but the rewards for bringing an extra sweater and rain gear are great: an abundance of wildflowers and very few tourists. The June–December period is the best time to visit Península Valdés—this is when you can see the whales. Tierra del Fuego has different charms year-round: in summer it's warm during the day and cool at night, which is ideal for outdoor activities but also means big crowds; in winter it's great for skiing, sledding, visiting dog-sledding camps, and hiking through beautifully desolate woods. If you want to whale-watch and do winter sports, consider combining a trip to Tierra del Fuego and Puerto Madryn sometime between June and September. Tierra del Fuego winters are not as harsh as you might think: the average temperature in August, the dead of winter, is about 36°F.

Eating & Sleeping

Restaurants reservations are seldom needed except during school, Easter, and summer holidays (July, January, and February). Attire is informal, and tipping is the same as in the rest of the country (about 10%).

Idyllic lake-view lodges, cozy *cabañas* (cabins), vast *estancias* (ranches), and inexpensive *hospedajes* or *residenciales* (bed-and-breakfasts) are found in towns and in the countryside throughout Patagonia. Luxurious hotels in the northern lake district and near the glaciers attract outdoor enthusiasts from all over the world, as do small family-run hostels, where backpackers squeeze five to a room. Fishing lodges on the lakes near Bariloche, San Martín de los Andes, and Junín de los Andes are not only for anglers; they make great headquarters for hiking, boating, or just getting away. In cities, avoid hotel rooms on lower floors that face the street. *Apart-hotels* have small, furnished apartments with kitchenettes. Local tourist offices are most helpful in finding anything from a room in a residence to a country inn or a downtown hotel. Patagonia has become such a popular tourist destination that advance reservations are highly recommended if you're traveling during peak times (December–March; July–August for the ski resorts). Note: lodging prices include tax; most include Continental breakfast as well, unless otherwise noted.

Staying at an estancia is a unique way to experience Patagonian life on the range. Sheep shearing, cattle round-ups, horseback riding, and sharing ranch chores are typical activities; a lamb asado is often an added attraction. Estancias are in remote areas, and accommodations are limited, so reservations are essential. For information on estancias in Santa

Cruz province, contact the **Centro de Información de la Provincia de Santa Cruz** (✉ Suipacha 1120, Buenos Aires ☏☏ 11/4325–3098 ⊕ www.estanciasdesantacruz.com). The regional tourist office, **Subsecretaría de Turismo de Santa Cruz** (✉ Av. Roca 1551, Río Gallegos ☏ 2966/422–702 ⊕ www.sectur.gov.ar) also has information on estancias.

For more general information, ⊕ www.interpatagonia.com has everything from ski resorts, to fishing lodges, restaurants to tourist attractions.

	WHAT IT COSTS In Argentine Pesos				
	$$$$	**$$$**	**$$**	**$**	**¢**
RESTAURANTS	over 35	25–35	15–25	8–15	under 8
HOTELS	over 400	250–400	150–250	80–150	under 80

Restaurant prices are for one main course at dinner. Hotel prices are for two people in a standard double room in high season.

Transportation 101

Traveling the length of Patagonia is a formidable task, especially if you're short on time. To put its size in perspective, Patagonia is 1,930 km (1,200 mi) long, a bit more than the distance from New York City to Miami. Driving on RN40 from Bariloche south to Río Gallegos appeals to Argentines and adventurous foreigners who have the time (one to two weeks). If you attempt that drive, don't leave without plenty of water, supplies, two spare tires, and camping equipment, because if you break down, cars and trucks might not pass for days.

A new airport in El Calafate, with direct flights from Buenos Aires and Bariloche, has made the far reaches of Patagonia much more accessible to tourists. Covering the great distances between Bariloche, in the north; Ushuaia, in the south; and El Calafate, Río Gallegos, and Trelew–Puerto Madryn in the middle, requires careful planning—air travel is essential. Tours to popular sights along the Atlantic coast, to the glaciers, or to the Lakes region, can be arranged in Buenos Aires or in each destination.

AIR TRAVEL   Airplanes will likely be your main form of transportation in Patagonia—distances between cities are vast, and roads are often desolate. Although many flights to and from Patagonian cities involve an extremely out-of-the-way change of planes in Buenos Aires, intra-Patagonian air service is slowly increasing; for instance, you can now travel nonstop between Bariloche and El Calafate.

BUS TRAVEL   With air service from the capital so convenient, and the bus trips so long, no one in their right mind travels to Patagonia from Buenos Aires by bus. However, buses are a useful form of transportation to get between the Lakes (El Bolsón or Bariloche) to Atlantic Patagonia (generally through Trelew), and they're the main way to travel between cities in southern Patagonia, including the Argentina–Chile border crossings.

CAR TRAVEL   In the Lakes region, a car is essential to enjoy the Circuito Chico and the Seven Lakes Road, among other sights, at your own leisure. A car is also a viable option to tour the Peninsula Valdés in Atlantic Patagonia. A car won't be as helpful in Southern Patagonia because of the long distances between cities; however, the proliferation of excellent tour operators and adventure outfitters across the region more than makes up for the inconvenience.

Border Crossings

U.S. citizens arriving into Chile by air to Santiago have to pay an entry fee of approximately US$60 (US$55 for Canadians, US$30 for Australians); you only have to pay this fee once for the lifetime of your passport. The fee is not assessed upon crossing the border overland. Either way, you'll get a 90-day tourist visa upon entry. The border crossings in southern Patagonia can be time-consuming because of long lines, but the process is quite straightforward for anyone with a passport from the United States, Canada, the UK, Australia, New Zealand, South Africa, or the EU. Keep the exit portion of your Argentine tourist visa for when you leave Chile; you'll get a new visa upon reentry. Be sure to keep the exit portion of your Chilean visa for the duration of your time in Chile, as you'll have to show it when you leave.

Other Practicalities

To call Chile from Argentina, dial 00, plus the country code of 56, plus the city code but *without* the initial 0 (e.g., 2 for Santiago). To call locally within Chile, simply dial the number (numbers of digits can vary) without either the initial 0 or "city code." To call from one region to another, dial the complete city code including the initial 0 (e.g., 02 for Santiago) and then the local number.

International-compatible ATMs are plentiful in Chile. Chilean peso coins come in denominations of 1 (rarely used), 5, 10, 50, 100, and 500; bills come in denominations of 500, 1,000, 2,000, 5,000, 10,000, and 20,000. Argentine pesos are not generally accepted anywhere in Chile, even just over the border. At press time, the exchange rate was approximately 550 Chilean pesos to the U.S. dollar, or 190 Chilean pesos to the Argentine peso.

Visitor Information

The comprehensive Inter Patagonia Web site is an excellent resource for tourist information for every city and region in Patagonia. Local tourist offices (Direcciónes de Turismo) are very helpful, easy to find, and usually open every day and into the evening.

🖪 **Inter Patagonia** ⊕ www.interpatagonia.com.

THE LAKE DISTRICT

Snow-packed peaks, a white volcano mirrored in a still lake, chalk-white glacial streams cascading over polished granite, meadows filled with chin-high pink and purple lupine, fast-flowing rivers, and thousands of lakes, with no houses, no piers, no boats: the northernmost end of Andean Patagonia, the lake district, seems like one big national park. Indeed, the Parque Nacional Lanín, just north of San Martín de los Andes in Neuquén Province, combined with the neighboring Parque Nacional

Nahuel Huapi, in Río Negro Province, with Bariloche as its headquarters, adds up to 2.5 million acres of natural preserve—about the size of New England. Furthermore, south of the Cholila Valley and northwest of Esquel is the Parque Nacional los Alerces, named for its 2,000-year-old *alerces,* which are similar to California redwoods. The park covers 1,610 square km (1,000 square mi) of true wilderness, with only one dirt road leading into it.

Along the eastern edge of the northern lake district, mountain streams flow into rivers that have carved fertile valleys into deep canyons. Welsh farmers have been growing wheat and raising sheep in the Chubut Valley, which includes the towns of Esquel and Trevelin in the Chubut province, since 1865. Rain diminishes as you move eastward, and the land flattens into a great plateau, running eastward into dry, desolate Patagonia. This is sheep-breeding country, and Benetton owns a large portion of it.

Bariloche & the Parque Nacional Nahuel Huapi

❶ *1,615 km (1,001 mi) southwest of Buenos Aires (2 hrs by plane), 432 km (268 mi) south of Neuquén on R237, 1,639 km (1,016 mi) north of Río Gallegos, 876 km (543 mi) northwest of Trelew, 357 km (221 mi) east of Puerto Montt, Chile, via lake crossing.*

Modern Bariloche is the gateway to all the recreational and scenic splendors of the northern lake district. However, as it's also the most popular vacation destination in Patagonia, with the region's busiest airport and one of the liveliest ski scenes in South America—particularly popular among the high-school party crowd—Bariloche has lost some of its luster. Although development in the area has maintained a sense of architectural restraint, it can be hard here, especially within the city itself, to experience the communion with nature that characterizes so much of Patagonia. As such, many people choose to base themselves outside the city—on Avenida Bustillo along the Circuito Chico, around the Peninsula Llao Llao, and in the nearby retreats of Villa La Angostura and San Martín de los Andes. But all is not lost in Bariloche: although planes, buses, trains, boats, and tour groups arrive daily, you can escape into the stunning wilderness of clear blue lakes, misty lagoons, rivers, waterfalls, mountain glaciers, forests, and flower-filled meadows on foot, mountain bike, or horseback or by boat. You can also fish peacefully in one of the 40 nearby lakes and countless streams. It's best to get around on your own with the help of a rental car, although myriad planned excursions are available with local tour companies.

The rustic gray-green stone-and-log buildings of the Centro Cívico (Civic Center) were designed by Alejandro Bustillo, the architect who also designed the Llao Llao Hotel and the National Park office in San Martín de los Andes. His Andean-Swiss style is recognizable in lodges and buildings throughout the lake district. The spacious square in front of the Civic Center, with an equestrian statue of General Roca (1843–1914) and a wide-angle view of the lake, is a good place to begin exploring Bariloche. Note that the Civic Center is Km 0 for measuring points from Bariloche.

The Lake District

CHILE

San Martín de los Andes
Junín de los Andes
Lago Lácar
Lago Escondido
Cerro Chapelco
Lago de los Cármenes
Lago Hermoso
Lago Miliquina
Lago Falkner
Lago Trafúl
Villa Trafúl
Cerro Bayo
Contuencia
El Cruce
Valle Encantado
Villa la Angostura
Lago Nahuel Huapi
Circuíto Chico
Braze de la Tristeza
Lago Moreno
Bariloche
Mte. Tronadór
Cerro Catedral
Cerro Otto
Pampa Linda
Lago Gutiérrez
R. Manso
Lago Mascardi
Lago J.H. Roca
TO EL BOLSÓN, ESQUEL, TREVELIN

The **Museo de la Patagonia** (Patagonia Museum) tells the social and geological history of northern Patagonia through displays of Indian and gaucho artifacts and exhibits on regional flora and fauna. The history of the Mapuche and the Conquista del Desierto (Conquest of the Desert) is also explained in detail. ⊠ *Centro Cívico, next to arch over Bartolomé Mitre* ☎ *2944/422–330* ⊠ *2.50 pesos* ☉ *Mon. and Sat. 10–1, Tues.–Fri. 10–12:30 and 2–7.*

The National Park

The **Parque Nacional Nahuel Huapi,** created in 1943, is Argentina's oldest national park, and Lago Nahuel Huapi is the sapphire in its crown. The park extends over 2 million acres along the eastern side of the Andes in the provinces of Neuquén and Río Negro, on the frontier with Chile. It contains the highest concentration of lakes in Argentina. The biggest is Lago Nahuel Huapi, a 897-square-km (346-square-mi) body of water, whose seven long arms (the longest is 96 km [60 mi] long, 12 km [7 mi] wide) reach deep into forests of *coihué* (a native beech tree), *cyprés* (cypress), and *lenga* (deciduous beech) trees. Intensely blue across its vast expanse and aqua green in its shallow bays, the lake meanders into distant lagoons and misty inlets where the mountains, covered with vegetation at their base, rise straight up out of the water. Every water sport invented and tours to islands and other extraordinarily beautiful spots can be arranged through local travel agencies, tour offices, and through hotels. Information offices throughout the park offer help in exploring the miles of mountain and woodland trails, lakes, rivers, and streams. ⊠ *Park entry 12 pesos.*

For information on mountain climbing, trails, *refugios* (mountain cabins), and campgrounds, visit the **Intendencia del Parque Nacional Nahuel Huapi** (⊠ Av. San Martín 24 ☎2944/423–111 ⊕www.parquesnacionales. gov.ar) at the Civic Center. Another source of information on local activities, excursions, lodging, and private and public campgrounds is the **Oficina Municipal de Turismo** (⊠ Centro Cívico, across from clock tower ☎ 2944/429–850), open daily 8:30 AM–9 PM.

The most popular excursion on Lago Nahuel Huapi is the 30-minute boat ride to **Isla Victoria** (Victoria Island), the largest island in the lake. A grove of redwoods transplanted from California thrives in the middle of the island. After a walk on trails that lead to enchanting views of emerald bays and still lagoons, the boat crosses to the tip of the Península Quetrihué for a visit to the **Parque Nacional los Arrayanes,** a unique forest of cinnamon-color myrtle trees. Like most boat trips on the lake, tours to Isla Victoria and Arrayanes begin at Puerto Pañuelo, on the Península Llao Llao. They run twice daily (more in high season), at 10 AM and 2 PM, by **Cau Cau** (⊠ Mitre 139, Bariloche ☎ 2944/431–372 ⊕ www.islavictoriayarrayanes.com) and **Turisur** (⊠ Mitre 219, Bariloche ☎ 2944/426–109 ⊕ www.bariloche.com/turisur).

The renowned ski area at **Cerro Catedral** (Mt. Cathedral) is 46 km (28½ mi) west of town on Avenida Ezequiel Bustillo (R237); turn left at Km 8.5 just past Playa Bonita. The mountain was named for the Gothic-looking spires that crown its peaks. Though skiing is the main activity here, the view from the top of the chairlift at 6,600 feet is spectacular any time of year. To the southwest, Monte Tronadór, a 12,000-foot extinct volcano, straddles the border with Chile, towering above lesser peaks that surround Lago Nahuel Huapi as it meanders around islands and disappears into invisible bays beneath mountains and volcanoes miles away. Lanín Volcano is visible on the horizon.

You can reach the summit of **Cerro Otto** (Mt. Otto; 4,608 feet), a small ski area, by hiking, mountain biking, or driving 8 km (5 mi) up a gravel road from Bariloche. Hiking to the top of the mountain takes you through a forest of lenga trees to Argentina's first ski area, at Piedras Blancas. Here Herbert Tutzauer, Bariloche's first ski instructor, won the first ski race by climbing the mountain, then skiing down it through the forest in 1½ hours. You can also take the **Teleférico Cerro Otto** (⊠ Av. de Los Pioneros ⬚ 30 pesos ☉ Daily 10–5), 5 km (3 mi) west of town; a free shuttle bus leaves from the corner of Mitre and Villegas, and Perito Moreno and Independencia. The ride to the top takes about 12 minutes. All proceeds go to local hospitals. At the top, a revolving cafeteria with a 360-degree panorama takes in Monte Tronadór, lakes in every direction, and Bariloche. In winter, skis and sleds are available for rent at the cafeteria. In summer, hiking and mountain biking are the main activities. For a real thrill, try soaring in a paraplane out over the lake with the condors. Call for **information** (☎ 2944/441–035) on schedules and sled or ski rentals.

A visit to **Monte Tronadór** (Thunder Mountain) requires an all-day outing of 170 km (105 mi) round-trip from Bariloche. The 12,000-foot extinct volcano, the highest mountain in the northern lake district, sits astride the frontier with Chile, with one peak on either side. Take R258 south along the shore of Lago Gutiérrez and Lago Mascardi. Between the two lakes the road crosses from the Atlantic to the Pacific watershed. At Km 35, turn off onto a road marked TRONADÓR and PAMPA LINDA and continue along the shore of Lago Mascardi, passing a village of the same name. Just beyond the village, the road forks and you continue on a gravel road, R254. Near the bridge the road branches left to Lago Hess and Cascada Los Alerces—a detour you might want to take on your way out.

As you bear right after crossing Los Rápidos Bridge, the road narrows to one direction only: it's important to remember this when you set out in the morning, as you can only go up the road before 2 PM and down it after 4 PM. The lake ends in a narrow arm (Brazo Tronadór) at the Hotel Tronadór, which has a dock for tours arriving by boat. The road then follows the Río Manso (Manso River) to **Pampa Linda,** which has a lodge, restaurant, park ranger's office, campsites, and the trailhead for the climb up to the Refugio Otto Meiling at the snow line. Guided horseback rides are organized at the lodge. The road ends 7 km (4½ mi) beyond Pampa Linda in a parking lot that was once at the tip of the now receding **Glaciar Negro** (Black Glacier). As the glacier flows down from the mountain, the dirt and black sediment of its lateral moraines are ground up and cover the ice. At first glance, it's hard to imagine the tons of ice that lie beneath its black cap.

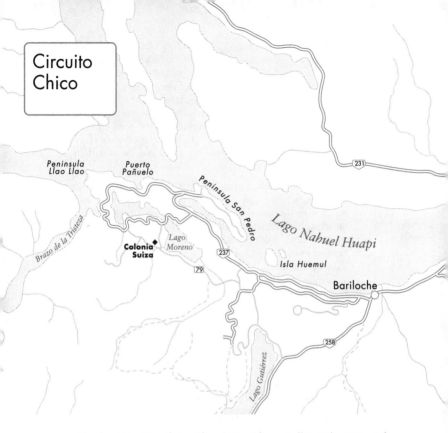

Circuito
Chico

Peninsula
Llao Llao

Puerto
Pañuelo

Península San Pedro

Lago Nahuel Huapi

231

Brazo de la Tristeza

Colonia
Suiza

Lago
Moreno

237

Isla Huemul

Bariloche

79

258

Lago Gutiérrez

The detour to **Cascada Los Alerces** (Los Alerces Falls), 17 km (10 mi) from the turnoff at the bridge near Mascardi, follows the wild Río Manso, where it branches off to yet another lake, Lago Hess. At this junction are a campground, refugio, restaurant, and trailhead for the 1,000-foot climb to the falls. The path through dense vegetation over wooden bridges crosses a rushing river as it spills over steep, rocky cliffs in a grand finale to a day of viewing nature at its most powerful and beautiful.

Scenic Routes

A possible excursion from Bariloche is the **Circuito Chico** (Small Circuit), a half-day, 70-km (43½-mi) scenic trip along the west shore of Lago Nahuel Huapi. You can do it by car, tour bus (trips cost 20 pesos–30 pesos), or mountain bike. First, head west on Avenida Bustillo (R237) toward Península Llao Llao. At Km 20, you can take a brief side trip on an 11-km-long (7-mi-long) dirt road to the **Península San Pedro,** then follow the coast road that passes some fine homes set back in the woods. Back on R237, continue west to **Puerto Pañuelo** (Km 25½) in a little bay on the right, on the Península Llao Llao; it's the embarkation point for lake excursions and for the boat crossing to Chile.

Across from the port, a long driveway leads up a knoll to the Hotel Llao Llao, which you'll only be able to admire from afar if you're not a guest.

The Circuito Chico then follows R77 to Bahía Lopez, winding along the lake's edge through a forest of ghostly, leafless lenga trees. After crossing the bridge that links Lago Moreno and Lago Nahuel Huapi at Bahía Lopez, the road crosses the Arroyo Lopez (Lopez Creek). Here you can stop for a hike up to a waterfall and then climb above Lago Moreno to Punto Panoramico, a scenic overlook well worth a photo stop. Just before you cross Lago Moreno, an unmarked dirt road off to the right leads to the rustic village of **Colonia Suiza,** a good spot to stop for tea or lunch. After passing Laguna El Trebol (a small lake on your left), R77 joins R237 from Bariloche.

The **Circuito Grande** (Large Circuit), a more ambitious excursion than the Circuito Chico that's particularly lovely in spring or fall, covers 250 km (155 mi). Along the way there are plenty of spots to stop and enjoy the view, have a picnic lunch, or even stay overnight. Tour buses do it as an all-day trip costing 30 pesos–40 pesos. Leaving Bariloche on R237 heading east, follow the Río Limay into the Valle Encantado (Enchanted Valley), with its magical red-rock formations. Before crossing the bridge at Confluéncia (where the Río Traful joins the Limay), turn left onto R65 to Lago Traful. Five kilometers (3 mi) beyond the turnoff, on a dirt road heading toward Cuyín Manzano, are some astounding sandstone rock formations. As you follow the shore of Lago Traful, a sign indicates a *mirador* (lookout) on a high rock promontory, which you can climb up to on wooden stairs. The road from Villa Traful dives into a dense forest until it comes to the intersection with the Seven Lakes Circuit (R237). Turn right if you want to add the Seven Lakes Circuit. Otherwise, turn left and follow the shore of Lago Correntoso to the paved road down to the bay at Villa La Angostura.

The **Circuito de los Siete Lagos** (Seven Lakes Circuit) is an all-day trip of 360 km (223½ mi) round-trip, which could be extended to include an overnight in San Martín de los Andes or Villa La Angostura. Drive north on R237 for 21 km (13 mi), and turn left on R231 to Villa La Angostura, 65 km (40 mi) from Bariloche. About 11 km (7 mi) farther along the same road is the Seven Lakes Road (R234), which branches right and along the way passes Lago Correntoso, Lago Espejo, Lago Villarino, Lago Falkner, and Lago Hermoso. After lunch or tea or an overnight in San Martín de los Andes, head south to Bariloche on the dirt road over Paso Córdoba, passing Lago Meliquina on the way. At Confluéncia, the road joins R237, following the Río Limay through Valle Encantado to Bariloche.

FodorśChoice ★ The **Cruce a Chile por Los Lagos** (Chile Lake Crossing) is a unique excursion by land and lakes that began in the 1930s when oxcarts used to haul people. These days you can do the tour in one or two days. Most people choose to do the crossing through an organized tour company, which generally stops for lunch in Puerto Blest and then continues on to Puerto Fríos on Laguna Frías. After docking at Puerto Fríos and clearing Argentine customs, you'll get on another bus that climbs through lush rain forest over a pass, then descends to Peulla, where Chilean customs is cleared (bring your passport). A little farther on is a comfort-

CLOSE UP

Crossing into the Chilean Lakes District

CROSSING INTO CHILE from Argentina's Lakes district is simple and efficient—provided you have your passport and are not carrying any fresh food (meat, cheese, fruits, or vegetables). Rental car companies should give you the proper documents for your car, but it's a good idea to double-check that you have all the necessary paperwork. It's also a good idea to have some Chilean pesos with you, as it can be expensive to change them at the border. Be aware of the weather, as lake crossings are not fun when you have to deal with driving rain and high waves. Snow may close some passes in winter.

There are seven border crossings in the Lakes district. Paso Pérez Rosales is part of the popular 12-hour bus and boat tour from Bariloche to Puerto Montt, Chile. The quickest way to return by paved road to Bariloche is via Osorno, crossing at Cardenal Samoré (aka Paso Puyehue) to Villa Angostura (125 km [78 mi] from the border to Bariloche on RN231).

Paso Hua Hum is the only crossing open year-round. It may be the shortest route—only 47 km (29 mi) from San Martín de los Andes on RP48—as the condor flies, but it's the longest journey by road, after factoring in the 1½-hour-long ferry

ride across Lake Pirehueico on the Chilean side. There are three ferries daily, and buses leave regularly from San Martín de los Andes. You can also make this crossing by raft in the river Hua Hum.

Farther north, and accessible via Junín de los Andes, are two passes that require a longer excursion. Mamuil Malal (aka Paso Tromen) is 67 km (41½ mi) northwest of Junín de los Andes on RP60. This dirt road crosses Lanín National Park and passes through a forest of ancient Arucaria trees as it heads for the foot of Lanín Volcano. Just before the park office, a road leads to good picnic and campsites on Lago Tromen. If you continue on to Chile, you'll see the Villarica and Quetupillán volcanoes to the south and Pucón to the north.

Paso Icalma is 132 km (82 mi) west of Zapala on RN13. Villa Pehuenia, 10 km (6 mi) before the pass, is a small village on the shore of Lake Alluminé with modern accommodations and restaurants. Rafting or fishing the Alluminé River, a visit to a Arucaria nursery, plus horse, bike, and raft rentals might tempt you to stay awhile.

—Eddy Ancinas

6

able lodge by Lago Todos los Santos. Early the next morning a catamaran sets out across the lake, providing views of the volcanoes Putiagudo (which lost its *punto* [peak] in an earthquake) and Osorno. The boat trip ends at the port of Petrohué. Another (and final) bus skirts Lago Llanquihue, stopping for a visit at the rockbound Petrohué waterfalls, passing through the town of Puerto Varas (famous for its roses) and arriving, at last, at the Chilean port town of Puerto Montt. Catedral Turismo specializes in this trip, which costs 140 pesos; you'll spend an additional 125 pesos–140 pesos for a night's stay at Blest and/or Peulla.

The Butterfly [handwritten]

Where to Stay & Eat

Accommodations range from family-run *residenciales* (bed-and-breakfasts) to resort hotels. If you don't have a car, it's better to stay in town. If you're looking for serenity, consider a lake-view hotel, inn, or cabins along the route to the Llao Llao Peninsula. They're really no more, or less, convenient to restaurants and activities than the places in town. Addresses for out-of-town dining and lodging properties are measured in kilometers from the Bariloche Civic Center. The most crowded time of the year is during school vacations (July and January). Of the many fine restaurants, most are casual and open noon–3 for lunch and 8–midnight for dinner.

Dunne known for rabbit + trout [handwritten marginalia]

$$$$ ✕ **Kandahar.** A rustic wood building with a woodstove and cozy window seats in alcoves around the bar is the perfect setting for a pisco sour, smoked meats, and guacamole. Start with unusual appetizers such as *tarteleta de hongos* (mushroom tart), followed by wild game and profiteroles with hot chocolate sauce. ⊠ *20 de Febrero 698* ☎ *2944/424–702* ▭ *AE, MC, V.*

$$$–$$$$ ✕ **Il Gabbiano.** "We don't serve lunch," the folks at this cozy, candlelit house out along the Circuito Chico boast, "because preparing dinner takes all day long." It's hard to argue with that philosophy after you sample the exquisite pastas, which change daily. Look for *tortelli* stuffed with wild boar, or pumpkin ravioli; they also have a way with fresh trout. With stucco, tile, and a beautiful wine cellar that's open to guests, the restaurant conjures up an easy feeling of rustic elegance. Bring a wad of cash, because in spite of the high prices, your plastic is no good here. ⊠ *Av. Bustillo, Km 24.3* ☎ *2944/448–346* ▭ *No credit cards* ⌘ *Reservations essential* ☉ *Closed Tues. No lunch.*

$$–$$$ ✕ **Don Molina.** There is always lamb *a la cruz* ("crucified," meaning vertically spit-roasted over an open fire) in the window at this immensely, and deservedly, popular eatery on the west end of Bariloche's main drag. This is a great opportunity to try this Patagonian specialty, but the products of the *parrilla* are also great. The owners and staff simply couldn't be any nicer, and an attractive mural and dim lighting add to the interior's appeal. ⊠ *Av. San Martín 607* ☎ *2944/436–616* ▭ *AE, DC, MC, V.*

Bill Clinton [handwritten marginalia]

$$–$$$ ✕ **El Patacón.** Constructed of local stone and wood, with large picture windows looking out over the lake, this restaurant is going for the log-cabin look. It's less than 10 minutes west of downtown toward the Llao Llao peninsula, and you'll find all manner of gaucho tools, local art, and weavings on its wooden walls. Leather and sheepskin furniture add to the country atmosphere. An organic garden with fresh herbs, berries, and vegetables enhances the menu of meats, game, and fish. Trout in leek sauce with risotto is a standout, homemade pastas are delicious, and the brownie with ice cream and red fruit sauce is extraordinary. Don't bother with the game carpaccio. ⊠ *Av. Bustillo, Km 7* ☎ *2944/442–800* ▭ *AE, DC, V.*

$–$$ ✕ **Berlina.** One of Bariloche's newest entries into the Patagonia microbrew craze, this modern brewpub always has at least six of their own beers on tap to complement the beer-themed cuisine, such as *trucha Berlina* (whole trout cooked with stout and chocolate malt), beef Wellington marinated in alt bier and orange juice, or a simple, well-executed grilled pizza. Best is the complex Belgian strong dark ale, whose notes of caramel are cut by an intense bitterness. They're serious about coffee, too, and the angular, two-floor interior is flooded with light and views of the surrounding mountains. ⊠ *Av. Bustillo, Km 11.7* ☎ *2944/523–336* ⊕ *www.cervezaberlina.com* ⊟ *AE, MC, V.*

$–$$ ✕**Cervecería Blest.** This warm, lively spot boasts that it was the first brewpub in Argentina. It's certainly one of the most atmospheric, too, with a relaxed bustle that hits the spot after a day on the slopes. Don't miss the excellent bock beer, with a toasty coffee flavor, or if you prefer hard cider, the Fruto Prohibido. You can come in just for an après-ski beer sampler, or stay for dinner, which might include *costillitas de cerdo ahumadas con chucrut* (smoked pork chops with sauerkraut—is there a more classic beer food than that?). Pizzas, steak potpies, and other Anglophilic options round out the menu. ⊠ *Av. Bustillo, Km 11.6* ☎ *2944/461–026* ⊟ *AE, MC, V.*

$–$$ ✕**Confitería La Alpina.** When a place is crowded all day long, there's usually something to it. At this restaurant on a busy corner of the main street, the reasons are at least threefold. First, there's a roaring fireplace right in the middle of the restaurant, illuminating and warming the dark wood tables, even the ones that are in cozy, private nooks. Second, there are the late hours; the place is essentially open all night. And finally, there's the food, which includes fondue—that ski-town classic—along with very competent preparations of local specialties, like Patagonian lamb *al ajillo* (with a savory, tomato-based garlic sauce). ⊠ *Moreno 98* ☎ *2944/425–693* ⊟ *AE, DC, MC, V.*

$ ✕**El Boliche de Alberto.** This local classic is always brightly lit, and always full. Just point at a slab of beef, chicken, lamb, or sausages, and have it grilled to your liking. It'll arrive sizzling on a wooden platter, accompanied by empanadas, salad, fried potatoes, and chimichurri sauce (slather it on the bread). ⊠ *Villegas 347* ☎ *2944/431–433* ⊠ *Bustillo 8800* ☎ *2944/462–285* ⊕ *www.elbolichedealberto.com* ⊟ *AE, DC, MC, V.*

¢–$ ✕**La Esquina.** This immensely popular *confitería* on the corner of Urquiza and Moreno serves all the standards—lamb, pastas, personal-sized pizzas, and such. Still, it's more notable as a place to sit and sip, or hang out by the bar, than to eat; their hot chocolate is delicious, and the wooden interior, full of knick-knacks and cheery music, has a pleasant bustle. ⊠ *Moreno 10* ☎ *2944/428–900* ⊟ *AE, DC, MC, V.*

★ **$$$$** ✕▦ **Hotel Edelweiss.** Fresh flowers from the owner's nursery are arranged throughout this excellent medium-size hotel, which is within walking distance of just about everything. The modern, spacious rooms and suites have lake views from their bay windows. Both lunch and dinner consist of good salads, grilled fish, fowl, game, and beef prepared with fresh vegetables and tasty sauces. Most ski and tour buses, whether arranged through the hotel or other travel agencies, pick up passengers at this hotel. ⊠ *Av. San Martín 202, 8400* ☎ *2944/445–500* ⊕ *www.edelweiss.com.ar* ⌖ *94 rooms, 6 suites* ⚐ *Restaurant, in-room safes, indoor pool, gym, hair salon, massage, sauna, bar, meeting room, travel services, free parking* ⊟ *AE, DC, MC, V* ⎟⊙⎟ *CP.*

Art Hotel: CASCO

$$$$ La Cascada. Named for its lovely waterfall plunging into an idyllic pool a few steps from the entrance, this lake-view hotel 6 km (4 mi) from Bariloche on the road to Llao Llao brings the outdoors inside through its floor-to-ceiling windows in the living room, dining room, and bar. Views through the trees of blue Nahuel Huapi Lake and distant peaks are enhanced by bay windows in most of the bedrooms. ⊠ *Av. E. Bustillo, Km 6, CC 279, 8400* ☎ *2944/441–088* ⊕ *www.lacascada.com* ↶ *25 rooms* ♧ *Restaurant, indoor pool, gym, sauna, bar* ⊟ *DC, MC, V* ⫪⊘ *CP.*

$$$$ Llao Llao Hotel & Resort. This masterpiece by architect Alejandro Bustillo sits on a grassy knoll surrounded by three lakes with a backdrop of rock cliffs and snow-covered mountains. Local wood—alerce, cypress, and hemlock—has been used for the walls along the 100-yard hallway, where paintings by local artists are displayed between fine boutiques. Service is formal, sometimes stuffy (other times rude), and prices are through the roof, but every room has a spectacular view, as does the restaurant. ⊠ *Av. Ezequiel Bustillo, Km 25, 25 km (15½ mi) west of Bariloche, 8400* ☎ *2944/448–530* ⊕ *www.llaollao.com* ↶ *153 rooms, 12 suites, 1 cabin* ♧ *2 restaurants, in-room safes, minibars, 18-hole golf course, tennis court, pool, fitness classes, gym, hair salon, hot tub, massage, sauna, spa, yoga, dock, windsurfing, boating, mountain bikes, archery, paddle tennis, piano bar, recreation room, babysitting, children's programs (ages 2–12), business services, convention center, meeting rooms, travel services, no-smoking rooms* ⊟ *AE, DC, MC, V* ⫪⊘ *CP.*

★ $$$$ Villa Huinid. This peaceful complex of cabins is lorded over by a grand hotel, opened in 2005, which has immaculate rooms featuring such modern amenities as 21-inch flat-panel TVs, as well as an impressive lake-view spa. Scattered on the lawns below the hotel is an older network of two-story log and stucco cottages (one, two, or three bedrooms). With their stone chimneys and wooden decks, the cabins look like private homes with well-tended gardens. Cypress plank floors with radiant heat, carved wooden counters, slate floors in the bathroom, and cozy plaids and prints in the bedrooms add to the total comfort—all this and a view of Nahuel Huapi Lake. ⊠ *Av. Bustillo, Km 2.6, 8402* ☎ *2944/523–523* ⊕ *www.villahuinid.com.ar* ↶ *46 rooms, 17 cabins* ♧ *Restaurant, bar, gym, indoor pool, hot tub, sauna, steam room, massage, IDD phones, kitchens, cable TV, library, playground* ⊟ *AE, MC, V.*

$$$–$$$$ Club Hotel Catedral. Popular with Argentine and Brazilian skiers (so book well in advance), this venerable stone-and-wood apart-hotel sits on a hill just beyond the tram building across the road from the Cerro Catedral ski area, 16 km (10 mi) from Bariloche. The gracious former dining room, with its large windows framing a perfect postcard view of the lake and surrounding mountains, has been reinvented as a living room. Apartments sleep up to four people. ⊠ *Base Cerro Catedral, 8400* ☎ *2944/460–006* ⊕ *www.clubhotel.com.ar* ⊠ *Av. Córdoba 1345, fl. 7, Buenos Aires, 1055* ☎ *11/4816–4811* ↶ *60 apartments* ♧ *3 restaurants, kitchenettes, 2 tennis courts, pool, sauna, bar, travel services, Internet* ⊟ *AE, DC, MC, V* ⊘ *Closed Apr.–May and Oct.–Nov.* ⫪⊘ *BP.*

$$$–$$$$ Hotel Tunquelen. Surrounded by 20 acres of woods and gardens, this châteaulike hotel outside Bariloche is visible from the lake but not from the road to Llao Llao. An uninterrupted view across the water to distant peaks—even from the indoor pool—has a calming effect. Rooms have whitewashed stucco and native wood, and they open onto the garden or overlook the lake (for an extra US$30 or so). A downstairs dining room serves breakfast and dinner, and cocktails are served in the garden, weather permitting. ⊠ *Av. Bustillo, Km 24.5, 24½ km (13 mi) west of Bariloche on the road to Llao Llao, 8400* ☎ *2944/448–600* ⊕ *www.maresur.com* ⌁ *31 rooms, 1 suite, 8 apartments* ⌂ *Restaurant, cable TV, indoor pool, gym, sauna, massage, dock, bicycles, piano bar, meeting rooms, travel services, free parking* ☰ *AE, DC, MC, V* ❑ CP.

$$ ⊞ **Aconcagua Hotel.** A tidy stucco building close to the Civic Center, this four-story hotel has weekly rates for its simple basic rooms, some of which have lake views. It's neither luxurious nor particularly attractive, but it provides reasonable comfort for little money. ⊠ *Av. San Martín 289, 8400* ☎ *2944/424–718* ⊕ *www.aconcaguahotel.com.ar* ⌁ *32 rooms* ⌂ *Snack bar, free parking* ☰ *AE, MC, V* ❑ CP.

$ ⊞ **Casita Suiza.** Swiss-owned and -operated since 1961, this charming downtown chalet exudes old-world hospitality. The owners have lovingly painted flowers on the walls. Rooms are well maintained, and rates include a hearty breakfast with homemade wheat bread, jams, and juices. In summer and spring the street-side terrace explodes with blossoming pansies and violets. ⊠ *Quaglia 342, 8400* ☎ *2944/426–111* ⊕ *www.casitasuiza.com* ⌁ *13 rooms* ⌂ *Restaurant, cable TV, bar, laundry service* ☰ *AE, DC, MC, V* ☉ *Closed July 10–23* ❑ CP.

Nightlife & the Arts

The **Map Room** (⊠ Urquiza 248 ☎ 2944/456–856 ⊕ www.themaproom.com.ar) is a delightfully dim haunt, lined with maps from the world travels of the friendly Canadian-Argentine couple that owns the place. The twenty-to-thirtysomething crowd comes for good local beer on tap and meals—including English breakfast—served in the restaurant downstairs.

Three of the town's most popular *discotecas* (discos) are all on the same street, Avenida J. M. de Rosas. Whole families—from children to grandparents—go to discos, though on Saturday night only people 25 years and older are admitted. The clubs are especially busy during school holidays and ski season. You can dance the night away at **Cerebro** (⊠ 405 Av. J. M. de Rosas ☎ 2944/424–948). Bariloche's oldest disco is **El Grisú** (⊠ 574 Av. J. M. de Rosas ☎ 2944/424–483). **Roket** (⊠ 424 Av. J. M. de Rosas ☎ 2944/431–940 ⊕ www.roket.com) has a cutting-edge sound system.

Patagonia has a thriving culture of microbrewed beer, and Bariloche is a natural center of the industry. The **Bariloche Microbrew Tour** (⊠ Information at The Map Room bar, Urquiza 248 ☎ Randy at 2994/1551–7677 or 2944/525–237, The Map Room 2944/456–856 ⊕ www.brewtour.com.ar ☒ 80 pesos ⌂ Reservations required) is a lively tour of four brewpubs around Bariloche, given in English and Spanish, that leaves at 7 PM each Wednesday and goes until midnight.

A Patagonian Feast

SINCE SHEEP AND CATTLE far outnumber humans in Patagonia, expect lamb and beef to appear on almost every menu. Often cooked on a *parrilla* (grill) before your eyes, beef, lamb, and *chorizos* (homemade sausages) are enhanced by a spoonful of *chimichurri* sauce (made from olive oil, garlic, oregano, and sometimes chopped tomatoes and onions). On ranches and in some restaurants, you may have the opportunity to try gaucho-style meat *al asador*, also known as *a la cruz*, where the lamb is attached to a metal cross placed in the ground over hot coals. The heat is adjusted by raking the coals as the meat cooks, and the fat runs down to create a natural marinade. Lamb (*cordero*) and goat (*chivito*) cooked in this manner are delicious, and the camaraderie of standing around the fire sipping *mate* (a traditional Argentine tea) or wine while the meat cooks is part of the gaucho tradition.

Throughout the northern Andean lake district, local farmed trout, salmon, and *abadejo* (a white fish) are grilled, fried, baked, smoked, and dried. Wild game such as *ciervo* (venison) and *jabalí* (wild boar) is prepared in a variety of ways, from carpaccio to grilled steaks. It's also often smoked; smoked fish (particularly trout) and game from the region are popular appetizers throughout Argentina. Farther south, in Tierra del Fuego, the seafood specialties are black hake (*merluza negra*), a rich white fish with

a texture similar to Patagonian toothfish—which is known in the U.S. as "Chilean sea bass"—and the legendary *centolla* (king crab or spider crab), which is, curiously, easier to find fresh in Buenos Aires than in Ushuaia. Pizza and empanadas are as popular here as elsewhere in the country, and as elsewhere, pasta also appears on every menu—look for *pasta casera* (homemade pasta)—and it's often served with sauces that are listed separately.

Beer and wine are both on the upswing in Patagonia, and you'll stumble across the rather unusual sight of a brewpub inside and outside of most of the region's cities. Dozens of microbreweries now dot the Lakes region in particular. Wine, too, is a growing industry in these parts, with the appropriately named Bodegas del Fin del Mundo, based in the Neuquén province, leading the way with some good Pinot Noirs and Cabernet-Malbec blends.

If the 10 PM dinner hour seems too far away from lunch, tea is a welcome break around 5 or 6 PM. Patagonia's Welsh teahouses, a product of Welsh immigration in the 19th century, serve delicious cakes, tarts, and cookies from recipes that have been handed down for generations. Jams made from local berries spread on homemade bread and scones are a welcome treat on a blustery day.

Sports & the Outdoors

FISHING Fishing season runs November 15–May 1. In some areas, catch-and-re-
lease is allowed year-around; in some places it's compulsory, and in some,
catches may be kept. Guides are available by the day or the week.
Nahuel Huapi, Gutiérrez, Mascardi, Correntoso, and Traful are just a
few of the many lakes in the northern lake district that attract fishing
fanatics from all over the world. If you're seeking the perfect pool or
secret stream for fly-fishing, you may have to do some hiking, particularly along the banks of the Chimehuín, Limay, Traful, and Correntoso
rivers. Near Junín de los Andes, the Río Malleo (Malleo River) and the
Currihué, Huechulafquen, Paimún, and Lácar lakes are also good fishing grounds. Near El Bolsón and Esquel in the Parque Nacional los Alerces,
many remote lakes and streams are accessible only by boat or seldom-
traveled dirt roads. Fishing lodges offer rustic comfort in beautiful settings; boats, guides, and plenty of fishing tales are usually included. Make
reservations early, as they're booked well in advance by an international
clientele of repeat visitors.

Fishing licenses allowing you to catch brown, rainbow, and brook trout
as well as perch and *salar sebago* (landlocked salmon) are available in
Bariloche at the **Direcciones Provinciales de Pesca** (⌂ Elfleín 10 ☎ 2944/
425–160). You can also get licenses at the Nahuel Huapi National Park
office and at most tackle shops. Boats can be rented at **Charlie Lake Rent-
A-Boat** (⌂ Av. Ezequiel Bustillo, Km 16.6 ☎☎ 2944/448–562).

Oscar Baruzzi at **Baruzzi Deportes** (⌂ Urquiza 250 ☎ 2944/424–922)
is a good local fishing guide. **Martín Pescador** (⌂ Rolando 257 ☎ 2944/
422–275) has a shop with fishing and hunting equipment. Ricardo
Almeijeiras, also a guide, owns the **Patagonia Fly Shop** (⌂ Quinchahuala
200, Av. Bustillo, Km 6.7 ☎☎ 2944/441–944).

HIKING Nahuel Huapi National Park has many forest trails that lead to hidden
lakes, tumbling streams, waterfalls, glaciers, and mountaintop vistas.
For maps and information in English on trails, distances, and degree of
difficulty, visit the **Parques Nacionales** (⌂ Av. San Martín 24 ☎ 2944/
423–111) office at the Civic Center. For ambitious treks, mountaineering, or use of mountain huts and climbing permits, contact **Club Andino
Bariloche** (⌂ 20 de Febrero 30 ☎ 2944/422–266 ⊕ www.clubandino.
com).

HORSEBACK *Cabalgatas* (horseback outings) can be arranged by the day or the week.
RIDING Argentine horses are sturdy and well trained, much like American Quarter Horses. *Tábanas* (horseflies) attack humans and animals in summer
months, so bring repellent. **El Manso** (☎ 2944/523–641 or 2944/441–
378) combines riding and rafting over the border to Chile. Tom Wes-
ley at the **Club Hípico Bariloche** (⌂ Av. Bustillo, Km 15.5 ☎☎ 2944/448–
193 ⊕ www.bariloche.org/twesley.html) does rides lasting from one
hour to a week.

MOUNTAIN The entire Nahuel Huapi National Park is ripe for mountain biking.
BIKING Whether you're a beginner or an expert, you can find a trail to suit your
ability. Popular rides are from the parking lot at the Cerro Catedral ski
area to Lago Gutiérrez and down from Cerro Otto. Local tour agencies

can arrange guided tours by the hour or day and even international excursions to Chile. Rental agencies provide maps and suggestions and sometimes recommend guides.

Adventure World (⊠ Base of Cerro Catedral ☎ 2944/460–164 or 2944/422–637) rents bikes at the ski area. From there you can ride off on your own or follow a guide down to Lago Guitérrez. **Alunco** (⊠ Moreno 187 ☎ 2944/422–283 ⊕ www.alcunoturismo.com.ar) is a full-service travel agency that arranges bike tours with local companies. **Dirty Bikes** (⊠ Vice Almirante O'Connor 681 ☎ 2944/425–616 ⊕ www.dirtybikes.com.ar) rents, repairs, and sells bikes and arranges local tours. **La Bolsa del Deporte** (⊠ Diagonal Capraro 1081 ☎ 944/433–111) rents and sells new and used bikes.

PARAGLIDING &
ZIPLINE TOURS
Parapente (paragliding) gives you the opportunity to soar with the condors through mountains and out over lakes, lagoons, and valleys. Cerro Otto and Cerro Catedral (both accessible by ski lifts) are popular launch sites. For equipment and guide information, contact **Parapente Bariloche** (☎ 2944/462–234, 2944/1555–2403 cell). **Canopy** (☎ 2944/1560–7191 ⊕ www.canopybariloche.com) allows you to zipline through (or, rather, above) the forest of Colonia Suiza.

SKIING
Cerro Catedral is the largest and oldest ski area in South America, with 29 lifts, mostly intermediate terrain, and a comfortable altitude of 6,725 feet. The runs are long, varied, and very scenic. Two ski areas share 4,500 acres of skiable terrain. Avoid Catedral during the first three weeks of July, when the slopes are absolutely packed with youngsters. **Lado Bueno** (The Good Side) has a vertical drop of 3,000 feet, mostly in the fall line. **Robles** goes about 300 feet higher, offering open bowls and better snow for beginners and intermediates at higher elevation. From the top of the second Robles chair, a Poma Lift transports skiers to a weather station at 7,385 feet, where a small restaurant, **Refugio Lynch,** is tucked into a wind-sculpted snow pocket on the edge of an abyss with a stupendous 360-degree view of Nahuel Huapi Lake, Monte Tronadór, and the Andes. **Villa Catedral,** at the base of the mountain, has ski retail and rental shops, information and ticket sales, ski school offices, restaurants, private ski clubs, an ice rink, and even a disco. Frequent buses transport skiers from Bariloche to the ski area. Adult lift tickets run 95 pesos in high season. For more information, contact **Catedral Alta Patagonia** (☎ 2944/423–776, 11/4780–3300 in Buenos Aires ⊕ www.catedralaltapatagonia.com).

For information and trail maps, contact **La Secretaría de Turismo de Río Negro** (⊠ 12 de Octubre 605 ☎ 2944/423–188). **Club Andino Bariloche** (⊠ 20 de Febrero 30 ☎ 2944/422–266) also has information and trail maps.

WHITE-WATER
RAFTING
With all the interconnected lakes and rivers in the national park, there's something for everyone—from your basic family float down the swift-flowing, scenic Río Limay to a wild and exciting ride down Río Manso (Class II), which takes you 16 km (10 mi) in three hours. If you're really adventurous, you can take the Manso all the way to Chile (Class IV) through spectacular scenery. Some tour companies organize a trip

down the Manso with return by horseback and a cookout at a ranch. **Adventure World** (✉ At the Base of Cerro Catedral ☎ 2944/460–164) does one-day and three-day raft trips on the Río Manso, with a combination horseback trip to the Chilean border available. **Alunco** (✉ Moreno 187 ☎ 2944/422–283 ⊕ www.alcunoturismo.com.ar) arranges rafting trips throughout the area. **Bariloche Rafting** (✉ Mitre 86, Room 5 ☎ 2944/435–708) offers trips along the Limay. **Cumbres Patagonia** (✉ Villegas 222 ☎ 2944/423–283) arranges trips on the Ríos Limay and Manso. **El Manso** (☎ 2944/523–641, 2944/1558–3114 cell) specializes in white-water rafting trips on the Manso River.

Villa La Angostura

❷ *In Neuquén Province, 81 km (50 mi) northwest of Bariloche (a 1-hr drive on R231 around the east end of Lago Nahuel Huapi; also accessible by boat from Bariloche); 90 km (56 mi) southwest of San Martín de los Andes on R234 (the Seven Lakes Rd., partly unpaved and closed for much of winter).*

Thoughtful planning and strict adherence to building codes have made this lakeside hamlet on a narrow isthmus off the shores of Lake Nahuel Huapi an attractive escape from the bustle of Bariloche. In the original Villa on the lake and elsewhere in town, log art abounds—over doorways, under window sills, on signposts, and on fences. There's even a large hand-carved wooden telephone on the street in front of the telephone office. Most of the shops and restaurants are in a commercial area called El Cruce (the Crossing). The name refers to the crossing of R231, which goes from Bariloche to the Chilean border, with the road to the port, Nahuel Huapi, and the Seven Lakes Road, R234, to San Martín de los Andes. The **Secretaría de Turismo y Cultura** (✉ Av. Siete Lagos 93 ☎ 2944/494–124) is at the southern end of Avenida Arrayanes.

In recent years, the wealthier set of Villa La Angostura—and the numerous skiers and snowbirds from the capital that frequent the area—have established an enclave called **Puerto Manzano**, 7 km (4½ mi) from El Cruce along R231. Its roads, which twist their way through idyllic woodsy scenery and beaches around a little bay, are now lined with elaborate vacation lodges half-buried in the forest and flashy modern hotels with indoor-outdoor swimming pools and elaborate spas. Puerto Manzano is also perfectly located for powder-hounds—it's nestled right next to the road that leads up to Villa La Angostura's small but popular ski area. **Cerro Bayo** (Bay-Color Mountain) is 9 km (5½ mi) northeast of town and open year-round for skiers (it's open to snowboarders in winter only), and also for mountain biking in the summer. Two chairlifts take you to the top (5,000 feet), where a 5-km (3-mi) panoramic trail wends its way around the mountain to a wide-angle view of Nahuel Huapi Lake. Six surface lifts transport skiers and snowboarders to easy and intermediate runs. The El Tronadór café at the mid-station serves, among other fare, waffles with local jams. El Refugio Chaltén, at the base of the mountain, serves goulash, lamb stew, snacks, and beverages.

6

The **Parque Nacional los Arrayanes** (⊠ 12 km [7½ mi] along a trail from the Península Quetrihué ☎ 2944/423–111) is the only forest of arrayanes in the world. These native trees absorb so much water through their thin skins that they force all other vegetation around them to die, leaving a barren forest of peeling cinnamon-color trunks. You can make this excursion by boat from Bariloche via Isla Victoria or from the pier at Bahía Brava in Villa La Angostura; or walk (three hours) or ride a bike or horse across the isthmus. A nice combination is to go by boat and return by bicycle (it's all downhill that way).

Where to Stay & Eat

$$–$$$$ ✕ **Tinto Bistró.** The hippest new spot in town is a confluence of form and function: it's not too trendy to serve great, carefully prepared food. The eclectic menu draws a lot of inspiration from Asia, while a spicy *cazuela* (stew) of fresh seafood with coconut milk also has a Brazilian bent. The wine list is also impressive, with many of Argentina's top labels poured at very fair prices. Avoid sitting by the dangerous heater in the back corner of the room. ⊠ *Bv. Nahuel Huapi 34* ☎ *2944/494–924* ▭ *AE, DC, MC, V.*

$$–$$$ ✕ **El Gusto Es Mío.** Customers of the popular pizzeria next door apparently demanded the opening of this new addition to Villa Angostura's lineup, and the eminently friendly owners happily obliged. The little white house could hardly be any cuter, with just a handful of intimate tables in low ambient lighting and the kitchen just visible in back. The cooking, however, is more haute than simple; a rainbow trout might be served with a delicate white wine sauce, or the filet mignon with a spill of earthy local mushrooms. ⊠ *Cerro Belvedere 69* ☎ *2944/495–515* ▭ *No credit cards.*

$–$$$ ✕ **Australis.** This is one of the best, and friendliest, microbreweries in Patagonia. The excellent cuisine integrates beer, all the way through to dessert— a memorable flan is made with chocolate and a delicious stout. The restaurant will cook up your own freshly caught fish if you bring it in. ⊠ *Av. Arrayanes (R231) 2490* ☎ *2944/495–645* ▭ *AE, DC, MC, V.*

¢–$ ✕ **La Casita de la Oma.** Between the bay and the main street, this teahouse serves homemade soups, sandwiches, salads, and a tempting array of cakes, pies, and scones. Jars of jams line the shelves. ⊠ *Cerro Inacayal 303* ☎ *2544/494–602* ▭ *MC, V* ⊗ *Closed May.*

$$$$ ✕▣ **Las Balsas.** A short drive down a secluded (and unpaved) road **Fodor'sChoice** brings you to this Relais & Châteaux hotel right at the edge of Lago ★ Nahuel Huapi. Every room has a different decor, but all have views of the woods or the lake. The relaxing spa features an indoor-outdoor pool framed by the lake. Afternoon tea and evening cocktails are served in the living room, a homey blend of wicker, natural wood, kilim rugs, and old photographs. In the candlelit dining room, fresh trout and spectacular game dishes are accompanied by vegetables and spices grown in the hotel's organic garden; don't miss the unbelievable venison ravioli. Dinner reservations are advised if you're not a guest. ⊠ *Bahía las Balsas, 8407* ☎ *2944/494–308* ⊕ *www.lasbalsas.com* ⤺ *13 rooms, 2 suites* ⌂ *Restaurant, pool, gym, hot tub, sauna, massage, beach, dock, bicycles, bar, recreation room, babysitting, laundry service, Internet, meeting rooms* ▭ *AE, MC, V* ⊗ *Closed May–Aug.* ⦿ *CP.*

★ **$$$$** ✕🏠 **Hotel Correntoso.** You can see the fish jump from your bedroom window, your dining table, through the glass panels of the encircling deck, or from the refurbished 100-year-old fishing bar down by the lake. Perched on a hill where the Correntoso River runs into Nahuel Huapi Lake, this landmark hotel celebrates its place in history with old photos, light fixtures made from coihué branches, hand-woven Mapuche fabrics, and custom-made furniture covered in leather and linen. The bar often has live music, and the restaurant overlooking the lake serves Patagonian specialties such as hare, wild boar, lamb, beef, and, of course, fish from local lakes and streams. ⊠ *RN 231 (Km 86), Puente Correntoso, 8407* 🕾 *2944/156–19727, 11/4803–0030 in Buenos Aires* ⊕ *www. correntoso.com* 🛏 *16 rooms, 16 suites* ⚖ *Restaurant, dining room, cable TV, marina, fishing, bar, pub, library, Internet* ⊟ *AE, MC, V.*

$$$$
Fodor'sChoice
★ 🏠 **Puerto Sur.** No hotel more perfectly embodies the new face of Puerto Manzano than this ingeniously designed masterpiece by architect Nora Larosa. Stone and wood flow together in harmony throughout the angular space built into the side of a hill. Views of the lake and mountains pour in from enormous picture windows and skylights. Every room is graced with a lakeview Jacuzzi and restrained modern art. The spa, indoor-outdoor pool, and private beach could hardly be any more elegant, service is impeccable, and owner Claudio is delightfully down-to-earth. What makes it all even harder to believe are the reasonable prices, at the very bottom of the $$$$ range. A scant 30 pesos extra gets you a private deck. ⊠ *Los Pinos 221, Puerto Manzano* 🕾 *2944/495–624* ⊕ *www.hosteriapuertosur.com.ar* 🛏 *7 rooms, 3 suites, 4 cabins* ⚖ *Restaurant, pool, private beach, movie theater, Wi-Fi, game room, health club, massage, sauna, steam room, bar* ⊟ *AE, DC, MC, V* ⟊ *CP.*

$$$–$$$$ 🏠 **Costa Serena.** Every room at this impressive complex in Puerto Manzano has a lake view—though they do border on being fancifully overdone, with bizarre glacier paintings. A-frame *cabañas* (cabins) sleep up to seven people. Suites have huge, wooden Jacuzzis with views straight out to the water. During high season a one-week minimum stay is required. ⊠ *Los Pinos 435, Puerto Manzano* 🕾 *2944/494–053* ⊕ *www. costaserenavla.com.ar* 🛏 *7 rooms, 3 suites, 4 cabins* ⚖ *Restaurant, pool, private beach, movie theater, game room, health club, sauna, steam room, bar* ⊟ *AE, DC, MC, V* ⟊ *CP.*

$$$–$$$$ 🏠 **Patagonia Paraíso.** This modern property overlooks a beach of volcanic sand. Rooms, which are all dubbed "suites," have balconies with lake views and deliciously soft and elegant linens. Larger deluxe suites, for a bit more, have two-person Jacuzzis that overlook the lake and rolling forested hills. ⊠ *Los Pinos 367, Puerto Manzano* 🕾 *2944/475–429* ⊕ *www.patagoniaparaiso.com* 🛏 *10 suites* ⚖ *Bar, minibars, meeting room, in-room safes, Jacuzzis* ⊟ *AE, DC, MC, V* ⟊ *CP.*

$$ 🏠 **Naranjo en Flor.** This tranquil mountainside retreat in Puerto Manzano looks like a Norman hunting lodge and feels like home, with a fireplace in the living room and a piano bar and playroom for bad-weather days. The restaurant offers interesting modern French cuisine. The modern carpeted bedrooms have big windows and tasteful antiques. ⊠ *Chucao 62, Puerto Manzano, 8407* 🕾 *2955/494–863* ⊘ *naranjoenflor@infovia. com.ar* 🛏 *8 rooms* ⚖ *Restaurant, pool, bar, travel services* ⊟ *AE, V* ⟊ *CP.*

$$ 🏠 **Pichi Rincón.** In a grove of trees just beyond the village, this simple two-story inn looks across a spacious lawn through the forest and to the lake. Two columns of gray river rock guard the comfortable sitting area, which has a fireplace. Natural wood dominates everywhere, from common areas to rooms, and hefty pine furniture decorates the rooms. ⊠ *Off Av. Quetrihué, 3 km (2 mi) south of town on R231; just before Correntoso, turn left on Av. Quetrihué, 8407* 🏠 *2944/494–186* ⊕ *www.pichirincon.com.ar* ⤳ *12 rooms, 3 cabins* ⚒ *Dining room, Internet, pool, game room, sauna, massage; no in-room TVs* 🖂 *MC, V* ⦿ *CP.*

Sports & the Outdoors

FISHING The bays and inlets of Lago Nahuel Huapi are ideal for trolling and spinning, and the mouth of the Río Correntoso (Correntoso River) is famous for its trout. For trolling, spinning, or fly-fishing equipment rental or purchase, or for guides, contact the **Banana Fly Shop** (⊠ Av. Arrayanes 282 ☎ 2944/494–634).

HORSEBACK RIDING Most trails used for hiking and mountain biking are also used for horseback riding. Picnic stops with a swim in a river, and an asado at the end of the ride are added attractions. Horses are available from **Los Saucos** (⊠ R231, Km 61.8 [Av. Arrayanes 2500] ☎ 2944/494–853). Another good riding outfit is **Cahuel Hueñi** (⊠ Av. Siete Lagos ☎ 2944/1561–4034). **Cabalgatas Correntoso** (⊠ Cacique Antriao 1850, on the road toward Mirador Belvedere ☎ 2944/1560–4903 or 2944/1551–0559 ⊕ www.cabalgatacorrentoso.com.ar) offers three day trips—a 2-hour lakeside jaunt, a 3½-hour waterfall riding-hiking trip, or a 9-hour circuit to the valley of Cajón Negro, which includes lunch and a swim; there are also two- to four-day trips into the mountains.

MOUNTAIN BIKING The area has more bike rental shops than gas stations. You can easily ride from the village to such places as Laguna Verde, near the port, or off the Seven Lakes Road to Mirador Belvedere and on to the waterfalls at Inacayal. The tourist office has a brochure, *Paseos y Excursiones,* with maps, distances, and descriptions (in Spanish) of mountain biking, hiking, and horseback-riding trails throughout the area. Maps, information, and rentals are available in Las Cruces at **Free Bikes** (⊠ Las Fucsias 268 ☎ 2944/495–047 ⊕ www.freebikes.com.ar). **IAN Bikes** (⊠ Topa Topa 102 and Las Fucsias ☎ 2944/495–005) rents bikes, too. Bikes are also available at the base of Cerro Bayo, at **Mountain Bike Cerro Bayo** (☎ 2944/495–047).

SKIING **Cerro Bayo** (🏠 2944/494–189 ⊕ www.cerrobayoweb.com), 9 km (5½ mi) from El Cruce via R66, has good skiing from July through September. There are 20 runs—nothing too challenging, but fun nonetheless. Day rates are less than at most other ski areas. Rental equipment and lessons are available at the base facility. You can cruise on skis in winter or mountain bike in summer down a long road with spectacular views of the lake and surrounding mountains.

Shopping

Shops along Avenida Arrayanes carry products that are typical of the area—chocolate, smoked meats, dried mushrooms, handicrafts, sporting goods, and knitwear. One of the best of the many chocolate shops is **En El Bosque** (✉ Arrayanes 218 ☎ 2944/495–738), a delicious artisanal producer where the smells of homemade sweets waft out onto the sidewalk; this one also doubles as a little teahouse. Delicious homemade jams (*dulces caseros*) are found in nearly every shop, at roadside stands, and at teahouses.

Villa Traful

❸ *60 km (37 mi) north of Villa La Angostura on R231 and R65, 100 km (60 mi) northwest of Bariloche on R237 and R65.*

Small log houses built by early settlers peek through the cypress forest along the way to Villa Traful, a village on Lago Traful. The town still feels untouched by the likes of American mogul Ted Turner (who has bought up a good bit of this part of Patagonia): it consists of a few dozen log cabins, horse corrals, two fishing lodges, shops for picnic and fishing supplies, and a park ranger's office. Less visited than those in neighboring villages, the fine ranches and private fishing lodges here are tucked back in the surrounding mountains. By day swimmers play on sandy beaches on the lake, a lone water skier cuts the still blue water, and divers go under to explore the mysteries of a submerged forest. Night brings silence, thousands of stars, and the glow of a lakeside campfire.

The **Oficina Municipal de Turismo** (✉ Across from municipal pier ☎ 2944/479–020) can assist you with planning excursions.

Only 3 km (2 mi) from the village is **Arroyo Blanco**, a waterfall that cascades 66 feet over the rocks into a natural pool. You can walk or ride (a bike or a horse) through 1,000-year-old forests above and beyond the village to this waterfall as well as to nearby caves and mountain lookouts.

Where to Stay & Eat

Besides staying in the resorts outside town, you can also pitch a tent and throw your sleeping bag down just about anywhere along the lake. Campsites with restrooms, benches, tables, and fire pits are plentiful along the southern shore of the lake. For exquisite beauty, look for Puerto Arrayanes at the western end of the lake. A large campground near the village is **Camping Vulcanche** (☎ 2944/479–061).

¢–$$$ ✗ **Ñancú Lahuén.** The carved-wood sign says TEAHOUSE, but it's much more. Sandwiches, omelets, homemade ice cream, tarts, pies, and anything chocolate are served from noon until sundown, when salmon, trout, and steak dinners are served in an adjacent log house with a hand-hewn thatched roof, an open fireplace, and a floor of trunk rounds. ✉ *R65* ☎ *2944/479–017* ⊕ *www.interpatagonia.com/nanculahuen* ▤ *AE, DC, MC, V.*

$ ✗▥ **Hostería y Cabañas Villa Traful.** Across the road from the lake is a large log house, constructed in the 1940s as a fisherman's inn. Cabins that sleep two to six people are also available for rent. Afternoon tea is served, as are dinners of trout and salmon. The hotel can arrange fishing guides and lake tours. ✉ *R65, 9006* ☎ *2944/479–006* ☎☎ *2944/479–005* ⊕ *www.hosteriavillatraful.com* ⇨ *5 cabins* ⚒ *Fishing, mountain bikes* ▤ *No credit cards* ☉ *May–Oct.*

Sports & the Outdoors

Trails through forests to lakes, lagoons, streams, and waterfalls are accessible on foot, horseback, or mountain bike.

You can dive to 30 meters (98 feet) in crystalline water and explore a submerged cypress forest. For information, contact **Cabañas Aiken** (☎ 2944/479–048).

This area is famous for its land-locked salmon and record-breaking-size trout in Lago Traful and the Laguna Las Mellizas (Twins Lagoon), 5 km (3 mi) north of town. Fishing season runs from November 15 to April 15. **Osvaldo Brandeman** (✉ Villa Traful ☎ 2944/479–048) is a local fishing guide.

Junín de los Andes

❹ *41 km (25 mi) northeast of San Martín on paved R234, 219 km (136 mi) north of Bariloche on paved R234, R40, and R237.*

The quickest route between Bariloche and San Martín de los Andes—and the only route for much of winter—is the paved road that runs through this typical agricultural town, where gauchos ride along the road, their dogs trotting faithfully behind. Once a fort in a region inhabited by the Mapuche, Junín de los Andes became a town during the last phase (1882–83) of the Conquista del Desierto, making it the oldest town in Neuquén Province. For centuries the valley where the town lies was the trading route of the Mapuche between mountainous Chile and the fertile plains of Argentina. Today Mapuche descendants sell their handicrafts and weavings in local shops and fairs. Junín also claims to be the trout capital of Patagonia, and you'll notice homages everywhere from a giant, kitschy statue of a fisherman hauling in his fresh catch (it's a classic photo op) to the street signs of the town, each of which are adorned with a little trout.

Where to Eat

The **Dirección Municipal de Turismo** (✉ Coronel Suárez and Padre Milanesio ☎ 2972/491–160) has information on lodging, dining, campgrounds, and nearby fishing lodges, which are open November–April.

$–$$ ✗ **Ruca Hueney.** For decades, this bustling joint on the corner of the main plaza has been Junín's classiest restaurant, and it's still the big trout in a small pond, teeming with local families on weekends. Don't expect culinary fireworks, but the service is extremely polite and the fish impeccably fresh—ask for it undercooked for best results. Pastas such as spinach-filled *canelones* are satisfying and surprisingly tasty, and there are even a few Middle Eastern specialties on the menu, such as *empanadas arabes* (beef empanadas). ✉ *Col. Suárez and Padre Milanesia* ☎ *2972/491–113* ⊕ *www.ruca-hueney.com.ar* ▭ *AE, MC, V.*

EN ROUTE The R237 north from Bariloche, which connects with the R40 farther north, isn't just the way to Junín de los Andes—it's also the way you'll be going to San Martín de los Andes during any season in which the Seven Lakes Road is closed. Although you may be distraught to miss the famous scenery of the Seven Lakes

Road, the R237 has some spectacular eye candy of its own, hugging the banks of the Río Limay, rising and dipping through colorful vistas of river flowing beneath hilly pine forests beneath craggy peaks. Most notable along the road as it rises toward Confluencia (the turn-off to Villa Traful) is the Valle Encantado (enchanted valley), which is studded with some remarkable rock formations that are evocative of Chile's Torres del Paine national park—or even Spain's Montserrat.

San Martín de los Andes

❺ *260 km (161 mi) north of Bariloche on R237, R40, and R234 via Junín de los Andes (a 4-hr drive), 158 km (98 mi) north of Bariloche on R237 and R63 over the Córdoba Pass (69 km [42 mi] is paved), 90 km (56 mi) northeast of Villa La Angostura on R234 (the Seven Lakes Rd., partly unpaved and closed for much of winter).*

Surrounded by lakes, dense forests, and mountains, including Cerro Chapelco, one of Argentina's top ski areas, San Martín de los Andes lies in a natural basin at the foot of Lago Lácar. It's the major tourist center in Neuquén Province and the gateway for exploring the Parque Nacional Lanín. Wide, flat streets run from the town pier on the eastern shore of Lago Lácar, along sidewalks lined with rosebushes, and near Plaza San Martín, the main square, two streets—San Martín and Gral. Villegas—teem with block after block of ski stores, chocolatiers, trinket shops, clothing boutiques, and cute hotels.

San Martín was founded in 1898; early Patagonian houses built with local timber and covered with corrugated metal to keep the wind out are still visible around the Plaza. But most of the city doesn't feel old at all; San Martín's longest-running restaurant, for instance, was founded in 1978—and founded by entrepreneurs who, like many of the city's 25,000 permanent residents, are Buenos Aires natives who moved down here to take part in the tourist industry.

One house of note, the **Obeid family mansion** (⊠ Roca and Coronel Perez), was built in 1903 with materials brought from Valdivia (Chile). For information on tours, lodging, and other services, contact the **Dirección Municipal de Turismo** (⊠ Av. San Martín and J. M. Rosas 790 ☎ 2972/427–347 ⊕ www.smandes.gov.ar); it's open daily 8 AM–9 PM.

If you've ever wondered how Patagonia's remarkable trout industry is sustained, the **Trampa de Peces** will give you a good idea. It's a publicly funded trout station, just outside of downtown along the lake, where trout are captured and reproduced to increase the trout population in Lago Lácar. ⊠ *Gral. Roca and Costanera* ☎ *2972/4222–927* 🕾 *Free* 🕙 *Dec.–Feb., Tues.–Sun. 10–1 and 4–7; guided tours at 11, noon, and 5. Mar.–Nov., Tues.–Sun. 11–4:30; guided tours at 11 and 3.*

The **Parque Nacional Lanín** (Lanín National Park), north of Nahuel Huapi National Park, runs north–south for 150 km (93 mi) along the Chilean border and covers 3,920 square km (1,508 square mi) of mountain lakes, rivers, and ancient forests. Giant *Araucaria araucana* (monkey puzzle trees) grow in thick groves in the northern region of the park. Towering over the entire park and visible from every direction, **Volcán Lanín** (Lanín Volcano) rises 12,378 feet in solitary snow-clad splendor—an imposing white cone on the western horizon.

The **Intendencia de Parques Nacionales** (National Park Office) building is a classic example of Andean-alpine architecture in the style of Bustillos, who did the Civic Center in Bariloche and the Llao Llao Hotel. Here you can get maps and information on all the parks and trails in the region, as well as fishing permits and information on big-game hunting. ⊠ *E. Frey 749* ☎ *2972/427–233* ⊙ *Weekdays 8–1:30.*

From town you can walk, mountain bike, or drive to the **Mirador de las Bandurrias** (Bandurrias Overlook), 8 km (5 mi) away, where you get a magnificent view of the town and the lake. To walk there, take Avenida San Martín to the lake, turn right, cross the bridge over Puahullo Creek, and then head uphill on a path around the mountain.

The rather long (200 km [124 mi] round-trip) but infinitely rewarding excursion to **Lago Huechulafquen** and **Lago Paimún** (Paimún Lake) can be made via Junín de los Andes. An overnight stay is recommended. From San Martín, take R234 north to Junín, and then take the dirt road (R61) west. As you speed across the open range following the **Río Chimehuín** toward the lake, Lanín Volcano plays hide-and-seek on the horizon. This is serious fishing country. Numerous beaches and campsites along the lakeshore make good picnic stops.

Where to Stay & Eat

Restaurants in San Martín are mostly parrillas, pizzerias, and simple cafés. As for lodging, though there are 5,000 hotel beds in town, surprisingly few of them are modern and luxurious. San Martín's fancy old hotels are noticeably dated these days, especially when compared with the spectacular spa complexes that have become commonplace farther south in the Lakes region. Rates are highest in July, when Argentine families take ski vacations, lower in August, and even lower December–March, which is summer and perhaps the best time to visit. There are two beach campgrounds with electricity, hot water, showers, restrooms, and a store at **Playa Catrite** (⊠ R234, Km 4 ☎ 2972/423–091). **Quila Quina** (⊠ R108, Km 12 ☎ 2972/426–919) also has a dining room and some water-sports equipment rental.

$$–$$$$ ✕ **La Reserva.** The name makes reference to the extensive regional and national wine list, but this elegant restaurant, a couple of blocks from the main drag, is much more than that. Elaborate place settings and proper service nod toward formality, but booth seating and warm lighting give the place a relaxed touch, too. Fresh trout is a treat, especially when spiked with preserved lemon, but you can skip the shellfish. Homemade pastas are more interesting than the norm—try the artichoke ravioli. ⊠ *Belgrano 940* ☎ *2972/428–734* ⊕ *www.lareservarestaurante.com.ar* ▭ *AE, DC, MC, V.*

$–$$$$ ✕ **La Tasca.** This is one of the traditional top-end standby choices in town, both for locals and tourists. With tables scattered about the black stone floor, and wine barrels, shelves, and every other imaginable surface stacked with pickled vegetables, smoked meats, cheese rounds, dried mushrooms and herbs, olive oils in cans and bottles, and wine bottles displayed 40 different ways, you might think you're in a Patagonian deli. The set-up encourages diners to be bold and try local wild game dishes; especially good is the "La Tasca" appetizer platter of smoked salmon, deer, boar, and trout pâté. ⊠ *Moreno 866* ☎ *2972/428–663* ⊟ *AE, MC, V.*

☼ **$$–$$$** ✗ **Fondue Betty.** It wouldn't be a ski town without a fondue place, but this one goes above and beyond the call of duty. Fondues are uniformly excellent; the cheese fondue is smooth and rich, while the meat fondue comes with cubes of Argentine beef in assorted cuts and up to twelve condiments. The wine list is also great. The two rooms are cozy and intimate, equally well suited to children and honeymooners; and there's warm, familiar service from a genial older couple. ⊠ *Villegas 586* ☎ *2972/422–522* ⊟ *DC, MC, V.*

$$–$$$ ✗ **El Regional.** This warm, cozy little restaurant has a dazzling array of *fiambres*, including wonderful smoked *jabalí* (wild boar) and pâté of trout. Accompany it with his own sweet artisanal beer—the *rubia* is light and fruity—or choose from a great selection of other Patagonian microbrews. ⊠ *Villegas 965* ☎ *2972/425–326* ⊟ *AE, DC, MC, V.*

$$ ✗ **El Almacén.** The name means "the grocery," and the shop here sells excellent regional wines and artisanal food products. The restaurant is very informal, but turns out some interesting concoctions, such as lamb stew with cayenne pepper, green couscous, and citrus confit. ⊠ *Capitán Drury 857* ☎ *2972/425–663* ⊕ *www.elalmacen.com.ar* ⊟ *DC, MC, V.*

★ **$–$$** ✗ **Kú.** Dark-wood tables and booths, a friendly staff, and a chalkboard: these are three good building blocks for a restaurant. Equally good for canoodling or carousing, this joint offers up Patagonian lamb *al asador*—on the open fire—plus a good assortment of *parrilla* classics. It's a couple of blocks past the main commercial strip, so the place draws a slightly more local crowd than some of its counterparts. ⊠ *Av. San Martín 1053* ☎ *2972/427–039* ⊟ *AE, DC, MC, V.*

$–$$ ✗ **Mendieta.** This may be the friendliest parrilla in Patagonia: cooks, waiters, and the owners scurry about with sizzling meats from the grill and fresh, steaming pasta with various sauces. By 2 PM the tables are filled with locals, who all seem to know each other. Pine racks around the dining room display a good selection of Argentina's fine wines, and you can watch three or more Patagonian lambs being slowly roasted *a la cruz* (on the cross) in the streetside window. ⊠ *Av. San Martín 713* ☎ *2972/429–301* ⊟ *DC, MC, V.*

☼ **$$$$** ⊞ **Le Châtelet.** The von Trapp family wouldn't feel out of place at this pricey but very comfortable downtown hotel that is definitely going for the old-world mountain lodge atmosphere. Standard rooms feel a bit worn, with pink rugs and aging TVs, but suites are a totally different experience, easily worth the extra 50 pesos or so—the Alpine theme is much better executed, and rooms have wooden eaves and working fireplaces. ⊠ *Villegas 650, 8370* ☎ *2972/428–294* ⊕ *www.hotellechatelet.com.ar* ⇌ *28 rooms, 4 suites* ⌂ *Bar, café, pool, room service, meeting rooms, gym, sauna, massage, Internet, free parking* ⊟ *AE, MC, V* ⓧ *CP.*

$$$$ ⊞ **Hotel la Cheminée.** Two blocks from the main street is this comfortable inn with pink-floral chintz and lace curtains. The front entrance could be described, charitably, as faux-chalet chic; still, it's inviting, and plump pillows, fresh flowers, and fireplaces in some rooms add to the coziness. A sumptuous breakfast and an afternoon tea of homemade breads, scones, cakes, cookies, and jams are served. ⊠ *M. Moreno and Gral. Roca, 8370* 🕾🕾 *2972/427–617* ✎ *lacheminee@smandes.com. ar* 🖎 *15 rooms, 3 suites, 1 cottage* ♤ *Café, pool, sauna, bar, free parking* ⊟ *AE, MC, V* ⦿ *CP.*

$$$ ⊞ **Hostería Anay.** *Anay* means "friendship" and that's what you feel when you step inside this small, white stucco–and–log house. Guests gather around the fireplace for tea, in the cozy sitting area or in the bright, cheerful breakfast room. Rooms have simple whitewashed walls, beamed ceilings, and carpeted floors. ⊠ *Cap. Drury 841, 8370* 🕾🕾 *2972/427–514* ⊕ *www.interpatagonia.com/anay* 🖎 *15 rooms* ♤ *Babysitting, laundry service, free parking* ⊟ *No credit cards* ⦿ *CP.*

$$–$$$ ⊞ **Hotel Caupolican.** In season, flowers cascade from the wooden window boxes of this hotel right on the main drag. In the reception and sitting area, locally carved wooden chairs are covered with sheepskin. The simple, comfortable rooms, done in bright colors, are far enough back from the street to be very quiet. The second-floor bar and lounge has a fireplace and windows that face the street. ⊠ *Av. San Martín 969, 8370* 🕾 *2972/427–658* ⊕ *www.interpatagonia.com/caupolican* 🖎 *43 rooms, 2 suites* ♤ *Café, sauna, bar, meeting room, free parking* ⊟ *AE, DC, MC, V* ⦿ *CP.*

Sports & the Outdoors

BEACHES **Playa Catrite,** 4 km (2½ mi) from San Martín on R234, on the south side of Lago Lácar, is a sandy beach with a campground, a store with picnic items, and a café. **Playa Quila Quina,** 18 km (11 mi) from San Martín, is reached by turning off R234 2 km (1 mi) before the road to Catrite and then getting on R108. On the 12-km (7-mi) drive to the lake you'll pass through Mapuche farmlands and forests. The soft, sandy beach and clear water attract both day-trippers and campers as well as residents with vacation homes. Both beaches can also be reached by boat.

BOATING You can rent small boats, canoes, and kayaks at the pier from **Lacar Nonthue** (⊠ Av. Costanera 🕾 2972/427–380). You can also rent a bicycle and take it with you on an all-day excursion to the other side of Lake Lácar.

FISHING During the fishing season (November 15–April 15, and sometimes extended to the end of May in certain areas), local guides can take you to their favorite spots on Lácar, Lolog, Villarino, and Falkner lakes and on the Caleufu, Quiquihue, Malleo, and Hermoso rivers, or farther afield to the Chimehuín River and Lakes Huechulafquen and Paimún. Permits are available at the **Parque Nacional Intendencia** (⊠ Emilio Frey 749 🕾 2972/427–233) or any licensed fishing stores along Avenida San Martín. Most stores can suggest guides. **Jorge Cardillo** (⊠ Villegas, behind the casino 🕾 2972/428–372) is a well-known local guide. **Augusto Matus** (🕾 2972/429–143, 2944/1556–3429 cell ⊕ tiempodepesca.com) offers guidance on wading and trolling for all levels of experience as well as fly-fishing trips for experts.

HORSEBACK RIDING
Horseback riding is a great way to see the areas you can't get to by car or boat. Hour-, day-, and week-long organized and guided rides, often with an *asado* (barbecue) included, can be arranged through local tour offices. **Abuelo Enrique** (⊠ Callejón Gingsins ☎ 2972/426–465) offers rides with a guide for two hours or all day, asado included. To get there, take Avenida Dr. Koessler (R234) toward Zapala, turn left at the polo field and head toward Lago Lolog, then take a right past the military barracks to Callejón Gingsins.

Adventure tour agencies in town can arrange canoeing, rafting, mountain bike, horseback riding, and fishing tours. **El Refugio** (⊠ Tte. Col. Perez 830 ☎☎ 2972/425–140 ⊕ www.elrefugioturismo.com.ar) is recommended. **Las Taguas Turismo** (⊠ Mascardi 892 ☎ 2972/427–423 ⊕ www.lastaguas.com) operates in both Lanín and Nahuel Huapi national parks. **Tiempo Patagónico** (⊠ Av. San Martín 950 ☎ 2972/427–113 ⊕ www.tiempopatagonico.com) offers excursions throughout the area.

MOUNTAIN BIKING
San Martín is flat, but everything goes up from it. Dirt and paved roads and trails lead through forests to lakes, waterfalls, and higher mountain valleys. In town you can rent bikes at **HG Rodados** (⊠ Av. San Martín 1061 ☎ 2972/427–345). Bikes are also available at **Enduro Kawa & Bikes** (⊠ Elordi and Perito Moreno ☎ 2972/427–093). **Chapelco Ski Area** has good trails and mountain-biking lessons.

SKIING
The ski area and summer resort of **Cerro Chapelco** (⊠ Information office: San Martín at Elordi ☎☎ 2972/427–845 ⊕ www.cerrochapelco. com) is 23 km (14 mi) from town—18 km paved and 5 km of dirt road. Ideal for families and beginning to intermediate skiers, the resort is one of Argentina's most popular ski areas. It has modern facilities and lifts, including a high-speed *telecabina* (gondola) from the base area. On a clear day, almost all the runs are visible from the top (6,534 feet), and Lanín Volcano dominates the horizon. Lift tickets run 55 pesos–96 pesos per day, and full equipment rental facilities are available at the base camp (32 pesos–51 pesos per day for skis, boots, and poles). On some days, cars need chains to get up to the mountain, so be sure to call and check the latest conditions before driving up. Taxis can also take you up or down for about 35 pesos each way. The summer Adventure Center has mountain biking for experts and classes for beginners, horseback rides, hiking, archery, a swimming pool, an alpine slide, and numerous other children's activities.

WHITE-WATER RAFTING
An all-day rafting trip that crosses into Chile on either Río Aluminé or Río Hua Hum can be arranged by **Tiempo Patagónico** (⊠ Av. San Martín 950 ☎ 2972/427–113 ⊕ www.tiempopatagonico.com).

El Refugio (⊠ Tte. Col. Perez 830 ☎ 2972/425–140 ⊕ www. elrefugioturismo.com.ar) leads rafting trips on nearby rivers. **Las Taguas Turismo** (⊠ Mascardi 892 ☎ 2972/427–423 ⊕ www.lastaguas.com) does combination rafting and mountain-biking trips.

El Bolsón

❻ *131 km (80 mi) south of Bariloche via R258.*

El Bolsón ("the purse"), in southwestern Río Negro Province, is so named because it's surrounded by high mountain ranges. This narrow mountain valley was first settled by Chilean farmers in the late 1800s and remained isolated until the 1930s, when a long, winding dirt road (often closed in winter) connected it to Bariloche. In the years since, Basque, Spanish, Polish, Arab, English, Swiss, and American hippies, attracted by the bucolic setting, pleasing (for Patagonia) microclimate, and the productive land, have all contributed to the cultural identity of the community. The first in Argentina to declare their town a non-nuclear zone, the forward-thinking citizens have preserved the purity of its air, water, and land, creating an environment that sustains the country's largest crops of hops—and for many of the above reasons, El Bolsón has also emerged as the nerve center of the exploding Patagonian microbrewed beer industry. There are now about a dozen beer producers in this city alone, although surprisingly, only two of them—Cerveceria El Bolsón and Otto Tipp—have actually opened establishments where you can sip their brews. Strawberries, raspberries, gooseberries, boysenberries, cherries, and plums also thrive here, and canneries export large quantities of jams and syrups.

As you travel here from Bariloche, the road passes Lago Gutiérrez and enters the Pacific watershed. Lago Mascardi flows into Lago Guillelmo just before the road climbs gently to a pass. Sixty-six kilometers (41 mi) from Bariloche, the first glimpse of the valley opens below you. As you descend into the valley and look south and west, the frozen glaciers of Perito Moreno and Hielo Azul (both more than 6,500 feet) appear on the horizon.

The **Secretaría de Turismo** (✉ Plaza Pagano and Av. San Martín ☎ 2944/492–604 or 2944/455–336 ⊕ www.bolsonturistico.com.ar) has information about lodging, activities, and excursions in the area.

The **Cascada de la Virgen** (Waterfall of the Virgin), 18 km (11 mi) north of El Bolsón, is not the most impressive of cascades, but it's visible from the road coming from Bariloche, so it doesn't demand much time. Nearby is a **campground** (☎ 2944/492–610 information) with cabins, grills, and a restaurant.

The **Cascada Mallín Ahogado** (Drowned Meadow Waterfall), 10 km (6 mi) north of El Bolsón on R258, makes a great picnic spot. The ski area at **Cerro Perito Moreno** is farther up the gravel road from the Cascada Mallín Ahogado.

A 39-km (24-mi) round-trip (mostly on dirt roads) to the **Parque Nacional Lago Puelo** (Puelo Lake National Park) is a good all-day excursion from El Bolsón. Information is available at the **park ranger's office** (☎ 2944/499–183), and picnic and fishing supplies can be purchased at the roadside store, 4 km (2½ mi) before you reach the sandy beach at Lago Puelo (Puelo Lake). Three launches, maintained by the Argentine navy, wait at the dock to take you on one- to three-hour excursions on the lake. The trip to El Turbio, an ancient settlement at the southern end of the lake on the Chilean border, is the longest. On the return trip, a branch to the right leads down a narrow arm to a river connecting Lago Puelo with Lago Epuyén (Epuyén Lake). A cruise along the shore of the Brazo Occidental (Western Arm) ends at the Chilean border, where the lake runs into a river bound for the Pacific Ocean. You can return by horse or on foot. One side of the lake is inaccessible, as the Valdivian rain forest grows on steep rocky slopes right down into the water. Campgrounds are at the park entrance by the ranger's station, in a bay on the Brazo Occidental, and at the Turbio and Epuyén river outlets.

Where to Stay & Eat

Though you'll have no trouble finding a good place to grab a bite to eat, the hotel selection in El Bolsón is woefully inadequate. At this writing, the Hotel Amancay, listed below, is truly the only full-service hotel worth recommending.

Many campgrounds line the banks of the Río Los Repollos (Los Repollos River), just before you enter town. More hotels and restaurants are being renovated or constructed along the rosebush-lined main street, and numerous small guest houses in and about the town take small groups. Lodges in the surrounding mountains open for fishing season in summer (November–April) and close in winter (May–October). Information about hotels, cabins, guest houses, and campgrounds is available at the **Secretaría de Turismo** (⊠ Plaza Pagano and Av. San Martín ☎ 2944/ 492–604).

$–$$ ✕ **Parrilla El Quincho.** About 10 minutes north of town, this is the place to try *cordero patagónico al asador* (lamb spit-roasted over a fire) in open air, along with sizzling platters of beef and entrails. You can get your classic country *asado* here, on the banks of the river Arroyo del Medio. Inside the rustic lodge, there are evocative wooden tables and chairs—it's all a welcome escape from the city streets. From El Bolsón, follow R258 north, and get off on the left exit for Catarata Mallín Ahogado. Follow that winding road north, then follow signs for El Quincho; you'll exit to the right after the Catarata exit (if you come to the Iaten K'aik museum, you've gone too far). ⊠ *Mallín Ahogado* ☎ *2944/ 492–870* ☲ *No credit cards.*

¢–$$ ✕ **Cervecería El Bolsón.** This is the brewery that started the Patagonia "cerveza artesanal" (artisanal beer) craze, and even if it's now the least artisanal of the bunch, it's a local landmark and fun place to check out. Every night from December through March, and Fridays and Saturdays for the rest of the year, the brewery's tasting room turns into a hopping bar and restaurant (there's also a campground here). There's a menu of beer-friendly foods like pizza, sausages with sauerkraut, and a hearty goulash. ⊠ *R258, Km 123.9, about 2 km (1 mi) north of town* ☎ *2944/ 492–595* ⊕ *www.cervezaelbolson.com* ☲ *AE, DC, MC, V* ☉ *Restaurant closed Wed. Apr.–Nov. No dinner Apr.–Nov.*

¢–$ ✕ **Otto Tipp.** Otto Tipp is named after a German immigrant who opened the first local brewery in 1890. Beers here include the classic triumvirate of Patagonian *cerveza artesanal*—blonde, red, and black—plus a fruity wheat beer. The menu includes *picadas* with local cheeses, salami, and so on, as well as pizza and other classic bar food, and you can watch the beer being brewed and bottled as you eat and drink. ⊠ *Islas Malvinas and Roca* ☎ *No phone* ⊟ *AE, DC, MC, V.*

¢–$ ✕ **Patio Venzano.** At this brightly lit, charming, friendly little restaurant on a busy downtown crossing, all the meat is cooked out on the backyard *parrilla*—even in winter, when a shivering *parrillero* whisks the platters in through the front door. The crowd is local and the food is good, especially the empanadas, which are some of Patagonia's best. ⊠ *Sarmiento and Hube* ☎ *No phone* ⊟ *No credit cards.*

$ ✕🏨 **Hotel Amancay.** A rose garden and masses of flowers greet you at the door of this pretty white-stucco hotel three blocks from the center of town. The warm, casual lobby has tile floors and dark-wood furniture with bright cushions. Rooms are clean but fairly basic, and showers are iffy, but this is about as well as you can do in humble downtown El Bolsón. At the Parilla Amancay restaurant, you can get beef, trout, lamb, and fresh vegetables cooked any way you like. Fresh pasta, pizzas, and a good fixed-price menu are also available. ⊠ *Av. San Martín 3217, 8430* ☎ *2944/492–222* 🛏 *15 rooms* ♿ *Restaurant, café, free parking* ⊟ *AE, DC, MC, V* ⦿ *CP.*

Sports & the Outdoors

Fishing in the lakes and streams that surround this area can be arranged with guides locally or in Bariloche. Hiking, rock climbing, mountain biking, and horseback riding (sometimes all combined in one trip) lead you to waterfalls, high mountain huts, deep canyons, and hidden lakes; trips can last a day or a week. Often you'll encounter a little teahouse or an asado at the end of your day. The tourist office can supply maps and directions or direct you to local outfitters. Both cross-country and downhill skiing are winter options at Cerro Perito Moreno, 22 km (13½ mi) north of town on R258. At the base is a refuge belonging to the Club Andino Piltriqitrón, as well as a restaurant and a rental shop. Three lifts service the trails for downhill skiing (3,000 feet–10,000 feet).

Shopping

At the local **mercado artesanal** (artisanal crafts fair), which takes place on the main plaza on Tuesdays, Thursdays, Saturdays, and Sundays from 10 AM to 5 PM, local artisans sell ceramics, leather goods, wood handicrafts, objects made from bone and clay, and agricultural products—plus the famous local artisanal beers. El Bolsón is known for its delicious small strawberries.

Esquel

❼ *180 km (112 mi) southeast of El Bolsón via R258 and R71, 285 km (177 mi) south of Bariloche via R259 and R40.*

In 1906 Esquel was a small village where sheep ranchers, many of them Welsh, came to buy supplies and visit with seldom-seen neighbors from the huge ranches, which still operate on the endless steppes east of the Andes. In 1910 the British owners of the approximately 2,538,202-square-km (980,000-square-mi) Leleque Ranch (now owned by Benetton) brought merino sheep from Australia to the region, establishing this breed in Patagonia. Although Esquel is now the most important town in northern Chubut Province and the gateway to unlimited recreational activities, it retains much of its frontier-town feeling. Along the roads outside town, for instance, you often see gauchos herding their sheep or "riding the fences" (checking to see that they aren't broken) of their vast ranches. Note that when you leave El Bolsón and enter the Province of Chubut, gas costs 40 percent less. For information about activities in the area, go to the **Secretaría de Turismo y Medio Ambiente** (⌂ Alvear and Sarmiento 📠 2945/451–927 ⊕ www.esquel.gov.ar).

In 1905, when Patagonia was still a territory, a railway project was conceived to facilitate the transport of wool, cattle, and lumber from the far-flung villages of El Maitén, Trevelín, and Esquel to Ingeniero Jacobacci, where it would link up with the national railway and the rest of the country. German and American companies worked with the Argentine railroad from 1922 until 1945, when the last section was completed. Today, **La Trochita,** also known as "el trencito" or the Great Patagonia Express, puffs clouds of steam and toots its horn as its 1922 Belgian Baidwin and German Henschell engines pull the vintage wooden cars 402 km (249 mi) between Esquel and Ingeniero Jacobacci (194 km [120 mi] east of Bariloche). Inside the cars, passengers gather around the woodstoves to add wood, sip mate, and discuss the merits of this rolling relic. The trip from Esquel to **Nahuel Pan** (20 km [12 mi] round-trip) leaves Esquel in summer Monday–Wednesday and weekends at 9 AM and 2 PM, returning at 12:30 and 4:30. The train to **El Maitén** to the north (165 km [102 mi] one-way) leaves Monday, Wednesday, and weekends at 3 (returning at 5:30), and includes a guided visit to the railroad museum and repair shop—a must for train buffs. For current schedules and reservations, contact the **Estación Esquel Train Station** (⌂ Brown and Roggero 📞 2945/451–403 ⊕ www.paginade/latrochita).

NEED A BREAK?

Homemade ice cream and pastries, coffee and tea, and two computers with Internet access will keep you busy for an afternoon at **Mayor** (⌂ Rivadavía 1943, at the corner of Sarmiento). **Marí Castaña** (⌂ 25 de Mayo and Rivadavía 1943 📞 2945/451–752), on one of Esquel's busiest street corners, is the classic Argentine *confitería;* locals and tourists flock to the place for its cool buzz, its whiskies and spiked coffee drinks, and its polite, friendly service.

The **Parque Nacional los Alerces** (Los Alerces National Park) is 50 km (30 mi) west of Esquel on R258 (and 151 km [94 mi] south of El Bolsón). The park is named for its 2,000- to 3,000-year-old *alerces (Fitzroya cupressoides)*, which are similar to redwoods. Covering 2,630 square km (1,012 square mi) of lakes, rivers, and forests, most of the park is accessible only by boats and trails. Wild, rugged, and astoundingly beautiful, this park is mostly untouched. The dirt road (the only one) into the park takes you to **Villa Futalaufquen** (Futalaufquen Village), on the lake of the same name. The park has only four small hotels and is the classic.

For camping and fishing information, visit the **park information office** (☎ 2945/471–020) in Villa Futalaufquen. Fishing in the 14 lakes and connecting rivers is legendary; licenses are available in the village at two small shops, Kiosco and Almacén, at the fishing lodges, and the campgrounds at Bahía Rosales.

A boat excursion from Puerto Limonao, the principal port on Lago Futalaufquen, takes you to **Lago Menendez** (Menendez Lake). Along the way you see the glaciers of the **Cerro Torrecillos** and stop at a grove of giant alerces. Tour operators in Esquel and lodges in the park can arrange lake excursions.

Where to Stay & Eat
Besides downtown hotels, there are hosterías, cabins, and campgrounds in the surrounding countryside. For information contact the tourist office. Food-wise, Esquel isn't quite cutting-edge, but there are lots of simple, characteristic *parrillas* around town.

¢–$$ ✕ **La Luna.** This terraced "resto bar," done up in evocative dark wood, is not just the ultimate lively *après-ski* spot—its vibe is also excellent for an intimate dinner. There's an Anglophile bent here, from the American classic-rock soundtrack to the J&B paraphernalia, but the food is Argentine to the core, with the occasional modern touch, such as a Guinness sauce on one of the 10 versions of *lomo* (beef tenderloin). Pastas, such as chicken lasagna, are homemade. Argentine-style pizzas include *fugazzeta* (mozzarella, onion, oregano, and green olives). Try the microbrewed Araucana beer, made in nearby El Bolsón. ⊠ *Rivadavía 1024* ☎ *2945/454–247* 🖃 *AE, DC, MC, V.*

$ ✕ **De Maria Parrilla.** Popular with local ranchers, fishermen, and town folk, this typical grill has a salad bar at dinner and Patagonian lamb is often cooked out back on an *asador*. The room is simple, narrow, and cute, with two rows of tables and an open kitchen in back. The owner, also a ski instructor, studied cooking in Buenos Aires and returned home to open this restaurant. The local lamb, pork, and game dishes are all prepared with a personal touch. ⊠ *Rivadavía 1024* ☎ *2945/454–247* 🖃 *AE, DC, MC, V.*

$$$$ ✕🖾 **Villa Futalaufquen.** From this stone-and-log lodge on top of a hill, you can look through tall alamo trees across miles of blue lake. Six-foot-tall lupines almost hide the little log cabins strewn across the lawn. Inside, worn leather, wicker furnishings, and wooden beams evoke a rustic elegance, reminiscent of an English hunting lodge. The rooms are simple—white walls, wood trim, a chair, and a bed—all you need, really, because the place to be is outside. In addition to offering equipment rentals, the hotel can arrange hiking and lake excursions. ⊠ *Villa Futalaufquen, 9200, 4 km (2 mi) from the village* ☎ *2945/471–008* 🛏 *12 rooms, 3 cabins* ♤ *Restaurant, waterskiing, fishing, bicycles, mountain bikes, horseback riding, bar* 🖃 *AE, DC, MC, V* ⏐◎⏐ *CP.*

$ 🖾 **Hostería Cumbres Blancas.** After a day of skiing, hiking, or exploring the nearby parks, the big carpeted rooms here exude unexpected extravagance. Most have views beyond the ample lawn to windswept plains and lonely mountains. The top-floor suite has a mountain view, balcony, and fireplace. A good restaurant adjoins the hotel. ⊠ *Av. Ameghino 1683, 9200* ☎ *2945/455–100* ⊕ *www.cpatagonia.com/esq/cblancas* ➟ *19 rooms, 1 suite* ♿ *Restaurant, room service, sauna, bar, recreation room, playground, free parking* ⊟ *AE, DC, MC, V* ¶⊙¶ *CP.*

$ ▦ **Hostería Cume Hué.** Owner Camilo Braese was born in this stucco-and-wood inn overlooking the lake. Having hiked and fished the area since he was a boy, Braese is much sought after as a guide. Breakfast, lunch, and tea are served in the living room, and dinner is eaten in the *quincho* (a room with a fireplace for asados). Rooms are basic, with small beds and lots of blankets. Some rooms have lake views. Most rooms share a bath, and there's only electricity at night. ⊠ *Off R71 on Lago Futalaufquen's north shore, 70 km (43½ mi) southwest from Esquel, 9200* ☎ *2945/453–639* ➟ *13 rooms (10 with shared bath)* ♿ *No a/c, no room phones* ⊟ *No credit cards* ⊘ *Closed May–Oct.* ¶⊙¶ *FAP.*

$ ▦ **Hotel Sol del Sur.** This large brick building right in downtown Esquel was a casino until 1987, when the top floor was converted into a large dining area and a meeting room and guest rooms were added on the floors in between. The building is still old and austere, as are the rooms. The convenience of having an adjoining tour agency and ski retail and rental shop makes up for the plain furnishings. ⊠ *9 de Julio and Sarmiento, 9200* ☎ *2945/452–189* ✉ *soldelsur@ar.inter.net* ➟ *50 rooms, 2 5-person apartments* ♿ *Restaurant, bar* ⊟ *AE, DC, MC, V* ¶⊙¶ *CP.*

Sports & the Outdoors

FISHING Fishing fanatics from the world over have come to battle with the stubborn trout or catch and release the wily rainbow in the remote lakes, tranquil lagoons, shallow rushing rivers or deep quiet ones of Los Alerces National Park. For fishing information on the Ríos Grande or Futaleufú (near Chile), and a list of licensed guides, contact the tourist office in Esquel. Permits are available at gas stations, fishing shops, and at the **Dirección de Pesca Continental** (⊠ Pasteur 538 ☎ 2945/42468).

RAFTING & The white-water rafting season begins in November, when the rivers are full and fast, BOATING and lasts into March. **Frontera Sur** (⊠ Avenida Alvear y Salmiento ☎ 2945/450–505 ⊕ www.fronterasur.net) organizes rafting trips for a day on the Corcovado or a week on the Futaleufú, ending in Chile; sometimes kayak and canoe instruction is included. **Sol del Sur** (⊠ 9 de Julio 1086 ☎⊞ 2945/42189 ⊕ www.hsoldelsur.com.ar) also offers rafting trips on the Corcovado and Futaeufú rivers.

SKIING Only 13 km (8 mi) from Esquel and generally blessed with a long ski season (July–mid-November), La Hoya is a popular ski resort for its reasonable prices and uncrowded slopes—2,200 acres of skiable terrain. For this reason, it tends to attract practicing junior ski teams from other countries. Four chairlifts and five surface lifts take you up 2,624 feet. Runs are long and above the tree line, and off-piste skiing is often possible. For information about the ski area, contact the Esquel tourist office, or **La Hoya Esquel** (⊠ Rivadavía 1003 ☎ 2945/453–018 ⊕ www.camlahoya.com.ar).

THE LAKE DISTRICT ESSENTIALS

Transportation

BY AIR

The best way to get to the Lakes region is by air from Buenos Aires. The country's major airline, Aerolíneas Argentinas, known locally simply as "Aerolíneas," flies (along with its subsidiary Austral) from Buenos Aires to Bariloche and San Martín's Chapelco airport. There is also direct service on Aerolíneas from Bariloche to Atlantic Patagonia (Trelew) and southern Patagonia (El Calafate), although those flights run as infrequently as once per week, so advance planning is essential. Aerolíneas Argentina's "Visit Argentina" pass allows you to fly to multiple destinations at a discount; it must be purchased outside of Argentina.

Southern Winds flies to Barlioche and Neuquén from Buenos Aires. Lan, formerly LanChile, a OneWorld member, now competes with Aerolíneas on the Buenos Aires–Bariloche route; check their Web site for specials, and you may find a cheaper fare than you do with Argentina's flag carrier.

For intra-Patagonia air travel, LADE (Líneas Aéreas del Estado) flies small planes, some jets and some propellers, from Bariloche, Chapelco (San Martín de los Andes), and El Bolsón across to Trelew and Puerto Madryn, and Comodoro Rivadavía in Atlantic Patagonia, and south to El Calafate, Río Gallegos, and Comodoro Rivadavía.

🛪 **Aerolíneas Argentinas** ☎ 0810/2228-6527 24-hr reservations and sales in Argentina, 11/4320-2000 in Buenos Aires, 2944/422-144 in Bariloche, 2972/427-636 in Chapelco, 2945/452-688 in Esquel. **LADE** ☎ 11/4361-7071 in Buenos Aires, 2944/423-562 in Bariloche, 2972/247-672 in Chapelco, 2944/492-206 in El Bolsón ⊕ www.lade.com.ar. **Lan** ☎ 2944/423-562 in Bariloche, 11/4378-2200 in Buenos Aires, 0800/222-2424 toll-free ⊕ www.lan.com. **Southern Winds** ☎ 0810/777-7979 ⊕ www.fly-sw.com.

BY BOAT

Traveling between Bariloche and Puerto Montt, Chile, by boat is one of the most popular excursions in Argentina. It requires three lake crossings and various buses and can be done in a day or overnight. Travel agents and tour operators in Bariloche and Buenos Aires can arrange this trip and many tour companies include it in their itineraries.

BY BUS

Buses arrive in Bariloche from every corner of Argentina—from Jujuy in the north, Ushuaia in the south, and everywhere in between. Several companies have daily service to Buenos Aires. Bariloche's Terminal de Omnibus is in the Estación de Ferrocarril General Roca (Railroad Station) east of town, where all bus companies have offices. Most have downtown offices, too, but your best bet is to go directly to the terminal. The following bus companies run comfortable and reliable overnight buses between Buenos Aires and Bariloche (the trip takes 22 hours): Chevallier, El Valle, and Via Bariloche. Buses also run daily between Bariloche and Chile (Osorno, Puerto Montt, Valdivia, and Santiago) via the Puyehue Pass; contact Tas–Choapa.

To travel from Bariloche south to El Bolsón and Esquel and across to Puerto Madryn, Trelew, and Gaiman, contact Don Otto, Andesmar at the bus terminal, and TAC. For travel north to Villa La Angostura, Traful, and San Martín de los Andes, contact TAC. Algarrobal has daily trips to Villa La Angostura.

Bus Companies **Algarrobal** ⊠ 9 de Julio 1800 Bariloche ☎ 2944/427–698. **Andesmar** ⊠ Mitre 385, Bariloche ☎ 2944/435–040. **Chevallier** ⊠ Moreno 105, Bariloche ☎ 2944/423–090, 11/4314–0111, 11/4314–5555 in Buenos Aires. **Don Otto** ⊠ At the bus terminal in Bariloche, B. Mitre 321 ☎ 2944/429–012. **El Pingüino** ☎ 11/4315–4438 in Buenos Aires, 2966/442–169 in Río Gallegos. **La Puntual** ☎ 11/4313–2441 in Buenos Aires. **TAC** ⊠ Moreno 138, Bariloche ☎ 2944/434–727, 2972/428–878 in San Martín de los Andes, 11/4313–3627 in Buenos Aires. **Tas-Choapa** ⊠ Moreno 138, Bariloche ☎ 2944/426–663, 562/697–0062 in Santiago. **El Valle** ⊠ 12 de Octubre 1884, Bariloche ☎ 2944/431–444, 11/4313–3749 in Buenos Aires. **Via Bariloche** ⊠ Mitre 321, Bariloche ☎ 2944/432–444, 2972/422–800 in San Martín de los Andes, 11/4663–8899 in Buenos Aires.

Bus Terminals **Bariloche** ⊠ Av. 12 de Octubre ☎ 2944/432–860. **San Martín de los Andes** ⊠ Villegas & Juez de Valle ☎ 2972/427–044.

BY CAR

Unless you're on a ski-only vacation, renting a car is essential in the spread-out Lakes region, giving you the freedom to stop when and where you want. This is especially true in Bariloche, where major sights lie largely outside of town along the Circuito Chico and Circuito Grande. Keep in mind that the Seven Lakes Road is closed for part of the year. For winter travel, it's a good idea to rent a 4x4, especially if you're traveling on dirt roads. Hiring a *remis* (car with driver) is another option; it costs more, however.

Driving to the Lakes region from Buenos Aires is a long haul (more than 1,500 km [930 mi] and at least three days) of interminable stretches without motels, gas stations, or restaurants. Fuel in Argentina is expensive and if you break down in the hinterlands, it's unlikely that you'll find anyone who speaks much English. Note, too, that what seem like towns marked on the map may just be private estancias not open to the public.

On the other hand, driving exposes you to the heart of the country (and roads are paved all the way to Bariloche). Planning is essential, and Automóvil Club Argentino can provide maps and advice. To get to Bariloche from Buenos Aires: take R5 to Santa Rosa (615 km [382 mi]), then R35 to General Acha (107 km [66 mi]), then R20 to Colonia 25 de Mayo, then R151 to Neuquén (438 km [272 mi]), and then R237 to Bariloche (449 km [279 mi]).

Local Agencies **Baricoche** ⊠ Moreno 115 piso 1 of 15, Bariloche ☎ 2944/427–638 ⊕ www.baricoche.com.ar. **Rent A Car Bariloche** ⊠ Rolando 258, Bariloche ☎ 2944/427–494 ⊕ www.rentacarbariloche.com.

Remis **Del Oscar** ⊠ Av. San Martín 1254, San Martín de los Andes ☎ 2972/428–774. **Patagonia Remises** ⊠ Av. Pioneros 4400, Bariloche ☎ 2944/443–700.

Auto Club **Automóvil Club Argentino** (ACA) ⊠ Av. del Libertador 1850, Buenos Aires ☎ 11/4802–6061 ⊕ www.aca.org.ar.

Contacts & Resources

BANKS & EXCHANGE SERVICES

BANKS **In Bariloche** Banco Frances ⊠ Av. San Martín 336 ☎ 2944/430–325. **Bansud** ⊠ Mitre 433 ☎ 2944/422–792.

In San Martín Banco de la Nación Argentina ⊠ Av. San Martín 687 ☎ 2972/427–292. **Bansud** ⊠ Av. San Martín 836 ☎ 2972/423–962.

EMERGENCIES

Coast Guard ☎ 106. **Fire** ☎ 100. **Forest Fire** ☎ 103. **Hospital** ☎ 107. **Police** ☎ 101.

HOSPITALS & **In Bariloche** Farmacia Avenida ⊠ Gallardo 395, Bariloche ☎ 2944/520-717. **Far-**
PHARMACIES **macia Zona Vital** ⊠ Moreno 301 and Rolando, Bariloche ☎ 2944/420-752. **Hospital Zonal Ramón Carillo** ⊠ Moreno 601 ☎ 2944/426-119. **Hospital Sanatorio del Sol** ⊠ 20 de Febrero 598 ☎ 2944/525-000.

In San Martín de los Andes Farmacia del Centro ⊠ San Martín 896 and Belgrano ☎ 2972/428-999. **Hospital Ramón Carillo** ⊠ San Martín and Rodhe ☎ 2972/427-211.

MAIL & SHIPPING

Post offices in bigger towns are usually open 10 AM to 6 PM; smaller towns generally make their own rules. Stamps can also be purchased at kiosks.

Post Office (Correo) Information Bariloche ⊠ Moreno 175. **San Martín de los Andes** ⊠ At the Civic Center, General Roca and Pérez.

TOUR OPTIONS

The English-speaking owners of Alunco, a very professional travel office specializing in trips in and around Bariloche, are third-generation Barilocheans, expert skiers, and outdoors enthusiasts who have explored the remotest corners of the northern lake district. The main focus of Catedral Turismo is the lake crossing from Bariloche to Chile. Andes Patagónicos also runs tours across to Chile, as well as a huge variety of tours in the Bariloche and Lakes area, including Cerro Catedral and other boat trips.

San Martín de los Andes's El Refugio and Tiempo Patagonico both run horseback riding, river rafting, mountain biking, lake, and land excursions in and around San Martín and to Lanín Volcano. Guided fishing, rafting, and horseback riding trips from El Bolsón and excursions to Lago Puelo National Park can be arranged by Patagonia Adventures and Quen Quen Turismo. Plan Mundo organizes fishing trips in Los Alerces National Park for about $1,200. The package includes round-trip airfare between Buenos Aires and Esquel, airport transfer on both ends, three nights with breakfast and dinner in the Hostería Futalaufquen in Esquel, and three full days of fishing, including launch, guide, permit, meals, and equipment. For organized white-water rafting trips to the Río Corcovado, near the Chilean border, contact Leo Tours.

Alunco ⊠ Moreno 187, fl. 1, Bariloche ☎ 2944/422-283 ⊕ www.alcunoturismo.com. ar. **Andes Patagónicos** ⊠ Mitre 125, Local 5, Bariloche ☎ 2944/431-777 or 2944/426-809 ⊕ www.andespatagonicos.com. **Catedral Turismo S.A.** ⊠ Palacios 263, Bariloche ☎ 2944/425-444 ⊕ www.hotelpuertoblest.com.ar. **Causana Viajes** ⊠ Moreno 390, Puerto Madryn ☎ 2965/455-044 ⊕ www.causana.com.ar. **Correntoso Travel** ⊠ Av. Arrayanes 21, Villa La Angostura ☎ 2944/494-803 ⊕ www.correntosotravels.com.ar.

El Refugio Turismo ✉ Col. Perez 830, San Martín de los Andes ☎ 2972/425–140
⊕ www.elrefugioturismo.com.ar. **Gador Viajes** ✉ Av. Santa Fe 1339, Buenos Aires ☎ 11/
4811–8498 or 11/4813–8696 ⊕ www.gadorviajes.com.ar. **Patagonia Adventures** ✉ Pablo
Hube 418, El Bolsón ☎ 2944/492–513. **Tiempo Patagónico** ✉ Av. San Martín 950, San
Martín de los Andes ☎☎ 2972/427–113 or 2972/427–114 ⊕ www.tiempopatagonico.com.

VISITOR INFORMATION

▉ Tourist Offices **Bariloche** ✉ Civic Center ☎ 2944/429–850 ⊕ www.barilochepatagonia.
info. **El Bolsón** ✉ Plaza Pagano and Av. San Martín ☎ 2944/492–604. **Junín de los
Andes** ✉ Padre Milanesia 590 ☎☎ 2972/491–160 ⊕ www.junindelosandes.gov.ar. **San
Martín de los Andes** ✉ San Martín and Rosas ☎ 2972/427–347 or 2972/427–695
⊕ www.sanmartindelosandes.gov.ar. **Trevelín** ✉ Plaza de la Fontana ☎ 2945/480–
120. **Villa la Angostura** ✉ Siete Lagos and Los Arrayanes ☎☎ 2944/494–124 ⊕ www.
villalaangostura.gov.ar. **Villa Traful** ✉ In center of town ☎ 2944/479–099.

ATLANTIC PATAGONIA

Traveling through Atlantic Patagonia is like being on an adventure
aboard Jacques Cousteau's boat. The aquatic life—from the famous southern right whales that flop around off the coast of the Peninsula Valdés
to penguin and sea elephant colonies—is some of the most extraordinary in South America. But the story of Atlantic Patagonia is also the
fascinating story of the Welsh who left Great Britain in 1865 as a result
of religious persecution and came here, often via the United States, and
often hauling elaborate farm machinery with them, to establish a colony
of their own in the Chubut Province.

But as elsewhere in Patagonia, it's also a tale of rugged, pioneering Ital-
ians, Spanish, Croats, Germans, Lebanese, and Portuguese, among others, who staked a claim in inhospitable, uncharted territories upon
invitation from the Argentine state beginning in the mid-19th century.
Argentina, in an effort to thwart Chilean and European ambitions for
the land and to quell the indigenous population, sought to settle the territory by actively courting European immigration, instituting customs
and tax incentives, and even shipping over hundreds of prisoners as col-
onizers. The settlers who came built water channels, ports, and chapels
while baking the breads and planting the crops of their homelands; these
cultural traditions still remain.

Puerto Madryn

❽ *67 km (41½ mi) north of Trelew, 450 km (279 mi) north of Comodoro
Rivadavía, 104 km (64 mi) west of Puerto Pirámides, 1,380 km (856
mi) south of Buenos Aires.*

The Welsh people, who came to Patagonia to seek refuge from religious
persecution in Great Britain, landed first in Puerto Madryn in 1865 (and
the anniversary of their arrival is celebrated every July 28 here and in
other Chubut towns). You can still find many of their descendants
today, but there isn't much evidence of the indigenous people who
helped the Welsh survive and become the first foreigners to unveil the
secrets of Patagonia's interior.

Atlantic Patagonia

Golfo San Matías

RIO NEGRO

Sierra Grande

Punta Buenos Aires

Punta Quiroga

Golfo San José

Punta Pirámide

Puerto Pirámide

47

52

47

Puerto Hurcules

9 Península Valdés

2

Puerto Delgada

Golfo San Nuevo

Punta Loma

Punta Ninfas

Punta León

Puerto Madryn 8

Carro Avanzado

3

1

Trelew 10

Rawson

Playa Union

Puerto Rawson

Gaiman 11

Dolavón

28 de Julio

12 Punta Tombo

32

Ameghino

1

Cabo Raso

25

3

ATLANTIC OCEAN

13 Camarones

CHUBUT

Arroyo Perdido

Rio Chubut

Rio Chico

El Sombrero

Bahía Bustamente

Golfo San Jorge

25

Astra

14 Comodoro Rivadavía

Lago Colhué Huapí

26

20

Sarmiento 15

3

0   50 miles

0   50 kilometers

Puerto Madryn's main hotels and residences are on or near the 3½-km-long (2-mi-long) Rambla, the pedestrian stretch that hugs Golfo Nuevo; it's also a favorite place for joggers and strollers. As recently as 1980, you could reliably see scores of southern right whales—the creatures for which Atlantic Patagonia is most famous—from the city streets and dock, but migration patterns have changed, and now the whale-watching has largely moved to sleepy Puerto Pirámides out on the peninsula. Still, many people choose to base themselves in livelier Madryn, with its myriad restaurants and nightlife, and see the whales on day-trips. In high whale-watching season—from September through December—the city's nearly 5,000 hotel rooms and its campgrounds usually fill up.

The **Museo Oceanográfico y Ciencias Naturales** (Oceanographic and Natural Science Museum) is worth a visit if you have the time. Housed in a lovely 1917 colonial building once owned by the Pujol family (original settlers), the museum focuses on marine life. You can see a giant squid preserved in formaldehyde and learn how fish breathe. ⊠ *Domecq García and Menéndez* ☎ *2965/451–139* ⊡ *Free* ☉ *Weekdays 9–7, weekends 2:30–7.*

Furthering Puerto Madryn's reputation as the eco-conscious center of Patagonia is the spectacular **EcoCentro,** a modern hands-on museum and research center that strives to promote the protection of the sea and its inhabitants through education. Exhibits provide background on local marine life, and the invertebrates "touch pool" allows visitors to get a real feel for the fish. The center is on a cliff at the north end of the city's beach. ⊠ *Julio Verne 3784* ☎ *2965/457–470* ⊕ *www.ecocentro.org. ar* ⊡ *15 pesos* ☉ *Wed.–Mon. 10–6.*

Where to Stay & Eat

$–$$$ ✕ **La Barra Bar y Comidas.** Usually it's not a good sign when a restaurant tries to do everything at once: *parrilla,* pizza, and elaborate meat and seafood dishes. However, La Barra does it all well, and the never-ending crowds at this restaurant, just steps from the shore, attest to the quality found here. Skip the mediocre fried calamari, however. ⊠ *Blvd. Brown and Lugones* ☎ *2965/455–550 or 2965/454–279* ⊟ *AE, DC, MC, V.*

$–$$ ✕ **Ambigú.** This stylish place to eat and drink is across the street from the beach. The menu has 60 pizzas to choose from, as well as entrées like sirloin medallion (medallón de lomo) with pumpkin puree. A clean, contemporary style complemented by well-mounted photographs documenting the history of the building (note the art deco detailing, including original iron cresting, on the exterior) lends the restaurant both authenticity and sophistication. ⊠ *Av. Roca at Av. Saénz Peña* ☎ *2965/ 452–541* ⊟ *AE, MC, V.*

$–$$ ✕ **Cantina El Náutico.** Don't let the corny, yellow-neon sign outside dissuade you; this local favorite run by three generations of a French Basque family serves fantastic homemade pasta and fresh seafood. Even the "butter" that accompanies the bread is a cut above—a mixture of mayonnaise with garlic, parsley, and pepper. For dessert, try the outstanding *macedonia* (fruit salad with ice cream). ⊠ *Av. Roca 790* ☎ *2965/471–404* ⊕ *www.elnauticocantina.com.ar* ⊟ *AE, DC, MC, V.*

$–$$ ✕ **La Gaviota Cocinera.** The secret of this restaurant from husband-and-wife team Pablo and Flavia Tolosa is the combination of cozy rooms and reliable food at extraordinarily reasonable prices. The three-course set-price meals might feature tenderloin with leek and mustard sauce, or grilled chicken stuffed with olives and dried tomatoes. ⊠ *Galles 32* ☎ *2965/456–033* ⊟ *AE, MC, V.*

$–$$ ✕ **Mr. Jones.** This brewpub is the closest thing to an Irish pub in Atlantic Patagonia, and it's packed every night. Although the beer is good, the food is not just an afterthought; offerings include potpies, sausages with kraut, pizzas, and other brew-happy food. ⊠ *9 de Julio 116 at 25 de Mayo* ☎ *2965/475–368* ⊟ *AE, MC, V.*

$–$$ ✕ **Restaurant Estela.** Run lovingly by Estela Guevara, who could easily pass for anybody's favorite aunt, this restaurant is a real pleasure. There are menus in English, German, French, and Italian; the postcards from all over the world sent by dinner guests and displayed on the walls attest to the owner's popularity. Ms. Guevara, who is of Ukrainian descent and speaks perfect English, tends to all her guests personally and will even offer travel advice. The restaurant serves hearty meals of beef, chicken, and fish at reasonable prices. ⊠ *R. S. Peña 27* ☎ *2965/451–573* ⊟ *AE, MC, V* ⊗ *Closed Mon.*

$$$ ✕🏠 **Estancia San Guillermo.** If you want to experience a Chubut farm filled with snorting pigs, overfriendly guanacos, and strutting roosters, head for Estancia San Guillermo. Just a few miles outside Puerto Madryn, owners Alfredo and Cristina Casado make you feel at home with their 1,200 sheep, which roam their 7,400-acre fossil-filled farm. Watch Alfredo shear a sheep or his helpers prepare the parrilla. Stay in roomy, comfortable villas with kitchens and bathrooms; rates include all meals. The estancia has a dining room, too, if you're just coming for the day. ⊠ *Contact info in Puerto Madryn: Av. 28 de Julio 90, 9120* ☎ *2965/452–150* ⊕ *www.san-guillermo.com* ♨ *Dining room, horseback riding* ⊟ *No credit cards* ⊗ *Closed mid-May–mid-June* ⫶⊙⫶ *FAP.*

$$$ 🏠 **Hotel Peninsula Valdés.** With nondescript white block architecture, this waterfront hotel may look bland from the outside, but it's simple, spotless, well-appointed rooms look out over the bay, and there's an elaborate spa hidden within. Ask for a room with a view on an upper floor for the best experience. ⊠ *Av. Roca 155, 9120* ☎ *2965/471–292* ⊕ *www.hotel-peninsula-valdes.com* ↩ *76 rooms* ♨ *Restaurant, bar, breakfast room, gym, sauna, health club, Internet, laundry service* ⊟ *AE, DC, MC, V* ⫶⊙⫶ *BP.*

$ 🏠 **Bahía Nueva Hotel.** This hotel on the bay has clean and spacious rooms and a great location. Only stay here if you can get a room facing the bay, however; the dark back rooms are not worth the price. The English-speaking staff are eager to please, and the eco-conscious literature and decor make guests aware of their awesome natural surroundings. The warm brick lobby area features a library, communal wired computers, comfortable armchairs, and a fireplace. ⊠ *Av. Julio A. Roca 67, 9120* ☎ *2965/450–045 or 2965/450–145* ⊕ *www.bahianueva.com.ar* ↩ *40 rooms* ♨ *Cable TV, bar, library, laundry service, Internet, business services* ⊟ *AE, DC, MC, V* ⫶⊙⫶ *CP.*

$ ⊡ **Hotel Aguas Mansas.** This hotel is one block from the beach in a pretty residential neighborhood and a few blocks from the center of town. It's nothing fancy—just clean, quiet rooms and good, personable service. It's one of the few lodgings with a pool, especially in this price range. ⊠ *José Hernandez 51, 9120* ☎ *2965/473–103* ⊕ *www.aguamansas.com* ⊑ *20 rooms* ⧫ *Cable TV, pool, bar, laundry service* ⊟ *MC, V* ⫶⊙⫶ *CP.*

Sports & the Outdoors

There are all sorts of sports in and around Puerto Madryn, ranging from bicycling and fishing to sand-boarding (basically, surfing on the sand). Puerto Madryn is also Argentina's scuba-diving capital. In an effort to further boost interest in scuba diving—by giving divers something else to explore—town officials sank the *Albatros,* a large fishing vessel, off the coast in Golfo Nuevo. Several scuba shops rent equipment and can arrange dives for you. Most of them are found on Boulevard Brown, which runs along the beach; almost all of them have small restaurants and bars complete with tiki huts, reclining chairs, and music. **Ocean Divers** (⊠ Blvd. Brown 700 ☎ 2965/472–569 or 2965/1566–0865) is a reliable place to find scuba equipment. **Scuba Duba** (⊠ Blvd. Brown 893 ☎ 2965/452–699) is an established dive shop.

Several companies rent bicycles for about 20 pesos a day, including **XT Mountain Bike** (⊠ Av. Roca 742 ☎ 2965/472–232).

Costas Patagonicas (☎ 2965/451–131) organizes fishing trips. **Jorge Schmid** (☎ 2965/451–511), a respected guide in the area, offers fishing trips, as well as whale-watching and dolphin-viewing trips.

Shopping

Puerto Madryn is one of the better shopping cities on the eastern coast of Patagonia. The best shopping is found on the streets that intersect with the Rambla, like **Avenida 28 de Julio,** at the corner of which is a pleasant, three-story upscale mall, Portal de Madryn. **Artesanias Mag** (⊠ Portal de Madryn, Av. Roca and Av. 28 de Julio ☎ 2965/474–700), makes its own pots and craft items from a local white clay known as *arcilla.* It also sells leather goods, hand-drawn postcards, and unique knives. **Barrika** (⊠ Av. Roca 109 ☎ 2965/450–454) is a lovely boutique wine shop. Its helpful staff will guide you to the choicest Argentine bottles. On the second floor of Portal de Madryn is **Yenelen,** which sells regional culinary goodies, such as torta *galetas,* chocolates, jellies made from wild Patagonian fruits, and teas. Yenelen runs a **chocolate factory** (⊠ Av. Roca 672 ☎ 2965/457–779), which is free and open to the public daily from 9:30 to 1 and 4:30 to 10. Yenelen also sells Welsh cakes and other local crafts.

Península Valdés

❾ *Puerto Pirámides is 104 km (64 mi) northwest of Puerto Madryn.*

Fodor'sChoice
★

The Península Valdés is one of Argentina's most important wildlife reserves. Its biggest attractions are the *ballenas francas* (southern right whales) that feed, mate, give birth, and nurse their offspring here. Each year, a few hundred whales come in to mate, rotating through from among a total population of about 2,000 (once 100,000-strong, the worldwide population of these giant mammals has declined drastically, a result of being hunted for their blubber). Each whale comes to the peninsula once every three or four years. One unique characteristic of these whales is that they have two external blowholes on top of their heads, and when they emerge from the water, they blow a V-shape water blast that can be seen for miles away. The protected mammals attract some 120,000 visitors every year from June, when they first arrive, through December. Especially during the peak season of September and October, people crowd into boats small and large to observe at close range as the 30- to 35-ton whales leap out of the water and blow water from their spouts.

Off-season the peninsula is still worth visiting: sea lions, elephant seals, Magellanic penguins, egrets, and cormorants as well as land mammals like guanacos, gray fox, and Patagonian *mara,* a harelike animal, all make their home here. Discovered by Spanish explorer Hernando de Magallanes in 1520 and named after Don Antonio Valdés, minister of the Spanish navy in the late 18th century, Península Valdés is a protected zone. The peninsula's animal population is so valued, it earned the area a UNESCO World Heritage site designation. It's also the lowest point on the South American continent, at 132 feet below sea level.

To get to the peninsula, you must drive along lonely roads surrounded by vast estancias dotted with sheep and a handful of cows. At the park gates, you must pass through the **Information Center and Museum** (☎ 2965/1556–5222 ☉ Daily 8–8), where you'll pay an entrance fee of 35 pesos. There, you can also get a map of the peninsula and check out a small but interesting display of peninsula lore.

Puerto Pirámides, the only village on Península Valdés, is a more tranquil, isolated base than Puerto Madryn from which to explore the area's natural attractions. For ecological reasons, only 350 people are allowed to live here, but there are a handful of campsites, hotels, and restaurants. Bring plenty of cash to the town with you, because there are often no working ATM machines. Aside from whale-watching and lounging around with a beer in hand and looking out on the pyramid-shape cliffs of Valdés Bay, the only activities in town are scuba diving and surfing. Whale-watching excursions leave from the little harbor, generally at 8:30 AM or 9 AM—check with your hotel to reserve with one of the local outfits. Smaller boats, such as the ones operated by Hydro Sport (⇨ Tour Options *under* Contacts & Resources *in* Atlantic Patagonia A to Z, *below*) are preferable to big ones, as they tend to get closer to the whales.

Although full-day tours from Puerto Madryn are available, the peninsula is really best seen by renting a car in Madryn and staying for a couple nights in Pirámides. Plan on at least two days and nights to see the sights of the peninsula, which should include at the least a one-hour boat trip from the harbor of Pirámides to see the whales (in season). For starters, the **Lobería Puerto Pirámides** is a sea lion colony 4 km (2½ mi) from the town (on the way to Punta Delgada). It's walkable if you don't have wheels. From June through November, whales can often be seen, just 30 meters offshore or so, from the **Observatorio de la Fundación Patagonia Natural** at Playa Faro, 12 km (7½ mi) from Pirámides toward Punta Flecha.

The most rewarding sights, however, come from driving all the way around the peninsula. Beginning in Pirámides, you can take an easy circuit route along the peninsula's desolate, unpaved roads (keep your speed below 60 kph at all times—the roads are notoriously slippery).

Begin by heading southeast (with a full tank of gas) along RP 2 for about 70 km (43 mi) to get to the elephant seals and sea lion colonies at **Punta Delgada,** on the southeastern tip of the peninsula. The elephant seals' breeding season starts in August when the males compete for beach space, after which females arrive, form harems, and give birth. The seals all head out to sea in November. There lies a starkly beautiful old lighthouse, which you can climb to the top of and appreciate the open-sea views, and guard's quarters that have been turned into an upmarket hotel and restaurant. You have to walk down a set of stairs and paths to get to the animal observation area, which is only open 9:30 AM–4:30 PM. From there, head up the eastern coast of the island (RP 47, though it's unmarked), another 70 km (43 mi) or so, toward **Caleta Valdés,** near which you can stop at Parador La Elvira), a complex with a restaurant, gift shop, and cliffside walkway to another impressive elephant seal beach, whose activity peaks in September. Head north to he northeastern corner of the island and **Punta Norte,** the most remote and largest sea lion settlement of all; here, orcas cruise through town from time to time, and Magellanic penguins roam the land from October through March. From Punta Norte, RP 3 is an inland shortcut that heads straight back southwest to Pirámides to complete this substantial, but eminently worthwhile, day trip.

Where to Stay & Eat

$–$$$ ✗ **Posada Pirámides.** This impossibly cute little restaurant, which feels like a living room, is across the street from the Hotel Paradise. Its kitchen and delightful staff proffer creative Argentine cuisine, with a spotlight on seafood—this is probably the best place to eat in town. Perhaps because the place doubles as a hostel (with very basic accommodation for youths or families), there's a young, informal attitude, but the preparations are serious; don't miss the signature *vieyras gratinados* (baked scallops with melted cheese) or a heavy but good preparation of *lenguado con salsa de camarones* (sole in shrimp sauce) with potatoes noisette. ✉ *Avda. de las Ballenas s/n* ☎ *2965/4950* ⊕ *www.posadapiramides. com* ➾ *AE* ☉ *Closed Apr.–May.*

$–$$ ✗ **Parador La Elvira.** This stop along the unpaved RP 47 might at first seem like a mirage: out of nowhere arises a complex with tour buses, gift shops, and a grand, picture-windowed restaurant that looks down the gentle arc of the peninsula's coastline. But the food is for real, in spite of the cafeteria-style self-service system. The crowning achievement is delectable *cordero al asador* (that classic Patagonian specialty of lamb spit-roasted "on the cross," which is hacked to pieces and served directly from the *asador*). The hearty soups and salad bar are a bit disappointing, however. ✉ *Near Caleta Valdés, along RP 47 on the Peninsula Valdés* ➾ *No credit cards.*

$ ✗ **La Estación Pub.** The coolest bar in Pirámides is also a simple but good restaurant. Specialties include delicious *milanesas* and vegetable-heavy pasta dishes. This is where all the town's twentysomethings congregate after hours; not surprisingly the restaurant is lively and funky with bizarre rock posters decorating the walls. ⊠ *Av. de las Ballenas s/n* ☎ *2965/495–047* ☰ *No credit cards.*

★ **$$$** ✗▥ **Punta Delgada.** This former lighthouse (along with a navy station, a post office, and a little school for the guards' families) is a sea-lion-colony observation station and elegant hotel. The Punta Delgada's luxuries are simple and aristocratically old-fashioned: comfortable beds, a tennis court, a pleasant pub with pool and darts, starry night skies, board games, and utter tranquillity. Excursions are organized by the staff. There are no telephones or even cell service, never mind television; there's no electricity 9–noon and 3–7. Nor are there water views from the rooms, unfortunately; the hotel sits too far inland on the knoll for that. Still, it's one of the most impressively isolated hotels in Patagonia. Dinner is served for hotel guests only, but nonguests who are day-tripping can lunch at the restaurant ($$–$$$$), which features chicken curry, king crab, and *cordero al asador* at midday. Tour groups tend to stop here for lunch in large numbers. ⊠ *Punta Delgada, Peninsula Valdés* ☎ *2965/458–444* ⊕ *www.puntadelgada.com* ⇆ *27 rooms* ⚐ *Restaurant, bar, tennis court, horseback riding; no TV, no phone* ☰ *AE, MC, V* ⊘ *Closed Apr.–July.*

$$ ✗▥ **The Paradise.** This hotel and restaurant is overpriced, but if you're seeking reliability, look no further. Rooms are clean and spare. Those on the second floor have a few more amenities like cable TV. The restaurant ($$–$$$) is one of the better ones in town, decorated with postcards and photographs left behind by visitors, and a fireplace in the back. Two bars create atmosphere enough to distract you from seafood dishes that lack flair. The hotel can organize scuba-diving tours and activities like sand surfing. ⊠ *Av. Julio A. Roca, 9121* ☎☎ *2965/495–030 or 2965/495–003* ⊕ *www.puerto-piramides.com.ar* ⇆ *12 rooms* ⚐ *Restaurant, some in-room hot tubs, fishing, bar, laundry service; no TV in some rooms* ☰ *AE, MC, V* ⦿| *CP.*

★ **$$$** ▥ **Las Restingas.** This is the most luxurious hotel in town; it's also the only place in town where you can view the whales from your hotel. Rooms boast crisp linens and huge picture windows from which you can watch the creatures bob in and out of the water on a good day. The harbor from which whale-watching trips leave is right at the property's border. ⊠ *Primera Bajada al Mar and Ribera Marítima* ☎☎ *2965/495–006 or 2965/495–101* ⊕ *www.lasrestingas.com* ⇆ *12 rooms* ⚐ *Restaurant, bar, laundry service, solarium, Internet, private beach* ☰ *AE, MC, V.*

$ ▥ **Cabañas en el Mar.** Families would do well to stay in one of these wooden cabañas that have small private balconies looking seaward. They come with small kitchens and can accommodate up to six people. Since the food options in town are limited, the cabañas are also popular with biologists on extended stays. ⊠ *Av. de las Ballenas s/n, 9121* ☎ *2965/495–049* ⊕ *www.piramides.net/cabanas* ⇆ *6 cabañas* ⚐ *Cafeteria, laundry service; no room TVs* ☰ *No credit cards.*

Sports & the Outdoors

For whale-watching, **Jorge Schmid** (📠 2965/295–012 or 2965/295–112) is a reliable operator, operating from the little harbor of Pirámides. They also rent scuba equipment. **Mar Patag** (📞 5411/5031–0756 ⊕ www.crucerosmarpatag.com) offers multiday luxury boat tours of Valdés Bay and the Atlantic Ocean. Its brand-new ship has seven well-equipped rooms and can accommodate up to 50 people. The all-inclusive cruises run two to three days and cost about $150 per person per day.

Trelew

⑩ *11 km (6 mi) east of Gaiman, 250 km (155 mi) north of Camarones, 1,800 km (1,116 mi) north of Ushuaia, 67 km (41½ mi) south of Puerto Madryn.*

Trelew (pronounced Tre-LEH-ew) is a commercial, industrial, and service hub with hotels, restaurants, gas stations, mechanics, and anything else you might need as you travel from point to point. Its biggest attractions are its paleontology museum and its proximity to the Punta Tombo Reserve and Península Valdés. Like Gaiman, Trelew has a strong Welsh tradition. If you come in the second half of October, you can participate in the Eisteddfod, a Welsh literary and musical festival, first held in Patagonia in 1875. Trelew itself was founded in 1886 as a result of the construction of the Chubut railway line, which joined the Chubut River valley with the Atlantic coast. It's named after its Welsh founder, Lewis Jones (Tre means "town" in Welsh, and Lew stands for Lewis), who fought to establish the rail line. For more information about the town, contact the **tourist office** (✉ Mitre 387 📠 2965/420–139 ⊕ www.trelewpatagonia.gov.ar).

The tourist office is in front of the town's main square, **Plaza Independencia,** which features a central gazebo with intricate woodwork and a steeple. In 1910 the plaza and gazebo were inaugurated in a spot formerly used for grazing by horses of the train station's employees.

The **Teatro Español** (Spanish Theater), on the north side of Plaza Independencia, was constructed by the city's Spanish immigrants in 1918. Today it's a cultural center that hosts drama, dance, and musical events. ✉ *Av. 25 de Mayo 237* 📞 *2965/434–336.*

The **Museo de Arte Visuales de Trelew** (Museum of Visual Arts) is east of the plaza and hosts good monthly contemporary art exhibitions. It's in a Flemish- and German-influenced building designed by a French architect in 1900. From 1913 to 1932, this was city hall. ✉ *Mitre 389* 📞 *No phone* ⊕ *http://ar.geocities.com/museotw* ☉ *Daily 8–8.*

☾ At Trelew's most prominent attraction, **Museo Paleontológico Egidio Feruglio (MEF),** the most modern display is 2 million years old. This state-of-the-art educational extravaganza features exhibits on extinct dinosaurs from Patagonia. There's a fossil of a 290-million-year-old spider with a 3-foot leg span and the 70-million-year-old petrified dinosaur eggs of a carnotaurus. The museum's tour de force is the bones of a 100-ton, 120-foot-long dinosaur. You can also glimpse into a workshop where

Fodor'sChoice

★

6

archaeologists study newly unearthed fossils. Tours in English are available. ⊠ *Av. Fontana 140* ☎ *2965/432–100 or 2964/420–012* 💶 *8 pesos* ⊙ *Daily 10–6.*

Across the street from MEF is Trelew's old train station, which operated from 1889 to 1961, when the government shut down the country's rail service. The national historic landmark now holds a small museum of town history, the **Museo Regional Pueblo de Luís** (Lewistown Regional Museum). It has a mishmash of displays on the European influence in the region, the indigenous populations of the area, and wildlife. ⊠ *Avs. 9 de Julio and Fontana* ☎ *2965/424–062* 💶 *2 pesos* ⊙ *Weekdays 8–8, Sun. 5–8.*

Where to Stay & Eat

$–$$ ✕ **El Viejo Molino.** It's fun to find a restaurant that outclasses its city. The
Fodor$Choice thoughtful design and ultramodern renovation of this 1886 mill have
★ set a new benchmark for dining on the Patagonian coast. Beneath the Alexander Calder–inspired mobiles that hang from the two-story-high ceilings, elegant hostesses and courteous waiters deliver cosmopolitan service. The interior's coup de grace is a glassed-in parrilla, where you can watch an attendant pour wine over the roast and attend to it lovingly. Old black-and-white photos on the wall document this location's history from a brick cube into an ivy-hung gem of a steak house. ⊠ *Mitre and Av. Galés 250* ☎ *2965/428–019* 🖃 *AE, MC, V.*

¢–$ ✕ **Margarita Resto-Bar.** This bar and restaurant, whose sister establish-
Fodor$Choice ment is in Puerto Madryn, has all the pretty young things of Trelew aflut-
★ ter. Creative mixed drinks like the Albano (rum, Dubonnet, Cointreau, Absolut Mandarin, and Angostura bitters) complement an eclectic, vegetarian-friendly menu, which might include chicken breast with olive and Dijon mustard, and a wide variety of salads. The place absolutely hops on weekend nights. ⊠ *Av. Fontana 19* ☎ *No phone* ⊕ *www. margaritapub.com* 🖃 *AE, MC, V.*

¢–$ ✕ **Touring Club.** This classic old *confitería* was founded in 1907 by the Chubut Railway Company as a restaurant and became Chubut's first hotel in 1926. In its heyday it was one of Patagonia's most luxurious options. Now, the hotel's rooms are too shabby to recommend, but the café staff is proud of its past; the spot is so old-world, the waiters will simply leave a bottle of liquor on your table after only charging you for one drink. Ask to see the old *salón* (dining room). ⊠ *Av. Fontana 240, 9100* ☎ *2965/433–997 or 2965/433–998* 🖃 *AE, DC, MC, V.*

$ 🛏 **Hotel Libertador.** This big hotel has seen better days, but because it caters to tour groups, the friendly, English-speaking staff is very reliable. Rooms are clean and light and reasonably modern. Fourteen "superior" rooms are more recently renovated and are worth the modest increase in price. ⊠ *Av. Rivadavia 31, 9100* ☎ *2965/420–220* ⊕ *www. hotellibertadortw.com* ⇦ *90 rooms* ⚙ *Restaurant, snack bar, cable TV, in-room data ports, laundry service, business services, car rental, free parking* 🖃 *AE, DC, MC, V* ⊙ *CP.*

$ 🛏 **Rayentray.** The nicest, and most expensive, hotel in Trelew is this 22-year-old building, part of an Argentine chain. Rayentray, which means "stream of flowers" in Mapuche, has more amenities than any other local hotel. It's a block from Plaza Independencia. ✉ *San Martín 101, 9100* ☎ *2965/434–702* ⊕ *www.cadenarayentray.com.ar* ⤳ *110 rooms* ⚭ *Restaurant, minibars, cable TV, pool, massage, sauna, laundry service, business services* ⊟ *AE, DC, MC, V* ⦿ *CP.*

Gaiman

⑪ *17 km (10½ mi) west of Trelew.*

The most Welsh of the Atlantic Patagonian settlements, Gaiman (pronounced GUY-mon) is far more charming than nearby Trelew and Rawson. The Welsh colony's history is lovingly preserved in museums and private homes; Welsh can still be heard on the streets (though residents speak accentless Spanish); and there continues to be a connection to Wales, with teachers, preachers, and visitors going back and forth frequently (often with copies of family trees in hand). Even the younger generation maintains an interest in the culture and language.

Perhaps the town's greatest draw is its five Welsh teahouses (*casas de te*)—Ty Gwyn, Plas-y-Coed, Ty Nain, Ty Cymraeg, and Ty Te Caerdydd. Although it would be hard, if not impossible, to find any such teahouses over in Wales itself—these establishments seem to be a purely Patagonian thing, catering exclusively to tourists, and all serve a similar menu of tea along with home-baked pastries, cakes, and breads for about the same price (around 18 pesos will buy a *completo* sampling, which should serve two). Still, the establishments each have different atmospheres. Teahouses are usually open daily 3–8; if you're anywhere nearby, they're worth a trip.

A tour guide at the **tourist office** (✉ Corner of Rivadavía and Belgrano Sts. ☎ 02965/491–152 ☉ Mon.–Sat. 9–8, Sun. 1–8) can hop in the passenger seat of your car to lead you through a few sights in town, including the now-unused 1904 train tunnel and the **Museo Antropológico de Gaiman,** a two-story brick house built in 1910 by the pioneering Nichols family (visiting the house costs 1 peso). Inside are pre-Hispanic skulls, Patagonian stone tools, and displays of other artifacts from the region. Note that this museum can only be visited with a tour guide. Call in advance for reservations.

The **Museo Histórico Regional de Gaiman** (Gaiman Regional Historical Museum) has photographs of Gaiman's original 160 settlers; stock certificates from the Companía Unida de Irrigación del Chubut (United Company for Chubut Irrigation), which was nationalized by Perón in the '40s; and other interesting memorabilia. Tegai Roberts, the English-speaking octogenarian who gives tours here, is the great-granddaughter of Michael D. Jones, one of the original settlers of the Patagonian colony. If you strike up a conversation with her, you're likely to get a complete oral history of Gaiman and its inhabitants. ✉ *Av. Sarmiento and Av. 28 de Julio* ▣ *1 peso* ☉ *Jan. and Feb., Tues.–Sun. 10–11:30 and 3–6; Mar.–Dec., Tues.–Sun. 3–6.*

★ Argentina's weirdest attraction is Gaiman's **Parque Desafío.** Colorful, kitschy, and entirely creative, the park is filled with recycled goods—

80,000 bottles, 15,000 tin cans, and the remains of several automobiles. Its mastermind is Joaquin R. Alonso, whose optimistic outlook on life is clearly conveyed in his artwork. Alonso and his wife Maria del Carmen Caballero, who live here, welcome you to the park and invite you to stroll the paths lined with Alonso's alternately pensive and humorous musings. One reads, "Cows affirm that artificial insemination is boring." A visit here is anything but. ✉ *Av. Brown 52 at Calle Espora* ☎ *2965/491–340* 💲 *5 pesos* ⊙ *Daily 10–7.*

The **Parque Paleontológico Bryn Gwyn** (Bryn Gwyn Paleontology Park), outside town, is the companion to the Museo Paleontológico Egidio Feruglio in Trelew. Here you can see 40 million years of geological history in a natural setting. Call ahead to make arrangements for getting into the park and going on a tour. ✉ *11 km (7 mi) south of town* ☎ *2965/1555–5014* ⊙ *Daily 11–5* 💲 *4 pesos.*

OFF THE BEATEN PATH

BOD IWAN FARM – Want to spend a day on the same farm where Bruce Chatwin stayed while researching his famed travelogue *In Patagonia*? Contact Waldo Williams at Bod Iwan Farm, a working Welsh farm 15 minutes east of Gaiman, where you can walk among cows, sheep, wagons, and tractors. Waldo will give you a tour of his century-old home, along with the grounds around the house, where he grows fields of alfalfa to feed the Hampshire Down sheep that populate the property. He and his families are encyclopedias of Gaiman lore. Stick around until dusk; watching the sunset in the Chubut River valley is quite an experience and you'll understand why Patagonia has been a source of both desperation and inspiration for so many. ☎ *2965/491–251 or 2965/1566–1816.*

Where to Stay & Eat

Dining options are limited in Gaiman. The town's true joy, however, is a visit to one—or all—of Gaiman's teahouses.

$$ ✕ **Ty Cymraeg.** Photographs of the Thomas family's ancestors hang proudly on the walls of the wood-paneled rooms in this teahouse on the banks of the Chubut River. An outdoor patio with tree-shaded benches is at your disposal. ✉ *Av. Matthews 74* ☎ *2965/491–010* ⊕ *www.cpatagonia.com/gaiman/cymraeg* ☐ *AE, DC, MC, V.*

★ **$$** ✕ **Ty Té Caerdydd.** Cypress trees, fountains, and sculpted gardens mark the grounds of Gaiman's largest teahouse, which looks like a mini palatial estate on the south bank of the Chubut River. It succeeds in impressing, though the dining rooms here are larger and less homey than the town's other teahouses. A separate *casa de artesanias* is the best place to pick up jams, handicrafts, and souvenirs. ✉ *Finca 202, Zona de Chacras* ☎ *2965/491–510* ☐ *AE, DC, MC, V.*

★ **$–$$** ✕ **La Vieja Cuadra.** Exposed brick adds warmth to the town's liveliest restaurant. Some come just to have a beer—the place stays lively well into the evening—while others come to dine on the house specialty: homemade pastas, like spaghetti or ham-and-cheese-stuffed *sorrentinos* (stuffed pasta) with bolognese meat sauce, or triangular pasta pillows with rabbit confit. Even better are the pizzas. If you crave sirloin, try the *lomo a los tres pimientos* (with three peppers). ✉ *M. D. Jones 418,* *at Tello on the plaza* ☎ *2965/1568–2352* ▤ *No credit cards* ⊙ *Closed Mon. No lunch Tues.–Sat. No dinner Sun.*

¢–$ ✕**El Ángel.** This mysterious restaurant, hidden inside a genteel old house down a silent side street, brings with it a bundle of unanswered questions: When is it open? What's on the menu today? The lack of set opening hours or set dishes may make this restaurant too much of a gamble for some, but rest assured that whatever they serve, when they deign to do so, is the best and most ambitious food in town. Try to reserve at least one day in advance, and don't plan on bringing the kids to this formal dining room. And don't be too shocked if, in spite of following all of the above instructions, you still can't get in. ✉ *Rivadavia 241* ☎ *2965/491–460* ▤ *No credit cards.*

★ $ ✕🏠**Ty Gwyn.** This wood-and-brick teahouse was opened in 1974 by Maria Elena Sanchez Jones, who still directs the kitchen. It serves delicious scones, breads, and jams lovingly made from local fruits, and other elaborate sweets, including the classic Argentine-Welsh tea accompaniment, *torta negra* (black cake), a kind of fruitcake. An interior garden leads to a staircase above which Ms. Sanchez Jones maintains four bedrooms that form the town's best lodging. The quarters are spotless, affordable, and have wood floors, soothing mint-colored walls, and small private balconies with river views. Room 4 has antique furnishings. ✉ *Av. 9 de Julio 147* ☎ *2965/491–009* ⊕ *www.cpatagonia.com/gaiman/ty-gwyn* ⇨ *4 rooms* ♿ *Restaurant, bar, laundry service; no room phones, no room TVs* ▤ *AE, MC, V* |O| *BP.*

$$ 🏠**Posada Los Mimbres.** An alternative to staying in town—and a great choice if you're seeking a little space and solitude—is this ranch on the Chubut River. Guests can choose to stay in one of two three-bedroom homes, one of which is a century old. You reach the ranch by following signs from town to the "Zona de Chacras," or farmhouse zone. It's a 5-km (3-mi) ride down a dirt road. ✉ *Chacra 211, 9105* ☎☎ *2965/491–299* ⊕ *www.posadalosmimbres.com.ar* ⇨ *2 houses* ♿ *Trekking, boating, biking; no a/c, no room phones* ▤ *No credit cards* |O| *BP.*

¢ 🏠**Hostería Gwesty Tywi.** Diego, the friendly owner, will really take care of you here, from helping you plan town and country visits to serving you a delicious breakfast each morning. Rooms are simple but immaculately well-kept, there's a delightful backyard, and the Gwesty Tywi has become something of a meeting place for itinerant travelers coming through Gaiman—Welsh and otherwise. Gaiman is small, and you can walk from the front door to any destination. ✉ *M. D. Jones 342, 9105* ☎☎ *2965/491–292* ⊕ *www.advance.com.ar/usuarios/gwestywi* ⇨ *6 rooms* ▤ *No credit cards* ♿ *Breakfast room; no room phones, no room TVs* |O| *CP.*

Punta Tombo

⑫ *120 km (74 mi) south of Trelew, 105 km (65 mi) north of Camarones.*

Fodor'sChoice The **Reserva Faunística Punta Tombo** (Punta Tombo Wildlife Reserve) has
★ the largest colony of Magellanic penguins in the world and one of the most varied seabird rookeries. Roughly 325,000 penguins live here from the middle of September through March. You can walk among them

(along a designated path) as they come and go along well-defined "penguin highways" that link their nests with the sea, and you can see them fishing near the coast. Other wildlife found here in abundance includes cormorants, guanacos, seals, and Patagonian hares. Although December is the best month to come—that's when the adult penguins are actively going back and forth from the sea to feed their newborns—anytime is good, except from April through August when the penguins feed at sea. Other than driving, the easiest way to get to Punta Tombo is with a tour guide from Trelew, Rawson, Gaiman, or even Puerto Madryn, the stopover points for the reserve.

Camarones

⑬ *252 km (156 mi) south of Trelew, 105 km (65 mi) south of Punta Tombo, 258 km (160 mi) north of Comodoro Rivadavía.*

Camarones is a tiny and dilapidated but charming fishing town whose main attractions are the particular blueness of the sea and the nearby nature reserve. Every year, on the second weekend in February, the town celebrates the Fiesta Nacional de Salmon (National Salmon Festival) with all kinds of events and a fishing contest. Camarones is difficult to reach by public transportation, though at least one bus company, Don Otto, passes through here on its 3½-hour trip from Trelew. The **Cabo Dos Bahías Fauna Reserve,** 30 km (19 mi) southeast of town, has all kinds of wildlife, including penguins, sea lions, birds, seals, guanacos, rheas, and foxes.

Where to Stay
Camping is free in the municipal campgrounds that front the Bay of Camarones; call the **Chubut Province Tourism Agency** (☎ 11/4432–8815 in Buenos Aires, 2965/481–113 in Rawson) for more information.

Comodoro Rivadavía

⑭ *1,854 km (1,149 mi) south of Buenos Aires, 1,726 km (1,070 mi) north of Ushuaia, 945 km (586 mi) north of Río Gallegos, 397 km (246 mi) south of Rawson.*

Argentina's answer to Houston, Comodoro Rivadavía is the town that oil built. Argentina's first oil discovery was made here in 1907 during a desperate search for water because of a serious drought. It was an event that led to the formation of Yacimientos Petroliferos Fiscales (YPF), among the world's first vertically integrated oil companies. After YPF's privatization in 1995, however, thousands were laid off, bringing hard times to Comodoro's 130,000 residents. Surrounded by dry hills and sheer cliffs off the Golfo San Jorge (San Jorge Gulf), Comodoro looks dramatic from a distance. Up close, it's a little frayed around the edges. The main commercial streets, where restaurants and bars can also be found, are San Martín and Comodoro Rivadavía. A relative urban newcomer, Comodoro has little of the old-world charm found in colonial Latin American cities, and it lacks a main central plaza with a traditional church. Residents congregate around the port, with its promenade, park, and basketball and volleyball courts.

Where to Stay & Eat

¢–$ ✕ **La Estancia.** This restaurant—made to look like a typical Argentine ranch—has been serving finely prepared, traditionally cooked meats for 34 years and is the city's oldest. Try the *cordero* (lamb) with chimichurri sauce and mashed potatoes, the seafood, or the homemade pasta. Desserts are extravagant, especially the pancakes with *dulce de leche* (sweet milk). The owners, the friendly Dos Santos family, provide excellent service. Unlike other restaurants, it has a menu in English. ✉ *Urquiza 863* ☎ *0297/447–4568* ⊟ *AE, DC, MC, V.*

$–$$ ✕☒ **Austral Plaza Hotel.** This is really two hotels in one: a 42-room luxury hotel with marble floors and plush towels in the rooms and a modest 108-room hotel adequate for its class. The older portion has the advantage of being cheaper while allowing access to some of the newer portion's amenities, such as fax and Internet services. The Austral also has perhaps the city's finest seafood restaurant, Tunet ($–$$). ✉ *Moreno 725, 9000* ☎ *0297/447–2200* ⊕ *www.australhotel.com.ar* ⤳ *150 rooms* ⚐ *Restaurant, gym, sauna, business services, free parking* ⊟ *AE, DC, MC, V* ⦿ *CP.*

Sarmiento & the Bosque Petrificado

⑮ *150 km (94 mi) west of Comodoro Rivadavía.*

Fodor's Choice
★
Sarmiento is a one-horse town of dirt and paved roads, with small, low structures—primarily houses, a couple of churches, a gas station, a few small restaurants, and some no-frills hotels. It's also the jumping-off point for the Bosque Petrificado José Ormaechea (José Ormaechea Petrified Forest), about 30 km (19 mi) from Sarmiento on R26. There, you can see trunks of petrified wood 65 million years old, with their colorful stratifications, and feel the overpowering wind. Let the park's resident attendant and self-professed "Patagonia fanatic," Juan José Balera, give you a whirl through the eerily lonely landscape in his Mercedes-Benz bus (just show up; he's usually there). If you rent a car, make it a four-wheel-drive vehicle because you'll have to drive half an hour on a rough, unpaved road once you leave Sarmiento. For more information about the park, contact the **tourist office** (☎0297/489–8220) in Sarmiento. While you're in the area, stop at **Lago Musters** (Musters Lake), 7 km (4 mi) from Sarmiento, and **Lago Olhue Huapi** (Olhue Huapi Lake), a little farther on. At Lago Musters you can take an isolated swim or go fishing.

ATLANTIC PATAGONIA ESSENTIALS

Transportation

BY AIR

The best way to get to Atlantic Patagonia is to fly from Buenos Aires, although the region is also connected by periodic flights to other parts of Patagonia. Trelew and Comodoro Rivadavía are the region's largest airports; the proximity of Trelew to Madryn and the Peninsula Valdés makes it the best option, generally speaking, although there is also a smaller, less well-connected airport in Puerto Madryn.

Aerolíneas Argentinas flies (along with its subsidiary Austral) from Buenos Aires to Trelew and Comodoro Rivadavía. From Trelew, Aerolíneas also flies direct, with varying frequency, to El Calafate and Ushuaia in southern Patagonia. LADE (Líneas Aéreas del Estado) connects Trelew, Puerto Madryn, and Comodoro Rivadavía to other parts of Patagonia, including Bariloche, Chapelco (San Martín de los Andes), and Esquel in the Lakes region, and El Calafate, Río Gallegos, and Ushuaia in southern Patagonia. Be aware that some of LADE's flights are on small propeller planes, and many routes only run once or twice per week.

🚩 **Aerolíneas Argentinas** ☎ 0810/2228-6527, 11/4320-2000 in Buenos Aires, 2965/420-060 in Trelew, 2974/548-126 in Comodoro Rivadavía ⊕ www.aerolineas.com.ar. **LADE** ☎ 0810/810-5233, 2965/451-256 in Puerto Madryn, 2965/435-740 in Trelew, 2974/470-585 in Comodoro Rivadavía ⊕ www.lade.com.ar.

BY BUS

In Atlantic Patagonia, it's difficult—but not impossible—to get around without a car. If you're based in Puerto Madryn or Puerto Pirámides to see the Peninsula Valdés, you should go with local tour operators rather than public buses for day excursions. However, buses do connect the cities of the region (Gaiman, Trelew, Puerto Madryn, and Comodoro Rivadavía, which is the best-connected city of all).

To travel from Atlantic Patagonia across to Bariloche and the Lakes region or down to southern Patagonia (a desperately long haul), you'll take Don Otto, Andesmar, or TAC. El Pingüino also has service between Trelew and Puerto Madryn and to Bariloche with a transfer in Comodoro Rivadavía. La Puntual is another major operator in the region, with a hub in Comodoro Rivadavía. To get to and from Buenos Aires, don't bother with the bus system—flying is quick and inexpensive.

🚩 **Andesmar** ✉ Urquiza and Lewis Jones, Trelew ☎ 2944/433-535 🚌 Terminal de Ómnibus, Puerto Madryn ☎ 2965/473-764. **Don Otto** ✉ Gales 35, Trelew ☎ 2965/423-943 🚌 Terminal de Ómnibus, Puerto Madryn ☎ 2965/451-675. **El Pingüino** ☎ 11/4315-4438 in Buenos Aires, 2965/427-400 in Trelew, 2965/456-256 in Puerto Madryn. **La Puntual** ☎ 11/4313-2441 in Buenos Aires, 2965/433-748 in Trelew, 297/429-176 in Comodoro Rivadavía. **TAC** ✉ Urquiza and Lewis Jones, Trelew ☎ 2965/431-452 🚌 Hipólito Yrigoyen 331, Puerto Madryn ☎ 2965/451-537.

BY CAR

The towns of Trelew and Gaiman are fairly self-contained, and the central area of Puerto Madryn is easily walkable, but unless you plan on doing a series of day excursions with tour operators, a car is the best way to see the natural wonders of Peninsula Valdés at a leisurely pace. Gas costs 30% less in the Chubut province, another boon for drivers. Hiring a *remis* (car with driver) is a pricier alternative.

Atlantic Patagonia is the closest part of Patagonia to Buenos Aires by road, but it's still a long haul across deserted stretches of road. It's best to rent a car in Puerto Madryn or Trelew. Within the Peninsula Valdés, roads are unpaved but straight and flat. On those roads, be on the lookout for sheep and other animals crossing, and do not exceed 60 kph, because the type of gravel makes skidding very easy.

🚘 Local Agencies **Aonik'Enk de Patagonia** ⊠ Av. Rawson 1190, Comodoro Rivadavía ☎ 0297/446-6768.

Contacts & Resources

BANKS & EXCHANGE SERVICES

BANKS 🚘 In Puerto Madryn **Banco de la Nación** ⊠ 9 de Julio 127 ☎ 2965/450-465. **Credicoop** ⊠ Roque Sanez Peña and 25 de Mayo ☎ 2965/455-139.

🚘 In Trelew **Banco de la Nación** ⊠ Belgrano and Julio A. Roca ☎ 2965/449-100. **Lloyds Bank** ⊠ 9 de Julio 102 ☎ 2965/434-264 or 2965/434-058.

EMERGENCIES

🚘 **Coast Guard** ☎ 106. **Fire** ☎ 100. **Forest Fire** ☎ 103. **Hospital** ☎ 107. **Police** ☎ 101.

MAIL & SHIPPING

🚘 Post Offices **Gaiman** ⊠ Juan C. Evans 110. **Puerto Madryn** ⊠ Belgrano and Maíz ⊠ Av. Julio A. Roca 223. **Trelew** ⊠ 25 de Mayo and Mitre.

TOUR OPTIONS

Carlos and Carol de Passera of Causana Viajes have 17 years of experience leading custom and special-interest trips—focusing, for example, on archaeology, birding, botany, natural history, or whale-watching—for American and Canadian adventure travel companies. Aiké Tour, Cuyun Co Turismo, and Factor Patagonia arrange all-day tours of the Península Valdés; reserve ahead, especially if you want an English-speaking guide. These companies also organize tours to Punta Tombo, Gaiman, the Dique Ameghino, and Camarones.

In the Peninsula Valdés, boat tours are the only way to see the Southern right whales up close. Jorge Schmid specializes in whale-watching tours; his boat has ample covered space in case it rains. Hydro Sport runs smaller whale-watching boats, which are particularly good for getting up close and personal with the whales. Zonotrikia leads treks through paleontological sites in the area. Aonik'Enk de Patagonia gives tours of Sarmiento, the Bosque Petrificado, and other nearby destinations; it also rents four-wheel-drive vehicles.

🚘 **Aiké Tour** ⊠ Av. Julio Roca 353, Puerto Madryn ☎ 2965/450-720. **Aonik'Enk de Patagonia** ⊠ Av. Rawson 1190, Comodoro Rivadavía ☎☎ 0297/446-6768 or 0297/446-1363. **Causana Viajes** ⊠ Moreno 390, Puerto Madryn ☎ 2965/455-044 ⊕ www.causana.com.ar. **Cuyun Co Turismo** ⊠ Julio A. Roca 165, Puerto Madryn ☎ 2965/454-950 or 2965/451-845 ⊕ www.cuyunco.com.ar. **Factor Patagonia** ⊠ 25 de Mayo, Puerto Madryn ☎ 2965/454-990 or 2965/454-991. **Hydro Sport** ⊠ Av. Julio A. Roca s/n, Puerto Madryn ☎ 2965/495-065 ⊕ www.hydrosport.com.ar. **Jorge Schmid** ⊠ Av. Julio A. Roca s/n, Puerto Pirámides ☎ 2965/495-112 or 2965/495-029. **Jose Luís Breitman** ☎ 2920/1560-5196. **Zonotrikia** ⊠ Av. Roca 536, Puerto Madryn ☎ 2965/451-427 or 2965/455-888.

VISITOR INFO

🚘 Tourist Offices **Comodoro Rivadavía** ⊠ Av. Rivadavía 430 ☎ 0297/446-2376. **Gaiman** ⊠ Belgrano 234 ☎ 2965/491-152. **Puerto Madryn** ⊠ Av. Roca 223 ☎ 2965/

453–504 or 2965/456–067 ⊕ www.turismomadryn.gov.ar. **Sarmiento** ⊠ Av. Reg. de Infanteria 25 ☎ 0297/489–8220. **Trelew** ⊠ Mitre 387 ☎☎ 2965/420–139.

SOUTHERN PATAGONIA

Imagine sailing across a tranquil blue lake full of icebergs, or traversing an advancing glacier, with crampons, in the shadow of the end of the Andes mountain range, literally watching a valley be formed before your eyes. A trip to southern Patagonia is like a trip back to the Ice Age. And above all else, it is that glacier—Perito Moreno—that is bringing tourists to Patagonia in unprecedented numbers. In spite of El Calafate's brand-new airport, experiencing southern Patagonia still means crossing vast, flat, windswept deserts to reach oases of isolated population centers. It means traveling to the end of the world—Tierra del Fuego (Land of Fire) and its dramatic Alps-like scenery of picturesque lakes, streams, mountains, and wildlife. It means being embraced by independent, pioneering souls just beginning to understand the importance of tourism as traditional industries—wool, livestock, fishing, and oil—are drying up.

The culture of southern Patagonia, like that of other parts of the region, is a hybrid of the cultures of primarily European immigrants, who came here in the 19th century, and the cultures of the indigenous peoples, mainly the Mapuche. The indigenous populations are long gone; they were wiped out by the four-year military campaign (1879–83) led by General Roca and known as the Conquest of the Desert. In summer (December–March), the towns of El Calafate and El Chaltén, in the southern lake district, come alive with the influx of visitors to the Parque Nacional los Glaciares and climbers headed for Cerro Torre and Cerro Fitz Roy.

El Calafate & the Parque Nacional los Glaciares

⑯ *320 km (225 mi) north of Río Gallegos via R5, 253 km (157 mi) east of Río Turbio on Chilean border via R40, 213 km (123 mi) south of El Chaltén via R40.*

Founded in 1927 as a frontier town, El Calafate is the base for excursions to the Parque Nacional los Glaciares (Glaciers National Park), which was created in 1937 as a showcase for one of South America's most spectacular sights, the Perito Moreno glacier. Because of its location on the southern shore of Lago Argentino, the town enjoys a microclimate much milder than the rest of southern Patagonia. During the long summer days between December and February (when the sun sets around 10 PM), and during Easter vacation, thousands of visitors come to see the glaciers and fill the hotels and restaurants. This is the area's high season, so be sure to make reservations well in advance. October, November, March, and April are less crowded and less expensive periods to visit. March through May can be rainy and cool, but also less windy and often quite pleasant. The only bad time to visit is winter, particularly June, July, and August.

To call El Calafate a boomtown would be to put it mildly. Between 2001 and 2005, the town's population exploded from 4,000 to 15,000, and

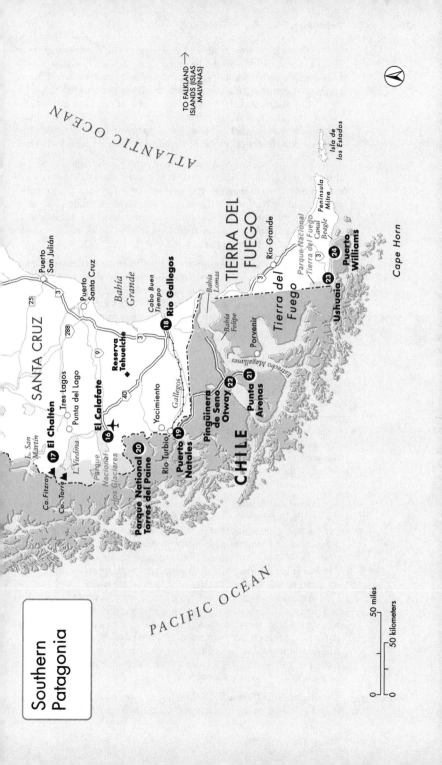

Southern Patagonia

ATLANTIC OCEAN

TO FALKLAND ISLANDS (ISLAS MALVINAS) →

Isla de los Estados

Cape Horn

PACIFIC OCEAN

SANTA CRUZ

Puerto San Julián

Puerto Santa Cruz

Bahía Grande

Cabo Buen Tiempo

18 Río Gallegos

TIERRA DEL FUEGO

Río Grande

Bahía Lomas

Reserva Tehuelche

Tres Lagos

Punta del Lago

17 El Chaltén

Co. Fitzroy

Co. Torre

L. San Martín

L. Viedma

Parque Nacional Los Glaciares

16 El Calafate

Yacimiento

Gallegos

Bahía Felipe

Porvenir

Tierra del Fuego

Parque Nacional Tierra del Fuego

Canal Beagle

23 Ushuaia

Peninsula Mitre

24 Puerto Williams

Estrecho de Magallanes

Río Turbio

19 Puerto Natales

20 Parque National Torres del Paine

Pingüinera de Seno Otway

22 Punta Arenas

21

CHILE

0   50 miles

0   50 kilometers

it shows no signs of slowing down; at every turn you'll see new construction. As such, the downtown has a very new feel to it, although most buildings are constructed of wood, with a rustic aesthetic that seems to respect the majestic natural environment. As the paving of the road between El Calafate and the Perito Moreno glacier nears completion, the visitors continue to flock in—whether luxury package tourists bound for the legendary Hostería Los Notros, backpackers over from Chile's Parque Nacional Torres del Paine, or *porteños* in town for a long weekend.

Daily flights from Buenos Aires, Ushuaia, and Río Gallegos, as well as direct flights from Bariloche, transport tourists in a few hours to El Calafate's 21st-century glass and steel airport—an island of modernity surrounded by the lonely expanse of Patagonia—with the promise of adventure and discovery in distant mountains and unseen glaciers. El Calafate is so popular that the flights are selling out weeks in advance, so don't plan on booking at the last minute.

Driving from Río Gallegos takes about four hours across desolate plains, enlivened occasionally by the sight of a gaucho, his dogs, and a herd of sheep, as well as *ñandú* (rheas), shy llamalike guanacos, silver-gray foxes, and fleet-footed hares the size of small deer. **Esperanza** is the only gas, food, and bathroom stop halfway between the two towns.

Avenida del Libertador San Martín (known as Libertador or San Martín) is the main street, with tour offices, restaurants, and shops selling regional specialities, sportswear, camping and fishing equipment, souvenirs, and food. A staircase in the middle of San Martín ascends to Avenida Julio Roca, where you'll find the bus terminal and a very busy **Oficina de Turismo** (⊠ Av. Julio Roca 1004 ☎🖨 2902/491–090 ⊕ www.elcalafate.gov.ar) with a board listing available accommodations and campgrounds; you can also get brochures and maps, and there's a multilingual staff to help plan excursions. It's open daily 7 AM–10 PM. The **Parques Nacionales** (⊠ Av. Libertador 1302 ☎ 2902/491–005), open weekdays 7–2, has information on the entire park, the glaciers, area history, hiking trails, and flora and fauna.

The Hielo Continental (Continental ice cap) spreads its icy mantle from the Pacific Ocean across Chile and the Andes into Argentina, covering an area of 21,700 square km (8,400 square mi). Approximately 1.5 million acres of it are contained within the **Parque Nacional los Glaciares**, a UNESCO World Heritage site. Extending along the Chilean border for 350 km (217 mi), the park is 40% covered with ice fields that branch off into 47 major glaciers that feed two lakes—the 15,000-year-old **Lago Argentino** (Argentine Lake, the largest body of water in Argentina and the third-largest in South America) in the southern end of the park, where you'll see the occasional group of flamingos, and **Lago Viedma** (Lake Viedma) at the northern end near **Cerro Fitz Roy**, which rises 11,138 feet. Plan on a minimum of two to three days to see the glaciers and enjoy the town—more if you plan to visit El Chaltén or any of the other lakes. Entrance to the park costs 30 pesos.

Fodor'sChoice
★ The **Glaciar Perito Moreno** lies 80 km (50 mi) away on R11, which is paved from El Calafate to the national park entrance. From there, a road that's

partly paved (it's scheduled to be entirely paved by the end of 2006) winds through hills and forests of lengas and ñires, until suddenly, the startling sight of the glacier comes into full view. Descending like a long white tongue through distant mountains, it ends abruptly in a translucent blue wall 3 km (2 mi) wide and 165 feet high at the edge of frosty green Lago Argentino.

Although it's possible to rent a car and go on your own, virtually everyone visits the park by day-trip tours that are booked through one of the many travel agents in El Calafate (unless, that is, you're staying in Los Notros, the only hotel inside the park itself; they arrange all the treks and such themselves). The most basic of these tours just take you to see the glacier up close from a viewing area composed of a series of platforms that are wrapped around the point of the Península de Magallanes. The viewing area, which might ultimately be the most impressive view of the glacier, allows you to wander back and forth, looking across the Canal de los Tempanos (Iceberg Channel). Here you listen and wait for nature's number one ice show—first, a cracking sound, followed by tons of ice breaking away and falling with a thunderous crash into the lake. Sometimes the icy water splashes onlookers across the channel! As the glacier creeps across this narrow channel and meets the land on the other side, an ice dam sometimes builds up between the inlet of Brazo Rico on the left and the rest of the lake on the right. As the pressure on the dam increases, everyone waits for the day it will rupture again. The last time was in March 2004, when the whole thing collapsed in a series of explosions that lasted hours and could be heard in El Calafate. You can look at photos of the event at the top of the "platforms."

Glaciar Upsala, the largest glacier in South America, is 60 km (37 mi) long and 10 km (6 mi) wide, and accessible only by boat. Daily cruises depart from Puerto Banderas (40 km [25 mi] west of El Calafate via R11) for the 2½-hour trip. While dodging floating icebergs (*tempanos*), some as large as a small island, the boats maneuver as close as they dare to the wall of ice rising from the aqua-green water of Lago Argentino. The seven glaciers that feed the lake deposit their debris into the runoff, causing the water to cloud with minerals ground to fine powder by the glacier's moraine (the accumulation of earth and stones left by the glacier). Condors and black-chested buzzard eagles build their nests in the rocky cliffs above the lake. When the boat stops for lunch at Onelli Bay, don't miss the walk behind the restaurant into a wild landscape of small glaciers and milky rivers carrying chunks of ice from four glaciers into Lago Onelli.

Where to Stay & Eat

$$$–$$$$ ✕ **Toma Wine Bar y Restó.** This hip restaurant represents the new, yuppie face of El Calafate, with creative preparations like *ojo de bife con calabazas confitadas* (ribeye with pumpkin confit) and *papas Toma* (french fries with melted cheese, smoked bacon, spring onion, and cream). Wine pairings are suggested with each main course, and to finish, there's good ol' apple pie à la mode, perhaps washed down by the port-style Malamado, made from Malbec grapes. The atmosphere is cool, dark, and trendy, and the service deferential. ⊠ *Av. del Libertador 1359* ☎ *2902/492–993* ▭ *AE, MC, V* ⊙ *No lunch. Closed Sun.*

$–$$$ ✕ **Casimiro Biguá.** This restaurant and wine bar is another one with a hipper-than-thou interior and an inventive menu serving such delectable delights as Patagonian lamb with *Calafate* sauce (Calafate is actually a local wild berry). The *cordero al asador* (spit-roasted lamb) displayed in the window, though, is the one throwback the place allows. There's an outdoor garden in the back, and a great wine list list. ✉ *Libertador 963* ☎ *2902/492–590* ⊕ *www.interpatagonia.com/casimiro* 🗖 *AE, DC, MC, V* ⊗ *No lunch. Closed Sun.*

$$ ✕ **La Cocina.** This casual café on the main shopping street serves homemade pasta, quiches, crepes, and hamburgers. Homemade ice cream and delicious cakes make good snacks any time of the day. "*Postre Chancho*" (Pig's Dessert) is ice cream with hot dulce de leche sauce. Note that there is a long siesta daily from 2 to 7:30. ✉ *Av. Libertador 1245* ☎ *2902/491–758* 🗖 *MC, V.*

★ **$$**   ✕ **Pura Vida.** Modernity merges with tradition at this hippieish, veggie-friendly restaurant a few blocks out of the center of El Calafate. It's a real treat to find such creative fare, funky decor, cool candles, and modern art in such a frontier town. The beef stew served inside a *calabaza* (pumpkin) has an irresistible flair to it and is excellently seasoned, although the beef isn't particularly tender. Even if, technically speaking, the cooking isn't quite top-flight, Pura Vida is more than the sum of its parts, drawing in backpackers and older folks alike with an almost mystical allure. ✉ *Libertador 1876* ☎ *2902/493–356* 🗖 *AE, MC, V.*

$$ ✕ **Rick's Café.** It's *tenedor libre* (all you can eat) for 22 pesos at this immensely popular *parrilla* in a big yellow building on El Calafate's main street. In part because of the value proposition, the place is packed full of locals and tourists day and night. The room is big and bustling, if not particularly interesting, and the spread includes lamb and *vacío* (flank steak). ✉ *Libertador 1091* ☎ *2902/492–148* 🗖 *MC, V.*

$–$$ ✕ **La Lechuza.** This cozy, bustling local place is known for having some of the best pizza in town. The brick oven and thin crust make for a more Italian-style taste and texture than at most spots. ✉ *Libertador and 1 de Mayo* ☎ *2902/491–610* 🗖 *No credit cards* ⊗ *No lunch Sun.*

$–$$ ✕ **La Tablita.** It's a couple of extra blocks away from downtown, across
FodorśChoice   a little white bridge, but this bustling parrilla is where all the locals go
★   for a special night out. You can watch your food as it's prepared: Patagonian lamb and beef ribs cook gaucho-style on an asador, or meat sizzling on the grill, including steaks, chorizos, and excellent *morcilla* (blood sausage). The enormous *parrillada* for two is an excellent way to sample it all, and the wine list is well-priced and well-chosen. ✉ *Coronel Rosales 28* ☎ *2902/491–065* ⊕ *www.interpatagonia.com/latablita* 🗖 *AE, DC, MC, V* ⊗ *No lunch Mon.–Thurs. June–July.*

$$$$ ✕🖭 **Hostería los Notros.** Weathered wood buildings cling to the moun-
FodorśChoice   tainside that overlooks the Perito Moreno Glacier as it descends into
★   Lago Argentino. This inn, seemingly at the end of the world, is 73 km (45 mi) west of El Calafate. The glacier is framed in the windows of every room. A path, through the garden and over a bridge spanning a canyon, connects rooms to the main lodge. Appetizers and wine are served in full view of sunset (or moonrise) over the glacier, followed by an absolutely spectacular menu that spotlights game, including delicious veni-

son and creative preparations of Argentine classics. Note that a two-night minimum stay is required. This property is extremely expensive (up to US$674 per night); prices include all meals, cocktails, park entry, and a glacier excursion. If you don't feel like spending that much, come just for a meal. ⊠ *Reservations in Buenos Aires: Arenales 1457, fl. 7, 1961* ☎ *11/4814–3934 in Buenos Aires, 2902/499–510 in El Calafate* ⊕ *www.losnotros.com* ⊅ *32 rooms* ♿ *Restaurant, fishing, hiking, horseback riding, bar, recreation room, playground, Internet, airport shuttle, travel services; no room phones; no room TVs* ☰ *AE, DC, MC, V* ⊘ *Closed June–mid-Sept.* ❑ *FAP.*

$$$ ✕❑ **Hotel Kau-Yatun.** Books, games, and magazines clutter the tables in the large living room of this former ranch house; guests congregate at the bar or in front of the fireplace. Rooms vary in size, shape, and decor, with all following a casual ranch theme. Country cuisine (meat, pasta, and vegetables) is served in the dining room, and wild game dishes are available at La Brida restaurant. On weekends, steaks and chorizos sizzle on a large open grill in the *quincho* (combination kitchen, grill, and dining room), while lamb or beef cooks gaucho style on an asador. ⊠ *25 de Mayo, 9405* ☎ *2902/491–059* ✉ *kauyatun@cotecal.com.ar* ⊅ *45 rooms* ♿ *Restaurant, horseback riding, bar, Internet, airport shuttle* ☰ *AE, MC, V* ⊘ *Closed May–Sept.* ❑ *CP.*

$$$$ ❑ **El Quijote.** Sun shines through picture windows onto polished slate floors and high beams in this modern hotel next to Sancho restaurant a few blocks from the main street. Rooms are carpeted and have plain white walls (which some readers have reported are paper thin) and wood furniture. ⊠ *Gregores 1155, 9405* ☎ *2902/491–017* ✉ *elquijote@cotecal.com.ar* ⊅ *80 rooms* ♿ *Café, bar, travel services* ☰ *AE, DC, MC, V* ⊘ *Closed June–July* ❑ *CP.*

$$$ ❑ **Kosten Aike.** The stone-and-brick accents and wood balconies outside, and the slate floors, wood-beamed ceilings, and unfailing attention to detail inside, will please aficionados of Andean Patagonian architecture. Tehuelche symbols and designs are used in everything from the curtains to the room plaques. A lobby bar and living room with fireplace, card tables, magazines, and a large TV is conducive to lounging about indoors anytime of day. ⊠ *G. Moyano y 25 de Mayo, 9405* ☎ *2902/492–424, 11/4811–1314 in Buenos Aires* ⊕ *www.kostenaike.com.ar* ⊅ *58 rooms, 2 suites* ♿ *Restaurant, gym, bar, shop, Internet, business services, meeting room, car rental* ☰ *AE, DC, MC, V* ⊘ *Closed May–Sept.*

$$$ ❑ **Posada los Alamos.** Surrounded by tall, leafy alamo trees and constructed of brick and dark *quebracho* (ironwood), this attractive country manor house uses rich woods, leather, and handwoven fabrics to produce conversation-friendly furniture groupings in the large lobby. Plush comforters and fresh flowers in the rooms, and a staff ready with helpful suggestions make this a top-notch hotel. Lovingly tended gardens surround the building and line a walkway through the woods to the restaurant and the shore of Lago Argentino. ⊠ *Moyano 1355 at Bustillo, 9405* ☎ *2902/491–144* ⊕ *www.posadalosalamos.com* ⊅ *140 rooms, 4 suites* ♿ *Restaurant, 3-hole golf course, tennis court, 2 bars, travel services* ☰ *AE, MC, V* ❑ *CP.*

6

$$ ⊞ **El Mirador del Lago.** The best thing about this hotel is not the zigzag brick facade offering all the front rooms a corner view of Lago Argentino, nor the cozy bar and sitting room, nor the collection of games, books, videos, and magazines to enjoy on stormy days. The best thing is the unfailingly friendly staff. They're all related and take great pride in helping their guests enjoy everything the region has to offer. They know the roads, the restaurants, and the best way to get to all the attractions. ⊠ *Av. Libertador 2047, 9405* ☎ *2902/493–213* ⊕ *www.miradordellago.com. ar* ⌁ *20 rooms* ⟀ *Dining room, sauna, bar, recreation room, travel services* ⊟ *AE, DC, MC, V* ☉ *Closed June* ⊚ *CP.*

$$ ⊞ **Michelangelo.** Bright red and yellow native flowers line the front of the low log-and-stucco building with its distinctive A-frames over rooms, restaurant, and lobby. A fine collection of local photographs is displayed on the walls next to a sunken lobby, where easy chairs and a banquette surround the fireplace. There's an excellent restaurant next door. ⊠ *Moyano 1020, 9405* ☎ *2902/491–045* ✑ *michelangelohotel@cotecal.com. ar* ⌁ *20 rooms* ⟀ *Restaurant, café, cable TV* ⊟ *AE, MC, V* ☉ *Closed June* ⊚ *CP.*

$ ⊞ **Calafate Hostel.** This hostel caters to every demographic, with dorm-style accommodations for backpackers in one building, and well-kept private rooms with private baths—and, believe it or not, Internet-connected desktop computers—in a separate structure next door. Both buildings share the bar-lounge and breakfast room. The bar is something of a hangout; this might not be the most upscale accommodation in town, but it's very comfortable, and it's right downtown. ⊠ *Gobernador Moyano 1226, 9405* ☎ *2902/492–450* ⊕ *www.calafatehostels. com* ⟀ *Internet, kitchen facilities, travel services* ⊟ *AE, MC, V.*

¢–$ ⊞ **América del Sur.** The only downside to this new hostel, which caters largely to younger backpackers, is its location (a 10-minute uphill walk from downtown), but there are beautiful views of the lake and mountains, and a free shuttle service to compensate for the distance. Otherwise, the place is simple but spectacular—sparklingly clean and legendarily friendly. There are rooms with 2 beds and 4 beds. It's a particularly cheap deal for groups of 4. ⊠ *Calle Pto. Deseado, 9405* ☎ *2902/493–525* ⊕ *www.americahostel.com.ar* ⟀ *Restaurant, bar, Internet, travel services; no TV* ⊟ *No credit cards.*

The Outdoors

BOAT TOURS The two most popular scenic boat rides in the Parque Nacional los Glaciares are the hour-long **Safari Náutico,** in which your boat cruises just a few meters away from the face of the Glaciar Perito Moreno, and the full-day **Upsala Glacier Tour,** in which you navigate through a more extensive selection of glaciers, including Upsala and Onelli, as well as several lakes within the park that are inaccessible by land. The Safari Náutico costs 60 pesos and includes transportation from El Calafate. The full-day Upsala trip, including lunch, costs around 175 pesos. **Upsala Explorer** (⊠ 9 de Julio 69, El Calafate ☎ 2902/491–034 ⊕ www. upsalaexplorer.com.ar) is the most popular operator of the boat tours. **René Fernández Campbell** (⊠ Avenida del Libertador 867, El Calafate ☎ 2902/491–155) is another local tour operator that runs boat tours around the glaciers.

HIKING You can hike anywhere in the Parque Nacional los Glaciares. Close to El Calafate are trails along the shore of Lago Argentino and in the hills south and west of town. El Chaltén is usually a better base than El Calafate for hikes up mountain peaks like Cerro Torre.

HORSEBACK RIDING Anything from a short day ride along Lago Argentino to a weeklong camping excursion in and around the glaciers can be arranged in El Calafate by **Gustavo Holzmann** (⊠ Av. Libertador 3600 ☎ 2902/493–203, 2966/1562–0935 cell) or through the tourist office. *Estancias Turísticas* (tourist ranches) are ideal for a combination of horseback riding, ranch activities, and local excursions. Information on **Estancias de Santa Cruz** is available in Buenos Aires at the **Provincial tourist office** (⊠ Suipacha 1120 ☎ 11/4325–3098 ⊕ www.estanciasdesantacruz.com). **Estancia El Galpón del Glaciar** (⊠ Ruta 11, Km 22 ☎☎ 2902/492–509 or 11/4774–1069 ⊕ www.estanciaalice.com.ar) welcomes guests overnight or for the day—for a horseback ride, bird-watching, or an afternoon program that includes a demonstration of sheep dogs working, a walk to the lake with a naturalist, sheep-shearing, and dinner in the former sheep-shearing barn, served right off the grill and the asador by knife-wielding gauchos. **Estancia Maria Elisa** (☎☎ 2902/492–583 or 11/4774–1069) is an upscale choice among estancias. Other estancias close to Calafate are **Nibepo Aike** (⊠ 50 km/31 mi from Calafate ☎ 2966/492–797 ⊕ www.nibepoaike.com.ar), **Alta Vista** (⊠ 33 km/20 mi from Calafate ☎ 2966/491–247), and **Huyliche** (⊠ 3 km/2 mi from Calafate ☎ 2902/491–025).

ICE TREKKING ★ A two-hour minitrek on the Perito Moreno Glacier involves transfer from El Calafate to Brazo Rico by bus and a short lake crossing to a dock and refugio, where you set off with a guide, put crampons over your shoes, and literally walk right across a stable portion of the glacier, scaling ridges of ice and ducking through bright blue ice tunnels. It is one of the most unique experiences in Argentina. The entire outing lasts about five hours. Hotels generally arrange minitreks through **Hielo y Aventura** (⊠ Av. Libertador 935 ☎ 2902/492–205 ⊕ www.hieloyaventura.com), which also organizes much longer, more difficult trips of eight hours to a week to other glaciers; you can also arrange the trek directly through their office in downtown El Calafate. Minitrekking runs about 250 pesos for the day.

MOUNTAIN BIKING Mountain biking is popular along the dirt roads and mountain paths that lead to the lakes, glaciers, and ranches. Rent bikes and get information at **Alquiler de Bicicletas** (⊠ Av. Libertador 689 and Comandante Espora ☎ 2902/491–398).

El Chaltén & Cerro Fitz Roy

⑰ *222 km (138 mi) north of El Calafate (35 km [22 mi] east on R11 to R40, then north on R40 on a dirt road to R23 north).*

The four-hour one-way bus or car trip to El Chaltén from El Calafate makes staying at least one night here a good idea. The only gas, food, and restroom facilities en route are at La Leona (110 km [68 mi] from El Calafate). As you follow the shore of Lago Viedma, look north for the glacier of the same name descending into the lake. Visible for hundreds of miles (weather permitting) on the northern horizon as you approach the frontier village of El Chaltén, the granite hulk of **Cerro Fitz Roy** (11,286 feet and named after the captain of the *Beagle,* on which Charles Darwin served as a naturalist) rises like a giant arrowhead next to the slender spires of **Cerro Torre** (10,174 feet). The Tehuelche called Cerro Fitz Roy Chaltén ("smoke") for the snow constantly blowing off its peak. The village was founded in 1985 as a hiking mecca at the base of the range. Before you cross the bridge to town over Río Gallegos, stop at the **Parque Nacional office** (🖃🖃 2962/493–004) for information on excursions and accommodations. Information is also available at the Río Gallegos and El Calafate tourist offices. Note: there is no ATM in town, so get plenty of money before you come in.

The **Laguna del Desierto** (Lake of the Desert), a lovely lake surrounded by forest, is 37 km (23 mi) north of El Chaltén on R23, a dirt road.

Where to Stay & Eat

$–$$$ ✕ **Zafarrancho.** This hip restaurant-bar has everything from storytelling to live music, and has become something of a local gathering place. The food is great, too: they make a mean *milanesa napoletana* (pounded, breaded, fried meat with tomato sauce and cheese). There's a more elaborate creative Patagonian menu, but it's only available in summer. In any season, though, you can slug beer until 2 AM, or surf the Web upstairs. ⊠ *Lionel Terray s/n* ☎ *2962/493–005* 🚫 *No credit cards.*

$–$$ ✕ **Ahumados Patagonia.** This small restaurant, in a grassy field next to the Albergue Patagonia hostel, serves smoked meats, hearty soups, chicken, lamb, beef kabobs, and fresh trout. ⊠ *Av. San Martín 493* ☎ *2962/493–019* 🚫 *MC, V.*

★ ¢–$ ✕ **El Bodegón.** This artisanal brewpub calls itself a "Hausbrauerei," but it's not just the beer that brings in the crowds. It's also the homey, warm atmosphere—you'll squeeze into one of just a couple of old wooden tables—and the delicious food, too. Pizza is made with loving care, but the tour de force is the delicious locro; traditionally a hearty northern Argentine stew, this is some of the best in southern Argentina. Prices are low, too. ⊠ *Av. San Martín s/n* ☎ *2962/493–109* 🚫 *No credit cards* ☉ *No lunch May–Sept.*

$$$$ ✕🖃 **Los Cerros.** From the high-end group that runs the legendary Hostería Los Notros at the Perito Moreno glacier comes this sparkling house upon a hill. The airy lobby has lovely wood details, a fireplace, and lamps that are like works of art. The restaurant ($$$$) is as artful as the hotel, with creative Patagonian cuisine; you can eat here and enjoy the view from a hill atop El Chaltén even if you're not staying. Prices are sky-high, but service from the young staff is impeccable, and for guests, excursions to Lago Viedma, Glaciar Torre, and Lago del Desierto are included. ⊠ *El Chaltén 9301* ☎ *0800/333–7282* ⊕ *www. loscerrosdelchalten.com* 🛏 *44 rooms* ⌂ *Restaurant, bar, lounge, Internet, laundry service; no room TVs* 🚫 *AE, DC, MC, V* ☉ *BP.*

$$ 🖃 **Kalenshen.** This delightful hotel, in a pink wooden house, has all the creature comforts—not always a given in this backpacker boomtown—plus a pleasant yellow lounge that is great for socializing. *Cabañas,* which sleep four people, are an even better deal than the clean, well-kept

rooms. The staff is friendly, and the location is perfect, right next to the town's little main street. ⊠ *Lionel Terray 50, 9301* ☎ *2962/493–108* ⊕ *www.kalenshen.com.ar* ➷ *9 rooms* ♿ *Restaurant, bar, living room* ▭ *AE, MC, V* ▮◯▮ *CP.*

¢ ▦ **Albergue Patagonia.** Just steps from hiking and mountain-biking trails stands this simple wood-frame farm house, with rooms that sleep two to six people. This is the true Chaltén style, popular with the legions of backpackers that trek through town, and it's a good place for solo travelers to meet others. You can cook your own meals here, prepare picnic lunches, peruse trail maps, and share information with fellow guests, all for under US$15. The hostel also arranges horseback riding, hiking, and biking excursions. ⊠ *Av. San Martín 493, 9301* ☎ *2962/493–019* ✎ *alpatagonia@infovia.com.ar* ➷ *7 rooms* ♿ *Restaurant, bicycles, horseback riding, bar, library, laundry facilities* ▭ *No credit cards.*

Sports & the Outdoors

HIKING Both long and short hikes on well-trodden trails lead to lakes, glaciers, and stunning viewpoints. A three-hour hike that includes all of the above takes you to El Mirador ("the lookout"). The six-hour hike to the base camp for Cerro Torre at Laguna Torre has (weather seldom permitting) dramatic views of Torres Standhart, Adelas, Grande, and Solo. The eight-hour hike to the base camp for Cerro Fitz Roy passes Laguna Capri, which mirrors the granite tower framed by ghostly lenga trees. Beyond El Chaltén (37 km [23 mi]), Lago del Desierto has an easy 5-km (3-mi) hike to Chorillo del Salto (Trickling Falls). Other hikes to and around Lago del Desierto are described in brochures and maps obtainable at the tourist office in El Chaltén or at the tourist office or national park office in El Calafate.

HORSEBACK Most of the hiking trails up, to, and around Fitz Roy are used to trans-
RIDING port mountaineering equipment by horse to base camps. Make arrangements for trail rides through local outfitters and guides, including **Rodolfo Guerra** (⊠ Northwest of town at Fitz Roy trailhead ☎ 2962/493–020).

Río Gallegos

⑱ *2,640 km (1,639 mi) south of Buenos Aires; 1,034 km (640 mi) south of Comodoro Rivadavia via R3; 319 km (197 mi) south of El Calafate; 596 km (370 mi) north of Ushuaia; and 251 km (157 mi) east of Puerto Natales, Chile, via R40.*

The administrative and commercial capital of Santa Cruz Province and perhaps the windiest town in the world (from September through November), Río Gallegos was founded in 1885 and served as a port for coal shipments from Río Túrbio (Túrbio River), on the Chilean border. Wool and sheepskins were its only other economic factors. As the gateway city to southern Patagonia, travelers en route south to Ushuaia, north to the Parque Nacional los Glaciares, or west to Chile, are often obliged to spend a night here. A desk at the airport has information on all the tourist attractions in the area, and helpful attendants will also make hotel reservations. More information is available at the **Subsecretaría de Turismo** (⊠ Av. Roca 863 ☎ 2966/438–725 ⊕ www.scruz.gov.ar) in town.

The End of the Chilean World

CROSSING FROM GLACIAL SOUTHERN PATAGONIA in Argentina to the Chilean side of the Patagonian South—home to Torres del Paine National Park—is an eminently worthwhile excursion, and it's an essential element of many travelers' itineraries. Crossing at Cancha Carrera is quick and simple. From Río Gallegos, it's 161 km (100 mi) northwest on RP5 to La Esperanza, then 129 km (80 mi) west on PR7 to Cancha Carrera.

From El Calafate, you can take a shortcut (closed in winter) on RN40 south to El Cerrito, which then runs 70 km (43 mi) southwest to RP7 at Estancia Tepi Aike, 78 km (48 mi) west of Esperanza. The longer but easier alternative is to drive 161 km (100 mi)

to La Esperanza on the main road to Río Gallegos, then west on PR7. As you approach the border, the grey granite spires of Torres del Paine are visible for miles across the empty plain. You will pass (and can stop and visit) the 100-year-old Tapi Aike ranch.

Río Túrbio, a coal-mining town with huge fields and a miner's museum, is 257 km (159 mi) west of Río Gallegos, and from there it's 30 km (19 mi) north to Puerto Natales, in a sound on the Chilean coast, the access city for Torres del Paine and Chilean coastal cruises. At Monte Aymond, 68 km (42 mi) south of Río Gallegos on RP68, you can cross into Tierra del Fuego via Punta Delgada in Chile.

—Eddy Ancinas

If you're into dinosaurs, visit the **Museo Regional Provincial Padre Manuel Jesus Molina** (Provincial Museum), which exhibits reconstructed skeletons excavated at sites in Patagonia. Exhibits on biology, geology, history, paleontology, and Tehuelche ethnology are displayed in different sections of the museum. ⊠ *Ramón y Cajal 51* ☎ *2966/423–290* 🎟 *Free* ⊙ *Weekdays 10–5, weekends 11–7.*

OFF THE BEATEN PATH

CABO VIRGENES – From September through April, this provincial nature preserve plays host to 150,000 mating Magellanic penguins—the second largest penguin colony in Patagonia. A lighthouse guarding the entrance to the Strait of Magellan has a tea house inside. You can go on an organized tour or on your own by following the signed interpretive trail. ⊠ *128 km (79 mi) south on RN3. At 17 km, branch left on to RP1, a dirt road, and continue past the ranches to the Reserva Faunística Provincial (Provincial Nature Preserve).*

Where to Stay & Eat

$$–$$$ ✕ **Bar Español El Horreo.** A well-heeled clientele begins to fill this rather classy Spanish-looking restaurant around 10:30 PM. Complimentary pisco sours begin your repast. It's hard to beat the local spring lamb, the steaks, or the mountain trout, crab, and seafood—grilled or in homemade sauces. ⊠ *Av. Roca 862* ☎ *2966/426–462* ▤ *MC, V.*

$ 🏨 **Hotel Santa Cruz.** Although the hotel looks old, rooms are comfortable, if a little utilitarian. Intimate seating areas, plants, and a friendly staff make the lobby bar a pleasant retreat on a windy day. Avoid rooms on the Avenida Roca side, as they can be noisy. ⊠ *Av. Roca 701, 9400* ☎ *2966/420–601* ⊕ *www.interpatagonia.com/hotelsantacruz* ⤳ *53 rooms, 1 suite* ⌔ *Restaurant, sauna, free parking* ⊟ *AE, DC, MC, V* ⍾⃝ *CP.*

Puerto Natales, Chile

⑲ *251 km (157 mi) west of Rio Gallegos, Argentina; 242 km (150 mi) northwest of Punta Arenas, Chile.*

Puerto Natales has seen a large increase in tourism in recent years; it's now rapidly emerging as the staging center for visits to Parque Nacional Torres del Paine, Parque Nacional Bernardo O'Higgins, and other attractions, including the Perito Moreno glacier across the border in Argentina. There is also a lot of tourism generated by the scenic **Navimag ferry/cruise** that comes in after the four-day journey from Puerto Montt. You can also take the ferry north from Natales to Puerto Montt, which leaves on Thursdays.

Aside from the numerous tour operators, everything here still feels more rustic and isolated than in cosmopolitan Punta Arenas. Hotels and restaurants are simpler, and shops older and more basic. On a clear day, an early morning walk along Avenida Pedro Montt, which follows the shoreline of the Seno Última Esperanza (or Canal Señoret, as it is called on some maps), can be a soul-cleansing experience. The rising sun gradually casts a glow on the mountain peaks to the west.

Serious hikers tend to spend four or five days—or more—hiking and camping in **Torres del Paine,** either before or after stopping in Puerto Natales. Others choose to spend a couple of nights in one of the park's luxury hotels, and take in the sights during day hikes from that base.

But if you have less time, it is quite possible to just spend one day touring the park, as many people do, with Puerto Natales as your base. In that case, rather than drive, you'll want to book a one-day Torres del Paine tour with one of the many tour operators in Natales. Most tours pick you up at your hotel between 8 AM and 9 AM, and most go along the same route, visiting several lakes and mountain vistas, seeing Lago Grey and its glacier, and stopping for lunch in Hostería Lago Grey or one of the other hotels inside the park. These tours return around sunset.

A few blocks east of the shore is the not-quite-central **Plaza de Armas.** An incongruous railway engine sits prominently in the middle of the square. ⊠ *Arturo Prat and Eberhard.*

Across from the Plaza de Armas is the squat little **Iglesia Parroquial.** The ornate altarpiece in this church depicts the town's founders, indigenous peoples, and the Virgin Mary all in front of the Torres del Paine.

A highlight in the small but interesting **Museo Historico Municipal** is a room of photos of indigenous peoples. Another room is devoted to the exploits of Hermann Eberhard, considered the region's first settler. ⊠ *Bulnes 285* ☎ *5661/411–263* ▱ *Free* ⊙ *Weekdays 8:30–12:30 and 2:30–6, weekends 2:30–6.*

In 1896, Hermann Eberhard stumbled upon a gaping cave that extended 200 meters (650 feet) into the earth. Venturing inside, he discovered the bones and dried pieces of hide of an animal he could not identify. It was later determined that what Eberhard had discovered were the extraordinarily well-preserved remains of a prehistoric herbivorous mammal, about twice the height of a man, which they called a *milodón*. The cave and a somewhat kitschy life-size fiberglass rendering of the creature are at the **Monumento Natural Cueva de Milodón.** ⊠ *Off Ruta 9, 28 km (17 mi) northwest of Puerto Natales* ☎ *No phone* 🎟 *1,500 pesos* ⊙ *Daily 8:30–6.*

Where to Stay & Eat

★ **$$–$$$** ✕ **Asador Patagónico.** This is a bright point of light in a rather bland Puerto Natales dining scene. The restaurant takes incredible care with the excellent *lomo* and other grilled steaks. A starter of steak tartare works well, too, as does a soupy *arroz con leche* (rice pudding) dessert. The wine list is serious, the atmosphere less so—it's perfectly relaxed, with good music, dim lighting, an open fire, and a friendly buzz. ⊠ *Prat 158* ☎ *5661/413–553* ⊕ *www.asadorpatagonico.cl* ⊟ *AE, DC, MC, V.*

$$ ✕ **Centro Español.** Tables swathed in bright red, and hardwood floors that would be perfect for flamenco dancing create this restaurant's subtly Spanish style. It's a bit formal, but never stuffy. There's a wide selection of simply prepared meat and fish entrées, including succulent squid, served in ample portions. ⊠ *Magallanes 247* ☎ *5661/411–181* ⊟ *AE, MC, V.*

$–$$ ✕ **El Rincón del Tata.** It's all about the atmosphere at this dim, funky little spot. In the evenings a strolling guitarist entertains with Chilean folk songs, encouraging diners to join in. Artifacts, mainly household items, from the town's early days fill the dining room, including a working wood-burning stove to keep you warm. Pizza is a specialty here, and it's not bad by Chilean standards; *salmón à la mantequilla* (salmon baked in butter and black pepper) is also decent, and the grilled lamb with garlic sauce is a Patagonian highlight. ⊠ *Arturo Prat 236* ☎ *5661/413–845* ⊟ *AE, DC, MC, V.*

$$$–$$$$ 🏨 **Hotel CostAustralis.** The peaked, turreted roof of this venerable three-story hotel dominates the waterfront. Designed by a local architect, it's considered one of the finest hotels in Puerto Natales. Rooms have wood-paneled entryways and Venetian and Czech furnishings. Some have a majestic view of the Seno Última Esperanza and the snowcapped mountain peaks beyond, while others look out over the city. ⊠ *Pedro Montt 262 and Bulnes* ☎ *5661/412–000* ⊕ *www.costaustralis.com* 🛏 *72 rooms, 2 suites* ⌂ *Restaurant, café, room service, in-room safes, mini-bars, cable TV, bar, laundry service, Internet, travel services* ⊟ *AE, DC, MC, V* ⅠⓄⅠ *BP.*

$$$ 🏨 **Hotel Martín Gusinde.** Part of Chile's modern AustroHoteles chain, this intimate inn possesses an aura of sophistication that contrasts with the laid-back atmosphere of Puerto Natales. Rooms have wood furniture and colorfully patterned wallpaper. It's across from the casino, a block south of the Plaza de Armas. In low season, prices drop by almost two-thirds. ⊠ *Carlos Bories 278* ☎ *5661/412–770* ⊕ *www.*

austrohoteles.cl/martingusinde.html ➥ *20 rooms* ⚴ *Restaurant, room service, in-room safes, cable TV, bar* ☰ *AE, MC, V* ⦿ *CP.*

$$ ⊞ **Hostal Lady Florence Dixie.** Named after an aristocratic English immigrant and tireless traveler, this modern hostel with an alpine-inspired facade is on the town's main street. Its bright, spacious lounge is a great people-watching perch. Guest rooms are a bit spartan—mostly just a bed and a bathroom—although the "superior" rooms are bigger. ⊠ *Bulnes 655* ☎ *5661/411–158* ⊕ *www.chileanpatagonia.com/florence* ➥ *18 rooms* ⚴ *In-room safes, Internet, café, living room, laundry service* ☰ *AE, MC, V* ⦿ *CP.*

$ ⊞ **Concepto Indigo.** Rooms in this restored old home have amazing views down the Canal Señoret stretching as far as the Mt. Balmaceda glacier and the Paine Grande. Ask for one of the corner rooms, which have windows along two walls. The walls are sponge-painted in bright reds, yellows, and blues, and hung with local art. The funky and friendly café downstairs has an eclectic collection of artifacts. ⊠ *Ladrilleros 105* ☎ *5661/413–609* ⊕ *www.conceptoindigo.com* ➥ *7 rooms* ⚴ *Restaurant, laundry service, Internet, travel services; no room phones, no room TVs* ☰ *MC, V* ⊘ *Closed in winter; months vary.*

Parque Nacional Torres del Paine

❷⓪ *125 km (75 mi) northwest of Puerto Natales, Chile.*

Fodor'sChoice
★

Some 12 million years ago, lava flows pushed up through the thick sedimentary crust that covered the southwestern coast of South America, cooling to form a granite mass. Glaciers then swept through the region, grinding away all but the ash-gray spires that rise over the landscape of one of the world's most beautiful natural phenomena, now the Parque Nacional Torres del Paine (established in 1959). Snow formations dazzle along every turn of road, and the sunset views are spectacular.

Among the 2,420-square-km (934-square-mi) park's most beautiful attractions are its lakes of turquoise, aquamarine, and emerald green waters. Don't bother looking for the Torres themselves from within the confines of the park—you can only see them from the outside on a clear day; but in any case, the name is misleading. It is the glaciers, mountain lakes, and snow-capped peaks—especially at sunset—that are the true highlights here.

Another draw is the park's unusual wildlife. Creatures like the guanaco (a woollier version of the llama) and the *ñandú* (resembling a small ostrich) abound. Predators like the gray fox make less frequent appearances. You may also spot the dramatic aerobatics of a falcon and the graceful soaring of the endangered condor. The beautiful puma is especially elusive, but sightings have grown more and more common.

Although considerable walking is necessary to take full advantage of Parque Nacional Torres del Paine, you don't have to be a hard-core backpacker. Many people choose to hike the so-called **"W" route**, which takes four days, but others prefer to stay in one of the comfortable lodges and hit the trails for the morning or afternoon. **Glaciar Grey,** with its

6

fragmented icebergs, makes a rewarding and easy hike; equally rewarding is the spectacular boat ride across the lake, past icebergs, and up to the glacier, which leaves from Hostería Lago Grey. Another great excursion is the 900-meter ascent to the sensational views from **Mirador Las Torres,** 4 hours one-way from Hostería Las Torres. Even if you're not staying at the Hostería, you can arrange a morning drop-off there, and a late afternoon pick-up, so that you can see the Mirador while still keeping your base in Puerto Natales or elsewhere in the park; alternatively, you can drive yourself to the Hostería and park there for the day.

Driving is another way to enjoy the park: most of the more than 100 km (62 mi) of roads leading to the most popular sites are safe and well maintained, though unpaved.

The vast majority of visitors come during the summer months, which means the trails can get congested. Early spring, when wildflowers add flashes of color to the meadows, is an ideal time to visit because the crowds have not yet arrived. The park is open all year, and trails are almost always accessible. Storms can hit without warning, however, so be prepared for sudden rain or snow. The sight of the Paine peaks in clear weather is stunning; if you have any flexibility in your itinerary, be sure to visit the park on the first clear day.

There are three entrances: Laguna Amarga, Lago Sarmiento, and Laguna Azul. You are required to sign in when you arrive at the park. *Guardaparques* (park rangers) staff six stations around the reserve. They request that you inform them when setting out on a hike. CONAF, the national forestry service, has an office at the northern end of Lago del Toro with a scale model of the park, and numerous exhibits (some in English) about the flora and fauna. ⊠ *CONAF station in southern section of the park past Hotel Explora* ☎ *5661/691–931* 🖼 *8,000 pesos* ☉ *Ranger station: Nov.–Feb., daily 8–8; Mar.–Oct., daily 8–12:30 and 2–6:30* ⊠ *Punta Arenas Branch, Av. Bulnes 0309* ☎ *5661/238–581* ⊠ *Puerto Natales Branch, O'Higgins 584* ☎ *5661/411–438.*

Where to Stay & Eat

$$ ✕🖼 **Posada Río Serrano.** A welcoming staff will show you a selection of rooms, including those with bunk beds and those with regular beds. Rooms are small, but clean, and a few actually have lake views. A salon with a fireplace is a great place to relax after a hike. Don't expect pampering—besides camping this is the cheapest place to stay in the park. The restaurant serves filling fish dishes *a lo pobre* (with fried eggs and french fries), as well as lamb; in summer there might be an outdoor *asado*. The inn also has a general store where you can find basic necessities such as batteries and cookies. ⊠ *Lago Toro* ☎ *5661/412–911 for reservations (Puerto Natales)* ⊕ *www.baqueanozamora.com* 🛏 *14 rooms, 4 with bath* ⚘ *Restaurant, bar, grocery; no a/c, no room phones, no room TVs* ▭ *No credit cards* ⍣⍥ *CP.*

$$$$ 🖼 **Hostería Lago Grey.** The panoramic view past the lake to the glacier beyond is worth the journey here, which doesn't change the fact that this older hotel is overpriced and not very attractive. Rooms are comfortable, but the materials are inexpensive, and baths small. There's a

TV with a VCR in the lounge. The view can also be enjoyed through the picture windows at the hotel's restaurant. Don't expect anything better than mediocre food, though; it's a captive audience, to say the least. Simple sandwiches are the best bet. The hotel operates its own sightseeing vessel, the *Grey II*, for close-up tours to Glaciar Grey. ✉ *Lago Grey* ☎ *5661/225–986* ⊕ *www.lagogrey.com* ⮌ *30 rooms* ⟋ *Restaurant, boating, fishing, hiking, horseback riding, bar, lounge, laundry service; no room TVs* ▤ *AE, DC, MC, V* ⦿ *BP.*

$$$$ 🏨 **Hostería Tyndall.** A boat ferries you from the end of the road the few minutes along the Serrano River to this wooden lodge. The simple rooms in the main building are small but cute, with attractive wood paneling. The lodge can be noisy, a problem solved by renting a log cottage (a great value for groups of 4). There's also a much more basic refuge for much less. Owner Christian is a wildlife enthusiast and bird-watcher; ask him for a tour of the grassy plain looking out toward the central cluster of snowy peaks. Or go fishing—they'll cook your catch for no additional charge. ✉ *Ladrilleros 256, Lago Tyndall; reservations: Puerto Natales* ☎ *5661/413–139* ⊕ *www.hosteriatyndall.com* ⮌ *24 rooms, 6 cottages* ⟋ *Restaurant, boating, fishing, hiking, horseback riding, lounge, laundry service; no room phones, no room TVs* ▤ *AE, DC, MC, V* ⦿ *CP.*

$$$$ 🏨 **Hotel Explora.** On the southeast corner of Lago Pehoé, this lodge is

Fodor'sChoice ★ one of the most luxurious—and the most expensive—in Chile. While there may be some debate about the aesthetics of the hotel's low-slung minimalist exterior, the interior is impeccable: it's Scandinavian in style, with local woods used for ceilings, floors, and furniture. No expense has been spared—even the bed linens were imported from Spain. A dozen full-time guides tailor all-inclusive park outings to guests' interests. A four-night minimum stay is required, for which you'll pay a minimum of US$3,120 for two people, including airport transfers, three meals a day, drinks, and excursions. Rooms with better views go up to almost double that. Nonguests may also enjoy a pricey prix-fixe dinner. ✉ *Lago Pehoé* ☎ *2/206–6060 in Santiago* ⊕ *www.explora.com* ⮌ *26 rooms, 4 suites* ⟋ *Restaurant, indoor pool, gym, outdoor hot tub, massage, sauna, boating, hiking, horseback riding, piano bar, library, shop, baby-sitting, laundry service, Internet, business services, meeting rooms, airport shuttle; no room TVs* ▤ *AE, DC, MC, V* ⦿ *All-inclusive.*

$$$–$$$$ 🏨 **Hostería Las Torres.** This is one of the (relatively) less expensive choices in the park, but it's still comfortable and the location couldn't be better. The day hike to the Mirador Torres is a highlight of the park. Rooms are simple, clean, and comfortable. The Hostería also offers hostel-style rooms for a bargain-basement 25 pesos, but they come without sheets and towels. ✉ *Lago Grey* ☎ *5661/710–050* ⊕ *www. lastorres.com* ⟋ *Restaurant, bar, spa, excursions* ▤ *AE, MC, V.*

Punta Arenas, Chile

㉑ *242 km (150 mi) southeast of Puerto Natales, Chile; 264 km (163 mi) southwest of Río Gallegos, Argentina.*

Founded a little more than 150 years ago, Punta Arenas (Point of Sands), easily accessible by international bus from Río Gallegos (with a ½-hour stop for passport control), was Chile's first permanent settlement in Patagonia. This port, no longer an important stop on trade routes, exudes an aura of faded grandeur. Great development in cattle-keeping, mining, and wood production carried out by European immigrants led to an economic and social boom at the end of the 19th century. Plaza Muñoz Gamero, the central square, is surrounded by evidence of that prosperity: buildings whose then-opulent brick exteriors recall a time when this was one of Chile's wealthiest cities.

The newer houses here have colorful tin roofs, best appreciated when seen from a high vantage point such as the Mirador Cerro la Cruz. Although the city as a whole may not be particularly attractive, look for details: the pink-and-white house on a corner, the bay window full of potted plants, parking attendants wearing the regional blue and yellow colors, and school children in identical naval pea coats that remind you that the city's fate is tied to the sea. Punta Arenas is also a major base for penguin-watchers and a key point of embarkation for travel to Antarctica—but don't overlook the city as a worthy destination unto itself.

What to See

Cementerio Municipal. The fascinating history of this region is chiseled into stone at the Municipal Cemetery. Bizarrely ornate mausoleums honoring the original families are crowded together along paths lined by sculpted cypress trees. In a strange effort to recognize Punta Arenas's indigenous past, there's a shrine in the northern part of the cemetery where the last member of the Selk'nam tribe was buried. Local legend says that rubbing the statue's left knee brings good luck. ⊠ *Av. Bulnes 949* ☏ *No phone* ✉ *Free* ⊙ *Daily dawn–dusk.*

Isla Magdalena. Punta Arenas is the launching point for a boat trip to see the more than 120,000 Magellanic penguins at the **Monumento Natural Los Pingüinos** on this island. A single trail, marked off by rope, is accessible to humans. The trip to the island, in the middle of the Estrecho de Magallanes, takes about two hours. To get here, you must take a tour boat: Comapa has service. If you haven't booked in advance, you can stop at any one of the local travel agencies and try to get on a trip at the last minute, which is often possible. You can only go from December through February; the penguin population peaks in January and February. However you get here, make sure to bring along warm clothing, even in summer; the island can be chilly, particularly if a breeze is blowing across the water.

☛ **Mirador Cerro la Cruz.** From a platform beside the white cross that gives this hill lookout its name, you have a panoramic view of the city's colorful corrugated rooftops leading to the Strait of Magellan. Stand with the amorous local couples gazing out toward the flat expanse of Tierra del Fuego in the distance. ⊠ *Fagnano and Señoret* ☏ *No phone* ✉ *Free* ⊙ *Daily.*

Museo Naval y Marítimo. The Naval and Maritime Museum extols Chile's high seas prowess, particularly concerning Antarctica. Its exhibits are worth a visit by anyone with an interest in ships and sailing, merchant and military alike. The second floor is designed in part like the interior

Patagonia's Penguins

AS THE FERRY SLOWLY APPROACHES Isla Magdalena, you begin to make out thousands of black dots along the shore. You catch you breath, knowing that this is your first look at the 120,000 seasonal residents of Monumento Natural Los Pingüinos, one of the continent's largest penguin sanctuaries, a population that is at its height during the breeding season, which peaks in January and February.

But the squat little birds are much closer than you think. You soon realize that on either side of the ferry are large groups of penguins catching their breakfast. They are amazingly agile swimmers, leaping almost entirely out of the water before diving down below the surface once again. A few swim alongside the boat, but most simply ignore the intrusion.

Several different types of penguins, including the Magellanic penguins found on the gentle hills of Isla Magdalena, make their homes along the Chilean coast. Although most favor cooler climates, small colonies can be found in the warmer waters north of Santiago. But for the thrill of seeing tens of thousands in one place, nothing beats Monumento Natural Los Pingüinos, open only from December to February. At this reserve, a two-hour trip by boat from Punta Arenas, the birds can safely reproduce and raise their young.

Found only along the coast of Chile and Argentina, Magellanic penguins are named for Spanish explorer Hernando de Magallanes, who spotted them when he arrived on these shores in 1520. They are often called jackass penguins because of the braying sound they make when

excited. Adults, with the characteristic black-and-white markings, are easy to distinguish from the adolescents, which are a mottled gray. Also gray are the chicks, which hide inside their burrows when their parents are searching for food. A good time to get a look at the fluffy little fellows is when their parents return to feed them regurgitated fish.

A single trail runs across Isla Magdalena, starting at the dock and ending on a hilltop at a red-and-white lighthouse. Ropes on either side keep humans from wandering too far afield. The penguins, however, have the run of the place. They waddle across the path, alone or in small groups, to get to the rocky beach. Familiar with the boatloads of people arriving two or three times a week, the penguins usually don't pay much attention to the camera-clutching crowds. A few of the more curious ones will walk up to people and inspect a shoelace or pants leg. If someone gets too close to a nest, however, they cock their heads sharply from side to side as a warning.

An easier way to see penguins in their natural habitat is to drive to Pingüinera de Seno Otway, on the mainland about an hour northwest of Punta Arenas. It's open longer than Isla Magdalena—from October to March. Founded in 1990, the reserve occupies 2 km (1 mi) of coastline. There are far fewer penguins here–only about 7,500–but the number is still astounding. The sanctuary is run by a nonprofit group, which can provide English-language guides. Travel companies from Punta Arenas arrange frequent tours to the reserve.

of a ship, including a map and radio room. Aging exhibits include an account of the 1908 visit to Punta Arenas by an American naval fleet. Ask for a tour or an explanatory brochure in English. ⊠ *Pedro Montt 981* ☎ *5661/205–558* 🖃 *700 pesos* ☉ *Tues.–Sat. 9:30–5.*

FodorśChoice **Museo Regional de Magallanes.** Housed in what was once the mansion
★ of the powerful Braun-Menéndez family, the Regional Museum of Magallanes is an intriguing glimpse into the daily life of a wealthy provincial family at the beginning of the 20th century. Lavish Carrara marble hearths, English bath fixtures, and cordovan leather walls are among the original accoutrements. The museum also has an excellent group of displays depicting Punta Arenas's past, from the moment of European contact to its decline with the opening of the Panama Canal. The museum is half a block north of the main square. ⊠ *Magallanes 949* ☎ *5661/244–216* 🖃 *1,000 pesos* ☉ *Oct.–Mar., Mon.–Sat. 10:30–5, Sun. 10:30–2; Apr.–Sept., daily 10:30–2.*

Palacio Sara Braun. This resplendent 1895 mansion, a national landmark and architectural showpiece of southern Patagonia, was designed by French architect Numa Meyer at the behest of Sara Braun. Materials and craftsmen were imported from Europe during the home's four years of construction. The city's central plaza and surrounding buildings soon followed, ushering in the region's golden era. Noteworthy are the lavish bedrooms, magnificent parquet floors, marble fireplaces, and hand-painted ceilings. Afterwards, head to the cellar tavern for a drink or snack. ⊠ *Plaza Muñoz Gamero 716* ☎ *5661/241–489* 🖃 *1,000 pesos, free Sun. and May* ☉ *Tues.–Fri. 10:30–1 and 6:30–8:30, Sat. 10:30–1 and 8–10, Sun. 11–2.*

Plaza Muñoz Gamero. A canopy of conifers shades this square, which is surrounded by splendid baroque-style mansions from the 19th century. A bronze sculpture commemorating the voyage of Hernando de Magallanes dominates the center of the plaza. Local lore has it that a kiss on the shiny toe of Calafate, one of the Fuegian people at the base of the monument, will one day bring you back to Punta Arenas. ⊠ *José Nogueira and 21 de Mayo.*

Where to Stay & Eat

$$$ ✕ **La Tasca.** In the Sociedad Española, on Punta Arenas's main square, comes this rustically elegant Spanish restaurant. The windows of the gracious space look out onto the plaza, while inside, wooden ceilings, relaxing music, and good lighting create a rarefied aura. Start things off right with a typical Chilean *vaina* (port, sherry, chocolate, cinnamon, and egg whites), and then try the paella *con centolla* (with king crab). Among fish mains, keep it simple; heavy cream sauces can be a bit much. ⊠ *Sociedad Española, Plaza Muñoz Gamero 771, 2nd floor* ☎ *5661/ 242–807* 🖃 *AE, DC, MC, V.*

★ $$–$$$ ✕ **Los Ganaderos.** Feel at home on the range in this enormous restaurant that resembles a rural *estancia* (ranch). The manager and waiters, dressed in gaucho costumes, serve up spectacular *cordero al ruedo* (spit-roasted lamb) cooked in the *salón de parrilla* (grill room); a serving comes with three different cuts. Wash down your meal with something from the long list of Chilean wines. The restaurant is several blocks north of the center of town, but it's worth the long walk or very short taxi ride. ⊠ *Bulnes 0977 at Manantiales* ☎ *5661/214–597* ⊕ *www. parrillalosganaderos.cl* ⊟ *AE, MC, V* ⊙ *Closed Sun.*

★ **$$–$$$** ✕ **Sotito's Bar.** A longtime favorite among locals, Sotito's is a virtual institution in Punta Arenas. The dining rooms are warm and cozy, with exposed brick and wood-beam ceilings. More importantly, it serves some of the best *centolla* (king crab) in the area. It's prepared five ways, including in an appetizer called *palta con centolla* (avocado with king crab). The restaurant is near the water a few blocks east of Plaza Muñoz Gamero. ⊠ *O'Higgins 1138* ☎ *5661/243–565* ⊕ *www.chileaustral.com/ sotitos* ⊟ *AE, DC, MC, V.*

$–$$ ✕ **El Estribo.** Centered around a large fireplace used to grill the meats, this narrow restaurant is filled with intimate little tables covered with white tablecloths. The name means The Stirrup, and the walls are adorned with tastefully arranged bridles, bits, lariats, and—of course—all manner of stirrups. The success of this longtime favorite, however, is due to its excellent regional food. There's also delicious spit-roasted lamb. For dessert try rhubarb pie—uncommon in these parts. ⊠ *Ignacio Carrera Pinto 762 at Magallanes* ☎ *5661/244–714* ⊕ *www. chileaustral.com/restaurantelestribo* ⊟ *No credit cards.*

★ **$–$$** ✕ **Taberna Club de la Unión.** A jovial, publike atmosphere prevails in this wonderful labyrinthine cellar down the side stairway of Sara Braun's old mansion on the corner of the main plaza. A series of nearly hidden rooms are walled in cozy stone and brick, and black-and-white photos of historical Punta Arenas adorn the walls. You're likely to hear ragtime and jazz on the stereo while enjoying beers served cold in frosted mugs, tapas-style meat and cheese appetizers, sandwiches, tacos, pizza, fajitas, and even carpaccio (it's more bar snacks than dinner). ⊠ *Plaza Muñoz Gamero 716* ☎ *5661/241–317* ⊟ *AE, DC, MC, V* ⊙ *Closed Sun. No lunch.*

¢–$ ✕ **Chocolatta.** Tea and coffee house, chocolate shop, and bakery, this *café* extraordinaire also has just the right atmosphere for plopping down in the middle of a hot—or cold—day of wandering Punta Arenas. The room is cozy, the staff friendly, and you can hang out, perhaps over a creamy hot chocolate, for as long as you'd like. ⊠ *Bories 852* ☎ *5661/268– 606* ⊟ *AE, DC, MC, V.*

★ **$$$$** ▦ **Hotel José Nogueira.** Originally the home of Sara Braun, wealthy widow of wool baron José Nogueira, this opulent 19th-century mansion also contains a museum. The location—steps off the main plaza—couldn't possibly be better. Carefully restored over many years, the building retains the original crystal chandeliers, marble floors, and polished bronze accents that were imported from France. Rooms are rather small—some smaller than others—but compensate with high ceilings, thick carpets, and period furniture. Suites have hot tubs and in-room faxes. ⊠ *Bories 959* ☎ *5661/248–840* ⊕ *www.hotelnogueira.com* ⌂ *25 rooms, 3 suites* ⚹ *Restaurant, in-room data ports, in-room safes, minibars, cable TV, bar, laundry service, business services* ⊟ *AE, DC, MC, V.*

$$$ ▦ **Hotel Finis Terrae.** A Best Western affiliate, this modern, comfortable hotel has a good location and a very professional staff. Small rooms are comfortable, with traditional floral-print bedcovers and overstuffed chairs, and the baths are spacious and modern. There's a pleasant lounge with a fireplace, and there are panoramic views from the sixth-floor restaurant and bar. Stick with the superior rooms or, better yet, the junior suites, and avoid the tiny standard rooms; if you need two beds in a room, look elsewhere. Discounts are considerable March–September. ⊠ *Av. Colón 766* ☎ *5661/228–200* ⊕ *www.hotelfinisterrae.com* ⇨ *60 rooms, 4 suites* △ *Restaurant, in-room safes, minibars, cable TV, 2 bars, Internet, business services, airport shuttle* ▤ *AE, DC, MC, V* ⑩ *BP.*

$$ ⊡ **Hotel Tierra del Fuego.** This very central hotel, a couple of blocks from the main plaza, is aging with grace. The place is clean and simple, with an old-world "pub" that serves sandwiches and drinks into the wee hours. Rooms benefit from nice rugs, and bathrooms feature marble sinks; some rooms have little kitchenettes. The prices are reasonable; it's a good value in this category, especially given the amount of space you get. ⊠ *Colón 716* ☎☎ *5661/226–200* ⊕ *www.puntaarenas.com/tierradelfuego* ⇨ *26 rooms* △ *Cable TV, minibars, pub, Internet, some kitchens* ▤ *AE, DC, MC, V* ⑩ *BP.*

$ ⊡ **Hostal Oro Fueguino.** On a slightly sloping cobblestone street near the observation deck at Cerro la Cruz, this funky little hostelry—tall, narrow, and rambling—welcomes you with lots of color. The first thing you notice is the facade, painted bright orange and blue. Inside are wall hangings and lamp shades made of eye-catching fabrics from as far off as India that create a hominess. The dining and living rooms are cheerful, and there's a wealth of tourist information. The warmth is enhanced by the personal zeal of the proprietor, Dinka Ocampo. ⊠ *Fagnano 365* ☎☎ *5661/249–401* ⊕ *www.orofueguino.cl* ⇨ *12 rooms* △ *Living room, breakfast room, cable TV, laundry service, Internet; no a/c* ▤ *AE, DC, MC, V* ⑩ *BP.*

Pingüinera de Seno Otway

㉒ *65 km (40 mi) northwest of Punta Arenas.*

Magellanic penguins, which live up to 20 years in the wild, return repeatedly to their birthplace to mate with the same partner. For about 2,000 penguin couples—no singles make the trip—home is this desolate and windswept land off the Otway Sound. In late September the penguins begin to arrive from the southern coast of Brazil and the Falkland Islands. They mate and lay their eggs in early October, and brood their eggs in November. Offspring are hatched mid-November through early December. If you're lucky, you may catch sight of one of the downy gray chicks that stick their heads out of the burrows when their parents return to feed them. Otherwise you might see scores of the ungainly adult penguins waddling to the ocean from their nesting burrows. They swim for food every eight hours and dive up to 100 feet deep. The penguins depart from the sound in late March.

The road to the sanctuary begins 30 km (18 mi) north of Punta Arenas, where the main road, Ruta 9, diverges near a checkpoint booth. A gravel road then traverses another fierce and winding 30 km (18 mi), but the rough trip (mud will be a problem if there's been a recent rain) should reward you with the sight of hundreds of sheep, cows, and birds, including, if you're lucky, rheas and flamingos. The sanctuary is a 1-km (½-mi) walk from the parking lot. It gets chilly, so bring a windbreaker.

If you don't have a car, Comapa, like many other tour companies based in Punta Arenas, offers tours to the Pingüinera. The tours generally leave from Punta Arenas and return about 3½ hours later. ⊠ *Off Ruta 9* 🕮 *1,200 pesos* ☉ *Oct.–Mar., daily 8:30–8:30.*

Ushuaia & the Tierra del Fuego

㉓ *230 km (143 mi) south of Río Grande, 596 km (370 mi) south of Río Gallegos, 914 km (567 mi) south of El Calafate, 3,580 km (2,212 mi) south of Buenos Aires.*

At 55 degrees latitude south, Ushuaia (pronounced oo-swy-ah; the Argentines don't pronounce the "h") is closer to the South Pole (2,480 mi) than to Argentina's northern border with Bolivia (2,540 mi). It is the capital and tourism base for Tierra del Fuego, an island at the southernmost tip of Argentina. Although its stark physical beauty is striking, Tierra del Fuego's historical allure is based more on its mythical past than on reality. The island was inhabited for 6,000 years by Yámana, Haush, Selk'nam, and Alakaluf Indians. But in 1902, Argentina, eager to populate Patagonia to bolster its territorial claims, moved to initiate an Ushuaian penal colony, establishing the permanent settlement of its most southern territories and, by implication, everything in between.

When the prison closed in 1947, Ushuaia had a population of about 3,000, made up mainly of former inmates and prison staff. Today, the Indians of Darwin's "missing link" theory are long gone—wiped out by disease and indifference brought by settlers—and the 50,000 residents of Ushuaia are hitching their star to tourism. The city rightly (if perhaps too loudly) promotes itself as the southernmost city in the world (Puerto Williams, a few miles south on the Chilean side of the Beagle Channel, is but a tiny town). Ushuaia feels a bit like a frontier boomtown, with the heart of a rugged, weather-beaten fishing village and the frayed edges of a city that quadrupled in size in the '70s and '80s. Unpaved portions of R3, the last stretch of the Panamerican Highway, which connects Alaska to Tierra del Fuego, are finally, albeit slowly, being paved. The summer months—December through March—draw 120,000 visitors, and the city is trying to extend those visits with events like March's Marathon at the End of the World.

Tierra del Fuego could be called picturesque, at a stretch. A chaotic and contradictory urban landscape includes a handful of luxury hotels amid the concrete of public housing projects. Scores of "sled houses" (wooden shacks) sit precariously on upright piers, ready for speedy displacement to a different site. Many of the newer homes are built in a Swiss-chalet style, reinforcing the idea that this is a town into which tourism has breathed new life. At the same time, the weather-worn pastel colors that dominate the town's landscape remind you that Ushuaia was once just a tiny fishing village, populated by criminals, snuggled at the end of the Earth.

As you stand on the banks of the Canal Beagle (Beagle Channel) near Ushuaia, as Captain Robert Fitz Roy—the captain who was sent by the English government in 1832 to survey Patagonia, including Tierra del Fuego—must have done, the spirit of the farthest corner of the world takes hold. What stands out is the light: at sundown the landscape is cast in a subdued, sensual tone; everything feels closer, softer, more human in dimension despite the vastness of the setting. The snowcapped mountains of Chile reflect the setting sun back onto a stream rolling into the channel, as nearby peaks echo their image—on a windless day—in the still waters.

Above the city, the last mountains of the Andean Cordillera rise, and just south and west of Ushuaia they finally vanish into the often stormy sea. Snow whitens the peaks well into summer. Nature is the principal attraction here, with trekking, fishing, horseback riding, and sailing among the most rewarding activities, especially in the Parque Nacional Tierra del Fuego (Tierra del Fuego National Park).

As Ushuaia converts to a tourism-based economy, the city seeks ways to utilize its 3,000 hotel rooms in the lonely winter season. Though most international tourists stay home to enjoy their own summer, the adventurous have the place to themselves for snowmobiling, dogsledding, and skiing at Cerro Castor.

The **tourist office** (⊠ Av. San Martín 674 ☎ 2901/432–000 or 0800/333–1476 ⊕ www.e-ushuaia.com) is a great resource for information on the town's and Tierra del Fuego's attractions. It's open weekdays 8 AM–10 PM, weekends 9–8. Several people on the cheerful staff speak English.

The **Antigua Casa Beben** (Old Beben House) is one of Ushuaia's original houses, and long served as the city's social center. Built between 1911 and 1913, Fortunato Beben is said to have ordered the house through a Swiss catalog. In the 1980s the Beben family donated the house to the city to avoid demolition. It was moved to its current location along the coast and restored, and is now a cultural center with art exhibits. ⊠ *Maipú and Pluschow* ☎ *No phone* 🎫 *Free* ☉ *Tues.–Fri. 10–8, weekends 4–8.*

Fodor'sChoice
★ Rainy days are a reality in Ushuaia, but two museums give you an avenue for urban exploration and a glimpse into Tierra del Fuego's fascinating past. Part of the original penal colony, the Presidio building was built to hold political prisoners, street orphans, and a variety of other social undesirables from the north. Today it holds the **Museo Marítimo** (Maritime Museum), within Ushuaia's naval base, which has exhibits on the town's extinct indigenous population, Tierra del Fuego's navigational past, Antarctic explorations, and life and times in an Argentine penitentiary. You can enter cell blocks and read the stories of the prisoners who lived in them while gazing upon their eerie effigies. Well-presented tours (in Spanish only) are conducted at 3:30 daily. ⊠ *Gobernador Paz and Yaganes* ☎ *2901/437–481* 🎫 *15 pesos* ☉ *Daily 10–8.*

At the **Museo del Fin del Mundo** (End of the World Museum), you can see a large stuffed condor, as well as other native birds, indigenous artifacts, maritime instruments, and such seafaring-related objects as an impressive mermaid figurehead taken from the bowsprit of a galleon. There are also photographs and histories of El Presidio's original inmates, such as Simon Radowitzky, a Russian immigrant anarchist who received a life sentence for killing an Argentine police colonel. The museum is in the 1905 residence of a Fuegonian governor. The home was later converted into a bank, and some of the exhibits are showcased in the former vault. ⊠ *Maipú 173 and Rivadavía* ☎ *2901/421–863* 🖅 *5 pesos* ⊙ *Oct.–Mar., daily 10–8; Apr.–Sept., daily noon–7.*

Tierra del Fuego was the last land mass in the world to be inhabited— it was not until 9,000 BC that the ancestors of those native coastal inhabitants, the Yamana, arrived. The **Museo Yamana** chronicles their lifestyle and history. The group was decimated in the late 19th century, mostly by European disease. (There is said to be, at this writing, one remaining Yamana descendant, who lives a few miles away in Puerto Williams.) Photographs and good English placards depict the unusual, hunched posture of the Yamana; their unusual, wobbly walk; and their hunting of cormorants, which were killed with a bite through the neck. ⊠ *Rivadavía 56* ☎ *2901/422–874* ⊕ *www.tierradelfuego.org.ar/ mundoyamana* 🖅 *5 pesos* ⊙ *Daily 10–8.*

The **Tren del Fin del Mundo** (End of the World Train) takes you to Estación Ande, inside the Parque Nacional Tierra del Fuego, 12 km (7½ mi) away. The train ride, which lasts about an hour each way, is a simulation of the trip on which El Presidio prisoners were taken into the forest to chop wood; but unlike them, you'll also get a good presentation of Ushuaia's history (in Spanish and English). The train departs daily at 9:30 AM, noon, and 3 PM in summer, and just once a day, at 10 AM, in winter, from a stop near the national park entrance. If you have a rental car, you'll want to do the round trip, but if not, one common way to do the trip is to hire a *remis* (car service) that will drop you at the station for a one-way train ride, pick you up at the other end, and then drive you around the Parque Nacional for two or three hours of sightseeing (which is more scenic than the train ride itself). ⊠ *Ruta 3, Km 3042* ☎ *2901/431–600* ⊕ *www. trendelfindelmundo.com.ar* 🖅 *95 pesos first-class ticket, 50 pesos tourist-class ticket, 20 pesos national park entrance fee (no park fee in winter).*

Tour operators run trips along the **Canal Beagle**, on which you can get a startling close-up view of all kinds of sea mammals and birds on **Isla de los Lobos, Isla de los Pájaros,** and near **Les Eclaireurs Lighthouse.** There are catamarans that make three-hour trips, generally leaving from the Tourist Pier at 3 PM, and motorboats and sailboats that leave twice a day, once at 9:30 AM and once at 3 PM (all of these weather allowing; few trips go in winter). Prices range 60 pesos–140 pesos; some include hikes on the islands. Check with the tourist office for the latest details; you can also book through any of the local travel agencies.

One good excursion in the area is to **Lago Escondido** (Hidden Lake) and **Lago Fagnano** (Fagnano Lake). The Panamerican Highway out of Ushuaia goes through deciduous beechwood forest and past beavers' dams, peat bogs, and glaciers. The lakes have campsites and fishing and are good spots for a picnic or a hike. This can be done on your own or as a seven-hour trip, including lunch, booked through the local travel agencies (75 pesos without lunch, 95 pesos with lunch). One recommended operator, offering a comfortable bus, a bilingual guide, and lunch at Las Cotorras, is **All Patagonia** (⊠ Juana Fadul 26 ☎ 2901/433–622 or 2901/430–725).

A rougher, more unconventional tour of the lake area goes to **Monte Olivia** (Mt. Olivia), the tallest mountain along the Canal Beagle, rising 4,455 feet above sea level. You also pass the **Five Brothers Mountains** and go through the **Garibaldi Pass,** which begins at the Rancho Hambre, climbs into the mountain range, and ends with a spectacular view of Lago Escondido. From here you continue on to Lago Fagnano through the countryside past sawmills and lumberyards. To do this tour in a four-wheel-drive truck with an excellent bilingual guide, contact **Canal Fun** (⊠ Rivadavía 82 ☎ 2901/437–395); you'll drive *through* Lago Fagnano (about 3 feet of water at this point) to a secluded cabin on the shore and have a delicious *asado,* complete with wine and dessert.

Estancia Harberton (Harberton Ranch; ☎ 2901/422–742) consists of 50,000 acres of coastal marshland and wooded hillsides. The property was a late-19th-century gift from the Argentine government to Reverend Thomas Bridges, officially considered the Father of Tierra del Fuego. Today the ranch is managed by Bridges's great-grandson, Thomas Goodall, and his American wife, Natalie, a scientist and author who has cooperated with the National Geographic Society on conservation projects. Most people visit as part of organized tours, but you'll be welcome if you arrive alone. They serve up a solid and tasty tea in their home, the oldest building on the island. For safety reasons, exploration of the ranch can only be done with a guide. Lodging is not available, but you can arrange to dine at the ranch by calling ahead for a reservation. Most tours reach the estancia by boat, offering a rare opportunity to explore the **Isla Martillo** penguin colony, in addition to a sea lion refuge on **Isla de los Lobos** (Island of the Wolves) along the way.

If you've never butted heads with a glacier, and especially if you won't be covering El Calafate on your trip, then you should check out **Glaciar Martial,** in the mountain range just above Ushuaia. Named after Frenchman Luís F. Martial, a 19th-century scientist who wandered this way aboard the warship *Romanche* to observe the passing of planet Venus, the glacier is reached via a panoramic *aerosilla* (ski lift). Take the Camino al Glaciar (Glacier Road) 7 km (4 mi) out of town until it ends (this route is also served by the local tour companies). Even if you don't plan to hike to see the glacier, it's a great pleasure to ride the 15-minute lift, which is open daily 10–5, weather permitting (it's often closed from mid-May until August) and costs 10 pesos round-trip. If you're afraid of heights, you can instead enjoy a small nature trail here, and a teahouse. You can return on the lift, or continue on to the beginning of a 1-km (½-mi) trail that winds its way over lichen and shale straight up the mountain. After a strenuous 90-minute hike, you can cool your heels in one of the many gurgling, icy rivulets that cascade down water-worn shale shoots or enjoy a picnic while you wait for sunset (you can walk all the way down if you want to wait until after the *aerosilla* closes). When the sun drops behind the glacier's jagged crown of peaks, brilliant rays beam over the mountain's crest, spilling a halo of gold-flecked light on the glacier, valley, and channel below. Moments like these are why this land is so magical. Note that temperatures drop dramatically after sunset, so come prepared with warm clothing.

Parque Nacional Tierra del Fuego

★ The pristine park, 21 km (13 mi) west of Ushuaia, offers a chance to wander through peat bogs; stumble upon hidden lakes; trek through native *canelo,* lenga, and wild cherry forests; and experience the wonders of wind-whipped Tierra del Fuego's rich flora and fauna. Everywhere, lichens line the trunks of the ubiquitous *lenga* trees, and "chinese lantern" parasites hang from the branches.

Everywhere, too, you'll see *castoreros* (beaver dams) and lodges. 50 beaver couples were first brought in from Canada in 1948 so that they would breed and create a fur industry. In the years since, however, the beaver population has grown to more than 50,000 and now represents a major threat to the forests, as the dams flood the roots of the trees; you can see their effects on the gnawed-down trees everywhere. Believe it or not, the government now pays hunters a bounty of 30 pesos for each beaver they kill (they need to show a tail and head as proof).

Visits to the park, which is tucked up against the Chilean border, are commonly arranged through tour companies. Trips range from bus tours to horseback riding to more adventurous excursions, such as canoe trips across Lapataia Bay. Another way to get to the park is to take the Tren del Fin del Mundo (⇨ *below*). **Transportes Kaupen** (☎ 2901/434–015), one of several private bus companies, has buses that travel through the park, making several stops within it; you can get off the bus, explore the park, and then wait for the next bus to come by or trek to the next stop (the service only operates in summer). Yet one more option is to drive to the park on R3 (take it until it ends and you see the famous sign indicating the end of the Pan-American Highway, which starts 17,848 km (11,065 mi) away in Alaska, and ends here). If you don't have a car, you can also hire a private *remis* to spend a few hours driving you through the park, including the Pan-American terminus, and perhaps also combining the excursion with the Tren del Fin del Mundo. Trail and camping information is available at the park-entrance ranger station or at the Ushuaia tourist office. At the entrance to the park is a gleaming new restaurant and teahouse set amidst the hills, **Patagonia Mia** (✉ Ruta 3, Entrada Parque Nacional ☎ 2901/1560–2757 ⊕ www.patagoniamia.com); it's a great place to stop for tea or coffee, or a full meal of roast lamb or Fuegian seafood.

A nice excursion in the park is by boat from lovely **Bahía Ensenada** to **Isla Redonda,** a wildlife refuge where you can follow a footpath to the western side and see a wonderful view of the Canal Beagle. This is included on some of the day tours; it's harder to arrange on your own, but you can contact the tourist office to try. While on Isla Redonda you can send a postcard and get your passport stamped at the world's southernmost post office. You can also see the Ensenada bay and island (from afar) from a point on the shore that is reachable by car.

Other highlights of the park include the spectacular mountain-ringed lake, **Lago Roca,** as well as **Laguna Verde,** a lagoon whose green color comes from algae at its bottom. Much of the park is closed from roughly June through September, when the descent to Bahía Ensenada is blocked by up to 6 feet of snow. Even in May and October, chains for your car are a good idea. There are no hotels within the park—the only one burned down in the 1980s, and you can see its carcass driving by—but there are three simple camping areas around Lago Roca. Tours to the park are run by **All Patagonia** (⌧ Juana Fadul 26 ☎ 2901/433–622 or 2901/430–725).

Where to Stay & Eat

Dotting the perimeter of the park are five free campgrounds, none of which has much more than a spot to pitch a tent and a fire pit. Call the **park office** (☎ 2901/421–315) or consult the ranger station at the park entrance for more information. **Camping Lago Roca** (⌧ South on R3 for 20 km [12 mi] ☎ No phone), within the park, charges 8 pesos per person per day and has bathrooms, hot showers, and a small market. Of all the campgrounds, **La Pista del Andino** (⌧ Av. Alem 2873 ☎ 2901/435–890) is the only one within the city limits. Outside of town, **Camping Río Pipo** (☎ 2901/435–796) is the closest to Ushuaia (it's 18 km [11 mi] away).

Choosing a place to stay depends in part on whether you want to spend the night in town or 3 mi uphill. Las Hayas Resort, Hotel Glaciar, Cumbres de Martial, and Los Yámanas have stunning views, but require a taxi ride to reach Ushuaia.

$$–$$$$ ✕ **Chez Manu.** *Herbes de provence* in the greeting room tip French
Fodor'sChoice owner-chef Manu Herbin's hand: he uses local seafood with a French
★ touch to create some of Ushuaia's most memorable meals. Perched a couple of miles above town, across the street from the Hotel Glaciar, this expensive restaurant has grand views of the Beagle Canal. The good wine list includes Patagonian selections. Don't miss the *trucha fueguina* (local trout) in white wine sauce, served with buttery rice cooked in fish stock or the *centolla* (king crab) au gratin. ⌧ *Camino Luís Martial 2135* ☎ *2901/432–253* ⊟ *AE, MC, V* ☺ *Closed Mon.*

$–$$$$ ✕ **Tia Elvira.** On the street that runs right along the Beagle Channel, this is an excellent place to sample the local catch. Garlicky shellfish appetizers and *centolla* (king crab) are delicious, and even more memorable is the dreamy, tender *merluza negra* (black sea bass). The room is decked out with nautical knick-knacks that are perhaps a bit tacky for such a pricey place. The service is friendly and familial. ⌧ *Maipú 349* ☎ *2901/424–725* ⊟ *AE, DC, MC, V* ☺ *Closed July.*

★ **$$–$$$** ✕ **Volver.** A giant plastic king crab sign beckons you into this red tin restaurant, which provides some major relief from Avenida San Martin's row of all-you-can-eat parrillas. The name means "return" and it's the kind of place that calls for repeat visits. Newspapers from the 1930s line the walls in this century-old home; informal table settings have placemats depicting old London landmarks; and fishing nets hang from the ceiling, along with hams, a disco ball, tricycles, and antique lamps. The culinary highlight is, of course, king crab (*centolla*), which comes served with a choice of five different sauces. ⊠ *Maipú 37* ☎ *2901/423–977* ⊟ *AE, DC, MC, V* ⊗ *No lunch May–Aug.*

$–$$$ ✕ **La Cabaña Casa de Té.** This cottage, in a verdant wood of lenga trees beside the surge of a powerful river, overlooks the Beagle Channel and provides a warm, cozy spot for tea or snacks before or after a hike to the Martial glacier—it's at the end of the Martial road that leads up from Ushuaia. Fondues are a specialty at lunchtime; at 8 PM the menu shifts to pricier dinner fare with dishes like salmon in wine sauce. ⊠ *Camino Luís Martial 3560* ☎ *2901/434–699* ⊟ *AE, DC, MC, V* ⊗ *Closed Mon.*

$–$$$ ✕ **La Estancia.** This restaurant in the center of town, set in a pleasant wooden A-frame room, is one of the classiest of the good-value "tenedor libre" (all-you-can-eat) parrillas on the main strip—nobody here orders à la carte. Skip the Italian buffet and fill up instead on the mouthwatering spit-roasted Patagonian lamb, grilled meats, and delicious *morcilla*. It's all you can eat for 21 pesos. Sit by the glass wall to see the *parrillero* artfully coordinate the flames and spits. ⊠ *Av. San Martín 257* ☎ *2901/1556–8587* ⊟ *AE, DC, MC, V.*

$$$$ ▦ **Cumbres de Martial.** This charming wood complex, painted fire-engine red, is high above Ushuaia at the foot of the ski lift that leads to the Martial glacier. Depending on your take, the *hostería* can seem desolate and removed from town, or a peaceful sanctuary close to glacier hiking. Each spacious room has an extremely comfortable bed and a small wooden deck with terrific views down to the Beagle Channel. The *cabañas* are beautiful self-contained log cabins. There are also a teahouse and a small nature trail beside the Martial River. There is, however, no complimentary shuttle service to town, so you'll need to take a (cheap) taxi to access Ushuaia. ⊠ *Camino Luís Martial 3560, 9410* ☎☎ *2901/ 424–799* ⊕ *www.cumbresdelmartial.com.ar* ⇨ *6 rooms, 4 cabins* ⚑ *Restaurant, tea shop, in-room safes, bar, lounge, laundry service, airport shuttle* ⊟ *AE, DC, MC, V* ⊗ *Closed Apr.–May* ⧖ *BP.*

$$$$ ▦ **Hotel del Glaciar.** Just above the Las Hayas hotel in the Martial Mountains, this hotel has the best views of Ushuaia and the Beagle Channel. The rooms are bright, clean, and very comfortable. After a long day in the woods, you can curl up on the large sofa next to the fire pit or make your way over to the cozy wood-paneled bar for a drink. Hourly shuttle buses take you to the town center. ⊠ *2355 Camino Glaciar Martial, Km 3.5, 9410* ☎ *2901/430–640* ⇨ *73 rooms, 4 suites* ⚑ *Restaurant, café, minibars, cable TV, bar, laundry service, Internet, convention center, airport shuttle, travel services* ⊟ *AE, DC, MC* ⧖ *CP.*

$$$$ ▦ **Hotel y Resort Las Hayas.** Las Hayas is in the wooded foothills of the
Fodor'sChoice Andes, overlooking the town and channel below. Ask for a *canal* view.
★ Rooms are all decorated differently, but all feature Portuguese linen, solid oak furnishings, and fabric-padded walls. A suspended glass bridge connects the hotel to a spectacular health spa, which includes a heated pool and even a squash court. The wonderful restaurant prepares an excellent version of *mollejas de cordero* (lamb sweetbreads) with scallops. Frequent shuttle buses take you into town. ⊠ *1650 Camino Luís*

Martial, Km 3, 9410 ☏ *2901/430710, 11/4393–4750 in Buenos Aires* ⊕ *www.lashayashotel.com* ⤳ *85 rooms, 7 suites* ⌂ *Restaurant, coffee shop, in-room safes, golf privileges, indoor pool, health club, hot tub, massage, sauna, spa treatments, squash, bar, laundry service, convention center, meeting rooms, airport shuttle, travel services* ☰ *AE, DC, MC, V* ⦿ *CP.*

$$$ ⊡ **Hotel Los Yámanas.** This cozy new hotel 4 km (2½ mi) from the center of town is named after the local tribe and blends a rustic mountain aesthetic with impeccable elegance. Some rooms have stunning views over the Beagle Channel, and all have wrought-iron bed frames, and are furnished with simple good taste. The expansive lobby and the second-floor restaurant are just as welcoming. ⊠ *Los Ñires 1850, Km 3, 9410* ☏ *2901/445–960* ⊕ *hotelyamanas.com.ar* ⤳ *18 rooms* ⌂ *Restaurant, bar, in-room safes, minibars, gym, Internet, laundry service, gift shop, game room* ☰ *AE, DC, MC, V* ⦿ *CP.*

★ **$$** ⊡ **Hostería Patagonia Jarké.** Jarké means "spark" in a local native language, and indeed this B&B is a vibrant addition to Ushuaia proper. This two-story lodge, on a dead-end street in the heart of town, is an amalgam of alpine and Victorian styles on the outside; inside, a spacious contemporary design incorporates a glass-roofed lobby, lounge, and breakfast room. Rooms have polished wood floors, peaked-roof ceilings, artisanal soaps, woven floor mats, and lovely views. ⊠ *Sarmiento 310, 9410* ☏ *2901/437–245* ⊕ *www.hosteriapatagoniaj.com* ⤳ *10 rooms* ⌂ *Café, in-room safes, cable TV, bar, laundry service, Internet, library* ☰ *AE, DC, MC, V* ⊘ *Closed Apr.–May* ⦿ *BP.*

$$ ⊡ **Hotel Cabo de Hornos.** Cabo de Hornos is a cut above other downtown hotels in the same price category. The rooms are clean and simple, and all have cable TV and telephones. The lobby-lounge is tacky and tasteful at the same time, decorated with currency and postcards from all over the world. Its old ski-lodge feel makes it a nice place to relax and watch *fútbol* with a cup of coffee or a beer. ⊠ *San Martín and Rosas, 9410* ☏ *2901/430–677* ⤳ *30 rooms* ⌂ *Restaurant, bar* ☰ *AE, MC, V* ⦿ *CP.*

Nightlife & the Arts

Ushuaia has a lively nightlife scene in summer, with its casino, discos, and cozy cafés all within close proximity of each other. The biggest and most popular restaurant-pub is **El Náutico** (⊠ Maipú 1210 ☏ 2901/430–415), which plays all kinds of music, from Latin to techno. It's pumping Thursday through Saturday nights from midnight to 6 AM.

A popular nightspot is **Lenon Pub** (⊠ Maipú 263 ☏ 2901/435–255), which serves drinks and food to those 21 and older. It's open 11 AM–6 AM. For more traditional Argentine entertainment, **Hotel del Glaciar** (⊠ 2355 Camino Glaciar Martial, Km 3.5 ☏ 2901/430–640) has tango shows Saturday at 11 PM. **Bar Ideal** (⊠ San Martín 393) is a cozy and historic bar and café. **Tante Sara** (⊠ San Martín 701 ☏ 2901/433–710 ⊕ cafebartantesara.com.ar) is a popular café-bar in the very heart of town, where locals kick back with a book or a beer (they pour Beagle, the local artisanal brew).

Sports & the Outdoors

FISHING The rivers of Tierra del Fuego are home to trophy-size freshwater trout—including browns, rainbows, and brooks. Both fly- and spin-casting are available. The fishing season runs November–March; fees range from 10 pesos a day to 40 pesos for a month. Fishing expeditions are organized by the following companies. Founded in 1959, the **Asociación de Caza y Pesca** (⊠ Av. Maipú 822 ☎ 2901/423–168) is the principal hunting and fishing organization in the city. **Rumbo Sur** (⊠ Av. San Martín 350 ☎ 2901/421–139 ⊕ www.rumbosur.com.ar) is the city's oldest travel agency and can assist in setting up fishing trips. **Wind Fly** (⊠ Av. 25 de Mayo 143 ☎ 2901/431–713 or 2901/1544–9116 ⊕ www.windflyushuaia.com.ar) is dedicated exclusively to fishing, and offers classes, arranges trips, and rents equipment.

FLIGHT-SEEING The gorgeous scenery and island topography are readily appreciated on a Cessna tour of the area. A half-hour flight (US$70 per passenger, US$100 for one passenger alone) with a local pilot takes you over Ushuaia and the Beagle Channel with views of area glaciers and snow-capped islands south to Cape Horn. A 60-minute flight crosses the Andes to the Escondida and Fagnano lakes. **Aero Club Ushuaia** (⊠ Antiguo Aerpuerto ☎ 2901/421–717 ⊕ www.aeroclubushuaia.org.ar) offers half-hour and hour-long trips.

MOUNTAIN BIKING A mountain bike is an excellent mode of transport in Ushuaia, giving you the freedom to roam without the rental car price tag. Good mountain bikes normally cost about 5 pesos an hour or 15 pesos–20 pesos for a full day. Bikes can be rented at the base of the glacier, at the **Refugio de Montaña** (⊠ Base Glaciar Martial ☎ 2901/1556–8587), or at **D. T. T. Cycles** (⊠ Av. San Martín 903 ☎ 2901/434–939). Guided bicycle tours (including rides through the national park), for about 50 pesos a day, are organized by **All Patagonia** (⊠ Fadul 26 ☎ 2901/430–725). **Rumbo Sur** (⊠ San Martín 350 ☎ 2901/421–139 ⊕ www.rumbosur.com.ar) is the city's biggest travel agency and can arrange trips. **Tolkeyén Patagonia** (⊠ San Martín 1267 ☎ 2901/437–073) rents bikes and arranges trips.

SKIING Ushuaia is the cross-country skiing (*esqui de fondo* in Spanish) center of South America, thanks to enthusiastic **Club Andino** (☎ 2901/422–335) members who took to the sport in the 1980s and made the forested hills of a high valley about 20 minutes from town a favorite destination for skiers. **Hostería Tierra Mayor** (☎ 2901/423–240), **Hostería Los Cotorras** (☎ 2901/499–300), and **Haruwen** (☎ 2901/424–058) are three places where you can ride in dog-pulled sleds, rent skis, go cross-country skiing, get lessons, and eat; contact the Ushuaia tourist office for more information. **Glaciar Martial Ski Lodge** (☎ 2901/243–3712), open year-round, Tuesday–Sunday 10–7, functions as a cross-country ski center from June through October. Skis can also be rented in town, as can snowmobiles.

For downhill (or *alpino*) skiers, Club Andino has bulldozed a couple of short, flat runs directly above Ushuaia. The area's newest downhill ski area, **Cerro Castor** (☎ 2901/422–244 ⊕ www.cerrocastor.com), is 26 km (17 mi) northeast of Ushuaia on R3, and has 19 trails and four high-speed ski lifts. More than half the trails are at the beginner level, six are intermediate, and three are expert trails, but none of this terrain is very challenging for an experienced skier. You can rent skis and snowboards and take ski lessons. **Transportes Kaupen** (☎ 2901/434–015) and other local bus companies run service back and forth from town.

Puerto Williams, Chile

㉔ *75-minute flight from Punta Arenas. 42 km (25 mi) west of Ushuaia.*

On a Chilean island southeast of Argentina's Ushuaia, the town of Puerto Williams is the southernmost permanent settlement in the world. Originally called Puerto Luisa, it was renamed in 1956 in honor of the military officer who took possession of the Estrecho de Magallanes for the newly founded nation of Chile in 1843. Most of the 2,500 residents are troops at the naval base, but there are several hundred civilians in the adjacent village. A tiny community of indigenous peoples makes its home in the nearby Ukika.

For a quick history lesson on how Puerto Williams evolved and some insight into the indigenous peoples, visit the **Museo Martin Gusinde,** named for the renowned anthropologist who traveled and studied in the region between 1918 and 1924. ⊠ *Aragay 1* ☎ *No phone* ⊠ *500 pesos* ☉ *Weekdays 10–1 and 3–6, weekends 3–6.*

Weather permitting, **Aerovías DAP** (⊠ O'Higgins 891, Punta Arenas ☎ 5661/223–340 ⊕ www.aeroviasdap.cl) offers charter flights over Cabo de Hornos, the southernmost tip of South America. Although the water looks placid from the air, strong westerly winds make navigating around Cape Horn treacherous. Hundreds of ships met their doom here trying to sail to the Pacific.

Where to Stay

When you arrive in Puerto Williams, your airline or ferry company will recommend a few of the hospedajes available, then take you around to see them. All are rustic inns that also serve meals.

¢ ☒**Hostal Pusaki.** Run with Chilean hospitality, this humble hospedaje has comfortable rooms with up to four beds (including bunks). The dining room serves fine local fare. Dinner is especially pleasant if the fresh *ensalada de centolla* (king crab salad) is on the changing menu. ⊠ *Piloto Pardo 242* ☎ *5661/621–020* ⇝ *3 rooms with shared bath* ⚿ *Restaurant; no a/c, no room phones, no room TVs* ☰ *No credit cards* ⦿ CP.

Nightlife

Permanently moored at the dock is a small Swiss freighter listing slightly to port called the *Micalvi.* It's home to the rustic **Club de Yates** (⊠ Dockside ☎ 5661/621–041). Sailors stop off here for good company, strong spirits, and hearty food as they travel between the Atlantic and Pacific around Cape Horn. Stop by and mingle with whomever is there at the time. You might meet Aussies, Brits, Finns, Russians, Swedes, or even the occasional American.

A world away from the cosmopolitan clubs of Santiago, **Pub El Pingüino** (⊠ Centro Commercial ☎ No phone) is a watering hole patronized by the town's civilians. Hours are irregular, but closer to the weekend it opens earlier and closes later.

Hiking

A hike to the top of nearby **Cerro Bandera** is well worth the effort if you have the stamina. The trail is well marked, but very steep. The view from the top toward the south to the Cordón Dientes del Perro (Dog's Teeth Range) is impressive, but looking northward over the Beagle Channel to Argentina—with Puerto Williams nestled below and Ushuaia just visible to the west—is truly breathtaking.

SOUTHERN PATAGONIA ESSENTIALS

Transportation

BY AIR

The best way to get to southern Patagonia is to fly from Buenos Aires. The country's major airline, Aerolíneas Argentinas, known locally simply as "Aerolíneas," flies (along with its subsidiary Austral) from Buenos Aires daily to Ushuaia, El Calafate, and Río Gallegos. Aerolíneas Argentina's "Visit Argentina" pass allows you to fly to multiple destinations at a discount; it must be purchased outside of Argentina. LADE (Líneas Aéreas del Estado), in small Fokker F-27 and F-28 and Twin Otter planes on a sparse schedule, connects Ushuaia and El Calafate with Puerto Madryn, Comodoro Rivadavia, and Río Gallegos, and even serves tiny Puerto Deseado. Chile-based Lan and its subsidiary Ladeco operate a number of flights daily between Punta Arenas, Chile, and Santiago, Chile, and LAN Argentina now offers service between Buenos Aires and Río Gallegos. Another Chilean airline, Aerovías DAP, has regularly scheduled flights between Punta Arenas, Porvenir, Puerto Williams, and Ushuaia.

Aerolíneas Argentinas ☎ 0810/2228-6527, 11/4320-2000 in Buenos Aires, 2966/422-020 in Río Gallegos, 2902/492-499 in El Calafate, 2901/436-586 in Ushuaia ⊕ www.aerolineas.com.ar. **Aerovías DAP** ☎ 5661/223-340 ⊕ www.aeroviasdap.cl. **LADE** ☎ 0810/810-LADE (5233) toll free, 2966/422-316 in Río Gallegos, 2902/491-262 in El Calafate, 2901/421-123 in Ushuaia ⊕ www.lade.com.ar. **Lan** ☎ 600/526-2000 in Chile, 11/4378-2200 in Argentina, 0800/222-2424 toll-free ⊕ www.lan.com.

BY BUS

More than anywhere else in Patagonia, buses are a major form of transportation in the South. They shuttle passengers across border crossings to Chile as well as between the major cities of Tierra del Fuego and southern Argentina. As elsewhere, Andesmar Autotransportes and La Puntual have a major presence.

The following bus companies connect Buenos Aires to Río Gallegos and El Calafate: Don Otto, Interlagos, El Pingüino, and TAC. In summer, Bus Sur, Cootra, and Turismo Zaahj make the 4½-hour run from Puerto Natales, Chile, to El Calafate. Cal Tur and Chaltén Travel run bus service between El Calafate and El Chaltén. El Pingüino also has service to Trelew and Puerto Madryn and to Bariloche with a transfer in Comodoro Rivadavia.

Tecni-Austral provides service between Ushuaia, Rio Grande, Rio Gallegos, and Punta Arenas, Chile. Buses Fernández is the main carrier between Punta Arenas and Puerto Natales. You'll probably want to fly to Ushuaia to make the most of your time in the Tierra del Fuego (besides being much faster, it's also cheaper to fly), but direct bus service between Buenos Aires and Ushuaia exists. Trans los Carlos and Turismo Ghisoni make the 12-hour run between Punta Arenas, Chile, and Ushuaia.

🚌 Bus Companies **Bus Sur** ✉ At the bus station, Av. Julio A. Roca 1004, Río Gallegos ☎ 2966/442–687, 2902/491–631 in El Calafate. **Buses Fernández** ✉ Armando Sanhueza 745, Punta Arenas, Chile ☎ 5661/221–812 ✉ Eleuterio Ramirez 399, Puerto Natales, Chile ☎ 5661/411–111 ⊕ www.busesfernandez.com. **Cal Tur** ✉ Terminal Ómnibus, El Calafate ☎ 2962/491–842. **Chaltén Travel** ✉ Guemes and Lago del Desierto, El Chaltén ☎ 2962/491–833 ⊕ www.chaltentravel.com. **Cootra** ✉ Terminal de Río Turbio ☎ 2902/421–448. **Don Otto** ✉ At the bus terminal in Bariloche, B. Mitre 321 ☎ 2944/429–012. **El Pingüino** ☎ 11/4315–4438 in Buenos Aires, 2966/442–169 in Río Gallegos. **Interlagos** ✉ At the bus terminals: ☎ 2902/491–179 in El Calafate, 2966/442–080 in Río Gallegos. **Tecni-Austral** ✉ L. Navarro 975, Punta Arenas, Chile ☎ 5661/222–078 or 5661/223–205 ✉ Terminal de Omnibus, Rio Gallegos ☎ 2966/442–477 ✉ Roca 157, Ushuaia ☎ 2901/431–408. **Trans los Carlos** ✉ Av. San Martín 880, Ushuaia ☎ 2901/22337. **Transportes Kaupen** ☎ 2901/434–015, **Turismo Ghisoni** ✉ Lautaro Navarro 975, Punta Arenas, Chile ☎ 5661/223–205. **Turismo Zaahj** ☎ 5661/412–260 in El Calafate. **El Valle** ✉ 12 de Octubre 1884, Bariloche ☎ 2944/431–444, 11/4313–3749 in Buenos Aires.

BY CAR

Car rental is not as much of a factor in southern Patagonia as in the rest of the region. Most travelers get between cities on planes or buses, and while in natural reserves such as Torres del Paine, Parque Nacional Los Glaciares, or Tierra del Fuego, get around with tour operators or by hiking. Still, rental options exist, and you can often take cars across the Chilean border (check with your rental agency). A car is perhaps most useful in Tierra del Fuego, for seeing the Parque Nacional. Hiring a *remis* (car with driver) is another, costlier option common for seeing that park.

🚗 Local Agencies **Cristina** ✉ Av. del Libertador 1711, El Calafate ☎ 2902/491–674 ✉ Libertad 123, Río Gallegos ☎ 2960/425–709. **Freelander** ✉ Av. del Libertador 1029, El Calafate ☎ 2902/491–446.

🚗 Remis **El Calafate** ✉ Av. Julio A. Roca ☎ 2902/492–005. **Centenario** ✉ Maipú 285, Río Gallegos ☎ 2966/422–320.

Contacts & Resources

BANKS & EXCHANGE SERVICES

BANKS 🏦 In El Calafate **Provincia de Santa Cruz** ✉ Av. Libertador 1285 ☎ 2902/492–320.

🏦 In Río Gallegos **Bancos de Galicia** ✉ Av. Roca 802. **Banco de Santa Cruz** ✉ Roca 802. **Hipotecario Nacional** ✉ Zapiola 49. **Nazionale de Lavoro** ✉ Fagnano off Av. Roca.

EMERGENCIES

🚨 **Coast Guard** ☎ 106. **Fire** ☎ 100. **Forest Fire** ☎ 103. **Hospital** ☎ 107. **Police** ☎ 101.

HOSPITALS & 🏥 In El Calafate **Farmacia El Calafate** ✉ Av. Libertador 1190 ☎ 9405/491–407. **Hospital Distrital** ✉ Av. Roca 1487 ☎ 2902/491–001.

PHARMACIES 🏥 In Río Gallegos **Hospital Regional** ✉ José Ingeniero 98 ☎ 2966/420–025 ☎ 2966/420–641.

MAIL & SHIPPING

Post offices in bigger towns are usually open 10 AM to 6 PM; smaller towns generally make their own rules. Stamps can also be purchased at kiosks.

🚩 Post Office (Correo) Information **El Calafate** ✉ Av. Libertador 1133. **Ushuaia** ✉ Belgrano 96.

TOUR OPTIONS

In El Calafate, most hotels arrange excursions to Moreno and Upsala glaciers. Hielo y Aventura specializes in glacier tours, with their show-stopping "minitrekking" (walking on the glacier with crampons) as well as the "*safari náutico*" (a boat ride next to the glacier). Upsala Explorer combines a day at an estancia and a boat trip to Upsala Glacier. Horseback riding can be arranged by Gustavo Holzman or through the tourist office. Alberto del Castillo, owner of El Calafate's E.V.T. Fitzroy Expeditions, has English-speaking guides and organizes both glacier and mountain treks.

Interlagos Turismo arranges tours between Río Gallegos and El Calafate and to the glaciers. Tur Aiké Turismo organizes tours in and around Río Gallegos. In El Chaltén, Cal Tur, Chaltén Travel, and Hielo y Aventura, and Upsala Explorer run local tours.

In Ushuaia and the Tierra del Fuego, All Patagonia, Canal Fun and Nature, Tiempo Libre, and Tolkar all offer a wide variety of adventurous treks through the Parque Nacional Tierra del Fuego and around the Canal Beagle. Tolkeyén Patagonia and Rumbo Sur organize tours of the Canal Beagle and bus trips that give an overview of the national park. All Patagonia organizes bus trips to Lago Escondido and other spots in the area. Sailing out to sea usually means contact with wide-eyed seals, sea elephants, and sea lions sunning on the rocks. All Patagonia and Rumbo Sur do sea excursions as well as trips to Antarctica. To charter a sailboat, head to Club Náutico, where locals gather to talk about fishing.

🚩**All Patagonia** ✉Juana Fadul 26, Ushuaia ☎2901/433–622 or 2901/1556–5758 ⊕www.allpatagonia.net. **Cal Tur** ✉ Libertador 1080, El Calafate ☎2902/491–368. **Canal Fun and Nature** ✉ Rivadavía 82, Ushuaia ☎2901/437–395 ⊕www.canalfun.com. **Chaltén Travel** ✉Guemes and Lago del Desierto, El Chaltén ☎ 2962/491–833 ⊕www.chaltentravel.com. **Club Náutico** ✉Maipú 1210, Ushuaia ☎No phone. **Fitzroy Expeditions** ✉Av. San Martín, El Chaltén ☎2962/493–017. **Gador Viajes** ✉Gob. Moyano 1082, El Calafate ☎2962/491–143. **Hielo y Aventura** ✉Av. Libertador 935, El Calafate ☎2902/492–205 ⊕www.hieloyaventura.com. **Interlagos Turismo** ✉Fagnano 35, Río Gallegos ☎2966/422–614 ✉Av. Libertador 1175, El Calafate ☎2902/491–175. **René Fernández Campbell** ✉Avenida del Libertador 867, El Calafate ☎2902/491–155. **Rumbo Sur** ✉Av. San Martín 350, Ushuaia ☎2901/421–139 ⊕www.rumbosur.com.ar. **Tiempo Libre** ✉25 de Mayo 260, Ushuaia ☎2901/431–374. **Tolkar** ✉Roca 157, Ushuaia ☎2901/431–408 or 2901/437–421. **Tolkeyén Patagonia** ✉ Maipú 237, Ushuaia ☎2901/437–073 or 2901/424–504. **Tur Aiké Turismo** ✉Zapiola 63, Río Gallegos ☎2902/422–436. **Upsala Explorer** ✉9 de Julio 69, El Calafate ☎2902/491–034 ⊕www.upsalaexplorer.com.ar.

VISITOR INFO

🚩Local Tourist Offices **El Calafate** ✉Terminal de Omnibus, Julio A. Roca 1004 ☎☎2902/491–090 ⊕www.elcalafate.gov.ar. **Río Gallegos** ✉Av. Roca 863 ☎2966/438–725 ⊕www.scru.gov.ar. **Sarmiento** ✉Av. Reg. de Infanteria 25 ☎0297/489–8220. **Tierra del Fuego Tourism Institute** ✉Av. Maipú 505, Ushuaia ☎2901/421–423. **Ushuaia** ✉Av. San Martín 674 ☎2901/432–000 or 0800/333–1476 ⊕www.e-ushuaia.com.

Adventure & Learning Vacations

WORD OF MOUTH

"In Iguazú we took a 20-minute ride in a 4x4 on a jungle trail to the river's edge, where we entered a speedboat. It flew downriver to the first set of falls, allowing us to take photos before moving forward into the spray, which drenched us head to toe."

—Nicci

"Trekking on the Perito Moreno glacier was too cool! We took a boat to the front of the glacier and then to its side, where we disembarked . . . off we went, through the woods to the glacier's edge. They strapped crampons on our feet, and we went onto the ice, walking up and down hills for two hours."

—Peep

By Joyce
Dalton

As in the past, today's travelers yearn to see the world's great cities, historic sites, and natural wonders. The difference is that far fewer are content to experience all this from the air-conditioned comfort of a huge coach. Even tour operators known not to skip on creature comfort have added hiking, canoeing, biking, or horseback riding to many itineraries and added "best available" lodgings to satisfy the increased demand for visits to more traditional locales. Operators specializing in sports-focused trips, adventurous journeys, or special-interest travel (traditional medicines or bird-watching safaris, for example) have witnessed such an upsurge in interest that they must continually seek out new destinations.

Choosing a tour package carefully is always important, but it becomes critical when the focus is adventure or sports. You can rough it or opt for comfortable, sometimes even luxurious, accommodations. You can select easy hiking and canoeing adventures or trekking, rafting, and climbing expeditions that require high degrees of physical endurance and technical skill. Study multiple itineraries to find the trip that's right for you. This chapter describes selected trips offered by some of the best adventure tour operators in today's travel world. Wisely chosen, special-interest vacations lead to distinctive, memorable experiences—just pack flexibility and curiosity along with the bug spray.

For additional information about a specific destination, contact the Argentina tourist board or the **South American Explorers Club** (☎ 607/277–0488 or 800/274–0568 ⊕ www.saexplorers.org). This company is a good source for current information regarding travel throughout the continent and it also has an office in Buenos Aires.

Choosing a Trip

With hundreds of choices for special-interest trips to Argentina and its neighbors, there are several factors to keep in mind when deciding which company and package will be right for you.

- **How strenuous a trip do you want?** Adventure vacations commonly are split into "soft" and "hard" adventures. Hard adventures, such as strenuous treks (often at high altitudes), Class IV or V rafting, or ascents of some of the world's most challenging mountains, generally require excellent physical conditioning and previous experience. Most hiking, biking, canoeing/kayaking, and similar soft adventures can be enjoyed by persons of all ages who are in good health and are accustomed to a reasonable amount of exercise. A little honesty goes a long way—recognize your level of fitness and discuss it with the operator before signing on.

- **How far off the beaten path do you want to go?** Although many trips described in this chapter might seem to be headed into uncharted territory, tour operators carefully check each detail before an itinerary goes into a brochure. Although you won't be vying with busloads of tourists for photo ops, you'll probably run into small groups of like-minded travelers. Journeys into truly remote regions typically involve camping or the simplest of accommodations, but they reward with more abundant wildlife and locals who are less accustomed to the clicking of cameras. Ask yourself if it's the *reality* or the *image* of roughing it that appeals to you.

- **Is sensitivity to the environment important to you?** If so, then determine if it's equally important to the tour operator. Does the company protect the fragile environments you'll be visiting? Are some of the profits designated for conservation efforts or put back into the communities visited? Does the company encourage indigenous people to dress up (or dress down) so that your group can get great photos, or does it respect their cultures as they are? Many of the companies included in this chapter are involved with environmental organizations and projects with indigenous communities visited on their trips. On ecotourism programs, check out the naturalist's credentials. A string of degrees can be less important than familiarity with the area.

- **What sort of group is best for you?** Do you enjoy a mix of companions or would you prefer similar demographics—for example, age-specific, singles, same sex? Inquire about the group size; many companies have a maximum of 10 to 16 members, but 30 or more isn't unknown. With large groups, expect little flexibility in deviating from the published itinerary and more time spent (or wasted) at rest stops, meals, and various arrivals and departures.

   If groups aren't your thing, most companies will customize a trip for you. In fact, this has become a major part of many tour operators' business. The itinerary can be as loose or as complete as you choose. Such travel offers all the conveniences of a package tour, but the "group" is composed of only you or you and those you've chosen as travel companions. Responding to a renewed interest in multigenerational travel, many tour operators offer designated family departures, with itineraries carefully crafted to appeal both to children and adults.

- **The client consideration factor—strong or absent?** Gorgeous photos and well-written tour descriptions go a long way in selling a company's trips. But the "client consideration factor" is important, too. Does the operator provide useful information about health (suggested or required inoculations, tips for dealing with high altitudes)? A list of frequently asked questions and their answers? Tips for photography under destination-specific conditions? Recommended readings? Equipment needed for sports trips? Packing tips when baggage is restricted? Climate info? Visa requirements? A list of client referrals? The option of using your credit card?

- **What is the refund policy if you must cancel?** Most often the options are no refund at all for cancellations 60 days or less before departure date and only a partial refund for cancellations earlier than 60 days. At least one company, however, offers 100% refund *after* the trip if expectations haven't been met and the company cannot resolve the complaint.

   If you're traveling alone and want to avoid the sometimes exorbitant single supplement, will the company match you up with another traveler? Does the company have a local office in the country you'll be visiting? Although it's not vital in most situations, it can lead to a speedier resolution of any problems that arise.

- **Are there hidden costs?** Know what is and isn't included in basic trip costs when comparing companies. Many factors affect the price, and the trip that looks cheapest in the brochure could well turn out to be the most expensive. And don't assume that roughing it will save you money: prices rise when limited access and a lack of essential supplies on-site require costly special arrangements.

International airfare is usually extra. Sometimes, flights within the country you are visiting are additional. Is trip insurance included or required? How much does it cost, and what situations are covered? Are airport transfers included? Visa fees? Departure taxes? Gratuities? Equipment? Meals? Bottled water? All excursions? Although some travelers prefer the option of an excursion or free time, many, especially those visiting a destination for the first time, want to see as much as possible. Paying extra for a number of excursions can significantly up the total trip cost.

Tour Operators

Below you'll find contact information for all tour operators mentioned in this chapter. For international tour operators, we list both the operator and their North American representative, so you can contact whichever company is easier for you. For example, Exodus is represented in North America by Adventure Center. While the list below hardly exhausts the number of reputable companies, these were chosen because they're established firms that offer a good selection of itineraries. Such operators are usually the first to introduce great new destinations, forging ahead before luxury hotels and air-conditioned coaches tempt less hardy visitors.

Abercrombie & Kent ✉ *1520 Kensington Rd., Oak Brook, IL 60523* ☎ *630/954–2944 or 800/323–7308* ⊕ *www.abercrombiekent.com.*
Adventure Center ✉ *1311 63rd St., Suite 200, Emeryville, CA 94608* ☎ *510/654–1879 or 800/227–8747* ⊕ *www.adventurecenter.com.*
Adventure Life ✉ *1655 S. 3rd St. W, Suite 1, Missoula, MT 59801* ☎ *406/541–2677 or 800/344–6118* ⊕ *www.adventure-life.com.*
Alpine Ascents International ✉ *121 Mercer St., Seattle, WA 98109* ☎ *206/378–1927* ⊕ *www.AlpineAscents.com.*
American Alpine Institute ✉ *1515 12th St., Bellingham, WA 98225* ☎ *360/671–1505* ⊕ *www.aai.cc.*
Andes Adventures ✉ *1323 12th St., Suite F, Santa Monica, CA 90401* ☎ *310/395–5265 or 800/289–9470* ⊕ *www.andesadventures.com.*
Arun Treks & Expeditions ✉ *301 E. 33rd St., Suite 3, Austin, TX 78705* ☎ *512/407–8314 or 888/495–8735* ⊕ *www.aruntreks.com.*
Austin-Lehman Adventures ✉ *Box 81025, Billings, MT 59108* ☎ *406/655–4591 or 800/575–1540* ⊕ *www.austinlehman.com.*
Australian & Amazonian Adventures ✉ *2711 Market Garden, Austin, TX 78745* ☎ *512/443–5393 or 800/232–5658* ⊕ *www.amazonadventures.com.*

Big Five Tours & Expeditions ✉ *1551 SE Palm Ct., Stuart, FL 34994* ☎ *772/ 287–7995 or 800/244–3483* ⊕ *www.bigfive.com.*

BikeHike Adventures ✉ *316 W. 5th Ave., Suite 13, Vancouver, BC V5Y 1J5 Canada* ☎ *604/731–2442 or 888/805–0061* ⊕ *www.bikehike.com.*

Boojum Expeditions ✉ *14543 Kelly Canyon Rd., Bozeman, MT 59715* ☎ *406/587–0125 or 800/287–0125* ⊕ *www.boojum.com.*

Butterfield & Robinson ✉ *70 Bond St., Toronto, Ontario M5B 1X3 Canada* ☎ *416/864–1354 or 800/678–1147* ⊕ *www.butterfield.com.*

Clipper Cruise Line ✉ *11969 Westline Industrial Dr., St. Louis, MO 63146* ☎ *314/655–6700 or 800/325–0010* ⊕ *www.clippercruise.com.*

Colorado Mountain School ✉ *341 Moraine Ave., Estes Park, CO 80517* ☎ *970/586–5758 or 888/267–7783* ⊕ *www.cmschool.com.*

Country Walkers ✍ *Box 180, Waterbury, VT 05676* ☎ *802/244–1387 or 800/464–9255* ⊕ *www.countrywalkers.com.*

Dragoman Overland This company is represented in North America by Adventure Center ⇨ *above* ✉ *Camp Green, Debenham, Suffolk IP14 6LA UK* ⊕ *www.dragoman.com.*

Earth River Expeditions ✉ *180 Towpath Rd., Accord, NY 12404* ☎ *845/ 626–2665 or 800/643–2784* ⊕ *www.earthriver.com.*

Earthwatch ✉ *3 Clocktower Pl., Suite 100, Maynard, MA 01754* ☎ *978/ 461–0081 or 800/776–0188* ⊕ *www.earthwatch.org.*

ElderTreks *Trips oriented toward age 50 and over.* ✉ *597 Markham St., Toronto, Ontario M6G 2L7, Canada* ☎ *416/588–5000 or 800/741– 7956* ⊕ *www.eldertreks.com.*

Equitours ✍ *Box 807, Dubois, WY 82513* ☎ *307/455–3363 or 800/ 545–0019* ⊕ *www.equitours.com.*

Exodus This company is represented in North America by Adventure Center ⇨ *above.* ✉ *9 Weir Rd., London SW12 OLT, England* ⊕ *www. exodustravel.com.*

Experience Plus! ✉ *415 Mason Ct., #1, Fort Collins, CO 80524* ☎ *970/ 484–8489 or 800/685–4565* ⊕ *www.ExperiencePlus.com.*

Explore! Worldwide This company is represented in North America by Adventure Center ⇨ *above.* ✉ *1 Frederick St., Aldershot, Hampshire GU11 1LQ UK* ⊕ *www.explore.co.uk.*

Fishing International ✉ *5510 Skylane Blvd., Suite 200, Santa Rosa, CA 95405* ☎ *707/542–4242 or 800/950–4242* ⊕ *www.fishinginternational. com.*

FishQuest ✉ *3375B Hwy. 76 West, Hiawassee GA 30546* ☎ *706/896– 1403 or 888/891–3474* ⊕ *www.fishquest.com.*

Fly Fishing And ✍ *Box 1719, Red Lodge, MT 59068* ☎ *406/446–9087* ⊕ *www.flyfishingand.com.*

Focus Tours ✉ *111 Malaga Rd., Santa Fe, NM 87505* ☎ *505/989–7193* ⊕ *www.focustours.com.*

Frontiers ✍ *Box 959, Wexford, PA 15090* ☎ *724/935–1577 or 800/ 245–1950* ⊕ *www. frontierstravel.com.*

G.A.P. Adventures ✉ *19 Charlotte St., Toronto, Ontario M5V 2H5 Canada* ☎ *416/260–0999 or 800/465–5600* ⊕ *www.gapadventures.com.*

Gecko's This company is represented in North America by Adventure Center ⇨ *above.* ✉ *258 Lonsdale St., Melbourne, V1C 3000 Australia* ⊕ *www.geckosadventures.com.*

Geographic Expeditions ✉ *1008 General Kennedy Ave., San Francisco, CA 94129* ☎ *415/922–0448 or 800/777–8183* ⊕ *www.geoex.com.*

Global Adventure Guide ✉ *14 Kennaway Rd., Unit 3, Christchurch, 8002 New Zealand* ☎ *800/732–0861 in North America* ⊕ *www. globaladventureguide.com.*

Hidden Trails ✉ *202–380 West 1st Ave., Vancouver, BC V5Y 3T7 Canada* ☎ *604/323–1141 or 888/987–2457* ⊕ *www.hiddentrails.com.*

Inca ✉ *1311 63rd St., Emeryville, CA 94608* ☎ *510/420–1550* ⊕ *www. inca1.com.*

International Expeditions ✉ *One Environs Park, Helena AL 35080* ☎ *205/428–1700 or 800/633–4734* ⊕ *www.ietravel.com.*

Joseph Van Os Photo Safaris ✇ *Box 655, Vashon Island, WA 98070* ☎ *206/463–5383* ⊕ *www.photosafaris.com.*

Journeys International ✉ *107 Aprill Dr., Suite 3, Ann Arbor, MI 48103* ☎ *734/665–4407 or 800/255–8735* ⊕ *www.journeys-intl.com.*

KE Adventure Travel ✉ *1131 Grand Ave., Glenwood Springs, CO 81601* ☎ *970/384–0001 or 800/497–9675* ⊕ *www.keadventure.com.*

Ladatco Tours ✉ *2200 S. Dixie Hwy., Suite704, Coconut Grove, FL 33133* ☎ *305/854–8422 or 800/327–6162* ⊕ *www.ladatco.com.*

Lindblad Expeditions ✉ *96 Morton St., New York, NY 10014* ☎ *212/ 765–7740 or 800/397–3348* ⊕ *www.expeditions.com.*

Mountain Madness ✉ *4218 SW Alaska, Suite 206, Seattle, WA 98116* ☎ *206/937–8389 or 800/328–5925* ⊕ *www.mountainmadness.com.*

Mountain Travel-Sobek ✉ *1266 66th St., Suite 4, Emeryville, CA 94608* ☎ *510/594–6000 or 888/687–6235* ⊕ *www.mtsobek.com.*

Myths and Mountains ✉ *976 Tee Ct., Incline Village, NV 89451* ☎ *775/ 832–5454 or 800/670–6984* ⊕ *www.mythsandmountains.com.*

Nature Expeditions International ✉ *7860 Peters Rd., Suite F-103, Plantation, FL 33324* ☎ *954/693–8852 or 800/869–0639* ⊕ *www.naturexp. com.*

Off the Beaten Path ✉ *7 E. Beall, Bozeman, MT 59715* ☎ *406/586–1311 or 800/445–2995* ⊕ *www.offthebeatenpath.com.*

OutWest Global Adventures *This company operates gay- and Lesbian-oriented tours.* ✇ *Box 2050, Red Lodge, MT 59068* ☎ *406/446–1533 or 800/743–0458* ⊕ *www.outwestadventures.com.*

PanAmerican Travel Services ✉ *320 E. 900 S, Salt Lake City, UT 84111* ☎ *801/364–4300 or 800/364–4359* ⊕ *www.panamtours.com.*

PowderQuest Tours ✉ *7108 Pinetree Rd., Richmond, VA 23229* ☎ *206/ 203–6065 or 888/565–7158* ⊕ *www.powderquest.com.*

Quark Expeditions ✉ *1019 Post Rd., Darien, CT 06820* ☎ *203/656– 0499 or 800/356–5699* ⊕ *www.quarkexpeditions.com.*

Remote Odysseys Worldwide (ROW) ✇ *Box 579, Coeur d'Alene, ID 83816* ☎ *208/765–0841 or 800/451–6034* ⊕ *www. ROWinternational.com.*

Rod & Reel Adventures ✉ *32617 Skyhawk Way, Eugene, OR 97405* ☎ *541/349–0777 or 800/356–6982* ⊕ *www.rodreeladventures.com.*

Small World Adventures ✇ *Box 1225, Salida, CO 81201* ☎ *970/309– 8913 or 800/585–2925* ⊕ *www.smallworldadventures.com.*

Snoventures ✉ *Cedar Ave., Huddersfield HD1 5QH UK* ☎ *775/586– 9133 in North America* ⊕ *www.snoventures.com.*

South American Journeys ✉ *9921 Cabanas Ave., Tujunga, CA 91042* ☎ *818/951–8986* ⊕ *www.southamericanjourneys.com and www. gosouthamerica.org.*
Southwind Adventures ✉ *Box 621057, Littleton, CO 80162* ☎ *303/972– 0701 or 800/377–9463* ⊕ *www.southwindadventures.com.*
Travcoa ✉ *2424 SE Bristol St., #310, Newport Beach, CA 92600* ☎ *949/ 476–2800 or 800/992–2003* ⊕ *www.travcoa.com.*
Victor Emanuel Nature Tours ✉ *2525 Wallingwood Dr., Suite 1003, Austin, TX 78746* ☎ *512/328–5221 or 800/328–8368* ⊕ *www.ventbird. com.*
Wilderness Travel ✉ *1102 9th St., Berkeley, CA 94710* ☎ *510/558–2488 or 800/368–2794* ⊕ *www.wildernesstravel.com.*
Wildland Adventures ✉ *3516 N.E. 155th St., Seattle, WA 98155* ☎ *206/ 365–0686 or 800/345–4453* ⊕ *www.wildland.com.*
WINGS ✉ *1643 N. Alvernon, Suite 109, Tucson, AZ 85712* ☎ *520/320– 9868 or 888/293–6443* ⊕ *www.wingsbirds.com.*
World Expeditions ✉ *580 Market St., Suite 225, San Francisco, CA 94104* ☎ *415/989–2212 or 888/464–8735* ⊕ *www.worldexpeditions. com.*
The World Outdoors ✉ *2840 Wilderness Pl., Suite D, Boulder, CO 80301* ☎ *303/413–0938 or 800/488–8483* ⊕ *www.theworldoutdoors.com.*
Zegrahm Expeditions ✉ *192 Nickerson St., #200, Seattle, WA 98109* ☎ *206/285–4000 or 800/628–8747* ⊕ *www.zeco.com.*

CRUISES

Antarctica Cruises

Founded to promote environmentally responsible travel to Antarctica, the **International Association of Antarctica Tour Operators** (☎ 970/704–1047 ⊕ www.iaato.org) is a good source of information, including suggested readings. Most companies operating Antarctica trips are members of this organization and display its logo in their brochures.

Season: November–March.
Location: Most cruises depart from Ushuaia, Argentina.
Cost: From $2,995 (triple-occupancy cabin) for 12 days from Ushuaia.
Tour Operators: Abercrombie & Kent; Adventure Center; Big Five Tours & Expeditions; Clipper Cruise Line; ElderTreks; G.A.P. Adventures; Lindblad Expeditions; Mountain Travel-Sobek; Quark Expeditions; Travcoa; Wilderness Travel; Zegrahm Expeditions.

Ever since Lars-Eric Lindblad operated the first cruise to the "White Continent" in 1966, Antarctica has exerted an almost magnetic pull for serious travelers. From Ushuaia, the world's southernmost city, you'll sail for two sometimes rough days through the Drake Passage and then on to the spectacular landscapes of Antarctica. Most visits are to the Antarctic Peninsula, the continent's most accessible region. Accompanied by naturalists, you'll travel ashore in motorized rubber crafts called Zodiacs to view penguins and seabirds. Some cruises visit research stations, and many call at the Falkland, South Orkney, South Shetland, or South

Georgia Islands. Expedition vessels have been fitted with ice-strengthened hulls; many originally were built as polar-research vessels. On certain Quark Expeditions itineraries you can travel aboard an icebreaker, the *Kapitan Khlebnikov,* which rides up onto the ice, crushing it with its weight. This vessel carries helicopters for aerial viewing. Quark has made two circumnavigations of Antarctica, a 21,000-km (13,000-mi) journey lasting almost three months, and may offer this trip again. Adventure Center and Big Five Tours & Expeditions offer sea kayaking and the chance to camp for one night on the ice at extra cost.

When choosing an expedition cruise, inquire about the qualifications of the onboard naturalists and historians; the maximum number of passengers carried; the ice-readiness of the vessel; onboard medical facilities; whether there's an open bridge policy, and the number of landings attempted per day.

Ocean Cruises

Season: October–April.

Locations: Cruise lines are finding South American ports of call increasingly popular among travelers. Bordered by long Atlantic and Pacific coasts, the continent offers an abundance of choices. Many itineraries visit Argentina (Buenos Aires and Ushuaia), Brazil (Belém, Fortaleza, Rio de Janeiro, and Salvador), and Chile (Antofagasta, Arica, Cape Horn, Coquimbo, Puerto Montt, Punta Arenas, and Valparaíso). Other typical port calls include Cartagena, Colombia; Guayaquil, Ecuador; Devil's Island, French Guinea; Callao (for Lima) and Paracas (for Nazca Lines), Peru; Punta del Este and Montevideo, Uruguay, and Caracas, Venezuela. Some ships set sail in the Caribbean and stop at one or two islands before heading south; a few transit the Panama Canal en route. West coast departures might include one or more Mexican ports before reaching South America. A partial navigation of the Amazon River, frequently as far as Manaus, is sometimes part of the program, as are the Falkland Islands. While a circumnavigation of the continent is possible (50 or more days), 14- to 21-day cruises are the norm. Most lines have multiple departures and operate several ships.

Vessels vary in the degree of comfort or luxury they offer as well as in what is or isn't included in the price. Such things as guided shore excursions, gratuities, dinner beverages, and port taxes are often extra. Peruse brochures carefully and ask questions to ensure your choice of vessel is the right one for you.

Cost: Prices vary according to the ship, cabin category, and itinerary. Figure $1,950 to $4,495 for a 14-day cruise, excluding international airfare.

Cruise Companies: The following operators offer cruises calling at various South American ports.

Celebrity Cruises (☎ 800/647–2251 ⊕ www.celebrity.com). **Clipper Cruise Line** (☎ 800/325–0010 ⊕ www.clippercruise.com). **Crystal Cruises** (☎ 800/446–6625 ⊕ www.crystalcruises.com). **Fred.Olsen Cruise Lines** (☎ 800/843–0602 ⊕ www.fredolsencruises.com). **Holland America Line** (☎ 877/724–5425 ⊕ www.hollandamerica.com). **Norwegian Cruise Line** (☎ 800/327–7030 ⊕ www.ncl.com). **Oceania Cruises** (☎ 800/254–5067

⊕ www.oceaniacruiseline.com). **Orient Lines** (☎ 800/333–7300 ⊕ www.orientlines.com). **Princess Cruises** (☎ 800/774–6237 ⊕ www.princess.com). **Radisson Seven Seas Cruises** (☎ 877/505–5370 ⊕ www.rssc.com). **Seabourn Cruise Line** (☎ 877/760–9052 ⊕ www.seabourn.com). **Silversea Cruises** (☎ 877/760–9052 ⊕ www.silversea.com).

Patagonia Coastal & Lake Cruises

Cruising the southern tip of South America and along Chile's western coast north to the lake district reveals some of Earth's most spectacular scenery: fjords, glaciers, lagoons, lakes, narrow channels, waterfalls, forested shorelines, fishing villages, penguins, and other wildlife. Many operators include a one- or two-day boating excursion as part of their Patagonia itineraries. The companies listed below offer from four to 12 nights aboard ship.

Argentina & Chile
Season: October–April.
Locations: Chilean fjords; Puerto Montt and Punta Arenas, Chile; Tierra del Fuego and Ushuaia, Argentina.
Cost: From $1,395 for 12 days from Buenos Aires.
Tour Operators: Abercrombie & Kent; Adventure Life; Big Five Tours & Expeditions; Clipper Cruise Line; Explore! Worldwide; International Expeditions; Lindblad Expeditions; Mountain Travel-Sobek; Off the Beaten Path; Wilderness Travel; Wildland Adventures.

Boarding your vessel in Punta Arenas, Chile or Ushuaia, Argentina, you'll cruise the Strait of Magellan and the Beagle Channel, visiting glaciers, penguin rookeries, and seal colonies before heading north along the fjords of Chile's western coast. All vessels used by the above companies are comfortable with baths en suite. Adventure Life and Lindblad Expeditions include the Chiloé Archipelago, a region rich in folklore about ghost ships, troll-like beings known as the Trauco, and magical sea creatures. With Abercrombie & Kent, Clipper Cruise Line, and Wildland Adventures, you'll savor the mountain scenery of Torres del Paine National Park for several days before or following the cruise, while Lindblad Expeditions, Mountain Travel-Sobek, and International Expeditions visit Tierra del Fuego National Park.

Several of the companies also include Cape Horn National Park. Wilderness Travel allows time for hiking at Volcano Osorno and in Alerce Andino National Park; the latter protects the second largest temperate rainforest ecosystem in the world. Following a five-day cruise, Off the Beaten Path travelers fly to Puerto Montt for a three-night stay at nearby Lake Llanquihue with opportunities for hiking in the mountains. Most itineraries begin or end with days in Santiago, Chile or Buenos Aires, Argentina.

LEARNING VACATIONS

Cultural Tours

Among the many types of travel, some find the most rewarding to be an in-depth focus on one aspect of a country's culture. This could mean exploring the archaeological remains of great civilizations, learning about the lives and customs of indigenous peoples, or trying to master culinary arts.

Argentina
Season: March–October.
Locations: Buenos Aires; Mendoza; northwest Argentina.
Cost: From $1,430 for nine days from Buenos Aires.
Tour Operators: Adventure Life; ElderTreks; Myths and Mountains.

Argentina's northwest is rich in cultural history as well as scenic beauty. With Adventure Life, spend seven days exploring this area. You'll visit Ischigualasto Provincial Park where 63 species of fossilized animals have been uncovered, Talampaya Provincial Park with ancient paintings and engravings on rock faces, the town of Tafi del Valle and its Neolithic remains, Quebrada de la Flecha where historic adobe huts stand atop sand dunes, and the city of Salta. Several hikes are on the itinerary. ElderTreks combines visits to several of the sites just mentioned with time in Bolivia and Chile; included is a three-day trek in western Argentina. For a literal taste of Argentina, join Myths and Mountains' 10-day Adventurous Cook's Tour. Led by a renowned Argentine gastronome, you'll take part in culinary workshops in Buenos Aires and wine-tastings in Mendoza; there's even a typical barbecue on a working *estancia* (ranch). The program includes some hiking and horseback riding, as well.

Scientific Research Trips

Joining a research expedition team gives you more than great photos. By assisting scientists, you can make significant contributions toward a better understanding of the continent's unique ecosystems and cultural heritages. Flexibility and a sense of humor are important assets for these trips, which often require roughing it.

Argentina
Season: September–October.
Locations: Catamarca Province; Ischigualasto Provincial Park.
Cost: $1,995 for 13 days from San Juan, Argentina.
Tour Operator: Earthwatch.

In Earthwatch's Triassic Park program you'll prospect rock formations for dinosaur fossils, excavate and map the finds, then collect and catalog them. Some fossils lie on the surface; others require chiseling. The remote northern valley where this work takes place holds the only unbroken record yet discovered spanning the entire Triassic period when dinosaurs first appeared. A second option involves working on a survey of archaeological resources on Mount Incahuasi high in the Andes, recording sites by GPS to create a comprehensive archaeological map. Fill out data sheets on structures and artifacts, take photographs, and make collections. A good level of fitness and experience with high altitudes is desirable.

THE OUTDOORS

Bird-Watching Tours

When selecting a bird-watching tour, ask questions. What species might be seen? What are the guide's qualifications? Does the operator work to protect natural habitats? What equipment is used? (In addition to binoculars, this should include a high-powered telescope, a tape recorder to record and play back bird calls [a way of attracting birds], and a spotlight for night viewing.)

Antarctica

Season: December.
Locations: Antarctic Peninsula; Falkland Islands; South Georgia Island.
Cost: From $10,580 for 23 days from Buenos Aires.
Tour Operator: Victor Emanuel Nature Tours.

Arguably the ultimate travel adventure, Antarctica exerts a strong pull on nature lovers. Now, a trip has been designed to focus on the special interests of serious birders. Traveling aboard the *Clipper Adventurer,* you'll view wandering, light-mantled, and royal albatrosses; snow petrels along with several other petrel species, and large colonies of king and Macaroni Penguins.

Argentina

Season: November–December.
Locations: Andes; Chaco; Iguazú; Pampas; Patagonia.
Cost: From $2,230 for eight days from Salta.
Tour Operators: Focus Tours; Victor Emanuel Nature Tours; WINGS.

More than 1,000 types of birds inhabit this vast country. Whatever part of Argentina you visit, expect to see a great variety of species, including many endemics. Focus Tours' 21-day program concentrates on the northern region, where feathered inhabitants such as the plumbeous sierra-finch, Salinas monjita, and Steinbach's canastero live. Calilegua National Park, with more than 400 bird species, is part of the itinerary. Victor Emanuel offers two Argentine programs, one to the central area for such endemics as Oustalet's and Cordoba cinclodes, and the other covering the Pampas and Patagonia with possible sightings including the Chaco pipit and Austral parakeet. WINGS' three itineraries visit the high Andes, the Pampas, and Iguazú Falls.

Chile

Seasons: October–November.
Locations: Atacama Desert; Lake District; Patagonia.
Cost: From $3,999 for 16 days from Santiago.
Tour Operators: Focus Tours; WINGS.

Chile spans a number of distinctive vegetational and altitudinal zones, ensuring a varied and abundant avian population. On a 16-day journey to the northern and central regions, Focus Tours participants visit the ski areas of Farellones and Valle Nevado to spot the rare crag chilia, an earthcreeper-like bird; Los Cipreses Reserve, stronghold of the burrowing parrot; La

Campana National Park, which holds five of Chile's eight endemic species; the Andes for the rare and threatened white-tailed shrike-tyrant, plus the arid Atacama and Lauca National Park. WINGS' itinerary covers the country from Patagonia in the south to the Atacama Desert in the north, also spending time in the lake district around Puerto Montt.

Natural History

Many operators have created nature-focused programs that provide insight into the importance and fragility of South America's ecological treasures. The itineraries mentioned below take in deserts, glaciers, rainforests, mountains, and rivers of this continent, as well as the impressive variety of its wildlife.

Argentina & Chile
Season: October–April.
Locations: Atacama Desert; Buenos Aires; Lake District; Patagonia; Santiago.
Cost: From $1,860 for nine days from Buenos Aires.
Tour Operators: Abercrombie & Kent; Adventure Life; Big Five Tours & Expeditions; ElderTreks; G.A.P. Adventures; Geographic Expeditions; Inca; Journeys International; Myths and Mountains; Nature Expeditions International; Off the Beaten Path; OutWest Global Adventures; PanAmerican Travel; South American Journeys; Southwind Adventures; Wilderness Travel; Wildland Adventures; World Expeditions.

Patagonia has long been a prime ecotourism destination, and nature lovers will find no lack of tour offerings for this region. You'll view the glaciers of Los Glaciares National Park where the Moreno Glacier towers 20 stories high, the soaring peaks of Torres del Paine, the fjords of the Chilean coast, and a Magellanic penguin colony. Most itineraries spend some days in the lake district, and a few visit Alerce Andino National Park and Orsorno Volcano. Many programs include day walks and, often, a one- to three-day cruise. Several operators feature a stay at a historic ranch, Estancia Helsingfors, on Lago Viedma. The Atacama Desert of northern Chile is nature of another sort. Abercrombie & Kent has a "Fire and Ice" itinerary, combining the deep south with this arid zone.

Overland Safaris

The brochure for a company that operates overland trips exclusively states in bold print: NOT YOUR EVERYDAY JOURNEY. While definitely not for everyone, this type of travel is sure to take you far from the beaten path. It's also a great way to immerse yourself in a number of cultures and landscapes. Expect to travel by truck, bus, train, boat, or custom-built expedition vehicles; no air-conditioned coach tours here. Occasionally, you may find yourself in lodges or inns, but much of the time you'll sleep outdoors. Know that you're expected to help pitch tents, cook, and do other chores. The camaraderie that evolves often sparks lifelong friendships. You should be tolerant of others, willing to forego some creature comforts, and be a good sport about taking part in group activities.

Companies often rank trip segments from easy to extreme. This type of trip generally attracts an international mix of physically fit adventurers between ages 18 and 50. Although the operators listed below don't have fixed upper age limits for participants, those over 60 will likely be asked to complete a health questionnaire. It should be noted that this practice isn't limited to overland journeys, but applies to many companies' programs that involve strenuous activities or roughing it.

Season: Year-round.
Locations: Throughout South America.
Cost: From $1,320 for 32 days (from La Paz), plus $390 for a "kitty," which funds such expenses as camp food, activities the group takes as a whole, and park entrance fees.
Tour Operators: Dragoman Overland; Exodus; G.A.P. Adventures; Gecko's.

These companies offer trips that cover most of South America and which range from four to 22 weeks. Itineraries typically are composed of segments, which you can take separately or combine into a longer trip. Most programs visit between three and nine countries.

Photo Safaris

A benefit of photo tours is the amount of time spent at each place visited. Whether the subject is a rarely spotted animal, a breathtaking waterfall, or villagers in traditional dress, you can focus both your camera and your mind on the scene before you. The tours listed below are led by professional photographers who offer instruction and hands-on tips. If you're not serious about improving your photographic skills, these trips might not be the best choice, as you could become impatient with the pace.

Antarctica
Season: October; February.
Locations: Antarctic Peninsula; Falkland, South Georgia, and South Orkney Islands.
Cost: From $8,495 for 16 days from Ushuaia.
Tour Operator: Joseph Van Os Photo Safaris; Lindblad Expeditions.

Photograph seabirds, Adélie and gentoo penguin colonies, albatross nesting areas, elephant and fur seals, plus the spectacular landscapes of Antarctic. With Joseph Van Os, you'll travel aboard the icebreaker *Kapitan Khlebnikov,* which carries its own helicopter. A high point of this trip is the chance to cruise the Weddell Sea and visit the Snow Hill colony of emperor penguins where some 4,000 breeding pairs are found. Lindblad Expeditions has one departure designated as a photo expedition where you can learn in the field with nature photographer Tom Mangelsen. This 14-day program calls at the islands listed above, as well as the Antarctic Peninsula.

Argentina & Chile
Season: March–April.
Locations: Central Pagagonia; Easter Island; Los Glaciares & Torres del Paine National Parks.

Cost: From $3,495 for 12 days from Santiago.
Tour Operators: Joseph Van Os Photo Safaris; Myths and Mountains.

Timed for vibrant fall colors among ice fields, snowcapped mountains, glaciers, and rushing streams, Joseph Van Os has 12- and 13-day departures during Patagonian fall (the northern hemisphere's spring). One trip visits the famed sites of Torres del Paine and Los Glaciares National Parks; the second concentrates on lesser known regions such as central Patagonia, including the Cavernas de Mármol, or Marble Caves. Led by photographer Bill Chapman, Myths and Mountains offers a 15-day program combining Torres del Paine National Park with the desolation and *moais* (giant stone statues) of Easter Island.

SPORTS

A sports-focused trip offers a great way to feel part of the country visited and to interact with local people. A dozen bicyclists entering a village, for instance, would arouse more interest and be more approachable than a group of 30 stepping out of a tour bus. Although many itineraries don't require a high level of skill, it is expected that your interest in the particular sport be more than casual, and some programs are designed for those with lots of experience. In either case, good physical conditioning, experience with high altitudes on certain itineraries, and a flexible attitude are important. Weather can be changeable, dictating choices of hiking or climbing routes. Companies that operate mountaineering programs usually build an extra day or two into their itineraries to allow for weather conditions. If you're not a particularly strong hiker or cyclist, determine if support vehicles accompany the group or if alternate activities or turn-around points are available on more challenging days.

Bicycling

Argentina & Chile
Season: October–March.
Locations: Atacama Desert; Lake District; Mendoza; Patagonia.
Cost: From $1,225 for eight days from Puerto Montt.
Tour Operators: Australian & Amazonian Adventures; Butterfield & Robinson; Experience Plus!; Global Adventure Guide; Southwind Adventures.

Global Adventure's 15-day journey, graded moderate with some uphill challenges and occasional singletrack riding, twice crosses the lower Andes as you ride along paved and dirt roads through forests and past volcanoes. The itinerary encompasses both the Lake District and Patagonia with occasional options for rafting, canyoning, or volcano climbing. Another tour combines biking in Chile and neighboring Bolivia. With Southwind, bike and hike the Lake District's gently rolling terrain, visiting Osorno Volcano, Puyehue and Huerquehue National Parks, and the resort town of Pucón. Nicknamed "a two-wheeled tango," Butterfield & Robinson's 9-day trip travels from Santiago, Chile, to Buenos Aires, Argentina (not totally by bike!), stopping in Chile's Atacama Desert and the Argentine wine country along the way. Starting in Bariloche,

Experience Plus! cycles up to 93 km (58 mi) a day around Lake Llan-quihue for views of Osorno and Calbuco volcanoes with the chance for Class III rafting on Río Petrohué. You can opt for a four-day extension on Chiloé Island. Choose from two biking journeys with Australian & Amazonian Adventures, one to Chile's Lake District, the other visiting a number of national parks, including Isluga, Surire, Vicuña, and Lauca. Most nights are spent camping.

Canoeing, Kayaking & White-Water Rafting

White-water rafting and kayaking can be exhilarating experiences. You don't have to be an expert paddler to enjoy many of these adventures, but you should be a strong swimmer. Rivers are rated from Class I to Class V according to difficulty of navigation. Generally speaking, Class I to III rapids are suitable for beginners, while Class IV and V rapids are strictly for the experienced. Canoeing is a gentler river experience.

Chile
Season: November–March.
Locations: Chiloé Archipelago; Northern Patagonia; Río Futaleufú.
Cost: From $680 for four days from Castro, Chiloé.
Tour Operators: Adventure Life; Australian & Amazonian Expeditions; Earth River Expeditions; Hidden Trails; PanAmerican Travel.

Chile has both scenic fjords for sea kayaking and challenging rivers for white-water rafting. With PanAmerican Travel, sea kayakers can spend nine days exploring the fjords, waterfalls, hot springs, and wildlife of the country's rugged coast, camping at night surrounded by splendid scenery. Australian & Amazonian Adventures offers three- to nine-day kayaking experiences. On the four-day itinerary, you'll discover the islands of the Chiloé Archipelago, a region rich in folklore, while the six-day program explores the fjords of northern Patagonia. For the experienced rafter, the Class IV and V rapids of Río Futaleufú offer many challenges. Its sheer-walled canyons boast such well-named rapids as Infierno and Purgatorio. Earth River's 10-day program here includes a rock climb up 98-meter (320-foot) Torre de los Vientos and a Tyrolean traverse where, wearing a climbing harness attached to a pulley, you pull yourself across a rope strung above the rapids. With tree houses and riverside hot tubs formed from natural potholes carved from the stone, overnight camping becomes an exotic experience. Earth River also offers a kayaking journey over a chain of three lakes, surrounded by snowcapped mountains. Access is by floatplane. Hidden Trails and Adventure Life have Futaleufú rafting trips; the latter's program, in addition to shooting the rapids, offers horseback riding in the mountains, kayaking, and fishing.

Fishing

Argentina & Chile
Season: September–March.
Locations: Chiloé Island; Lake District; Patagonia.
Cost: From $2,975 for seven days from Balmaceda, Chile.

Tour Operators: Fishing International; FishQuest; Fly Fishing And; Frontiers; PanAmerican Travel; Rod & Reel Adventures.

For anglers, Argentina and Chile are the southern hemisphere's Alaska, offering world-class trout fishing in clear streams. A bonus is the availability of landlocked salmon and golden dorado, known as the "river tiger." Bilingual fishing guides accompany groups, and accommodations are in comfortable lodges with private baths. While November is the usual opening date for freshwater fishing, the season begins two months earlier at Lago Llanquihue due to the large resident fish population. Rod & Reel takes advantage of this, basing participants at a lodge near Osorno Volcano.

With Fly Fishing And, your 10 days will be divided between two lodges, meaning you can fish several rivers and creeks, while PanAmerican's seven-day program breaks up lodge stays with a night of riverside camping. Fishing International offers an Argentina program fishing the Ibera Marshes for dorado and a Chile trip based at an *estancia* (ranch) where you can fish two rivers for brown trout weighing up to 15 pounds. FishQuest has four offerings, fishing a variety of rivers for brown and rainbow trout, dorado, giant catfish, and salmon. With Frontiers, choose from a great variety of lodges and rivers in both Argentina and Chile.

Hiking, Running & Trekking

South America's magnificent scenery and varied terrain make it a terrific place for trekkers and hikers. The southern part of Argentina and Chile, known as Patagonia, and Peru's Inca Trail are especially popular. Numerous operators have hiking and trekking trips to these regions, so study several offerings to determine the program that's best for your ability and interests. The trips outlined below are organized tours led by qualified guides. Camping is often part of the experience, although on some trips you stay at inns and small hotels. Itineraries range from relatively easy hikes to serious trekking and even running.

Argentina & Chile
Season: October–April.
Locations: Atacama Desert; Lake District; Patagonia.
Cost: From $1,065 for 12 days from Salta, Argentina.
Tour Operators: Adventure Life; American Alpine Institute; Andes Adventures; Australian & Amazonian Adventures; BikeHike Adventures; Butterfield & Robinson; Country Walkers; Geographic Expeditions; KE Adventure Travel; Mountain Travel-Sobek; Southwind Adventures; The World Outdoors; Wilderness Travel; Wildland Adventures; World Expeditions.

Patagonia may be the most trekked region in South America. All of the above companies have programs here, ranging from relatively easy hikes (Butterfield & Robinson, Country Walkers) to serious treks involving daily elevation gains up to 800 meters (2,625 feet) and ice and snow traverses using crampons (American Alpine Institute). Highlights include Torres del Paine, Los Glaciares, and/or Tierra del Fuego National

Parks and crossing the Patagonian Ice Cap. Adventure Life's program lets you overnight in igloo-shape tents at EcoCamp in Torres del Paine.

In addition to its hiking trip, Andes Adventures offers an 18-day running itinerary with runs covering as much as 31 km (19 mi) per day. Other options include an Atacama Desert trek with KE Adventure Travel, which includes an ascent of Licancabur Volcano or a Futaleufú Canyon trek with Wilderness Travel. Adventure Life, Australian & Amazonian Adventures, and Southwind Adventures each offer four different itineraries, while American Alpine Institute, KE Adventure Travel, and Wilderness Travel have three.

Horseback Riding

Argentina

Season: Year-round, lower elevations; November–March, Andes.
Locations: Corrientes; Nahuel Huapi National Park; Lake District; Patagonia; Tunuyan Valley.
Cost: From $649 for six days from Mendoza.
Tour Operators: Australian & Amazonian Adventures; Boojum Expeditions; Equitours; Hidden Trails.

Few countries have a greater equestrian tradition than Argentina. Equitours introduces you to the country's gaucho culture at a 15,000-acre *estancia* (cattle ranch). You ride through the grasslands and beech forests of Lanin National Park and spend several nights camping. Hidden Trails offers eight itineraries in Argentina, exploring the forests, mountains, and lakes of Patagonia, the vast wilderness around Canyon del Diabolo and the Serrucha mountain range, or several *estancia*-based adventures where you'll ride more than 32 km (20 mi) a day and perhaps, join the gauchos as they round up cattle and horses. With Boojum Expeditions, ride sure-footed Criollo horses high in the mountains and along rugged trails. As the company warns, "This is not a place to learn to ride." On Australian & Amazonian Adventures' six-day trip, ride in the Río Tunuyan area, crossing the border into Chile. On both this trip and Boojum's, nights are spent camping.

Chile

Season: October.–April; year-round, Atacama.
Locations: Atacama Desert; Patagonia; Río Hurtado Valley.
Cost: From $1,450 for seven days from Calama.
Tour Operators: Equitours; Hidden Trails.

On Equitours' 12-day "Patagonia Glacier Ride" you cross the pampas to Torres del Paine National Park, a region of mountains, lakes, and glaciers. Nights are spent camping or in lodges. Hidden Trails has six itineraries: you can opt for a ride in southern Chile through lonely valleys, along historic mule trails created by gold diggers, and into the Andes; join an Atacama Desert adventure riding over the crusted salt of the Salar de Atacama and across expanses of sand, visiting ancient ruins and petroglyphs, or choose from four Patagonia programs, camping or staying at *estancias,* depending on the itinerary selected. If getting off the beaten path appeals to you, consider the company's "Glacier Camping Ride" which ventures into remote areas accessible only by foot or horse.

Uruguay

Season: Year-round.
Locations: Laguna Negra.
Cost: From $1,850 for 15 days from Montevideo.
Tour Operators: Boojum Expeditions; Hidden Trails.

Uruguay's coastline boasts wide beaches dotted with small communities of artists and fishermen. With Boojum Expeditions, explore this area on mixed Criollo and Spanish Barb horses accompanied by gaucho helpers. You'll overnight both at an estancia and a castle-like hotel atop a hill. This is a comfortable trip with no camping. Those with more time might combine this ride with Boojum's Patagonia journey for a "Coastline to Condors" adventure.

Hidden Trails operates two rides in Uruguay. A nine-day itinerary includes eight days of riding across a traditional cattle breeding area to the coast with time to discover the diversity of wildlife at the UNESCO-designated Bañados del Este Biosphere Reserve. You'll stay in some of Uruguay's oldest and best-preserved haciendas. A second itinerary, based at two estancias, offers the chance to learn about rural activities and ride through a forest of *ombúes,* strange trees with thick, twisting branches spreading over the ground.

7

Mountaineering

Only the most towering peaks of Asia vie with the Andes in the challenges and rewards awaiting mountaineers. This is no casual sport, so choose your tour operator carefully, ask questions, and be honest about your level of fitness and experience. Safety should be the company's, and your, first priority. Are the guides certified by professional organizations, such as the American Mountain Guides Association? Are they certified as Wilderness First Responders and trained in technical mountain rescue? What is the company's safety record? What is the climber-to-guide ratio? Are extra days built into the schedule to allow for adverse weather? Is there serious adherence to "leave no trace" environmental ethics? Several of the tour operators mentioned below have their own schools in the U.S. and/or other countries which offer multilevel courses in mountaineering, ice climbing, rock climbing, and avalanche education.

Antarctica

Season: November–January.
Location: Mount Vinson.
Cost: $26,500 for 22 days from Punta Arenas.
Tour Operator: Alpine Ascents International; Mountain Madness.

If you have a solid mountaineering background and are accustomed to cold weather camping, this could be the ultimate mountaineering adventure. A short flight from Patriot Hills in Antarctica brings you to the base camp. With loaded sleds, move up the mountain, establishing two or three camps before attempting the 4,897-meter (16,077-foot) summit of Mt. Vinson. Although the climb itself is considered technically moderate, strong winds and extreme temperatures (as low as -40F), make this a serious challenge. The two companies above will help you achieve this mountaineering goal. Additionally, Alpine Ascents offers the chance to ski from the 89th parallel to the 90th. Aircraft will bring you within 70 miles of the South Pole; then, ski the rest of the way. This unique adventure can be made independently or as an extension of the Vinson climb.

Argentina & Chile

Season: November–February.
Locations: Mt. Aconcagua; Cerro Marconi Sur; Gorra Blanca; Patagonian Ice Cap.
Cost: From $2,980 for 11 days from Calafate, Argentina.
Tour Operators: Alpine Ascents International; American Alpine Institute; Arun Treks & Expeditions; Colorado Mountain School; KE Adventure Travel; Mountain Madness; World Expeditions.

Argentina's Mt. Aconcagua is 6,960 meters (22,835 feet)—no lightweight on the list of the world's highest peaks. Though some routes aren't technically difficult, Aconcagua is demanding physically and requires the use of ice axes, crampons, and ropes. All of the above operators offer climbs of Aconcagua, some via the more difficult Polish glacier route. Frequent high winds and ice make this route very challenging and only for those with extensive mountaineering experience at high altitudes. American Alpine Institute has a second expedition with ascents of Cerro Marconi Sur and Gorra Blanca in southern Patagonia. On this program, you'll also traverse part of the Patagonian ice cap.

Multisport

Not long ago, multisport offerings were so sparse that the topic didn't merit inclusion in this chapter. Since then, such trips now form an important part of many adventure tour operators' programs. Innovative itineraries combine two or more sports, such as biking, fishing, canoeing, hiking, horseback riding, kayaking, rafting, and trekking.

Argentina & Chile

Season: November–April.
Locations: Lake District; northern Chile; Patagonia; Río Futaleufú, Chile.
Cost: From $765 for five days from Puerto Montt, Chile.
Tour Operators: American Alpine Institute; Austin-Lehman Adventures; Australian & Amazonian Adventures; BikeHike Adventures; Earth River Expeditions; Fishing International; Hidden Trails; Mountain Madness; Mountain Travel-Sobek; Nature Expeditions International; The World Outdoors; Wilderness Travel; World Expeditions.

Whether you choose the Lake District or Patagonia, the scene for your active vacation will be one of great beauty. Both regions offer superb trekking, kayaking, horseback riding, and biking. Hidden Trails combines horseback riding with sea kayaking in Patagonia, while Mountain Madness offers hut-to-hut trekking in the Torres del Paine area along with kayaking on the Río Serrano and an optional ice climb. With Nature Expeditions, you'll have soft adventure options most days, such as hiking, rafting (Class II and III rapids), and horseback riding. BikeHike has two multisport trips in Argentina and Chile; you can hike, raft, sea kayak, bike, and ride horses in the Lake District or hike, ride horses, and sand board in northern Chile. On Austin-Lehman's Pagatonia and Lake District itinerary, rest at night in five-star hotels and upscale lodges after horseback riding, biking, rafting, kayaking, and hiking during the day. If you want to try serious rafting, consider one of the Río Futaleufú trips, such as those run by Earth River Expeditions and The World Outdoors; these programs also include hiking and horseback riding.

Skiing & Snowboarding

When ski season's over in the northern hemisphere, it's time to pack the gear and head for resorts in Argentina or Chile. Advanced and expert skiers will find seemingly endless terrain, and powder hounds will discover the ultimate ski. If your present level leans more toward beginner or intermediate, not to worry. Adventures aplenty await you, too. Snowboarders, also, will find the southern mountains much to their liking. In addition to marked trails, there's off-piste terrain, often with steep chutes and deep powder bowls, plus backcountry areas to try. Those with strong skills could opt for heli-skiing on peaks reaching 4,200 meters (13,600 feet) as condors soar above. As hard as it might be to break away from the slopes, a day of hiking or snowshoeing would be well-spent.

Many of the resorts exude a European ambience with a lively nightlife scene. Everywhere, you'll be surrounded by some of Earth's grandest natural beauty. The operators mentioned below have created all-inclusive ski packages covering airport/hotel and hotel/ski mountain transfers, accommodations, two meals daily, and lift tickets for a number of mountains and resorts in both Argentina and Chile; many packages combine the two countries. Costs vary with the accommodations selected. Prices quoted are per person double; costs are even lower if four people share a room. Be aware that less expensive packages, while providing the services mentioned, generally aren't guided tours. Eight-day guided packages start around $1,795.

Argentina

Season: June–October.
Locations: Catedral Bariloche; Cerro Bayo; Chapelco; La Hoya-Esquel; Las Leñas.
Cost: From $880 for an eight-day nonguided inclusive package from Buenos Aires.
Tour Operators: Ladatco Tours; PowderQuest Tours; Snoventures.

Argentina's Bariloche, an alpine-style resort town nicknamed "Little Switzerland," is 13 km (8 mi) from the slopes of Cerro Catedral. This ski area offers more than 1,500 skiable acres with 105 km (65 miles) of trails and is a good choice for skiers of all levels. The resort is in the midst of a several-year expansion project that will double lift capacity and open new terrain. Your lift ticket is valid for skiing both at Catedral and the adjacent resort of Robles. Also accessed by a flight to Bariloche, the ski center of Cerro Bayo on the northwestern tip of Lake Nahuel Huapi is generally not crowded and offers steep powder runs and excellent backcountry hiking. Some packages combine Catedral, Cerro Bayo, and La Hoya; the latter is a government-owned and -operated resort near the town of Esquel where easy hikes lead to steep bowls and chutes, some reaching 60 degrees.

With 56 km (35 mi) of downhill trails and a vertical drop of 1,219 meters (4,000 feet), plus more than 100 couloirs (steep gullies) and vast off-piste and backcountry areas, Las Leñas is considered by many to be South America's premier ski destination. Appealing especially to the expert, Las Leñas has served as summer training ground to several Olympic ski teams. Situated between Bariloche and Las Leñas near the resort town of San Martin de los Andes, Chapelco offers challenges for skiers and riders at all levels. The mountain claims a high-speed quad, a gondola, and access to great backcountry bowls. Ladatco Tours has a seven-day package to Catedral Bariloche, while PowderQuest and Snoventures have multiple offerings for all ski destinations mentioned with a wide variety of accommodations choices to suit most budgets. Many of their packages combine stays at two or more ski areas.

Chile

Season: June–October.

Locations: El Colorado; La Parva; Portillo; Pucón; Termas de Chillán; Valle Nevado.

Cost: From $730 for a seven-day nonguided inclusive package from Santiago.

Tour Operators: Ladatco Tours; Myths and Mountains; PowderQuest; Snoventures.

A short drive from Santiago, Valle Nevado has more than 300 acres of groomed runs and a 792-meter (2,600-foot) vertical drop. Famous for powder, it's also home to the Andes Express, a chair lift so super-fast, you can get in extra runs each day. From Valle Nevado you can interconnect with the slopes of nearby El Colorado and La Parva, making for a vast amount of skiable terrain. First-rate heliskiing, heliboarding, and even hang gliding can be taken out of Valle Nevado; the off-piste is excellent, as well. A snowboard camp is based here coached by North American AASI level-three certified instructors. Participation in the seven-day program, divided into first-time and advanced groups, can be arranged by PowderQuest.

Near the base of Mt. Aconcagua, the western hemisphere's highest mountain, Portillo, serviced by 12 lifts, ranks as one of the top 10 ski resorts in the world on numerous lists. Several national ski teams have their off-season training here. While there's terrain for all ability levels, 43% is designated expert. The heliskiing is enviable, and Portillo's lively aprés-ski life is a bonus.

Yet another world-class resort, Termas de Chillán, has what one tour operator terms "killer slopes," plus a network of forest tracks for cross-country skiers. Its 28 runs along 35 km (22 mi) of groomed trails include South America's longest at 13 km (6 mi). Boasting one of Chile's deepest snow packs, the resort offers varied terrain on two volcanoes for skiing or snowboarding, plus a thermal area comprised of nine pools for end-of-the-day relaxation. The trails are fairly evenly divided among skill levels. Termas de Chillán presents some of the best off-piste adventures on the continent plus fine hiking opportunities.

At the small resort of Pucón, situated on the edge of Lago Villarrica, ski on the side of Chile's most active volcano. You can hike to the crater to gaze at molten magma, then ski or snowboard back down. Bordering two national parks plus a national reserve, Pucón offers great snowshoeing as well as such sports as rafting and caving. PowderQuest and Snoventures offer inclusive packages to all resorts mentioned. Ski weeks without guides run in the $730 to $800 range. PowderQuest's main focus is guided tours of eight to 16 days with time spent at as many as seven resorts in both Argentina and Chile. Myths and Mountains has an 11-day trip to Portillo led by Rusty Crook, a former World Cup skier, while Ladatco offers packages to Valle Nevado, Portillo, and Chillán.

V O C A B U L A R Y

Words and Phrases

English	Spanish	Pronunciation

Basics

English	Spanish	Pronunciation
Yes/no	Sí/no	see/noh
Please	Por favor	por fah-**vor**
Thank you (very much)	(Muchas) gracias	(**moo**-chas) **grah**-see-ass
You're welcome	De nada	deh **nah**-da
Excuse me	Con permiso	con pehr-**mee**-so
Pardon me	¿Perdón?	pehr-**don**
Could you tell me...?	¿Podría decirme...?	po-**dree**-ah deh-**seer**-me
	¿Podrías decirme...?	po-**dree**-as deh-**seer**-me
I'm sorry	Lo siento/Perdón	lo see-**en**-to/ pehr-**don**
Hello!/Hi!	¡Hola!	**o**-la
Good morning!	¡Buen día!	bwen **dee**-a
Good afternoon!	¡Buenas tardes!	**bwen**-as **tar**-des
Good evening/ Good night!	¡Buenas noches!	**bwen**-as **no**-ches
Goodbye!	¡Chau!/¡Adiós!	chow/a-dee-**os**
Mr./sir	Señor	sen-**yor**
Mrs./madam	Señora	sen-**yor**-a
Miss	Señorita	sen-yo-**ri**-ta
Pleased to meet you	Mucho gusto	**moo**-cho **goos**-to
How are you?	¿Cómo está usted?	**ko**-mo es-**ta** oos-**ted**
	¿Cómo estás?	**ko**-mo es-**tas**
Very well, thank you.	Muy bien, gracias.	**mwee** bi-**en**, **grah**-see-ass
And you?	¿Y usted?	ee oos-**ted**
	¿Y vos?	ee voss
Hello (on the telephone)	Hola	**o**-la

Numbers

0	Cero	**seh**-ro
1	Un, uno	oon, **oo**-no
2	Dos	doss

3	Tres	tress
4	Cuatro	**kwah**-troh
5	Cinco	**sin**-koh
6	Seis	**say**-iss
7	Siete	see-**yet**-eh
8	Ocho	**och**-oh
9	Nueve	**nweh**-veh
10	Diez	dee-**ess**
11	Once	**on**-seh
12	Doce	**dos**-seh
13	Trece	**tres**-seh
14	Catorce	kat-**or**-seh
15	Quince	**keen**-seh
16	Dieciséis	dee-**ess**-ee-**say**-iss
17	Diecisiete	dee-**ess**-ee-see-**yet**-eh
18	Dieciocho	dee-**ess**-ee-**och**-oh
19	Diecinueve	dee-**ess**-ee-**nweh**-veh
20	Veinte	**vain**-the
21	Veintiuno	**vain**-tee-**oo**-no
30	Treinta	**train**-tah
32	Treinta y dos	traint-tah-ee-**doss**
40	Cuarenta	kwah-**ren**-tah
43	Cuarenta y tres	kwah-**ren**-tah-ee-**tress**
50	Cincuenta	sin-**kwen**-tah
54	Cincuenta y cuatro	sin-**kwen**-tah-ee-**kwah**-tro
60	Sesenta	seh-**sen**-tah
65	Sesenta y cinco	seh-**sen**-tah-ee-**sin**-koh
70	Setenta	seh-**ten**-tah
76	Setenta y seis	seh-**ten**-tah-ee-**say**-iss
80	Ochenta	oh-**chen**-tah
87	Ochenta y siete	oh-**chen**-tah-ee-see-**yet**-eh
90	Noventa	no-**ven**-tah
98	Noventa y ocho	no-**ven**-tah-ee-**och**-oh
100	Cien	see-**en**
101	Ciento uno	see-**en**-to-**oo**-no
200	Doscientos	doh-see-**en**-toss

500	Quinientos	kin-ee-**en**-toss
700	Setecientos	set-eh-see-**en**-toss
900	Novecientos	nov-eh-see-**en**-toss
1,000	Mil	meel
2,000	Dos mil	doss meel
1,000,000	Un millón	un mi-**shon**

Days of the Week

Sunday	domingo	doh-**ming**-oh
Monday	lunes	**loo**-ness
Tuesday	martes	**mar**-tess
Wednesday	miércoles	mee-**er**-koh-less
Thursday	jueves	**hweh**-vess
Friday	viernes	vee-**er**-ness
Saturday	sábado	**sah**-bad-oh

Months

January	enero	eh-**neh**-ro
February	febrero	feb-**reh**-ro
March	marzo	**mar**-soh
April	abril	ab-**reel**
May	mayo	**mah**-shoh
June	junio	**hoo**-nee-oh
July	julio	**hoo**-lee-oh
August	agosto	ah-**gos**-toh
September	septiembre	sep-tee-**em**-breh
October	octubre	ok-**too**-breh
November	noviembre	nov-ee-**em**-breh
December	diciembre	diss-ee-**em**-breh

Useful Phrases

Do you speak English?	¿Habla usted inglés? ¿Hablás inglés?	**ab**-la oo-**sted** ing-**less** **ab**-las ing-**less**
I don't speak Spanish	No hablo castellano	No **ab**-loh cas-**teh**-sha-no
I don't understand	No entiendo	No en-tee-**en**-doh
I understand	Entiendo	en-tee-**en**-doh
I don't know	No sé	No seh
I am... American	Soy... estadounidense	soy ess-**tah**-doh-oo-nee-**den**-seh

English	inglés(a)	ing-**less**(ah)
Scottish	escocés(a)	ess-koss-**sess**(-ah)
Irish	irlandés(a)	eer-lan-**dess**
Australian	australiano(a)	ow-stra-**lee**-ah-noh(nah)
from New Zealand	neo-celandés(a)	nay-oh-seh-lan-**dess**(ah)
What's your name?	¿Cómo se llama usted?	ko-mo seh **shah**-mah oo-**sted**
	¿Cómo te llamás?	ko-mo teh **shah**-mass
My name is...	Me llamo...	meh **shah**-moh...
What time is it?	¿Qué hora es?	keh **o**-rah ess
It's one o'clock	Es la una	ess la **oo**-na
It's two/three/four... o'clock	Son las dos/tres/ cuatro	son lass doss/ tress/**kwah**-troh
Yes, please/	Sí, gracias.	see, **grah**-see-ass
No, thank you	No, gracias.	noh, **grah**-see-ass
How?	¿Cómo?	**ko**-mo
When?	¿Cuándo?	**kwan**-doh
This/next week	Esta semana/	**ess**-tah sem-**ah**-nah/
	La semana que viene	la sem-**ah**-nah keh vee-**en**-eh
This/next month	Este mes/El mes que viene	**ess**-teh mess/ el mess keh vee-**en**-eh
This/next year	Este año/El año que viene	**ess**-teh **an**-yoh/ el **an**-yoh keh vee-**en**-eh
Yesterday/today/ tomorrow	Ayer/hoy/mañana	**ah**-share/oy/ man-**yan**-ah
This morning/ afternoon	Esta mañana/tarde	**ess**-tah man-**yan**-ah/ **tar**-deh
Tonight	Esta noche	**ess**-tah **noch**-eh
What?	¿Qué?	keh
What is this?	¿Qué es esto?	keh ess **ess**-toh
Why?	¿Por qué?	por **keh**
Who?	¿Quién?	kee-**yen**
Telephone	teléfono	tel-**eff**-on-oh
I am ill	Estoy enfermo(a)	ess-**toy** en-**fer**-moh(mah)
Please call a doctor	Por favor, llame a un médico	Por fah-**vor**, **shah**-meh a oon **meh**-dik-oh
Help!	¡Auxilio!	owk-**see**-lee-oh
Fire!	¡Incendio!	in-**sen**-dee-oh
Look out!	¡Cuidado!	kwee-**dah**-doh

I'd like...	Quiero...por favor	kee-**eh**-roh... por fah-**vor**
a room	un cuarto	oon **kwar**-toh
the key	la llave	la **shah**-veh
a newspaper	un diario	oon dee-**ah**-ree-oh
to send this letter to...	mandar esta carta a...	man-**dar** ess-tah **kar**-tah a...

Out and About

Where is...?	¿Dónde está...?	**don**-deh ess-**tah**...
the train station	la estación de tren	la ess-tah-see-**on** deh tren
the subway station	la estación de subte	la ess-tah-see-**on** deh **soob**-teh
the bus stop	la parada del colectivo	la pah-**rah**-dah del col-ek-**tee**-voh
the post office	el correo	el cor-**reh**-yoh
the bank	el banco	el **ban**-koh
the hotel	el hotel	el oh-**tel**
the store	la tienda	la tee-**en**-dah
the cashier	la caja	la **cah**-ha
the museum	el museo	el moo-**seh**-yoh
the hospital	el hospital	el oss-pee-**tal**
the elevator	el ascensor	el ass-**en**-sor
the bathroom	el baño	el **ban**-yoh
the entrance/exit	la entrada/salida	la en-**trah**-dah/ **sal**-ee-dah
Here/there	acá/allá	ah-**kah**/ah-**shah**
Open/closed	abierto/cerrado	ab-ee-**er**-toh/ seh-**rah**-do
Left/right	izquierda/derecha	iss-kee-**er**-dah/ deh-**rech**-ah
Straight ahead	derecho	deh-**rech**-oh
Is it near/far?	¿Está cerca/lejos?	ess-**tah ser**-kah/ **leh**-hoss
Avenue	avenida	av-en-**ee**-dah
City street	calle	**cah**-sheh
Highway	carretera/ruta	cah-ret-**eh**-rah
Waterfront promenade	costanera	cost-an-**eh**-rah
Cathedral	catedral	cat-**eh**-dral
Church	iglesia	ig-**less**-ee-ah
City Hall	municipalidad	moo-niss-ee-**pal**-ee-dad
Door, gate	puerta, portón	**pwer**-tah/por-ton
Tavern or rustic restaurant	bodegón	bod-eh-**gon**

Restaurant	restaurante/restorán	rest-ow-**ran**-teh/ rest-oh-**ran**
Main square	plaza principal	**plass**-ah prin-see-**pal**
Market	mercado	mer-**kah**-do
Neighborhood	barrio	**bah**-ree-oh
Traffic circle	rotunda	rot-**oon**-dah

Shopping

How much is it?	¿Cuánto cuesta?	**kwan**-toh **kwes**-tah
It's expensive/cheap	Es caro/barato	ess **kah**-roh/bah-**rah**-toh
A little/a lot	Un poquito/mucho	oon pok-**ee**-toh/ **mooch**-oh
More/less	Más/menos	mass/**meh**-noss
Enough/too much/ too little	Suficiente/dem asiado/muy poco	soo-fiss-ee-**en**-teh/ dem-ass-ee-**ah**-doh/ mwee **poh**-koh
I'd like to buy...	Quiero comprar... por favor.	kee-**eh**-roh kom-**prar**... por fah-**vor**
cigarrettes	cigarrillos	sig-eh-**ree**-yoss
matches	fósforos	**foss**-for-oss
a dictionary	un diccionario	oon dik-see-on-**ah**-ree-oh
soap	jabón	hah-**bon**
sunglasses	anteojos de sol	an-tee-**oh**-hoss deh sol
suntan lotion	protector solar	proh-tek-**tor** sol-**ar**
a map	un mapa	oon **map**-ah
a magazine	una revista	**oo**-na rev-**eess**-tah
paper	papel	pap-**el**
envelopes	sobres	**sob**-ress
a postcard	una tarjeta postal	**oo**-na tar-**het**-ah **poss**-tal
I'd like to try on...	Me gustaría probarme...	meh goos-tah-**ree**-ah proh-**bar**-meh...
this T-shirt	esta remera	**ess**-tah rem-**eh**-rah
these trousers/jeans	este pantalón/jean	**ess**-teh pan-tah-**lon**/ sheen
this skirt	esta pollera	**ess**-tah posh-**eh**-rah
this shirt	esta camisa	**ess**-tah kam-**ee**-sah
this sweater	este suéter	**ess**-teh **swet**-er
this overcoat	este abrigo	**ess**-teh ab-**ree**-goh
this jacket	este saco	**ess**-teh **sak**-oh
this suit	este traje	**ess**-teh **trah**-heh
these shoes	estos zapatos	**ess**-toss sah-**pat**-oss
these sneakers	estas zapatillas	**ess**-tass sah-pat-**ee**-shass

Have you got it in a bigger/smaller size?	¿Lo tenés en un talle más grande/chiquito?	loh ten-**ess** en oon **tah**-sheh mass **gran**-deh/chee-**kee**-toh
Does it come in another color?	¿Lo tenés en otro color?	loh ten-**ess** en ot-roh kol-**or**
I'll take this.	Me llevo éste.	meh **sheh**-voh **ess**-teh

Colors

Black	Negro	**neg**-roh
Blue/light blue/ navy blue	Azul/celeste/ azul marino	ah-**sool**/sel-**ess**-teh/ ah-**sool** mah-**ree**-noh
Brown	Marrón	mah-**ron**
Gray	Gris	greess
Green	Verde	**ver**-deh
Pink	Rosa	**ross**-ah
Purple	Violeta	vee-ol-**et**-ah
Orange	Naranja	nah-**ran**-hah
Red	Rojo	**roh**-ho
White	Blanco	**blan**-koh
Yellow	Amarillo	am-ar-**ee**-shoh

Dining Out

Please could you bring me...	Me podrías traer... por favor	me pod-**ree**-ass trah-er... por fah-**vor**
a bottle of...	una botella de...	**oo**-na bot-**eh**-shah deh...
a cup of...	una taza de...	**oo**-na **tass**-ah deh
a glass of...	un vaso de...	oon **vah**-soh deh
an ashtray	un cenicero	oon sen-ee-**seh**-roh
the bill/check	la cuenta	la **kwen**-tah
some bread	pan	pan
some butter	manteca	man-**tek**-ah
the menu	la carta	la **kar**-tah
a knife	un cuchillo	oon koo-**chee**-shoh
a fork	un tenedor	oon ten-eh-**dor**
a spoon	una cuchara	**oo**-na koo-**chah**-rah
a napkin	una servilleta	**oo**-na ser-vee-shet-ah
salt/pepper	la sal/la pimienta	la sal/la pim-ee-**en**-tah
sugar	el azúcar	el ass-**oo**-kar
Breakfast	el desayuno	el dess-ah-**shoo**-noh
Cheers!	¡Salud!	sal-**ood**
Cocktail	un aperitivo/ un trago largo	oon ap-er-it-**ee**-voh/ oon **trah**-goh **lar**-goh
Dinner	la cena	la **sen**-ah

Dish	un plato	oon **plat**-oh
Enjoy!	¡Buen provecho!	bwen proh-**vech**-oh
Fixed-price menu	Un menú fijo/ ejecutivo	oon men-**oo fee**-hoh/ eh-hek-oo-**tee**-voh
Lunch	el almuerzo	el al-**mwer**-soh
Selection of cold cuts	una picada	oo-na pik-**ah**-dah
Tip	una propina	oo-na prop-**ee**-nah
Waiter/Waitress	mozo/moza	**moss**-oh/**moss**-ah

MENU GUIDE

With so much meat on the menu, you'll need to know how to order it: *jugoso* (juicy) means medium rare, *vuelta y vuelta* (flipped back and forth) means rare, and *vivo por adentro* (alive inside) is barely warm in the middle. Argentines like their meat *bien cocido* (well cooked).

aceite de olivo: olive oil

alfajores: Argentine cookies, usually made with *dulce de leche* and often covered with chocolate, though there are hundreds of varieties

arroz: rice

bife de lomo: filet mignon

bife de chorizo: like a New York strip steak, but double the size (not to be confused with *chorizo,* which is a type of sausage)

budín de pan: Argentine version of bread pudding

cabrito: roasted kid

cafecito: espresso

café con leche: coffee with milk

centolla: King crab, a Patagonian specialty

chimichurri: a sauce of oil, garlic, and salt, served with meat

chinchulines: small intestines

chorizo: thick, spicy pork-and-beef sausages, usually served with bread (*choripan*)

churros: baton-shaped donuts for dipping in hot chocolate

ciervo: venison

Chivito: kid

cordero: lamb

cortado: coffee "cut" with a drop of milk

dulce de leche: a sweet caramel concoction made from milk and served on pancakes, in pastries, on cookies, and on ice cream

empanadas: pockets stuffed with meat—usually beef—chicken, or cheese

ensalada de fruta: fruit salad (sometimes fresh, sometimes canned)

estofado: beef stew

facturas: small pastries

huevos: eggs

humitas: steamed cornhusks wrapped around cornmeal and cheese

jamón: ham

lechón: roast suckling pig

lengua: tongue

licuado: milk shake

locro: local stew, usually made with hominy and beans, that's cooked slowly with meat and vegetables; common in northern Argentina

medialuna: croissant

mejillones: mussels

merluza: hake

milanesa: breaded meat cutlet, usually veal, pounded thin and fried; served as a main course or in a sandwich with lettuce, tomato, ham, cheese, and egg

milanesa a la napolitana: a breaded veal cutlet with melted mozzarella cheese and tomato sauce

mollejas: sweetbreads; the thymus glands, usually of the cow but also can be of the lamb or the goat

morcilla: blood sausage

pejerrey: a kind of mackerel

pollo: chicken

provoleta: grilled provolone cheese sprinkled with olive oil and oregano

puchero: boiled meat and vegetables; like pot-au-fen

queso: cheese

salchichas: long, thin sausages

sambayon: an alcohol-infused custard

tamales: ground corn stuffed with meat, cheese, or other fillings and tied up in a corn husk

tenedor libre: all-you-can-eat meat and salad bar

tinto: red wine

trucha: trout

INDEX

404 < Index

PHOTO CREDITS

Cover Photo *(Andes Mountains, Patagonia)*: John Warden/Superstock. F10, *Walter Bibikow/viestiphoto.com.* F11 (left), *Joe Viesti/viestiphoto.com.* F11 (right), *Joe Viesti/ viestiphoto.com.* F12, *Andy Christodolo/Cephas Picture Library/Alamy.* F13, *Popperphoto/Alamy.* F14, *Ignacio Alvarez/age fotostock.* F15 (left), *Walter Bibikow/ viestiphoto.com.* F15 (right), *P. Narayan/age fotostock.* F23, *Joe Viesti/viestiphoto.com.* F24, *Ignacio Alvarez/age fotostock.* Color Section: *Feeling small at Perito Moreno Glacier, Parque Nacional Los Glaciares, Patagonia: Alan Kearney/viestiphoto.com. Gaucho festival: Carlos E. Hermet/age fotostock. Iguazú Falls: Philip Coblentz/Brand X Pictures. Magellanic penguins, Reserva Faunística Punta Tombo, Patagonia: R. Matina/age fotostock. Typical architecture in Ushuaia, Tierra del Fuego, Patagonia: Joe Viesti/ viestiphoto.com. La Boca district, Buenos Aires: Philip Coblentz/Brand X Pictures. Llamas: Ignacio Alvarez/age fotostock. Tango dancers in La Boca, Buenos Aires: Alvaro Leiva/age fotostock. El Diego de la Gente: soccer legend Diego Maradona: Popperphoto/Alamy. Straight up in Parque Nacional Talampaya, the northwest: Ignacio Alvarez/age fotostock. 18th-century Iglesia San Francisco, Salta: Peter Purchia/viestiphoto. com. Evita's tomb, Cementerio de la Recoleta, Buenos Aires: Adrian Reynolds/age fotostock. Malbec harvest, Bodega Terrazas de los Andes, Mendoza: Andy Christodolo/ Cephas Picture Library/Alamy. Along a road less traveled, Jujuy Province: Ignacio Alvarez/age fotostock.*

NOTES

More Magazine 4/08

Buenos Vinos $250
buenos-vinos.com
Wine + Tango
Piazzolla Tango
piazzollatango.com
Cabana Las Lilas
laslilas.com -steak

Museo de Arte Latin Americano
de B.A
o MALBA   malba.org.ar

NOTES

NOTES

NOTES

NOTES

NOTES

NOTES

NOTES

NOTES

ABOUT OUR WRITERS

Eddy Ancinas, one of the authors of the first edition of *Fodor s Argentina,* wrote the new Wine Regions chapter and updated Smart Travel Tips and for this edition. Eddy met an Argentine ski racer at the 1960 Winter Olympics; after they were married in 1962, they traveled and lived in Argentina. Since then, she has led ski and horseback trips in Peru, Argentina, and Chile, and has written about skiing and adventure travel in these countries.

Brian Byrnes, who updated the Where to Stay, Nightlife, and Essentials sections of Buenos Aires as well as the Northwest chapter, first arrived in Argentina in 2001 to update the Patagonia chapter of *Fodor's Argentina.* He liked the country so much that he decided to stay. He has since married a *porteña* and settled in Buenos Aires, where he reports for CBS News, NPR, *Newsweek,* and other media outlets. His company, Tierra Productions, produces feature television programming about South America for clients around the world.

Although **Robin S. Goldstein** is trained in philosophy at Harvard and law at Yale, his heart has always been in travel and food writing. His credits include many editions of *Fodor's Italy* as well as stints in Chile, Ecuador, Mexico, and Spain. He has also been food critic for *Metro New York* and the *New Haven Advocate,* and co-authored *Fearless Critic* restaurant guide to Austin, Texas, among other books. He updated the Patagonia chapter and covered Buenos Aires restaurants.

Victoria Patience, who updated the Exploring, Where to Eat, Where to Stay, and Shopping sections of the Buenos Aires chapter as well as the Excursions and Córdoba chapters, has been hooked on the city since she first laid eyes on it. She studied Spanish and Latin American literature at the University of London and traveled throughout Mexico, Colombia, Peru, Bolivia, and Chile before going to Argentina to spend a year at the University of Buenos Aires. Five years later, she's still in the city—and has no plans to leave.